INTERNATIONAL ENVIRONMENTAL LAW AND THE GLOBAL SOUTH

The unprecedented degradation of the planet's vital ecosystems is among the most pressing issues confronting the international community. Despite the proliferation of legal instruments to combat environmental problems, conflicts between rich and poor nations (the North–South divide) have compromised international environmental law, leading to deadlocks in environmental treaty negotiations and non-compliance with existing agreements. This volume examines both the historical origins of the North–South divide in European colonialism as well as its contemporary manifestations in a range of issues including food justice, energy justice, indigenous rights, trade, investment, extractive industries, human rights, land-grabs, hazardous waste, and climate change. Born out of the recognition that global inequality and profligate consumerism present threats to a sustainable planet, this book makes a unique contribution to international environmental law by emphasizing the priorities and perspectives of the global South.

SHAWKAT ALAM is an Associate Professor of Law and Director of the Centre for Environmental Law at Macquarie University, Sydney, Australia.

SUMUDU ATAPATTU is Director of Research Centers at the University of Wisconsin Law School and lead counsel for human rights at the Center for International Sustainable Development Law, Montreal, Canada.

CARMEN G. GONZALEZ is a Professor of Law at Seattle University School of Law and has published widely on international environmental law, environmental justice, trade and the environment, and food security

JONA RAZZAQUE is a Professor of Environmental Law at Bristol Law School, University of the West of England, where she specializes in the intersection of human rights and the environment.

International Environmental Law and the Global South

Edited by

SHAWKAT ALAM
Macquarie University Law School

SUMUDU ATAPATTU
University of Wisconsin Law School

CARMEN G. GONZALEZ
Seattle University School of Law

JONA RAZZAQUE
University of the West of England

CAMBRIDGE
UNIVERSITY PRESS

32 Avenue of the Americas, New York, NY 10013-2473, USA

Cambridge University Press is part of the University of Cambridge.

It furthers the University's mission by disseminating knowledge in the pursuit of
education, learning, and research at the highest international levels of excellence.

www.cambridge.org
Information on this title: www.cambridge.org/9781107055698

© Cambridge University Press 2015

This publication is in copyright. Subject to statutory exception
and to the provisions of relevant collective licensing agreements,
no reproduction of any part may take place without the written
permission of Cambridge University Press.

First published 2015

A catalog record for this publication is available from the British Library.

Library of Congress Cataloging in Publication Data
International environmental law and the Global South / edited by Shawkat Alam, Macquarie University
Law School; Sumudu Atapattu, University of Wisconsin Law School; Carmen G. Gonzalez,
Seattle University School of Law; Jona Razzaque, University of the West of England, Bristol.
pages   cm
Includes index.
ISBN 978-1-107-05569-8 (Hardback)
1. Environmental law–Developing countries.   2. Environmental policy–Developing
countries.   3. Environmental law, International.   I. Alam, Shawkat, editor.   II. Atapattu, Sumudu
A., editor.   III. Gonzalez, Carmen G., editor.   IV. Razzaque, Jona, editor.
K3585.I5775 2016
344.04′6–dc23   2015004867

ISBN 978-1-107-05569-8 Hardback

Cambridge University Press has no responsibility for the persistence or accuracy
of URLs for external or third-party Internet Web sites referred to in this publication
and does not guarantee that any content on such Web sites is, or will remain,
accurate or appropriate.

Contents

Author Biographies	*page* ix
Acknowledgments	xix
Foreword	xxi
Judge Christopher Weeramantry	

1   The North–South Divide in International Environmental
Law: Framing the Issues   1
Sumudu Atapattu and Carmen G. Gonzalez

**PART I HISTORY OF THE NORTH–SOUTH DIVIDE AND
GLOBAL ENVIRONMENTAL GOVERNANCE**

2   History of the North–South Divide in International Law:
Colonial Discourses, Sovereignty, and Self-Determination   23
M. Rafiqul Islam

3   Unsustainable Development   50
Ruth Gordon

4   The Significance of International Environmental Law
Principles in Reinforcing or Dismantling the North–South
Divide   74
Sumudu Atapattu

5   The Stockholm Conference and the Creation of the
South–North Divide in International Environmental Law
and Policy   109
Karin Mickelson

Contents

6   Global Environmental Governance and the South   130
Ved P. Nanda

7   Quest for International Environmental Institutions:
Transition from CSD to HLPF   152
Bharat H. Desai and Balraj K. Sidhu

PART II SELECTED INTERNATIONAL ENVIRONMENTAL LAW EXAMPLES

8   Human Rights, the Environment, and the Global South   171
Louis J. Kotzé

9   Access and Benefit-Sharing: North–South Challenges in
Implementing the Convention on Biological Diversity and
Its Nagoya Protocol   192
Jorge Cabrera Medaglia

10   Emerging Powerful Southern Voices: Role of BASIC
Nations in Shaping Climate Change Mitigation
Commitments   214
Rowena Maguire and Xiaoyi Jiang

11   Sustainable Development in the Era of Bioenergy and
Agricultural Land Grab   237
Chidi Oguamanam

12   Trade in Hazardous Waste   256
Zada Lipman

13   The Right to Water: Constitutional Perspectives from the
Global South   277
Carlos Bernal

PART III TRADE, INVESTMENT, AND SUSTAINABLE DEVELOPMENT

14   Trade and the Environment: Perspectives from the
Global South   297
Shawkat Alam

15   From a Divided Heritage to a Common Future?
International Investment Law, Human Rights, and
Sustainable Development   317
Shyami Puvimanasinghe

Contents

16	Project Finance and Sustainable Development in the Global South Shalanda H. Baker	338
17	International Environmental Law and Sovereign Wealth Funds Benjamin J. Richardson	356
18	Transnational Corporations and Extractive Industries Sara L. Seck	380

PART IV ENVIRONMENTAL JUSTICE AND VULNERABLE GROUPS

19	Food Justice: An Environmental Justice Critique of the Global Food System Carmen G. Gonzalez	401
20	A Justice Paradox: Climate Change, Small Island Developing States, and the Absence of International Legal Remedy Maxine Burkett	435
21	South of South: Examining the International Climate Regime from an Indigenous Perspective Elizabeth Ann Kronk Warner	451
22	Water Wars: Anti-Privatization Struggles in the Global South Jackie Dugard and Elisabeth Koek	469
23	Natural Disaster and Climate Change Paul J. Govind and Robert R. M. Verchick	491
24	International Law, Cultural Diversity, and the Environment: The Case of the General Forestry Law in Colombia Daniel Bonilla Maldonado	508
25	The Contours of Energy Justice Lakshman Guruswamy	529

PART V CHALLENGES AND OPTIONS

26	South–South Cooperation: Foundations for Sustainable Development Koh Kheng-Lian and Nicholas A. Robinson	553

viii *Contents*

27 Public Participation in International Negotiation and Compliance 572
Lalanath de Silva

28 Access to Remedies in Environmental Matters and the North–South Divide 588
Jona Razzaque

29 Sustainable Development versus Green Economy: The Way Forward? 609
Shawkat Alam and Jona Razzaque

Index 625

Author Biographies

Shawkat Alam is an Associate Professor of Law and Director of the Centre for Environmental Law at Macquarie University, Sydney, Australia, where he teaches and researches in the areas of international law, environmental law, trade, and sustainable development. Shawkat is currently Acting Dean of Macquarie Law School. He has previously been an academic in the Department of Law at Dhaka University, and he also taught at Rajshahi University, Bangladesh. Shawkat holds an LLB (Hons) from Rajshahi University, an LLM from Dhaka University, and a PhD from Macquarie University. He has published scholarly books and articles on international trade, the environment, and sustainable development.

Sumudu Atapattu, LLM, PhD (Cambridge), Attorney-at-Law (Sri Lanka), is Director of Research Centers at the University of Wisconsin Law School, where she teaches seminar courses on international environmental law and climate change, human rights, and the environment. She has published widely; her first book, *Emerging Principles of International Environmental Law*, was published by Transnational Publishers in 2006. Her second book, *Human Rights Approaches to Climate Change*, is forthcoming from Routledge. She is the Lead Counsel for Human Rights at the Centre for International Sustainable Development Law and was an Associate Professor at the University of Colombo Law School from 1995 to 2002.

Shalanda H. Baker teaches courses in international environmental law, renewable energy law, and sustainable development, as well as related courses in energy, business law, and international development, at the University of Hawai'i School of Law. Her research explores large energy and infrastructure project development, indigenous rights, and the effect of development on the environment. Shalanda is the Faculty Advisor to the Environmental Law Program and the founding director of an energy law project at the law school. She received her JD from Northeastern

University School of Law and her LLM from the University of Wisconsin Law School while completing a William H. Hastie Fellowship.

Carlos Bernal is an Associate Professor at Macquarie Law School, Sydney, Australia. He holds an LLB, an MA, an SJD, and a PhD (in philosophy). He teaches and researches in the fields of constitutional comparative law, jurisprudence, and torts. His scholarship, published in various languages, undertakes a critical analysis of the adjudication of human and constitutional rights in Latin America. He has also investigated and appraised the active role of current constitutional courts of that part of the world in conducting judicial review of legislation, constitutional amendments, administrative action, and actions and omissions by private stakeholders.

Daniel Bonilla Maldonado is Associate Professor of Law and Director of the Public Interest Law Group at the Universidad de los Andes in Bogota, Colombia. He holds a PhD and an LLM from Yale Law School and a law degree from Universidad de los Andes. He has been a visiting professor or lecturer at a number of institutions, including Yale Law School, Fordham Law School, Oñati International Institute for the Sociology of Law, University of Texas School of Law, Georgia State University College of Law, University of Puerto Rico, and Universidad Nacional de Colombia.

Maxine Burkett is an Associate Professor of Law at the University of Hawai'i. An expert in the law and policy of climate change, she has presented research on diverse areas of climate law throughout the United States and in West Africa, Asia, Europe, and the Caribbean. From 2009 to 2012 Maxine also served as the inaugural Director of the Center for Island Climate Adaptation and Policy. She attended Williams College and Exeter College, Oxford University, and received her law degree from Boalt Hall School of Law at the University of California, Berkeley. In 2010, Maxine served as the youngest recipient of the Wayne Morse Chair of Law and Politics at the Wayne Morse Center, University of Oregon.

Jorge Cabrera Medaglia is an internationally recognized expert in biodiversity and biosafety law. He holds a JD and postgraduate and LLM degrees in environmental, agricultural, and trade law. He is currently a Professor of Environmental Law at the University of Costa Rica, a legal advisor to the National Biodiversity Institute of Costa Rica, and Lead Counsel for the Biodiversity Program at the Centre for International Sustainable Development Law based in Montreal, Canada. Jorge is also a member of the Access and Benefit-Sharing (ABS) Expert Group established by the FAO Commission on Genetic Resources to advise the Commission working groups on ABS issues (2013–2015), was a negotiator of the Convention on Biological Diversity (CBD) and the *Nagoya Protocol* for the government of Costa Rica (which included acting as chair of some expert groups on ABS created by the CBD), and was a member of the drafting commissions for the Biodiversity Law of Costa Rica (1998) and of several ABS laws and regulations in different regions. He has published widely on issues of biodiversity, ABS, IP rights, trade, and environment, including the *IUCN Guide to the Nagoya Protocol on ABS* (IUCN, 2012). Jorge has more than twenty-two years' experience in international environmental law.

Bharat H. Desai holds the prestigious Jawaharlal Nehru Chair in International Environmental Law as well as being a Professor of International Law and Chairman of the Centre for International Legal Studies in the School of International Studies at Jawaharlal Nehru University in New Delhi. He serves as an associate editor of the *Yearbook of International Environmental Law* (Oxford), a governing board member of the International Union for the Conservation of Nature Academy of Environmental Law (Ottawa), and Chairman of the Centre for Advanced Study on Courts and Tribunals (Amritsar).

Jackie Dugard, BA (Hons), LLB (Wits), MPhil and PhD (Cambridge), LLM (Essex), is an Associate Professor at the School of Law, University of the Witwatersrand, where she teaches property law. She is a cofounder and former executive director of the Socio-Economic Rights Institute of South Africa, where she is an honorary senior researcher. With a background in social sciences and law, Jackie is a human rights activist and scholar and has published widely on the role of law and courts in effecting social change, as well as on socio-economic rights, access to courts, protest, and social movements.

Carmen G. Gonzalez is a Professor of Law at Seattle University School of Law and writes in the areas of international environmental law, environmental justice, trade and the environment, and food security. She has been a Fulbright Scholar in Argentina, a Fellow at the US Supreme Court, a visiting professor at the Hopkins-Nanjing Center in China, and a visiting Fellow at the Lauterpacht Centre for International Law at Cambridge University in the United Kingdom. She has also worked on USAID-funded environmental law capacity-building projects in Latin America and in the former Soviet Union. Carmen currently serves as cochair of the Research Committee of the International Union for the Conservation of Nature Academy of Environmental Law. She holds a BA in political science from Yale University and a JD from Harvard Law School.

Ruth Gordon has taught at Villanova University School of Law since 1990. She is a graduate of New York University School of Law as well as the London School of Economics and Political Science. Her scholarly work generally focuses on the global South and its encounters with myriad facets of international law, including the environment, the impact of race and racism, the global economy, colonialism, and development. She taught the law of contracts between 1990 and 2008 and now teaches in the areas of international business transactions, international trade and investment, and public international law, as well as teaching a seminar on international environmental law.

Paul J. Govind is currently a lecturer in environmental law and policy at the Centre for Environmental Law, Macquarie University, Australia, where he is also Program Director for Environmental Law Studies. He is editor of the *Australian Journal of Environmental Law,* and his research interests include climate change adaptation law and policy, climate change and disaster risk reduction, and climate finance and its relationship to development. Paul is currently completing his PhD at Australian National University, exploring the role of the right to development in the context of climate change adaptation funding and resilience. His recent publications have examined the relationship between funding channels for climate change adaptation and disaster risk reduction, the relationship between climate change adaptation and disaster risk reduction in the context of global North–South relations, and the importance of social vulnerability in the allocation of climate finance.

Lakshman Guruswamy, the Nicholas Doman Professor of International Environmental Law at the University of Colorado at Boulder, was born in Sri Lanka and is a recognized expert in international environmental and energy law. Lakshman teaches courses on international environmental law, energy justice, and oil and international relations. He is also the Director of International Energy Programs at the Getches Wilkinson Center of the University of Colorado. He has authored books traversing crucial aspects of international environmental and energy law and has published widely on the subjects of international energy and environmental law in legal and scientific journals.

M. Rafiqul Islam is a Professor of Law at Macquarie University. He obtained his PhD and LLM from Monash University and his MA in Economics, BA (Hons), and LLB (first class) from the University of Rajshahi. His teaching and research interests are in the area of public international law. He has published extensively on international law, international trade law, human rights, and the constitutional law of Bangladesh. He was awarded the Macquarie University Outstanding Teacher Award 2000 for his excellence in teaching and in higher degree research supervision. His recent books include *An Introduction to International Refugee Law* (2013) and *International Law: Current Concepts and Future Directions* (2014).

Xiaoyi Jiang is currently an Associate Professor of Environmental Law at the Wuhan University China Institute of Boundary and Ocean Studies (CIBOS), China. She holds a PhD from the University of Western Sydney, Australia, on the topic of legal issues for implementing the Clean Development Mechanism. Her scholarship focuses on international, comparative, and national environmental law and policy, and her research and publications emphasize climate change issues. Since joining the CIBOS, which is supported by the Ministry of Foreign Affairs of the People's Republic of China, in 2010, she has also worked on maritime environment issues.

Koh Kheng-Lian is Emeritus Professor of the Law Faculty, National University of Singapore. She was a founding member and former Director of the Asia-Pacific Centre for Environmental Law from 1996 to 2013 and is now its Honorary Director. She was the IUCN CEL Regional Vice Chair for South and East Asia, and a member of its Steering Committee, from 1996 to 2004. The author of many publications and conference papers in environmental law, including *ASEAN Environmental Law, Policy and Governance: Selected Documents* (two volumes, 2009 and 2012), she has also published books and articles on criminal law, commercial transactions, and straits in international navigation. She is the 2012 recipient of the Elizabeth Haub Prize in Environmental Law and an honoree in the Singapore Women's Hall of Fame 2014.

Elisabeth Koek is a PhD candidate at the Irish Centre for Human Rights, NUI Galway, and is currently based in Gaza City, where she works for the Norwegian Refugee Council. Previously, Elisabeth worked in Monrovia for the UN peacekeeping mission in Ramallah for Palestinian human rights organization Al-Haq, in Johannesburg on socio-economic rights issues, and in Amsterdam and New York in corporate law. Elisabeth holds an LLM in public international law from King's College London and an LLM in corporate law from the University of Leiden Law School in the Netherlands.

Louis J. Kotzé is Research Professor at the Faculty of Law, North-West University, South Africa (Potchefstroom Campus). He previously served as Professor of Environmental Law at that institution. He is also Visiting Professor of Environmental Law at University of Lincoln, United Kingdom, and the author, coauthor, or coeditor of various publications related to South African, regional, and global environmental law. His research focuses on environmental constitutionalism, on human rights and the environment, and on global environmental governance. His latest books include *Global Environmental Governance: Law and Regulation for the 21st Century* (Edward Elgar, 2012) and *Transboundary Governance of Biodiversity* (with Thilo Marauhn; Brill Nijhoff, 2014). He is a co-editor of the *Journal of Human Rights and the Environment* and assistant editor of *Transnational Environmental Law*. Louis is an Alexander von Humboldt Foundation Fellow, Deputy Director of the Global Network for Human Rights and the Environment, and a National Research Foundation–rated researcher.

xiv *Author Biographies*

Elizabeth Ann Kronk Warner currently serves as an Associate Professor and Director of the Tribal Law and Government Center at the University of Kansas School of Law. She also serves as an acting Chief Judge of the Sault Ste. Marie Tribe of Chippewa Indians Court of Appeals. She has written extensively in the field of climate change and its impacts on indigenous peoples, including several law review articles and a chapter in the book *Climate Change and Indigenous Peoples: The Search for Legal Remedies*, which she also co-edited. She is a tribal citizen of the Sault Ste. Marie Tribe of Chippewa Indians.

Zada Lipman is an Emeritus Professor of Law at Macquarie University. She has co-authored five books, the most recent being *Environmental and Planning Law in New South Wales* (with Lyster, Franklin, Pearson, and Wiffen; 3rd edn, Federation Press, 2012). Her recent publications include "Pollution Control and the Regulation of Chemicals and E-Waste," in *Routledge Handbook of International Environmental Law* (eds Alam, Bhuiyan, Chowdhury, and Techera; Routledge, 2012), and "Compliance and Enforcement of International Conventions in Australia," in *Compliance and Enforcement in Environmental Law* (eds Paddock, Qun, Kotze, Markell, Markowitz, and Zaelke; Edward Elgar, 2011).

Rowena Maguire is a senior lecturer and co-chair of the International Law and Global Governance Research Program within the Faculty of Law at the Queensland University of Technology, Australia. Her doctoral research focused on the international regulation of sustainable forest management and was published by Edward Elgar in 2013 as *Global Forest Governance*. Her research work post–PhD completion has centered on the international climate regime, with a focus on issues of equity within the regime, and she is currently part of a research team working on a funded Australian Research Council project examining integrity issues within the UNFCCC.

Karin Mickelson is an Associate Professor at the University of British Columbia, Faculty of Law. Her research has focused on the South–North dimension of international law, with a particular focus on international environmental law. She has been involved in Third World Approaches to International Law since the late 1990s.

Ved P. Nanda is John Evans University Professor at the University of Denver and Thompson G. Marsh Professor of Law and Director of the Nanda Center for International and Comparative Law at the University of Denver, Sturm College of Law. From 1994 to 2008, he also served as Vice Provost for Internationalization at the university. Former students and friends of Ved established the Nanda Center and the Ved Nanda Professorship in International Law at the College of Law.

He has authored or co-authored more than two dozen books on international law and policy, and he has written more than 200 book chapters and law review articles.

Chidi Oguamanam is a full Professor in the Faculty of Law at the University of Ottawa. He is called to the Bar in Nigeria and Canada and is affiliated with the Centre for Law, Technology and Society and the Centre for Environmental Law and Global Sustainability at the University of Ottawa. Chidi was formerly Director of the Law and Technology Institute at the Schulich School of Law, Dalhousie University; his publications include *International Law and Indigenous Knowledge* (University of Toronto, 2010), *Intellectual Property in Global Governance* (Routledge, 2012), and *Innovation and Intellectual Property: Collaborative Dynamics in Africa* (co-editor; University of Cape Town, 2014).

Shyami Puvimanasinghe is a Human Rights Officer at the Office of the High Commissioner for Human Rights, Geneva, Switzerland. She previously served as a senior lecturer at the University of Colombo, Sri Lanka, and worked in the non-governmental sector in Botswana. Her publications on sustainable development include *Foreign Investment, Human Rights and the Environment* (Brill, 2007). A graduate of the University of Colombo and Attorney-at-Law of the Supreme Court of Sri Lanka, she holds an LLM from Harvard Law School and a PhD in development studies from the Institute of Social Studies, The Hague, the Netherlands.

Jona Razzaque, Professor of Environmental Law at Bristol Law School, University of the West of England (UWE), is a barrister and holds a PhD in law from the University of London. Prior to joining the UWE, she worked as a staff lawyer with the Foundation for International Environmental Law and Development and previously taught at the School of Oriental and African Studies, University College London, and Queen Mary University of London. She is a member of the editorial board of the *Journal of Environmental Law* and serves as a member of the IUCN World Commission on Environmental Law. She has researched widely on access to justice and participatory rights in environmental matters.

Benjamin J. Richardson is a Professor at the University of Tasmania's Faculty of Law and the Institute for Marine and Antarctic Studies. He previously worked abroad for more than eighteen years, in law faculties in New Zealand, Canada, and the United Kingdom. His last such position was at the University of British Columbia, where he held the Canada Research Chair in Environmental Law and Sustainability and was Director of its Centre for Law and Environment. Benjamin's teaching and scholarship are diverse, including climate change law, socially responsible investment, corporate social responsibility, and Aboriginal legal issues.

Author Biographies

Nicholas A. Robinson is the University Professor for the Environment at Pace University, Gilbert and Sarah Kerlin Distinguished Professor of Environmental Law Emeritus at Pace University School of Law, and Adjunct Professor at the Yale University School of Forestry and Environmental Studies. He is also the co-director of the Pace Global Center for Environmental Legal Studies. He founded Pace's environmental law programs, edited the proceedings of the 1992 United Nations Earth Summit in Rio de Janeiro, Brazil, and is the author of several books and numerous articles. He teaches a number of environmental law courses and is former Chair of the Commission on Environmental Law and Legal Advisor to the International Union for the Conservation of Nature and Natural Resources.

Sara L. Seck (LLB, Toronto; PhD, Osgoode Hall) is an Associate Professor at the Faculty of Law at Western University, Ontario, Canada, which she joined in July 2007. Her research explores corporate social responsibility, international sustainable mineral development law, international human rights and environmental law, climate change, and indigenous law, as well as international and transnational legal theory. Theoretically, she is interested in the relationship between TWAIL and international legal process theories informed by constructivist understandings of international relations. Sara has published widely, including in the *Yale Human Rights and Development Law Journal* and the *Canadian Yearbook of International Law*.

Balraj K. Sidhu holds a PhD in international law from Jawaharlal Nehru University, New Delhi. Balraj is Executive Director of the Centre for Advanced Study on Courts and Tribunals, Amritsar, which is dedicated to the study of the role and function of courts and tribunals in global governance; international justice; rule of law; and the promotion of transjudicial dialogue between international courts and national courts. Balraj has contributed extensively to research papers in journals of international repute on issues concerning arbitration, international environmental dispute settlement, green courts and tribunals, transboundary water resources governance, polar regions, natural resource management, and conservation issues.

Lalanath de Silva is the Director of the Environmental Democracy Practice at the World Resources Institute and has more than thirty years of experience in the fields of environmental law, human rights, and international law. He was a public interest lawyer for more than two decades, co-founding two leading NGOs in Sri Lanka. He worked as a legal consultant to Sri Lanka's Ministry of Environment and as a legal officer in the Environmental Claims Unit of the UN Compensation Commission. He has a PhD from the University of Sydney and an LLM from the University of Washington, Seattle, and he graduated from Sri Lanka Law College with honors.

Robert R. M. Verchick holds the Gauthier–St. Martin Chair in Environmental Law at Loyola University New Orleans. He is also Senior Fellow in Disaster Resilience Leadership at Tulane University. As an official at the US Environmental Protection Agency (EPA) in 2009 and 2010, Robert helped develop climate adaptation policy for the EPA and served on President Barack Obama's Interagency Climate Change Adaptation Task Force. He holds a JD degree from Harvard University and an AB degree from Stanford University.

Christopher Weeramantry is a former vice-president of the International Court of Justice, a former judge of the Supreme Court of Sri Lanka, Professor of Law Emeritus at Monash University, Australia, and a counsellor of the World Future Council. A prolific writer, he has published many books and articles on a wide range of issues. He won the UNESCO Prize for Peace Education in 2006, the Right Livelihood Award in 2007, and the Lifetime Achievement Award of the Lawyers Committee on Nuclear Policy in 2008. He established the Weeramantry International Centre for Peace Education and Research in Sri Lanka in 2001.

Acknowledgments

This project would not have been possible without the collaboration of many people. We would like to thank all our contributors, who produced their chapters amid many demands on their time. They were very gracious about the editorial comments and suggestions and worked with us to ensure that the central theme of the book was highlighted in their chapters.

We owe a particular debt of gratitude to Dilara Reznikas, who worked tirelessly to ensure that all the chapters were formatted properly and were ready by the deadline. Without her, we would have been lost. Her dedication and attention to detail, as well as her editorial skills, were invaluable.

We are most grateful to Professor Benjamin J. Richardson and Judge Christopher Weeramantry for their support with this challenging project. We would also like to acknowledge the support of Cambridge University Press, especially John Berger, in publishing this manuscript.

Finally, we would all like to thank our families. This work would not have been possible without their continuing patience and ongoing support.

Foreword

It is not commonly realized that the damage presently being done to the environmental rights of future generations is unprecedented in human history.

The environment is being damaged not merely on a global scale but also across all barriers of time, for the damage now being done will last for thousands of years. Indeed, we are damaging it not merely for thousands of years but for thousands of generations, as can be seen when we consider the after-effects of nuclear activity. This is sufficiently established, for the half-life of some products of nuclear activity is around 25,000 years and there is no known method for disposal of the resulting radioactive waste.

Moreover, the environmental damage we are now causing is largely irreversible and will accumulate over years to produce the most disastrous effects. Among these are climate change, which may negate many of the basic assumptions in accordance with which humanity has planned its lifestyle and ordered its affairs from the commencement of civilization.

In contemplating environmental damage of this magnitude, my mind goes back to the arguments heard by the International Court of Justice in the cases relating to nuclear weapons that came before the Court in my time.

In one of them, a lawyer appearing for one of the antinuclear powers argued that if prehistoric men had been able to damage the environment in a manner that affects us today, we would condemn them in the strongest terms as primitive brutes who did not know what they were doing. One fears to think what words could be used by future generations to describe those who have damaged their environment, with full knowledge of what they were doing. And what would future generations think of a legal system that permits this to happen?

It is a sobering thought, in the midst of all this devastation, that concern for future generations was uppermost in the minds of all cultures and civilizations in generations past. Native Americans considered the impact of their decisions for seven generations to come. African cultures thought that any decision should take account of past, present, and future as inextricably linked to each other. Native Australians thought of all people as linked by an umbilical cord to Mother Earth, whom it was their duty to protect, because if Mother Earth suffered damage in any way, they would be damaged themselves. All religions likewise made the interests of children one of the foremost considerations of any society, and the trusteeship of the environment a special duty.

In this situation, lawyers, judges, and legislators across the world are under a special duty to prevent this betrayal of our trusteeship duties toward future generations. However, international environmental law has, until recently, been a much neglected branch of international law. That omission is now being remedied, but even today the problems resulting from the North–South divide lack the attention received by other areas of international environmental law.

The appearance of a volume throwing fresh light on these neglected areas is, therefore, to be greatly welcomed. It is a significant step forward in an area of great importance to the human future, and its value is all the greater because it assembles together the vast experience and learning of internationally recognized scholars from both North and South.

The editors of this volume are a group of scholars who are eminently suited to the task. Each of them has a distinguished range of publications, a dedicated record of service to environmentally escalated causes, and membership in various international groups and committees that have dealt with such topics as sustainable development, environmental justice, law and society, environmental education, environmental governance, and human rights relating to the environment.

The contributors likewise are all distinguished scholars who have made significant contributions in various areas of international environmental law. They are drawn from nations across the North–South divide and bring to bear on their studies a depth of philosophical learning that greatly enhances their presentation of the problems involved. They also bring to bear on their work a considerable body of experience from international organizations in which they have served with distinction.

I congratulate the editors and contributors on the work they have produced, which throws much needed light on both the causes of the problems addressed and the avenues toward their solution.

This volume alerts lawyers, legislators, and concerned citizens to the fact that we are slowly but surely moving toward the abyss of environmental destruction – that is, unless we all join actively in the crucial task of addressing the causes of this frontal attack upon the rights of posterity. Time for such remedial action is fast running out, and any step stimulating further action in this direction is most opportune.

A special feature of this volume is that it throws light on such topics as the history of the North–South divide, various relevant international conventions and declarations, climate change, food justice, bioenergy, cultural diversity, extractive industries, energy justice, the trade in hazardous wastes, the right to water, green energy, and South–South cooperation. It is a fascinating list, and indeed a treasure trove of environmentally related information.

Thus far, international environmental law has not sufficiently addressed the problem that the global South is at the receiving end of – namely, some of the most devastating environmental damage being caused in our time. It is therefore a welcome addition to the literature of contemporary international environmental law.

The inequality in economic power between the global North and the global South tends, all too often, to result in a violation of some of the basic principles of international law, while preserving the appearance of compliance with them. This volume adds considerably to the contemporary literature of international environmental law.

One is reminded, in this context, of President Eisenhower's celebrated farewell address to the American people, warning them of the growing power of the military-industrial complex, which could intrude into every aspect of their daily life. This warning applies *a fortiori* to the people of the developing world, who do not even have the protections on which citizens of the western world can rely against such encroachment upon their rights. The economic power of corporations is growing by the day, and many of them have revenue far exceeding that of more than 150 of the world's nation states. Worst of all, the military of the global North has used territories of the global South for the testing of nuclear weapons, and the effects of these are painfully felt in the form of disfigurements, excruciating agonies, and birth deformities.

One reality of a world scene dominated by large multinational economic conglomerates is that they operate in countries whose entire national income is much less than theirs. They operate on contractual terms contained in an agreement between them – a contract very often drawn up in circumstances in which the weaker contracting party has to accept the terms dictated to it by the multinational, because it has no other realistic option. Thereafter, the work proceeds on the basis of the contractual arrangement, with the more powerful party relying on the letter of the written contract. The poorer party has no option but to submit, and there is no international tribunal to which it can take any problems of environmental damage that may occur as a result. Consequently, the denigration of its atmosphere, the pollution of its water, damage to its soil, and even radioactivity of its land occur without principles, procedures, or institutions in the field of international law that can prevent this.

Moreover, conglomerates of economic power are constantly indulging in conduct that is damaging to the environment of people of the developing world, most of whom are in no position to prevent this. For example, industrial organizations, pharmaceutical companies, mining operations, chemical factories, and the like have been discharging pollutants into the environment of developing countries for some time. They do this by relying on the letter of the contract and ignoring the fact that the poorer contracting parties are unable to resist the terms they offer.

The authors included in this publication have earned the gratitude of the legal profession and the international public by filling an important gap in legal literature and bridging the gap between the theory and practice of international environmental law. They have also brought a futuristic vision into their discussion of the problems addressed. This adds greatly to the value of the publication, which will take its place as one of the important contributions toward making international environmental law more universally applicable and practically effective.

Economic justice between the global North and the global South includes the concept of environmental justice, for the pollution of the environment is a major denial of justice – not only to present generations but also to the future. The Rio Declaration carried this concept very far and this volume carries it further still.

Areas that should receive the attention of international law include the creation of new institutions to handle these matters, adoption of new concepts to give them a firm theoretical foundation and a greater public awareness, and participation in all these matters by the people of the North and the South. All these objectives are promoted by this book, which should make a contribution toward the solution of these problems at all levels – administrative, judicial, academic, educational, economic, and managerial, as well as at the level of public activity. Without activity in all these areas, these problems cannot be solved. This volume is structured to promote activity at every level mentioned.

For all these reasons, publication of this volume at a time when the issues it addresses are coming to the forefront of international affairs can help greatly to illuminate current discussion on this matter. The book contains an abundance of little-known factual material and a refreshing panorama of arguments and viewpoints that will bring home the urgency and importance of the matters under discussion.

The distinguished editors and authors have rendered a significant service to the development of international law in one of its most crucial areas.

Judge Christopher Weeramantry

1

The North–South Divide in International Environmental Law: Framing the Issues

Sumudu Atapattu and Carmen G. Gonzalez

1. INTRODUCTION

The unprecedented degradation of the planet's vital ecosystems is one of the most pressing issues confronting the international community today. From the 1972 Stockholm Conference on the Human Environment[1] through the 2012 Rio +20 United Nations Conference on Sustainable Development,[2] the international community has responded to this crisis by adopting numerous treaties, declarations, UN General Assembly resolutions, customary rules, and judicial decisions that address specific environmental threats.

Despite the proliferation of laws and legal instruments to combat environmental degradation, the global economy continues to exceed ecosystem limits, thereby jeopardizing the health and well-being of present and future generations and threatening the integrity of the planet's biodiversity.[3] States differ in their contribution to global ecological destruction, their vulnerability to environmental harm, their capacity to address environmental problems, and the economic and political power they wield in multilateral environmental negotiations. While international cooperation is necessary to address global environmental degradation, the global environmental agenda has often been dominated by the priorities and concerns of affluent countries (such as nature conservation). The concerns of poor countries (such as social and economic development and poverty alleviation) are frequently marginalized.[4]

---

[1] UN, *Report of the United Nations Conference on the Human Environment*, Stockholm, Sweden, 5–16 June 1972, UN Doc. A/Conf.48/14/Rev. 1.

[2] UN, *Report of the United Nations Conference on Sustainable Development*, Rio de Janeiro, Brazil, 20–22 June 2012, UN Doc. A/Conf.216/16.

[3] United Nations Millennium Ecosystem Assessment, *Ecosystems and Human Well-Being: Synthesis* (Washington, DC: Island Press, 2005), pp. 1–24.

[4] R. Anand, *International Environmental Justice: A North-South Dimension* (Hampshire: Ashgate, 2004), pp. 3–6; C. G. Gonzalez, "Beyond Eco-Imperialism: An Environmental Justice Critique of Free Trade" (2001) 78 *Denver University Law Review* 979 at 985–986.

The North–South Divide in International Environmental Law

Because environmental issues are closely intertwined with economic issues, international environmental law has been and continues to be the site of intense contestation over environmental priorities, over the allocation of responsibility for current and historic environmental harm, and over the relationship between economic development and environmental protection. These conflicts have often resulted in inadequate compliance with existing environmental agreements as well as deadlocks in ongoing treaty negotiations, most notably climate change negotiations.[5]

2. SIGNIFICANCE OF THE VOLUME

This volume examines the ways in which the North–South divide has compromised the effectiveness of international environmental law and proposes a variety of strategies to bridge the divide. In this volume, the terms *North* and *South* distinguish wealthy industrialized nations (including the United States, Canada, Australia, New Zealand, Japan, and the member states of the European Union) from their generally less prosperous counterparts in Asia, Africa, and Latin America. Despite its heterogeneity, the global South shares a history of Northern economic and political domination, and Southern nations have often negotiated as a bloc (the Group of 77 plus China) to demand greater equity in international economic and environmental law.[6]

However, this volume also recognizes the conflicts and tensions *within* the North and the South. As the negotiations over climate change illustrate, the environmental priorities of certain Southern states, such as India and China, often diverge from those of more ecologically vulnerable nations, such as the small island states.[7] Furthermore, China's growing economic clout in the global South and middle-income Southern nations' acquisition of agricultural lands in Asia, Africa, and Latin America for biofuels production and to satisfy domestic food needs (the so-called land grabs) have generated South–South debates about sustainable investment.[8] Similarly, the European Union and the United States have frequently clashed over environmental policy, most notably over the regulation of genetically modified organisms and toxic chemicals and over efforts to address climate change.[9]

---

[5] Anand, note 4, pp. 5–9, 126–131.

[6] C. G. Gonzalez, "Environmental Justice and International Environmental Law," in S. Alam, M. J. H. Bhuiyan, T. M. R. Chowdhury, and E. J. Techera (eds.), *Routledge Handbook of International Environmental Law* (New York: Routledge, 2013), 77–97, p. 81.

[7] See chapter 20, M. Burkett, "A Justice Paradox: Climate Change, Small Island Developing States, and the Absence of International Legal Remedy"; and chapter 10, R. Maguire and X. Jiang, "Emerging Powerful Southern Voices: Role of BASIC Nations in Shaping Climate Change Mitigation Commitments."

[8] T. Ferrando, "Land Grabbing Under the Cover of Law: Are BRICS–South Relationships any Different?" September 2014, www.tni.org. See chapter 11, C. Oguanaman, "Sustainable Development in the Era of Bioenergy and Agricultural Land Grab."

[9] D. E. Adelman, "A Cautiously Optimistic Appraisal of Trends in Toxics Regulation" (2010) 12 *Washington University Journal of Law and Public Policy* 377; C. G. Gonzalez, "Genetically

A systematic examination of international environmental law from a North–South perspective has never been conducted, and this volume seeks to fill that void. While some scholars have analyzed the North–South divide in relation to particular environmental problems[10] or principles[11] and have investigated how the colonial encounter shaped the doctrines and institutions of international law,[12] this is the first volume that examines the North–South divide in international environmental law in its historical context.

This book also acknowledges the important role of non-state actors in this field. For example, transnational corporations can serve as a significant source of financing for climate change mitigation and adaptation,[13] and corporate environmental and social responsibility initiatives have proliferated in recent years.[14] However, multinational companies headquartered in the North have been responsible for many of the environmental and human rights violations in the South,[15] as demonstrated by the *Ogoniland* case in Nigeria[16] and the litigation against Chevron in Ecuador.[17] Since they operate in the gray zone between international law and national law, transnational corporations have traditionally escaped scrutiny and accountability at the international level.[18] International trade, investment, and financial institutions (such as the World Bank, the World Trade Organization,

---

Modified Organisms and Justice: The International Environmental Justice Implications of Biotechnology" (2007) 19 *Georgetown Environmental Law Review* 583; see Chapter 10 R. Maguire and X. Jiang, "Emerging Powerful Southern Voices: Role of BASIC Nations in Shaping Climate Change Mitigation Commitments".

[10] Anand, note 4 (examining the North–South divide in relation to climate change, ozone depletion, and the hazardous water trade); K. Mickelson, "Leading Toward a Level Playing Field, Repaying Ecological Debt, or Making Environmental Space: Three Stories About International Environmental Cooperation" (2005) 43 *Osgoode Hall Law Journal* 138; K. Mickelson, "Competing Narratives of Justice in North–South Environmental Relations: The Case of Ozone Layer Depletion," in J. Ebbesson and P. Okowa (eds.), *Environmental Law and Justice in Context* (Cambridge: Cambridge University Press, 2009).

[11] L. Rajamani, *Differential Treatment in International Environmental Law* (Oxford: Oxford University Press, 2006).

[12] R. Falk, B. Rajagopal, and J. Stevens (eds.), *International Law and the Third World: Reshaping Justice* (New York: Routledge-Cavendish, 2008).

[13] United Nations Framework Convention on Climate Change (UNFCCC) Secretariat, "Investment and Financial Flows to Address Climate Change," 2007, http://unfccc.int.

[14] L. Catá Backer, "Multinational Corporations, Transnational Law: The United Nation's Norms on the Responsibility of Transnational Corporations as Harbingers of Corporate Social Responsibility as International Law" (2006) 37 *Columbia Human Rights Law Review* 287.

[15] B. Stephens, "The Amorality of Profit: Transnational Corporations and Human Rights" (2002) 20 *Berkeley Journal of International Law* 45 at 49–53.

[16] See *Social and Economic Rights Action Center and Center for Economic and Social Rights v. Nigeria* (the *Ogoniland Case*), Case No. ACHPR/COMM/AO44/1,OAUDoc.CAB/LEG/67/3 (2001), www.achpr.org/files/sessions/30th/comunications/155.96/achpr30_155_96_eng.pdf.

[17] M. A. Gómez, "The Global Chase: Seeking Recognition and Enforcement of the Lago Agrio Judgment Outside of Ecuador" (2013) 1 *Stanford Journal of Complex Litigation* 429; S. Romero and C. Krauss, "Ecuador Orders Chevron to Pay $9 Billion," *New York Times*, 14 February 2011.

[18] P. Simons, "International Law's Invisible Hand and the Future of Corporate Accountability for Violations of Human Rights" (2012) 3 *Journal of Human Rights and the Environment* 5.

4   *The North–South Divide in International Environmental Law*

and the International Monetary Fund) and sovereign wealth funds have likewise influenced both economic and environmental policy in the global South.[19] Finally, the book discusses the impact of indigenous mobilization, grassroots social movements, and transnational networks on the evolution of international environmental law.[20] These examples illustrate that the international community includes a range of actors and that it has moved away from the state-centric notion of traditional international law.

Virtually all areas of environmental concern display North–South divisions, and this volume has chosen some of these issues for in-depth analysis: water conflicts,[21] access to food,[22] forests and indigenous peoples,[23] trade,[24] investment,[25] energy,[26] extractive industries,[27] human rights,[28] climate change,[29] biodiversity,[30] land grabs,[31] and the hazardous waste trade.[32] While it is impossible to cover all environmental issues that give rise to the North–South divide in one volume, the

[19] See chapter 17, B. J. Richardson, "International Environmental Law and Sovereign Wealth Funds"; chapter 14, S. Alam, "Trade and the Environment: Perspectives from the Global South"; chapter 15, S. Puvimanasinghe, "From a Divided Heritage to a Common Future? International Investment Law, Human Rights, and Sustainable Development"; chapter 19, C. G. Gonzalez, "Food Justice: An Environmental Justice Critique of the Global Food System"; and chapter 28, J. Razzaque, "Access to Remedies in Environmental Matters and the North–South Divide."

[20] See chapter 18, S. L. Seck, "Transnational Corporations and Extractive Industries"; chapter 21, E. A. Kronk Warner, "South of South: Examining the International Climate Regime from an Indigenous Perspective"; chapter 22, J. Dugard and E. Koek, "Water Wars: Anti-Privatization Struggles in the Global South"; and chapter 24, D. Bonilla Maldonado, "International Law, Cultural Diversity, and the Environment: The Case of the General Forestry Law in Colombia."

[21] See chapter 22, J. Dugard and E. Koek, "Water Wars: Anti-Privatization Struggles in the Global South."

[22] See chapter 19, C. G. Gonzalez, "Food Justice: An Environmental Justice Critique of the Global Food System."

[23] See chapter 24, D. Bonilla Maldonado, "International Law, Cultural Diversity, and the Environment: The Case of the General Forestry Law in Colombia."

[24] See chapter 14, S. Alam, "Trade and the Environment: Perspectives from the Global South."

[25] See chapter 15, S. Puvimanasinghe, "From a Divided Heritage to a Common Future? International Investment Law, Human Rights and Sustainable Development."

[26] See chapter 25, L. Guruswamy, "The Contours of Energy Justice."

[27] See chapter 18, S. Seck, "Transnational Corporations and Extractive Industries."

[28] See chapter 8, L. J. Kotze, "Human Rights, the Environment and the Global South."

[29] See chapter 20, M. Burkett, "A Justice Paradox: Climate Change, Small Island Developing States, and the Absence of International Legal Remedy"; chapter 10, R. Maguire and X. Jiang, "Emerging Powerful Southern Voices: Role of BASIC Nations in Shaping Climate Change Mitigation Commitments"; chapter 21, E. A. Kronk Warner, "South of South: Examining the International Climate Regime from an Indigenous Perspective"; and chapter 23, P. Govind and R. R. M. Verchik, "Natural Disaster and Climate Change."

[30] See chapter 9, J. Cabrera Medaglia, "Access and Benefit Sharing: North–South Challenges in Implementing the Convention on Biological Diversity and its Nagoya Protocol."

[31] See chapter 11, C. Oguanaman, "Sustainable Development in the Era of Bioenergy and Agricultural Land Grab."

[32] See chapter 12, Z. Lipman, "Trade in Hazardous Waste."

book highlights several significant examples where the divide is apparent and also where positive developments and contributions have helped bridge the divide. In short, the book introduces this rich yet hitherto uncharted area of scholarship. It seeks to provide an illustrative, rather than an exhaustive, list of issues that have been particularly contentious from a North–South perspective. It differs from the traditional environmental law textbook, research handbook, or treatise because it takes the perspective of the South, and emphasizes the need to address historical inequities and inadequacies in the international environmental law regime in order to improve its effectiveness and to reduce the gap between the global North and the global South. The book also recognizes the influential role of countries such as China that straddle the North–South divide. China sometimes replicates the trade and investment patterns of Northern countries (in the land grabs, for example) while at the same time maintaining its "developing country" status by negotiating with the G-77.[33] China's rise can produce strategic alliances that enhance the bargaining power of the South or, conversely, alliances that marginalize vulnerable states, such as the small island states and least developed countries.[34]

Recognizing the urgent need for North–South collaboration to address the grave environmental problems confronting the international community, this volume does not restrict itself to identifying obstacles and roadblocks. On the contrary, the book discusses some of the concessions that the South has been successful in winning from the North, such as transfer of technology and establishing international funds to help the Southern countries fulfill their international obligations. However, the book recognizes that these ostensibly positive developments may create additional opportunities for the North to control the South by withholding funds or placing conditions on their use.

3. COLONIAL AND POSTCOLONIAL ORIGINS OF THE NORTH–SOUTH DIVIDE

The persistent mistrust between the global North and the global South is grounded in colonial and postcolonial economic law and policy. The European conquest of Asia, Africa, and Latin America paved the way for contemporary economic and social inequality by transforming self-sufficient economies into economic satellites of Europe, promoting slavery and indentured servitude, and wreaking havoc on the

---

[33] See generally Ferrando, note 8; J. T. Gathii, "Beyond China's Human Rights Exceptionalism in Africa: Leveraging Science, Technology and Engineering for Long-Term Growth" (2013) 51 *Columbia Journal of Transnational Law* 664; C. G. Gonzalez, "China's Engagement with Latin America: Partnership or Plunder?", in E. Blanco and J. Razzaque (eds.), *Natural Resources and the Green Economy: Redefining the Challenges for People, States, and Corporations* (Leiden: Martinus Nijhoff Publishers, 2012), pp. 37–79.

[34] See chapter 10, R. Maguire and X. Jiang, "Emerging Powerful Southern Voices: Role of BASIC Nations in Shaping Climate Change Mitigation Commitments."

6   *The North–South Divide in International Environmental Law*

livelihoods, ecosystems, cultures, and lifeways of indigenous peoples.[35] Over time, Northern countries came to specialize in capital-intensive goods and to enjoy high standards of living while the colonized territories produced minerals, agricultural products, and other raw materials for the benefit of their colonial overlords.[36]

Most Southern countries were under colonial rule when the global North created the legal architecture for contemporary globalization. The World Bank, the International Monetary Fund (IMF), and the 1947 General Agreement on Tariffs and Trade (GATT) were designed to erode state sovereignty in order to facilitate the free flow of goods, services, and capital across national borders.[37] This legal framework enabled the North to fuel its economic expansion through the continued exploitation of the South's natural resources, trapping Southern countries in vicious cycles of poverty and environmental degradation and widening the North–South economic divide.[38] Moreover, the economic policies pursued by the North resulted in global environmental harms such as acid rain, ozone depletion, and climate change, with impacts not just on the present generation but also on generations to come.[39]

Despite commonalities in the colonial experience, it is difficult to define the "postcolonial era" because it does not include just one history and one set of countries, but rather ongoing relationships among multiple countries from the North and South.[40] However, in spite of the varied political and economic trajectories of the global South in the decades following political independence, most Southern countries were integrated into the global economy as exporters of raw materials and importers of manufactured goods.[41] This economic specialization rendered Southern countries vulnerable to the declining terms of trade for primary commodities relative to manufactured goods[42] and to the efforts of foreign investors to curtail national sovereignty in order to safeguard the profitability of their investments in resource-extractive industries.[43]

Newly independent countries of the South banded together in the decades following World War II to create a more equitable postcolonial world order. In 1955, representatives of twenty-nine newly independent nations of Africa and Asia met in Bandung, Indonesia and vowed to promote economic cooperation, human

---

[35] C. Ponting, *A Green History of the World: The Environment and the Collapse of Great Civilizations* (New York: Penguin Books, 1991), pp. 128–140, 194–212.

[36] Ibid, p. 222.

[37] See chapter 2, R. Islam, "History of the North–South Divide: Colonial Discourses, Sovereignty and Self-Determination."

[38] Ponting, note 35, pp. 194–223.

[39] Ibid, pp. 383–392.

[40] P. Childs and P. Williams, *An Introduction to Post-Colonial Theory* (New York: Routledge, 1997).

[41] L. Young, *World Hunger* (New York: Routledge, 1997), p. 41.

[42] Ibid, p. 42.

[43] K. Miles, *The Origins of International Investment Law: Empire, Environment and the Safeguarding of Capital* (Cambridge: Cambridge University Press, 2013), pp. 78–100.

rights, and self-determination, and to condemn new forms of imperialism.[44] The Bandung conference served as the catalyst for the coalition of Asian, African, and Latin American states (later known as the Group of 77 plus China) that would articulate its demands for economic justice and national self-determination through a variety of legal doctrines,[45] including permanent sovereignty over natural resources,[46] the right to development,[47] and the common heritage of mankind principle.[48] Southern countries used their numerical majority in the United Nations General Assembly to attempt to establish a New International Economic Order (NIEO) that would vindicate these demands and provide debt relief, preferential access to Northern markets, and the stabilization of primary commodity export prices.[49] Southern countries also sought to redress the enduring inequalities arising from the colonial encounter through the differential and more favorable treatment of Southern countries in both international economic law (special and differential treatment) and international environmental law (common but differentiated responsibility principle).[50]

The debt crisis of the 1980s and the rise of the free market model known as the Washington Consensus marked the untimely death of the NIEO.[51] The structural adjustment policies imposed by the IMF and the World Bank as conditions for debt relief required Southern nations to adopt a standard package of economic reforms that included privatization, deregulation, trade liberalization, reduction or elimination of social safety nets, and expansion of export production to service the foreign debt.[52]

In order to earn badly needed foreign exchange, debt-ridden Southern countries flooded world markets with minerals, timber, and agricultural products, thereby driving down prices and enabling the North to live beyond the constraints of its

---

[44] C. J. Lee, "Introduction: Between a Moment and an Era: The Origins and Afterlives of Bandung," in C. J. Lee (ed.), *Making a World After Empire: The Bandung Moment and Its Political Afterlives* (Athens: Ohio University Press, 2010), pp. 1–32.

[45] Ibid.

[46] UN General Assembly, *Resolution Adopted by the General Assembly: 1962 General Assembly Resolution on Permanent Sovereignty over Natural Resources*, 14 December 1962, GA Res. 1803 (XVII) / 17 UN GAOR Supp. (No.17) at 15; UN Doc. A/5217 (1962).

[47] UN General Assembly, *Declaration on the Right to Development*, 4 December 1986, UN Doc. A/Res/41/128.

[48] For a discussion of this principle, see J. Noyes, "Common Heritage of Mankind: Past, Present and Future" (2011–2012) 40 *Denver Journal of International Law and Policy* 447. See Chapter 4, S. Atapattu, "The Significance of International Environmental Law Principles in Reinforcing or Dismantling the North–South Divide," which discusses the role of this and other principles of international environmental law in relation to the North–South divide.

[49] R. Gordon, "The Dawn of a New, New International Economic Order?" (2009) 72 *Law and Contemporary Problems* 131 at 142–145; UN General Assembly, *Declaration of the Establishment of a New International Economic Order*, 1 May 1974, A/Res/S-6/3201.

[50] F. Ismail, "Rediscovering the Role of Developing Countries in GATT Before the Doha Round" (2008) 1 *Law and Development Review* 49 at 58–59; L. Rajamani, *Differential Treatment in International Environmental Law* (Oxford: Oxford University Press, 2006).

[51] Gordon, note 49 at 145–150.

[52] Ibid; Gonzalez, note 6, p. 82.

8   *The North–South Divide in International Environmental Law*

natural resource base.[53] Much of the environmental degradation experienced by Southern countries has been caused by export-oriented production to satisfy Northern demand, rather than by local consumption.[54] Indeed, communities in the South have traditionally led more sustainable lives than the consumerist societies of the North, as discussed by Judge Weeramantry in his separate opinion in the *Case Concerning the Gabcíkovo-Nagymaros Project.*[55]

The Washington Consensus exacerbated the North–South divide by reinforcing the South's dependence on the export of raw materials rather than facilitating the development of more dynamic economic sectors.[56] The World Trade Organization agreements that succeeded the 1947 GATT nominally granted Southern countries special and differential treatment (such as additional time to comply with WTO obligations), but failed to dismantle the subsidies and import barriers of greatest concern to Southern nations (particularly Northern agricultural subsidies that enabled Northern exporters to undercut Southern farmers).[57] The WTO also restricted the ability of Southern countries to use tariffs and subsidies to strategically promote potentially dynamic industries; dismantled the import barriers that protected nascent Southern industries from more technologically advanced Northern competitors; and imposed onerous new obligations in the areas of intellectual property, services, and investment.[58] Scholars of economic history have recognized that the United States, Japan, Germany, the United Kingdom, South Korea, and Taiwan achieved economic prosperity through protectionism. By depriving Southern countries of the tools used by the global North and by certain middle-income Southern countries to diversify and industrialize their economies while enhancing the protection of investors and intellectual property, the international economic order institutionalizes Southern poverty.[59]

The primary beneficiaries of the Washington Consensus have been the powerful transnational corporations that dominate the global economy. The reluctance of

[53] Ponting, note 35, p. 223.

[54] W. E. Rees and L. Westra, "When Consumption does Violence: Can There Be Sustainability and Environmental Justice in A Resource-Limited World?", in J. Agyeman, R. D. Bullard, and B. Evans (eds.), *Just Sustainabilities: Development in an Unequal World* (Cambridge: MIT Press, 2003), pp. 99–124, at 105, 110.

[55] *Case Concerning the Gabcíkovo-Nagymaros Project* (Hungary v. Slovakia) [1997] ICJ Reports 228.

[56] Gordon, note 49 at 149–150.

[57] F. J. Garcia, "Beyond Special and Differential Treatment" (2004) 27 *Boston College International and Comparative Law Review* 291. See chapter 19, C. G. Gonzalez, "Food Justice: An Environmental Justice Critique of the Global Food System."

[58] Garcia, note 57 at 298; Y. S. Lee, *Reclaiming Development in the World Trading System* (Cambridge: Cambridge University Press, 2006), pp. 41–42.

[59] H. Chang, *Good Samaritans: The Myth of Free Trade and the Secret History of Capitalism* (New York: Bloomsbury Press, 2008); H. Chang, *Kicking Away the Ladder: Development Strategy in Historical Perspective* (London: Anthem Press, 2002); A. Amsden, *The Developing World's Journey through Heaven and Hell* (Cambridge: MIT Press, 2009); E. Reinert, *How Rich Countries Got Rich... and Why Poor Countries Stay Poor* (New York: Caroll and Graf, 2007).

states to regulate the extraterritorial activities of their corporations and the difficulty of holding parent companies liable for the actions of their subsidiaries have resulted in corporate impunity for human rights and environmental abuses in Southern countries.[60] While some attempt has been made over the years to make corporate actors more socially responsible, these attempts have resulted in soft law measures without any real sanctions. International investment law has enhanced corporate power by requiring host governments to compensate foreign investors when efforts to regulate in the public interest diminish the profitability of the investment.[61] Even where Southern victims can assert a claim for relief against Northern states or corporations, these victims are hesitant to resort to legal action for fear of reprisal and withholding of aid, thereby reinforcing the North's domination of the South.[62] In addition, as explained in this volume, a form of financing called "project finance" has exacerbated corporate impunity with regard to human rights and environmental harms caused by large-scale energy and infrastructure projects, by facilitating the externalization of social and environmental risks.[63]

In sum, the persistence of extreme poverty in the global South is attributable not to random misfortune, but to a global economic order that systematically benefits the wealthy and disenfranchises the poor. As philosopher Thomas Pogge candidly observes:

> Our new global economic order is so harsh on the global poor, then, because it is formed in negotiations where our representatives ruthlessly exploit their vastly superior bargaining power and expertise, as well as any weakness, ignorance, or corruptibility they may find in their counterpart negotiators, to tune each agreement for our greater benefit. In such negotiations, the affluent states will make reciprocal concessions to one another, but rarely to the weak. The cumulative result of many such negotiations and agreements is a grossly unfair global economic order under which the lion's share of the benefits of global economic growth flows to the most affluent states.[64]

4. INTERNATIONAL ENVIRONMENTAL LAW AND THE NORTH–SOUTH DIVIDE

North–South conflicts originating in the economic realm have profoundly shaped the evolution of international environmental law and policy. The global North

---

[60] Gonzalez, note 6, pp. 92–94.

[61] Ibid, pp. 94–95.

[62] See chapter 28, J. Razzaque, "Access to Remedies in Environmental Matters and the North–South Divide"; chapter 20, M. Burkett, "A Justice Paradox: Climate Change, Small Island Developing States, and the Absence of International Legal Remedy."

[63] See chapter 16, S. H. Baker, "Project Finance and Sustainable Development in the Global South."

[64] T. Pogge, *World Poverty and Human Rights* (Cambridge: Polity Press, 2008), p. 27.

10   *The North–South Divide in International Environmental Law*

industrialized and developed by exploiting the planet's natural resources without regard for the environmental consequences. Northern consumption patterns, which are increasingly emulated by Southern elites, have brought the planet's ecosystems to the brink of collapse and will constrain the development of options of present and future generations, particularly in the global South.[65] Indeed, some observers have argued that the North owes an ecological debt to the South for "resource plundering, unfair trade, environmental damage, and the free occupation of environmental space to deposit waste."[66]

As natural resources become increasingly scarce, Southern countries are concerned about harnessing them to promote social and economic development. Many Southern nations view Northern demands for environmental protection as hypocritical, given the North's enormous ecological footprint, and as a threat to Southern efforts to eradicate poverty and provide citizens with the basic necessities of life.[67]

The global North and the global South also have conflicting environmental priorities and concerns. While the North has historically prioritized global environmental problems (such as ozone depletion and protection of endangered species), the South has often emphasized environmental problems with more immediate impacts on vulnerable local populations, including the hazardous waste trade, desertification, food security, access to safe drinking water and sanitation, and indoor air pollution caused by lack of access to sustainable energy.[68]

As the South has pressed the North to shoulder primary responsibility for major environmental problems (such as climate change) in light of the North's disproportionate contribution to global environmental degradation,[69] the North has resisted responsibility for past wrongs, and has reluctantly accepted the principle of common but differentiated responsibility on the basis of the North's superior financial and technical resources rather than that of historic responsibility.[70] While the North has unilaterally imposed environmental requirements on Southern products in order to combat "eco-dumping," the South has perceived these requirements as disguised protectionism, and as arbitrary and inequitable given the North's voracious consumption of the planet's natural resources and unwillingness

---

[65] K. Mickelson, "Leading Toward a Level Playing Field, Repaying Ecological Debt, or Making Environmental Space: Three Stories About International Environmental Cooperation" (2005) 43 *Osgoode Hall Law Journal* 138 at 150–154. See chapter 3, R. Gordon, "Unsustainable Development."

[66] E. Paredis, G. Geominne, W. Vanhove, F. Maes, and J. Lambrecht, *The Concept of Ecological Debt: Its Meaning and Applicability in International Policy* (Ghent: Academia Press, 2007), p. 7.

[67] See chapter 3, R. Gordon, "Unsustainable Development."

[68] Gonzalez, note 4 at 1008–1009; Anand, note 4, p. 6.

[69] Anand, note 4, p. 5.

[70] Gonzalez, note 6, pp. 91–92. See also chapter 4, S. Atapattu, "The Significance of International Environmental Law Principles in Reinforcing or Dismantling the North-South Divide."

to provide Southern nations with the financial and technical resources necessary to comply with these environmental requirements.[71]

The North–South divide is further exemplified in the realms of trading toxic chemicals and waste. Due to increased scientific understanding of the risks posed by toxic chemicals, the North has at times prohibited the sale of certain chemicals within its territory, but has nevertheless permitted the export of these chemicals to countries in the South. The concern is the South's lack of capacity to make informed decisions about the safe handling and disposal of such chemicals, especially considering that sustainable management of chemicals can generate significant economic benefits.[72] Another related issue is the North's export of toxic waste to the South on the ground that such disposal is more "cost-effective." A prime example is the export of end-of-life ships containing toxic materials from the United States and the European Union to Asia for breaking and recycling.[73] Again, the North's export of such waste despite the South's limited capacity to manage it in an environmentally sound manner reinforces the historical divide, which has led to allegations of "toxic colonialism" by the global South.[74]

Of course, the North–South divide is an oversimplification, and this book explores the complexity and heterogeneity within the broad categories of *North* and *South*. Climate change provides an excellent example of alliances and tensions that transcend the traditional North–South binary. Facing the potential loss of territory, the Alliance of Small Island States (AOSIS) favors deep cuts in greenhouse gas emissions, while BASIC countries generally want Northern states to take the lead in climate change mitigation, adaptation, financing, and technology transfer. Low-lying countries such as Bangladesh have joined forces with the AOSIS; least developed countries and members of the African group have also intervened from time to time.[75] Concerned that deforestation will distract attention from the need to reduce emissions, Brazil and other countries of the Amazon basin have resisted efforts to regulate the Amazon rainforest under the climate change

---

[71] Gonzalez, note 4 at 1004–1009; chapter 14, S. Alam, "Trade and the Environment: Perspectives from the Global South."

[72] P. S. Chasek and D. L. Downie, *Global Environmental Politics* (Boulder: Westview Press, 2013), pp. 131–151.

[73] M. S. Karim, "Environmental Pollution from the Shipbreaking Industry: International Law and National Legal Response" (2010) 22 *Georgetown International Environmental Law Review* 185.

[74] See chapter 12, Z. Lipman, "Trade in Hazardous Waste."

[75] See chapter 10, R. Maguire and X. Jiang, "Emerging Powerful Southern Voices: Role of BASIC Nations in Shaping Climate Change Mitigation Commitments"; chapter 20, M. Burkett, "A Justice Paradox: Climate Change, Small Island Developing States, and the Absence of International Legal Remedy." Climate-vulnerable Southern countries, including Bangladesh, Nepal, Vietnam, Rwanda, and Ghana, have worked with small island nations to establish the Climate Vulnerable Forum – a group of nations seeking rapid and ambitious action on climate change. See Climate Vulnerable Forum, "CVF Declarations," www.thecvf. org (setting forth the declarations of the Climate Vulnerable Forum).

12 *The North–South Divide in International Environmental Law*

regime. However, recognizing that there could be significant financial support for forest conservation and management, the Alliance of Rainforest Nations is actively supporting the Reducing Emissions from Deforestation and Forest Degradation (REDD) mechanism.[76] Oil-exporting countries form yet another group, while the European Union seems to be increasingly isolated among Northern countries in its support for significant emission reductions. Deep divisions between the United States and the European Union have led to loose coalitions of non-EU Northern countries, such as the JUSCANZ group (Japan, United States, Canada, Australia, and New Zealand).[77] These loose alliances and divisions within the global North and the global South complicate the treaty-negotiating process and, ultimately, international law-making.

5. THEORETICAL PERSPECTIVES AND APPROACHES

This volume explores the past, present, and future of international environmental law through a different lens – that of the priorities and concerns of the global South. Despite the pervasive North–South conflicts in international environmental law, much of the scholarly literature published in the global North fails to fully appreciate and address the tensions between Northern environmental priorities and Southern needs and aspirations. While some texts refer to these tensions, particularly in relation to climate change negotiations, they rarely place it in historic context. This book seeks to fill the gap in the existing literature and inform the research agenda by discussing the history of the North–South divide and its contemporary manifestations in a variety of areas of international environmental law and policy. Without an understanding of North–South tensions in historical context, it is impossible to understand the current state of international environmental law, let alone address the tensions. The contributors to this volume are scholars from the global North and the global South who approach the topic from a variety of theoretical and practical perspectives and approaches.

Although the individual chapters reflect the heterogeneous backgrounds and perspectives of the contributors, the volume as a whole owes an intellectual debt to the scholarship of the Third World Approaches to International Law (TWAIL) movement.[78] While this movement is by no means monolithic, TWAIL scholarship largely examines the ways in which the colonial legacy underpins contemporary international law.[79] TWAIL scholars explain how international law was used to

[76] See D. Hunter, J. Salzman, and D. Zaelke, *International Environmental Law and Policy*, 4th ed. (New York: Foundation Press, 2011), p. 675; S. Oberthur and H. E. Ott, *The Kyoto Protocol: International Climate Policy for the 21st Century* (Berlin: Springer, 1999), pp. 13–32.

[77] Oberthur and Ott, note 76, pp. 13–32.

[78] M. Mutua, "What is TWAIL?", American Society of International Law, Proceedings of the 94th Annual Meeting (5–8 April 2000), pp. 31–38.

[79] O. C. Okafor, "Newness, Imperialism, and International Legal Reform in our Time: a TWAIL Perspective" (2005) 34 *Osgoode Hall Law Journal* 171 at 176.

justify the conquest of nature and of non-European peoples in the name of "civilization" and "development," and expose and critique the contemporary uses of international law to legitimate Northern hegemony.[80] TWAIL's goal is to make real "the promise of international law to transform itself into a system based, not on power, but justice."[81] This volume draws upon TWAIL scholarship but seeks to go further by exploring both the emancipatory and hegemonic role of international law and discourse in the context of a wide range of North–South environmental disputes.

This volume is also influenced by the work of scholars who view the North–South divide in international environmental law through the framework of environmental justice.[82] The environmental justice movement arose in the United States as a grassroots response to the disparate exposure to environmental hazards of low-income communities and communities of color.[83] Environmental justice has since been adopted as the language of resistance by a variety of local and transnational environmental movements in both the North and the South – including movements for climate justice, water justice, food justice, and energy justice.[84]

The environmental justice framework provides a compelling moral narrative with justice at its core as an antidote to the technocratic, ahistorical approach that dominates much of mainstream environmental discourse. The objective is to reconceptualize environmental problems as manifestations of social, economic, and environmental injustice between and within nations and to place them in historical context rather than treating them as technical problems to be overcome by scientific innovation or more effective planning.[85] As Part IV of the volume demonstrates, many of the contributors to this volume draw explicitly or implicitly on the concept of environmental justice to frame their discussion of North–South environmental inequities as well as grassroots environmental struggles.[86]

---

[80] A. Anghie, *Imperialism, Sovereignty and the Making of International Law* (Cambridge: Cambridge University Press, 2005).

[81] A. Anghie, "What Is TWAIL: Comment," American Society of International Law, Proceedings of the 94th Annual Meeting 39–40 (5–8 April 2000), p. 40.

[82] Gonzalez, note 6, pp. 77–97; J. Ebbesson and P. Okowa (eds.), *Environmental Law and Justice in Context* (Cambridge: Cambridge University Press, 2009); Anand, note 4.

[83] Gonzalez, note 6, pp. 79–80.

[84] J. Martinez-Alier, I. Angulelovski, P. Bond, D. Del Bene, F. Demaria, J. Gerber, L. Greyl, W. Haas, H. Healy, V. Marin-Burgos, G. Ojo, M. Porto, L. Rijnhout, B. Rodriguez-Labajos, J. Spangeberg, R. Warlenius, and I. Yanez, "Between Activism and Science: Grassroots Concepts for Sustainability Coined by Environmental Justice Organizations" (2014) 21 *Journal of Political Ecology* 19 at 27–42.

[85] Ibid at 84.

[86] See chapter 19, C. G. Gonzalez, "Food Justice: An Environmental Justice Critique of the Global Food System"; chapter 20, M. Burkett, "A Justice Paradox: Climate Change, Small Island Developing States, and the Absence of International Legal Remedy"; chapter 25, L. Guruswamy, "The Contours of Energy Justice"; chapter 22, J. Dugard and E. Koek, "Water Wars: Anti-Privatization Struggles in the Global South"; chapter 21, E. A. Kronk Warner, "South of South: Examining the International Climate Regime from an Indigenous

14   *The North–South Divide in International Environmental Law*

The concept of environmental justice is grounded in international human rights law, but has clear connections to several international environmental law principles based on notions of equity and justice, including common but differentiated responsibility (CBDR), inter- and intragenerational equity, and sustainable development.[87] According to Hunter, Salzman, and Zaelke, the CBDR principle – which continues to create intense North–South debate – highlights the need for coordinated action by both the North and the South, with each nation's responsibility adjusted according to the level of capacity and contribution to global environmental problems.[88] Furthermore, they point out that while the principle remains a cornerstone of international environmental law and policy, it continues to be a point of debate for both the North and South.[89] Indeed, as Atapattu points out in her chapter in this volume, the debates surrounding the adoption of this principle proved explosive, as the United States in particular sought to cast this principle as a reflection of the North's "superior" technical and financial capacity rather than its duty to provide redress for past harm, thereby reinforcing colonial patterns of domination.[90]

Another common thread that runs through the volume is the notion of sustainable development, which many contributors use as an overarching framework to situate their analysis of various environmental issues identified for in-depth discussion. The Johannesburg Declaration emphasized that sustainable development comprises three pillars: economic development, social development, and environmental protection.[91] Southern countries have utilized the three pillars of sustainable development to demand economic and social justice for their citizens in addition to environmental protection. The adoption of the Millennium Development Goals and the focus on sustainable development since its explicit emergence in *Our Common Future* emphasize the need for a collective approach that involves all stakeholders, including both the North and South. International environmental law relies upon consensus, and this volume highlights the South's historic and potential contribution to its development. However, further integration of the South and of non-elite stakeholders, particularly vulnerable communities, is needed, and this volume illustrates the positive practices that can be implemented within the international environmental law regime to incorporate Southern perspectives.

Perspective"; chapter 24, D. Bonilla Maldonado, "International Law, Cultural Diversity, and the Environment: The Case of the General Forestry Law in Colombia"; chapter 18, S. Seck, "Transnational Corporations and Extractive Industries."

[87] Gonzalez, note 6, pp. 85–87, 90–92.

[88] Hunter et al., note 76, p 464.

[89] Ibid, p. 465.

[90] See chapter 4, S. Atapattu, "The Significance of International Environmental Law Principles in Reinforcing or Dismantling the North–South Divide."

[91] *Johannesburg Declaration on Sustainable Development: Report of the World Summit on Sustainable Development*, Johannesburg, 4 September 2002, UN Doc. A/CONF. 199/20, Resolution 1, Annex, pp. 1–5.

6. OVERVIEW OF THIS VOLUME

The volume proceeds in five parts: Part I addresses the history of the North–South divide and global environmental governance; Part II discusses selected environmental law examples; Part III examines trade, investment, and sustainable development; Part IV addresses environmental justice and vulnerable groups; and finally, Part V is devoted to a discussion of options and challenges.

6.1 History of the North–South Divide and Global Environmental Governance

Part I lays the groundwork for the entire volume by exploring the theory and history of the North–South divide in international law, including its colonial underpinnings. It then undertakes a critical examination of the concept of sustainable development, followed by a discussion of the role of international environmental law principles in reinforcing or dismantling the North–South divide. One of the themes explored in the volume is the South's contribution to the development of international law generally, and international environmental law in particular.

Part I also examines global environmental governance (including its institutional framework) from a Southern perspective. The dominance of the North in global environmental governance can negatively impact the contributions of the South. It follows that reform will be required to enhance the South's participation in the development and implementation of international environmental law. Capacity-building, for example, is essential because Southern countries often lack the technical expertise and the resources to participate effectively in global environmental negotiations, such as the highly technical negotiations regarding, for example, climate change, biodiversity, and the hazardous waste trade.

6.2 Selected International Environmental Law Examples

While the North–South divide is apparent in all areas of international environmental law, Part II of this volume examines the divide in practice (and the ways in which it might be overcome) by using selected international environmental law issues as examples. Perhaps the most pressing environmental issue facing the globe today is climate change (although localized problems in the South, such as poverty and access to water, energy, and food, also demand immediate attention). Four chapters of this volume are devoted to climate change, while several other chapters refer explicitly to it.[92] Climate change is an issue that both the North and South

---

[92] See chapter 21, E. A. Kronk Warner, "South of South: Examining the International Climate Regime from an Indigenous Perspective"; chapter 20, M. Burkett, "A Justice Paradox: Climate Change, Small Island Developing States, and the Absence of International Legal Remedy"; chapter 10, R. Maguire and X. Jiang, "Emerging Powerful Southern Voices: Role of BASIC

16 *The North–South Divide in International Environmental Law*

have a vested interest in addressing, and the recent lack of progress at the global level is indicative of continued division between the goals of the North and of the South. For example, the Rio+20 report acknowledges the importance of addressing climate change (for its own sake and for the benefits it may have in addressing sustainable development), and also highlights the vulnerability of the South, particularly small island developing states.[93] Given the urgency of the issue, the report concludes that the current actions of the states are inadequate. As Hunter et al. note, "[a]t times, divisions between blocs of countries over the negotiations of the climate change regime have been as intense as any issues outside war and national security."[94] The international community will have to come up with a solution to the plight of small island states when they are no longer able to sustain their populations due to sea-level rise and the consequent inundation of their land. Climate policy may converge with migration policy and national security policy as climate refugees from small island nations and other vulnerable locations are compelled to migrate across national borders to protect their lives and livelihoods.[95]

6.3 *Trade, Investment, and Sustainable Development*

A unique feature of the volume is its discussion of international economic law and its relationship to specific environmental issues from a North–South perspective. Part III of the volume contains chapters on trade,[96] investment,[97] project finance,[98] sovereign wealth funds,[99] and extractive industries,[100] which highlight several issues: (a) the relationship between international economic law and sustainable development; (b) the role of Northern states in perpetuating the North–South divide through international trade, finance, and investment law; (c) the impunity of corporate actors with regard to human rights and environmental violations; (d) the advantages and drawbacks of social responsibility initiatives as a means of enhancing the human rights and environmental performance of transnational corporations,

Nations in Shaping Climate Change Mitigation Commitments"; chapter 23, P. Govind and R. R. M. Verchik, "Natural Disaster and Climate Change."

[93] UN, note 2.

[94] Hunter et al., note 76, p. 674.

[95] M. Burkett, "Climate Refugees", in S. Alam, M. J. H Bhuiyan, T. M. R. Chowdhury, and E. J. Techera (eds.), *Routledge Handbook of International Environmental Law* (New York: Routledge, 2013), pp. 717–729.

[96] See chapter 14, S. Alam, "Trade and the Environment: Perspectives from the Global South."

[97] See chapter 15, S. Puvimanasinghe, "From a Divided Heritage to a Common Future? International Investment Law, Human Rights and Sustainable Development."

[98] See chapter 16, S. H. Baker, "Project Finance and Sustainable Development in the Global South."

[99] See chapter 17, B. J. Richardson, "International Environmental Law and Sovereign Wealth Funds."

[100] See chapter 18, S. Seck, "Transnational Corporations and Extractive Industries."

sovereign wealth funds, and other lenders and investors; and (e) conflicts among the Northern "green" agenda, Southern demands for social and economic development, and the aspirations of historically marginalized communities.

6.4 *Environmental Justice and Vulnerable Groups*

As noted earlier in this chapter, a significant number of contributors to this volume use environmental justice as a normative framework. Part IV of the volume is devoted to a discussion of vulnerable groups (and states) through the lens of environmental justice. Thus, indigenous peoples, small island states, those affected by inequitable access to food, energy, and water, and those disproportionately affected by natural disasters related to climate change are the subject of Part IV. One of the lessons of Part IV and of other chapters in this volume is that international environmental law has been shaped not just by states and international institutions, but also by the organized resistance of indigenous peoples, vulnerable states, and transnational social movements.[101] These chapters also emphasize the legal and moral obligations of all states, both affluent and poor, to respect, protect, and fulfill the human rights of marginalized populations within and beyond their own borders.[102]

6.5 *Challenges and Options*

Part V discusses challenges that transcend many of the issues identified in this book, including the enforcement of international environmental obligations, particularly given the South's limited capacity for environmental reporting and review. Inadequate enforcement is a significant obstacle to the success of international environmental law, and the problem could be addressed, at least in part, through the greater involvement of the South in the development of environmental practices, policies, and mechanisms. This section also discusses participation in environmental governance by the communities most directly impacted by environmental degradation to

---

[101] See, e.g., chapter 24, D. Bonilla Maldonado, "International Law, Cultural Diversity, and the Environment: The Case of the General Forestry Law in Colombia"; chapter 21, E. A. Kronk Warner, "South of South: Examining the International Climate Regime from an Indigenous Perspective"; chapter 22, J. Dugard and E. Koek, "Water Wars: Anti-Privatization Struggles in the Global South"; chapter 20, M. Burkett, "A Justice Paradox: Climate Change, Small Island Developing States, and the Absence of International Legal Remedy"; chapter 19, C. G. Gonzalez, "Food Justice: An Environmental Justice Critique of the Global Food System"; chapter 18, S. Seck, "Transnational Corporations and Extractive Industries."

[102] See e.g. chapter 25, L. Guruswamy, "The Contours of Energy Justice"; chapter 19, C. G. Gonzalez, "Food Justice: An Environmental Justice Critique of the Global Food System"; chapter 21, E. A. Kronk Warner, "South of South: Examining the International Climate Regime from an Indigenous Perspective"; chapter 20, M. Burkett, "A Justice Paradox: Climate Change, Small Island Developing States, and the Absence of International Legal Remedy"; chapter 18, S. Seck, "Transnational Corporations and Extractive Industries."

18   *The North–South Divide in International Environmental Law*

ensure that the environmental discourse is infused with the needs and concerns of the most vulnerable, rather than being co-opted by elites.[103] Finally, the section situates international environmental law within the broader corpus of international law (including international economic law and international human rights law) and discusses the need to harmonize and integrate these areas of law from a Southern perspective.

One way of overcoming the North–South divide is to promote South–South cooperation.[104] As one of the chapters in Part V explains, South–South cooperation emerged when the decolonization process ended. Despite the many divisions within the South, Southern countries often negotiate with the North as a bloc to enhance their ability to secure concessions. The adoption of the CBDR principle amid opposition from the North is a good example.

Part V also discusses remedies available under international law from a North–South perspective[105] and concludes that while many remedies are ostensibly available to victims from the South (both individuals and states), in practice they are reluctant to avail themselves of these remedies due to fear of reprisals from the North, including the withholding of development aid. By way of illustration, when Tuvalu, a small island state in the Pacific which is facing the prospect of losing its territory due to rising seas, threatened to file legal action against the United States for its contribution to climate change, the United States threatened to withhold development assistance to Tuvalu. These power imbalances and the threat of sanctions prevent Southern states from seeking remedies from powerful Northern states, a dynamic reminiscent of past colonial patterns of domination.

The final chapter compares sustainable development with the emerging discourse on the green economy.[106] It cautions against unraveling the gains made with regard to sustainable development by ignoring the three pillars of sustainable development and the principle of integration and taking us back to the old development paradigm with its profligate consumerism, which has proven to be totally unsustainable.

7. AREAS FOR FURTHER RESEARCH

We acknowledge that the issues we have chosen for analysis in this volume represent only the tip of the iceberg and that there are many more issues that

---

[103] See chapter 27, L. De Silva, "Public Participation in International Negotiation and Compliance."

[104] See chapter 26, K.L. Koh and N. Robinson, "South–South Cooperation: Foundations for Sustainable Development."

[105] See chapter 28, J. Razzaque, "Access to Remedies in Environmental Matters and the North–South Divide."

[106] See chapter 29, S. Alam and J. Razzaque, "Sustainable Development versus Green Economy: The Way Forward?"

require analysis from a North–South perspective. These include migration associated with environmental degradation, particularly climate change, biosafety, oceans and marine resources, hazardous chemicals, shipbreaking, electronic waste, and projects under the REDD mechanism.

In addition, the following issues arise in many of the chapters in the volume and are worth highlighting. These issues require a major reorienting of the global economic system if we are serious about addressing the disparities in the global community: (a) regulation of transnational corporations; (b) restructuring of international economic law and its interface with sustainable development; (c) the need to reconceptualize development; (d) the danger that the BASIC countries will reproduce the patterns of unsustainable development and patterns of economic domination that created the North–South divide; and (e) the need to ensure environmental justice and the protection of human rights, particularly of the most vulnerable, including ensuring gender equality. While sustainable development was advanced as an alternative paradigm to the existing "development at any cost" trajectory, many states have paid only lip service to sustainability. Exceeding ecological limits is ultimately catastrophic for all, especially the most vulnerable. We can learn from communities that have managed to live within ecological limits. One of the major obstacles to overcoming the problems discussed in the book is that the South often seeks to emulate the Northern example of what constitutes a decent standard of living, despite the fact that the planet cannot sustain that kind of "development" within its ecological limits.

Finally, we would like to offer some suggestions as to how this volume might be used. We had multiple constituencies in mind when we embarked upon this project and our vision was to ensure that this book would be useful to all these constituencies, both in the North and in the South. This volume is offered as a supplement to the existing scholarly literature on international environmental law, much of which does an excellent job of articulating the issues. However, we felt that a crucial part of the story was missing, and we have tried in this volume to supply the missing pieces – offering a North–South perspective grounded in the colonial encounter with environmental justice and sustainable development as overarching frameworks. Thus, we hope that environmental law scholars, policy-makers, treaty negotiators, TWAIL scholars, and scholars of international law and international relations across the world – whether they are based in the North or the South – will use this volume in their teaching, research activities, policy work, and treaty negotiations.

We have been fortunate to have a wide group of scholars and practitioners contributing to this volume. While the majority of contributors are from academia, we have included chapters from practitioners affiliated with international organizations, highly respected civil society organizations, and think tanks. We strongly believe that the diverse group of contributors enriches our volume by providing multiple viewpoints and approaches to the issues under discussion. Furthermore, we strove hard to include as many contributors from the global South as possible and to ensure that the contributors from the global North appreciated the central theme of the book. Without an understanding of the North–South tensions that underscore many of the current environmental issues, it is often difficult to appreciate the full extent of the environmental challenges facing the global community today. We hope that this publication will contribute to the existing literature on international environmental law, providing a different lens through which to understand its evolution, the compromises, the political debates, the limitations and nuances, and the present state of the law.

We do not pretend that the path ahead of us is easy. The problems we face are large and can often seem insurmountable. In order to solve them, we need all voices at the table and all hands on deck. These problems are urgent. The clock is ticking and the landscape is more complicated than ever. However, legal and policy frameworks that do not adequately reflect the interests of the global South have no chance of succeeding. An ecologically sustainable planet is impossible in a world plagued with significant and growing inequalities.

PART I

History of the North–South Divide and Global Environmental Governance

2

History of the North–South Divide in International Law: Colonial Discourses, Sovereignty, and Self-Determination

M. Rafiqul Islam

1. INTRODUCTION

International law is a product of an evolutionary process that has been in effect since the dawn of history. An examination of its historic origin, subsequent development, and contemporary manifestation reveals the decisive influence of asymmetric power and economic inequality in shaping its normative standards and direction. It is this quest for power and economic clout that has resulted in conflicts of competing interests dubbed variously over history as "civilized" and "primitive," "west" and "east," "developed" and "developing," and "clash of civilizations." This division is currently called the North–South divide, in reference to geostrategic and economic power imbalances, including the digital divide in the context of technology. The "North" is a group of developed, industrialized, and technologically advanced states, often known as the First World, and the "South" represents developing, least developed, and technologically impoverished states, also called the Third World. International relations are littered with conflicts of interest between these two groups. The root of this North–South divide lies in the very creation, nature, features, and orientation of international law from its antiquity to the present context.

This chapter is an historic account of the genesis, conceptual justification, and metamorphosis of the North–South divide in a number of areas of international law, including international environmental law. It highlights certain historic international events and features that have contributed to the skewing of international law toward the North. Although the North–South divide confronts increasing challenges from emerging new powers and players (the media and NGOs) calling for the reconfiguration of the balance of power and distributive justice to bridge the divide, its dominant role continues unabated in the twenty-first century.

2. INTERNATIONAL LAW JUSTIFYING COLONIALISM: SEEDS OF THE NORTH–SOUTH DIVIDE

International law dates back prior to the 1648 Treaty of Westphalia,[1] when the law of nations required no particular form of societal/political organization to become an international entity and actor. The constituting elements of international law in antiquity were communities, tribes, peoples, and individuals, which enjoyed sovereignty, rights, duties, and international legal personality. Their intersocietal diplomatic relations shaped classical international law.[2]

Ever since the Spanish discovery and conquest of the Americas in the fifteenth century, a number of international legal concepts and principles have been devised by European conquerors and invaders to justify their conquests and subsequent colonization. This was possible because these powers were dominant enough to regulate the shaping of international law in their favor. They used military conquest to justify the establishment of European governing authority without Native Americans' consent. The first international law of colonialism was the doctrine of discovery that legitimized European Christian powers' exploration, claims, and occupation of non-Christian native lands and properties that they "discovered" beyond Europe. The doctrine regarded European civilization, religions, race, and ethnicity as superior to that of non-European and non-Christian people and used European laws to extinguish native ownership and title to lands. When a discovered land was found unoccupied, or even occupied but not in accordance with European laws, the discovered land was considered *terra nullius* (empty or unoccupied) and subject to discovery claims. Thus, the right of non-Christian natives to land, sovereignty, and self-determination was made subservient to that of European Christians, who thought they were ordained by God to play a paternalistic and guardian role in the civilization, education, and conversion to Christianity of "primitive" native people.[3]

European juristic opinions afforded intellectual support. Vitoria, a Spanish canonist and jurist, enunciated the doctrine of guardianship to explain the nature of relationship between indigenous peoples and Spain following the Spanish conquest

---

[1] Concluded on October 24, 1648, ending two prolonged European wars; D. Croxton, *Westphalia: The Last Christian Peace* (New York: Palgrave Macmillan, 2013); D. Croxton, "The Peace of Westphalia of 1648 and the Origins of Sovereignty" (1999) 21 *International History Review* 569; L. Gross, "The Peace of Westphalia, 1648–1948" (1948) 42 *American Journal of International Law* 20.

[2] M. Alfonso Martinez, Special Rapporteur, *Study on Treaties, Agreements and Other Constrictive Arrangements Between States and Indigenous Populations*, 25 August 1992, E/CN.4/Sub.2/1992/32, chapter 3.

[3] A. Anghie, *Imperialism, Sovereignty, and the Making of International Law* (Cambridge: Cambridge University Press, 2005), pp. 3–31; J. Pitts, "Political Theory of Empire and Imperialism" (2010) 13 *Annual Review of Political Science* 211; A. Serra, "The Discovery of the New World and International Law" (1971) 3 *University of Toledo Law Review* 308; R. Miller et al., *Discovering Indigenous Lands: The Doctrine of Discovery in the English Colonies* (East Lansing: Michigan State University Press, 2010).

of the New World. He relied on the dynamics of diversity, observed indigenous peoples fell short of European norms and standards, and declared that the relationship was that of a ward to a guardian.[4] Vattel reinforced the pre-eminence of Eurocentric positivism in international law by maintaining that only entities with centralized, hierarchical forms of governance, and control over territory, could be regarded as states.[5] Therefore indigenous societal entities lacked the attributes of states in the European sense. But critics have asserted that "indigenous governance in the Americas was far more refined than that evidenced across the Atlantic [and] it is often overlooked that the European societies that first encountered indigenous nations were themselves only in the early stages of civilization in the contemporary sense."[6]

The colonial international law doctrines were motivated partly by the need and greed of European settlers for local land and resources, and partly by the colonial arrogance of civilizing non-European people through European universal civilization. Economic greed established automatic legal claims over native lands, assets, and properties, including the sole pre-emption right to buy lands, which could not be sold to anyone except discovering Europeans. This rule diminished indigenous property value to the great economic benefit of European colonists, who also dominated indigenous diplomatic and political activities. Indigenous treaty-making authority was taken away by new European rules that deprived indigenous communities of their sources of income from international trade and commerce.[7]

The colonial doctrines justified the domination and subordination of indigenous political entities and proposed certain duties on invaders toward improving the moral and material conditions of the invaded. The judiciary failed to identify any legally enforceable indigenous rights emanating from these doctrines. European legislative and judicial actions, as well as international adjudication and arbitration, prevented any international juridical status being accorded to indigenous communities.[8] The autonomous status and rights of these self-defined and self-controlled distinct communities, with social cohesion and a passionate desire for

---

[4] J. Scott, *The Spanish Origin of International Law* (Oxford: Clarendon Press, 1928).

[5] G. Morris, "In Support of the Right of Self-Determination for Indigenous Peoples Under International Law" (1986) 29 *German Yearbook of International Law* 277; D. Sanders, "The Re-Emergence of Indigenous Questions in International Law" (1983) *Canadian Human Rights Yearbook* 3.

[6] R. Robbins, "Self-Determination and Subordination: The Past, Present, and Future of American Indian Governance," in M. James (ed.), *The State of Native America – Genocide, Colonization, and Resistance* (Boston: South End Press, 1992), p. 87; see also H. Berman, "Perspectives on American Indian Sovereignty and International Law, 1600 to 1776," in O. Lyons and J. Mohawk (eds.), *Exiled in the Land of the Free: Democracy, Indian Nations and the U.S. Constitution* (Santa Fe: Clear Light Publishers, 1992), p. 130.

[7] E. Kades, "The Dark Side of Efficiency: Johnson v M'Intosh and the Expropriation of American Indian Lands" (2000) 148 *University of Pennsylvania Law Review* 1078 at 1110.

[8] R. Barsh, "Indigenous Peoples and Right to Self-Determination in International Law," in B. Hocking (ed.), *International Law and Aboriginal Human Rights* (Sydney: Law Book Co, 1988), pp. 79, 98; Morris, note 5, p. 294.

survival, was interrupted by alien invasion and dispossession. The international law of colonialism thus served as an instrument to spread and universalize European norms, economic interests, and political domination, the vestiges of which still continue unabated "today to restrict the human, property, and sovereign rights of Indigenous Nations and peoples by the settlers in Australia, Brazil, Canada, Chile, New Zealand and the US."[9]

Excessive Eurocentrism in the law of nations virtually universalized the European norms and standards. The influence of the Westphalia Treaty provided a new framework of European state-centric order in which the intellectual basis of international law drifted apart from natural law and morality toward positivism and national self-interest, within a single value-laden Eurocentric identity. It devised a number of positivist principles of absolute sovereignty, consent, and recognition of the state to control the claim of new statehood and deny international legal status to any other entities.[10] This European monocultural bias of international law in the plural world composed of diverse stakeholders lies at the root of discrimination and division between the North and South today.

The Congress of Vienna (1815) put in place a new international order based on the European balance of power. International law became exclusively Eurocentric and sought to preserve the values and civilization of European and Christian states. Colonization and the global trading system worked to disseminate, expand, and internationalize European values and law throughout the rest of the world, with any resistance being suppressed by force.[11] The proliferation of treaties between European and non-European states typically endowed the former with territorial gains, diplomatic relations, and new trading opportunities. In return, non-European states received entry into the international system, which was conditional upon the consent of, and on terms specified by, the European powers and acquiescence to the thoroughly Eurocentric character of international law.[12]

---

[9] R. Miller, "The International Law of Colonialism: A Comparative Analysis" (2011) 15 *Lewis and Clark Law Review* 847. The judgment of *Delgamuuk et al v Queen* in 1990 by the British Columbian Supreme Court (Canada) shows these deeply rooted western views today, as McEachern CJ held: "[t]he plaintiff's ancestors had no written language, no horses or wheeled vehicles, slavery and starvation was not uncommon [...] and there is no doubt, to quote Hobbs that aboriginal life in the territory was, at best, nasty, brutish and short," Smithers Registry, No. 0843, p. 13, quoted from Martinez, note 2, p. 22, para. 130.

[10] A. Watson, *The Evolution of International Society: A Comparative Historical Analysis* (New York: Routledge, 1992), pp. 192–193; H. McNeill, 'Contemporary Practice of Public International Law: An Overview,' in E. Schaffer and R. Snyder (eds.), *Contemporary Practice of Public International Law* (New York: Oceana, 1997), p. 1.

[11] For example, Great Britain waged the opium war in 1842 to secure Chinese markets after facing resistance to its expansionist policies and secured Hong Kong and other Chinese islands to establish captive colonial markets pursuant to an unequal treaty under which Great Britain had no obligation to return these territories to China: The Treaty of Peace, Friendship and Commerce (Nanking Treaty) between Great Britain and China, August 29, 1842.

[12] The European empire expanded in North and South America and Turkey became the first non-Christian state by the mid-nineteenth century: H. Bull and A. Watson (eds.), *The*

Until the end of the nineteenth century, the age of discovery necessitated the evolution of rules governing the acquisition of territory and resources, such as *terra nullius*, which was used in international law to describe indigenous land in order to dispossess indigenous ownership and sovereignty through the occupation and acquisition of European state sovereignty.[13] International law explicitly used racial and cultural criteria to determine who would be allowed into the community of states and reflected the hegemony of Europe. The character of statehood advanced by Hugo Grotius in the seventeenth century and recognized by European states was based on two conditions: that the new state entity was European and Christian. Limited non-European entities were recognized as states in the eighteenth and nineteenth centuries, provided they were Christian (Haiti in 1804 and Liberia in 1847). Turkey was the first non-Christian state recognized, in 1856.[14] Absolute sovereignty with unlimited prerogatives eventually turned the positivistic political structure into anarchic, self-serving pursuit of racial supremacy, national interests, and militarized security ventures.[15]

Conceptually, international law became parochial, pragmatic, and permissive, allowing European states to bend the law to their advantage. For example, the principle of sovereign equality of states helped powerful European states to obscure the inherent structural inequality, hierarchical influence, and power realities in gaining undue advantage in interstate negotiations and relations. The international law of colonialism was neither timeless nor universal, but created and imposed by the prevailing European balance of power that dominated international law since the fifteenth century and flourished through the 1648 Westphalia Treaty in the seventeenth and eighteenth centuries. The domination of Eurocentric international law received a further boost from the Congress of Vienna, which lasted for almost a century (1815–1919) until the First World War. Through these historical developments, Eurocentric ideals, morals, and standards cascaded in every sphere of the normative character of international law that lies at the root of the North–South polarization of the world.

Expansion of International Society (Oxford: Clarendon Press, 1992); O. Osternd, "The Narrow Gate: Entry into the Club of Sovereign States" (1997) 23 *Review of International Studies* 168.

[13] British settlers used *terra nullius* in Australia, which was overturned by the High Court of Australia in *Mabo v Queensland* (No. 2) (1992) 175 CLR 42; the International Court of Justice (hereinafter the ICJ) rejected the Spanish claim of *terra nullius* over Western Sahara in *Western Sahara Opinion* (1975) ICJ Reports 12.

[14] H. Grotius, *De Jure Et Gentium Libri Octo*, Ch 1, s XIV, translated by F. Kelsey, *Classics of International Law Series*, vol. 12 (New York: Oxford University Press, 1925), p. 1646; N. Wallace-Bruce, *Claims to Statehood in International Law* (New York: Carlton Press, 1994), p. 24.

[15] D. Philpott, "A Brief History of International Sovereignty" (1955) 48 *American Journal of International Law* 353; L. Wildhaber, "Sovereignty and International Law," in R. Macdonald and D. Johnston (eds.), *The Structure and Process of International Law* (The Hague: Martinus Nijhoff, 1983), p. 438; S. Dubow, "Ethnic Euphemisms and Racial Echoes" (1994) 20 *Journal of South African Studies* 355.

3. INTERNATIONAL INSTITUTIONAL LAW OF COLONIALISM: EMBELLISHER OF THE NORTH–SOUTH DIVIDE

The evolution of international law in the interwar and postwar periods continued to be a Eurocentric enterprise, affording legal rationales for the continuation of colonialism, universality of European norms, and control over natural resources to benefit from non-Europeans. Two relevant developments in this period were the mandate system of the League of Nations (hereinafter the LN) and the trusteeship system of the United Nations (hereinafter the UN).

The mandate system: The mandate system was created to govern the territories of the defeated German and Ottoman Empires in the 1920s. It classified these territories as "backward" and mandated them to the winning "advanced" powers for governance with a view to promoting their self-rule. The system was hailed a "sacred trust of civilization," which effectively institutionalized the exclusion and economic exploitation of the "uncivilized." It took the international legitimacy and the influence of European colonialism to their apex, particularly by legitimizing British and French mandates in Africa and the Middle East. The LN never took any initiatives to end these colonial empires, though mandated territories were accorded international status with minimum supervision.[16]

The trusteeship system: The postwar international law and the UN Charter also justified colonialism by way of establishing a *trusteeship system* to supervise the former possessions of the defeated Axis Powers in the 1940s to 1950s. It regarded these territories and their people as non-self-governing and placed them under the governance of some western metropolitan powers under trusteeship agreements (Charter of the United Nations, Chapters 11, 12, and 13).[17] It created a superior–subordinate relationship between a dominant western power and a dependent non-western people separate from and subordinate to the ruling power. Despite the evil of domination and exploitation inherent in this relationship, trusteeship was praised as "a civilizing mission" to remove the political, economic, and social primitiveness of colonial people – a preparatory ground for their full self-rule, free political institutions, and well-being.[18] That perception and purpose soon became frustration when trusteeship was transformed into an institution of alien political subjugation, economic exploitation, social discrimination, and cultural imperialism. The international community witnessed flagrant abuses of trusteeship and

---

[16] A. Anghie, "Colonialism and the Birth of International Institutions: Sovereignty, Economy and the Mandate System of the League of Nations" (2001) 34 *New York University Journal of International Law and Politics* 513; N. Matz, "Civilization and the Mandate System under the League of Nations as Origin of Trusteeship" (2005) 9 *Max Planck Yearbook of United Nations Law* 47.

[17] *Charter of the United Nations,* San Francisco, 26 June 1945, in force 24 October 1945, (1945) ATS 1 / 59 Stat. 1031; TS 993; 3 Bevans 1153 (hereinafter the UN Charter).

[18] J. Engers, "From Sacred Trust to Self-Determination" (1977) 24 *Netherlands International Law Review* 85.

rampant utilization of colonial resources for the benefit of metropolitan powers. South Africa's profound human rights abuses of its Namibian (South West Africa) trust territory and Australia's continuous exploitation of Nauruan phosphate to produce cheap fertilizer for Australian agriculture when Nauru was under the former's trusteeship administration have been well documented in two ICJ cases.[19]

The mandate and trusteeship systems palpably prevented the political independence, economic emancipation, and sociocultural development of colonial people, which led to a strong sense of antipathy toward colonialism and a surge of nationalistic feeling. Nonetheless, the international status of these territories in the LN Covenant and UN Charter and their institutional supervisory role were the beginning of an end to European colonialism. The monopoly of sovereign states as the sole subjects and persons in international law ended following the emergence of the LN and UN, which became international legal subjects and persons in their own right. While the effect of the international status of mandated territories on their colonial powers was extremely limited, the role of the UN Trusteeship Council contributed to the internationalization of the marginalized plight of colonial people, which triggered a strong decolonization sentiment throughout the world in the 1950s to challenge the legitimacy of imperialism as a doctrine of international law.[20]

Gross violations of human rights and the common suffering of colonial people at the hands of their colonial powers intruded upon the world's conscience to reassess the validity of international law of colonialism. When the international community fully realized that colonialism was an institution in which the domination of colonial powers over colonial people could not be eradicated, only then did the UN start to explore strategies to abolish colonialism in all forms and manifestations. European colonists attempted – in vain – to resist decolonization in a bid to protect their interests in colonial possessions. Finally, colonialism was stripped of its legitimacy by the UN General Assembly Declaration on the Granting of Independence to Colonial Countries and Peoples (1960), providing colonial peoples an inalienable right of self-determination to freely pursue their political destiny and economic development.[21] Thus, the right to colonialism was replaced by the right

[19] *Namibia Opinion* (1971) ICJ Reports 16 and *Certain Phosphate Lands in Nauru (Nauru v Australia)* (1992) ICJ Reports 240 (preliminary judgment of 26 June 1992).

[20] These systems influenced Indian nationalism and Gandhi with an "ethical language" and vocabulary: K. Grant and L. Trivedi, "A Question of Trust: The Government of India, the LN, and Mahandas Gandhi," in R. Douglas et al. (eds.), *Imperialism on Trial: The International Oversight of Colonial Rule in Historical Perspective* (Lanham: Lexington Books, 2006), pp. 21–43, xi–xii; J. Darwin, "Decolonisation and the End of Empire," in R Winks and W. Louis et al. (eds.), *The Oxford History of the British Empire: Volume V: Historiography* (Oxford: Oxford University Press, 1999), p. 215.

[21] *Declaration of the Granting of Independence to Colonial Countries and Peoples*, 14 December 1960, 1960 UN Yearbook 40; GA Res. 1514 (XV), 15 UN GAOR Supp. (No. 16) at 66, UN Doc. A/4684 (1961).

to colonial self-determination. Many former colonies became independent states and UN members. But international relations soon drifted from decolonization commitments to Cold War concerns in the 1950s, when the Trusteeship Council became a tool for Cold War geopolitics marked by western resistance to Soviet support for colonial self-determination as a means of establishing a pro-Soviet bloc in the expanding UN.[22] This conflict gave rise to Cold War geoeconomics in international law, which institutionalized an economic distinction between new states as "developing" and former colonial powers as "developed," once again reinforcing the dynamics of difference in the postcolonial era.

The economic impact of colonialism: The international law of colonialism substantially contributed to the creation and continuation of lopsided distribution of economic wealth by allowing European colonial powers to prosper at the expense of the colonized, who now comprise the South. Economies of the world prior to the Industrial Revolution (around 1760–1840) were by and large at similar levels of development; a glaring disparity was then dramatically created due to the colonialism-led Industrial Revolution in Europe. Some of these colonial powers, notably the United Kingdom, undertook rapid industrialization by accessing and exploiting colonial natural resources and raw materials and utilizing the labor force from colonies at the minimal wage possible and under conditions of slave labor. As a result, their cost of production was very low, but they exported these industrial products to their captive colonial markets at an artificially high price to maximize profit.[23] Most Southern states did not exist during colonialism, and now have no access to foreign natural and human resources and new markets for exclusive exploitation. They can no longer expand their limited capital reserves beyond the creation of wealth through value adding to their natural resources. This historic legacy of economic disparity continues unabated under current international economic law, which requires the South to compete with the North that has accumulated wealth through a method no longer available.[24]

International law-making: The institution of colonialism received a further boost in a new political guise in the UN through its primary *international law-making sources*: treaties, customary state practices, and general principles of law

---

[22] R. Whitcomb, *The Cold War in Retrospect: The Formative Years* (New York: Greenwood Publishing, 1998); M. Bradley, "Decolonization, the Global South and the Cold War, 1919–1962," in M. Leffler and O. Westad (eds.), *The Cambridge History of the Cold War: Volume 1: Origins* (New York: Cambridge University Press, 2010), pp. 464–485; J. Yu, "African Decolonization and Cold War Politics in the UN," 2006, www.zum.de.

[23] D. Tussie, *The Less Developed Countries and the World Trading System: A Challenge to the GATT* (London: Printer Publishers, 1987), p. 137; P. Cain and A. Hopkins, "The Political Economy of British Expansion Overseas, 1750–1914" (1980) 33 *The Economic History Review* 463–490; P. Cain and A. Hopkins, "New Imperialism 1850–1945" (1987) 40 *The Economic History Review* 1.

[24] M. R. Islam, *International Trade Law* (Sydney: Law Book Company, 1999), pp. 168–169; Tussie, note 23.

recognized by civilized nations, embodied in Article 38(1) of the *Statute of the International Court of Justice* (hereinafter the ICJ Statute).[25]

Treaties are based on reciprocal and voluntary consents and common goals of the state parties. Their binding force emanates from the maxim *pacta sunt servanda* (promises must be kept), which is a source of international law. Although negotiating states enjoy full freedom in making treaties, their power differentials dictate treaty terms. In the past, colonial powers made treaties for their colonies and colonial resources that benefited metropolitan territories. Treaty negotiations are inherently diplomatic and adversarial in nature, where power politics and maximizing self-interest play a dominant, if not decisive, role. This self-serving approach circumscribes the opportunity for any level playing field for weaker states, which have too much to lose to seriously pursue their legal rights in negotiations. Many Southern states lack adequate legal knowledge about their rights and duties, as well as the necessary experts and financial resources to keep pace with the phases of treaty negotiations. Powerful states often manipulate negotiations by trade-offs and arm-twisting through promises of foreign investments, special trade terms, increased market access, aid, and loans as incentives, and threats of aid withdrawal and retaliation to coercively ensure their interests are protected. This underdog status of weak states in negotiations masks the sacrifice of their legitimate rights. This reflection of the relative power position is evident in many international law-making treaties, from past petroleum extractive concessionary agreements to the present UN Convention on the Law of the Sea 1982 (hereinafter the UNCLOS) and its associated 1994 agreement on deep-seabed mining (see section 5) and World Trade Organization trade agreements (see section 6).[26] International law created through these treaties represents and protects, more often than not, the interests of Northern states.

Customary international law is premised on the idea of law being the descriptive of accepted state practice. The normative value of the pre–World War II practice of some fifty relatively equal and homogenous western states was largely uniform and functionally less problematic because of their common cultural background and ideological unity. The whole corpus of customary international law lacked the institutional framework required for the development of a formal process of law-making.[27]

---

[25] San Francisco, 26 June 1945, in force 24 October 1945, 3 Bevans 1179; 59 Stat. 1031; T.S. 993; 39 *American Journal of International Law* Supp. 215 (1945).

[26] B. Kingsbury, "Sovereignty and Inequality" (1998) 9 *European Journal of International Law* 599; S. Scott, "International Law as Ideology: Theorizing the Relationship between International Law and International Politics" (1994) 5 *European Journal of International Law* 313; F. Jawara and A. Kwa, *Behind the Scenes at the WTO: The Real World of International Trade Negotiations* (London: Zed Books, 2001).

[27] P. Kelly, "The Twilight of Customary International Law" (2000) 40 *Virginia Journal of International Law* 450; A. Roberts, "Traditional and Modern Approaches to Customary International Law: A Reconciliation" (2001) 95 *American Journal of International Law* 757; M. Byers, "Customs, Power and the Power of Rules: Customary International Law from an Interdisciplinary Perspective" (1995) 17 *Michigan Journal of International Law* 109.

32   *History of the North–South Divide in International Law*

Its fluid, unwritten, imprecise, and passive nature makes it easily manipulable by dominant states to their advantage, while disadvantaging the vast majority of states that emerged after World War II whose values, traditions, and practices are not reflected.[28] Customary international law recognized the European claim of civilization and a mission to elevate non-Europeans, whose values and traditions were denied, suppressed, and constructed as primitive, paving the way for the institution of colonialism. It allowed imperial politics to distort the coercive realities of the superior–inferior relationship between European colonial powers and non-European colonial people as a sacred civilizing mission. Customary international law thus provided a suitable legal framework within which colonial and imperialist aspirations to an unequal and subservient relationship between hegemonic and newly born states advanced, exemplified by the continuing economic and military dependency of many Afro-Asian states on their former colonial powers.[29] For example, as explained in section 4, customary international law was invoked by Northern states in the decades following the Second World War to override UN General Assembly resolutions that favored Southern states in disputes over the proper compensation for the nationalization of foreign resource-extractive enterprises, thereby limiting the ability of Southern nations to exercise sovereign control over their natural resources. Where there is no treaty and/or customary international law, "the general principles of law recognized by civilized nations" are to be used as a source of international law. This provision overtly discriminates in favor of the national laws of "civilized" states and against the national laws of states which fall short of being "civilized." The first institutionalized international law-making process in Article 38 of the Statute of the Permanent Court of International Justice[30] included "civilized nations," excluding non-state entities, colonial peoples, and tribal civilizations as subjects of international law. The ICJ Statute in 1945 found the imperial remnant of 1921 a handy tool to establish the dominance of the Allied Powers and their allies over the Axis Powers and non-state entities in international law-making.[31]

Being the only UN plenary organ, the General Assembly is represented by the highest state authorities, and is where all states meet together to exchange views and adopt decisions through a democratic process. Although it has a general role to play

---

[28] E. Kwakwa, "Emerging International Development Law and Traditional Law – Congruence or Cleavage?" (1987) 17 *Georgia Journal of International & Comparative Law* 432; V. Fon and F. Parisi, "Stability and Change in International Customary Law" (2009) 17 *Supreme Court Economic Review* 279.

[29] T. Muller, "Customary International Law" (2009) 15 *Indian Journal of Global Legal Studies* 58; A. Cassese, *International Law in a Divided World* (Oxford: Clarendon Press, 1984), pp. 34–54, 181; J. Gathii, "International Law and Eurocentricity" (1998) 9 *European Journal of International Law* 184.

[30] Geneva, 16 December 1920, in force 20 August 1921, 6 *League of Nations Treaty Series* (hereinafter LNTS) 379, 390; 114 BFSP 860; 17 *American Journal of International Law* Supp. 115 (1923).

[31] M. R. Islam, *International Law: Current Concepts and Future Directions* (Australia: Lexis-Nexis, 2014), p. 83.

in the "progressive development of international law" (UN Charter, Article 13), its resolutions are largely recommendatory and devoid of any binding legal effect, falling short of becoming authoritative evidence of international law. This soft law-making creates soft international obligations, which often go unheeded for want of mandatory enforcement. This lack of enforceability generates false expectations of legal regulation that soft law cannot deliver. For example, General Assembly resolutions on the New International Economic Order 1974 (hereinafter NIEO) and the Charter of Economic Rights and Duties of States 1974 (hereinafter CERDS) proved to be symbolic in the face of strong Northern resistance at their implementation stages (see section 4).

Resolutions of the Security Council, being the UN executive organ composed of only fifteen states and represented at the bureaucratic level, are binding on states[32] despite the Council's undemocratic decision-making, systemic manipulation, and rampant abuses by the five permanent members with veto power. The sole purpose is to dictate and control the course of international events, peace, and security in the best interest of powerful states, to the exclusion and grave detriment of the overwhelming majority states that emerged through decolonization. Hence the formal sources of international law prior and after the world wars remained largely Eurocentric, reflecting the interests of the Northern states that dominate international law-making despite a substantial increase in the number of non-European states constituting the majority in the UN.[33]

4. POSTCOLONIAL LEGAL LANDSCAPE: NORTH–SOUTH TENSIONS IN INTERNATIONAL LAW REFORM

The dynamics of North–South competing interests remained influential in international law-making, reform, and implementation in the second half of the twentieth century. Decolonization created many new Southern states, which believed that the application of Eurocentric international law to them was contrary to their legal equality and disadvantageous.[34] By virtue of their UN membership and numerical strength in the General Assembly, they brought to bear political pressure for law reform. But this pressure proved inadequate to transform international law.[35] Northern states supported only cosmetic changes to the status quo and blocked, through their superior economic and political clout, any substantive reform. The subordination of the South as law-makers was

[32] UN Charter, note 17, chapter 7.

[33] M. Sornarajah, "Power and Justice: Third World Resistance in International Law" (2006) 10 *Singapore Yearbook of International Law* 19; G. Abi-Saab, *The International Legal System in Quest of Equity and Universality* (Leiden: Brill, 2001).

[34] Kwakwa, note 28.

[35] O. Hathaway, "Between Power and Principle: An Integrated Theory of International Law" (2005) 72 *University of Chicago Law Review* 494; G. Abi-Saab, "Whither the International Community" (1998) 9 *European Journal of International Law* 248.

34   *History of the North–South Divide in International Law*

evident in the non-binding nature of soft law created through the overwhelming majority vote in the General Assembly.

4.1 *Permanent Sovereignty over Natural Resources*

Newly decolonized Southern states found their natural resources had already been exploited by the colonial powers to such an extent that their economic viability as sovereign states was at risk. In reclaiming their right to natural resources free from any external interference, these states relied on the positivistic international law prerogatives of states, such as their territorial sovereignty and sovereign equality, to determine and apply laws and policies pertaining to the exploitation and development of their natural resources. In this pursuit, General Assembly Resolution 1803 (XVII) on Permanent Sovereignty over Natural Resources (1962)[36] aimed at promoting the economic emancipation of colonially dependent peoples and newly independent Southern states. Natural resource exploitation in many newly born Southern states was still dominated by foreign multinational corporations (MNCs) that maximized their profits at the expense of the former's national interests. Resolution 1803 introduced a public and national interest dimension in natural resources exploitation and development in these states. It was premised on the positivistic territorial "sovereignty" of a state to possess, utilize, and freely dispose of its natural resources, which was deemed "permanent" as ownership and control always remain in the state to which they belong. It purported to end the colonial system of foreign ownership of natural resources and production facilities by granting decolonized Southern states ownership of and control over their natural resources to be used for nation-building purposes. In some instances, the full enjoyment of economic sovereignty necessitated the transfer of ownership through nationalization, expropriation, and requisition of properties.[37]

Resolution 1803 also recognized indigenous sovereignty over natural resources used by indigenous peoples since time immemorial, before these resources came under alien domination.[38] The European colonization of indigenous peoples, their lands, and their resources forced many indigenous communities to move to rugged inland terrains containing untapped natural resources susceptible to exploitation by

---

[36] 14 December 1962, GA Res. 1803 (XVII), 17 UN GAOR Supp. (No.17) at 15; UN Doc. A/5217 (1962).

[37] M. R. Islam, "Permanent Sovereignty over Natural Resources: Its Changing Landscape and Continuing Relevance in a Globalised World" in M. Rahman (ed.), *Sovereignty over Natural Resources and Human Rights: Empowerment through Law of the Common People* (Dhaka: ELCOP, 2010), pp. 1–21; P. De Waart, "Permanent Sovereignty over Natural Resources as a Cornerstone for International Economic Rights and Duties" (1977) 24 *Netherlands International Law Review* 22.

[38] E-I. Daes, *The UN Human Rights Commission, Prevention of Discrimination and Protection of Indigenous Peoples, Indigenous Peoples' Permanent Sovereignty Over Natural Resources*, UN Doc. E/CN.4/Sub.2/2002/23 (30 July 2002), p. 3, para. 7.

extractive industries. Indeed, extractive activities in indigenous traditional lands and territories have increased significantly in recent decades. These activities may cause disruptions to indigenous rights to ancestral land, societal structures, and cultural identity, as was the case in Ecuador when a planned oil exploration project impacted profoundly on local indigenous communities.[39] This is why natural resources linked to indigenous peoples are regarded as their property and attempts have been made to ensure a relatively responsible approach to the use and development of natural resources to protect indigenous people from activities harmful to their environment, culture, and society.[40] Environmental protection is also required to prevent the overexploitation of these resources. With their holistic knowledge and practice of environmentally friendly natural resource management, the active participation of indigenous peoples in resource exploitation is a prerequisite for a cleaner and greener environment and sustainable development.[41] Devoid of their right to natural resources, indigenous peoples would continue to be deprived of their economic self-determination, right to develop, means of subsistence and poverty alleviation, enjoyment of human rights, and physical and socio-cultural survival.

4.2 *Economic Self-Determination*

Ownership of, and control over, natural resources has always been critical in the pursuit of economic emancipation of dependent peoples. The UN Charter considers the achievement of self-determination (Articles 1(2) and 55) to be an inherent human right of all peoples to freely determine their political destiny and pursue economic, social, and cultural development.[42] All UN members have willfully

---

[39] W. Shutkin, "International Human Rights Law and the Earth: The Protection of Indigenous Peoples and the Environment" (1991) 31 *Virginia Journal of International Law* 494.

[40] The *United Nations Declaration on the Rights of Indigenous Peoples*, New York, 12 September 2007, A/61/L.67, Annex, Art. 26(3) (hereinafter UNDRIP); E.-I. Daes, *The Protection of the Cultural and Intellectual Property of Indigenous Peoples*, UN Doc. E/CN.4/Sub.2/1993/28 (28 July 1993); *The World Conference on Human Rights*, Vienna, UN Doc. A/Conf.157/23 (1993).

[41] UNDRIP, note 40, Art. 27; *Rio Declaration on Environment and Development*, Rio de Janeiro, 13 June 1992, UN Doc. A/CONF.151/26 (vol. I); 31 *International Legal Materials* 874 (1992), Principle 22; *Recognizing and Strengthening the Role of Indigenous People and Their Communities*, Report of the UN Conference on Environment and Development, 3–14 June 1992, UN Doc. A/CONF.15/26/Rev. 1, vol. I, p. 385; *Plan of Implementation of the World Summit on Sustainable Development*, 4 September 2002, UN Doc. A/CONF.199/20 (2002), pp. 14–15; Report of the UN Conference on Sustainable Development (Rio+20) 2012, Rio de Janeiro, 20–22 June 2012, UN Doc. A/CONF.216/16 (hereinafter Rio+20 Report).

[42] *International Covenant on Civil and Political Rights*, New York, 16 December 1966, in force 23 March 1976, GA Res. 2200A (XXI), 21 UN GAOR Supp. (No. 16) at 52; UN Doc. A/6316 (1966); 999 *United Nations Treaty Series* (hereinafter UNTS) 171; 6 *International Legal Materials* 368 (1967), Art. 1; *Declaration on Principles of International Law Concerning Friendly Relations and Co-operation in Accordance with the Charter of the United Nations*, GA Res. 2625, 25 UN GAOR Supp. 18 122; 65 *American Journal of International Law* 243 (1971), Principle V.

36   *History of the North–South Divide in International Law*

assumed specific obligations to adopt joint and separate measures for the realization of economic self-determination embodied in Article 55 of the UN Charter, which has further been reinforced by the expression "pledge" in Article 56, entailing precise legal obligations for UN members. The General Assembly reiterated and reaffirmed that denial of the right of peoples to their economic resources is inconsistent with economic self-determination. Its Resolution 1314(XIII) explained the nature of permanent sovereignty of peoples and nations over their natural resources as a constituent element of the right to self-determination.[43] The interface between sovereignty over natural resources and economic self-determination lies in the fact that the latter becomes meaningless without the former. The right to economic self-determination therefore inevitably includes the right to permanent sovereignty over natural resources. This relationship has received the greatest endorsement from the Decolonization Declaration 1960 and Resolution 1803, which has been consolidated further in successive UN resolutions.[44] Hence, Resolution 1803 is not a mere political statement of distant economic goals but an embodiment of an inalienable right of all peoples to economic self-determination.[45]

4.3 *New International Economic Order (NIEO)*

The General Assembly sought to implement Resolution 1803 through a number of subsequent resolutions, notably the establishment of an action program for a NIEO in May 1974 and the creation of a Charter of Economic Rights and Duties of States (CERDS) in December 1974.[46] It also adopted two related resolutions in 1977 and 1979 to augment the capacity-building of Southern states in the exploration of natural resources through multilateral development assistance.[47] The CERDS unequivocally confirmed states' right to full ownership of and permanent control over their natural resources, with further guidelines for nationalization and compensation in Article 2.[48]

---

[43] Establishing the Commission on Permanent Sovereignty over Natural Resources (12 December 1958).

[44] GA Res. 2158(XXI) (25 November 1966); GA Res. 2386(XXIII) (19 November 1968); GA Res. 3171(XXVIII) (17 December 1973); GA Res. 2692(XXV) (11 December 1970); GA Res 3016 (XXVII) (18 December 1972).

[45] M. R. Islam, "The Dispute between Nauru and Australia over Rehabilitation: A Test Case for Economic Self-Determination" (1992) 8 *Queensland University of Technology Law Journal* 147; Waart, note 37.

[46] *Declaration on the Establishment of a New International Economic Order*, UN Doc. A/Res/s-6/3201 (1 May 1974); *Programme of Action on the Establishment of a New International Economic Order*, UN Doc. A/Res/s-6/3202 (1 May 1974); *Charter of Economic Rights and Duties of States*, UN Doc. A/Res/29/3281 (12 December 1974).

[47] UN Doc. A/RES/32/176 (19 December 1977) and UN Doc. A/RES/33/194 (29 January 1979).

[48] S. Chatterjee, "The Charter of Economic Rights and Duties of States: An Evaluation after 15 Years" (1991) 40 *International and Comparative Law Quarterly* 669; B. Weston, "The Charter

4.4 North–South Tensions over the Implementation of Soft Law

Overwhelming support in the General Assembly led most members to recognize Resolution 1803 as a *jus cogens* (peremptory) principle of international law and hold "that the resolution was intended to express existing law."[49] Yet its implementation encountered objections and non-cooperation from most Northern states, which either voted against or abstained from voting in NIEO and CERDS resolutions. Growing nationalistic feeling regarding the realization of economic self-determination led many newly decolonized Southern states to nationalize foreign properties engaged in exploiting their natural resources in the extractive sectors. Nationalization is an established sovereign legal act of the host state in international law in compliance with certain legal requirements, also mentioned in Resolution 1803: namely, public purposes and national security and interests, and the payment of "appropriate compensation" according to domestic and international law. [50] The nationalization move resulted in retardation of FDI flows to Southern states, leading to economic slowdown. The necessity of FDI for development and the comparatively weak bargaining clout of Southern states in negotiations with FDI–exporting Northern states forced the former to adopt a promotional policy to attract, and not to police, FDI, which eroded their decisive say in the exploitation of their natural resources guaranteed under Resolution 1803.[51]

Northern states continued to follow the Hull formula of "adequate, effective and prompt" compensation that international law created in the first half of the twentieth century.[52] No UN resolution ever endorsed and followed the Hull principle,

---

of Economic Rights and Duties of States and the Deprivation of Foreign-Owned Wealth" (1981) 75 *American Journal of International Law* 437.

[49] K. Gess, "Permanent Sovereignty over Natural Resources: An Analytical Review of the UN Declaration and its Genesis" (1964) 13 *International and Comparative Law Quarterly* 409; see also K. Hossain and S. Chowdhury (eds.), *Permanent Sovereignty Over Natural Resources in International Law: Principle and Practice* (New York: St. Martin's Press, 1984), pp. 28–32; N. Schrijver, *Sovereignty over Natural Resources: Balancing Rights and Duties* (Cambridge: Cambridge University Press, 2008), pp. 4–6, 36.

[50] A. Maniruzzaman, "State Contracts with Aliens: The Question of Unilateral Change by the State in Contemporary International Law" (1992) 9 *Journal of International Arbitration* 141; E. Penrose et al., 'Nationalization of Foreign-Owned Property for a Public Purpose: An Economic Perspective on Appropriate Compensation' (1992) 55 *Modern Law Review* 355; P. Norton, "A Law of the Future or a Law of the Past? Modern Tribunals and the International Law of Expropriation" (1991) 85 *American Journal of International Law* 475.

[51] This situation led to the establishment of Multilateral Investment Guarantee Agency in 1985, a World Bank initiative to protect the FDI interest of Northern states: see Islam, note 24, pp. 253, 255; M. Sornarajah, *The International Law on Foreign Investment* (Cambridge: Cambridge University Press, 2010), pp. 334–358.

[52] Cordell Hull, U.S. Secretary of State, claimed full compensation in the US-Mexico dispute over the Mexican agrarian nationalization in 1938: see Exchange of Letters between U.S. Secretary of State Cordell Hull and Mexican Minister of Foreign Relations Eduardo Hay, reprinted in (1938) 32 *American Journal of International Law* 181; the Hull formula was also

38 *History of the North–South Divide in International Law*

which skewed heavily in favor of foreign investors. The Hull formula required *full*, as opposed to *fair*, compensation. Foreign investors enjoyed unfettered freedom of choice in their policies regarding the contracted areas and paid very little royalties or revenues to host states.[53] CERDS Article 2(c) purported to address this imbalance by conferring on nationalizing states the right to determine the amount of "appropriate compensation to be paid [...] taking into account the relevant laws and regulations and all circumstances that the state considers pertinent."[54] Article 2 (c) provided for appropriate compensation under the domestic laws of host states to the exclusion of international law, which was supported by Southern states as a legitimate exercise of their sovereignty over natural resources, but opposed by Northern states that claimed it gave host states *carte blanche* to ascertain the payable amount of compensation.[55]

In *Texaco Petroleum Co.* v *Libya*, the sole Arbitrator Dupuy rejected the Libyan invocation of CERDS Article 2 on the ground that it was no more than a General Assembly recommendation and valid only "in the eyes of States which have adopted it" and "supported only by non-industrialized States."[56] This reasoning lacked objectivity and impartiality in view of the circumstances of CERDS adoption and the voting pattern, which was supported by 120 votes, with six against and ten abstentions. Yet its legal status was denied, in total disregard of the overwhelming support of Southern states. Judicial settlements of major compensation disputes in the twentieth century reveal that "partial," not full, compensation has become more norm than exception, paid in a lump sum or installments.[57] CERDS reformed the partisan and outdated Hull formula as the standard of compensation payment for nationalization in NIEO; yet Northern states regarded the majority-made CERDS a non-binding soft law and the minority-made Hull formula a binding hard customary international law.

---

practiced in nineteenth century colonization; M. Bulajic, *Principles of International Development Law* (Dordrecht: Martinus Nijhoff, 1992), p. 264.

[53] N. Di Mascio and J. Pauwelyn, "Nondiscrimination in Trade and Investment Treaties: Worlds Apart or Two Sides of the Same Coin?" (2008) 102 *American Journal of International Law* 53.

[54] United Nations Conference on Trade and Development, Res. 88(XII), October 1972, para. 2 empowers states an exclusive right to determine compensation.

[55] A. Akinsanya, *The Expropriation of Multinational Property in the Third World* (New York: Praeger, 1980), pp. 45–55.

[56] Award in *Texaco v Libya* (19 January 1977), 17 *International Legal Materials* 1, paras. 88–90 (1977).

[57] D. Gantz, "Marcona Settlement" (1977) 71 *American Journal of International Law* 474; F. Dawson and B. Weston, "Prompt, Adequate and Effective: A Universal Standard of Compensation?" (1961–1962) 30 *Fordham Law Review* 738; C. Amerasinghe, "Issues of Compensation for the Taking of Alien Property in the Light of Recent Cases and Practice" (1992) 41 *International and Comparative Law Quarterly* 41; M. Mendelson, "Discussing Compensation for Expropriation: The Case Law" (1985) 79 *American Journal of International Law* 415.

5. STATE SOVEREIGNTY IN THE POST–COLD WAR ERA: SOME SOVEREIGNS MORE EQUAL THAN OTHERS?

The post–Cold War era in the 1990s witnessed the advent of certain pressing issues transcending the sovereign power of any single state and forging interdependence and collaboration in their regulation. Rapid advances in technologies and an abundance of global common issues have been reconstructing sovereignty, taking "the internal form of fragmentation and poly-centricity and the external form of 'network governance'."[58] The conventional conception and construction of state sovereignty linked to exclusive territorial authority is neither theoretically tenable nor empirically serviceable in the face of globalization, which has been transforming the world's states from independent to interdependent. It is no longer feasible for international law grounded in the principle of absolute and independent territorial jurisdiction to be able to deal with new cross-border issues, including the exchange of goods, services, technology, and information. Sovereignty as a discrete political order is now being diffused across a range of state and non-state authorities coordinating national policies and activities to represent and pursue the legitimate interests of national constituencies in line with responsibilities owed to the global community.[59] Sovereignty has become a tool for international cooperation and engagement rather than a shield providing isolation and insulation from international interference.

The effect of this growing internationalism on state sovereignty has become a concern for many Southern states due to its North–South implications. The collapse of the former Soviet Union in the late 1980s radically altered the balance of power, resulting in the triumph of Northern liberalism over the epistemological understanding of diverse systemic orientations of states in this plural world. This global environment rendered the space for unilateral and autonomous exercise of national sovereignty asymmetrical, with new opportunities and benefits for some states and new risks and threats for others. This asymmetry has consolidated the sovereign power of Northern states and eroded the sovereign power of Southern states. For example, many Southern states play only a marginal role in the national allocation and utilization of resources, which are often dictated by outside forces and requirements, irrespective of domestic socio-economic needs and priorities.

---

[58] K. Jayasuriya, "Globalization, Law and the Transformation of Sovereignty: The Emergence of Global Regulatory Governance" (1999) 6 *Indiana Journal of Global Legal Studies* 426; see also J. Goodman, "Myths of Globalization: Power, Legitimacy and Sovereignty" (2007–2008) 5 *New Zealand Yearbook of International Law* 522; G. Wang, "The Impact of Globalization on State Sovereignty" (2004) 3 *Chinese International Law Journal* 473.

[59] W. Nagan and C. Hammer, "The Changing Character of Sovereignty in International Law and International Relations" (2005) 43 *Columbia Journal of Transnational Law* 141; S. Krasner, "The Hole in the Whole: Sovereignty, Shared Sovereignty, and International Law" (2004) 25 *Michigan Journal of International Law* 1075; H. Stacy, "Relational Sovereignty" (2005) 99 *American Society of International Law Proceedings* 396–400.

40   *History of the North–South Divide in International Law*

The role of international law in ensuring and regulating peaceful coexistence between Northern and Southern states based on the sovereign equality of states has been weakened by the advent of a unipolar world dominated by a single superpower in pursuit of "assertive multilateralism"[60] to advance its foreign policy, strategic goals, and economic interests. The United States and its powerful allies enjoy a self-perpetuating image of benevolent leader in international rule-making and standard-setting. The assertion of, and monopoly over, totally unrestrained and unregulated exclusive rights to pre-emptive self-defense under the guise of the so-called "war on terror" and actions against "rogue regimes" has become a new vocabulary for establishing imperialistic control over the post–Cold War "new world order," which has serious marginalizing effects on the sovereignty of many weak states, international law, and the UN Charter.[61] For the protection of their economic interests, both NAFTA and the EU set import standards for rules of origin, trade in agriculture and pharmaceuticals, TRIPS-Plus, and quarantine arbitrarily above the WTO requirements, which impairs or nullifies the legitimate exporting interests of Southern states (discussed in section 6). These rules and standards are implemented selectively only in response to U.S. strategic interests through the support of sheer military might, economic coercion, sanctions, and veto power in the UN Security Council.[62] Interstate conflicts over human rights, immigration, the environment, and nuclear, chemical, and other weapons are increasingly dictated by cultural and religious diversities, in what has been termed "the clash of civilizations."[63] The United States has continually exonerated itself from abiding by the international legal principles it promotes for others. It refuses to be bound by international obligations due to the belief that its political pre-eminence and superpower status have elevated it to an exceptionalist state above international law.[64]

---

[60] Statement of Ambassador Madeleine Albright at the U.S. Congress, House Committee on Foreign Affairs, Hearings before the Subcommittee on International Security, International Organizations and Human Rights, 103rd Congress, 2nd Session, 24 June 1994, pp. 3–21.

[61] Pre-emptive self-defence and wars on terror violate the *jus cogens* prohibition on uses of force (UN Charter, Art. 2(4) and the ICJ in *Military and Paramilitary Activities in and against Nicaragua* (1986) ICJ Reports 94, rules of permissible use of force in self-defence in UN Charter, Art. 51, and international humanitarian law; stockpiling of "Weapons of Mass Destruction" undermines the UN agenda of disarmament; see Islam, note 31, chapters 8, 9, 19; Anghie, note 3, chapter 6.

[62] For example, Iran and North Korea have been singled out as rogue states and untrustworthy to possess nuclear weapons, which nuclear states have taken for granted, particularly when the United States remains the first and only state to have used nuclear weapons; see also C. Wall, "Human Rights and Economic Sanctions: The New Imperialism" (1998) 22 *Fordham International Law Journal* 3; D. Rieff, "Humanitarianism in Crisis" (2002) 81(6) *Foreign Affairs* 111.

[63] Former U.S. President Bush, in his "Remembering September 11" address, said that the war on terror "is more than a military conflict. It is the decisive ideological struggle of the 21st century [...] and it is a struggle for civilization," *The Washington Post*, 11 September 2006; S. Huntington, "The Clash of Civilizations?" (1993) 72(3–5) *Foreign Affairs* 22.

[64] Former U.S. President Bush asserted that "the UN Charter is dead and the United States is not bound by international law," quoted in *The Observer*, July 14, 2002, p. 14; P. Sands, "Lawless World: International Law after September 11, 2001 and Iraq" (2005) 6 *Melbourne*

Concurrently, the United States is a major advocate of a just world and a contributor to its downfall.[65] Its non-ratification of many treaties it negotiated, including most human rights and environmental treaties, exposes its arrogant unilateralism in zealously guarding its self-interest.[66] Its hard-nosed tactics over the ratification of the UNCLOS[67] are a case in point. The Convention treated deep-sea natural resources as the common heritage of humankind, to be utilized for the benefit of humankind through a just and equitable international order of distributive economic justice.[68] This objective led to the creation of a centralized international regime for the exploration of deep-seabed resources to develop and transfer marine technology for capacity-building of human resources in Southern states under Part XI (Arts 268 and 269) of the Convention. The United States expressed its reservations regarding this regime and declined to ratify the Convention predominantly due to the treaty's: (a) restriction on the ability of the United States and its corporations to monopolize deep-seabed mining by virtue of their advanced technological capability, (b) requirement to disclose the technology to be used in mining and transfer of technology to Southern coastal states, and (c) non-assurance of perpetual U.S. membership of the International Seabed Authority (ISA).

The United States' uncompromising approach prevented the implementation of the Convention, which was eventually modified to achieve "universal participation" by concluding an agreement between the United States and the UN in 1994. This agreement favors U.S. interests and demands in deep-seabed mining, and its free-market approach to technology transfer requires Southern states to buy technology at commercial prices. Developed coastal states now have increased control over the ISA through their decisive authority in the ISA Council, which regulates

---

Journal of International Law 448; E. Venisti, "The U.S. and the Use of Force: Double-Edge Hegemony and the Management of Global Emergencies" (2004) 14 European Journal of International Law 688.

[65] J. Hathaway, "America, Defender of Democratic Legitimacy?" (2000) 11 European Journal of International Law 134.

[66] It refused to ratify the Vienna Convention on the Law of Treaties, Vienna, 23 May 1969, in force 27 January 1980, UN Doc. A/Conf.39/27; 1155 UNTS 331; 8 International Legal Materials 679 (1969); 63 American Journal of International Law 875 (1969); Rome Statute on the International Criminal Court, Rome, 17 August 1998, in force 1 August 2002, UN Doc. A/CONF. 183/9; 37 International Legal Materials 1002 (1998); 2187 UNTS 90; Convention on the Prohibition of the Use, Stockpiling, Production and Transfer of Anti-Personnel Mines and on their Destruction, Ottawa, 18 September 1997, in force 1 March 1999, 056 UNTS 241; 36 International Legal Materials 1507 (1997); and Convention on Cluster Munitions, Dublin, 30 May 2008, CCM/77; A. Bradford and E. Posner, "Universal Exceptionalism in International Law" (2011) 52 Harvard International Law Journal 53.

[67] Montego Bay, 10 December 1982, in force 16 November 1994, 1833 UNTS 3; 21 International Legal Materials 1261 (1982).

[68] C. Joyner, "Legal Implications of the Concepts of the Common Heritage of Mankind" (1986) 35 International and Comparative Law Quarterly 193; E. Guntrip, "The Common Heritage of Mankind: An Adequate Regime for Managing the Deep Seabed?" (2003) 4 Melbourne Journal of International Law 384.

tenders for seabed mining. Transfer of technology to developing and least developed coastal states is no longer mandatory; nor is there a requirement to assess and address the impacts of prospecting and mining on the rich biological life of the deep seabed. All these changes are contrary to the original provisions in Part XI of the UNCLOS and legitimize the lopsided distribution of benefits from and control over the management of deep-seabed resources to Northern states, to the grave economic detriment of Southern states.[69]

The United States and the other four permanent members of the Security Council use their veto power to pursue their geopolitical strategies in a manner that camouflages the decisive role of power in the idealistic rhetoric of global peace and security, exemplified by their military intervention in Iraq in 2003 to promote "democracy." These exceptionalist states are often part of the problem of international law violations and inadequate enforcement and democratic deficit in international institutional law-making. While persistent violations of international law and obligations impact decisively on small and weak Southern states, exceptionalist states use such violations as tactics to create fear. They adopt a "my way or the highway" attitude to serve their self-interest and weather whatever international criticisms and rebukes that come their way.[70] The problem lies not in their elite status per se, but in the enabling power of this status to manipulate and contravene international law with impunity and exempt themselves from international obligations and standards whenever necessary.

The sovereign equality of states as one of the founding pillars of international law is meant to address global power imbalance and afford opportunities for weak and small states to pursue their sovereign rights. This legal equality of statehood was conceived as the enforcer of behavioral obligations on all states with regard to mutual respect, collective security, and the protection of the vulnerable from the powerful.[71] This ideological basis of international order is being routinely eroded by a hierarchy of powerful states which hold a pervasive anachronistic view of international law that can be stretched, twisted, and sidelined at will and with impunity; and which deem international legal obligations subservient to political agendas, economic interests, and military strategies. The power gap has grown so

---

[69] B. Oxman, "Law of the Sea Forum: The 1994 Agreement on Implementation of the Seabed Provisions of the Convention on the Law of the Sea" (1994) 88 *American Journal of International Law* 687; M. Hayashi, "The 1994 Agreement for the Utilization of the Law of the Sea Convention" (1996) 27 *Ocean Development & International Law* 31; Islam, note 31, pp. 471–475; E. Egede, "African States and Participation in Deep Seabed Mining: Problems and Prospects" (2009) 24 *International Journal of Marine and Coastal Law* 683.

[70] R. Putnam, "Diplomacy and Domestic Politics: The Logic of Two-Level Games" (1993) 4 *International Organization* 431; R. Keohane, "International Law and International Obligations: Two Optics" (1997) 38 *Harvard International Law Journal* 499.

[71] J. Fitzpatrick, "Speaking Law to Power: The War against Terrorism and Human Rights" (2003) 14 *European Journal of International Law* 264; I. Simonovic, "State Sovereignty and Globalization: Are Some States More Equal?" (2000) 28 *Georgia Journal of International & Comparative Law* 382.

exponentially that powerful states have gained the reputation of being bullies, and this has become an accepted custom.[72] The continued existence and operation of NATO, a remnant of Cold War military hostility, is a tangible manifestation of the presence of hard power diplomacy. This is how the rise of exceptionalist states has disrupted and depleted the effectiveness of the principle of sovereign equality of states. The North's maintenance of the privileged world leadership position through reliance on military and economic superiority has reinforced a neocolonial hierarchical reality of the North–South order, in which Northern states continue to assert and enjoy their status as more equal than others. Most Southern states, which are not enamored with Northern hierarchical power, have become less sovereign and encounter greater difficulty in exercising their sovereignty. Their limited powers are overwhelmed by the organized predatory power of the Northern hegemonic international order in the post–Cold War era.

6. DILUTED SOVEREIGNTY UNDER ECONOMIC GLOBALIZATION: WINNERS AND LOSERS[73]

Globalization is a reality in many facets of modern national and international life. One of its important manifestations is the erosion of state sovereignty to facilitate the free movements of goods, services, and capital across national borders pursuant to multilateral legal and institutional frameworks. Its main features are trade liberalization, privatization, and financial deregulation. The Bretton Woods economists in 1944 advanced the intellectual framework for the contemporary global economy by establishing the International Monetary Fund (IMF) and the World Bank to assist in the recovery of the war-ravaged world economy, and particularly the reconstruction and development of Europe. They envisioned a world economy driven by profit maximization through comparative advantage and dominated by industrialized states. The plight of Southern states, most of which were under colonial rule in 1944, was not in the minds of the postwar economic policy-makers.[74]

Economic globalization yields lopsided economic benefits – substantial new opportunities for some states, and limited benefits with new risks and threats for others. Southern states with rudimentary physical infrastructure, low levels of industrialization, and a mostly unskilled work force lack the economic clout

---

[72] R. Brewster, "Unpacking the State's Reputation" (2009) 50 *Harvard International Law Journal* 232, 268.

[73] This section provides a brief account of the economic, particularly economic sovereignty, aspect of the North South divide. The environmental aspects are explored in subsequent chapters in Part I of this volume. (see L. J. Kotze, "Human Rights, the Environment and the Global South").

[74] Islam, note 24, p. 96; G. Strange, "Global Economic Governance Institutions and the Developing World: From Bretton Woods to Beijing?," Research-to-Teaching/Teaching-to-Research Working Paper No. 7 (2011), p. 5.

44 *History of the North–South Divide in International Law*

necessary to take the advantage of new opportunities and benefits created by globalization, resulting in their unequal and limited access to the world market. Southern states sought to address their economic weaknesses by pursuing national development plans and strategies such as import substitution industrialization (ISI); but the free market doctrines espoused by Northern states and international financial institutions left almost no scope for state intervention and autonomous national economic policies in Southern economies. The U.S., European Commission, and Japan preached "free trade" and "free market" only after they became economically powerful through protectionist trade and monopolistic market control. Modest progress in industrialization achieved through import substitution industrialization in Latin America was suddenly hamstrung by the effects of the debt crisis of the 1980s and IMF/World Bank loan conditionalities and structural adjustments. The asymmetric economic development in Northern and Southern states is largely attributable to inconsistencies between the rhetoric and reality of "free trade" and the doctrinal framework of the free market and its actual operation.[75]

IMF and World Bank loan conditionalities are set only for borrowers, mostly Southern states, which are invariably forced to undertake austerity measures (such as cutting public welfare spending) and structural reforms that reduce state intervention in the economy. These loan conditionalities have increased IMF–World Bank control over indebted Southern states, whose sovereignty to pursue developmental goals, alternative economic policies, and regulation of trade, investment, and finance is now circumscribed. Northern creditor states, however, retain their right to determine their own national economic policies. Although the harshness of the economic reforms imposed by the IMF and the World Bank has been tempered by greater heed to poverty alleviation, healthcare, education, environmental protection, labor standards, social safety nets, and good governance,[76] the pace of progress has been slow, piecemeal, and inadequate given the needs of the South. Mounting worldwide calls for substantive change and comprehensive regulation amid successive global financial crises since 2008 appear to be gradually weakening the calls for strict regulation.

---

[75] H-J. Chang, *Kicking Away the Ladder: Development Strategies in Historical Perspective* (London: Anthem Press, 2002); H-J. Chang, "Kicking Away the Ladder: How the Economic and Intellectual Histories of Capitalism Have Been Re-Written to Justify Neo-Liberal Capitalism" (2002) 15 *Post-Autistic Economics Review*, article 3 www.btinternet.com/~pae_news/review/issue15.htm; W. Ruigrok, "Paradigm Crisis in International Trade Theory" (1991) 25 *Journal of World Trade* 77.

[76] World Bank, *Development and Human Rights: The Role of the World Bank* (Washington: World Bank, 1998); IMF, "Review of the 2002 Conditionality Guidelines," 3 March 2005, www.imf.org; H. Morris, "The Globalization and Human Rights Law and the Role of International Financial Institutions in Promoting Human Rights" (2000) 33 *George Washington International Law Review* 85; for a criticism of the Poverty Reduction Strategy Programme, see J. Hickel, "The World Bank and Development Delusion," Al-Jazeera, 27 September 2012.

The 1947 GATT reduced tariff barriers only on manufactured goods, which benefited Northern states mostly due to their industrial and technological superiority. Agriculture, the main export of Southern states, and non-tariff barriers were excluded from the scope of the GATT. This trading arrangement allowed Northern states to monopolize global trade in manufactured goods and protect their inefficient agriculture by erecting tariff and non-tariff barriers to agricultural imports from Southern states. After nearly seventy years of institutionalized and structured trade liberalization, agricultural trade is yet to be liberalized. The WTO Agreement on Agriculture failed to liberalize trade in agricultural products, and the Doha Round of WTO negotiations has faltered primarily due to North–South conflicts over agricultural trade.[77]

The WTO TRIPS Agreement ensures mandatory protection for trade-related intellectual property rights in technology-importing Southern states with no guarantee of technology transfer, which is voluntary for technology-exporting Northern states.[78] The TRIPS Agreement has serious restraining effects on the modernization and development of many Southern economies. The UN Sub-Commission for the Promotion and Protection of Human Rights Report 2000 raised serious human rights concerns over the TRIPS Agreement and termed the WTO trading rules a "veritable nightmare" for Southern states and their citizens.[79] The TRIPS pharmaceutical patent permits branded prescription drugs used for fatal contagious diseases (HIV, AIDS, malaria, tuberculosis, and other epidemics) to be patented, rendering accessibility and affordability almost impossible for Southern states. Equivalent non-branded generic drugs, which are cheap and available, can be produced and used only as a last resort in response to public health crises, under stringent conditions. The WTO Doha Declaration on Public Health 2001 and its Generic Drug Waiver Accord 2003 allow states facing public health crises to produce generic drugs exclusively for their own use, not for export to be used in

---

[77] C. G. Gonzalez examines the issue in detail in Chapter 19 of this book (see "Food Justice: An Environmental Justice Critique of the Global Food System"). Agriculture remains the most protective, subsidized, and distorted trade in the WTO, WTO Secretariat press release of April 27 2001. According to the World Bank, agricultural trade liberalization would boost the income of Southern states by US$44 billion, helping millions escape poverty: D. Laborde, W. Martin, and D. van der Mensbrugghe, "Implications of the Doha Market Access Proposals for Developing Countries," World Bank Policy Research Working Paper 5697 (2011); N. Hoekman, "The WTO and the Doha Round: Walking on Two Legs' Economic Promise," World Bank Poverty Reduction and Economic Management Network Paper No. 68 (2011).

[78] M. R. Islam, *International Trade Law of the WTO* (New York: Oxford University Press, 2006), pp. 410–413.

[79] J. Oloka-Onyango and D. Udagama, *The Realization of Economic, Social and Cultural Rights: Globalization and Its Impact on the Full Enjoyment of Human Rights*, UN Sub-Commission for the Promotion and Protection of Human Rights, 15 June 2000, agenda item 4, E/CN.4/Sub.2/2000/13.

46 History of the North–South Divide in International Law

public health crises in other states – many of whom lack drug manufacturing capacity and are thus deprived of the waiver.[80]

The WTO General Agreement on Trade in Services (GATS) liberalizes skilled, managerial, and professional services to the exclusion of unskilled and semi-skilled labor, where Southern states enjoy a comparative advantage. While Northern states, with their advanced technology and education, freely export skilled, managerial, and professional services to Southern states under the GATS, the cross-border movement of semi-skilled and ordinary labor from Southern to Northern states faces restrictions based on sovereignty and immigration law. This selective liberalization of trade in services, requiring Southern states to open up their markets for services from Northern states without any reciprocation for semi-skilled and unskilled labor, deprives Southern states of their comparative advantage in cheap labor. Through this double standard in service trade, the WTO has boosted the earnings and bargaining power of Northern states and their MNCs through incursions into the global South at the expense of local companies. The mobility of capital investment and immobility of unskilled labor enables MNCs to pit workers against each other, depressing the wages, working conditions, safety and security, labor rights, and collective bargaining power of unskilled workers in both Southern and Northern states. Bewildered by the market power of MNCs in a deregulatory environment, Southern workers in service trade are exposed to plummeting employment opportunities as a result of service trade liberalization, the true beneficiaries of which are the transnational elites of the global North.[81]

International law governing the operation of foreign direct investment (FDI) has been uncertain and controversial in the absence of any multilateral convention and substantive rules or principles.[82] In this vacuum, capital-exporting states and the World Bank have developed various guidelines, dispute settlement arbitration, and bilateral investment treaties (BITs) for the protection of investment. The World Bank Guidelines on the Treatment of FDI 1992[83] prescribe standards of protection and treatment of FDI that host states are obliged to guarantee. Its International Centre for the Settlement of Investment Disputes 1965 (ICSID)[84] offers protection of FDI primarily against nationalization and allows foreign investors to gain direct access to an international dispute settlement forum by bypassing the national dispute settlement of host states. BITs are premised on reciprocal encouragement and protection of each other's investment flow, which in reality is one-sided,

---

[80] M. R. Islam, "Generic Drugs: Doha to Cancun – A Peripheral Response to a Perennial Conundrum" (2004) 7 *Journal of World Intellectual Property* 675.

[81] B. S. Chimni, "International Institutions Today: An Imperial Global State in the Making" (2004) 15 *European Journal of International Law* 22; B. S. Chimni, "A Just World Under Law: A View from the South" (2007) 22 *American University International Law Review* 199.

[82] Sornarajah, note 51, chapter 1; *Barcelona Traction case (Belgium v Spain)* (1970) ICJ Reports 3, pp. 42–47.

[83] 21 September 1992, 31 *International Legal Materials* 1363 (1992).

[84] 18 March 1965, 4 *International Legal Materials* 63 (1965).

predominantly from the capital-exporting North to the capital-importing South and from former colonial powers to newly decolonized states. The inequality of BIT parties is apparent in negotiated bargaining and trade-off powers of inducements (aid promises) and coercions (covert trade sanctions) leading to exoneration from liability and the rigid FDI protection regime.[85] Hence the existing international investment protection regime is skewed to protect foreign investors, mostly MNCs – which in effect consolidates Northern economic and political clout in Southern states, which lose sovereignty over natural resources and the ability to regulate FDI in the pursuit of national policies of sustainable development, environmental protection, and public interest.

Economic globalization has diluted state sovereignty in a manner that produces winners and losers. The winners, mostly Northern states, have benefited from the liberalization of trade in manufactured goods and in services and from the enhanced protection of investor rights and intellectual property. The exclusion of agricultural trade, transfer of technology, and the cross-border movement of people from the WTO framework has produced losers – predominantly Southern states, which encounter economic and political dislocations and loss of sovereignty. Their scarce resources are being increasingly used to satisfy the demands of Northern consumers in order to earn the foreign currency necessary to service the foreign debt, while many of their citizens are impoverished and undernourished.[86] The ability of Southern states to provide the basic necessities of life (including foodstuffs, health services, clothing, housing, drinking water, a healthy environment, social security, and education) is eroding as power becomes concentrated in the hands of strong market players, predominantly MNCs. Globalization has rendered markets more monopolistic than competitive. The North's domination of institutions such as the World Bank, the IMF, and the WTO has accorded Northern states unfettered and easy access to the national wealth, natural resources, cheap labor, and billions of new consumers in Southern states. It has turned the "free" market into "a form of market colonialism [which] subordinates people and governments through the seemingly neutral interplay of market forces."[87]

---

[85] Sornarajah, note 51, pp. 187, 232–233; K. Miles, *The Origins of International Investment Law: Empire, Environment and Safeguarding of Capital* (New York: Cambridge University Press, 2013); M. R. Islam and I. Prihandono, "Political Strategies of TNCs for Corporate Interest in Indonesian Public Interest Litigation: Lessons for Developing Countries Hosting FDIs" (2011) 12 *Journal of World Investment & Trade* 701; J. Siqueiros, "Bilateral Treaties on the Reciprocal Protection of Foreign Investment" (1994) 24 *California Western International Law Journal* 255.

[86] K. Sauvant, "From Economic to Socio-Cultural Emancipation: The Historical Context of the New International Economic Order and the New International Socio-Cultural Order" (1981) 3 *Third World Quarterly* 58; J. Collins, "World Hunger: A Scarcity of Food or a Scarcity of Democracy?" in M. Klare and D. Thomas (eds.), *World Security: Challenges for a New Century* (New York: Wordsworth Publishing, 1994), pp. 356, 358; R. Litan, "The 'Globalization' Challenge" (2000) 18 *Brookings Review* 35.

[87] M. Chossudovsky, "Global Impoverishment and the IMF-World Bank Economic Medicine," 1994, www.corpwatch.org.

7. INTERNATIONAL ENVIRONMENTAL LAW: A VICTIM OF THE NORTH–SOUTH DIVIDE[88]

International environmental law has a strong North–South dimension. Northern states exploited their resources for industrialization and development for decades, without any concern for environmental degradation. Southern states still have vast amounts of natural resources and biological diversity. But the benefits flowing from these ecological assets have been concentrating in the North due to its superior scientific, technical, economic, and investment capabilities.[89] As worldwide scarcity of natural resources increases, so does Southern states' concern to control their resource exploitation for economic development. The exploitation of natural resources for development and poverty alleviation has become a paramount priority in many Southern states, which perceive environmentalism as a means of undermining their sovereignty and enabling Northern states to gain access to Southern untapped resources. Relying on the inseparable nexus between environmental protection and social and economic development, Southern states emphasize poverty alleviation through development as the first key step in addressing environmental protection. Southern and Northern concerns over green economy and poverty eradication have been embodied in the Rio+20 Declaration with a commitment to promote economically, socially, and environmentally sustainable development to free humanity from poverty and hunger as a matter of urgency.[90] This Southern preoccupation with development is a reflection of glaring economic disparities between the North and South, and threatens to undermine the possibility of collective North–South action to protect the environment.

The principle of common but differentiated responsibilities has emerged as one mechanism to bridge the North–South divide.[91] This principle imposes on Northern and Southern states common responsibilities for environmental protection, but Northern states will bear greater burdens than Southern states. The rationale is that Northern states are largely responsible for past environmental

---

[88] This section provides a brief account of the environmental aspect of the North–South divide, which is examined in: Chapter 1, S. Atapattu and C. G. Gonzalez, "The North–South Divide in International Environmental Law: Framing the Issues" Chapter 3, R. Gordon, "Unsustainable Development" Chapter 4, S. Atapattu, "The Significance of International Environmental Law Principles in Reinforcing or Dismantling the North–South Divide" Chapter 5, K. Mickelson, "The Stockholm Conference and the Creation of the South–North Divide in International Environmental Law and Policy" Chapter 6, V. P. Nanda, "Global Environmental Governance and the South" Chapter 7, B. H. Desai and B. K. Sidhu, "Quest for International Environmental Institutions: Transition from CSD to HLPF".

[89] A. Crawford, "International Environmental Law and State Sovereignty: An Irreconcilable Tension" (1999) 40 *International Law News* 65.

[90] UN, *Report of the United Nations Conference on Sustainable Development*, Rio de Janeiro, Brazil, 20–22 June 2012, UN Doc. A/Conf.216/16, Parts I and III.

[91] *Rio Declaration on Environment and Development*, Rio de Janeiro, 13 June 1992, UN Doc. A/CONF.151/26 (vol. I); 31 *International Legal Materials* 874 (1992).

degradation, continue to consume an overwhelming proportion of the planet's resources, and possess superior technological and financial capabilities to protect the environment. However, many Northern states have refused to accept responsibility for their historic contribution to global environmental degradation.[92] They interpret the principle as imposing only future, not past, responsibilities. This North–South conflict has prevented a global consensus on environmental protection.[93] As the planet teeters on the brink of collapse and economic inequality between and within nations intensifies, addressing the North–South divide in international environmental law becomes increasingly urgent.

8. CONCLUSION

The North–South divide in international law hamstrings its capacity to deliver a just, participatory, and inclusive world order to collectively address pressing global issues of common interest, such as environmental degradation, of the twenty-first century. Any bid to address these issues must be mindful of the historic legacy of the North–South divide, which continues unabated. Striving for a more universal and less Northern/Eurocentric approach to global governance appears to be the best hope for a collaborative and reasoned internationalism in this plural world.

[92] D. French, "Developing States and International Environmental Law: The Importance of Differentiated Responsibilities" (2000) 49 *International and Comparative Law Quarterly* 39; C. Stone, "Common but Differential Responsibilities in International Law" (2004) 98 *American Journal of International Law* 276.

[93] For the development of international environmental law amid the North–South divide, see chapter 5, K. Mickelson, "The Stockholm Conference and the Creation of the South–North Divide in International Environmental Law and Policy".

3

Unsustainable Development

Ruth Gordon

Humanity has to make development sustainable to ensure that it meets the needs of the present, without compromising the ability of future generations to meet their own needs[1].

1. INTRODUCTION

Economic development, at least thus far, has been decidedly unsustainable. As the Industrial Revolution unfolded in the global North it gradually improved the lives of human beings, but its impact on the natural world has been quite abysmal; the seas, skies, and earth deteriorated, as did many of the species that inhabited them. Over time the notion of protecting the natural environment and addressing environmental degradation emerged in England, the United States, and other Northern countries, and in 1972 the United Nations Conference on the Human Environment marked the official inauguration of international environmentalism. This Conference led to the creation of the United Nations Environment Programme (UNEP) and the adoption of the Stockholm Declaration, which avowed that the international community would now address the many environmental problems that transcended international borders, and would do so through international institutions, law, and cooperation.

Many of the low-income nations of the global South, however, had yet to fully realize the benefits or the burdens of industrialization, or to engage in environmentalism. Instead, they were steadfastly pursuing economic development, which seemed to conflict with international environmentalism. Having fully subscribed to the development narrative of industrialization and economic growth, addressing environmental concerns threatened to slow or impede this process, and to many this scenario was unacceptable. Some viewed environmentalism as a luxury that

---

[1] World Commission on Environment and Development, *Our Common Future* (New York: Oxford University Press, 1987), p. 8 [hereinafter *Our Common Future*].

low-income countries (LICs) could ill afford and as presenting yet another hurdle imposed by the countries in the global North which they themselves did not have to face as they became wealthy;[2] besides, environmental degradation and destruction were primarily due to the excesses of the global North, and thus remedying it was their responsibility. Still international environmental norms and law were posed as universal undertakings, and thus had to include and accommodate the nations of the global South; this was accomplished by way of "sustainable development," which purported to reconcile economic growth and environmental protection.[3] This concept appeared to mollify everyone because its proponents identified poverty and underdevelopment as major causes of environmental degradation and thus offered development and growth as the solution; indeed, more, not less, growth and industrialization were needed if the environment was to be protected and saved. The industrialized profligate global North, however, was not adequately held to answer for its role in environmental degradation or, more importantly, for the reality that at the core of our contemporary conundrum is the unsustainability of modern industrial life, which has been unsustainable as it pertains to the global North and is utterly unrealizable when extended to the entire global community.

As sustainable development emerged in international discourse it did not effectively examine the development paradigm of the global North, which developers posited as a model for the South; nor did it seriously interrogate the role of the global economy and global institutions in the economic and environmental plight of the global South. Given the lack of progress at "progress," however, this was never a pressing issue, as it seemed the global South would never industrialize, or at least not any time soon. Thus, having to reconcile the type of modernization prevailing in the global North with environmental sustainability was not a significant issue. With the rise of "the Rest" – that is, an industrializing global South – the international community faces the prospect of a world engaged in an unsustainable existence that may literally be destroying the planet. As broad swathes of humanity stand on the precipice of Northern-style "development," the planet appears to be on the threshold of environmental disaster. Climate change and other forms of severe environmental degradation may prove that development as defined by the global North will ultimately devastate the global environment, leaving future generations struggling to endure. At the same time, freezing current levels of inequality, which would leave many destitute, is just as unacceptable, thus

[2] H-J. Chang, *Kicking Away the Ladder: Development Strategy in Historical Perspective* (London: Anthem Press, 2002), discussing how development in the global North differed radically from the methods and practices that have been forced upon the nations of the global South.

[3] Sustainable development was initially and most famously defined as development that "meets the needs of the present, without compromising the ability of future generations to meet their own needs": see World Commission on the Environment and Development, note 1, p. 8.

52 Unsustainable Development

underscoring the need for more innovative notions of sustainability based on different sensibilities. Hopefully this evolving vantage point will emanate from the global South – although in all honesty, it does not look particularly promising for either the earth or the impoverished, as development in all of its guises usually seems to prevail over the environment in both the global North and South, while inequality and poverty persist.

This chapter begins with a brief examination of "development" in both the global North and the global South. The environmental damage caused by development was not initially a concern in the global North, and the global South merely followed the North's lead. Eventually environmentalism emerged in Europe and then America, and as international themes tend to emanate from Northern discourses, international environmentalism soon materialized. However, the advent of international environmentalism came at a particularly inauspicious time for the global South, which feared environmentalism would slow its development. Thus, the concepts of development and environmentalism had to be reconciled. Sustainable development was the solution and is the focus of the second section. The third section turns to interrogating sustainable development from the vantage point of both the global South and global North, concluding that it is the unsustainability of the North that has not been adequately addressed and is responsible for the vast majority of the environmental degradation now facing the global community. Finally, the chapter offers some concluding thoughts on avoiding the environmental collapse that Northern economic development and priorities portend, but within a framework of global justice and fairness.

2. DEVELOPMENT AND THE ENVIRONMENT

2.1 Development

2.1.1 Development in the Global North

If not for the Industrial Revolution, I would not be writing these words, nor would you be reading them; it is at the core of life as we know it.[4] Before the Industrial Revolution, economies were stagnant, and while there was a small merchant class, there was little social and economic mobility. In the mid-eighteenth century new mechanized forms of production began to emerge in England that inexorably and completely altered the economies and societies of Europe, its offshoots, and

---

[4] J. A. Montagna, "The Industrial Revolution," http://www.yale.edu. While the period is appropriately labeled a "revolution," in that it comprehensively destroyed the former social and economic order, the term is inapposite because it connotes abrupt change. The changes that are termed the Industrial Revolution actually unfolded gradually, taking place between 1760 and 1850.

eventually the world.[5] People began moving from rural areas to cities, incomes climbed, the nature of work changed, life expectancies rose, and eventually there was higher demand for leisure goods and services as at least some individuals could devote fewer hours to work.[6] Yet, as populations and the industrial base that sustained them expanded, natural resources became strained. Lands and waterways were polluted by industrial discharge, mining operations, and human sewage; urban air pollution rose steeply; and species of flora and fauna vanished, as undeveloped land was devoted to agricultural and other purposes or was degraded by various forms of pollution.[7] This environmental disorder was duplicated, in varying degrees, throughout Europe and often, through colonial conquest, was exported to Africa and Asia. In America, it reached extraordinary heights.

The American Industrial Revolution progressed on an unprecedented scale, against a milieu of a more limited labor force and an almost extreme capitalist ethos. Moreover, unlike in Europe, it occurred against the backdrop of seemingly unlimited land and natural resources, and this notion of unbounded abundance undoubtedly shaped American perspectives toward the environment.[8] Species were hunted to extinction, forests were razed for agriculture and other uses, and rivers were dammed to generate hydroelectric power. Eventually, substances that deplete the ozone layer were developed; other industrial chemicals were introduced that despoiled the landscape and raised concerns regarding hazardous and nuclear waste disposal;[9] and the waste generated reached immense levels.

---

[5] T. Schrecker, "Sustainability, Growth and Distributive Justice: Questioning Environmental Absolutism," in J. Lemons, L. Westra, and R. Goodland (eds.), *Ecological Sustainability and Integrity: Concepts and Approaches* (Dordrecht: Kluwer Academic Publishers, 1998), p. 221, discussing the length, tensions, and burdens of the industrial revolution. On the rise of the merchant class, the weakening of traditional European political structures, and the rise of the West, see C. A. Kupchan, *No One's World: The West, The Rising Rest, and the Coming Global Turn* (Oxford: Oxford University Press, 2012), pp. 13–75.

[6] R. Socolow, C. Andrews, F. Berkhout, and V. Thoma (eds.), *Industrial Ecology and Global Change* (New York: Cambridge University Press, 1994), pp. 60–61.

[7] I. G. Simmons, *An Environmental History of Great Britain: From 10,000 Years to the Present* (Edinburgh: Edinburgh University Press, 2001), p. 174.

[8] J. H. Lienhard, "Engines of Our Ingenuity," No. 181: American Industrial Revolution, www. uh.edu; C. J. Madoc, *Environmental Issues in American History: A Reference Guide with Primary Documents* (Westport: Greenwood Press, 2006), p. 36. M. Teich and R. Porter (eds.), *The Industrial Revolution in National Context: Europe and the USA* (Cambridge: Cambridge University Press, 1996), p. 355.

[9] Although the use of nuclear power began in the United States, the disposal of nuclear waste has proven to be an international problem: see e.g. World Nuclear Association, "International Nuclear Waste Disposal Concepts," April 2012, www.world-nuclear.org. Other environmental problems indicating environmental disorder include the dustbowl of the 1930s Depression (see University of Illinois, "About the Dust Bowl," http://www.english.illinois.edu) and the use of pesticides (see North Carolina Cooperative Extension, "Pesticide Usage in the United States: History, Benefits, Risks, and Trends," 1996, http://ipm.ncsu.edu).

54 *Unsustainable Development*

2.1.2 Development in the Global South

Growth in the global North also meant transferring energy and material from the periphery to the industrial center, and thus the Northern model of environmental exploitation was eventually brought to the global South.[10] Asia, Africa, and the Americas were viewed by European colonizers as a source of natural wealth to be exploited for short-term gain, and this natural wealth was extracted with impunity. Examples abound of colonial governments consuming the environmental resources of their colonies by means of policies that promoted extraction with little regard for the environmental consequences.[11] The blatant exploitation of the colonial era, however, was about to be supplanted with a new paradigm more in keeping with a new world order led by the United States.

In the aftermath of World War II the industrialized world was in the throes of economic expansion and growth. A robust and unrivaled United States cemented its leadership of the global North as it restored a war-torn Europe and Japan (whose revival and reconstruction were essential), and set about establishing the international institutions that would manage the global economy.[12] Thus, the newly created Bretton Woods institutions focused on trade, the international monetary system, and financing the restoration of Europe;[13] the peoples and nations of the global South were to be included in this grand transformation by way of "development."

---

[10] W. E. Rees and L. Westra, "When Consumption Does Violence: Can There Be Sustainability and Environmental Justice in a Resource-Limited World?," in R. J. Agyeman, R. D. Bullard, and B. Evans (eds.) *Just Sustainabilities: Development in an Unequal World* (London: Earthscan, 2002), p. 104.

[11] For instance, Australian colonial administrators sold gold-prospecting rights in Papua New Guinea to multinational corporations without consulting local communities. The result was toxic sediments that destroyed river ecosystems, fish, and birds, and devastated the livelihoods of people living downstream. In French West Africa colonial administrators deforested local forests to build and fuel railroads. Similar policies prevailed in British colonies where, for example, deforestation took place to plant cash crops for the benefit of the colonial administration; local communities had little input into such policies. In the Belgian Congo the colonial government extracted rubber, ivory, and minerals: K. Harper and S. R. Rajan, "International Environmental Justice: Building the Natural Assets of the World's Poor" (2005) 71 *Political Economy Research Institute University of Massachusetts Amherst: Anthropology Department Faculty Publication Series* 2.

[12] W. Sachs (ed.), "Environment," in *The Development Dictionary: A Guide to Knowledge as Power* (London: Zed Books, 2001), p. 26, noting that the unfettered enthusiasm for economic growth in 1945 reflected the West's desire to restart the economic machine after a devastating war.

[13] The International Monetary Fund (IMF), the International Bank for Reconstructions and Development (the World Bank), and the stillborn International Trade Organization, established in 1945, were to manage the world economy, with the United States at the de facto helm. Indeed, when the United States did not join the International Trade Organization, it foundered and the General Agreement on Tariffs and Trade (GATT) had to fill in until 1994, when the World Trade Organization (WTO) was launched.

In his 1949 inaugural address, U.S. President Harry Truman redefined the global South as the undeveloped areas of the world whose underdevelopment was an international problem to be remedied by industrialization and a "higher standard of living,"[14] which would be realized under the guidance of the World Bank and other international institutions. The global South was to advance along the inevitable trajectory of progress[15] and catch up to the high-income nations that already had a high gross national product (GNP).[16] Traditions at odds with the development paradigm were discarded and cultures that were not based on material accumulation were overwhelmed, for development meant adopting the Northern ethos of production and consumption,[17] which included the relationship between industrialized states and the environment.[18] The World Bank, IMF, and other international institutions lent funds, devised policies, and eventually prescribed increasingly onerous and intrusive policy edicts and proscriptions in pursuit of development.[19] Joining the global economy became essential as domestic institutions

---

[14] A. Gillespie, *The Illusion of Progress: Unsustainable Development in International Law and Policy* (London: Earthscan, 2001), p. 1. Truman was referring to the nations and peoples emerging from colonialism, which had yet to industrialize and were primarily in the Southern hemisphere, meaning Africa, South and Central America, and Asia. These nations were also collectively referred to as the Third World, a term that emerged during the Cold War as these nations sought to define themselves as distinct from the Western First World and the Communist Second World. See R. E. Gordon, "Katrina, Race, Refugees, and Images of the Third World," in J. Levitt and M. C. Whitaker (eds.), *Hurricane Katrina: America's Unnatural Disaster, Justice and Social Inquiry* (Lincoln: University of Nebraska Press, 2009). The role of colonialism in the global South's presumed "underdevelopment" was conveniently ignored – rather, it was the people themselves who were regarded as underdeveloped. See also R. Gordon, "Saving Failed States: Sometimes a Neocolonialist Notion" (1997) **12** *American University Journal of International Law and Policy* 930.

[15] W. Sachs, "Global Ecology in the Shadow of Development," in W. Sachs (ed.), *Global Ecology: A New Arena of Political Conflict* (London: Zed Books, 1993), p. 5.

[16] Ibid, p. 7.

[17] Gillespie, note 14, p. 1, stating that this process simultaneously diminished traditions, hierarchies, and habits – that is, it devalued "the whole texture of societies"; Sachs, note 15, pp. 5–6, observing that development increasingly came to encompass a broad range of ideas that swamped societies and cultures.

[18] L. K. Caldwell, "The Concept of Sustainability: A Critical Approach,' in J. Lemons, L. Westra, and R. Goodland (eds.), *Ecological Sustainability and Integrity: Concepts and Approaches* (Dordrecht: Kluwer Academic Publishers, 1998), p. 1, asserting, for example, the modern proclivity to work against rather than with nature and that the disregard for nature follows from a mindset that sees human achievement as being limited only by human will and imagination.

[19] Although the World Bank (WB) was originally created to rebuild Europe and the IMF was charged with coordinating and supporting international monetary policy, the functions and focus of these institutions evolved over time. The WB turned to developing nations after the U.S. Marshall Plan provided the necessary funds to rebuild Europe. The IMF's focus did not narrow quite as much, but it has played a crucial role in global South development. R. E. Gordon and J. H. Sylvester, "Deconstructing Development" (2004) **22** *Wisconsin International Law Journal* 23.

56 *Unsustainable Development*

were shattered, undercutting the ability to survive and thrive outside of it;[20] global North views of production and productivity are now so dominant and ingrained that alternatives are almost impossible to imagine, even as environmental decline makes alternatives all the more urgently needed.[21]

2.2 *Encountering Ecology*

2.2.1 The Emergence of Environmentalism in the Global North

Given the environmental destruction wrought by industrialization, the notion of protecting the natural environment eventually materialized in European countries, and then the U.S.. European environmental movements emerged in the 1880s, expanded and declined throughout the early twentieth century,[22] and then reemerged in force during the 1960s at the behest of an increasingly educated, postindustrial Europe that no longer had to focus on meeting basic needs.[23] Even so, the resolve to protect the environment waned during economic recessions, when environmental protection was viewed as a possible threat to economic recovery and prosperity – a pattern that has persisted[24] and that mirrors tensions between development and environmental protection in the global South. Environmental disasters and catastrophes made an indefinite retreat impossible, however, as oil spills, acid rain, chemical plant explosions, and other environmental calamities continued to unfold, culminating in perhaps the ultimate environmental disaster – the 1986 Chernobyl nuclear reactor explosion and meltdown. Thus, by

---

[20] Sachs, note 15, p. 4.

[21] Ibid, p. 4. For discussions of possibilities in the wake of what appears to be the waning of western hegemony, see e.g. Kupchan, note 5, pp. 75–146 and E. B. Ziegler, "China's Cities, Globalization and Sustainable Development: Comparative Thoughts on Urban Planning, Energy and Environmental Policy" (2006) 5 *Washington University Global Studies Law Review* 5.

[22] R. J. Dalton, "The Environmental Movement in Western Europe," in S. Kamieniecki (ed.), *Environmental Politics in the International Arena* (Albany: State University of New York Press, 1993), p. 41. As the environmental consequences of the Industrial Revolution became more noticeable and scientific knowledge more convincing, the possibilities of potential ecological harms became increasingly apparent. The European upper class began to challenge the idea of progress popularized by the Enlightenment. See Dalton, pp. 40–42. Conservation groups flourished during times of European affluence, as at least some members of the public had more leisure time and there was more economic mobility. When these periods were interrupted by war and economic recession, however, these movements lost steam. C. Rootes, "1968 and the Environmental Movement in Europe," in M. Klimke and J. Scharloth (eds.), *1968 in Europe: A Handbook on National Perspectives and Transnational Dimensions of 1960/ 70s Protest Movements* (New York: Palgrave Macmillan, 2008), p. 295.

[23] Rootes, note 22, p. 296.

[24] For instance, during the global economic recession of 1974–1975, governments focused on their economies and environmental concerns receded in importance; indeed at times environmental protection was viewed as an economic threat: ibid, p. 39. Thus leaders either lacked enthusiasm for environmental reform or were hostile to it: Dalton, note 22, p. 56.

the late 1980s, environmental concerns were a prominent and permanent part of European policy-making.[25]

While the origins of American environmentalism can be traced to Henry David Thoreau's 1854 classic, *Walden*, which lamented human destruction of the environment in the name of capitalist expansion,[26] the modern environmental movement is widely viewed as commencing with the 1962 publication of Rachel Carson's *Silent Spring*, which documented the devastating effects of pesticides on wildlife and human beings.[27] In the wake of *Silent Spring*, there was some reexamination of how the industrial world was negatively affecting nature and both human and non-human life.[28] Inspired by the social justice protests of the 1960s, the first Earth Day was held on April 22, 1970, and it marked the beginning of environmentalism as a "mass social movement."[29] The U.S. Environmental Protection Agency was established soon thereafter,[30] myriad environmental groups emerged,[31] and by the late 1970s the environmental movement had evolved from a grassroots campaign to a fully institutionalized presence with a stake in the American political process.[32]

[25] By 1992, 85 per cent of European Union (EU) citizens believed reducing pollution and protecting the environment were of "immediate concern": K. Hillstrom and L. C. Hillstrom (eds.), *Europe: A Continental Overview of Environmental Issues* (Santa Barbara: ABC Clio, 2003), p. 235. Given these views and that Europe's geography exacerbated the "transboundary nature" of environmental problems, EU institutions increasingly became more involved in environmental policy and were eventually given authority to act on behalf of member states on environmental issues: Hillstrom and Hillstrom (eds.), pp. 235–236.

[26] P. Shabecoff, *A New Name for Peace: International Environmentalism, Sustainable Development, and Democracy* (Hanover: University Press of New England, 1996), p. 18, noting that many philosophies found in contemporary environmental movements can be traced to Thoreau's values and ideals. In his now classic 1854 book, *Walden: Or Life in the Woods*, Thoreau decried the destruction of nature, which human beings were destroying in the interest of capitalist expansion: Shabecoff, p. 18.

[27] R. N. L. Andrews, *Managing the Environment, Managing Ourselves: A History of American Environmental Policy* (London: Yale University Press, 1999), p. 202. See also, Sachs, note 15, p. 9; N. Hildyard, "Foxes in Charge of the Chickens," in W. Sachs (ed.), *Global Ecology: a New Arena of Political Conflict* (London: Zed Books, 1993), pp. 22, 25.

[28] Shabecoff, note 26, p. 27.

[29] On 22 April 1970 millions of Americans demonstrated in the streets and on campuses: W. Manes, *Green Rage: Radical Environmentalism and the Unmaking of Civilization* (Boston: Little, Brown & Co., 1990), p. 45. It precipitated a larger interest in quality-of-life and environmental issues. Shabecoff, note 26, p. 27; R. Gottlieb, *Forcing the Spring: The Transformation of the American Environmental Movement* (Washington: Island Press, 1993), p. 105.

[30] The U.S. Environmental Protection Agency (EPA) was created in December 1970 and fourteen major federal environmental statutes were enacted in the 1970s. Many federal laws and regulatory initiatives to control pollution followed as public sentiment and awareness evolved: Andrews, note 27, p. 233.

[31] Principal environmental groups include the Environmental Defense Fund, the National Audubon Society, the National Wildlife Federation, the Natural Resources Defense Council, Friends of the Earth, and the Sierra Club.

[32] In the late 1970s, the environmental movement employed effective litigation strategies and managed to get important and significant legislation enacted. Over the ensuing two decades, the movement successfully defended these advances, but did not make much headway in building upon its initial victories: C. Coglianese, "Social Movements, Law,

2.2.2 The Emergence of International Environmentalism

As environmentalism gained salience in the global North, it was bound to be exported to the international sphere, as international paradigms tend to follow Northern concepts and discourses.[33] Moreover, there was also growing recognition that some environmental problems, such as acid rain and other forms of pollution,[34] truly do transcend national boundaries, and those nations experiencing damage due to such harms began to seek some measure of redress. The modern international environmental era is widely viewed as commencing in 1972 with the United Nations Conference on the Human Environment held in Stockholm, Sweden.[35] What has become known as the Stockholm Conference was the first major international conference on the environment and laid the foundation for international environmental law and policy-making. It propelled the founding of the UN Environment Programme[36] and adopted the Stockholm Declaration, whose twenty-six principles sought to inaugurate a common framework for the international environmental initiatives that were to follow.[37] While other significant and exceptionally important environmental conferences followed Stockholm,[38] it is the reaction to the evolving environmental discourse that emerged from Stockholm that drove the need for the concept of sustainable development, which was to emerge soon thereafter.[39]

---

and Society: The Institutionalization of the Environmental Movement," John F. Kennedy School of Government Harvard University Faculty Research Working Papers Series (2001), p. 7.

[33] Gordon and Sylvester, note 19, p. 15.

[34] L. Wenner, "Transboundary Problems in International Law," in S. Kamieniecki (ed.), *Environmental Politics in the International Arena Movements, Parties, Organizations and Policy* (Albany: State University of New York Press, 1993), pp. 165–176, discussing the international legal response to transboundary air and water pollution.

[35] In 1968, Sweden suggested convening a conference on the environment to the United Nations Economic and Social Council, one of the principal organs of the United Nations.

[36] The United Nations General Assembly established UNEP on 15 December 1972. See UN General Assembly, *Resolution Adopted by the General Assembly: Institutional and Financial Arrangements for International Environmental Cooperation*, 15 December 1972, A/RES 2997. For a critique of international environmental institutions and the lack thereof, see "Excerpt from the Johannesburg Memo: Fairness in a Fragile World," in K. Conca and G. D. Dabelko (eds.), *Green Planet Blues: Environmental Politics From Stockholm to Johannesburg*, 3rd ed. (Boulder: Westview Press, 2004), pp. 172–178.

[37] See *Declaration of the United Nations Conference on the Human Environment*, Stockholm, 16 June 1972, UN Doc. A/Conf.48/14/Rev. 1 (1973); 11 ILM 1416 (1972) [hereinafter Stockholm Declaration]. The most famous principle contained in the Stockholm Declaration is Principle 21.

[38] See chapter 5, K. Mickelson, "The Stockholm Conference and the Creation of the South–North Divide in International Environmental Law and Policy."

[39] For a comprehensive legal analysis of sustainable development, see N. Schrijver, *Evolution of Sustainable Development in International Law: Inception, Meaning and Status* (Leiden: Martinus Nijhoff, 2008).

3. RECONCILING DEVELOPMENT AND ECOLOGY

3.1 *Precursors to Accommodation*

A major contention at Stockholm was whether economic growth and development were inherently damaging to the environment,[40] and fervent disagreements emerged between the global North and the global South, as well as among growth-oriented governments and more environmentally sensitive Northern NGOs.[41] As the global North asserted that environmental protection was an obligation to be assumed by all states, nations in the global South generally resisted this mandate.[42] The Stockholm Declaration proclaimed that environmental problems in developing countries were due to underdevelopment, and thus developing countries and their industrialized counterparts should focus on development.[43] Yet, the development paradigm continued to affirm the viability of the development model of the global North, which had industrialization and economic expansion at its core,[44] and environmental concerns as secondary at best.

The evolving international focus on the environment did not seem to bode well for those seeking economic development, and it emerged just as global South demands for economic justice and a more equitable economic order were growing more insistent. The 1970s were marked by turbulent North–South debates that gave rise to global South demands for a New International Economic Order,[45] the adoption of a Charter of Economic Rights and Duties of States,[46] and the espousal of other global South entreaties for a more equitable international economic order that would facilitate its economic development;[47] protecting the natural environment most definitely was not part of these demands. The global South did insist upon permanent sovereignty over its natural resources, but this privilege was more in the interest of sovereign prerogatives to exploit and profit from these resources,

---

[40] K. Conca and G. D. Dabelko (eds.), *Green Planet Blues: Four Decades of Global Environmental Politics*, 3rd ed. (Boulder: Westview Press, 2004), p. 229.

[41] NGOS were more concerned with the ecological consequences of constantly expanding economic activity than governments in both the global North and global South: ibid, p. 229.

[42] Schrijver, note 39, p. 49 (noting that environmentalism was regarded as contrary to global South efforts to mitigate poverty); Sachs (ed.), note 12, pp. 47–48.

[43] Stockholm Declaration, note 37, Principle 9. See also Gillespie, note 14, p. 6.

[44] Gillespie, note 14, p. 5.

[45] UN General Assembly, *Resolution Adopted by the General Assembly: 3201 (S-VI). Declaration on the Establishment of a New International Economic Order*, 1 May 1974, A/Res/s-6/3201.

[46] UN General Assembly, *Resolution Adopted by the General Assembly: 3281(XXIX). Charter of Economic Rights and Duties of States*, 12 December 1974, A/RES/29/3281.

[47] R. Gordon, "The Dawn of a New, New International Economic Order?" (2009) **72** *Duke Journal of Law and Contemporary Problems* 142.

60   *Unsustainable Development*

rather than to conserve or protect them. Indeed, it seemed as if the new environmental ethos would only impede Southern progress.[48]

In the decade following Stockholm a succession of UN meetings endeavored to alter the perception of an unbounded natural world in which each nation could independently maximize economic growth.[49] Efforts were made to foster awareness of ecological limits and constraints, even if nature was not accorded an "absolute value," which might have hindered its utilization.[50] There were also undertakings to raise environmental awareness in the global South by focusing on environmental problems that were particularly salient in the Southern hemisphere, such as deforestation and desertification.[51] But many in the global South believed that to the extent that there was environmental degradation, it was largely due to the practices of the affluent inhabitants of Northern industrialized nations,[52] and it was their responsibility to address the problem and assume the costs of any necessary mitigation. North–South conflict over environmental protection became one of the outstanding issues blocking agreement at international fora.[53] Nonetheless, environmental concerns remained an increasingly important and permanent part of international political and legal discourse, and it thus had to be determined how developing countries and development would be incorporated into this paradigm.

3.2 *Making Development Sustainable*

In 1983, the UN General Assembly appointed the World Commission on Environment and Development (WCED), under the chairmanship of Gro Harlem Brundtland. The General Assembly charged the Brundtland Commission with devising strategies for sustainable development;[54] that is, with somehow reconciling two

---

[48] The global South also insisted that environmental issues be dealt with at the national level. Principle 21 of the Stockholm Declaration reflects the compromise between the principle of permanent sovereignty and the principle of not causing damage beyond national borders.

[49] Sachs (ed.), note 12, p. 27.

[50] Schools of thought emerged in the United States during the 1960s that suggest that there may be ecological limits. Professor Sachs cites conferences during the 1970s on population, food, human settlements, water, desertification, science and technology, and renewable energy: ibid, pp. 27–28.

[51] Ibid.

[52] The impoverished citizens of the global South were at best "future claimants to the industrial lifestyle": ibid.

[53] The global South contended that the wealthy countries of the global North should pay for the damage they caused and also demanded additional development funding: D. A. Brown, "The Need to Face Conflicts between Rich and Poor Nations to Solve Global Environmental Problems," in L. Westra and P. H. Werhane (eds.), *The Business of Consumption: Environmental Ethics and the Global Economy* (New York: Rowman & Littlefield Publishers, 1998), p. 31. Common but differentiated responsibilities reflect the notion of greater global North responsibility for environmental harm. Schrijver, note 39, pp. 178–179.

[54] UN General Assembly, *Resolution Adopted by the General Assembly: Process of Preparation of the Environmental Perspective to the Year 2000 and Beyond*, 19 December 1983, A/RES/38/161,

seemingly disparate and antagonistic concepts: protecting the environment, as opposed to human activities in both the global North and South that are synonymous with development and tend to generate environmental degradation.[55] While this seemed to be a nearly unattainable goal, it was just as inconceivable to, in effect, freeze global inequality under the guise of protecting the environment.[56] Their report, *Our Common Future*, purported to align the desire for development with concerns for the environment in a manner that allowed them to co-exist;[57] to wit, humanity had only to "make development sustainable – to assure that it meets the needs of the present, without compromising the ability of future generations to meet their needs."[58] "Development" in both the North and South was vindicated and actually emerged stronger, while sustainability became less about ecology and more about the needs, wants, and priorities of human beings.[59]

While conventional development theory expanded to encompass environmentalism, development in essence barely changed at all.[60] According to the *Brundtland Report*, the foremost adversary of the environment was not industrialization but rather poverty, as impoverishment reduced the ability to use resources in a sustainable manner.[61] Overpopulation, often associated with poverty, was yet another enemy of the environment, for, according to the *Brundtland Report*, global population growth rates were unsustainable, thus putting untenable pressures on both natural and human resources.[62] While populations were universally rising, making overpopulation a global problem, this quandary was "concentrated in the developing regions of Asia, Africa, and Latin America" and thus at the core of this particular part of the mosaic were the nations and peoples of the global South.[63]

---

which established WECD and charged it with proposing environmental strategies to achieve sustainable development. See also Schrijver, note 39, pp. 64–65.

[55] G. Rist, *The History of Development from Western Origins to Global Faith*, 2nd ed. (New York: Zed Books, 2004), p. 180.

[56] Ibid, p. 181.

[57] Sachs, note 12, p. 29.

[58] *Our Common Future*, note 1, p. 8.

[59] The concept of "sustainable development" altered both sustainability and development, steadily shifting sustainability away from giving priority to nature towards according primacy to human beings, often at the expense of nature. Caldwell, note 18, p.1.

[60] For more on the capacity of development theory to absorb narratives and theories, see Gordon and Sylvester, note 19 at 15–18.

[61] *Our Common Future*, note 1, pp. 28–31. Given their limited options the poor had to exploit and often degrade natural resources for their short-term survival: ibid; S. M. Lèlè, "Sustainable Development, A Critical Review," in K. Conca and G. Dabelko (eds.), *Green Planet Blues: Environmental Politics from Stockholm to Johannesburg*, 3rd ed. (Boulder: Westview Press, 2004), p. 258 (questioning the connection between poverty and environmental degradation).

[62] WCED suggested that rising populations inevitably strained natural resources. It did acknowledge, however, that each additional person from the industrialized world placed more burden on the environment that an additional person in the global South: *Our Common Future*, note 1, pp. 95–102.

[63] Ibid, pp. 236–238. The Report predicted that by the millennium the global South would add three quarters of a billion individuals to the total global population while the global North

WCED did consider such matters as energy, pollution, the global economy, and manufacturing – endeavors that more fully engaged the policies and practices of the Global North.[64] Yet, the concept of sustainable development was conceived in large part to engage the global South in ecological discourse, not to fundamentally question global North understandings of development and economic growth and their bearing on the environment. Accordingly, the substantial impact of poverty on the environment, and the conjecture that development would eradicate that poverty, made economic growth essential. The problem was not economic growth per se, but the environmentally destructive character of current development undertakings and incentives.[65] Rather than critically interrogating the dominant paradigms of trade and production,[66] *Our Common Future* called for a new era of economic growth[67] that was both socially and environmentally sustainable, meaning global South growth had to also restrain the myriad environmental problems that seemed to be looming for future generations.[68] Thus developers were now tasked with a new set of objectives that included meeting food, energy, water, and sanitation requirements; ensuring sustainable population levels while simultaneously conserving and enhancing the resource base; reorienting technology and managing risk; and merging the environment and economics in decision-making.[69] These prescriptions were entirely in accordance with traditional development methods and doctrine, which unwaveringly rely on Northern expertise and intervention to determine policies and priorities. Hence as the environment and development became intertwined, the "environment" was easily and swiftly welcomed and absorbed into the established paradigm of development.[70]

would only contribute an added 110 million persons: ibid. A range of policies were needed in the global South to bring down fertility rates: ibid, pp. 105–107.

[64] Ibid, pp. 168–177 (energy and fossil fuels); 178–181 (air pollution); 181–189 (nuclear energy); 206–232 (industry). Indeed, the *Brundtland Report* has been characterized as providing an "exhaustive list of threats to the planet's equilibrium": Rist, note 55, p. 180.

[65] Lèlè, note 61, p. 259 (critiquing negative and somewhat more positive aspects of economic growth).

[66] S. Alam, M. J. H. Bhuiyan, T. M. R. Chowdhury, and E.J. Techera (eds.). note 5, p. 230.

[67] According to *Our Common Future*, a rise in per capita incomes was necessary, albeit not sufficient to eliminate absolute poverty.

[68] Sachs, note 12, p. 28. Such problems include climate change, pollution, deforestation, desertification, and overfishing which depletes fish stocks among others. See also C. Gonzalez, "Environmental Justice and International Environmental Law," in S. Alam, M. J. H. Bhuiyan, T. M. R. Chowdhury, and E. J. Techera (eds.). *Routledge Handbook of International Environmental Law* (London: Routledge, 2013), p. 77 (noting myriad environmental problems facing the global community).

[69] Lèlè, note 61, pp. 252, 256.

[70] Sachs, note 12, p. 29. Professor Sachs notes: "the way was thus clear for the marriage between 'environment' and 'development': the newcomer could be welcomed to the old-established family."

Sustainable development became a "metafix" of sorts that could unite all the relevant participants, and most especially the international business community.[71] It met the requisites of the global South as it entailed development, and it retained the norms of Northern developers as it could be achieved through an assortment of expert interventions in poor, environmentally damaged countries. Perhaps sustainable development can be embraced to the extent that it has terminated or modified projects and practices that harmed populations and habitats and thus hindered outsider interventions.[72] Nonetheless, the concept is deeply flawed for it fails to adequately address the deeper roots of our collective distress: The unsustainability of global North development that is characterized by an ethos and economic system that views the environment as an externality that is to be conquered, and which almost always comes second to economic growth.

4. INTERROGATING SUSTAINABLE DEVELOPMENT

The notion of "sustainable development" can be difficult to challenge. It is a particularly appealing concept that makes it seem possible for humankind to both have its cake and eat it too[73] – that humanity can continue along the current path of economic development and growth, while simultaneously sustaining the environment. Sustainable development appears to address what is essentially an enigma without meaningfully challenging existing power structures or the impact that the modern quest for a higher material standard of living has had on the natural world.[74] Indeed, in many respects it only reinforces these constructs, as it essentially negates the view that environmental conservation inevitably constrains development or that development, as currently fashioned in the global North, unavoidably

---

[71] Sustainable development soon devolved into a "collection of quick fixes that included modifying economic dogma to incorporate environmental considerations and yet still achieve economic growth": Lèlè, note 61, pp. 257–258. Of course, there was still the problem of who would pay for development that relied on more environmentally sound methods, and thus initially, sustainable development discourse often entailed demonstrating its viability to low-income countries that asserted these costs should be borne by the global North. In 1991, the Global Environmental Facility (GEF) was established to fund sustainable development initiatives; see Global Environment Facility, 'What is the GEF,' http://www.thegef.org; see also Schrijver, note 39, p. 69. For critical assessments of the GEF see V. Shiva, 'The Greening of the Global Reach,' in W. Sachs (ed.), *Global Ecology: A New Arena of Political Conflict* (London: Zed Books, 1993), pp. 149, 151. Hildyard, note 27, pp. 22, 32.

[72] C. Gonzalez, "Markets, Monocultures, and Malnutrition: Agricultural Trade Policy Through an Environmental Justice Lens" (2006) 14 *Michigan State University Journal of International Law* 362 (discussing unsustainable and destructive agricultural practices).

[73] Lèlè, note 61, p. 618.

[74] D. McLaren, "Environmental Space, Equity and the Ecological Debt," in J. Agyeman et al. (eds.), *Just Sustainabilities: Development in an Unequal World* (London: Earthscan, 2002) pp. 19, 30–32 (examining the environmentally harmful impact of various commercial practices). For a particularly critical assessment of UNCED, see Hildyard, note 27, p.22.

64   *Unsustainable Development*

means an unacceptable level of environmental degradation.[75] As rising economic activity is associated with either improvement or deterioration in environmental quality, there is little need to limit economic output as long as natural resource consumption is contained.[76] Thus, the environment often became a matter of management, meaning that with sufficient management, development could continue and the environment would be preserved.[77] Also unresolved is what is to be sustained and for how long, as most conceptions of sustainability require a degree of long-term consciousness that is largely absent from most modern societies.[78] *Our Common Future* proclaimed that international trade was the engine of the growth that was necessary for a more equitable distribution of wealth and in various guises this claim has persisted.[79] But proposed policies for growth that would reduce poverty and stabilize the ecosystem have not differed very much from the policies that have caused global inequality and threaten the environment.[80]

4.1 *Critiquing Sustainable Development: A View From the Global South*

Modern elites have a remarkable capacity to weather any storm with their power firmly intact, and the global environmental predicament has not been an exception.[81] In constructing the concept of sustainable development, rather than examining the environmental destruction endemic in economic growth, the responsibility for environmental degradation was essentially laid at the feet of the world's most impoverished people, whose poverty was destroying the environment. Of course there is some truth to such assertions, as people will do whatever is necessary to survive.[82] Yet,

---

[75] L. Lohmann, "Whose Common Future?," in K. Conca and G. D. Dabelko (eds.), *Green Planet Blues: Environmental Politics From Stockholm to Johannesburg*, 3rd ed. (Boulder: Westview Press, 2004), p. 246 (citing the depression, New Deal, Marshall Plan, and Bretton Woods).

[76] Caldwell, note 18, p. 259.

[77] Rees and Westra, note 19, p. 105.

[78] Caldwell, note 18, p. 254. For example, one articulation of a sustainable society envisions an entity that can persist over generations and is judicious and sufficiently visionary and malleable to not degrade its physical or social systems of support. Another conceptualizes characteristics of a steady or homeostatic state. These definitions imply and seem to require a degree of foresight, coherence, and steadfastness that is generally not an attribute of most contemporary societies: ibid.

[79] Rist, note 55, pp. 149–150 (contending that the New International Economic Order and other indicators of global South revolt actually reinforced the prevailing international economic order).

[80] Ibid, p. 186; P. Elkins, "Making Development Sustainable," in W. Sachs (ed.), *Global Ecology: A New Arena of Political Conflict* (London: Zed Books, 1993), p. 91 (noting that development means imposed modernization while growth means a higher GNP); McLaren, note 74, pp. 32–34 (discussing how globalization has exacerbated economic degradation and attempts to bring equity to sustainable development).

[81] Lohmann, note 75, p. 246 (citing the depression, New Deal, Marshall Plan, and Bretton Woods). See also Hildyard, note 27, pp. 22, 23–25.

[82] Lohmann, note 75, p. 247.

neither *Our Common Future* nor most subsequent reports[83] fundamentally challenged the forces responsible for this rampant poverty, or for the many environmental problems in the global South that far surpass the activities of indigent people struggling to meet their most basic needs.[84] The global economy and global institutions profoundly influence the economies and ecologies of the global South. For example, the need for foreign exchange earnings to pay international debt obligations has led to producing cash crops for export, utilizing damaging farming methods,[85] and allowing overexploitation of forestry and mineral resources primarily for the benefit of multinational corporations.[86] Structural adjustment programs mandated by the World Bank and IMF have frequently had quite devastating environmental effects locally and have also furthered urbanization.[87] Trade and the restructuring of rural economies have often displaced people from productive landscapes to overcrowded cities, primarily to supply urban industrial constituencies that are mainly in the global North. This has contributed to impoverishment, urban migration, and local ecological decay. International development models and debt-financed development have furthered the depletion of natural capital in the global South and have led to the net transfer of wealth to the global North, while simultaneously furthering poverty and ecological decline in the global South.[88]

Of course, the concept of sustainable development evolved beyond *Our Common Future*; indeed, development became a more prominent aspect of the calculation. As the political strength and size of the global South continued to grow and mature, it was increasingly realized by the international community that global South cooperation would be needed to resolve such complex environmental challenges as climate change, depletion of the ozone layer, and the loss of biological diversity. The global South continued to insist on development as its main priority, however, and this sensibility essentially prevailed. Major environmental conferences now explicitly and directly focus on achieving sustainable development; indeed, development now takes center stage in international environmental discourse. Legal canons evolved, such as common but differentiated responsibility, which acknowledged the global North's primary responsibility for many global environmental harms and their greater access to mechanisms to

---

[83] Sachs, note 12, p. 3; Hildyard, note 27, p. 22; Elkins, note 80, p. 91.

[84] Rist, note 55, p. 182 (noting that the new era of development did not look very different from the previous one).

[85] Rees and Westra, note 19, p. 105. See also C. Gonzalez, "The Global Food Crisis: Law, Policy, and the Elusive Quest for Justice" (2010) 13 *Yale Human Rights and Development Law Journal* 65; C. Gonzalez, note 72 at 362–370.

[86] McLaren, note 74, p. 21.

[87] Rees and Westra, note 19, p. 105 (noting traditional farmers and agricultural workers are often driven from rural areas as their markets are undercut by corporate producers or imports).

[88] Rees and Westra, note 19, p. 106; T. Juniper, "Presentation to the World Trade Organization Symposium," in K. Conca and G. D. Dabelko (eds.), *Green Planet Blues: Environmental Politics From Stockholm to Johannesburg*, 3rd ed. (Boulder: Westview Press, 2004), pp. 190, 191, 193 (critically assessing global North trade policies).

66 *Unsustainable Development*

mitigate those harms.[89] Sustainable development as it pertains to the global South has been the subject of numerous critiques – indeed, far too many to recount here. But then, the development this chapter seeks to more critically interrogate is not the sustainability of development in the global South, which was the focus of *Our Common Future* and much of the development discourse that followed; rather, it is to challenge sustainability in the global North, which has been the template for development in the global South and whose development paradigm has pushed the planet to the brink of ecological breaking point.

4.2 *Critiquing Sustainable Development: A View From the Global North*

The *Brundtland Report* indicated that bringing the entire world up to the standard of living enjoyed in industrialized countries would require a 5–10 percent increase in industrial output.[90] The problem is that development on such a scale is biophysically impossible, as the standard of living in industrialized countries is unsustainable even when limited to the 20 percent of the global population where it currently exists.[91] These living standards were never decisively questioned – indeed, they were the template – because in fashioning the concept of sustainable development, WCED failed in one of its primary missions: to seriously and critically interrogate the lifestyles and ecological ethos of the affluent in both the global North and global South,[92] including the oversized consumption patterns common in the global North. With respect to both present and future needs, Our Common Future did not adequately distinguish between the vastly different "needs" of the global North and the global South; essentially, between the human needs found in much of the global South versus the consumer wants that are at the core of much of the consumption in the global North.[93] While recognizing that "painful choices had to be made," there was insufficient discussion of the processes that industrialized countries might undertake to modify their problematic consumption patterns.[94] In 1992 UNCED adopted Agenda 21,[95] which recognized the

---

[89] Schrijver, note 39, p. 179 (noting the concept is found in numerous treaties and documents). However, differentiated responsibility has caused some controversy with respect to the treaties to address climate change. At least in the United States, the concept has been relied upon to eschew any action to address climate change, citing rising GHG emissions by developing countries such as China. See e.g. S. Tiezzi, "The United States and China Play Chicken Over Climate Change, U.S.–China Cooperation on Climate Change Could Literally Save the World – So Why Aren't They Cooperating?," November 26, 2013, for *The Diplomat* http://thediplomat.com.

[90] *Our Common Future*, note 1, p. 213; cf. Schrecker, note 5, p. 219 (discussing studies demonstrating that such growth may indeed be possible).

[91] Schrecker, note 5, p. 219.

[92] Rist, note 55, p. 181.

[93] Elkins, note 80, p. 91. See also McLaren, note 74.

[94] Rist, note 55, p. 181.

[95] *Agenda 21: Programme of Action for Sustainable Development*, Rio de Janeiro, 14 June 1992, U.N. GAOR, 46th Sess., Agenda Item 21, UN Doc. A/Conf.151/26 (1992) [hereinafter Agenda 21].

outsized global footprint of the global North and called for measures to remedy this state of affairs.[96] Similar calls were made in Johannesburg in 2002 and yet again in Rio in 2012.[97] Yet, Agenda 21 and its progeny failed to change consumption levels, despite a number of initiatives and increasing awareness of the issue. Indeed, a 2012 study, *Back to Our Common Future: Sustainable Development in the 21st Century*,[98] found that Agenda 21 had little if any impact on unsustainable consumption.[99] Ecological footprint analysis makes clear that the global North utilizes an unsustainable amount of global resources, that it is responsible for much of the environmental degradation in the world, and that its contemporary consumption patterns are profoundly inequitable.[100] A population's ecological footprint is the area of land and water required to produce the resources that the population consumes and to assimilate the wastes that it produces.[101] The residents of the global North require an average of 5–10 hectares (12–25 acres) of productive land and water to support their lifestyles, while the citizens of the world's poorest countries have average eco-footprints of less than one hectare (2.47 acres). The North is appropriating far more than its equitable share of the planet's resources.[102] Quantifying the North's

[96] Agenda 21 was to be a "blueprint for action" that the international community would undertake to make development sustainable. Chapter 4(3) of Agenda 21 centered on shifting consumption patterns. It stated: "[t]he major cause of the continued deterioration of the global environment is the unsustainable pattern of consumption and production, particularly in industrialized countries." Agenda 21 also addressed the high consumption patterns found in particular areas of the world: see chapter 4(5), Agenda 21.

[97] At the 2012 United Nations Conference on Sustainable Development (Rio+20), the global community reaffirmed its commitment to the Rio Principles and Agenda 21, as well as the Plan of Action and the Declaration on Sustainable development from the 2002 World Summit on Sustainable Development: UN General Assembly, Resolution Adopted by the General Assembly, *The Future We Want*, 27 July 2012, A/RES/66/288 [hereinafter *The Future We Want*]).

[98] Sustainable Development, *Back to our Common Future*, May 2012, http://sustainabledevelop ment.un.org [hereinafter *Back to Our Common Future*].

[99] Sustainable Development, "Review of Implementation of Agenda 21 and the Rio Principles," January 2012, http://sustainabledevelopment.un.org. Prior to Rio+20, the European Commission funded a study to take stock of progress on sustainable development. The report, entitled *Back to Our Common Future*, found that the goals of the Earth Summit had not been fulfilled and private consumption has only continued to expand: *Back to Our Common Future*, note 99, p. iii.

[100] Unless otherwise noted all ecological footprint analyses and data can be found in Rees and Westra, note 19, p. 99. See also McLaren, note 74, pp. 20–25.

[101] Ecological footprinting estimates human demand (or load) on the earth in terms of the ecosystem required to provide basic material support for any defined population. Rees and Westra, note 19, p. 109.

[102] Even China's per capita eco-footprint is only 1.2 hectares. The United States, Western Europe, and even Canada arrogate two to five times their equitable share of the planet's productive land and water, much of it through trade, while the lower income nations of the global South, such as India and China, use only a fraction of their equitable population-based allocation. The enormous purchasing power of the world's richest countries enables them to finance massive "ecological deficits" by appropriating the unused productive capacity of other nations and the global commons: Rees and Westra, note 19, p. 110.

68 *Unsustainable Development*

ecological excesses helps demonstrate that much of the ecological damage afflicting the global South is caused by export-oriented production to fulfill global North demands and wants, rather than by global South consumption to meet local needs. Although it is global North consumption that is responsible for the vast majority of the world's ecological destruction, distance and wealth tend to make these consequences invisible to its beneficiaries.

Ecological footprint analysis also makes evident that the global economy has already exceeded the planet's ecological limits. With an estimated average eco-footprint of 2.8 hectares per capita, the present human population already has a total eco-footprint of almost 17 billion hectares. However, there are only approximately 12 billion productive hectares on Earth,[103] suggesting that we are exceeding our planet's long-term human-carrying capacity by as much as 40 per cent. Yet, it is the global North – only a fifth or so of humanity – that consumes more than 80 per cent of the total global economic output, and thus the affluent alone effectively "appropriate" the entire ecological carrying capacity of the Earth, dooming efforts to achieve sustainability with justice through material growth.[104] To wit, the unsustainable development is to be found in the global North.

There are inadequate ecological goods and services to support the global North, much less the existing world population, at Northern material standards.[105] Indeed, one wonders whether either development or environmentalism could have been taken very seriously given these profound limits; either broad swathes of humanity were never expected to "develop" or environmental degradation was not a priority, for it is clear they could not co-exist. Nonetheless, more than several billion people are poised to realize global North-type existence, as a number of very large countries in the global South stand on the precipice of development. It is quite apparent that the global South cannot follow the global North's path of material excess, at least not using prevailing technologies. If humanity cannot safely expand its way to sustainability, it is imperative that we realize other ways of relieving the material impoverishment of half of humanity, beginning with the global North reducing its inflated ecological footprint to create the ecological space for growth in the global South.

5. CONCLUSION: CHALLENGING UNSUSTAINABILITY

[The Global North's] exploitation of 'ecological resources threaten to exhaust, poison or unalterably disfigure forests, soils, water and air'. The opposite of overconsumption,

---

[103] These 12 billion hectares are comprised of 9 billion hectares of productive cropland, pasture and forest and about 3 billion hectares of shallow oceans – the marine area that supplies about 96 per cent of the global fish catch: ibid, p. 111.

[104] Ibid, p. 109.

[105] This also does not take into account the habitat needs of the millions of species with which we share the planet: ibid.

destitution – is also unacceptable as it is damaging for both people and the environment. It seems environmental harm results when people have too little and too much.[106]

Discussions of both the environment and development are imbued with Northern goals and aspirations that are posed as being universal.[107] Human welfare is equated with income growth, and the unrestrained marketplace is pressed as the "wellspring and arbiter of social values."[108] But within the contemporary market model distributive inequity is disregarded and the environment is greatly undervalued, at least in practice.[109] Within the global capitalist system that undergirds the economies of the global North and thus the development paradigm, it seems economic growth *persistently* trumps environmental concerns. Indeed, several particularly striking examples from the global North illustrate this mindset quite starkly.

Throughout most of the summer of 2010, an oil well located more than five miles beneath the ocean floor steadily and continually discharged oil into the Gulf of Mexico. It devastated coastlines, oceans, marine life, and the countless livelihoods that depend on the Gulf for recreation, fishing, and myriad other activities that hinge on natural resources.[110] Neither BP, the rig's lessee, nor the U.S. federal government had a ready solution that could be achieved in less than three to four months.[111] In the midst of this debacle, President Barack Obama imposed a freeze on offshore drilling until the system could be examined and adequate safeguards assured.[112] This seemed prudent to many, but there were howls of protest, even as thousands of gallons of oil spilled into the Gulf with no viable solution to stop it.[113] It seemed that such an interruption could mean the loss of jobs, and the crisis had already caused the loss of enough jobs. The United States is also weighing whether to build a pipeline across the entire country to transport oil from Canada to the Gulf of Mexico.[114] In the age of climate change this seems particularly unwise, given the greenhouse gas emissions that will be emitted from burning the fossil

---

[106] A. Durning, "How Much is Enough?," in K. Conca and G. D. Dabelko (eds.), *Green Planet Blues: Environmental Politics From Stockholm to Johannesburg*, 3rd ed. (Boulder: Westview Press, 2004), p. 275.

[107] Sachs (ed.), note 12, pp. 26, 36.

[108] Rees and Westra, note 19, p. 104.

[109] Ibid, p. 104. The environment is often deemed invaluable to humankind. Yet in practice it is often undervalued when it must compete with the economic needs of an international economy shaped by global capital and the global North.

[110] "Gulf Oil Spill: The Effect on Wildlife," *New York Times*, August 16, 2010.

[111] "BP Oil Time Line," *The Guardian*, June 22, 2010.

[112] U.S. Department of the Interior, "Press Release: Interior Issues Directive to Guide Safe, Six-Month Moratorium on Deepwater Drilling," May 30, 2010, http://www.doi.gov.

[113] "Interior Secretary Says He Will Impose New Drilling Moratorium," CNN, June 23, 2010 (discussing different views on drilling moratorium).

[114] The Keystone Pipeline would pump oil from Canada to the Gulf of Mexico and is quite controversial. For articles recounting the Keystone pipeline chronicle, see The *New York Times*, "Keystone XL Pipeline," http://topics.nytimes.com; S. Wheaton, "Hundreds Face Arrest at Anti-Pipeline Protest," *The Caucus*, March 2, 2014.

70 *Unsustainable Development*

fuels that will be piped through this pipeline. But it is strenuously argued that this project will create jobs and no matter how short-term those jobs may be or how few jobs may be generated, when measured against the environmental damage such a pipeline may cause, as of this writing it is a very open question as to whether it will be built. Again concerns regarding the economy, jobs, and growth could prevail.

Making choices between environmental harm and the economic sustainability of the broader community is challenging and is made more difficult by a system that abounds in inequality and is dominated by global capital and multinational corporations. To further complicate matters, environmental degradation and regulation, like many problems, often weighs most heavily on the poorest segments of almost all societies; in other words, in many respects we are *not* all in this together.[115] For example, if higher emissions standards are imposed, it is often those that are the most economically vulnerable who suffer the most dire consequences because they have the least fuel efficient cars and, in rural or suburban areas, may be the most dependent on automobiles because they live furthest from their place of employment.[116] Poor communities in the global North and South are also much more likely to live near environmental hazards.[117] Thus, inequality in both the global North and global South generally means that both environmental harm and the measures adopted to address that harm weigh most heavily on the poorest segments of society.

While the industrializing global South has differed from the global North in some respects, it has also been far too imitative in the quest for that ever-seductive life style enjoyed by many in the global North. And in all honesty, why should there not be a yearning for an existence we take for granted? It normally means housing, year-round controlled indoor temperatures, running water, perhaps door-to-door transportation, and a range of comforts we take for granted.[118] But it comes at a huge cost to human health and the environment, including: a changing climate; polluted air and waterways; exhausted fish stocks; oceans used as garbage dumps;

[115] J. Agyeman, R. Bullard, and B. Evans (eds.), *Just Sustainabilities: Development in an Unequal World* (London: Earthscan, 2002) (for essays examining the numerous facets of the nature and need for environmental justice).

[116] Schrecker, note 5, p. 218 (noting conflicts between employment and environmental protection in industrialized countries is a more complex illustration of tradeoffs).

[117] The environmental justice movement emerged in the United States as links between race or class and local environmental harm were identified. Low income and people of color were much more likely to be located near environmental hazards than whites and the more affluent. The movement merged "civil rights and environmental advocacy to address these disparities": K. M. Gast, "Environmental Justice and Indigenous Peoples in the United States: An International Human Rights Analysis" (2004) 14 *Transnational Law and Contemporary Problems* 256. Environmental justice has also achieved international significance as the impoverished have again been disproportionately affected by environmental harms: A. R. Jahiel, 'Globalization and the Violation of Environmental Justice,' February 22, 2003, http://www.hrichina.org. For a nuanced discussion of environmental justices, see Gonzalez, note 68, p. 77.

[118] Durning, note 106, p. 275.

almost unimaginable quantities of waste and overflowing landfills; ubiquitous chemical contamination; and myriad other environmental problems.[119] Yet, perpetual destitution is surely not the answer, and thus the eradication of poverty must remain at the top of our collective agendas. Instead, the principal change must come from a global North that must begin to question and give up its prodigality. One scholar suggests that we begin to question how much is enough – as we try to discern the difference between our needs and our wants. We must consider the level at which the global ecology and humanity can co-exist over the long term, and justice necessitates that there be some measure of equity and equality in how those ecological resources are shared. There are currently three broad ecological classes: High-income consumers;[120] the middle-income class;[121] and the impoverished.[122] The living conditions of the poor are unacceptable, while those of high-income consumers are just as unacceptable as they further acute economic inequity and are unsustainable; thus perhaps our salvation exists somewhere in the middle. Genuine sustainability, along with some semblance of equity and justice, may lie somewhere between the high-consumption, wasteful lifestyle of the global North and the destitution that characterizes many communities in the global South (and the poorest, such as the homeless, in the global North).

There are some signs of a shift in the newly emerging global South, whose populations are living more in the middle, and where some governments are at least attempting to promote sustainability as they build infrastructure and cities. While the severe pollution in major cities in China, Mexico, and other nations

[119] Of course, the nature and extent of these problems varies between, and sometimes within, states in the global North. States have also undertaken differing measures to address environmental problems over the past fifty years. It can fairly be said that almost all countries are more conscious of environmental harm and damage, and have done more to protect the environment, than was the case before environmental protection became part of national policies.

[120] Professor Durning defines the global consumer class as households with incomes above US $7,500, with most enjoying a previously unknown lifestyle in which they commonly eat meat; spend most of their time in climate-controlled buildings that are equipped with hot water, refrigerators, clothes washers and dryers and a plethora of other electric-powered devices; travel in private autos and airplanes; and are surrounded by disposable goods. As a class, they possess 64 percent of the world income, which is thirty-two times that of the poorest. Most members of the global consumer class reside in North America, Western Europe, Japan, Australia, Hong Kong, Singapore, and the oil sheikdoms of the Middle East: Durning, note 106, p. 275.

[121] The middle-income class: earns between US$700 and US$7,500 per family member; generally eats a grain-based diet; has running water; lives in moderate buildings with electricity for lights, radios, and increasingly refrigerators, clothes washers and the like; travels by bus, rail, and bicycle and maintains a modest stock of durable goods. They mostly reside in Latin America, China, East Asia, and the Middle East, and collectively claim about one third of the world's income: ibid.

[122] The world's 1.1 billion poor people: earn less than US$700 a year per household; live in substandard housing; travel by foot; eat only grains, root vegetables, beans, and other legumes; and may only have access primarily to unclean water. This segment of the world population earns just 2 percent of the world's income: ibid.

demonstrates that there are definitely problems, there are also positive examples, such as Brazil, where ethanol has displaced fossil fuels; India and Mexico, which are developing smaller and smarter cars; and even China, which is building cities that are less dependent on cars and is becoming a leader in green technology.[123] These global South initiatives are not a panacea, but perhaps might offer environmental respite and an emergent model for a global North seeking a new sensibility.

Thus far that awareness has eluded the United States, as the BP disaster amply demonstrates. The global North appears to be betting on technology for ecological salvation; that we will find technological solutions to the ecological problems we currently confront.[124] Our refusal to change even as we confront climate change attests to this belief – and to the profound appeal of how we live. Given the absolutely astounding rate of technological change,[125] perhaps reliance on technology is not completely irrational. But perhaps we would have a better chance of avoiding environmental ruin if the international community could escape the clutches of global capital. While the fervent free-market neoliberal U.S. model has been largely rejected, whether state-led capitalism is an improvement or will be an adequate alternative remains to be seen.[126]

The broader international community must begin to determine the level of consumption our planet can support and how the entire global population can live comfortably without severe environmental harm. It will inevitably mean living below the consumer lifestyle of the global North but above the level of the most impoverished, whether in the global North or South. It is impossible to say exactly how this will play out, but the rising global South seems to be a more plausible model than that of the global North. Many of the most important transformations, however, must come from the global North whose lifestyle is at the root of unsustainability. It may begin with awareness, although globalization has made it more difficult to see the ecological impact of one's actions. It may also mean asking hard questions, including when more is not necessarily better and, having fully met

---

[123] R. Gordon, "The Environmental Implications of China's Engagement with Sub-Saharan Africa" (2012) **42** *Environmental Law Reporter News and Analysis* 11109.

[124] Caldwell, note 18, p. 1 (noting what might be an overreliance on technology and an unwarranted presumption that technology can solve most human problems, and that humanity is betting its future on technological ingenuity). Caldwell also observes that for politicians a technological fix is often preferable to making well-thought-out policies.

[125] E. Brynjolfsson and A. McAfee, *Race Against the Machine: How the Digital Revolution is Accelerating Innovation, Driving Productivity and Irreversible Transforming Employment and the Economy* (Lexington: Digital Frontier Press, 2011) (for a fascinating discussion of the rapidly accelerating rate of technological change). That younger Americans are even contemplating forgoing cars in favor of public transportation attests to the possibilities of cultural change. Such a possibility would have been deemed impossible only five years ago.

[126] Many industrializing middle-income countries, such as South Korea, China, Japan, and Brazil, are decidedly capitalist, but the state plays a much larger role in the economy through explicit industrial policies: S. S. Cohen and J. Bradford DeLong, *The End of Influence: What Happens When Other Countries Have the Money* (New York: Basic Books, 2010). The United States, on the other hand, has pursued one of the more extreme types of market-driven capitalism.

our material needs, whether there are perhaps non-material sources of fulfillment, as it may be the case that we must eat, travel, and use energy and materials more like those in the middle.[127] We must change our priorities and examine our needs versus our wants, which may already be being driven by economic collapse and technological change. If there is one thing that is certain, it is that things often unfold in unimaginable and unpredictable ways.

[127] Durning, note 106, p. 275. Perhaps the "sharing economy" which is in its infancy might presage such a change. Technology is allowing people to share automobiles, vacation housing and other consumer goods. While not viewed as an environmental initiative, it may portend a more ecologically sustainable ethos.

4

The Significance of International Environmental Law Principles in Reinforcing or Dismantling the North–South Divide

Sumudu Atapattu

1. INTRODUCTION

The field of international environmental law has blossomed into a separate branch of international law despite its slow start, and is now replete with principles that govern environmental issues.[1] While their legal status varies, these principles are important for several reasons.[2] First, they provide a framework to negotiate new environmental treaties and implement existing ones. Thus, for example, the UN Framework Convention on Climate Change (UNFCCC), quite unprecedentedly, devotes a whole article to "principles" that should guide the parties to the Convention to achieve its objectives and to implement its provisions.[3] Second, they provide

---

[1] For a discussion of general principles in the field of environmental protection see D. Hunter, J. Salzman and D. Zaelke *International Environmental Law and Policy*, 4th ed. (New York: Foundation Press, 2011), chapter 8; P. Sands and J. Peel, *Principles of International Environmental Law*, 3rd ed. (Cambridge: Cambridge University Press, 2012), chapter 6; P. Birnie, A. Boyle and C. Redgwell, *International Law and the Environment*, 3rd ed. (New York: Oxford University Press, 2009), chapter 3; S. Atapattu, *Emerging Principles of International Environmental Law* (New York: Transnational Publishers, 2006); N. de Sadeleer, *Environmental Principles: From Political Slogans to Legal Rules* (New York: Oxford University Press, 2002).

[2] See Hunter et al., note 1, p. 440.

[3] New York, 9 May 1992, in force 21 March 1994, 1771 UNTS 107; S. Treaty Doc No. 102–38; UN Doc. A/AC.237/18 (Part II)/Add.1; 31 ILM 849 (1992), Art. 3. The *Cartagena Protocol on Biosafety to the Convention on Biological Diversity*, Cartagena, 29 January 2000, in force 11 September 2003, 2226 UNTS 208; 39 ILM 1027 (2000); UN Doc. UNEP/CBD/ExCOP/1/3 at 42 (2000) specifically incorporates Principle 15 of the *Rio Declaration on Environment and Development*, Rio de Janeiro, 13 June 1992, UN Doc. A/CONF.151/26 (vol. I); 31 ILM 874 (1992) (hereinafter Rio Declaration) on the Precautionary Principle (see discussion later in the chapter). See also D. French, "Developing States and International Environmental Law: The Importance of Differentiated Responsibilities" (2000) 49 *International and Comparative Law Quarterly* 35 at 41: French believes that Article 3 provides a written constitution which the Conference of Parties is under an obligation to apply in fulfilling the obligations under the Convention. Moreover, "Article 3 is an excellent example of how a treaty can not only guide the future implementation of its own provisions, but also the subsequent development of future protocols." However, even the inclusion of Article 3 gave rise to North–South divisions.

74

guidance to various judicial bodies to resolve environmental disputes. Thus, in the Pulp Mills Case, the ICJ referred to transboundary environmental impact assessment as part of customary international law.[4] Third, they provide a framework for the development of national environmental law and have also influenced judicial decisions at the national level. Thus, the Indian Supreme Court has applied the precautionary principle, the polluter pays principle, sustainable development, and the intergenerational equity principle in many of the cases before it.[5] Finally, some principles may be useful in integrating environmental issues with other branches of international law. This cross-fertilization[6] is particularly evident in relation to international trade law and international human rights law and vice versa: Trade sanctions have been used successfully in environmental regimes. The ozone regime is a good example. Moreover, some principles embodied in soft law instruments can shape state practice and result in crystallizing a customary international law principle over time, or they could be incorporated into a treaty. Principle 21 of the Stockholm Declaration[7] is a good example of a soft law principle becoming part of customary international law, while participatory rights being incorporated into a treaty, albeit regional, is an example of soft law becoming part of treaty law.[8]

These principles can be divided into several categories: Those that have been borrowed from general international law (such as the principle of good neighborliness, state responsibility, and many procedural principles); those that have been borrowed from specialized areas of international law (such as human rights principles, particularly participatory rights); and those that are specific to the international environmental law field (such as the common but differentiated responsibility principle, sustainable development, the precautionary principle, the polluter pays principle, and the intergenerational equity principle).

See C. Wold, David Hunter, and Melissa Powers, *Climate Change and the Law* (Newark: LexisNexis, 2009), pp. 150–151.

[4] *Pulp Mills on the River Uruguay Case* (Argentina v Uruguay) [2010] ICJ Reports 113 [hereinafter *Pulp Mills* case]. Similarly in the *Case Concerning the Gabcikovo Nagymaros Project* (Hungary v Slovakia) [1997] ICJ Reports 228 [hereinafter *Case Concerning the Gabcikovo Nagymaros Project*], the ICJ spoke of the emergence of several new international environmental law principles and the need to take them into account.

[5] See S. Atapattu, "The Role of Human Rights Law in Protecting Environmental Rights in South Asia," in L. Haglund and R. Stryker (eds.), *Closing the Rights Gap: From Human Rights to Social Transformation* (Berkeley: University of California Press, 2015).

[6] See P. Sands, "Treaty, Custom and the Cross-fertilization of International Law" (1998) 1 *Yale Human Rights and Development Law Journal* 85.

[7] *Declaration of the United Nations Conference on the Human Environment*, Stockholm, 16 June 1972, UN Doc. A/Conf.48/14/Rev. 1(1973); 11 ILM 1416 (1972) [hereinafter Stockholm Declaration].

[8] Many other examples can be found – the Cairo Guidelines being the foundation for Basel Convention on Hazardous Waste, and Bonn Guidelines being the foundation for the Nagoya Protocol on Access to Genetic Resources and Benefit Sharing.

76   *International Environmental Law Principles and the North–South Divide*

Southern countries often contend that they did not participate in the creation of international law principles.[9] They posit that at the time these principles were emerging they were not fully-fledged members of the international community, although they are no strangers to the idea of international law.[10] Since their independence, however, they have been active in influencing the development of international law, and their influence can be seen[11] in relation to the emergence and adoption of many principles in the environmental field, although there is still an asymmetry in relation to negotiations at the international level.[12] Mickelson, for example, argues that *as a discipline*, international environmental law "has failed to respond to Third World concerns in a meaningful fashion. Indeed, it has accommodated these concerns at the margins, as opposed to integrating them into the core of the discipline and its self-understanding."[13]

The 1972 Stockholm Conference on the Human Environment[14] is the foundation of modern international environmental law, and thus has a rather recent history as compared with other areas of international law.[15] However, action relating to the environment pre-dates the Stockholm Conference[16] and, as the ICJ noted in the Case Concerning the Gabcikovo-Nagymaros Project,[17] "[t] hroughout the ages mankind has, for economic and other reasons, constantly

---

[9] See K. Mickelson, "South, North, International Environmental Law and International Environmental Lawyers" (2000) 11 *Yearbook of International Environmental Law* 52; B. S. Chimni, "Third World Approaches to International Law: A Manifesto" (2006) 8 *International Community Law Review* 3; A. Anghie and B. S. Chimni, "Third World Approaches to International Law and Individual Responsibility in Internal Conflicts" (2003) 2(1) *Chinese Journal of International Law* 77; K. Mickelson, "Rhetoric and Rage: Third World Voices in International Legal Discourse" (1998) 16(2) *Wisconsin International Law Journal* 353.

[10] Third World Approaches to International Law (TWAIL) is identified as a critique of international law and is a distinct way of thinking about international law and what it should be. "For TWAIL scholars, international law makes sense only in the context of the lived history of the peoples of the Third World": See Anghie and Chimni, note 9 at 78. See also Mickelson, note 9 at 353, who notes that the conventional view among international legal scholars is that there is no coherent and distinctive "Third World approach" to international law.

[11] See J. Ntambirweki, "The Developing Countries in the Evolution of an International Environmental Law" (1990) 14 *Hastings International and Comparative Law Review* 905 who notes that "despite the initial reluctance to convert to the banner of environmental conservation, the Third World states have continued to play a large role in the evolution of a new international law of the environment."

[12] See chapter 7, L. de Silva, "Public Participation in International Negotiation and Compliance."

[13] See Mickelson, note 9 at 54. She contends that the colonial background of international law is shared by international environmental law.

[14] UN, *Report of the United Nations Conference on the Human Environment*, Stockholm, Sweden, 5–16 June 1972, UN Doc. A/Conf.48/14/Rev. 1.

[15] Areas such as humanitarian law and law of the sea have evolved over centuries.

[16] See Mickelson, note 9, who laments the way the history of international environmental law (IEL) is discussed in leading textbooks on the subject, treating the latter half of the twentieth century as when the "real story" of IEL began.

[17] See *Case Concerning the Gabcikovo Nagymaros Project*, note 4.

interfered with nature."[18] Judge Weeramantry's separate opinion in that case is particularly insightful:

> There are some principles of traditional legal systems that can be woven into the fabric of modern environmental law. They are specially pertinent to the concept of sustainable development which was well recognized in those systems. Moreover, several of these systems have particular relevance to this case, in that they relate to the harnessing of streams and rivers and show a concern that these acts of human interference with the course of nature should always be conducted with due regard to the protection of the environment. In the context of environmental wisdom generally, there is much to be derived from ancient civilizations and traditional legal systems in Asia, the Middle East, Africa, Europe, the Americas, the Pacific and Australia – in fact, the whole world. This is a rich source which modern environmental law has left largely untapped.[19]

It is no coincidence that the examples Judge Weeramantry chose to draw inspiration from in his separate opinion all come from the global South: Irrigation systems in ancient Ceylon (now Sri Lanka); the ancient cultures of sub-Saharan Africa – *Sonjo and Chagga*, both Tanzanian tribes;[20] *Qanats* of Iran;[21] and the irrigation works of China and the Inca civilization. He noted that many more instances can be cited "which accorded due importance to environmental considerations and reconciled the rights of present and future generations."[22] He noted that modern environmental law can learn from practices and principles of traditional systems and referred specifically to the following principles: (a) trusteeship of earth resources (b) intergenerational rights (c) integration of development and environmental conservation (d) duty to preserve the integrity and purity of the environment (e) collective ownership of natural resources which should be used for the maximum service to people.[23]

We are very familiar with these principles in modern environmental law.[24] Rather than treat Southern countries as peripheral and sometimes grudging actors in the field of environmental law,[25] Northern states should draw inspiration from traditional practices and learn from them, just like Judge Weeramantry did in his separate opinion. Southern states, for their part, must learn from the practices of their ancestors and lead a more sustainable way of life.

If we fast-forward to the present era, a very different picture emerges. At Stockholm, Southern countries opposed international regulation of the environment, arguing that

---

[18] Ibid, p. 78.
[19] Ibid (Separate Opinion of Vice-President Weeramantry), p. 95.
[20] Ibid.
[21] Ibid.
[22] Ibid, p. 100. He stated that this is sustainable development *par excellence*.
[23] Ibid.
[24] Inter- and intragenerational equity principle, environmental impact assessment procedure, public trust doctrine, eco-system services, etc. See Hunter et al., note 1.
[25] See Mickelson, note 9 at 60.

78   *International Environmental Law Principles and the North–South Divide*

such issues are best handled at the national level.[26] For them, environmental pollution associated with industrialization did not pose an immediate threat, and they were concerned with more pressing issues relating to poverty.[27] They have consistently maintained that the environmental agenda should incorporate their concerns relating to poverty and underdevelopment.[28] Even with regard to the creation of environmental issues, one can see the North–South divide: While global environmental issues are caused by affluence, local environmental issues are primarily caused by poverty and underdevelopment.[29]

Discussing the history of international environmental law, Mickelson concedes that while a great deal of attention has been paid to the South, it is different from paying attention to "how international environmental law and policy might be conceptualized in order to represent an inclusive framework that represents the interests and *perspectives* of the South and North alike."[30] She is of the view that Southern countries are treated as grudging participants rather than as active partners.[31]

The Stockholm Conference[32] and later the Rio Conference gave birth to many international environmental law principles. This chapter seeks to discuss the most pertinent principles that have either contributed to reinforcing the North–South divide or succeeded in dismantling it. While a discussion of all the international

[26] See UN General Assembly Resolution on Development and Environment, UN Doc. A/RES/ 2849 (XXVI); ILM 1972; reproduced in Hunter et al., note 1, p. 141.

[27] See Mickelson, note 9 at 61. See also J. Ntambirweki, note 11 at 906, where he quotes the Prime Minister of India, Indira Gandhi, who noted the dilemma between environmental protection and poverty alleviation: "[w]e do not wish to impoverish the environment any further and yet we cannot for a moment forget the grim poverty of large numbers of people. [. . .] The environment cannot be improved in conditions of poverty. Nor can poverty be eradicated without the use of science and technology."

[28] UN General Assembly Resolutions relating to sovereignty over natural resources reflect the root of the South's insecurity toward the Northern agenda. The South also feared that strict environmental standards would be harmful to their exports and these standards could be used as trade protectionist measures by the North: see Hunter et al., note 1, p. 1227.

[29] See J. Goldensberg, referred to in Mickelson (2000), note 9 at 69. However, as discussed later, the situation changed as Southern countries started to feel the negative impact of global environmental problems locally. They have become vocal advocates of action relating to climate change, hazardous waste, and GMOs. See the following chapters in this book: chapter 20, M. Burkett, "A Justice Paradox: Climate Change, Small Island Developing States, and the Absence of International Legal Remedy"; chapter 21, E. A. Kronk Warner, "South of South: Examining the International Climate Regime from an Indigenous Perspective"; chapter 23, R. Verchik and P. Govind, "Natural Disaster and Climate Change"; chapter 10, R. Maguire and X. Jiang, "Emerging Powerful Southern Voices: Role of BASIC Nations in Shaping Climate Change Mitigation Commitments"; chapter 12, Z. Lipman, "Trade in Hazardous Waste." See also Ntambirweki, note 11 at 927, where he refers to lost opportunities for concrete action on environmental issues important to the South.

[30] See Mickelson (2000), note 9 at 60.

[31] Ibid.

[32] See Mickelson, note 9 at 62, where she refers to Stockholm as "the single most significant event in the history of international environmental law."

environmental principles is beyond the scope of this chapter, the principles that are most relevant from a North–South perspective are: Permanent sovereignty over natural resources; common heritage of mankind; common but differentiated responsibility; prior informed consent; benefit-sharing; and sustainable development (which includes the inter-and intragenerational equity principle). Principles such as the precautionary principle and the polluter pays principle will be discussed briefly because their adoption also gave rise to North–South divisions. While principles such as environmental impact assessment and participatory rights seem well entrenched in both national and international law,[33] and accepted by both Northern and Southern states as an important tool in the decision-making process,[34] in practice there is often a mismatch between what the law says and how it is implemented. Thus, the implementation of procedural rights such as access to information, participation, and access to remedies will be discussed briefly.

The aforementioned principles can be broadly divided into two categories: Pre–Rio principles and post–Rio principles. Sustainable development has had a huge impact on the development of international environmental law principles post–Rio, while national sovereignty remained the dominant feature of the pre–Rio principles.

2. PRE–RIO PRINCIPLES

An important feature of principles in the pre–Rio era is that they originated mainly out of "first generation" environmental issues – i.e. transboundary environmental issues. They also adopted a reactionary approach rather than an anticipatory approach.[35] These environmental issues were clearly not as complex as those issues that are intrinsically linked to the global economy. Another commonality is the increasing participation by newly decolonized countries that were keen to assert their sovereignty in the international arena.[36] The clear divisions between Northern countries and Southern countries particularly in relation to environmental issues were apparent in almost all the debates surrounding them. These divisions resulted in the polarization of these two groups, which eventually led to the establishment of the World Commission on Environment and Development in 1983 by the

---

[33] See S. Atapattu, note 1, chapter 4.

[34] Over 100 states have national laws governing environmental impact assessments, see N. Craik, *The International Law of Environmental Impact Assessment: Process, Substance and Integration* (Cambridge: Cambridge University Press, 2008), p. 23.

[35] The principle of prevention, closely related to Principle 21 of the *Stockholm Declaration*, requires states to prevent environmental damage even in the absence of a transboundary impact: see Sands et al., note 1, p. 200. The principle of prevention was also confirmed in the *Pulp Mills* case, see note 4.

[36] The New International Economic Order (NIEO)–era resolutions and the adoption of the resolution on the right to development are clear examples of the dominance by Southern countries in the UN General Assembly. See Hunter et al., note 1, p. 141.

80   *International Environmental Law Principles and the North–South Divide*

UN General Assembly. The mandate given to the Commission was, inter alia, to find ways to reconcile this impasse.[37] This section will discuss some of the principles that were particularly contentious from a North–South perspective during the pre–Rio era.

2.1 *Permanent Sovereignty Over Natural Resources*

One of the early examples of Southern countries' influence in the global arena is the adoption of the permanent sovereignty over natural resources (PSNR) principle.[38] While this principle has a more general application, PSNR has wide implications for environmental law. It is closely linked to decolonization as newly independent states were keen to assert their sovereignty over their resources, particularly oil.[39] Latin American states took up the issue at the UN, which culminated in the adoption of a General Assembly resolution on the subject[40] as a basic component of the right to self-determination.[41] It was a follow-up to Resolution 1314 of 1958, which established the Commission on Permanent Sovereignty over Natural Resources. Referring to the "inalienable right of all States freely to dispose of their natural wealth and resources in accordance with their national interests," the resolution stated: "[t]he right of peoples and nations to permanent sovereignty over their natural wealth and resources must be exercised in the interest of their national development and of the well-being of the people of the State concerned."[42]

---

[37] World Commission on Environment and Development, *Our Common Future* (Oxford: Oxford University Press, 1987), p. ix [hereinafter *Our Common Future*]. See also chapter 3, R. Gordon, "Unsustainable Development."

[38] See U. Beyerlin, "Bridging the North-South Divide in International Environmental Law" (2006) 66 *Zeitschrift für ausländisches öffentliches Recht und Völkerrecht* 259. However, some of his assertions are incorrect and misleading. For example, he states that "[a] number of international environmental agreements at the outset preclude the Sorthern states from membership" (at 266). The examples he cites are regional treaties adopted by the ECE, which is a regional organization comprising Northern states. Moreover, the *Convention on Access to Information, Public Participation in Decision-Making and Access to Justice in Environment Matters*, Aarhus, 28 June 1998, in force 30 October 2001, 2161 UNTS 447; 38 ILM 517 (1999) [hereinafter Aarhus Convention] which is cited as an example of such exclusion, explicitly allows accession by any member of the UN with the approval of the Meeting of Parties (Article 19(2)).

[39] For a comprehensive discussion of the emergence of the principle, see N. Schrijver, *Sovereignty Over Natural Resources* (Cambridge: Cambridge University Press, 1997).

[40] UN General Assembly, *1962 General Assembly Resolution 1803 on Permanent Sovereignty over Natural Resources*, 14 December 1962, A/5217 (1962).

[41] Ibid, Preamble. The two human rights treaties that followed the *Universal Declaration of Human Rights* include this right as an aspect of the right of self-determination.

[42] Ibid, art. 1. Note, by contrast, that the subsequent General Assembly Resolution 2158 (XXI) on Permanent Sovereignty over Natural Resources, refers only to the inalienable right of countries and omits any reference to "people."

The resolution further noted that the violation of this right "is contrary to the spirit and principles of the Charter of the United Nations and hinders the development of international co-operation and the maintenance of international peace."[43] It is interesting that a link was made with international peace: This probably referred to the tensions that were running high as a result of the wave of expropriations that was taking place in newly independent countries.[44]

North–South divisions were evident in the debates on permanent sovereignty in the General Assembly. The United Kingdom, for example, stated that self-determination was a political rather than a legal principle and that there was "no such thing as permanent sovereignty over natural resources."[45] It further noted that if it was a mere affirmation of the sovereignty principle, that was acceptable, but it is quite distinct from permanent sovereignty and had nothing to do with self-determination.[46] The U.S., for its part, was of the view that the resolution was a "serious error."[47] Southern countries, on the other hand, maintained that it was necessary as the right of self-determination was essential for the enjoyment of all other rights.[48]

PSNR has crept into early environmental instruments including the Stockholm Declaration and is at odds with environmental principles and the emergence of sustainable development as a principal objective of the international community.[49] With the emergence of major environmental issues such as acid rain it became clear that both underdevelopment and overconsumption created environmental problems. These environmental issues challenged the PSNR principle directly: States may have sovereignty over their resources but such sovereignty is not unlimited. Slowly the realization dawned that limits have to be imposed on how states use their resources, at least with regard to their transboundary impact. The

---

[43] Ibid, art. 7.

[44] See Schrijver, note 39, p. 41 where he refers to the nationalization by Iran of the Anglo-Iranian Oil Company in 1951 as "the first major economic 'North–South clash in the post-war period'." One of the contested issues related to the amount of compensation to be awarded for the expropriated property – it has ranged from "appropriate" to "prompt, effective and adequate" compensation. See also R. Islam's chapter, "History of North–South Divide: Colonial Discourses, Sovereignty, and Self-Determination," in this book.

[45] See Schrijver, note 39, p. 51.

[46] Ibid.

[47] Ibid.

[48] Ibid.

[49] While states still retain some measure of discretion as to how to use their natural resources, limits have been placed on their ability to do so by the international environmental obligations that they have accepted. Thus, principles such as environmental impact assessment, public participation, sustainable development, the precautionary principle, the polluter pays principle, the principle of prevention, have all had the effect of restricting the (internal) sovereignty of states, and this applies equally to both Southern and Northern countries. From this perspective, these principles have had a neutralizing and harmonizing effect. However, as the later discussion shows, their implementation leaves much to be desired in many instances.

82   *International Environmental Law Principles and the North–South Divide*

Stockholm Conference resulted in the adoption of the Stockholm Declaration on the Human Environment.[50] However, developing countries strongly opposed any attempt to impose restrictions on their quest for economic development. They argued that poverty was the biggest polluter and environmental protection would place restrictions on their ability to pursue economic development. Moreover, they feared that this would impose conditionalities on their ability to receive development aid, particularly from the World Bank. They also feared trade protectionism by Northern states and did not want Northern standards imposed on them.[51] Northern countries, by contrast, were beginning to experience negative consequences of environmental degradation and were keen to take action to protect the environment.[52] Principle 21 reflects a delicate balance between rights and responsibilities:

> States have, in accordance with the Charter of the United Nations and the principles of international law, the sovereign right to exploit their own resources pursuant to their own environmental policies, and the responsibility to ensure that activities within their jurisdiction or control do not cause damage to the environment of other States or of areas beyond the limits of national jurisdiction.[53]

This principle, commonly referred to as "Principle 21," has since become part of customary international law[54] and constitutes the foundation of modern international environmental law. The origins of this principle can be traced to the old Roman Law principle of *sic utere tuo ut alienum non laedas* (the principle of good neighborliness) and is rooted in the principle of sovereignty itself.[55] Over the years the emergence of the principle of prevention as well as sustainable development has put fetters on the ability of states to exercise full sovereignty over their natural resources, even in the absence of a transboundary impact. This seems to have further reinforced the North–South divide as experience has shown that despite these developments, Southern countries do not have full sovereignty over their resources, particularly in relation to issues of "biopiracy."[56]

---

[50] See Stockholm Declaration, note 7.

[51] This concern found its way into the Rio Declaration, note 3, Principle 11.

[52] For a detailed discussion of the North–South divisions at Stockholm, see chapter 5, K. Mickelson, "The Stockholm Conference and the Creation of the South–North Divide in International Environmental Law and Policy." In contrast to the Rio conference that came twenty years later, there was very little participation by civil society groups at Stockholm. See Hunter et al., note 1, p. 162.

[53] Stockholm Declaration, note 7, Principle 21.

[54] See Hunter et al., note 1; Sands et al., note 1.

[55] See "Sic Utere Tuo ut Alienum Non Laedas, Note and Comment" (1907) 5(8) *Michigan Law Review* 673 ("[t]he rightful use of one's property cannot be a legal wrong to another"); Schrijver, note 39, p. 243. It was applied in the often quoted *Trail Smelter* (USA v Canada) Award of 1941, III RIAA 1911 at 1965 as early as 1941.

[56] See discussion later.

2.2 *The Common Heritage of Mankind Principle*

Another principle that has caused considerable controversy is the common heritage of mankind principle (CHMP). According to this principle, resources of the global commons belong to mankind as a whole.[57] The freedom of the high seas, one of the oldest principles of international law, was premised on the belief that the resources of the oceans were so vast that states could not possibly exhaust them. However, with the overexploitation of resources and some fish species even facing extinction, it soon became clear that some rules were necessary to govern its use.

One of the contested issues relating to the law of the sea involved the resources of the deep seabed. Southern countries had neither the financial wherewithal nor the technology to exploit these resources. However, because the resources are part of the global commons, Southern states were of the view that Northern states should not be entitled to benefit from all the resources exclusively, and that some form of sharing was equitable. In 1966, U.S. President Johnson stated: "[w]e must ensure that the deep seas and the ocean bottom are, and remain, the legacy of all human beings."[58]

In 1967, Ambassador Pardo of Malta proposed to the General Assembly to declare the seabed and the ocean floor to be the common heritage of mankind.[59] In 1970, the General Assembly did so in its Declaration of Principles Governing the Sea-Bed and the Ocean Floor and the Subsoil Thereof, Beyond the Limits of National Jurisdiction.[60] Noting that the area is to be used exclusively for peaceful purposes, the Declaration recognized the needs of developing countries: "[t]he exploration of the area and the exploitation of its resources shall be carried out for the benefit of mankind as a whole, irrespective of the geographical location of States, whether land-locked or coastal, and taking into particular consideration the interests and needs of the developing countries."[61]

The Declaration further stated that the exploitation of these resources should be done in accordance with the legal regime to be established for the safe development and the rational exploitation of resources and to "ensure the equitable sharing by States in the benefits derived therefrom, taking into particular consideration the interests and needs of the developing countries, whether land-locked or coastal."[62]

---

[57] For an extensive discussion of the common heritage principle, see K. Baslar, *The Concept of the Common Heritage of Mankind in International Law* (The Hague: Martinus Nijhoff, 1998); J. Noyes, "Common Heritage of Mankind: Past, Present and Future" (2011) 40 *Denver Journal of International Law and Policy* 447.

[58] Referred to in Schrijver, note 39, p. 216.

[59] See Schrijver, note 39, p. 216. Although Ambassador Pardo is credited with coining this principle, it was first proposed by Thailand during the 1958 *Conference on the Law of the Sea*, Geneva, 29 April 1958, in force 30 September 1962, 13 UST 2312; 450 UNTS 11, but there was no support for it.

[60] 12 December 1970, A/RES/25/2749.

[61] Ibid, para. 7.

[62] Ibid, para. 9.

84   *International Environmental Law Principles and the North–South Divide*

Thus, this Declaration refers to the equitable sharing of benefits derived from exploiting the deep seabed. The common heritage principle is considered to comprise five components: International management;[63] use for peaceful purposes; benefit-sharing; non-appropriation; and preservation for future generations. Of these, benefit-sharing proved to be the most controversial.[64]

This principle was incorporated into the 1982 UN Law of the Sea Convention (UNCLOS), which adopted an elaborate legal regime governing deep-seabed mining.[65] However, Northern states refused to ratify the Convention mainly due to the inclusion of the common heritage principle, mandatory technology transfer, and the supranational authority of the "UN Enterprise."[66] In an effort to get universal participation, particularly the support of Northern states, Part XI of the Convention on deep-seabed mining was amended in 1994 by the adoption of the Agreement Relating to the Implementation of Part XI of the UN Law of the Sea Convention.[67] The earlier formulation of the section governing deep-seabed mining had provisions on mandatory technology transfer and production limitations in favor of those Southern countries that produced minerals from land-based sources whose economies could have been affected in the event that deep-seabed mining became commercially viable. Southern countries insisted that the resources of the "Area"[68] are the common heritage of mankind, a principle that has given rise to much controversy at the international level, particularly due to its benefit-sharing idea.[69] The earlier formulation of this provision read as follows:

> The Area and its resources are the common heritage of mankind. [...] No state shall claim or exercise sovereignty or sovereign rights over any part of the Area or its resources. [...] All rights in the resources of the Area are vested in mankind as a

[63] See H. Tuerk, *Reflections on the Contemporary Law of the Sea* (Boston: Martinus Nijhoff, 2012), who notes that international management also gave rise to a North–South debate.

[64] See Schrijver, note 39, p 215. See also, H. Tuerk, note 63, p. 45, who believes that at least the components relating to international management, peaceful use, and protection of the environment have been accepted by the international community.

[65] *United Nations Convention on the Law of the Sea*, Montego Bay, 10 December 1982, in force 16 November 1994, 1833 UNTS 3; 21 ILM 1261 (1982), art. 136 [hereinafter UNCLOS]: "the Area and its resources are the common heritage of mankind."

[66] See Schrijver, note 39, pp. 217–218.

[67] This section was amended by UN General Assembly, *Resolution Adopted by the General Assembly: Agreement Relating to the Implementation of Part XI of the United Nations Convention on the Law of the Sea of 10 December 1982*, 28 July 1994, A/RES/48/263. Although the resolution is titled "Agreement Relating to the Implementation of Part XI of the United Nations Convention on the Law of the Sea," it was in fact an amendment. This raises interesting questions about the legality of hard law being amended by soft law and itself raises North–South issues. Southern countries lobbied hard to get Part XI into UNCLOS but if the international community can amend these binding provisions by a non-binding resolution to appease Northern countries that can undermine the whole legitimacy of the system.

[68] The "Area" is defined as "the sea-bed and ocean floor and subsoil thereof beyond the limits of national jurisdiction:" UNCLOS, note 65, art. 1(1).

[69] It is interesting to compare this with the benefit sharing provisions in the biodiversity legal regime that came ten years later. See discussion in section 3.3.

whole. [...] The Authority shall provide for the equitable sharing of financial and other economic benefits derived from activities in the Area.[70]

Although the Convention still retains reference to the common heritage principle, mandatory technology transfer provisions were watered down in favor of an obligation to cooperate, as were the provisions relating to the powers of the supranational mining company, the Enterprise, which seemed to have appeased Northern countries.[71] Ironically, the United States has so far not ratified the Convention, despite the international community's efforts to accommodate its wishes.

The legal status of the common heritage principle remains unresolved.[72] While some scholars have accorded it the status of a peremptory norm of international law,[73] others consider that as a legal principle it is now dead.[74] Yet, others contend that the truth may lie somewhere between these two extremes and the common heritage principle has some legal significance.[75] Not all global commons regimes adopt this principle either: While the Moon Treaty[76] incorporates it, the Antarctic regime[77] does not. It would seem that PSNR applies to resources within states and the common heritage principle applies to resources beyond the limits of national sovereignty. Noting that both principles play a valuable role, Schrijver concludes:

> Both principles are pillars underpinning the same movement in international law to strengthen the strategic position of developing countries in response to the intensifying exploitation of their resources by other States and foreign companies and to prevent this happening with the resources of the deep sea-bed. The developing countries advocated these two new principles in an effort to promote a redistribution of global wealth in order to be in a better position to realize their development plans.[78]

However, consistent state practice is lacking and it remains one of the principles that has given rise to a huge North–South controversy over its application and legal

---

[70] UNCLOS, referred to in Hunter et al., note 1, p. 455.
[71] For a discussion of the revisions to Part XI of UNCLOS, see H. Tuerk, note 63, p. 41.
[72] See Schrijver, note 39, p. 221. See also H. Tuerk, note 63, p. 48, who believes that the common heritage of mankind principle has become an important principle of international law with regard to conservation and transmission of a heritage to future generations. In this regard, it shares features with sustainable development.
[73] See Schrijver, note 39, p. 221.
[74] See B. C. Brennan and B. Larschan, "The Common Heritage of Mankind Principle in International Law" (1983) 21 *Columbia Journal of International Law* 305; referred to in Schrijver, note 39, p. 221.
[75] See Schrijver, note 39, pp. 221–222, where he identifies several factors on which the legal merits of the principle depend, including whether it will attract widespread and representative participation in the future. See also H. Tuerk, note 63.
[76] *Agreement Governing the Activities of States on the Moon and Other Celestial Bodies*, New York, 18 December 1979, in force 11 July 1984, 1363 UNTS 21; 18 ILM 1434 (1979); 18 UST 2410.
[77] *Antarctic Treaty*, Washington, 1 December 1959, in force 23 June 1961, 12 UST 794; 402 UNTS 71; 19 ILM 860 (1980).
[78] See Schrijver, note 39, p. 229.

86 *International Environmental Law Principles and the North–South Divide*

status. Thus, for example, the Moon Treaty, which includes the common heritage principle, has a mere fifteen ratifications.[79] None of the space-faring nations have ratified it.[80] The experience with UNCLOS indicates that while Southern countries may have been successful in getting this principle included in treaties, its application has been watered down in order to get the participation of Northern countries.[81] It is no accident that later treaties such as UNFCCC and the Biodiversity Convention adopt the rather neutral, albeit ambiguous, term "common concern of mankind"[82] rather than the more controversial common heritage principle.[83] Interestingly, as discussed later, in the case of biodiversity, Southern countries also opposed the adoption of the common heritage principle because they feared that it would mean free access to their biological resources by Northern states.

3. POST–RIO

The publication of the report of the World Commission on Environmental Development (WCED) in 1987 and its emphasis on the need to adopt a path of sustainable development for both Northern and Southern countries had a significant impact on the Rio Declaration. In the run-up to the conference as well as

---

[79] See M. Listner, "The Moon Treaty: Failed International Law or Waiting in the Shadows?" www.thespacereview.com.

[80] For a list of signatory countries, see United Nations Office for Disarmament Affairs, "Agreement Governing the Activities of States on the Moon and Other Celestial Bodies," http:// disarmament.un.org.

[81] Oceans and Law of the Sea, "Agreement Relating to Implementation of Part XI of the United Nations Convention on the Law of the Sea of 10 December 1982: Overview," 21 July 2010, www.un.org. Hunter et al., note 1, p. 457, note that PSNR and common heritage are "obviously related." To some extent, one starts where the other ends. Both derived from the New International Economic Order in the 1960s and 1970s "in which developing countries sought to assert their numerical superiority in the United Nations that would reverse the era of colonialism."

[82] See Hunter et al., note 1, p. 459. It is interesting to note that neither camp wanted the CHMP included in these treaties. Southern countries did not want too much international control over their natural resources while Northern countries did not want to share benefits arising from their exploitation: Hunter et al., note 1, p. 460.

[83] See the discussion in section 3.3 on the negotiations surrounding the *Convention on Biological Diversity*, Rio de Janeiro, 5 June 1992, in force 20 December 1993, 1760 UNTS 79; 31 ILM 818 (1992) [hereinafter CBD], during which Southern countries, in stark contrast to their position during the Law of the Sea negotiations, *opposed* the application of the CHMP to biological diversity. One of the reasons for the failure to adopt a convention on forests at Rio was because heavily forested countries like Brazil feared the internationalization of their forests. See Hunter et al., note 1, p. 157. Nonetheless, the international community adopted a nonbinding set of principles, which in effect reiterate the sovereignty of states in relation to their forests. See UN General Assembly, *Report of the United Nations Conference on Environment and Development: Non-Legally Binding Authoritative Statement of Principles for a Global Consensus of the Management, Conservation and Sustainable Development of all Types of Forests*, 3–14 June 1992, A/CONF.151/26 (vol. III).

during it, North–South divisions could not have been more pronounced. As Hunter et al. point out, Southern countries brought a developmental agenda to the table while Northern countries brought an environmental one. Southern countries were interested in poverty alleviation and local environmental issues while Northern countries were interested in global environmental issues such as climate change. Southern countries wanted to know how the sustainable development agenda was going to be financed and Northern countries were not willing to make firm commitments.[84] Given these deep divisions, it is surprising that two treaties and three non-binding instruments were even adopted at Rio.

The Rio Declaration is an important juncture in the evolution of international environmental law and marks the consolidation of support for sustainable development. Instead of trying to improve the definition of sustainable development in the WCED report, the Rio Declaration sought to give it content. It identified substantive and procedural components of sustainable development; it contained several tools that can be used to achieve sustainable development, and it also identified linkages.[85] However, the compromise language reflecting the North–South divisions is evident throughout the Declaration. Of the principles that were contentious at Rio, the common but differentiated responsibility principle (CBDR) stands out. Sustainable development itself was also contentious, particularly since some Southern countries felt that it applied only to them, as Northern countries were already "developed."[86]

3.1 Sustainable Development

Next to globalization, sustainable development has perhaps attracted most scholarly debate in recent history. The WCED defined sustainable development as "development that meets the needs of the present without compromising the ability of future generations to meet theirs."[87] From this rather vague definition, sustainable development has developed into an umbrella concept embodying both substantive and procedural components some of which now have normative quality. The Johannesburg Declaration took this one step further by articulating that the three pillars of sustainable development are economic development, environmental protection, and social development.[88] While this emphasizes the

---

[84] Hunter et al., note 1, p. 155. For a sharp critique of the Rio Conference, see P. Chatterjee and M. Finger, *The Earth Brokers: Power, Politics and World Development* (London: Routledge, 1994).

[85] See S. Atapattu, note 1, p. 89. See also "ILA New Delhi Declaration on Principles of International Law Relating to Sustainable Development" (2002) 2 *International Environmental Agreements: Politics, Law and Economics* 211.

[86] For a detailed discussion of sustainable development see chapter 3, R. Gordon, "Unsustainable Development."

[87] *Our Common Future*, note 37, p. 43.

[88] UN, *Report of the World Summit on Sustainable Development*, 26 August-4 September 2002, A/CONF.199/20, Annex, pp. 1–5 [hereinafter Johannesburg Declaration]. See also W. Sachs,

88   *International Environmental Law Principles and the North–South Divide*

interconnectedness of these three issues, there is no agreement as to how a balance should be struck between these three areas.[89] Although sustainable development has been included in almost all the treaties and soft law instruments adopted since the WCED report and has attracted broad acceptance from the international community,[90] deep divisions remain. The main objective of Southern countries is poverty alleviation and improving the standard of living of their population. Many are grappling with malnutrition and disease and many still consider environmental protection a luxury they can ill afford. Rajamani refers to the divisions at Rio as follows:

> The notion of sustainable development around which consensus swirled at Rio, however, was an ambiguous creature. While it presented the illusion of having something for everyone, in seeking to keep its definitional scope as broad as possible, it lost significantly not just in its subjective content and coherence but also in its ability to present a genuine compromise position between the needs and desires of the developing and industrial countries. It is no surprise then that in post-Rio environmental battles both developing and industrial countries employ the common language of sustainable development, which suggests a consensus in values, yet they differ drastically in their approach, focus, method, and aims.[91]

Sustainable development has been interpreted in various ways:[92] As an objective,[93] a concept,[94] a legal principle,[95] a legal term,[96] an interstitial norm,[97] a principle of reconciliation,[98] an umbrella concept encompassing both substantive and

---

"Rio+10 and the North-South Divide," World Summit Papers No. 8 Heinrich Boll Foundation (2001).

[89] See L. Rajamani, *Differential Treatment in International Environmental Law* (Oxford: Oxford University Press, 2006), p. 66, who notes that in the run-up to the WSSD, Northern and Southern countries were not in agreement as to where the balance should be struck between economic development, social development, and environmental protection.

[90] Hunter et al., note 1, p. 148 attribute this in part to its "brilliant ambiguity."

[91] See L. Rajamani, note 89, p. 61.

[92] See J. Ellis, "Sustainable Development as A Legal Principle: A Rhetorical Analysis," in H. Fabri, R. Wolfrum, and J. Gogolin (eds.) *Selected Proceedings of the European Society of International Law* (Oxford: Hart, 2008).

[93] The United States has taken the view that development is a goal, although it has adopted sustainable development as an objective. See EPA, "Toward Sustainability: Building a Better Understanding of Ecosystem Services," http://www.epa.gov.

[94] ICJ's view in *Case Concerning the Gabcikovo Nagymaros Project,* note 4.

[95] See Vice-President Weeramantry in his separate opinion in *Case Concerning the Gabcikovo Nagymaros Project,* note 4.

[96] See P. Sands, "International Law in the Field of Sustainable Development" (1994) 65 *British Yearbook of International Law* 203 at 379.

[97] See V. Lowe, "Sustainable Development and Unsustainable Arguments," in A. Boyle and D. Freestone (eds.), *International Law and Sustainable Development: Past Achievements and Future Challenges* (New York: Oxford University Press, 1999), p. 26.

[98] See Vice-President Weeramantry in his separate opinion in the *Case Concerning the Gabcikovo Nagymaros Project,* note 4.

procedural components,[99] a concept with legal implications,[100] an ambiguous creature,[101] and, at the other extreme, as giving rise to its own body of law, called international sustainable development law.[102] It has also been pointed out that sustainable development provides a framework for national governance[103] and that for the first time, a state's development policy became subject to international scrutiny.[104] Furthermore, it provides coherence and an organizing conceptual framework to other international environmental law principles that have developed on a rather ad hoc basis.[105] Both Northern and Southern countries are also divided on its interpretation. Southern countries have generally emphasized the economic development component of sustainable development while Northern countries tend to emphasize the environmental protection component, perhaps because they are already developed.[106] This unfortunately ignores the need for the North to curb its unsustainable consumption and production patterns to achieve sustainable development, as reflected in Principle 8 of the Rio Declaration.[107] The following is a sharp critique of sustainable development from an activist from the global South:

> While the WCED focused on environment and development as two faces of the same coin, subsequent debates have been on the basis that environment (protection) is something related to the North and sustainable development to the South.
>
> The latter concept has now been pushed to the point of making it the burden of the South to ensure that it pursues policies that will not compromise the ability of future generations or worsen the burden on the environment with consequence for the North whose concerns have become identified as global environmental issues.

[99] See Atapattu, note 1, chapter 7.

[100] See Birnie et al., note 1, p. 127.

[101] See Rajamani, note 89, p. 61.

[102] See MC. C. Segger and A. Khalfan, *Sustainable Development Law: Principles, Practices, and Prospects* (New York: Oxford University Press, 2004).

[103] See J. Dernbach, "Sustainable Development as a Framework for National Governance" (1998) 49 *Case Western Reserve Law Review* 1.

[104] See Birnie et al., note 1, p. 127.

[105] See Hunter et al., note 1, p. 147.

[106] See Hunter et al., note 1, p. 155 where they note that in the run up to the Rio Declaration: "[t]he South was concerned that the term sustainable development might only apply to them, as the North was already developed." See also I. Porras, "The Rio Declaration: A New Basis for International Cooperation," in P. Sands (ed.), *Greening International Law* (London: Earthscan, 1994), 20 at 27, where she notes that because sustainable development refers to development as opposed to growth or economy, "it appears to apply exclusively to developing countries. Industrialized countries rarely refer to their activities as development activities, and, therefore, seem to be outside the scope of the term."

[107] Principle 8 reads as follows: "to achieve sustainable development and a higher quality of life for all people, States should reduce and eliminate unsustainable patterns of production and consumption and promote appropriate demographic policies." Porras, note 106 at 27, believes that with the adoption of Principle 8 "developed countries became full partners in the quest for sustainable development." The Rio Declaration reminds us that intra-generational equity can only be achieved if industrial countries cease to benefit from their unsustainable practices.

The WCED report accepted the imperatives of growth for poverty eradication and development of the South. But since "political realism" seemed to rule out North–South income distribution and changes in consumption and lifestyles in the North, the commission interpolated existing models and argued for a continued 3 per cent growth in the North to enable the South to grow, and showed great faith in the ability of technology to solve the problems.[108]

This indicates that a sustainable development path implies that the status quo remains the same for Northern countries: Sustainable development means that the needs of the North will be met without compromising the needs of future generations.[109] The main threat to sustainable development posed by Northern countries arises from consumption and production patterns, while the main threat from Southern countries is poverty.[110] Given that Northern countries, with about 20 percent of the world's population, consume 80 percent of the world's resources,[111] one can see that addressing poverty alone cannot solve the problem. The bigger threat comes from overconsumption of resources. While the Stockholm Conference made no reference to consumption and production patterns, the Rio Declaration refers to this in Principle 8 in a rather half-hearted manner[112] combining it with "appropriate demographic policies." Unlike Principle 7, which specifically refers to developed countries, Principle 8 makes no such reference in relation to consumption and production.

While notions of fairness and justice underlie many of the international environmental law principles, including sustainable development,[113] the gap between the rich and the poor keeps on widening. The Johannesburg Declaration identified the link between sustainable development, poverty and consumption patterns:

> We recognize that poverty eradication, changing consumption and production patterns, and protecting and managing the natural resource base for economic and social development are overarching objectives of and essential requirements for sustainable development. [...] The deep fault line that divides human society

---

[108] C. Raghavan quoted in Hunter et al., note 1, p. 154.

[109] Raghavan, quoting a report from the South Centre, in Hunter et al., note 1, p. 154.

[110] See also UN General Assembly, *Resolution Adopted by the General Assembly: Rio+20 The Future We Want*, 27 July 2012, A/Res/66/288 [hereinafter Rio+20]; Third World Network, "North-South Divide Over Rio+20 Outcome Document," www.twnside.org.sg.

[111] See "Consumption by the United States," 2008, http://public.wsu.edu. See also WRI, "State of Consumption Today," www.worldwatch.org.

[112] Note the use of word "should" rather than "shall" in Principle 8. See Chatterjee and Finger, note 84, p. 40 who note that many issues were left untouched at Rio, including Northern consumption, global economic reform, the role of transnational corporations, and nuclear energy, while "the military was totally left off the agenda."

[113] See D. French, "'From Seoul with Love' – The Continuing Relevance of the 1986 Seoul ILA Declaration on Progressive Development of Principles of Public International Law Relating to a New International Economic Order" (2008) 55 *Netherlands International Law Review* 27.

between the rich and the poor and the ever-increasing gap between the developed and developing worlds pose a major threat to global prosperity, security and stability."[114]

This indicates that the gap between Northern countries and Southern countries is a major threat to achieving sustainable development, and in particular the intragenerational equity component. Pointing out that the interplay between fairness, equity, and sustainability is central to the discourse on sustainable development, Duncan French observes:

> And whether the marginalized are the poor – often ethnic minority – communities within affluent states... or, at the macro level, the global South *en bloc*, the plea for greater fairness in the distribution of environmental benefits (and equally important, a reduction in the disproportionate allocation of negative environmental externalities), is always very similar. Justice will sometimes be a demand for preferential treatment, but often it is simply a call to be treated fairly and on a par with more powerful groups within a society."[115]

He distinguishes between three variations of justice – corrective justice, distributive justice and procedural fairness – and notes that corrective justice can be used to correct past injustices:

> It is the belief that the law can be used to offset, or prevent, the continuing unfairness of historical wrongs; certainly the argument has been most conspicuous in the environmental sphere where the historical exploitation of natural resources, damage to the natural environment and over-use of natural sinks by the North is now viewed as being at the expense of the current and future claims of the global South."[116]

However, it is unlikely that Northern states will ever accept legal liability for past wrongs, as is evident from the debates surrounding the common but differentiated responsibility principle and climate change.[117]

Equity, justice and fairness all play a role in relation to sustainable development, although none of these terms are fully defined. Equity is an important component of sustainable development and underlies the CBDR principle. Here, too, one can see the North–South divide. Although it is not possible to generalize, Northern countries tend to emphasize intergenerational equity,[118] while Southern states tend

---

[114] Johannesburg Declaration, note 88.
[115] See D. French, "Sustainable Development and the Instinctive Imperative of Justice in the Global Order," in D. French (ed.), *Global Justice and Sustainable Development* (Leiden: Martinus Nijhoff, 2010), p. 8.
[116] Ibid, p. 16.
[117] See discussion later in the chapter.
[118] The seminal work on this is by E. B. Weiss, *In Fairness to Future Generations: International Law, Common Patrimony and Intergenerational Equity* (New York: Transnational, 1989); *cf.* D. B. Gatmaytan, "The Illusion of Intergenerational Equity: Oposa v. Factoran as Pyrrhic Victory" (2002) 15 *Georgetown International Environmental Law Review* 457 who contends that the Oposa case has attained celebrity status all over the world except in the Philippines.

to emphasize intragenerational equity: "[d]espite its conceptual over-use, intragenerational equity is a fundamental idea. It is firmly premised on two interwoven ideas: First, that disparities in wealth and power continue to exist between developing and developed States and, second, a moral-political assertion that these disparities must be addressed if long-term solutions are to be found."[119]

A related issue that gave rise to considerable North–South debate surrounded the adoption of the General Assembly Resolution on the Right to Development.[120] According to the Office of the UN High Commissioner for Human Rights, the right to development includes: "full sovereignty over natural resources; self-determination; popular participation in development; equality of opportunity; and the creation of favorable conditions for the enjoyment of other civil, political, economic, social and cultural rights."[121] Each of these components is fairly uncontroversial, yet the resolution itself became a highly contentious issue. While Southern countries pushed for the adoption of the resolution, several Northern countries opposed its adoption. In fact, the United States appended an interpretative statement stating that, in its opinion, development was a goal, not a right.[122] When the right to development was being debated during the Rio Conference, Northern states wanted Principles 3 and 4 combined into a right to sustainable development. Southern states opposed this and wanted sustainable development separated from the right to development.[123] However, given that sustainable development encompasses economic development, this apprehension seems rather redundant now.[124]

Southern countries often contend that inequities within the current generation must be addressed before one can talk about equity among generations.[125] While this has some merit, it does not mean that Southern countries should follow the same destructive path that Northern countries followed in their pursuit of economic development. Sustainable development requires *both* intra- and intergenerational equity – not achieving one at the expense of the other. Noting that at Rio, two of the greatest issues of our times – environment and poverty – converged, Lester Brown

---

[119] See French, note 115, p. 20. However, within the South itself, vast disparities exist as exemplified by the debates surrounding climate change with least developed countries and small island states emphasizing inter-generational equity particularly because their very survival as a sovereign state is at stake. See W. N. Adger, J. Paavola, and Saleemul Huq (eds.), *Fairness in Adaptation to Climate Change* (Cambridge: MIT Press, 2006).

[120] UN General Assembly, *Declaration on the Right to Development*, 4 December 1986, A/RES/41/128.

[121] United Nations Human Rights, "Declaration on the Right to Development at 25," www.ohchr.org.

[122] See Schrijver, note 39, p. 79.

[123] See Porras, note 106, p. 25. She argues that while environment and development are equal partners of sustainable development, the right to development comes before sustainable development in the Rio Declaration; thus, it seems to give pre-eminence to development.

[124] For a detailed discussion of the right to development, see chapter 15, S. Puvimanasinghe, "International Investment Law, Human Rights and Sustainable Development".

[125] See Ntambirweki, note 11, p. 924.

stresses the need to address the current global inequality in wealth: "[i]n poor countries, where the overwhelming concern is survival to the next harvest, it is difficult to elicit support for protecting the ozone layer or stabilizing climate. The bottom line may well be the realization that we can no longer separate the future habitability of the planet from the current international distribution of wealth."[126]

Despite the uncertainty surrounding sustainable development with regard to its meaning and legal status, it holds important lessons for both camps. It requires both groups to incorporate environmental concerns into the development process and, more importantly, requires Northern states to curb their unsustainable consumption and production patterns.[127] By identifying sustainable development as a concept that requires development decisions to be the outcome of a particular procedure,[128] by subjecting development decisions to international scrutiny by integrating environmental concerns and social concerns into the economic development process, it plays an important role at both international and national levels.[129] It has progressed from a slippery concept[130] to an umbrella concept encompassing both substantive and procedural components with normative force and widespread endorsement by the international community.[131]

3.2 *The Common but Differentiated Responsibility Principle (CBDR)*

An exception to the cardinal principle of sovereign equality of states,[132] the CBDR principle refers to the need to adopt differential norms in certain circumstances

---

[126] See L. Brown, "Time is Running Out on the Planet," Earth Summit Times, June 2, 1992, p. 13, referred to in Hunter et al., note 1, p. 161. French, note 115, makes a similar argument when he notes that intragenerational equity must be achieved if sustainable development is to be achieved.

[127] Rio Declaration, note 3, Principle 8. See also Rio+20, note 110, para. 4.

[128] See Birnie and Boyle, note 1, p. 96 who believe that international law requires development decisions to be the outcome of a process that promotes sustainable development. Thus, it requires the carrying out of environmental impact assessments, public participation, integration of environmental concerns into the decision-making process, etc. See also Sands et al., note 1, p. 217. For the procedural dimension of sustainable development, see section 3.5.

[129] See A. Boyle and D. Freestone (eds.), *International Law and Sustainable Development: Past Achievements and Future Challenges* (New York: Oxford University Press, 1999) 1 at 6, who note: "[i]ts most potentially revolutionary aspect, however, is that it makes a state's management of its own domestic environment and resources a matter of international concern for the first time in a systematic way."

[130] See R. J. Araujo, "Rio+10 and the World Summit on Sustainable Development: Why Human Beings are at the Center of Concerns" (2004) 2 *Georgetown Journal of International Law and Public Policy* 201.

[131] See A. Dobson, *Fairness and Futurity* (Oxford: Oxford University Press, 1999) referred to in Hunter et al., note 1, p.175, who believes that the "extraordinary thing about sustainable development in many ways is that it has acquired such widespread endorsement." See also S. Atapattu, note 1, chapter 7; Birnie et al., note 1. See also Segger and Khalfan, note 102.

[132] This forms the cornerstone of international law and is embodied in the UN Charter, San Francisco, 26 June 1945, in force 24 October 1945, 59 Stat. 1031; TS 993; 3 Bevans 1153 as one of its principles, namely Article 2(1). See, however, Bodansky, who is of the view that there is no

94 *International Environmental Law Principles and the North–South Divide*

given the heterogeneity of the global community.[133] Principle 7 of the Rio Declaration embodies the CBDR principle and comprises several components:[134] First, it refers to the common responsibility of states to protect the environment; second, it refers to different contributions to global environmental problems by developing and developed countries; third, it acknowledges the greater pressures that Northern countries place on the global environment without referring to their historic responsibility;[135] finally, it refers to the capacity of Northern countries to address global environmental problems due to the superior financial resources and technology that they command. However, Southern countries were not successful in their attempt to include a specific reference to the historic responsibility of Northern states that, no doubt, have greater responsibility in creating them. On the face of it, the adoption of this principle is a victory for the Southern countries. With the advent of global environmental problems such as climate change and ozone depletion it became increasingly clear that adopting a legal regime with uniform obligations for both Northern and Southern countries was neither feasible nor equitable, because the contribution of the two groups to their creation was anything but equal. Similarly, the ability of these groups to address the issues also differs considerably.

While several environmental legal regimes embody differential obligations, the climate regime is noteworthy for the significant North–South, South–South, and North–North conflicts and cleavages that it has produced.[136] In 2007, the president of Uganda called climate change an "act of aggression" by Northern countries against Southern countries.[137]

The continued application of the CBDR principle based on Annex I and non-Annex I countries in the climate change regime has given rise to controversy.

> reason to treat states as equal and questions why Nauru should have the same say as India or China: D. Bodansky, "The Legitimacy of International Governance: A Coming Challenge for International Environmental Law?" (1999) 93 *American Journal of International Law* 596 at 614.

[133] See Beyerlin, note 38, p. 277 who states that *prima facie*, CBDR appears to be a "promising conceptual approach for bridging the North-South divide in international environmental relations."

[134] Rio Declaration, note 3, Principles 6 (which refers to the need to take account of the special situation of developing countries, particularly those of least developed countries), 9 (which refers to the need to transfer technology, although it does not specifically mention developing countries), and 11 (which requests states to enact necessary environmental legislation but notes that standards applied in some countries may be inappropriate in others and may incur unwarranted economic and social costs in other countries, particularly, developing countries).

[135] See Rajamani, note 89, p. 72 who refers this to as the "culpability and entitlement premise."

[136] See chapter 10, R. Maguire and X. Jiang, "Emerging Powerful Southern Voices: Role of BASIC Nations in Shaping Climate Change Mitigation Commitments."

[137] See J-A. van Wyk, "The African Union's Response to Climate Change and Climate Security in Climate Change and Natural Resource Conflicts" in D. A. Mwiturubani and J-A. van Wyk (eds.), *Africa* (Pretoria: Institute for Security Studies, 2010), p. 6.

Emissions from countries such as China, India, and Brazil are increasing[138] and the distinction made between developing and developed countries in 1992, when the UNFCCC was adopted, is becoming increasingly difficult to justify. Thus, some scholars have argued that a more precise interpretation of the CBDR will be central to post-Copenhagen negotiations.[139]

If the basic premise of differential norms is facilitating universal participation, what happened with Part XI of the UNCLOS seems to turn the notion of universal participation on its head. Differential treatment and benefit-sharing that favored Southern states was *removed* in order to ensure participation by Northern countries.[140] While we generally strive for universal participation, it is not absolutely necessary for the success of treaties; however, the participation of key players is. We have seen this the hard way with regard to the climate change regime. The United States, the biggest emitter of greenhouse gases at the time, withdrew from the Kyoto Protocol in 2001.[141] Without the biggest player in the game, the Kyoto Protocol has limped along thanks to the heroic efforts of the EU and other Northern countries.[142] With the emergence of other key players in the game – China, India, Brazil – the non-participation of the U.S. has become a thorny issue. China, now the biggest emitter of CO_2, refuses to accept binding obligations unless the United States too changes its position.[143] Under the current legal regime, Southern countries do not have any binding emission reduction obligations, although many have made voluntary commitments under the Copenhagen Accord.[144] They cling to the CBDR as a lifeline and refuse to accept binding obligations unless major emitters in the global North also do so. Their argument is simple: Northern countries created the problem and benefited in the process, so they must bear the burden of addressing the problem.[145] However, the issue is getting more complex as

---

[138] China overtook the United States in 2007 in relation to CO_2 emissions: see "China Overtakes the U.S. in Greenhouse Gas Emissions," *New York Times*, June 20, 2007.

[139] See J. Whalley and S. Walsh, "Post-Copenhagen Negotiation Issues and the North-South Divide" (2010) 8 *Seattle Journal for Social Justice* 773; J. Pauwelyn, "The End of Differential Treatment for Developing Countries? Lessons from the Trade and Climate Change Regimes" (2013) 22(1) *Review of European Comparative and International Environmental Law* 29 at 41, who contends that "treating all developing countries as a single group is neither effective nor equitable."

[140] See Rajamani, note 89, p. 33.

[141] See Hunter et al., note 1, p. 684. Canada, on the other hand, withdrew from Kyoto in 2012 after having ratified it. See "Canada to Withdraw from Kyoto Protocol," BBC News, 13 December 2011.

[142] See S. Oberthur and H. E. Ott, *The Kyoto Protocol: International Climate Policy for the 21st Century* (Berlin: Springer, 1999), chapter 2.

[143] Ibid.

[144] See Natural Resources Defense Council, "From Copenhagen Accord to Climate Action," www.nrdc.org.

[145] See M. Weisslitz, "Rethinking the Equitable Principle of Common but Differentiated Responsibility: Differential versus Absolute Norms of Compliance and Contribution in the Global Climate Change Context" (2002) 13(2) *Colorado Journal of International Environmental Law and Policy* 473.

96   *International Environmental Law Principles and the North–South Divide*

emissions from Southern countries are increasing rapidly, and amid this bickering, the global climate and, especially, vulnerable communities suffer.

While flexibility built into a treaty regime may promote participation, there are disadvantages that must be taken into consideration. Can the treaty itself be undermined with too many differential obligations, making it hard to monitor the obligations[146] and thereby affecting the overall legitimacy of the treaty regime? Another challenge is to decide whether differentiation is based on needs or on past wrongs. If it is the latter, the focus shifts from Southern countries' needs to the Northern countries' wrongs:

> Rio principle 7, in calling for the assignment of heavier contributions to developed countries in response to "the pressures their societies place on the global environment," shifts the focus from Poor's needs to Rich's wrongs. If we agreed to put the principle into action, it would mean that the Rich (and everyone else) should be confronted with the full social costs of their emissions. Thus understood, the principle is no more controversial, or peculiarly equitable, than declaring that the polluter should pay.[147]

Although the CBDR principle seems to favor Southern countries, if you dig a little deeper into the politics governing its adoption, a different picture emerges. The G-77 proposal for the CBDR, which specifically referred to historic responsibility, was rejected at Rio:

> The major cause of the continuing deterioration of the global environment is the unsustainable patterns of production and consumption particularly in developed countries. [...] In view of their main historical and current responsibility for global environmental degradation and their capability to address this common concern, developed countries shall provide adequate, new and additional financial resources and environmentally sound technologies on preferential and concessional terms to developing countries to enable them to achieve sustainable development.[148]

This formulation gave rise to deep North–South debates. From the beginning, the United States opposed the adoption of this principle, even going to the extent of entering an interpretative statement to Principle 7:[149]

> The United States understands and accepts that principle 7 highlights the special leadership role of the developed countries, based on our industrial development,

---

[146] See A. Halvorssen, *Equality among Unequals in International Environmental Law: Differential Treatment for Developing Countries* (Boulder: Westview Press, 1999), p. 106. See also A. Halvorssen, "Common, but Differentiated Commitments in the Future Climate Change Regime – Amending the Kyoto Protocol to include Annex C and the Annex C Mitigation Fund" (2007) 18 *Colorado Journal International Environmental Law and Policy* 247.

[147] C. Stone, "Common but Differentiated Responsibilities in International Law" (2004) 98 *American Journal of International Law* 276.

[148] Referred to in French, note 3 at 36.

[149] See Hunter et al., note 1, p. 466.

our experience with environmental protection policies and actions, and our wealth, technical expertise and capabilities.

The United States does not accept any interpretation of principle 7 that would imply a recognition or acceptance by the United States or any international obligations or liabilities, or any diminution in the responsibilities of developing countries.[150]

This is a significant departure from attributing historic responsibility to Northern countries for their past polluting activities. Far from acknowledging liability for past activities, it in effect reinforces Northern superiority, which resembles the justifications for past colonial domination – in relation to its wealth, its technical expertise, and the resources at its command. It seems like a slap in the face for Southern states, particularly those who have to bear a disproportionate burden due to global environmental problems created by Northern countries. The dire fate of small island states affected by climate change comes to mind:

The industrial countries have benefitted disproportionately from the industrialization process that led to the accumulation of greenhouse gases in the atmosphere, yet since the damage is universal, the costs are borne by everyone. Equity herein would demand that those who have benefitted the most from the process that led to the creation of the problem bear an unequal burden for addressing the problem. It is this equity that the measure of historical responsibility within the principle of common but differentiated responsibility aims to achieve.[151]

Finally, a much watered-down version in the form of the current Principle 7 was adopted, which left both groups dissatisfied: Southern countries were not happy because any reference to historic responsibility was removed and Northern countries were not happy that Southern countries were given preferential treatment.[152] Despite these differences, its adoption signifies a delicate balance struck and a compromise reached by the international community.

The disproportionate contribution to environmental problems as well as disproportionate benefits derived from them lies at the heart of the North–South debates

---

[150] Referred to in Hunter et al., note 1, p. 466. See also D. French (ed.), *Sustainable Development and the Instinctive Imperative of Justice in the Global Order in Global Justice and Sustainable Development* (Leiden: Martinus Nijhoff, 2010), p. 16.

[151] L. Rajamani, "The Principle of Common but Differentiated Responsibility and the Balance of Commitments under the Climate Regime" (2000) 9(2) *Review of European Comparative International Environmental Law* 120 at 123. With regard to CBDR and the climate regime, Rajamani argues that mitigation is based on historic responsibility while adaptation is based on pressing needs. Mitigation costs are high in Northern countries while adaptation costs are high in Southern countries.

[152] See French, note 3, pp. 37–38. The United States in particular was unhappy that developing countries may have lesser obligations than developed countries. French notes that despite criticisms by both groups of states, "there is little doubt that Principle 7 is a major new contribution to international environmental law" (p. 38) and "its significance is likely to increase as Southern states continue to take an active role in environmental policy and law-making" (p. 59).

98 *International Environmental Law Principles and the North–South Divide*

surrounding the CBDR. Northern countries' disproportionate participation cannot be discounted from either account. While it can be argued that CBDR combines all of the earlier components (historic responsibility, disproportionate benefits, ability to address the problems, availability of technological and other resources), it is not clear which aspect should be emphasized. As Mickelson questions, "[i]s it a question of *ability* to pay or *responsibility* to pay?"[153] The adoption of CBDR broke new ground in international environmental law and is a victory for the Southern states, yet some of the interpretations surrounding it and the experience with Part XI of the UNCLOS suggests the contrary.

3.3 *Benefit-sharing and Prior Informed Consent*

Access to resources and benefit-sharing is another principle that has given rise to controversy along North–South lines. The earlier articulation of this principle was made in relation to the common heritage of mankind principle (CHMP) previously discussed. Due to the inclusion of this principle in the UNCLOS, the entire section on deep-seabed mining had to be amended after the Convention was opened for signature.

However, this is not the end of the story. Barely ten years after the adoption of the UNCLOS, Southern countries succeeded in including benefit-sharing in the Convention on Biological Diversity (CBD).[154] In fact, the entire Convention is a good case study of compromises along North–South divisions. The CBD represents an instance where the global South realized its potential in terms of negotiating a treaty where it had the upper hand. While on the surface the North seemed to advocate for conservation of biological diversity, what it actually wanted was *access* to biological resources in the South. Southern nations also wanted to ensure that they derived economic benefit from the exploitation of these resources, not simply conserving them.[155] While they lacked the technology to exploit genetic resources, they were not going to sit back while Northern biotech and pharmaceutical companies exploited these as well as their traditional knowledge.[156] Thus, the ensuing Convention is both a conservation and economic document. During the negotiating process, Southern countries insisted that the Convention should be broad enough to address sustainable use of biodiversity.[157] When the Convention was opened for signature it was signed by every country represented at UNCED with the notable exception of the United States, which particularly objected to the

[153] See Mickelson, note 9, p. 70.

[154] CBD, note 83.

[155] See D. Downes, "New Diplomacy for the Biodiversity Trade: Biodiversity, Biotechnology, and Intellectual Property in the Convention on Biological Diversity" (1993) 4 *Touro Journal Transnational Law* 1.

[156] Ibid.

[157] See Hunter et al., note 1, p. 999.

use of intellectual property rights, the provisions on sharing benefits, and technology transfer.[158] Although President Clinton later signed the Convention, it has never been ratified.[159]

The preamble affirms several principles: (a) that biological diversity is a common concern of mankind, (b) that states have sovereign rights over their biological resources, (c) the precautionary principle, (d) the principle of anticipation and prevention of the causes of significant loss of biological diversity, (e) that the special situation of developing countries must be taken into account, (f) that the special situation of least developed countries and small island states should be taken into account, (g) that economic and social development and poverty eradication are overriding priorities for developing countries, and (h) the principle of conserving biological diversity for present and future generations.[160] The preamble recognizes "[t]he close and traditional dependence of many indigenous and local communities embodying traditional lifestyles on biological resources, and the desirability of sharing equitably benefits arising from the use of traditional knowledge, innovations and practices relevant to the conservation of biological diversity and the sustainable use of its components."[161]

The objectives of the Convention are threefold: (a) conservation of biological diversity, (b) sustainable use of its components, and (c) fair and equitable sharing of benefits arising out of the utilization of genetic resources.[162] Article 8 on in-situ conservation again articulates the need to encourage the equitable sharing of benefits arising from the utilization of traditional knowledge, innovations, and practices.

Article 15 emphasizes that access to genetic resources shall be subject to the prior informed consent of the party providing such resources. This is another important principle and has been incorporated in several other legal regimes.[163] Article 15 further calls upon parties to the Convention to adopt legislative, administrative, and policy measures "with the aim of sharing in a fair and equitable way the results of research and development and the benefits arising from the commercial and other utilization of genetic resources"[164] with the parties providing such resources on mutually agreed terms.

The Convention avoids any reference to CHMP; instead it refers to biodiversity as a "common concern of mankind."[165] During the negotiating process neither the

---

[158] Ibid, p. 1000.
[159] Ibid.
[160] CBD, note 83, Preamble.
[161] Ibid.
[162] CBD, note 83, art. 1.
[163] *Basel Convention on the Control of Transboundary Movement of Hazardous Wastes and Their Disposal*, Basel, 22 March 1989, in force 5 May 1992, 1673 UNTS 126; 28 ILM 657 (1989); *Convention on the Prior Informed Consent Procedure for Certain Hazardous Chemicals and Pesticides in International Trade*, Rotterdam, 10 September 1998, in force 24 February 2004, 2244 UNTS 337; 38 ILM 1 (1999) are some examples.
[164] CBD, note 83, art. 15.
[165] CBD, note 83, Preamble.

South nor the North wanted the CHMP included as a principle: Southern countries did not want the CHMP included because it implied providing free access to the resources, while Northern countries opposed it because it required sharing of the benefits resulting from exploiting these resources.[166] In an effort to avoid this controversy and to justify international action, the negotiators opted for the rather neutral concept of "common concern of mankind," which, incidentally, is also the term used in relation to climate in the UN Framework Convention on Climate Change.[167] The Biodiversity Convention makes a distinction between *biological diversity* and *biological resources* – the former is a common concern of mankind and to be conserved, while the latter is subject to the state's sovereignty and is to be used sustainably: "[i]n this way, an uneasy compromise was reached between the North's interests in conservation and the South's interest in benefiting from the biological resources within their borders."[168]

Despite Northern states' objections to the benefit-sharing component of the CHMP, Southern states succeeded in including it as a substantive requirement in the CBD in relation to benefits arising from the utilization of traditional knowledge[169] as well as in relation to genetic resources.[170] The latter is also subject to the prior informed consent of the party providing such resources. The Convention breaks new ground in international environmental law by incorporating substantive provisions on benefit-sharing and requiring approval in relation to traditional knowledge held by indigenous and community groups, and suggests "a major shift in power first toward developing countries and then toward local communities."[171] These innovative provisions cannot, unfortunately, mask the reality on the ground. Obtaining the consent of these groups is not easy as they are not homogenous and language and culture may provide an additional layer of complexity to the problem. Where there are multiple groups involved, it is not clear which group or groups should give consent or receive compensation. In addition, even though access to genetic resources and benefit-sharing is to be done upon mutually agreed terms and conditions, parties to these negotiations are rarely equal. While some success stories exist,[172] most often these negotiations are skewed

---

[166] See Hunter et al., note 1, p. 1001. Legally, too, adopting the CHMP to resources within states was problematic. CHMP is generally applied in relation to resources outside the jurisdiction of states, while the PSNR is applied in relation to resources within states.

[167] *United Nations Framework Convention on Climate Change*, 9 May 1992, in force 21 March 1994, 1771 UNTS 107; S. Treaty Doc No. 102–38; UN Doc. A/AC.237/18 (Part II)/Add.1; 31 ILM 849 (1992).

[168] See Hunter et al., note 1, p. 1001.

[169] CBD, note 83, art. 8(j).

[170] Ibid, art. 15. For a detailed discussion of the negotiations leading up to the CBD and the North–South divide, see Downes, note 155.

[171] See Hunter et al., note 1, p. 1013.

[172] See e.g. the contract signed between Merck Pharmaceutical Company and the Costa Rican National Institute for Biodiversity, and the agreement between six indigenous communities and Peru's International Potato Centre, referred to in Hunter et al., note 1, p. 1013.

and there have not been a significant number of contracts between pharmaceutical companies and developing countries.[173] Moreover, the real stakeholders – indigenous and rural communities – are often left out of these negotiations and Southern countries do not necessarily act in the best interest of these vulnerable communities.[174]

In an effort to strike a balance between access to resources and benefit-sharing, the parties to the CBD adopted a set of voluntary guidelines in 2002. Called the Bonn Guidelines on Access to Genetic Resources and Fair and Equitable Sharing of the Benefits Arising out of their Utilization,[175] these guidelines call the parties to establish a national focal point for access and benefit-sharing and make such information available through the clearing house mechanism.[176] The focal point is required to inform applicants for access to genetic resources of the procedures for obtaining prior informed consent and mutually agreed terms, including benefit-sharing, the competent national authorities, relevant indigenous and local communities, and relevant stakeholders.[177]

The Bonn Guidelines paved the way for the adoption of the Nagoya Protocol on Access to Genetic Resources[178] in 2010, which incorporates both fair and equitable sharing of benefits and the prior informed consent principles. Article 5 provides that benefits arising from the utilization of genetic resources and its subsequent applications and commercialization shall be shared in a fair and equitable way with the party providing such resources upon mutually agreed terms. Access to genetic resources is subject to the prior informed consent of the party providing such resources. Article 7 specifically embodies prior and informed consent and approval of indigenous or local communities in relation to traditional knowledge associated with genetic resources held by such communities. The Nagoya-Kuala Lumpur Supplementary Protocol[179] offers another instance of the North–South divide. At

---

[173] Ibid, p. 1014.

[174] For example, see the story of the Neem tree in India, see Hunter et al., note 1, p. 1021. A coalition of about 200 organizations filed a petition in the U.S. Patent Office seeking to invalidate the patent granted to Grace Co.

[175] Secretariat of the Convention on Biological Diversity, "Bonn Guidelines on Access to Genetic Resources and Fair and Equitable Sharing of the Benefits Arising out of their Utilization," www.cbd.int.

[176] Ibid.

[177] Ibid.

[178] "Nagoya Protocol on Access to Genetic Resources and the Fair and Equitable Sharing of Benefits Arising from their Utilization to the 1992 Convention on Biological Diversity," www.cbd.int. See Nijar, "The Nagoya Protocol on Access and Benefit Sharing of Genetic Resources: Analysis and Implementation Options for Developing Countries," South Centre Research Papers 36 (2011). See chapter 9, J. Cabrera Medaglia, "Access and Benefit-Sharing: North–South Challenges in Implementing the Convention on Biological Diversity and its Nagoya Protocol."

[179] "Nagoya-Kuala Lumpur Supplementary Protocol on Liability and Redress to the Cartagena Protocol on Biosafety," New York, 6 March 2012 (not yet in force), http://bch.cbd.int. See G. S. Nijar, "The Nagoya-Kuala Lumpur Supplementary Protocol on Liability and Redress to

the time the Biosafety Protocol was adopted, the parties were not able to agree on a liability regime. Article 27 of the Protocol envisages the adoption of a liability regime within four years of the Protocol; it took the parties ten years to do so. During the negotiations for the Biosafety Protocol, Southern countries, concerned that they would be used as laboratories for the release of GMOs without proper testing or impact assessment, became ardent supporters of the Protocol, along with Europe. They wanted to ensure that the Protocol incorporated the following: Prior informed consent before GMOs could be released; the precautionary principle in managing the transfer, use, and disposal of GMOs; liability and compensation for damage from such releases; and environmental and risk assessment. Northern states, particularly the U.S., opposed any system of liability and compensation and sought to restrict the scope of the Biosafety Protocol to intentional releases.[180] In the end, both sides compromised and deferred the adoption of a liability regime to a later date. On the whole, international law avoids specific liability regimes, so the fact that the supplementary Protocol was adopted is an achievement for Southern states.

Both fair and equitable sharing and prior informed consent are quite revolutionary developments in international environmental law. Lack of fair and equitable sharing of benefits is often lamented by Southern countries. Biopiracy[181] is among their biggest complaints, and it is no surprise that Southern states worked hard to include these principles in the legal regime governing biological diversity. Some argue that the exploitation of Southern biological resources is a form of colonialism by Northern countries and that "intellectual property rights are simply a vehicle for legalizing the theft of knowledge or resources from the South."[182] Not all Northern countries support biopiracy, however; the EU, for example, is contemplating legislation regulating biopiracy.[183] Under the proposed law, which is based on the CBD and the Nagoya Protocol, pharmaceutical industries will need the written consent of local or indigenous people before exploring genetic resources or making use of their traditional knowledge. Laudable as the draft law is, getting the written consent of these indigenous groups might be problematic, given that some of these

---

the Cartagena Protocol on Biosafety: An Analysis and Implementation Challenges" (2012) 13 (3) *International Environmental Agreements: Politics, Law and Economics* 271.

[180] See Hunter et al., note 1, p. 1039. See also G. S. Nijar, note 179, who observes that: "[t]he resistance by developed countries, backed by the biotechnology industry, to avoid any civil liability provisions increased the resolve of developing countries to insist on the inclusion of such provisions."

[181] Biopiracy is defined as "the commercial development of naturally occurring biological material [...] by a technologically advanced country or organization without fair compensation to the peoples or nations in whose territory the materials were originally discovered," in The Free Dictionary, www.thefreedictionary.com. It must be noted that this is not a legal definition.

[182] See Hunter et al., note 1, p. 1018.

[183] M. Hall, "EU Debate Biopiracy Law to Protect Indigenous People," *The Guardian*, May 1 2001.

groups are illiterate or may not speak the language of the majority, or it may not be clear whose consent is required if many indigenous groups are involved. Furthermore, shouldn't they derive some benefit from these resources or from sharing their traditional knowledge?

In a harsh critique of the CBD, Ashish Kothari of India argues that biodiversity should be considered as a global heritage that should include not just genetic resources but also biodiversity-related knowledge and biotechnologies:

> A victim of the North-South conflict during the run-up to the signing of the Convention at the Earth Summit was the ethically superior position of biodiversity as a global heritage. [...] In an unequal world, a common heritage has every chance of being misused. Thus, the last two centuries have seen the countries of the North, themselves poor in biodiversity, literally looting the resources of the biologically-rich nations of the South while creating protectionist systems to monopolize the technologies and benefits arising out of these resources. A common heritage has been turned into a colony for the North.[184]

Traditional knowledge has been another area of contention, and here too we see the adoption of prior informed consent as a guiding principle.[185] Of the fifty ratifications needed for the Nagoya Protocol to enter into force, it has so far received only twenty-nine, and all of them are from the global South.[186] Pharmaceutical companies in the North are unhappy about sharing benefits with local communities but if the proposed EU law is adopted, they will be required to compensate indigenous communities for using their traditional knowledge in developing marketable products. According to Green MEP Sandra Belier, "90% of genetic resources are in the south and 90% of the patents are in the north."[187] She cites as an example, the German company Schwab's activities in South Africa, where the company made huge profits from a product they developed from the geranium plant. These patents were later cancelled due to appeals by the African Center for Biosafety based in South Africa, which called the patents "an illegitimate and illegal monopolisation of genetic resources derived from traditional knowledge and a stark opposition to the convention on biodiversity."[188] Ms. Belier noted: "[i]n order to participate in the conservation of biodiversity, the people and knowledge that are associated with it, we must ensure today that the benefits arising

---

[184] See Hunter et al., note 1, p. 1018, quoting A. Kothari, "Beyond the Biodiversity Convention: A View from India," in V. Sanches and C. Juma (eds.), *Biodiplomacy: Genetic Resources and International Relations* (Nairobi: ACTS Press, 1994), pp. 67–72.

[185] In 2013, the EU contemplated the need to adopt legislation on biopiracy to protect traditional knowledge. See M. Hall, "EU Debate Biopiracy Law to Protect Indigenous People," *The Guardian*, May 1, 2001.

[186] United Nations Decade on Biodiversity, "Three New Ratifications Edge Landmark Treaty on Genetic Resources Towards Entry into Force," January 31, 2014, www.cbd.int.

[187] See Hall, note 185.

[188] Ibid.

104   *International Environmental Law Principles and the North–South Divide*

from the utilisation of genetic resources and the associated traditional knowledge are shared in a fair and equitable manner."[189]

The CBD, in addition to giving rise to deep North–South divisions,[190] is also an example of Southern states seeking to gain control of their natural resources at the expense of local communities that depend on these resources for their survival. State authorities rarely enter into consultations with these communities, who become further marginalized when they face the prospect of being evicted from lands they have lived on for generations if these lands hold promise of oil or other lucrative resources.[191] While there are a few success stories of multinational companies entering into agreements with local groups,[192] oftentimes the case is one of neglect, marginalization, and even violence where the local communities oppose efforts by multinational companies to exploit their resources.[193]

3.4 *The Precautionary Principle*

Principle 15 of the Rio Declaration advocates the adoption of the precautionary approach in the face of scientific uncertainty. The controversy surrounding the precautionary "principle" was about whether it was in fact a principle, an approach, or a guideline. This principle reflects both North–South divisions as well as North–North divisions. At the time the Rio Declaration was adopted, the United States objected to the language of Principle 15 on the ground that precaution was not a principle, but rather an approach.[194] This language was eventually adopted in the

---

[189] Ibid.

[190] See Chatterjee and Finger, note 84, p. 43 who argue that the CBD clearly favors the North.

[191] Some of the cases decided by the Inter-American Commission and Court of Human Rights are relevant here. See *Saramaka People* v *Suriname*, Inter-American Court of Human Rights, Judgment of 28 November 2007, Series C No. 174 where the principle of free, prior, and informed consent was adopted at least in situations that involve the survival of indigenous peoples. See also *Kichwa People of Sarayaku* v *Ecuador*, Inter-American Court of Human Rights, Judgment of 27 June 2012, Series C No. 245 where the Inter-American Court held that the state must consult with Sarayku people in a prior, adequate, and effective manner in relation to activities and projects involving extraction of natural resources. In *Maya Communities of the Toledo District* v *Belize*, Inter-American Court of Human Rights, Report No. 96/03, Case 12.0053, October 24 2003, the Commission held that Belize had violated the communal property rights of these indigenous peoples by granting concessions without consulting them and obtaining their consent.

[192] See earlier discussion.

[193] This often happens with the collusion of the state in question. The *Ogoni* case is a good example. See *The Social and Economic Rights Action Center and the Center for Economic and Social Rights* v *Nigeria*, African Commission on Human and Peoples" Rights, Comm. No. 155/96 (2001).

[194] See H. Meyer, "The Precautionary Principle and the Cartagena Protocol on Biosafety: Development of a Concept," in T. Traavik and L. Li Ching, *Biosafety First – Holistic Approaches to Risk and Uncertainty in Genetic Engineering and Genetically Modified Organisms* (Trondheim: Tapir Academic Press, 2007).

Rio Declaration with the added caveat that such measures should also be cost-effective.[195] While the Convention on Biological Diversity did incorporate a rather stricter version of the precautionary principle at the insistence of the EU and some Southern countries, this was only possible in the preamble. The Biosafety Protocol, on the other hand, reflects precautionary decision-making in several instances and incorporates Principle 15 of the Rio Declaration as its objective. Again, the U.S., Australia, and several Northern states objected to the adoption of the precautionary "principle," fearing that it would have legal implications. The African group – which had represented the "like-minded group"[196] since 1999 – demanded the inclusion of the precautionary principle in the Protocol and was supported by the EU.[197]

The issue came to a head in the *Beef Hormones* case before the WTO[198] and reflects a classic North–North division.[199] The case was brought by the United States and Canada against the European Union. The European Union banned the importation of hormone-treated beef and other meat products from North America on the ground that there is no scientific consensus regarding the health effects of such products. On the basis of the precautionary principle, which is incorporated in the Maastricht Treaty, the EU banned its importation into Europe.[200] The main argument hinged on the binding nature of the precautionary approach/principle. While the EU argued that it is part of customary international law, the United States argued that it was an approach, not a principle. Moreover, the United States argued that EU had not conducted an adequate risk assessment to determine that hormone-treated beef posed a health risk. Canada, interestingly, argued that the precautionary principle could be considered as part of general principles of law.[201] In the end, the WTO did not pronounce on the issue but maintained that the United States could continue its sanctions while the EU could continue its ban.[202]

Major divisions surfaced during the negotiations leading up to the liability regime under the Cartagena Protocol on Biosafety, but not along traditional North–South divisions as one might expect. Strange alliances were made here: New Zealand and Brazil, no doubt making a strange pair, worked together to block virtually everything; the Miami group – major exporter countries and their allies, the U.S., Canada, Australia, Argentina, Uruguay, and Chile – tried to exclude LMOs intended for direct use as food or feed or for processing; and the "like-minded

---

[195] See Rio Declaration, note 3, Principle 15.
[196] Composed largely of Southern states that favored strict liability provisions.
[197] See H. Meyer, "Socio-Economic Considerations Under the Cartagena Protocol on Biosafety: Insights for Effective Implementation," September 28, 2012, www.twnside.org.sg.
[198] WT/DS48/AB/R, referred to in Hunter et al., note 1, p. 1254.
[199] See Hunter et al., note 1, p. 479 who note that "the precautionary principle has emerged as perhaps the most controversial of all international environmental law principles."
[200] See R. Johnson and C. Hanrahan, "The US–EU Beef Hormone Dispute" Congressional Research Service (2010).
[201] Ibid.
[202] Ibid.

106   *International Environmental Law Principles and the North–South Divide*

group," composed largely of Southern countries, wanted strict liability provisions included in the Protocol and expressed frustration at the slow pace of progress.[203] The Nagoya-Kuala Lumpur Supplementary Protocol on Liability and Redress was finally adopted in 2012 and incorporates Principles 13[204] and 15[205] of the Rio Declaration in the preamble.[206]

3.5 *The Polluter Pays Principle*

The polluter pays principle originated from the Organisation for Economic Co-operation and Development (OECD), hence from the global North. A sound economic principle that requires polluters to internalize their externalities and the users of natural resources to bear full environmental and social costs also saw North–South divisions. Despite its inclusion in the Rio Declaration[207] as Principle 16, the principle remains controversial, "particularly in developing countries where the burden of internalizing environmental costs is perceived as being too high."[208] Nonetheless, it plays an important role in harmonizing environmental standards and the risk of certain countries lowering their environmental standards in order to attract investors. This is the "race to the bottom" argument raised by many people. The principle requires allocating costs of pollution prevention and encourages rational use of scarce natural resources.

Several tools are available to implement the principle – imposing taxes or fees or eliminating subsidies for pollution control as well as using liability regimes. The polluter pays principle has been applied mainly in relation to allocating costs between states and private operators and has rarely been applied in interstate disputes.[209] A good example of imposing strict liability on polluters regardless of fault is the 1980 Comprehensive Environmental Response, Compensation, and Liability Act (CERCLA) in the US, commonly known as Superfund legislation.[210] It imposed liability on those responsible for releasing hazardous waste from chemical and petroleum industries and introduced a tax that was credited to a trust fund whose monies were used to clean up abandoned sites when no responsible party

---

[203] See Third World Network, "Liability and Redress for Damage Resulting from GMOs: The Negotiations under the Cartagena Protocol on Biosafety," 2012, www.twnside.org.sg.

[204] Principle 13 calls upon parties to develop national law regarding liability and compensation for victims of pollution and other environmental damage.

[205] Principle 15 embodies the precautionary approach.

[206] For a discussion of the Protocol, including its negotiating history, see Nijar, note 179.

[207] Principle 16. The soft language here is very striking. See S. Gaines, "The Polluter-Pays Principle: From Economic Equity to Environmental Ethos" (1991) 26 *Texas International Law Journal* 463.

[208] See Hunter et al., note 1, p. 484.

[209] This may be due to the fact that not many environmental cases have come before international courts.

[210] See United States Environmental Protection Agency, "CERCLA Overview" www.epa.gov.

could be identified.[211] The main objective of the legislation is environmental remediation, rather than compensating victims. Interestingly, the Indian Supreme Court took this one step further and held, in *Indian Council for Enviro-Legal Action v Union of India*,[212] that the polluter pays principle extends to compensating the victims of pollution: "[r]emediation of the damaged environment is part of the process of 'Sustainable Development' and as such the polluter is liable to pay the cost to the individual sufferers as well as the cost of reversing the damaged ecology."[213]

3.6 Participatory Rights

As was discussed, sustainable development embodies both substantive and procedural components. The procedural components – access to information, right to participate in the decision-making process, and access to remedies[214] – are part of international human rights law. These rights entered into the environment discourse originally through the environmental impact assessment process and are now codified in the Aarhus Convention adopted in 1998.

While these rights are designed to empower communities and are part of democratic participation and good governance, in actual practice the situation is quite different. Often, poor and marginalized communities, including indigenous communities, are not provided with necessary information or afforded the opportunity to participate in the decision-making process.[215] Many of these communities are illiterate and cannot access the relevant information, even if such information is publicly available.[216] They may not speak the language of the majority or may be unable to participate due to poverty and other pressing daily challenges. While in many countries environmental impact assessment processes provide for public participation, poor people often cannot or do not participate due to lack of access, lack of education, or language issues. Moreover, these communities lack access to experts who can decipher highly technical reports, as well as lawyers who will represent them in the event that their rights have been violated.

---

[211] Ibid.

[212] (2011) 8 SCC 161.

[213] See Hunter et al., note 1, p. 487.

[214] See chapter 27, L. de Silva, "Public Participation in International Negotiation and Compliance."

[215] See S. Kravchenko, "The Myth of Public Participation in a World of Poverty" (2009) 23 *Tulane Environmental Law Journal* 33 at 46–47, who argues that while access rights are available to the poor they are often not in a position to use those rights. Many reasons have been identified as barriers to participation, including literacy, costs, personal and property risk from participation, lack of legal identity, and insufficient property registration.

[216] Cf. chapter 16, S. Baker "Project Finance and Green Energy", where wind energy projects in Oaxaca, Mexico have been implemented without the participation of affected community members, including indigenous groups.

108 International Environmental Law Principles and the North–South Divide

With regard to indigenous communities, issues become more complex – often there are several different indigenous groups, who may or may not represent the majority. If we are to apply FPIC, which group's consent is required? Do the proponents need to obtain each group's consent? Do they have a right of veto? A good example of a regime in which the participation of indigenous groups is institutionalized is provided by the Arctic Council. While not without its critics, the Council, a high-level intergovernmental forum established in 1996, provides for the participation of indigenous communities as permanent participants.[217]

4. CONCLUSION: REINFORCING THE DIVIDE OR DISMANTLING THE DIVIDE?

The principles selected for discussion here have revealed deep North–South divisions surrounding their adoption and application. While history will judge how both sets of groups fared, at the present time it is safe to say that the report card is rather mixed, with no clear winner. The North and the South will continue to be engaged in this battle and, unfortunately, the clear loser will be the environment. Future generations are also set to lose, particularly when it comes to issues like climate change.

Although divisions are largely based on the historic division between the North and the South, the earlier discussion showed that this line is not very clear-cut: States will make alliances strategically based on their interests, the issue in question, and which alliance would be most beneficial to them. A good example is the strange alliance made during the negotiations of the Nagoya-Kuala Lumpur Protocol between Brazil, which was once part of the like-minded group, and New Zealand, which does not commercially produce or export GMOs.

Northern countries cannot continue to ignore the legitimate concerns of Southern countries, particularly when it comes to poverty alleviation. Southern countries, for their part, cannot continue to blame the North for all of the planet's ills. They, particularly the emerging economies, must accept their share of responsibility for global environmental problems. Otherwise, our children and grandchildren will judge both groups as failures, leaving them to cope with the irreversible consequences of the problems that we have created in the name of "development."

---

[217] See S. Atapattu, "Climate Change, Indigenous Peoples and the Arctic: The Changing Horizon of International Law" (2013) 22 *Michigan State International Law Review* 377 at 398.

5

The Stockholm Conference and the Creation of the South–North Divide in International Environmental Law and Policy

Karin Mickelson

1. INTRODUCTION

This chapter situates the emergence of a South–North divide in relation to environmental concerns in the process leading up to the United Nations (UN) Conference on the Human Environment, held in Stockholm, Sweden in June 1972. The Stockholm Conference represented the first attempt on the part of the international community to understand and address environmental problems in a broad, holistic, and comprehensive fashion.[1] One could argue that it marked the beginning of international environmental law and policy in a true sense.[2] If so, it is not much of a stretch to argue that international environmental law begins with – and needs to be understood in light of – South–North tensions.[3]

The chapter begins by exploring South–North tensions during the Stockholm Conference process and its immediate aftermath. It then briefly discusses how these tensions have continued to play a central role at the major international gatherings on environmental protection held since: The 1992 United Nations Conference on Environment and Development (UNCED or Earth Summit); the

---

[1] With the exception of the socialist states, which were not represented for unrelated political reasons, this was a global gathering. Their lack of involvement was a response to a decision that effectively excluded the German Democratic Republic from participation, and did not represent an objection to the Conference or its goals. See the discussion in P. Stone, *Did We Save the Earth at Stockholm?* (London: Earth Island, 1973), pp. 89–95.

[2] While many commentators might take issue with this characterization, few would dispute the Conference's status as a major milestone. Philippe Sands and Jacqueline Peel, for example, while identifying four distinct periods in the evolution of international environmental law, use the Stockholm Conference as a marker to identify the beginning of a period during which the UN attempted to create "a system for co-ordinating responses to international environmental issues": P. Sands and J. Peel, *Principles of International Environmental Law*, 3rd ed. (Cambridge: Cambridge University Press, 2012), p. 22.

[3] On Southern engagement with the Stockholm Conference, see generally, T. E. J. Campbell, "The Political Meaning of Stockholm: Third World Participation in the Environment Conference Process" (1973) 8 *Stanford Journal of International Studies* 138.

The Stockholm Conference and the Creation of the South–North Divide

2002 World Summit on Sustainable Development (WSSD); and finally the 2012 "Rio+20" United Nations Conference on Sustainable Development. In so doing, the chapter aims to provide a broad overview of the impact of the South–North divide on the development and scope of international environmental law and policy, and to demonstrate that many if not most of the concerns raised by developing countries in current environmental debates have been at issue since the early stages of the discipline.

While any attempt to provide a broad historical survey of this kind requires a choice of focus, it also requires an acknowledgment of the extent to which this choice is necessarily limited and partial. There are obvious and significant dangers in focusing on landmark events rather than on the ebb and flow of ongoing discussions and negotiations.[4] However, these events have represented opportunities to debate fundamental questions regarding global environmental problems and their solutions, and therefore provide invaluable focal points for tracing the development of international environmental law and policy, and the role that the global South has played in that process.

Another caveat should be kept in mind. The Southern approach to environmental law and policy cannot be fully understood outside of the broader context of Southern engagement with international law more generally. In fact, a significant proportion of South–North tensions that run through this field might be said to stem from the unwillingness of the global South to treat environmental concerns as separate from other global problems, and the frustration of many Northern governments and commentators who have seen this unwillingness as an indication of either intransigence or a lack of understanding of the severity of the environmental challenge. I would argue that this frustration runs both ways: that many Southern governments and commentators have been equally discouraged by the unwillingness to fully comprehend an alternative vision of international environmental law as part of a much broader struggle to find models of global governance that reflect concerns about equity, equality, and human well-being.

2. THE PROPOSAL FOR A UNITED NATIONS CONFERENCE ON THE HUMAN ENVIRONMENT AND INITIAL RESISTANCE

The idea of a global gathering on environmental matters was first put forward by Sweden in 1967, and formally proposed at the UN Economic and Social Council

---

[4] In fact, these so-called "mega-conferences" themselves are often criticized for consuming resources, time and energy that might better be devoted to more concrete responses to environmental degradation, but can also be seen as serving important functions including global agenda setting. See e.g. G. Seyfang, "Environmental Mega-Conferences—From Stockholm to Johannesburg and Beyond" (2003) 13(3) *Global Environmental Change* 223.

the next year.[5] In December 1968, the UN General Assembly decided to convene a conference in terms that reflected a relatively narrow understanding of environmental concerns, highlighting the dangers associated with "modern scientific and technological developments."[6] Developed countries generally took the lead in the early stages of preparation for the Conference, with developing countries playing a relatively minor role although they often expressed support for the conference initiative.[7] As time went by, however, an increasingly skeptical attitude began to emerge, and a potential boycott of the conference by developing countries became a significant concern.[8] Mustering their support came to be a central aspect of the lead-up to Stockholm, and was made a top priority by the Secretary-General of the Conference, Maurice Strong.[9]

Prior to working for the UN, Strong had spent five years as the head of the Canadian International Development Agency (CIDA). He was not only comfortable with the discourse of development; he also knew many of the key diplomatic players and was able to build on those contacts. By all accounts, he worked tirelessly to bring the developing countries on board, criss-crossing the globe and leaving much of the day-to-day planning of the conference to those working under him. However, the challenge he faced went beyond normal diplomatic maneuvering; as he explained in his memoirs, "I knew the conference would fail if we couldn't persuade the developing countries to take part, and I knew they'd never agree to come unless their concerns were addressed. The draft conference agenda I'd inherited didn't even attempt to do so."[10] As Strong describes it, the revised agenda that he proposed reflected one key concept: "a redefinition and expansion of the concept of environment to link it directly to the economic development process and the concerns of developing countries."[11]

While the Preparatory Committee, including its developing country participants, seemed willing to accept this new approach, Strong remained concerned that it needed to be further refined and tested. With the assistance of Barbara Ward, a well-known writer on international development issues, Strong organized a meeting of development experts to discuss his thesis. Among them was Mahbub ul Haq, a Pakistani economist, at that time Director of Policy Planning at the

---

[5] See H. Selin and B-O. Linnér, *The Quest for Global Sustainability: International Efforts on Linking Environment and Development* (Cambridge: Science, Environment and Development Group, Center for International Development, Harvard University, 2005), pp. 19–20.

[6] UN General Assembly, *Problems of the Human Environment*, 3 December 1968, A/RES 2398 (XXIII).

[7] See the discussion in D. E. Luchins, "The United Nations Conference on the Human Environment: A Case Study of Emerging Political Alignments, 1968–1972," PhD dissertation, City University of New York (1977), pp. 87–107.

[8] Ibid, pp. 111–113.

[9] Strong had been appointed to replace Jean Mussard in November 1970. See the discussion in A. E. Egelston, *Sustainable Development: A History* (New York: Springer, 2012), p. 62.

[10] M. Strong, *Where on Earth Are We Going?* (Toronto: Alfred A. Knopf Canada, 2000), p. 121.

[11] Ibid.

112   *The Stockholm Conference and the Creation of the South–North Divide*

World Bank. Haq was known for his willingness to criticize the traditional development paradigm, having gone so far as to state at a meeting of the Society for International Development in 1971 that what was required was a "basic re-examination of the existing theories and practice of development. It is time we stand economic theory on its head and see if we get any better results."[12] However, he was equally and openly skeptical about the newfound concern about the environment, and articulated a host of reasons why developing countries should resist participating in the conference on terms set by the developed countries.[13] Strong describes Haq's position as "devastating and simple":

> [I]ndustrialization had given developed countries disproportionate benefits and huge reservoirs of wealth and at the same time had caused the very environmental problems we were now asking developing countries to join in resolving. The cost of cleaning up the mess, therefore, should be borne by the countries that had caused it in the first place. If they wanted developing countries to go along, they'd have to provide the financial resources to enable them to do so.[14]

Two other economists that Strong consulted, Gamani Corea from Sri Lanka and Enrique Iglesias from Uruguay, agreed with Haq. Strong felt that the concerns raised were valid, and recognized that the success of the conference depended on finding ways to address them.[15] As he puts it, he challenged Haq to participate in a "rigorous, objective process of evaluating the concept"[16] of redefining the environmental challenge to determine whether it could serve as "a new basis for South–North cooperation."[17] Along with Corea and Ward, Strong and Haq undertook the task of evaluation.

3. OVERCOMING RESISTANCE THROUGH REDEFINITION: THE FOUNEX MEETING ON ENVIRONMENT AND DEVELOPMENT

The process culminated in a Meeting of Experts on Environment and Development held in Founex, Switzerland in June 1971, with Corea chairing and Haq acting as rapporteur. Most of the participants were from developing countries, and the majority worked in the field of development; the meeting was criticized by one contemporary commentator as being "long on economists but short on the ecological

---

[12] Cited in M. ul Haq, *The Poverty Curtain: Choices for the Third World* (New York: Columbia University Press, 1976), p. 34. See generally K. Haq and R. Ponzio (eds.), *Pioneering the Human Development Revolution: An Intellectual Biography of Mahbub ul Haq* (New Delhi: Oxford University Press, 2008).

[13] Strong, note 10, p. 123.

[14] Ibid.

[15] Ibid.

[16] Ibid.

[17] Ibid, p. 124.

side."[18] Participants thus shared an overarching commitment to development, and many were to go on to play leading roles in international development policy both within and outside the UN system.

The Founex Report on Development and Environment[19] that was the outcome of the meeting starts by recognizing that "the current concern with environmental issues has emerged out of the problems experienced by the industrially advanced countries,"[20] and points out that those problems were to a large extent the result of development itself. The report emphasizes that these problems are serious, and that in some ways the "dangers extend beyond national boundaries and threaten the world as a whole."[21] It goes on to assert that developing countries had an obvious interest in these issues, both because of the impacts on the global environment and because they "would clearly wish to avoid, as far as is feasible, the mistakes and distortions that have characterized the patterns of development of the industrialized societies."[22]

The report then articulates its fundamental premise:

> [T]he major environmental problems of developing countries are essentially of a different kind. They are predominantly problems that reflect the poverty and very lack of development of their societies. They are problems, in other words, of both rural and urban poverty. In both the towns and in the countryside, not merely the "quality of life", but life itself is endangered by poor water, housing, sanitation and nutrition, by sickness and disease and by natural disasters. These are problems, no less than those of industrial pollution, that clamour for attention in the context of the concern with human environment. They are problems which affect the greater mass of mankind.[23]

What is being posited here is not a contrast between the environmental problems of the North and the developmental problems of the South; instead, it is the existence of different *kinds* of environmental problems. And while development can be seen as the cause of environmental degradation in the North, it is seen as "a cure for [the] major environmental problems"[24] facing the South. Development must therefore be seen as an imperative; as the report puts it, "concern for environment must not and need not detract from the commitment of the world community – developing and more industrialized nations alike – to the overriding task of development of the developing regions of the world."[25]

---

[18] See Stone, note 1, pp. 102–103.

[19] *Founex Report on Development and Environment, Submitted by a Panel of Experts Convened by the Secretary-General of the United Nations Conference on the Human Environment, 4–12 June 1971* (Paris: Mouton, 1972), pp. 7–36 [hereinafter Founex Report].

[20] Ibid, p. 10.

[21] Ibid.

[22] Ibid.

[23] Ibid.

[24] Ibid, p. 11.

[25] Ibid.

114   *The Stockholm Conference and the Creation of the South–North Divide*

To this point, the report could perhaps be seen as evidence in support of the dominant representation of the global South's prioritization of development over environment. However, the report does not stop there. It goes on to specify that while development is the overriding priority, what development entails needs to be redefined in order to focus on the "dire poverty which is the most important aspect of the problems which affect the environment of the majority of mankind."[26] The incorporation of environmental concerns is seen as part of a broader rethinking of development itself:

> In the past, there has been a tendency to equate the development goal with the more narrowly conceived objective of economic growth as measured by the rise in gross national product. It is usually recognized today that high rates of economic growth, necessary and essential as they are, do not by themselves guarantee the easing of urgent social and human problems. Indeed in many countries high growth rates have been accompanied by increasing unemployment, rising disparities in income both between groups and between regions, and the deterioration of social and cultural conditions. A new emphasis is thus being placed on the attainment of social and cultural goals as part of the development process. The recognition of environmental issues in developing countries is an aspect of this widening of the development concept.[27]

Despite having redefined both environment and development so as to highlight how they dovetail, the report does not shy away from acknowledging the potential tension between them that may confront planners and policy-makers. While it may be relatively easy to incorporate environmental objectives "[t]o the extent that these objectives support or reinforce economic growth," there will also be conflicts, and these will involve "difficult choices [. . .] regarding the 'trade off' between these and the narrower growth objectives."[28] The report takes it as a given that "[t]hese choices can only be made by the countries themselves in the light of their own situations and development strategies and cannot be determined by any rules established *a priori*."[29] The report also stresses that "the extent to which developing countries pursue a style of development that is more responsive to social and environmental goals must be determined by the resources available to them,"[30] and, while recognizing the possibility of "better allocation of the presently available resources,"[31] makes it clear that more resources are required.

It is generally agreed that the Founex meeting and report played a crucial role in generating developing-country support for the Conference. Strong characterized it

---

[26] Ibid.
[27] Ibid.
[28] Ibid.
[29] Ibid.
[30] Ibid, p. 14.
[31] Ibid.

as "the most important single event in the lead-up to Stockholm,"[32] and emphasized its "profound influence both on the Stockholm Conference and on the evolution of the concept of the environment-development relationship."[33] Many of the concerns discussed at the meeting went on to inform the preparatory process and the debate at the Conference itself.[34]

4. SOUTH–NORTH TENSIONS AT THE STOCKHOLM CONFERENCE

While Founex contributed a great deal to the prospects of success of the conference, Strong did not overlook the need for more direct lobbying, continuing to consult with key developing countries. In June of 1971, the same month as the Founex meeting, he was able to secure a commitment from Indian Prime Minister Indira Gandhi to attend the conference, having suggested that the absence of developing countries would allow the industrialized countries to control how environmental issues were addressed internationally, and that she was uniquely well placed to represent the views of the developing world.[35] Her decision to attend ensured that India played a central role in the preparatory process, and in Strong's view made it far more likely that other developing countries would participate as well.

Indira Gandhi was in fact the only head of government to attend the conference apart from Swedish Prime Minister Olof Palme, and her speech was regarded by many as encapsulating the differences in perception between South and North. Mrs. Gandhi began by seeking common ground, invoking Indian history for concepts of wildlife and forest preservation and, in so doing, implicitly rejecting the notion that environmental responsibility is a western and/or modern idea.[36] She expressed concern about the problem of environmental degradation both in India and around

---

[32] Strong, note 10, p. 124.

[33] Ibid, p. 125.

[34] Even after the Conference, the report continued to be seen as critically important in helping to shed light on developing country concerns. Adil Najam, a leading expert on South–North international environmental relations, sees it as "one of the most authentic and articulate enunciations of the South's collective interests on issues of environment and development." See A. Najam, "Why Environmental Politics Looks Different from the South," in P. Dauvergne (ed.), *Handbook of Global Environmental Politics* (Cheltenham: Edward Elgar, 2005), pp. 111–126. The Report is, of course, not without its critics. According to Steven Bernstein, Founex "fostered an expanded notion of development beyond economic growth that included other social and cultural goals" but "it established no clear definition of development nor did it specify the relationship between broader social goals and economic growth. The achievement of this inclusive notion of development seemed to be taken as an article of faith": see S. F. Bernstein, *The Compromise of Liberal Environmentalism* (New York: Columbia University Press, 2001), p. 39. Anne Egelston goes further, disputing both the Report's status as an "enlightened precursor to sustainable development" and its impact on the Conference, which she regards as limited "because development represented a small portion of the overall agenda": see Egelston, note 9, pp. 63–64.

[35] Strong, note 10, p. 127.

[36] I. Gandhi, 'The Unfinished Revolution' (1972) 28 *Bulletin of the Atomic Scientists* 35 at 35.

116 *The Stockholm Conference and the Creation of the South–North Divide*

the world, stating that "[i]t is sad that in country after country, progress should become synonymous with an assault on nature. We, who are a part of nature and dependent on her for every need, speak constantly about 'exploiting' nature."[37] However, Mrs. Gandhi insisted that poverty has its own environmental impacts, in a statement that is frequently quoted but perhaps almost as frequently misunderstood:

> We do not want to impoverish the environment any further and yet we cannot for a moment forget the grim poverty of large numbers of people. Are not poverty and need the greatest polluters? For instance, unless we are in a position to provide employment and purchasing power for the daily necessities of the tribal people and those who live in or around our jungles, we cannot prevent them from combing the forest for food and livelihood; from poaching and from despoiling the vegetation. When they themselves feel deprived, how can we urge the preservation of animals? How can we speak to those who live in villages and in slums about keeping the oceans, rivers and the air clean when their own lives are contaminated at the source? The environment cannot be improved in conditions of poverty. Nor can poverty be eradicated without the use of science and technology.[38]

Mrs. Gandhi then turned to a discussion of the need to think critically about mainstream understandings of development. She acknowledged that while early experiences with industrialization tended to copy the developed countries, there was a growing sense of a need to re-prioritize and move away from a unidimensional model of development as growth.[39] She offered a strong critique of the mainstream economic understanding of development, asserting that the "inherent conflict is not between conservation and development, but between environment and the reckless exploitation of man and earth in the name of efficiency."[40] She went on to identify the root causes of environmental degradation in "[a]ll the 'isms' of the modern age – even those which in theory disown the private profit principle – [that] assume that man's cardinal interest is acquisition."[41] Pollution, she insisted, is not a technical problem but a problem of values.[42] Having acknowledged the need to think critically about development, however, Mrs. Gandhi nevertheless insisted that it need not and cannot be abandoned. Instead, it is essential to show that the emerging concern for the environment will not sideline the interests of the most vulnerable: "[w]e have to prove to the disinherited majority of the world that ecology and conservation will not work against their interest but will bring an improvement in their lives."[43]

---

[37] Ibid.
[38] Ibid at 36.
[39] Ibid.
[40] Ibid at 37.
[41] Ibid.
[42] Ibid.
[43] Ibid.

Toward the end of her presentation, in a statement that is particularly fascinating because it runs counter to the common portrayal of Southern leaders as focusing all blame on the North while reserving none for themselves, she again invoked common responsibilities and the need to face the new challenges collectively, pointing out that "[i]t serves little purpose to dwell on the past or to apportion blame, for none of us is blameless,"[44] and insisting that "[t]here is no alternative to a cooperative approach on a global scale to the entire spectrum of our problems."[45]

While developing countries did not represent a united front in the context of the Conference (Brazil, for example – a vocal opponent of the conference initiative from the outset – largely maintained its hardline stance at the Conference itself),[46] one could argue that Indira Gandhi's statement appears to have been a more accurate reflection of the stance of the South at the Conference; guarded and somewhat skeptical, but at least willing to enter into dialogue. Such an attitude was reflected in the final text of the Stockholm Declaration itself, as were many of the concerns emerging from the Founex meeting. Portions of the Declaration are drawn more or less verbatim from the Founex Report; for example, the preamble contains one paragraph that begins by asserting that "[i]n the developing countries most of the environmental problems are caused by under-development,"[47] and goes on to emphasize the need for developing countries to focus on development and for developed countries to reduce the South–North gap. Principles 8 through 14 deal specifically with various aspects of the relationship between environment and development, and the particular needs and concerns of developing countries are given pride of place. But the attention to development and developing countries is far more extensive, encompassing nearly half of the total of twenty-six principles. The preamble is replete with references to these matters as well, some of them introduced at the last minute to reflect the discussion at the conference itself.

Against this backdrop, then, the Stockholm Conference and Declaration could be seen as having a dual purpose: expanding the Northern view of the environmental crisis to encompass the negative effects of poverty as well as those of prosperity, and expanding the Southern view of the developmental crisis to include environmental concerns.[48] It is difficult to say with any degree of certainty whether

---

[44] Ibid at 38.

[45] Ibid.

[46] For a brief summary of the Brazilian position see W. Rowland, *The Plot to Save the World: The Life and Times of the Stockholm Conference on the Human Environment* (Toronto: Clarke, Irwin & Co., 1973), pp. 53–54.

[47] *Declaration of the United Nations Conference on the Human Environment*, Stockholm, 16 June 1972, UN Doc. A/Conf.48/14/Rev. 1(1973); 11 ILM 1416 (1972), preambular para. 4 (Report of the United Nations Conference on the Human Environment, A/CONF.48/14/Rev.1) [hereinafter Stockholm Declaration].

[48] I have made this point previously; see K. Mickelson, "South, North, International Environmental Law and International Environmental Lawyers" (2000) 11 *Yearbook of International Environmental Law* 52 at 62–63.

118   *The Stockholm Conference and the Creation of the South–North Divide*

either of these aims were fully met at Stockholm. With regard to the former, a fairly typical assessment is that "[d]evelopment issues, though included in the conference's agenda and addressed in the Action Plan recommendations and declaration principles, were clearly of secondary priority and never seriously addressed in the follow-up efforts after the Stockholm conference."[49] With regard to the latter, while the important short-term goal of ensuring developing country participation in the conference had been achieved, both the proceedings and the Declaration reflected ongoing tensions. Arguably, however, those tensions were often overstated by much of the press coverage and academic commentary on the conference, which appeared to equate the stance of developing countries with that articulated by Brazil rather than the considerably more nuanced stance taken by India and other states.[50] This portrayal of the South as an unwilling participant in global environmental policy-making has proven to be extraordinarily long-lasting and difficult to dislodge.

5. THE NEW INTERNATIONAL ECONOMIC ORDER AND THE COCOYOC DECLARATION

Part of the reason for the portrayal of developing countries as having taken a hardline stance at the Conference was the general atmosphere in international politics at the time. The period following Stockholm, from 1973 to 1975, is widely regarded as the peak of Southern optimism regarding the possibility of bringing about fundamental change in the international system. The set of proposals that were put forward by the South at around this time came to be known as the New International Economic Order (NIEO). Although few if any of the specific proposals were actually new, given that developing countries had been seeking changes in the international system for a decade, the NIEO was notable because of the attempt to assemble a broad and coherent program of reform of the international economic system. The South demanded a more equitable distribution of world industrial production, a restructuring of international markets, increased financial support, and the establishment of new international governance structures.[51] The NIEO proposals also reflected a significantly more radical way of conceptualizing international economic and legal relations between states. This reflected, at least in part, the growing influence of theories of dependency and neocolonialism that explained the developmental dead end that many of the

---

[49] P. M. Haas et al., "Appraising the Earth Summit: How Should We Judge UNCED's Success?" (1992) 34(8) *Environment* 6 at 9.

[50] See e.g. Campbell, note 3 at 148–150.

[51] H. O. Bergeson, H.-H. Holm and R. D. McKinlay, "The Origins of the NIEO Debate," in H. O. Bergeson et al. (eds.), *The Recalcitrant Rich: A Comparative Analysis of the Northern Responses to the Demands for a New International Economic Order* (London: Frances Pinter, 1982), p. 3.

Southern countries seemed to be facing in terms of structural inequality that served the interests of powerful states.[52]

In 1974, at the height of this tense but somewhat exhilarating time in international relations, UNEP and UNCTAD convened a joint Symposium on Patterns of Resource Use, Environment, and Development Strategies in Cocoyoc, Mexico. Intended to be a gathering of the same character as the Founex meeting,[53] with participants acting in their private capacities, the symposium in fact reunited many of those who had been at Founex. Barbara Ward again played a key role, serving as chair and rapporteur for resource use and the environment. The Cocoyoc Declaration adopted by the participants exemplifies a shift in perspective that clearly reflected the prevailing intellectual and political climate.[54] While Founex had hinted at the sense of frustration regarding the lack of progress on the development front, Cocoyoc expressed outrage:

> Thirty years have passed since the signing of the United Nations Charter launched the effort to establish a new international order. Today, that order has reached a critical turning point. Its hopes of creating a better life for the whole human family have been largely frustrated. It has proved impossible to meet the "inner limit" of satisfying fundamental human needs. On the contrary, more people are hungry, sick, shelterless and illiterate today than when the United Nations was first set up.

> At the same time, new and unforeseen concerns have begun to darken the international prospects. Environmental degradation and the rising pressure on resources raise the question whether the "outer limits" of the planet's physical integrity may not be at risk.[55]

The notion of "inner" and "outer" limits was the conceptual thread that tied the Declaration together, as it called for a new system that could operate within those limits: meeting human needs while respecting ecological constraints. It proceeded to delineate three requirements for the new system: the need to "redefine the whole purpose of development," the need to recognize the possibility of "many different roads of development," and the importance of self-reliance.[56] With respect to the first, the Declaration asserted that economic growth that does not meet basic needs for food, shelter, clothing, health and education but instead "maintains or even increases the disparities between and within countries is not development. It is exploitation."[57] However, and importantly, the Declaration also insisted that

---

[52] C. Murphy, *The Emergence of the NIEO Ideology* (Boulder: Westview Press, 1984), p. 92.

[53] J. Ekenberger, "The Cocoyoc Declaration," (1975) 4(2) *Ambio* 105.

[54] The Cocoyoc Declaration adopted by the participants in the UNEP/UNCTAD Symposium on "Patterns of Resource, Environment, and Development Strategies' held at Cocoyoc, Mexico, from 8 to 23 October 1974," reproduced in "The Cocoyoc Declaration: A call for the Reform of the International Economic Order" (1975) 31(3) *Bulletin of the Atomic Scientists* 6 [hereinafter Cocoyoc Declaration].

[55] Ibid, p. 6.

[56] Ibid, p. 8.

[57] Ibid, p. 8.

development must go beyond the satisfaction of basic needs to take into account "a deep social need to participate in the shaping of one's own existence, and to make some contribution to the fashioning of the world's future."[58] With respect to the second, the Declaration was crystal clear about the limitations of mainstream assumptions regarding a single path to development:

> We reject the unilinear view which sees development essentially and inevitably as the effort to imitate the historical model of the countries that for various reasons happen to be rich today. For this reason, we reject the concept of "gaps" in development. The goal is not to "catch up", but to ensure the quality of life for all with a productive base compatible with the needs of future generations.[59]

Finally, the Declaration expressed the conviction of the Cocoyoc participants that "one basic strategy of development will have to be increased national self-reliance," and went on to explain what this would entail:

> It does not mean autarky. It implies mutual benefits from trade and cooperation and a fairer redistribution of resources satisfying the basic needs. It does mean self-confidence, reliance primarily on one's own resources, human and natural, and the capacity for autonomous goal-setting and decision-making... It excludes exploitative trade patterns depriving countries of their natural resources for their own development... It implies decentralization of the world economy, and sometimes also of the national economy to enhance the sense of personal participation. But it also implies increased international cooperation for collective self-reliance. Above all, it means trust in people and nations, reliance on the capacity of people themselves to invent and generate new resources and techniques to increase their capacity to absorb them, to put them to socially beneficial use, to take a measure of command over the economy, and to generate their own way of life.[60]

Like the NIEO proposals, the Declaration could be seen as a radical critique of existing paradigms, and it includes a fierce denunciation of the injustices that continued to characterize the international system. However, it concluded with a statement that reflected another important aspect of those proposals – a deep-seated conviction that fundamental change was in fact possible:

> We have faith in the future of mankind on this planet. [...] The road forward does not lie through the despair of doom watching or through the easy optimism of successive technological fixes. It lies through a careful and dispassionate assessment of the "outer limits", through cooperative search for ways to achieve the "inner limit" of fundamental human rights, through the building of social structures to express those rights, and through all the patient work of devising techniques and styles of development which enhance and preserve our planetary inheritance.[61]

[58] Ibid.
[59] Ibid.
[60] Ibid, p. 9.
[61] Ibid, p. 10.

At the end of the Symposium, the Cocoyoc Declaration was adopted with considerable fanfare, and attracted immediate and sometimes critical attention.[62] It was cited with approval at UNEP Governing Council meetings and was specifically mentioned as having important linkages with the NIEO.[63] And it may well be that as the drive for the NIEO began to lose momentum, those linkages might have led to a gradual decline in interest in the kind of radical critique that the Declaration represented. Nevertheless, particularly when read against the backdrop of the Founex Report, it demonstrates the extent to which understandings of development and of its relationship with environmental protection among prominent representatives of the global South and their intellectual allies was far more nuanced and multifaceted than is generally acknowledged.

6. REDEFINING INTERNATIONAL ENVIRONMENTAL LAW AS INTERNATIONAL SUSTAINABLE DEVELOPMENT LAW? THE BRUNDTLAND COMMISSION AND THE EARTH SUMMIT

The years that followed the Stockholm Conference and the Cocoyoc Symposium were critical for the development of environmental law at both national and international levels, years of institutional growth and entrenchment of environmental concerns as an important aspect of governmental responsibility. From the outset, the interface between environmental and developmental concerns was an important element of the emerging field of international environmental law and policy. However, this interrelationship was always contested, and was frequently not reflected in either environmental or development policy. In 1982, when a UNEP Governing Council Session of a Special Character (sometimes referred to as "Stockholm+10") was held in Nairobi, UNEP Executive Director Mostafa Tolba stated that underdevelopment "is still the principal cause of the environmental problems we have to solve."[64] While the Stockholm Conference had established that the solution was "environment-based development which enhances rather than damages the environment," and there was a plethora of "strategies, action plans [and] guidelines" that could provide guidance as to how this could be accomplished, Tolba asserted, "Governments have not matched this developing

[62] According to Johan Galtung, who was the Rapporteur for Development Strategies, the U.S. State Department sent a 3ft long cable signed by then Secretary of State Henry Kissinger "rejecting the Declaration entirely": J. Galtung, "The Cocoyoc Declaration," 29 March 2010, www.transcend.org.

[63] During the Governing Council meeting in 1976, for example, the representative of Mexico asserted that "the Cocoyoc Declaration contained not only ideas that were important from an environmental viewpoint, but also an extremely useful plan of action, and should be studied by the Secretariat and by delegations as a guide to future action in the area of environment and development:" D. S. Zalob, 'The UN Environment Programme: Four Years After Stockholm' (1976) 2 *Environmental Policy and Law* 50 at 59.

[64] UNEP, "Session of a Special Character" (1982) 9 *Environmental Policy and Law* 2 at 2.

122 *The Stockholm Conference and the Creation of the South–North Divide*

environmental knowledge with deeds."[65] In the meantime, "[o]n virtually every front there has been a marked deterioration in the quality of our shared environment."[66]

During this same time period, economic recession in the North and the impacts of the debt crisis in the South had also led to significant concern that development had stalled. The work of the World Commission on Environment and Development (chaired by Gro Harlem Brundtland of Norway, and often referred to as the Brundtland Commission) can thus be understood in part as an attempt to address gaps in achieving both environmental and developmental objectives.[67] The Commission was established in 1983 and presented its report, entitled *Our Common Future*, in 1987.[68] This popularized the term "sustainable development," which it defined as "development that meets the needs of the present without compromising the ability of future generations to meet their own needs."[69] In its insistence that environment and development were interrelated and inseparable, the Commission reiterated a longstanding theme, but was able to bring it to the forefront of international environmental diplomacy. However, as is discussed in the chapters by Ruth Gordon and Sumudu Atapattu,[70] many were deeply skeptical about the Commission's work, with some critics alleging that its articulation of sustainability was "deliberately ill-defined"[71] so as to preclude meaningful objections, while others attacked its reformulation of the "by-now old development myth [. . .] of unlimited industrial development."[72]

Despite these types of criticisms, the decision to convene a follow-up to the Stockholm Conference, to be known as the "United Nations Conference on Environment and Development" (UNCED), seemed to indicate that there was now a consensus about the convergence of environment and development, as reflected in the official title of the conference itself. The ambitious agenda for the Conference reflected this broad view, including issues that had not been part of the discussions at Stockholm, such as unsustainable consumption patterns.[73]

---

[65] Ibid.

[66] Ibid.

[67] The Commission was not the only body to address the latter; Willy Brandt, former Chancellor of West Germany, chaired the International Commission on International Development Issues, which had released a report in 1980 and a follow-up three years later.

[68] World Commission on Environment and Development, *Our Common Future* (Oxford: Oxford University Press, 1987).

[69] Ibid, p. 43.

[70] See chapter 3, R. Gordon, "Unsustainable Development"; Chapter 4, S. Atapattu, "The Significance of International Environmental Law Principles in Reinforcing or Dismantling the North–South Divide."

[71] N. Middleton and P. O'Keefe, *Redefining Sustainable Development* (London: Pluto Press, 2001), p. 2.

[72] P. Chatterjee and M. Finger, *The Earth Brokers: Power, Politics and World Development* (London: Routledge, 1994), p. 27.

[73] See D. A. Fuchs and S. Lorek, "Sustainable Consumption Governance: A History of Promises and Failures" (2005) 28 *Journal of Consumer Policy* 261 at 264: Fuchs and Lorek characterize

However, the lead-up to UNCED revealed ongoing and fundamental divergences of perspective between South and North.[74] While specific differences emerged on issues ranging from forests to biodiversity to climate change,[75] one leading commentator, Martin Khor, has highlighted two overarching concerns from the point of view of the South. First, there was little sense that the North, or at least certain key states within it, was willing to curtail its own consumption, or to re-evaluate long-held notions of economic well-being and prosperity.[76] U.S. President George Bush's proclamation that "the American lifestyle is not negotiable"[77] at least had the virtue of honestly acknowledging the limits within which the UNCED negotiations took place. Second, according to Khor, "the North as a whole was not prepared to seriously commit itself to helping the South carry out the transition to sustainable development,"[78] and the specific measure of Northern commitment in the form of new and additional financial resources was clearly lacking.[79]

Despite the hopes of many Southern representatives that the conference would provide an opportunity to fashion a global consensus regarding poverty alleviation, this proved to be difficult to achieve. As Brazilian negotiator José Goldemberg later pointed out, "[t]he industrialized countries were not particularly interested in addressing the root causes of poverty, which had been the focus of South-North confrontation for the [previous] thirty years."[80] A normative commitment was certainly reflected in the Rio Declaration on Environment and Development. Principle 5 specifically provided that "[a]ll States and all people shall cooperate in the essential task of eradicating poverty as an indispensable requirement for

the UNCED process as having "firmly established [sustainable consumption] on the global governance agenda."

[74] South–North tensions featured prominently in both media and scholarly commentary on the preparations for the conference and the conference proceedings themselves. See the discussion in M. A. L. Miller, *The Third World in Global Environmental Politics* (Boulder: Lynne Rienner Publishers, 1995), pp. 8–9; R. R. White, *North, South and the Environmental Crisis* (Toronto: University of Toronto Press, 1993), pp. 179–180; R. Panjabi, "The South and the Earth Summit: The Development/Environment Dichotomy" (1992) 11 *Dickinson Journal of International Law* 77.

[75] Clear South–North splits emerged in relation to the desirability of a treaty dealing with forests (with most developing countries resisted the calls for a treaty on this issue), the protection of intellectual property rights in the context of biological diversity, and the question of whether there ought to be binding emissions reductions commitments for developed countries in the climate change regime. These were only a few of the more contentious and visible faultlines.

[76] M. Khor, *Reaffirming the Environment-Development Nexus of UNCED 1992* (Penang: Third World Network, 2012).

[77] A. Rogers, *The Earth Summit: A Planetary Reckoning* (Los Angeles: Global View Press, 1993), p. 139.

[78] Khor, note 76, p. 5.

[79] Ibid.

[80] J. Goldemberg, "The Road to Rio," in I. L. Mintzer and J. A. Leonard (eds.), *Negotiating Climate Change: The Inside Story of the Rio Convention* (Cambridge: Cambridge University Press, 1994), p. 177.

124   *The Stockholm Conference and the Creation of the South–North Divide*

sustainable development, in order to decrease the disparities in standards of living and better meet the needs of the majority of the people of the world."[81] Furthermore, a recognition of developmental aspirations ran throughout the Declaration, particularly in the references to the right to development,[82] the need to give "special priority" to the needs of developing countries,[83] and the concept of common but differentiated responsibilities.[84] Nevertheless, significant questions about the way forward remained. As Khor argued:

> The UNCED process was able to generate the perspective that environment and development were inextricably linked, and that a new South-North partnership would also be required if the world is to be saved from ecological disasters. Many individuals, from governments, NGOs or international agencies, taking part in UNCED could agree intellectually to these propositions. However, transforming the rhetoric into principle, policies and social change is the difficult part, and by the end of the Rio Conference it was evident that political will was still lacking in the North.[85]

At a deeper level, the UNCED process, outcomes, and understanding of sustainable development, like the Brundtland report, have been criticized by activists and scholars for remaining enmeshed in mainstream (and arguably discredited) understandings of economic well-being. In one particularly scathing critique, Pratap Chatterjee and Matthias Finger characterized the UNCED process as an exercise in co-optation and rationalization, as a result of which:

> [...] old thinking about economic growth prevails, old institutions promoting such growth persist, and the old development establishment that had made a living out of such economic growth has repackaged itself in green and miraculously represented itself as the new global environmental leaders.[86]

This perpetuation of old ways of thinking can also be seen as perpetuating existing power imbalances. As Vandana Shiva has noted:

> Solutions to the global environmental problems can come only from the global, that is, the North. Since the North has abundant industrial technology and capital, if it has to provide a solution to environmental problems, they must be reduced to a currency that the North dominates. The problem of ecology is transformed into a problem of technology transfer and finance. What is absent from the analysis is that the assumption that the South needs technology and finances from the North is a major cause of the environmental crisis, and a major reason for the drain of

---

[81] *Rio Declaration on Environment and Development*, Rio de Janeiro, 13 June 1992, UN Doc. A/CONF.151/26 (vol. I); 31 ILM 874 (1992), Principle 5.

[82] Ibid, Principle 3.

[83] Ibid, Principle 6.

[84] Ibid, Principle 7.

[85] Khor, note 76, p. 10.

[86] Chatterjee and Finger, note 72, p. 162.

resources from South to North [...]. The old order does not change through the environmental discussions, rather it becomes more deeply entrenched. [87]

7. TAKING STOCK IN JOHANNESBURG: THE WORLD SUMMIT ON SUSTAINABLE DEVELOPMENT

The World Summit on Sustainable Development (WSSD), held in Johannesburg in 2002, struck a very different tone from that of the Rio and Stockholm conferences before it. The Johannesburg Declaration on Sustainable Development,[88] instead of being a statement of principles, is an unusual amalgam: a diagnosis of prevailing ills and proclamation of sweeping aspirations, coupled with a reiteration of existing goals. This was in keeping with an overarching emphasis on implementation – specifically, the implementation of Agenda 21[89] and the host of commitments that had been made at Rio, as well as the Millennium Development Goals[90] that had been adopted by the UN General Assembly in 2000. While some commentators saw this focus on implementation as pragmatic and appropriate,[91] particularly given the failure on the part of the international community to fulfill the promises made at Rio, others lamented the missed opportunity to strengthen or deepen existing commitments. Friends of the Earth International proclaimed that the Summit "barely begins to deal with the scale of the problems the world faces. It is a betrayal of hundreds of millions of poor and vulnerable people and their communities around the world. Governments have failed to set the necessary social and ecological limits to economic globalisation."[92]

This reference to globalization highlights an important aspect of the WSSD discussions, which were taking place several years after the establishment of the World Trade Organization and the ascendance of economistic thinking that might be said to have accompanied it. Globalization had not even been mentioned in the Rio Declaration; in the Johannesburg Declaration it is acknowledged as having "added a new dimension" to both the developmental and environmental challenges facing the international community. On the one hand, the declaration notes that "[t]he rapid integration of markets, mobility of capital and significant increases in investment flows around the world have opened new challenges and opportunities for the pursuit of sustainable development."[93] On the other, it points out that

---

[87] V. Shiva, "The Greening of the Global Reach," in W. Sachs (ed.), *Global Ecology: A New Arena of Global Conflict* (Halifax: Fernwood Books, 1993), p. 153.

[88] *Johannesburg Declaration on Sustainable Development*, Johannesburg, 4 September 2002, UN Doc. A/CONF. 199/20), pp. 1–5 [hereinafter Johannesburg Declaration].

[89] *Agenda 21: Programme of Action for Sustainable Development*, Rio de Janeiro, 14 June 1992, U.N. GAOR, 46th Sess., Agenda Item 21, UN Doc. A/Conf.151/26 (1992).

[90] UNDP, "The Millennium Development Goals," www.undp.org.

[91] See e.g. H. French, "From Rio to Johannesburg and Beyond: Assessing the Summit," World Summit Policy Brief No. 12, Worldwatch Institute (2002).

[92] Friends of the Earth International, "Betrayal ... But See You All in Mexico!," www.foei.org.

[93] Johannesburg Declaration, note 88, para. 14.

126   *The Stockholm Conference and the Creation of the South–North Divide*

"the benefits and costs of globalization are unevenly distributed, with developing countries facing special difficulties in meeting this challenge."[94] This ambivalent assessment expresses concern about the differential impacts of globalization without calling into question its fundamental premises, and thus seems to reflect an acceptance of a changed political and economic landscape, with the full implications for the understanding of sustainable development left unclear.[95]

A key feature of this changed landscape was the emphasis on market-based solutions to environmental problems. While this could already be discerned during the Rio process, it reached a new level at Johannesburg. The emphasis on public-private partnerships and an expanded role for the business sector in helping to meet sustainable development objectives was openly acknowledged by UNDP administrator Mark Malloch Brown, who described the WSSD as "the world's biggest trade fair."[96] The United States had been a particularly enthusiastic proponent of the partnership concept, and the Special Representative for Sustainable Development at the U.S. State Department was later to laud the positive effects of the partnership approach in terms of an increased emphasis on results, enhanced "transparency based accountability" and improved reporting.[97] Despite assurances that such partnerships were not intended to detract from the role (and obligations) of government, and efforts to develop standards for partnership arrangements, civil society groups raised significant concerns; the Third World Network queried whether the partnership approach could signal "the wholesale corporatization of the UN."[98] The Delhi-based Centre for Science and Environment emphasized the ways in which the partnerships suited the interests of the United States in particular:

> They are voluntary; involve no firm multilateral commitments for funds or deadlines on part of the US government; bring corporations firmly into the picture giving them a free hand to promote their interests through such partnerships; and best of all, ensure that responsibilities remain fuzzy. There are no rules to govern partnerships — only a set of flimsy guidelines that were not even discussed in Johannesburg.[99]

---

[94] Ibid.

[95] The Plan of Implementation also contains a section on "sustainable development in a globalizing world," which affirms that "[g]lobalization should be fully inclusive and equitable" but is limited to a fairly technical discussion of issues such as trade and "narrowing the digital divide": UN, *Report of the World Summit on Sustainable Development*, 26 August–4 September 2002, A/CONF.199/20, resolution 2, annex (Plan of Implementation of the World Summit on Sustainable Development), paras. 47–52.

[96] Quoted in Centre for Science and Environment, "The World's Biggest Trade Fair," Down to Earth, September 30, 2002.

[97] See discussion in S. J. Scherr and R. J. Gregg, "Johannesburg and Beyond: The 2002 World Summit on Sustainable Development and the Rise of Partnerships" (2006) 18(3) *Georgetown International Environmental Law Review* 425 at 445.

[98] S. R. Iyer, "Partnerships" that Raise More Questions than Answers," Third World Network Briefing Paper 13, October 2003.

[99] Centre for Science and Environment, note 96.

While Southern governments also raised concerns about the partnerships concept, they seemed resigned to accepting them. As the Centre for Science and Environment noted, "[i]n many ways, these partnerships were the only hope for funds in a conference where it was otherwise clear that no further financial commitments would be forthcoming from the industrialised world."[100]

Some commentators characterized the WSSD as a "step backward" from the Stockholm and Rio outcomes; as the authors of a recent text on international environmental law put it, "Johannesburg may stand for a critical shift from 'sustainability' to development'."[101] Paul Wapner, a (Northern) academic commentator, has suggested that South and North appeared to have "swapped" interests,[102] with a greater degree of concern for environmental protection being voiced by Southern governments and Northern governments "increasingly letting these concerns fall by the wayside in favor of, ironically, economic development."[103] While I would take issue with the assumption that the South and North had in fact espoused this neat environment versus development dichotomy, Wapner's assessment raises important questions. Did the common ground that appeared to have been forged in the years between Rio and Johannesburg represent a genuine consensus regarding the interrelationship between environmental and economic prosperity? Or had the balance tilted in the direction of traditional understandings of economic prosperity that would always leave both the environment and broader conceptions of human well-being as lesser priorities? And did this shift to pragmatism simply highlight the contradictions and limitations inherent in the sustainable development paradigm itself?[104]

8. THE FUTURE WE WANT OR SAME AS IT EVER WAS? RIO+20

The most recent of the large gatherings on international environmental policy mentioned at the beginning of this chapter, the 2012 United Nations Conference on Sustainable Development, brings us up to date in our historical survey. Rio+20, as it is usually known, was intended "to secure renewed political commitment for sustainable development, assessing the progress to date and the remaining gaps in the implementation of the outcomes of the major summits on sustainable development and addressing new and emerging challenges."[105] In convening the

---

[100] Ibid.

[101] U. Beyerlin and T. Marauhn, *International Environmental Law* (Oxford: Hart, 2011), p. 26.

[102] P. Wapner, "World Summit on Sustainable Development: Toward a Post-Jo'burg Environmentalism" (2003) 3(1) *Global Environmental Politics* 1 at 4.

[103] Ibid at 5.

[104] R. D'Souza, "Sustainable Development or Self-Determination? Asking Hard Questions About the World Summit on Sustainable Development (WSSD)" (2002) 33(1) *Social Policy* 23.

[105] UN General Assembly, *Resolution Adopted by the General Assembly: Implementation of Agenda 21, the Programme for the Further Implementation of Agenda 21 and the Outcomes of the World Summit on Sustainable Development*, 31 March 2010, A/RES 64/236, para. 20(a).

conference the UN General Assembly also identified two themes: "a green economy in the context of sustainable development and poverty eradication and the institutional framework for sustainable development."[106] The "green economy" proved to be a particularly intense site of South–North debate, as the tensions that emerged during the Stockholm process, and that resurfaced at both UNCED and the WSSD, continued to play a prominent role.

UNEP had begun a "Green Economy Initiative" following the global economic crisis of 2008, amid concerns that a focus on economic recovery could compromise the commitment to both environmental protection and development. Defined as an economy "that results in improved human well-being and social equity, while significantly reducing environmental risks and ecological scarcities,"[107] the "green economy" came to be a focal point of discussion within UNEP and the United Nations system more generally. Despite the breadth of the definition and what some considered to be the potentially transformative potential of the concept,[108] however, much of the discussion centred on specific and fairly technical questions regarding how to promote investment in "green sectors" and how to "green" sectors that had traditionally been either pollution- or resource-intensive.

Given this relatively narrow interpretation of the green economy that was carried into the Rio+20 deliberations, it might be seen as surprising that this turned out to be a focal point of South–North disagreement. It could have led to a feel-good consensus that would have required relatively little in the way of fundamental change. Instead, while the European nations championed the concept, many developing countries, and the larger ones in particular, were resistant, and the final conference document, "The Future We Want," simply noted that the state representatives consider the green economy "as one of the important tools available for achieving sustainable development" and that it "could provide options for policy-making but should not be a rigid set of rules."[109] While Southern resistance could be characterized as a knee-jerk reaction against having restrictions imposed on their development trajectories, the reality was much more complex. There were specific concerns that the green economy might be used to justify unilateral trade restrictions, or to insist on market access for "environmentally friendly" goods.[110] More generally, concerns were raised that an embrace of the green economy could represent a departure from the normative consensus around the concept of sustainable development that had been achieved in 1992 and reiterated in 2002, which

---

[106] Ibid.

[107] United Nations Environment Programme, *Towards a Green Economy: Pathways to Sustainable Development and Poverty Eradication* (UNEP, 2011), p. 16.

[108] See S. Bernstein, "Rio+20: Sustainable Development in an Era of Multilateral Decline" (2013) 13(4) *Global Environmental Politics* 12.

[109] *Report of the United Nations Conference on Sustainable Development*, Rio de Janeiro, 20–22 June 2012, UN Doc. A/CONF.216/16), p. 10, para. 56.

[110] M. Khor, "Risks and Uses of the Green Economy Concept in the Context of Sustainability, Poverty and Equity," South Centre, Research Paper No. 40 (2011).

emphasized the interconnectedness of environmental, social, and economic factors as the three pillars of sustainable development.[111] And at a deeper level, long-standing concerns about the ability of states to make their own choices also played an important role. According to the Earth Negotiations Bulletin, "Bolivia summed up the opposition, asserting that no single development model – whatever its color – should be imposed, and that the rights of developing states to pursue their own development paths must be upheld."[112]

Both in response to the green economy proposals and more generally, there have been an increasing number of calls for a willingness to look beyond prevailing models, the formulation of local solutions, and, above all, the need to stop looking northward for either models or solutions. In expressing its rejection of the Rio+20 outcomes, the Bolivian Climate Change Platform noted:

> It is wrong to assume that deepening the neo-liberal model via a green economy will simultaneously lead to sustainable economic development, the eradication of poverty and the maintenance and management of ecosystems. As peoples of the world we know this is the same neo-liberal model – even more inhuman – that will exacerbate social inequalities that have destroyed and harmed Mother Earth and nature.[113]

Similarly, Sunita Narain of the Centre for Science and Environment argued:

> It is not possible to emulate the lifestyle of the already industrialised without compromising the survival of the planet. [...] They have no real answers to the future because they want to keep tinkering with the present. They are looking to find small solutions to the massive problem of increased emissions, linked to growth.[114]

These impassioned pleas echo calls from around the world for new ways of thinking about environment and development, and resonate with many of the sentiments expressed at Founex and Cocoyoc decades earlier. It remains to be seen whether these calls will be any more successful in reorienting the international systems toward a more equitable relationship between South, North, and the natural world upon which both depend.

---

[111] Such concerns were raised during the first session of the Preparatory Committee for Rio+20, at which Yemen, speaking for the G-77 China, argued that "there is no clear and agreed definition of what "green economy' entails and no need to redefine sustainable development or replace it with an abstract concept": Earth Negotiations Bulletin, "Summary of the First PrepCom for the UN Conference on Sustainable Development," www.iisd.ca, p. 5.

[112] Earth Negotiations Bulletin, "Summary of the United Nations Conference on Sustainable Development," June 13–22, 2012, www.iisd.ca, p. 21.

[113] Bolivian Climate Change Platform, "Rio+20: This Is Not the 'Future We Want'," June 21, 2012, http://climate-connections.org.

[114] S. Narain, "Building a True Green Economy," June 5, 2012, www.downtoearth.org.in.

6

Global Environmental Governance and the South

Ved P. Nanda

1. INTRODUCTION

Systematic, coherent, and effective global environmental governance at all levels (multilateral, regional, subregional, and national) is a prerequisite for meeting the ongoing and emerging environmental challenges facing the international community. And there has been wide recognition for several decades now that, because the existing environmental governance architecture is fragmented and incoherent, it has failed to effectively and efficiently address environmental issues on a global scale, and hence the global environment has continued to decline. There is wide recognition, as well, that unless the environmental dimension of sustainable development is given attention on par with the economic and social dimensions, it will be hard to realize the goal of sustainable development.

Environmental deterioration has continued notwithstanding the goal to "defend and improve the human environment for present and future generations,"[1] as proclaimed at the first UN Conference on the Human Environment in Stockholm in 1972. The Stockholm Conference provided the framework for the establishment by the General Assembly of the United Nations Environment Program (UNEP) as the primary environmental body within the UN system. The UNEP was tasked with acting as a catalyst and focal point for coordinating activities in the UN system.

This chapter focuses on global environmental governance structures and the challenges of the existing structure for the global South. Section 2 highlights environmental challenges the world community is facing. The efforts undertaken thus far to reform international environmental governance are reviewed in section 3. This will be followed by a discussion of the implications of these developments for the South in section 4. Section 5 concludes by discussing the additional steps

---

[1] This goal was proclaimed in the Stockholm Declaration. See the *Report of the United Nations Conference on the Human Environment*, Stockholm, 16 June 1972, UN Doc. A/CONF.48/14 & Corr. 1.

Ved P. Nanda 131

required to integrate the fragmented international environmental governance system and to facilitate the achievement of sustainable development in the global South.

2. ENVIRONMENTAL CHALLENGES FOR THE WORLD COMMUNITY

In June 1992, the United Nations convened a conference to mark the twentieth anniversary of the Stockholm Conference, entitled the UN Conference on Environment and Development (UNCED or Rio Conference), in Rio de Janeiro.[2] During the twenty years since the Stockholm Conference, the planet's environmental health, and especially that of developing countries, had continued to decline. Maurice Strong, Secretary-General of both the Stockholm and Rio conferences, reflected on the seriousness of the situation after his extensive worldwide travels preceding the Rio Conference: "the extent and nature of environmental degradation and its tragic human consequences were everywhere. The cities of the developing countries [...] are now among the world's most polluted, many of them headed for environmental and social breakdown." [3] He added that the "appalling destruction of natural resources, loss of forest cover, erosion and degradation of soils, and deterioration of supplies and quality of water are visible throughout the developing world [...] threatening a massive human ecotragedy beyond any ever before witnessed."[4]

Another ten years had passed when, in September 2002, the Johannesburg World Summit on Sustainable Development (WSSD) warned: "[t]he global environment continues to suffer. Loss of biodiversity continues, fish stocks continue to be depleted, desertification claims more and more fertile land, the adverse effects of climate change are already evident, natural disasters are more frequent and more devastating and developing countries more vulnerable, and air, water and marine pollution continue to rob millions of a decent life."[5]

A growing world population, technological advances, and the expanding production and consumption of goods and services continued to cause unprecedented environmental changes, including global warming, air pollution, loss of biodiversity, overexploitation of aquatic ecosystems, and land degradation. These changes are reported in the 2007 study by UNEP entitled *Global Environment Outlook: Environment for Development* (GEO-4),[6] part of a series of the organization's science-based, comprehensive, and in-depth assessment reports. The GEO-4

---

[2] UN General Assembly, *Report of the United Nations Conference on Environment and Development*, 3–14 June 1992, A/CONF.151/26 [hereinafter UNCED Report].

[3] M. Strong, "Beyond Rio: Prospects and Portents" (1993) 4 *Colorado Journal of International Environmental Law and Policy* 21 at 23.

[4] Ibid.

[5] *Johannesburg Declaration on Sustainable Development: Report of the World Summit on Sustainable Development*, Johannesburg, 4 September 2002, UN Doc. A/CONF. 199/20.

[6] UNEP, *Global Environment Outlook: Geo 4* (Malta: Progress Press, 2007).

report led the UN General Assembly to adopt a resolution in December 2008 expressing deep concern for potential negative implications of these environmental changes for economic and social development, especially for the poor and vulnerable groups all over the world.[7]

UNEP also publishes annual Year Books that examine emerging environmental issues while undertaking a review of environmental developments during the preceding year. UNEP Year Book 2013 acknowledges that the year 2012 "witnessed failures to protect the environment, including increased emissions of greenhouse gases and other types of air pollutants, growth in unsustainable consumption and production, and increased biodiversity loss. [...] Many of the world's ongoing and emerging environmental issues identified during the past decade still persist and must be addressed."[8]

Another UN publication, *Keeping Track of Our Changing Environment: From Rio to Rio+20 (1992–2012)*,[9] chronicled the environmental changes since the 1992 Rio Conference. In the foreword to the report, UNEP Executive Director Achim Steiner noted that rapid environmental changes have taken place, ranging "from the accumulating evidence of climate change and its very visible impacts on our planet, to biodiversity loss and species extinctions, further degradation of land surfaces and the deteriorating quality of oceans."[10] The study warned that "[w]ith limited progress on environmental issues achieved, and few real 'success stories' to be told, all components of the environment – land, water, biodiversity, oceans and atmosphere – continue to degrade."[11]

As a final highlight of environmental challenges, the latest edition in UNEP's GEO series, *Global Environment Outlook (GEO) 5: Environment for the Future We Want*,[12] warns that the world's seven billion people "are collectively exploiting the Earth's resources at accelerating rates and intensities that surpass the capacity of its systems to absorb wastes and neutralize the adverse effects on the environment," leading to the depletion or degradation of several key resources.[13]

The realization that the existing international environmental mechanisms are unable to halt environmental degradation has prompted serious consideration to enhancing the governance structure. The efforts undertaken toward this goal are considered next.

---

[7] UN General Assembly, *Resolution Adopted by the General Assembly: Report of the Governing Council of the United Nations Environment Programme on Its Tenth Special Session*, 19 December 2008, A/RES/63/220.

[8] UNEP, *UNEP Year Book 2013: Emerging Issues in Our Global Environment* (Nairobi: United Nations Environment Programme, 2013) [hereinafter 2013 Year Book].

[9] UNEP, *Keeping Track of Our Changing Environment: From Rio to Rio+20 (1992-2012)* (Nairobi: United Nations Environment Programme, 2011).

[10] Ibid, p. ii.

[11] Ibid, p. 90.

[12] UNEP, *GEO 5: Environment for the Future We Want* (Malta: Progress Press, 2012).

[13] Ibid, p. xviii.

3. EFFORTS TO REFORM INTERNATIONAL ENVIRONMENTAL GOVERNANCE

The 1972 Stockholm Conference produced an action plan for environmental management and established a framework for the first international environmental institutional mechanism, UNEP, to implement it. UNEP consists of a Governing Council (GC), comprising fifty-eight members representing all regions and mandated to give general policy guidance to the UN; the Environmental Secretariat; the Environmental Fund to finance environmental activities across the entire UN system; and the Environment Coordination Board (now the Environment Management Group) to promote interagency cooperation within the UN system.

Since the Stockholm Conference several institutional mechanisms have been created and the existing ones strengthened to protect the environment. To illustrate, in response to several proposals for governance reform, a number of institutions were established and initiatives taken on the road to the 1992 Rio Conference and in connection with it. These included the Global Environment Facility (GEF)[14] and the Commission on Sustainable Development.[15]

One of the conference's signature accomplishments was the adoption of Agenda 21,[16] a comprehensive action plan for managing the environment in the twenty-first century. The document contains numerous policies, plans, programs, processes, and other guidance for intergovernmental organizations and national governments to follow in implementing the international legal documents produced at the conference. The conference also adopted by consensus the Rio Declaration on Environment and Development,[17] of which several principles elaborate on the environment–development linkage, giving "special priority" to the needs of developing countries, "particularly the least developed and those most environmentally vulnerable."[18]

The Rio Declaration explicitly recognized the principle of "common but differentiated responsibilities" among states in the following terms: "[i]n view of the

---

[14] The Global Environment Facility was created as a pilot program by the World Bank in 1991 to assist in the protection of the global environment and to promote environmentally sustainable development; it has provided developing countries and countries with economies in transition more than US$11 billion in grants and has leveraged US$57 billion in co-financing for more than 3,200 projects in over 165 countries. It has also made more than 16,000 small grants directly to civil society and community-based organizations, totaling more than US$653 million: Global Environment Facility, "What is the GEF," www.thegef.org. According to its website it serves 183 countries to address global environmental issues in partnership with other institutions and the private sector: Global Environment Facility, "What is the GEF," www.thegef.org.

[15] Sustainable Development, "Commission on Sustainable Development," http://sustainabledevelopment.un.org.

[16] UNCED Report, note 2, p. 14.

[17] *Rio Declaration on Environment and Development*, Rio de Janeiro, 13 June 1992, UN Doc. A/CONF.151/26 (vol. I); 31 ILM 874 (1992) [hereinafter Rio Declaration].

[18] Ibid, Principle 6.

134   *Global Environmental Governance and the South*

different contributions to global environmental degradation, States have common but differentiated responsibilities. The developed countries acknowledge the responsibilities that they bear in the international pursuit of sustainable development in view of the pressures their societies place on the global environment and of the technologies and financial resources they command."[19]

Principle 10 of the Rio Declaration, significant to developing countries as well as developed, embodied all three facets of public participation – access to information, access to participation in decision-making, and access to justice. It calls for individuals to have "appropriate access to information [...] held by public authorities," information on hazards in their communities, "and the opportunity to participate in decision-making processes."[20] States are obligated to make "information widely available" and to provide "[e]ffective access to judicial and administrative proceedings."[21]

The following discussion focuses on selected reform efforts among the large number of proposals from governments, scholars, and the United Nations itself.

The Malmö Declaration,[22] adopted at the first meeting of the Global Ministerial Environment Forum (GMEF) held in Sweden in May 2000, focused, inter alia, on major environmental challenges of the twenty-first century. After expressing deep concern about the increasing rate of deterioration of the environment and the natural resource base, governments agreed that the 2002 WSSD "should review the requirements for a greatly strengthened institutional structure for environmental governance [...] that has the capacity to effectively address wide-ranging environmental threats in a globalizing world."[23] Noting "an alarming discrepancy between commitments and action," governments urged the international community to implement in a timely fashion those goals and targets regarding increased support to developing countries.[24]

In December 2001, then UNEP Executive Director Klaus Toepfer submitted a report to the GC/GMEF on international environmental governance.[25] He presented an overview of the state of international governance, beginning with the Stockholm Conference and noting developments since that time. The report highlighted the establishment of several new institutional arrangements and the creation of more than 500 multilateral environmental agreements (MEAs).[26]

---

[19] Ibid, Principle 7.

[20] Ibid, Principle 10.

[21] Ibid.

[22] UNEP, "Malmö Ministerial Declaration," http://unep.org.

[23] Ibid, para. 24.

[24] Ibid, para. 2.

[25] UN Governing Council of the United Nations Environment Programme, *Global Ministerial Environment Forum, International Environmental Governance: Report of the Executive Director*, 13–15 February 2002, UNEP/GCSS.VII/2.

[26] Ibid, paras. 20–60. As of the beginning of 2012, more than 600 MEAs were registered with the United Nations – 61 related to atmosphere, 155 to biodiversity, 179 to chemicals and waste, 46 to land, and 197 to water. See Executive Director of UNEP Governing Council, Discussion

The report noted among problem areas inadequate international institutional arrangements, incoherent decision-making structures, limitations in access and participation, lack of meaningful coordination, and inadequate authority of UNEP.[27] It pointed to a particularly heavy burden that developing countries must carry because of stress on the current system, and the difficulty they have in meeting the demands of the growing number of environmental institutions, issues, and agreements. The problem is further exacerbated as developing countries are not equipped to participate fully in the development of international environmental policy.[28] And there is no common framework to increase their capacity either to have meaningful participation or the means to implement and monitor agreements at the national level. The framework to assist them with the needed technical capabilities is also lacking.[29]

Toepfer's report found sources of financing for environmental activities insufficient to meet the needs of the developing countries, and it discussed in this regard the roles of the GEF, the Global Mechanism of the Convention to Combat Desertification, and the Multilateral Fund for the Implementation of the Montreal Protocol.[30] It also discussed the financing of UNEP itself.[31] The report especially recommended that the needs and constraints of developing countries be considered in any reform model pertaining to environmental compliance, enforcement, and liability.[32] It also emphasized the need for improving capacity and providing adequate financial resources so that developing countries can implement MEAs effectively.[33]

Toepfer found a lack of coordination among MEAs to be responsible for the lack of implementation of MEAs.[34] Problem areas include: too many MEAs; the differing locations of secretariats for conventions and venues for conferences of parties and their subsidiary bodies; the large number of meetings posing difficulties in both participation and implementation, especially for developing countries; and national reports required by MEAs being so burdensome that they are frequently submitted either late or not at all.[35] Insufficient finances, uncertainty of appropriate technology transfer, and lack of adequate alternate dispute mechanisms cause additional problems, resulting in ineffective implementation and monitoring.

Paper by the Executive Director, *Background Paper for the Ministerial Consultations – Global Environment Outlook and Emerging Issues: Setting Effective Global Environmental Goals*, 5 January 2012, UNEP/GCSS.XII/13/Jan. 5, 2012.

[27] UNEP, note 25, para. 71.

[28] P. Sands, *Principles of International Environmental Law*, 3rd ed. (Cambridge: Cambridge University Press, 2012), p. 663.

[29] UN Governing Council of the United Nations Environment Programme, note 25, para. 74.

[30] Ibid, paras. 98–112.

[31] Ibid, paras. 113–122.

[32] Ibid, paras. 124, 133(d).

[33] Ibid, para. 138.

[34] See generally ibid, paras. 135–139.

[35] UN Governing Council of the United Nations Environment Programme, note 25, para. 137.

In addition, the tendency of MEA secretariats to act as autonomous bodies and further expand their work, with the resulting proliferation of more subsidiary bodies and ad hoc working groups within MEAs, leads to institutional congestion.[36]

In February 2002, the UNEP Governing Council at its Seventh Special Session in Cartagena, Colombia, proposed a number of reforms to be transmitted to the Preparatory Committee for the WSSD.[37] These recommendations were the work of an open-ended intergovernmental group of ministers established to undertake a comprehensive, policy-oriented assessment of existing institutional arrangements of the environmental governance system, as well as future needs and options for strengthening it.[38]

Recommendations regarding the role and structure of the GC/GMEF included a call for universal membership in the body, and for the body to effectively impart broad policy advice and guidance in addition to promoting international cooperation in the field of the environment.[39] Other recommendations related to the following: Strengthening the role and financial situation of the UNEP;[40] improved coordination among and effectiveness of MEAs;[41] and the efficient functioning and enhanced role of the Environmental Management Group (EMG) to ensure enhanced coordination across the UN system.[42] Of special interest to developing countries were recommendations on capacity-building, technology transfer, and country-level coordination.[43]

At the WSSD, the Johannesburg Plan of Implementation (JPOI)[44] contained several commitments on strengthening environmental governance. For example, Article 139(f) was aimed at increasing effectiveness and efficiency by limiting overlap and duplication of activities of international organizations, within and outside the United Nations, based on their mandates and comparative advantages. Article 140(b) urged strengthening collaboration within and between the UN

---

[36] A. Najam and M. Papa, *Global Environmental Governance: A Reform Agenda* (International Institute for Sustainable Development, 2006), p. 30, citing H. French, "Reshaping Global Governance," in L. Starke (ed.), *State of the World* (London: Earthscan, 2002), pp. 176–183.

[37] United Nations Environment Programme (UNEP), *Report of the Governing Council, Seventh Special Session (13–15 February 2002)*, 15 February 2002, A/57/25, Decision SS.VII/i. International Environmental Governance.

[38] This group was established pursuant to the UNEP Governing Council decision. UNEP, *Proceedings of the Governing Council at its Twenty-First Session*, 14 February 2001, UNEP/GC21/9.

[39] UNEP, note 37, paras. 11, 11A. The first meeting of the Global Ministerial Environmental Forum took place on May 29–31, 2000: UNEP, "UNEP Governing Council: New York," http://unep.org.

[40] UNEP, note 37, paras. 12–25.

[41] Ibid, paras. 26–30.

[42] Ibid, paras. 36–37.

[43] Ibid, paras. 31–35.

[44] World Summit on Sustainable Development, *Johannesburg Declaration on Sustainable Development and Plan of Implementation of the World Summit* (New York: United Nations Department of Public Information, 2003).

system, the international financial institutions, the GEF, and the World Trade Organization (WTO), utilizing the various coordinating bodies, which would be of special assistance to developing countries. The strengthened interagency collaboration was especially aimed at supporting the efforts of developing countries in implementing Agenda 21. And Article 140(d) called for full implementation of the Governing Council's recommendation.

Further reflection on the existing institutional framework of UN environmental work took place at the September 2005 World Summit of Heads of State and Government at the UN Headquarters in New York. The outcome was the adoption of a General Assembly resolution entitled "2005 World Summit Outcome,"[45] covering the following areas: "enhanced coordination, improved policy advice and guidance, strengthened scientific knowledge, assessment and cooperation, and better integration of environmental activities in the broader sustainable development framework at the operational level, including through capacity-building."[46]

The heads of state and government gathered at the Summit supported the achievement of "stronger system-wide coherence within the United Nations system" by implementing the necessary measures. This led to the initiation of two review processes, one of which resulted in the report "Delivering As One,"[47] in the areas of development, humanitarian assistance, and the environment. The message was that the United Nations was to "deliver as one," at the country level, and not in a fragmented fashion by the various UN bodies working separately. The second initiative led to the formation of an informal consultative process on the institutional framework for UN environmental activities.[48]

The next major development took place in October 2009 when a regionally representative group of high officials appointed by the UNEP GC presented a set of options for improving international environmental governance. This set of opinions re-emphasized scientific discourse in framing environmental policy responses.[49] Agreed via what came to be known as the "Belgrade process," the group's recommendations were endorsed at the GC's 2010 Special Session.[50]

---

[45] UN General Assembly, *Resolution Adopted by the General Assembly: 2005 World Summit Outcome*, 24 October 2005, A/RES/60/1.

[46] Ibid, para. 169.

[47] UN General Assembly, *Note by the Secretary General: Follow-up to the Outcome of the Millennium Summit*, 20 November 2006, A/61/583.

[48] See UN General Assembly, "Informal Consultative Process on the Institutional Framework for the United Nations' Environment Activities: Co-Chairs' Options Paper," 14 June 2007, www.un.org.

[49] For the group's report, see UN Governing Council of the UNEP, *International Environmental Governance: Outcome of the Work of the Consultative Group of Ministers or High-Level Representatives*, 24–26 February 2010, UNEP/GCSS.XI/4, Annex.

[50] For the UNEP Governing Council's decision endorsing the group's report, see UN Governing Council of the UNEP, *International Environmental Governance: Outcome of the Work of the Consultative Group of Ministers or High-Level Representatives*, 2 December 2009, UNEP/GCSS.XI/11, Annex 1.

The group identified five objectives of an international environmental governance system: (1) creating a strong, credible, and accessible science base and policy interface; (2) developing a global authoritative voice for environmental sustainability; (3) achieving effectiveness, efficiency, and coherence within the United Nations system; (4) securing sufficient, predictable, and coherent funding; and (5) ensuring a responsive and cohesive approach to meeting the needs of countries.[51]

These objectives were identified with their respective functions. To illustrate, the first objective's corresponding functions are:

a) Creating a strong, credible and accessible science base and policy interface.
    i.   Acquisition, compilation, analysis and interpretation of data and information.
    ii. Information exchange.
    iii. Environmental assessment and early warning.
    iv. Scientific advice.
    v.   Science-policy interface.[52]

Subsequently, the GC formed another consultative group of high officials to build on the work done by the earlier consultative group. This group met in Nairobi, Kenya and Espoo, Finland, in July and November 2010, respectively, and after considering the objectives and functions identified by the former group, it listed in its report[53] six potential systemwide responses to the current international environmental governance system. These options are: (1) strengthen the science–policy interface with the full and meaningful participation of developing countries' (2) develop a systemwide strategy for environment in the UN system, (3) encourage synergies between compatible MEAs, (4) create a stronger link between global environmental policy-making and financing, (5) develop a systemwide capacity-building framework for the environment, and (6) continue to strengthen strategic engagement at the regional level.[54]

After taking account of these responses, the group "considered institutional forms that would best serve to implement these responses" and achieve the objectives and functions mentioned previously. Generally accepting that "form should follow function and that UNEP should be strengthened and enhanced," it then identified as a key outcome of the international environmental governance system

---

[51] UNEP GC/GMEF, *International Environmental Governance: Outcome of the Work of the Consultative Group of Ministers or High-Level Representatives,* 2 December 2009, UNEP/GCSS.XI/4, Annex, para. 10. For incremental reform options, see para. 12, and for broader reform options, see para. 13.

[52] Ibid, para. 10.

[53] UNEP, "Consultative Group of Ministers or High-Level Representatives, Nairobi-Helsinki Outcome," 23 November 2010, www.unep.org.

[54] Ibid, para. 7(a)–(f).

"[s]trengthening the global authoritative voice, as well as other voices, for the environment.[...] providing credible, coherent and effective leadership for environmental sustainability under the overall framework of sustainable development."[55] The group presented five options for "broader institutional reform": (1) enhance UNEP; (2) establish a new umbrella organization for sustainable development, (3) establish a specialized agency such as a world environment organization, (4) reform the UN Economic and Social Council and the UN Commission on Sustainable Development, and (5) enhance institutional reforms and streamline existing structures.[56] The group suggested that the second and fourth options would best be addressed in the context of wider sustainable development,[57] and that options 1, 3, and 5 were potential options for "strengthening the form of the environment pillar in the context of sustainable development."[58]

However, it must be noted that while the reforms seek to address the need for increased clustering and synchronization between substantive MEA obligations, the view of coordination *alone* as a matter of improving global environmental governance is largely misplaced. Indeed, while coordination is of central importance to these rounds of institutional reform, the plethora of coordinating bodies – including the UNEP, GEF, Commission on Sustainable Development, Environmental Management Group (EMG), and Global Ministerial Environment Forum (GMEF) – adds additional bureaucratic burdens that also consume substantial resources.

Finally, the 2012 Rio+20 UN Conference on Sustainable Development responded to the various reports, studies, and proposals for reform.[59] Heads of state and government reaffirmed the need "to strengthen international environmental governance within the context of the institutional framework for sustainable development, in order to promote a balanced integration of the economic, social and environmental dimensions of sustainable development as well as coordination within the UN system."[60]

Preceding the conference, the Executive Director, Achim Steiner, presented a discussion paper for the ministerial consultations on international environmental governance in January 2012.[61] He acknowledged the consensus regarding gaps in the current system which do not allow it to adequately respond to the changing

---

[55] Ibid, para. 11.

[56] Ibid, para. 11(a)–(e).

[57] Ibid, para. 12.

[58] Ibid, para. 13.

[59] See UN General Assembly, *Rio+20, The Future We Want*, 11 September 2012, A/Res/66/288 [hereinafter *The Future We Want*].

[60] Ibid, para. 87.

[61] UN Governing Council of the UNEP, *Report of the Executive Director: International Environmental Governance*, 24 January 2012, UNEP/GCSS.XII/13/Add. 2.

environmental situation or to countries' growing concerns and that, hence, the status quo is no longer an option.[62] He listed the gaps, including:

(a) Lack of an authoritative voice to guide environmental policy effectively at the global level;
(b) Lack of coherence among global environmental policies and programs;
(c) High degree of financial fragmentation;
(d) Lack of coherence in the governance and administration of multilateral environmental agreements;
(e) Lack of a central monitoring, review and accountability system for commitments made under multilateral environmental agreements;
(f) Lack of sufficient, secure and predictable funding; and
(g) Implementation gaps experienced at the country level.[63]

Steiner then reviewed the developments pertaining to reform under the auspices of UNEP until January 2012, and discussed in detail the implications of selecting one of the following two options: (1) strengthening the capacity of UNEP with universal membership and stronger finance or (2) transforming UNEP into a specialized agency for the environment with adequate financing and universal membership.[64] The first option could be achieved through a UN General Assembly resolution. The current institutional structure and reporting arrangements to the General Assembly through the Economic and Social Council would remain unchanged. The second option would require an independently negotiated treaty to form a specialized agency.

Steiner compared the advantages and disadvantages of each.[65] The advantages of the first option include access to the UN regular budget and adoption of negotiated reforms through a General Assembly resolution without necessity of member states' ratifications. The disadvantages include lack of autonomy for environmental decision-making in the UN system because General Assembly approval would be required for the UNEP Governing Council decisions, and the inability to establish treaties. On the other hand, the advantages of option two would be to enable UNEP to adopt treaties and other instruments and have a clear relationship between UNEP and other specialized agencies, including financial relationships. Disadvantages include that UNEP would not have access to the UN regular budget, and that negotiation of UNEP's founding instrument would require an independent negotiation process with the outcome being reliant upon countries ratifying in accordance with their domestic laws.

---

[62] Ibid, para. 2.
[63] Ibid.
[64] Ibid, para. 13–53.
[65] Ibid, para. 54–58.

At the Governing Council's special session preceding the Rio+20 Conference, in February 2012, the Council took note of the work done by consultative groups it had established, as well as of the Executive Director's note regarding the incremental reforms, and recalled the prior commitments to strengthen UNEP's role "as the leading global environmental authority that sets the global environmental agenda, promotes the coherent implementation of the environmental dimension of sustainable development within the United Nations system and serves as an authoritative advocate for the global environment."[66] It invited the General Assembly to examine the possibility of developing, for the environment, a systemwide strategy.[67]

In the President's summary of the discussions by ministers and heads of delegation, he stated that while there was broad support for strengthening the environmental component of the international framework for sustainable development, consensus was lacking on the future structure, as views were mixed on whether UNEP should be strengthened or a specialized agency for the environment be established.[68] Among the recommendations for reform were the following: (1) an endorsement of the prior consultations' outcomes, (2) the establishment of an anchor organization with universal membership, and (3) assessed member contributions to enhance available resources.[69]

At Rio+20, in the outcome document, heads of state and government expressed their commitment to strengthen and upgrade UNEP. They affirmed the prior UN resolutions that reinforced UNEP's mandate and invited the UN General Assembly to adopt a resolution providing for:

- The establishment of universal membership in the Governing Council of UNEP;
- Having secure, stable, adequate and increased financial resources both from the regular UN budget and voluntary contributions to fulfill UNEP's mandate;
- Enhancing UNEP's voice and ability to fulfill its coordination mandate within the UN system;
- Promoting a strong science–policy interface;
- Disseminating and sharing evidence-based environmental information and raising public awareness on environmental issues;
- Providing capacity-building to countries and supporting and facilitating access to technology;

---

[66] UNEP, *Decisions Adopted by the Governing Council/Global Ministerial Environment Forum at its Twelfth Special Session*, 8 March 2012, Advance Copy, Decision SS.XII/3, Preamble.

[67] Ibid, para. 6.

[68] Ibid, para. 37.

[69] Ibid, para. 41.

142 *Global Environmental Governance and the South*

- Progressively consolidating headquarters functions in Nairobi, as well as strengthening its regional presence to assist countries in the implementation of their national environmental policies; and
- Ensuring the active participation of all relevant stakeholders.[70]

Heads of state and government recognized MEAs' "significant contributions to sustainable development" and, acknowledging the work already done for enhancing synergies among the Basel,[71] Rotterdam,[72] and Stockholm Conventions[73] in the chemicals and waste cluster, they encouraged parties to MEAs "to consider further measures, in these and other clusters ... to promote policy coherence at all relevant levels, improve efficiency, reduce unnecessary overlap and duplication, enhance coordination and cooperation among MEAs, including the three Rio Conventions as well as with the UN system in the field."[74] They also decided to establish a universal intergovernmental high-level political forum to subsequently replace the Commission on Sustainable Development,[75] with its format and organizational aspects to be determined by the General Assembly.[76]

In the follow-up to the Rio+20 Conference, the UN General Assembly, recalling its decision to have secure, stable, adequate, and increased financial resources for UNEP and the need to consider UNEP's "administrative and management costs" in the context of the regular budget of the UN, adopted a resolution on 21 December 2012.[77] Reiterating that technology support to developing countries and capacity-building for them in environment-related fields are important

---

[70] *The Future We Want*, note 59, para. 88.

[71] *Basel Convention on the Control of Transboundary Movements of Hazardous Wastes and Their Disposal*, Basel, 22 March 1989, in force 5 May 1992, 1673 UNTS 126; 28 ILM 657 (1989).

[72] *Convention on the Prior Informed Consent Procedure for Certain Hazardous Chemicals and Pesticides in International Trade*, Rotterdam, 10 September 1998, in force 24 February 2004, 2244 UNTS 337; 38 ILM 1 (1999).

[73] *Stockholm Convention on Persistent Organic Pollutants*, Stockholm, 22 May 2001, in force 17 May 2004, 2256 UNTS 119; 40 ILM 532 (2001).

[74] Ibid, para. 89. MEA clustering (by thematic areas, functions, geographic regions, etc.) greatly impacts participation of developing countries in the decision-making process. For a discussion of various aspects of MEA clusters, see generally K. von Moltke, "On Clustering International Environmental Agreements," 2001, www.iisd.org; K. von Moltke, "Clustering Multilateral Environment Agreements as an Alternative to a World Environment Organization," in F. Biermann and S. Bauer (eds.), *A World Environment Organization: Solution or Threat for Effective Environmental Governance?* (Aldershot: Ashgate, 2005), pp. 173–202; S. Oberthur, "Clustering of Multilateral Environmental Agreements: Potentials and Limitations" (2002) 2 *Politics, Law and Economics* 317; J. Wehrli, "Clustering Assessment: Enhancing Synergies among Multilateral Environmental Agreements," Governance and Sustainability Issue Brief Series (January 2012). A. Najam and M. Papa, *Global Environmental Governance: A Reform Agenda* (International Institute for Sustainable Development, 2006), p. 34.

[75] *The Future We Want*, note 59, para. 84.

[76] Ibid, para. 86.

[77] UN General Assembly, *Report of the Governing Council of the United Nations Environment Pogramme on Its Twelfth Session and on the Implementation of Section IV.C, Entitled "Environmental Pillar in the Context of Sustainable Development", of the Outcome Document of the*

components of UNEP's work,[78] the General Assembly decided to strengthen and upgrade UNEP as requested in the outcome document, *The Future We Want.*[79] It made several other decisions as well, including establishing universal membership in UNEP's Governing Council[80] and requesting UNEP's Executive Director "to continue to provide support for the full and effective participation of representatives of developing countries in the Governing Council meeting and invite the Governing Council to consider further arrangements in this regard."[81] It also urged donors to increase their voluntary funds.[82]

Under the new structure, the UNEP GC met in Nairobi for its first universal session in February 2013. In his policy statement at the opening of the session, with its theme *Rio+20: From Outcome to Implementation,* Executive Director Achim Steiner called for a coherent and systemic approach to environmental protection, saying "[w]e cannot continue to 'save the planet,' one species, one ecosystem, one policy, one issue, one law, one treaty at a time. Our challenge at the beginning of the 21st century has become a systemic one."[83] He added: "[t]he current framework of international environmental governance is characterized by institutional fragmentation and the lack of a holistic approach to environmental issues. [...] UNEP could do more to support national policy development, build capacity for implementing multi-lateral agreements and catalyze large-scale change at the global level."[84]

This expression from Steiner not only reveals the difficulty of consolidating institutional fragmentation, but further provides an important insight into how this develops. To this extent, the plethora of different characterizations of the environmental pillar mirrors the direct impact of different epistemic communities operating within the international environmental policy space.[85] What Steiner describes is the increasing difficulty of engaging the diversity of different epistemic communities without resort to a single conceptualization of the issue; it is the role of UNEP to gather varying epistemic communities in order to achieve large-scale change under a discourse of sustainable development.

The GC recommended that the UN General Assembly rename it the United Nations Environment Assembly of the United Nations Environment Programme,[86]

United Nations Conference on Sustainable Development, 21 December 2012, A/RES/67/213 [hereinafter UNGA resolution 67/213].

[78] Ibid, Preamble.

[79] Ibid, para. 4(a). The reference is to para. 88 of *The Future We Want,* note 59.

[80] Ibid, para. 4(b).

[81] Ibid, para. 4(c).

[82] Ibid, para. 5(b).

[83] UNEP, "Policy Statement by Achim Steiner," 23 June 2014, http://unep.org, p. 5.

[84] Ibid, p. 17.

[85] P. Haas, "Introduction: Epistemic Communities and International Policy Coordination" (1992) 46(1) *International Organization* 1 at 3.

[86] UN Governing Council of the United Nations Environment Programme, *Proceedings of the Governing Council/Global Ministerial Environment Forum at its First Universal Session,* 18–22 February 2013, UNEP/GC.27/17, Decision 27/2, para. 1.

144 *Global Environmental Governance and the South*

with its first session to be held in June 2014.[87] It decided to discontinue the Global Ministerial Environment Forum and bolstered environmental law in requesting UNEP's Executive Director to lead the UN system and support national governments in the development and implementation of the environmental rule of law, "with attention at all levels to mutually supporting governance features, including information disclosure, public participation [...] as well as environmental auditing and [...] independent dispute resolution."[88] This request built on the UNEP-convened World Congress on Justice, Governance and Law for Environmental Sustainability held during Rio+20, and the Executive Director's report about recent developments related to environmental law in the context of the outcome of that Congress.[89]

Subsequently, based on the GC's decisions taken at its first universal session, the Second Committee of the General Assembly recommended that the General Assembly adopt the following draft resolution: "Report of the Governing Council of the United Nations Environment Programme on its first universal session and the implementation of section IV.C, entitled 'environmental pillar in the context of sustainable development,' of the outcome document of the United Nations Conference on Sustainable Development."[90] It also reiterated the importance of Nairobi as the location of UNEP's headquarters and requested the Secretary-General to meet the body's resource needs.[91] On 20 December 2013, the General Assembly adopted, without a vote, the draft resolution recommended by the Second Committee.[92]

Finally, the first meeting of the high-level political forum on sustainable development took place on 24 September 2013. In his statement, Salman Khurshid, Minister of External Affairs of India, called for meaningful global partnership which would provide enhanced means of implementation to developing countries for the development agenda to succeed.[93] In the summary of the inaugural 2004 meeting, of which the overall theme was "[b]uilding the future we want: From Rio+20 to the post-2014 development agenda," the president of the UN General Assembly called the forum a guardian of the sustainable development agenda.

---

[87] Ibid, para. 3.

[88] Ibid, para. 4, Decision 27/9: Advancing justice, governance and law for environmental sustainability.

[89] Ibid; UN Governing Council of the United Nations Environment Programme, *Report of the Executive Director: Justice, Governance and Law for Environmental Sustainability*, 18–22 February 2013, UNEP/GC.27/13.

[90] UN General Assembly, *Sustainable Development: Report of the Governing Council of the United Nations Environment Programme on Its First Universal Session*, 9 December 2013, A/68/438/Add.7.

[91] Ibid, para. 13.

[92] UN General Assembly, note 77.

[93] Sustainable Development, "Statement by Salman Khurshid at the Inaugural Meeting of the High-Level Political Forum on Sustainable Development," 24 September 2014, http://sustainabledevelopment.un.org.

He said that "participants recognize the particular vulnerabilities and challenges of least developed countries, small island developing states, landlocked countries and African countries and reaffirmed the commitment to devote greater attention to these challenges in the future work of the high-level political forum."[94]

4. IMPLICATIONS OF THESE DEVELOPMENTS FOR THE GLOBAL SOUTH

As discussed previously, world leaders who gathered at Rio+20 responded to the growing realization that the existing global environment governance structure was inadequate to maintain and improve the global environment. Developing countries have been under special constraints because they are unable to fully and meaningfully participate in setting the global environmental policy and agenda and take effective action to implement and enforce their international and regional environmental obligations.

To illustrate, a 2008 UNEP report by the Executive Director noted that between 1992 and 2007, there were a total of 540 meetings by conferences of parties of major MEAs, in which 5,084 decisions were taken, requiring preparation and follow-up.[95] The time and effort needed to participate in these decisions, for implementation and to follow up, illustrate the burden on developing countries. As each MEA maintains its own administrative system – including costs for the secretariat, financing of meetings, and procurements – there is huge cost involved in administration, which could otherwise be used for capacity-building or for implementation of agreements.[96] The combined annual cost of financing of MEAs is reported roughly at US$445 million, compared with the annual consolidated budget of the World Trade Organization at US$222 million in 2010 and that of the International Labor Organization at US$726.7 million as its biennium budget.[97] Both the WTO and ILO have authority over all multinational agreements within their areas of expertise.[98]

The report aptly concluded: "[i]ncoherence and complexity in the international environmental governance system can lead to both transaction costs and [...]

[94] Note by the president of the UN General Assembly, *Summary of the First Meeting of the High-Level Political Forum on Sustainable Development*, 13 November 2013, A/68/588, paras. 2, 8, 24.

[95] UN Governing Council of the United Nations Environment Programme, *Note by the Executive Director, Efforts to Meet International Agreed Environmental Goals and Objectives: Demands and Outputs of Selected Multilateral Environmental Agreements for the Period 1992–2007*, 29 December 2008, UNEP/GC.25/INF/16/Add.1, Annex.

[96] P. Chaesk, "NGOs and State Capacity in International Environmental Negotiations: The Experience of the Earth Negotiations Bulletin" (2001) 10(2) *Review of European Community and International Environmental Law* 168 at 168–169.

[97] UNEP Division of Environmental Law and Conventions (DELC), "Issues Brief #2, the Environmental Dimension of IFSD: Fragmentation of Environmental Pillar and Its Impact on Efficiency and Effectiveness," www.unep.org, p. 3.

[98] Ibid.

146   *Global Environmental Governance and the South*

discourage developing country participation in the system, giving rise to questions on whether the system [...] provides coherent support to [developing] countries" so that they can meet their environmental and developmental objectives.[99]

To reiterate, the primary needs of developing countries in the environmental realm – adequate financing, technology, and capacity – are not met by the existing international environmental governance system. A report of the UNEP Division of Environmental Law and Conventions (DELC) appropriately notes that capacity-building for the implementation of MEAs extends beyond technical assistance to include "strengthening of institutional structures, mechanisms, procedures, as well as the creation of an enabling environment with adequate policies and laws."[100]

According to the report, in the pursuit of implementing international policies, many developing countries lack capacity to:

- build and maintain strong environmental institutions;
- create a strong scientific knowledge base for environmental policy-making;
- effectively integrate environmental concerns into national economic and development planning processes; and
- set up effective environmental monitoring and implementation schemes.[101]

The report further observes that many of the decisions on capacity-building undertaken by the Conference of Parties of several conventions are fairly general and are often not based on the specific capacity needs of individual countries or regions.[102]

Based upon analysis undertaken in prior studies, the report lists the following capacity-developing needs expressed by countries to achieve global environmental commitments: (1) capacity to incorporate convention obligations into national policy, legislation, and institutions; (2) economic instruments and financing mechanisms to ensure sustainability; (3) information collection, management, and exchange; and (4) public awareness and environmental education.[103]

This discussion demonstrates the need of a plan for technology support and capacity-building in developing countries.[104] In response to this need, UNEP's

---

[99] Ibid.

[100] UNEP, Division of Environmental Law and Conventions, "Issues Brief #3: The Environmental Dimension of IFSD – Country Responsiveness: Implementation and Capacity Support for the Environmental Pillar of IFSD," www.unep.org, p. 1.

[101] Ibid, p. 2.

[102] Ibid.

[103] Ibid.

[104] See Organization of American States, "Manual on Compliance with and Enforcement of Multilateral Environmental Agreements," www.oas.org, p. 208. See also S. Kravchenko, "The Aarhus Convention and Innovations in Compliance with Multilateral Environmental Agreements" (2007) 18(1) *Colorado Journal of International Environmental Law and Policy* 1 at 28.

Governing Council took the initiative to formulate a comprehensive strategy, as it set up a high-level working group which adopted the Bali Strategic Plan for Technology Support and Capacity-building (Plan) in December 2004 in Bali, Indonesia. Subsequently, UNEP's Executive Director submitted the Plan to the twenty-third session of the GC/GMEF, held in Nairobi in February 2005,[105] and the Governing Council adopted it.[106]

The Plan's objectives, which remain currently valid, included strengthening the capacity of developing countries' governments at all levels so they can: fully participate in the development of coherent international environmental policy; implement their obligations at the national level under international agreements; achieve their environmental goals; use and sustain the capacity or technology after training or other capacity-building efforts; and develop national research, monitoring, and assessment capacity which would support national institutions aimed at ensuring sustainability of capacity-building efforts.[107]

Other objectives are, inter alia, related to: undertaking systematic measures for providing technology support and capacity-building to ensure the effective participation of developing countries in negotiations concerning MEAs; ensuring integration of principles of transparency and accountability; providing specific gender-mainstreaming strategies in formulating relevant policies and promoting the participation of women in environmental decision-making to enhance UNEP's delivery of technology support and capacity-building to developing countries; and promoting, facilitating, and financing access to and support of environmentally sound technologies and corresponding know-how, especially for developing countries.[108]

Under the Bali Plan, each country is encouraged to identify its own needs in these areas to meet its environmental priorities.[109] The Plan was to be consistent with regional and subregional strategies as defined by regional and subregional bodies, and it encompassed promotion and support of South–South cooperation.[110] It especially underscored the importance of South–South cooperation and stressed the need to promote exchange of information, expertise, and experiences between the institutions of the South, aimed at strengthening those institutions and developing human resources.[111]

---

[105] UN Governing Council of the United Nations Environment Programme, *Note by the Executive Director: International Environmental Governance – Bali Strategic Plan for Technology Support and Capacity-Building*, 23 December 2004, UNEP/GC.23/6/Add.1 and Corr. 1, Annex [hereinafter Bali Plan].

[106] UN Governing Council of the United Nations Environment Programme, *Proceedings of the Governing Council/Global Ministerial Environment Forum at Its Twenty-Third Session*, February 21–25, 2005, UNEP/GC.23/11.

[107] Ibid, para. 3.

[108] Bali Plan, note 105, para. 3.

[109] Ibid, para. 10.

[110] Ibid, paras. 12–15.

[111] Ibid, para. 21.

148 *Global Environmental Governance and the South*

Since the adoption of the Plan by UNEP's Governing Council in 2005, the Governing Council and the UN General Assembly have frequently referred to it.[112] In December 2012, UNEP's Executive Director reported the body's contribution to promoting South–South cooperation through partnership building and the exchange of experiences, knowledge, and best practices between the South's experts and institutions.[113] However, notwithstanding some progress toward the Plan's implementation, due to a lack of resources it has yet to be fully implemented.

It should be noted that as early as 1972, when the UN General Assembly established the Environmental Secretariat, the Environmental Fund, and the UNEP Governing Council, the General Assembly recognized:

> [...] the need for processes within the United Nations system which would effectively assist developing countries to implement environmental policies and programmes that are compatible with their development plans and to participate meaningfully in international environmental programmes.[114]

But in the forty years since then, UNEP has never had adequate resources or capacity to meet the demands from developing countries.

As to the lack of sufficient financial resources, UNEP Executive Director Klaus Toepfer's 2001 report acknowledging this situation was mentioned previously.[115] Notwithstanding the establishment of the GEF, the Multilateral Fund for the Implementation of the Montreal Protocol, and the Global Mechanism of the Convention to Combat Desertification, these financing mechanisms are dispersed and not coordinated. For example, GEF, which primarily finances environmental projects related to MEAs, functions independently from financing operations of the World Bank, UNEP, and the United Nations Development Programme (UNDP), its three implementing agencies. In addition, each treaty body operates its own financing structures and many convention secretariats have their own institutional structures.

One of the emerging issues of special concern to the South – chemicals and waste management – provides an apt illustration of the problems faced by developing countries. The 2013 UNEP Year Book calls for "the need for better information

---

[112] See e.g. UN General Assembly, *Resolution Adopted by the General Assembly: Report of the Governing Council of the United Nations Environment Programme on Its Twenty-Sixth Session*, 22 December 2011, A/RES/66/203; UNEP Governing Council, Decision 26/2, GA resolution 67/213.

[113] UN Governing Council of the United Nations Environment Programme, *Report by the Executive Director: Progress Reports Mandated by the Governing Council at Previous Sessions*, 18-22 February 2013, UNEP/GC.27/15, para. 38. See generally paras. 36–56.

[114] UN General Assembly, *Resolution Adopted by the General Assembly: Institutional and Financial Arrangements for International Environmental Cooperation*, 15 December 1972, A/RES/27/2997.

[115] See UN Governing Council of the United Nations Environment Programme, note 25.

and sound management to minimize chemical risks."[116] The implications for developing countries are enormous; a shift in the production and use of chemicals continues from developed to developing countries, causing a growing economic and health burden, according to a 2012 UNEP report entitled "Global Chemicals Outlook Synthesis Report for Decision-Makers," which focuses especially on the challenges and opportunities for developing countries.[117]

Commenting on the report, UNEP Executive Director Achim Steiner said: "alerting [m]inisters and decision-makers on the most pressing challenges related to the changes and trends in the production and use of chemicals, the Global Chemicals Outlook makes a convincing economic case for investing in sound chemicals management."[118] And in the outcome document, *The Future We Want*,[119] heads of state and government expressed deep concern that "many countries, in particular least developed countries, lack the capacity for sound management of chemicals and waste throughout their life-cycle."[120]

They further called for additional efforts "to enhance work towards strengthening capacities, including through partnerships, technical assistance and improved governance structures." They encouraged "countries and organizations which have made progress toward achieving the goal of sound management of chemicals by 2020 to assist other countries by sharing knowledge, experience and best practices,"[121] and called for further progress across countries and regions aimed at filling the gaps in implementation of commitments.[122]

Acknowledging that "sustainable and adequate long-term funding is a key element for the sound management of chemicals and waste, in particular in developing countries,"[123] they welcomed the consultative process "initiated to consider the need for heightened efforts to increase the political priority accorded to sound management of chemicals and waste and the increased need for sustainable, predictable, adequate and accessible financing for the chemicals and waste agenda."[124]

Subsequently, in November 2012, in his report to UNEP's Governing Council on chemicals and wastes management,[125] the Executive Director stated that UNEP

---

[116] UNEP, note 8, p. 37. For the discussion, see pp. 37–51.
[117] See generally UNEP, "Global Chemicals Outlook: Toward Sound Management of Chemicals – Synthesis Report for Decision-Makers," September 5, 2012, www.unep.org [hereinafter GCO Synthesis Report].
[118] Ibid, p. 44.
[119] *The Future We Want*, note 59.
[120] Ibid, para. 215.
[121] Ibid.
[122] Ibid, para. 213.
[123] Ibid, para. 223.
[124] Ibid.
[125] UN Governing Council of the United Nations Environment Programme, *Report of the Executive Director: Chemicals and Wastes Management*, February 18–22, 2013, UNEP/GC.27/4.

150 Global Environmental Governance and the South

had initiated regional projects "to build the capacity of participating countries to tackle the human health and environmental challenges from the use of mercury in artisanal and small-scale gold mining."[126]

Then, in February 2013, the UNEP Governing Council/Global Ministerial Environmental Forum at its first universal session recognized "the significance of the findings of the Global Chemicals Outlook, which highlighted the significant increase in the manufacture and use of chemicals globally, their importance to national and global economies and the costs and negative effects on human health and the environment of unsound chemicals management and made recommendations for future action."[127] It also welcomed the outcome document's call "relating to the sound management of chemicals and waste and the reaffirmation of the aim to achieve by 2020 the sound management throughout their life cycle and of hazardous waste."[128]

Such, in short, is the impact of the lack of effective environmental governance on developing countries.

5. CONCLUSION

As discussed earlier in the chapter, the Summit of World Leaders at Rio+20 took promising steps to reform the international environmental governance architecture. Since then, the UN General Assembly has adopted implementation measures for strengthening and upgrading UNEP pursuant to the Rio+20 outcome document. The General Assembly established universal membership in UNEP's Governing Council and requested UNEP's support to developing countries for their full and effective participation in the GC meetings and hence in the decision-making process for formulating international environmental policy and agenda. It also supported increased financial resources for UNEP from the regular budget of the UN and urged donors to increase their contributions. This, indeed, is progress in reforming and strengthening the environmental dimension, which has often been described as the foundation of the economic and social dimensions of sustainable development.

Will this change in structure suffice to bring the much needed coherence and effectiveness to the fragmented international environmental governance system? To illustrate, the need is obvious to enhance synergies among MEAs, whether by clustering them, having their secretariats work together, or adopting any other means to accomplish this goal. Change in the UNEP structure alone is not likely to accomplish it. Specific mechanisms will have to be devised, such as joint

---

[126] Ibid, para. 40.
[127] UN Governing Council of the United Nations Environment Programme, *Decision 27/12: Chemicals and Waste Management*, February 18–22, 2013, UNEP/GC.27/17, para. 13.
[128] Ibid, para. 1.

financing; managerial and secretariat functioning among MEAs; and ensuring cooperation among their advisory bodies.[129]

Developing countries need to integrate their environmental sustainability priorities into development and economic policies. there is no mystery about what they need to achieve environmental sustainability: they need assistance to enable them to comply with, implement, and monitor their internationally agreed commitments, along with their own national priorities. All of this requires adequate finances, human resources, technical and policy expertise, and institutional capacity. To provide the needed assistance, the restructured UNEP must expand its regional offices and work even more closely than it currently does with the UNDP and UN country teams at the national level.

UNEP has certainly undertaken some commendable initiatives and projects, such as the joint UNEP/UNDP Poverty and Environment Initiative (PEI), a global program that supports countries in bringing poverty and environment linkages into the forefront of their national and subnational planning at all levels of projects.[130] PEI brings financial and technical support to environmental stakeholders as well as government decision-makers to properly manage the environment. The goal is to "bring about lasting institutional change and to catalyze key actors to increase investment in the pro-poor environment and natural resource management,"[131] and thus sustainable growth.

The Rio+20 outcome document was the necessary first step toward the needed reforms. Much work remains to be done, and the stakes could not be higher.

---

[129] See e.g. Wehrli, note 74.
[130] UN PEI, "About PEI," www.unpei.org/.
[131] Ibid.

7

Quest for International Environmental Institutions: Transition from CSD to HLPF

Bharat H. Desai and Balraj K. Sidhu

1. INTRODUCTION

In our quest for interdependence as well as coexistence and cooperation, there has been a remarkable effort to attain a balance between idealistic notions of international cooperation and practical constraints emanating from assertions of sovereignty as well as the national interests of states. Since the establishment of the United Nations (UN), international institutions have provided useful fora for international cooperation on a variety of issues. The growth of international organizations (specialized agencies) and commissions, as well as other programs within the UN system, are a testament to the craving for the *institutionalization* of international cooperation.

This web of institutionalization has also been spreading in the past four decades in the field of international environmental law. The international law-making process in the environmental field is generally shaped by international institutions, which act as catalysts, stimulators, and sometimes even active participants in the process. The growing corpus of multilateral environmental agreements (MEAs)[1] has significantly contributed to the proliferation of institutions specific to the field. They cater to regulatory requirements under the relevant MEAs. As compared to these regime-specific institutions, several specialized environmental institutions (IEIs), such as the United Nations Environment Program (UNEP),[2] Global Environment Facility (GEF),[3] and Commission on Sustainable Development (CSD or

---

[1] For a detailed examination of the phenomenon of MEAs, see B. H. Desai, *Multilateral Environmental Agreements: Legal Status of the Secretariats* (Cambridge: Cambridge University Press, 2010).

[2] See UN General Assembly, *Resolutions Adopted on the Report of the Second Committee: Institutional and Financial Arrangements for International Environmental Co-operation*, 15 December 1972, A/RES/2997 (XXVII).

[3] The Global Environment Facility was launched as a pilot project just prior to the 1992 Rio Earth Summit. However, due to issues concerning democratic structure and transparency, it

Commission)[4] – now replaced by the High-Level Political Forum on Sustainable Development (HLPF)[5] – have come onto the international scene.

As a plenary organ of the United Nations, the General Assembly has provided crucial impetus to the whole process, even as the technique of "global conferencing" has become increasingly popular.[6] In the environmental arena, the General Assembly has acted as "conductor of a grand orchestra" that provides political guidance to states, notwithstanding the inbuilt Charter limitation that it can only make "recommendations" through its resolutions.[7] The Assembly has adopted, often without a vote, resolutions comprising constituent instruments for specialized environmental institutions such as UNEP and CSD. The power and legitimacy of the Assembly's actions and initiatives are derived from the member states. The increasing interdependence among states has laid solid foundations for international environmental cooperation. This cooperation has also been facilitated by the changes in the post–World War II international legal order. With the surrender of old colonial possessions and the assertion of the principle of self-determination by nations and peoples, a host of new states appeared on the international horizon. This has required international law to adapt to the needs and aspirations of what has now come to be known as the global South. International law has evolved into a protector, to some extent, of the small and weak states, rather than serving only as the handmaiden of powerful states.[8]

> led to its restructuring in 1994. See Global Environment Facility, *Instrument for the Establishment of the Restructured Global Environment Facility* (Washington: Global Environment Facility, 2004).
>
> [4] See UN General Assembly, *Resolutions Adopted by the General Assembly: Institutional Arrangements to Follow up the United Nations Conference on Environment and Development,* 29 January 1993, A/RES/47/191[hereinafter General Assembly resolution 47/191].
>
> [5] See UN General Assembly, *Resolution Adopted by the General Assembly: Forum and Organizational Aspects of the High-level Political Forum on Sustainable Development,* 9 July 2013, A/Res/67/290.
>
> [6] See generally, P. M. Haas, "UN Conferences and Constructivist Governance of the Environment" (2002) 8 *Global Governance* 73.
>
> [7] There has been a great debate concerning the nature and legal effect of the resolutions of the UN General Assembly. It has been observed that the records of the United Nations Conference on International Organization (UNCIO) at San Francisco do not provide an authoritative interpretation of what exactly was envisaged by the use of the word "recommendations" in Articles 10–14 of the Charter. See F. B. Sloan, "The Binding Force of a 'Recommendation' of the General Assembly of the United Nations" (1948) 25 *British Yearbook of International Law* 7 at 10. See also R. Higgins, "The Development of International Law by the Political Organs of the United Nations" (1965) 59 *ASIL Proceedings* 116 at 117; W. Friedmann, "Preface," in O. Y. Asamoah (ed.), *The Legal Significance of the Declarations of the General Assembly of the United Nations* (The Hague: Martinus Nijhoff, 1966), p. v; S. M. Schwebel, "The Effect of Resolutions of the UN General Assembly on Customary International Law" (1979) 73 *ASIL Proceedings* 301.
>
> [8] For more detail see R. P. Anand, *Confrontation or Co-operation: International Law and the Developing Countries* (New Delhi: Banyan Publications, 1987), p. 267; R. P. Anand, *Asian States and the Development of a Universal International Law* (New Delhi: Vikas Publications, 1972), p. 245.

Recent developments reveal a growing trend of replacing outdated international institutions, as well as former commitments (such as Northern financial commitments that remain largely unfulfilled), with new structures and commitments. Key examples include the recent replacement of CSD with HLPF, as well as the ongoing negotiation of the Sustainable Development Goals that will supersede the Millennium Development Goals in 2015. These new structures and commitments are welcome steps to the extent that they address new development and environment challenges faced by the global South and place additional pressure on the global North to honor its commitments. This chapter examines the replacement of the CSD by the HLPF, and analyzes the potential of the HLPF to help bridge the historical faultlines with respect to sustainable development that continue to divide the global South and the North.

2. LOCATING THE GLOBAL SOUTH

The growing institutionalization is inextricably linked to an increase in the number of states on the international scene. The participation of a large number of states in multilateral environmental negotiations underscores their desire to be part of the law-making and institution-building processes, and has injected much needed legitimacy into international environmental law. Nevertheless, Southern states are often reluctant participants in a process which they perceive as of remote concern to them and as impinging upon their much cherished sovereignty. Multilateral environmental negotiations have also brought into sharp focus North–South conflicts over justice and equity, such as conflicts over climate change, access to genetic resources, and the hazardous waste trade.[9] International environmental institutions have been pressed to make their functioning democratic, transparent, and reflective of the needs and aspirations of disadvantaged Southern countries.

In order to meet pressing global and local environmental challenges, all states, both industrialized and developing, need to cooperate as closely as possible.[10] However, even after four decades, efforts to develop a sound environmental and developmental partnership between the North and the South have been hampered seriously by economic disparities and by differing perspectives on the link between

---

[9] See the following chapters in this book: Chapter 20, M. Burkett, "A Justice Paradox: Climate Change, Small Island Developing States, and the Absence of International Legal Remedy"; Chapter 21, E. A. Kronk Warner, "South of South: Examining the International Climate Regime from an Indigenous Perspective"; Chapter 23, R. Verchik and P. Govind, "Natural Disaster and Climate Change"; Chapter 10, R. Maguire and X. Jiang, "Emerging Powerful Southern Voices: Role of BASIC Nations in Shaping Climate Change Mitigation Commitments"; Chapter 12, Z. Lipman, "Trade in Hazardous Waste."

[10] See B. H. Desai, "Environment and Development: Making Sense of Predicament of the Developing Countries" (2013) World Focus 1 at 3. See also B. H. Desai, "Managing Ecological Upheavals: A Third World Perspective" (1990) 30(10) Social Science and Medicine 1065; B. H. Desai, "Threats to the World Eco-System: A Role for Social Scientists" (1992) 35(4) Social Science and Medicine 589.

environment and development.[11] Bridging the North–South divide is a prerequisite for any successful global environmental cooperation. Most of the people in the global South are acutely aware that there are "two worlds, two planets, two humanities." As Mahbubul Haq had prophesized, "our two worlds, while they touch and meet, they rarely communicate. And it is that process of real communication, real dialogue, that we have to encourage today in case we have to equip ourselves to deal with the problems of this world."[12]

In this context, the UN General Assembly took cognizance of the report of the World Commission on Environment and Development (WCED), *Our Common Future*, which recognized that environment and development are inextricably intertwined.[13] The General Assembly subsequently decided to convene[14] a United Nations Conference on Environment and Development (UNCED) in Brazil, to coincide with World Environment Day on 5 June 1992. The enabling resolution of the General Assembly set up a Preparatory Committee (PrepCom) to address an ambitious agenda. One of the important mandates given to the UNCED was:

> To promote the further development of international environmental law, taking into account the declaration of the United Nations Conference on the Human Environment, as well as the *special needs and concerns of the developing countries*, and to examine in this context the feasibility of elaborating general rights and obligations of States, as appropriate, in the field of the environment, and taking into account relevant existing international legal instruments.[15]

One of the basic objectives of the UNCED was to "promote the development or strengthening of appropriate institutions." Following the biggest ever coming together of heads of state and governments on an environment and development platform, the UNCED adopted a draft resolution on institutional arrangements. Essentially, it relied upon the chapter on international institutional arrangements[16] in Agenda 21 and endorsed the recommendation for the establishment of a high-level Commission on Sustainable Development (CSD).[17] The UNCED draft resolution IV[18] (for adoption by the Assembly) as well as the Secretary-General's

---

[11] See chapter 5, K. Mickelson, "The Stockholm Conference and the Creation of the South–North Divide in International Environmental Law and Policy."

[12] See Desai (2013), note 10 at 4.

[13] See UN Secretary-General, *Report of the World Commission on Environment and Development: Our Common Future (Brundtland Report)*, 4 August 1987, A/42/427, Annex.

[14] UN General Assembly, *United Nations Conference on Environment and Development*, 22 December 1989, A/RES/44/228, para.151 [hereinafter UNCED Resolution].

[15] Ibid, Part I, para. 15(d). [emphasis added]

[16] See chapter 38 of *Agenda 21* in N. A. Robinson (ed.), *Agenda 21: Earth's Action Plan* (New York: Oceana 1993), pp. 604–619.

[17] See generally T. Doyle, "Sustainable Development and Agenda 21: The Secular Bible of Global Free Markets and Pluralist Democracy" (1998) 19(4) *Third World Quarterly* 771.

[18] UN General Assembly, *Report of the United Nations Conference on Environment and Development*, 12 August 1992, A/CONF.151/26, Vols. I, II and Corr. I and III.

156 *Quest for International Environmental Institutions*

report[19] recommended that ECOSOC set up the proposed CSD as one of its functional commissions in accordance with Article 68 of the UN Charter in order to enhance international cooperation and rationalize intergovernmental decision-making capacity for the integration of environment and development issues. The Assembly took note of the UNCED report[20] and quickly adopted[21] the proposed draft resolution. This gave ECOSOC the mandate to establish the CSD as one of its functional commissions. The creation of this new UN environmental institution has been viewed by scholars as indirectly contributing to the dilution of UNEP's authority as regards institutionalized international environmental cooperation.[22]

In hindsight, Rio indirectly contributed to UNEP's weakening, while adding a CSD that failed to raise the profile of the international environmental agenda. The implications of this institutional weakness have become increasingly apparent, while the state of much of the environment has kept on deteriorating. The proliferation of environmental secretariats for individual conventions, located in different parts of the world, has highlighted the lack of a forceful central institution. Fragmentation and lack of coordination grew, rather than the integrated approach which has rightly become the hallmark of the modern environmental paradigm.[23]

By 1998, as part of an overall effort to reform the UN system, the UN Secretary-General established a Task Force on Environment and Human Settlements, which was headed by UNEP's then Executive Director, Klaus Töpfer.[24] The Töpfer task force identified as problematic the "proliferation"[25] of environmental institutions

---

[19] See UN General Assembly, *Resolution Adopted by the General Assembly: Institutional Arrangements to Follow Up the UNCED*, 22 December 1992, A/47/598 & Add.1.

[20] The General Assembly resolution 47/190 [22 December 1992] took note of the Report of the United Nations Conference on Environment and Development on 22 December 1992. It also decided to include in the provisional agenda of the forty-eighth session and subsequent sessions an item entitled "[i]mplementation of decisions and recommendations of the United Nations Conference on Environment and Development": see *Yearbook of the United Nations* (1992) 46, 675.

[21] General Assembly resolution 47/191, note 4.

[22] B. H. Desai, "UNEP: A Global Environmental Authority?" (2006) 36(3–4) *Environmental Policy and Law* 137 at 142. See also B. H. Desai, "UNEP: Coming Out of Coma" (2001) 9(2) *Down To Earth* 49.

[23] R. Dolzer, "Time for Change," *Our Planet: United Nations Environment Programme Magazine*, vol. 9, (1997) 19.

[24] In early 1998, the UN Secretary-General set up a high-level 21-member United Nations Task Force on Environment and Human Settlements. It comprised ministers, government advisors, and members of civil society as well as representatives from the UN Secretariat. It was headed by Klaus Töpfer, who was the executive director of UNEP. The task force presented its report to the Secretary-General on 15 June 1998. See UN Task Force on Environment and Human Settlements, *Report to the Secretary-General*, 15 June 1998 [on file with the author] [hereinafter Task Force Report]. See also UN General Assembly, *Report of the Secretary-General: Environment and Human Settlements*, 6 October 1998, A/53/463, Annex at 11–28; and UN General Assembly, *Report of the Secretary-General: Environment and Human Settlements*, 6 January 1999, UNEP/GC.20/ INF/13.

[25] There has been a proliferation of environmental institutions in the post-UNCED period, including the Commission on Sustainable Development [hereinafter CSD], the Inter-Agency

that changed the UN's environmental governance structure and led to the creation of institutional structures parallel to UNEP and CSD.[26] In the view of the Töpfer task force, this proliferation gave rise to "substantial overlaps, unrecognized linkages and gaps."[27] The task force expressed the concern that "these flaws are basic and pervasive. They prevent the UN system from using its scarce resources to best advantage in addressing problems that are crucial to the human future; harm the credibility and weight of the United Nations in the environmental arena; and damage the UN's working relationship with its partners in and outside of Government."[28]

A variety of reasons can be found for this multiplicity of institutions, including the growth in ad hoc, piecemeal and sectoral environmental law-making, which was represented by the MEAs; periodic efforts at "global conferencing"[29] on the environment and sustainable development, represented by the Rio and Johannesburg summits; and the creation of more permanent structures with mandates that overlap with UNEP's existing or potential mandate, such as the Global Environment Facility (GEF) and the Commission on Sustainable Development (CSD).

The proliferation of environmental institutions has often resulted in overlapping jurisdictions working at cross-purposes, turf wars, and wasted resources.[30] Cumulatively, these institutions have not succeeded in efficiently and effectively realizing the goal of international environmental cooperation. At the same time, the multiplicity of institutions has also made the task of coordination very difficult. In fact, lack of coordination has emerged as one of the major challenges of international environmental governance. Recent academic studies have concluded that the current system of international environmental governance is "not only too

---

Committee on Sustainable Development, and the Global Environment Facility. Similarly, considerable "greening" of other development-oriented international institutions can be seen within the UN system, such as the World Health Organization, the World Meteorological Organization, the Food and Agriculture Organization, the United Nations Educational, Scientific and Cultural Organization [hereinafter UNESCO], as well as the UN's regional economic commissions (the Economic Commission for Africa, the Economic Commission for Europe, the Economic Commission for Latin America and the Caribbean, the Economic and Social Commission for Asia and the Pacific, and the Economic and Social Commission for Western Asia).

[26] B. H. Desai, "Revitalizing International Environmental Institutions: The UN Task Force and Beyond" (2000) 40 *Indian Journal of International Law* 455 at 471.

[27] See UN Task Force on Environment and Human Settlements, *Report to the Secretary-General*, 15 June 1998 (on file with the author) at 29–30. See also, UN General Assembly, *Report of the Secretary-General: Environment and Human Settlements*, 6 October 1998, A/53/463, Annex at 85.

[28] Ibid.

[29] For details of a series of UN convened global conferences, see United Nations, *The World Conferences: Developing Priorities for the 21st Century* (New York: United Nations, 1997).

[30] B. H. Desai, "Strengthening International Environmental Governance: Some Reflections," in S. Kothari, I. Ahmad, and H. Reifeld (eds.), *The Value of Nature: Ecological Politics in India* (New Delhi: Konrad Adenauer Stiftung, Rainbow Publishers, 2000), pp. 221–242.

158   *Quest for International Environmental Institutions*

complicated, but it is also steadily getting worse."[31] In this context, the replacement of the CSD by the HLPF raises questions about the new institution's ability to effectively promote international cooperation and to address the needs and demands of the global South.

3. CURTAINS COME DOWN ON CSD

One of the primary functions[32] of CSD was to oversee the implementation of Agenda 21. It was firmly placed within the UN system as a functional commission of ECOSOC. As such, the task of the CSD was to assist, advise, and make recommendations and reports to the ECOSOC concerning the mandate assigned to it. In a sense, CSD remained primarily a monitoring body for the Rio mandate. It was also regarded as a "facilitator with the potential to harness public support to influence the course of governments and institutional programmes."[33] Over a period of twenty years, CSD has dealt with various contentious issues that saw deep fissures between the North and the South, including conflicts over environment and development and over finance and transfer of technology. Given the lack of coordination, it appears that the CSD has not achieved success in resolving these problems.

In addition, CSD's mandate generated uncertainty regarding the place of UNEP within the UN hierarchy. For instance, CSD duties included the following:

> To monitor progress in the implementation of Agenda 21 and activities related to the integration of environmental and developmental goals throughout the United Nations system through *analysis and evaluation of reports from all relevant organs, organisations, programmes and institutions of the United Nations system* dealing with various issues of environment and development, including those related to finance.[34]

Thus, CSD's mandate required UNEP to report to CSD. This presented an unusual legal situation wherein a subsidiary organ of the General Assembly was required to report to another subsidiary organ created by ECOSOC. It may not be a coincidence that international institutional arrangements under Agenda 21 first dealt with the mandate and structure of CSD, and only later recognized the need

---

[31] See United Nations University, *International Sustainable Development Governance: The Question of Reform: Key Issues and Proposals* (Tokyo: UNU/IAS, 2002), pp. 4–48.

[32] General Assembly resolution 47/191; as an instrument constituting CSD, see below note 34; ibid.

[33] R. Ismail, *Agenda 21 and the UN Commission on Sustainable Development*, Massachusetts Institute of Technology (Cambridge: MIT, 1997), p. 30.

[34] General Assembly resolution 47/191, para. 3 (a); see *Yearbook of the United Nations* (1992) 46, p. 676. Also see *Agenda 21: Programme of Action for Sustainable Development*, Rio de Janeiro, 14 June 1992, U.N. GAOR, 46th Sess., Agenda Item 21, A/Conf.151/26, chapter 38, para. 13(a) [hereinafter Agenda 21]. [emphasis added]

for an "enhanced and strengthened role for UNEP and its Governing Council."[35] This suggests that during the Rio process and its aftermath, the UN member states had less confidence in UNEP than in the high-profile CSD.

CSD comprised fifty-three members elected by the ECOSOC for a period of three years. It also had a small Bureau[36] consisting of a chairperson, three vice-chairpersons, and a rapporteur to be elected from each of the regional groups, as well as a High-Level Advisory Board of eminent persons having recognized expertise in the field. Though there has been representation in the Commission from Southern countries, this has not brought transparency and acceptability in its decisions. Consistent with Agenda 21, CSD could also provide for the effective participation of non-governmental organizations and other major groups[37] in its deliberations.

At the CSD-11[38] an agreement was reached on its future program and organization of work for a fifteen-year period from 2004–2005 to 2016–2017.[39] The program envisaged seven two-year cycles with a review year and a policy year. The review year would discuss specific themes while the policy year would adopt policy decisions. The Commission was able to complete only four cycles before it was replaced by the High-Level Political Forum (HLPF) on Sustainable Development.[40] Nevertheless, the platform provided by the Commission remained ineffective in resolving these problems and giving concrete future policy direction. The countries of the global South, particularly those located closer to Nairobi (UNEP) than New York (CSD) quickly lost confidence in the CSD. In addition, the member states found the two-year cycles of the CSD excessively rigid and an obstacle to addressing critical contemporary challenges as well as new or emerging issues. The CSD was criticized for being an environmental body, and for ignoring the social and economic dimensions of sustainable development. The cluttering of too many disparate issues often prevented in-depth discussions. As a result, the

---

[35] Agenda 21, note 34, paras. 11–13, 21–23. See also Desai (2006), note 22.

[36] See General Assembly resolution 47/191, note 4, para. 11.

[37] Agenda 21 has earmarked roles for various major groups consisting of women, children, and youth; indigenous people and their communities; non-governmental organizations; local authorities, workers, and trade unions; business and industry; the scientific and technological community; and farmers; see Agenda 21, note 34, chapters 24–32.

[38] The eleventh session of the CSD took place in New York on April 28–May 9, 2003. An estimated forty ministers, senior representatives of the governments, heads of the UN agencies, and other international organizations, as well as more than 900 representatives of non-governmental organizations and other stakeholders, took part in this session of CSD; see UN Economic and Social Council, Commission on Sustainable Development, *Report on the 11th Session*, 27 January 2003, E/2003/79; E/CN.17/2003/6.

[39] At its eleventh session the CSD decided that its multiyear program of work beyond 2003 would be organized on the basis of seven two-year cycles, with each cycle focusing on selected thematic clusters of issues.

[40] See UN General Assembly, *Draft Resolution Submitted by the President of the General Assembly: Format and Organizational Aspects of the High Level Political Forum on Sustainable Development*, 27 June 2013, A/67/L.72.

160   *Quest for International Environmental Institutions*

outcome of CSD negotiations was often disappointing. Consensus proved elusive, and pending issues remained unresolved.

CSD's task was generally based upon national reports to be submitted by the states. In fact, reporting was used as a tool to provide input for the annual sessions of the CSD. However, the task of reporting was "voluntary" for all the entities apart from states, such as multilateral financial institutions, convention secretariats, international organizations, and non-governmental organizations. The CSD's experience with national reports was mixed.[41] Most states regarded the submission of reports as a *voluntary exchange of information* rather than any obligation per se. The Commission was unable to secure Northern funding to establish a transparent and robust data-tracking mechanism or to enhance the reporting capacity of Southern countries. Even after twenty years of existence, the CSD had failed to develop any guidelines for reporting. The Commission did succeed in spurring the development of national sustainable development strategies (NSDS) as well as sustainable development indicators; however, it was unable to undertake any systematic monitoring and review of such measures. The lack of effective mechanisms to review country progress reports and commitments and the lack of data on compliance with its own decisions hampered the functioning of the CSD. As a result, the Commission's ability to monitor the implementation of the sustainable development agenda was highly compromised.

The mandate[42] given by the UN General Assembly was that CSD, as a preparatory committee,[43] undertake the comprehensive review and assessment of progress achieved in implementation of Agenda 21 (1992) and the Program for the Further Implementation of Agenda 21 (1997). In this capacity, as a PrepCom for the Johannesburg Summit, the CSD organized four meetings during a period of one year where the central thrust was the implementation of the commitments that

---

[41] The number of national reports received by CSD during initial years were as follows: 152 (1992), 53 (1994), 59 (1995), 41 (1996), and 97 (1997). The largest number of national reports came in the wake of the organization of UNCED and there were no reports in 1993 as it was CSD's organizing year. It is quite revealing as to how seriously countries have been taking the reporting task to annual CSD meetings; for details see F. Yamin, "The CSD Reporting Process: A Quiet Step Forward for Sustainable Development," in *Yearbook of International Co-operation on Environment and Development* (London: Earthscan Publications Ltd, 1998), p. 58.

[42] While adopting the resolution at its fifty-fifth session, the General Assembly expressed deep concern that "despite the many successful and continuing efforts of the international community since the Stockholm Conference and the fact that some progress has been achieved, the environment and the natural resource base that support life on earth continue to deteriorate at an alarming rate", see UN General Assembly, *Resolution Adopted by the General Assembly: Ten Year Review of Progress Achieved in the Implementation of the Outcome of the United Nations Conference on Environment and Development*, 5 January 2001, A/Res/55/199, paras. 2, 16, 17.

[43] UN General Assembly, *Report of the Commission on Sustainable Development Acting as a Preparatory Committee for the World Summit on Sustainable Development*, 20 June 2011, A/56/19.

states had already made, rather than undertaking any new commitments. The Johannesburg Plan of Implementation also underscored the need to undertake institutional reforms including promoting and facilitating partnerships involving governments, international organizations, major groups, and relevant stakeholders.[44]

During the twenty-year history of the CSD, Southern states came to rely upon it as a crucial dialogue forum on issues concerning not only sustainable development but also finance and transfer of technology. CSD became an important platform for raising awareness about sustainable development and contributed to "pushing the envelope" in the areas of forests, chemicals, energy, and oceans.[45] However, CSD was less successful at injecting the sustainability agenda into the national policy-making process. Southern countries became disenchanted with the Commission's inability to translate the commitments undertaken by Northern countries into reality.[46] The cumbersome agenda of the Commission also increased the difficulties encountered by the South, such as grappling with numerous and complex issues, undertaking and understanding scientific assessments, obtaining funding for domestic implementation, preparing national reports, and getting enough funding to attend CSD meetings in New York.[47] Moreover, CSD contributed to the fragmentation of the environmental and sustainable development agenda by further marginalizing the UNEP and undermining its authority to set the global environmental agenda.[48] Member states finally decided on 21 December 2012[49] that

---

[44] Ibid.

[45] CSD did help in forging a new partnership between the North and the South on the issue of forests. In order to build upon this, CSD initially launched an intergovernmental panel on forests (1995–1997), which was followed up by an intergovernmental forum on forests (1997–1999). It was decided to establish yet another forum to continue debate on the issue. CSD-8 handed over the matter of establishment of UN Forum on Forests (UNFF) to ECOSOC. In addition to this, CSD also recommended the General Assembly to establish a UN Informal Consultative Process on Oceans to review developments in ocean affairs: Report of the Secretary General to the Commission for Sustainable Development, *Oceans and Seas*, E/CN.17/1999/4 (8 February 1999). The recommendation of the second session of CSD also led to processes to establish the Rotterdam Convention on Prior Informed Consent (PIC) and the Stockholm Convention on Persistent Organic Pollutants (POPs).

[46] See generally UN General Assembly, *Report of the Secretary-General: Lessons Learned from the Commission on Sustainable Development*, 26 February 2013, A/67/757.

[47] F. Dodds, R. Gardiner, D. Hales, M. Hemmati, and G. Lawrence, "Post-Johannesburg: The Future of the Commission on Sustainable Development," Stakeholder Forum Paper, No. 9 (November 2002).

[48] B. H. Desai, "The Quest for a United Nations Specialized Agency for the Environment" (2012) 101(2) *The Roundtable: The Commonwealth Journal of International Affairs* 167. See also Desai (2006), note 22.

[49] See UN General Assembly, *Resolution Adopted by the General Assembly: Implementation of Agenda 21, the Programme for the Further Implementation of Agenda 21 and the Outcomes of the World Summit on Sustainable Development and of the United Nations Conference on Sustainable Development*, 21 December 2012, A/RES/67/203.

162 *Quest for International Environmental Institutions*

the CSD would have its last session immediately prior to the convening of the first meeting of the HLPF on sustainable development in order to ensure a smooth institutional transition. CSD-20, which was designated as the last session of the Commission, took place on Friday 20 September 2013.[50] This effectively brought the curtain down on a UN entity whose continuation no one was probably any longer willing to support.

4. ADVENT OF THE HIGH-LEVEL POLITICAL FORUM

In the run-up to Rio+20, discussions on the sustainable development framework focused on whether to transform the CSD into a Sustainable Development Council (SDC) or to abolish it altogether.[51] The governments eventually decided to close down the Commission and replace it with a High-Level Political Forum (HLPF). The HLPF is a hybrid body that will operate under the auspices of both the Economic and Social Council (ECOSOC) and the General Assembly. The establishment of the HLPF on Sustainable Development was called for by the UN Conference on Sustainable Development[52] (UNCSD or Rio+20) in June 2012 in its outcome document, *The Future We Want*.[53] In fact, the president of the sixty-seventh session of the General Assembly asked the ambassadors from Brazil and Italy to conduct informal consultations on the format and organizational modalities of HLPF.[54] These consultations began in January 2013 and concluded with the adoption of Resolution 67/290 on 9 July 2013.[55]

Though the new body will replace the CSD, it draws upon the strengths, experiences, resources, and inclusive participation modalities of the CSD.[56] The HLPF will start its work where the CSD left off. Nevertheless, it has been specially

---

[50] See UN Economic and Social Council, *Draft Resolution Submitted by the Vice-President of the Council, Martin Sajdik (Austria): Conclusion of the Work of the Commission on Sustainable Development*, 22 July 2013, E/2013/L.38.

[51] M. Ivanova, "Reforming the Institutional Framework for Sustainable Development," Outreach, September 2013.

[52] The United Nations Conference on Sustainable Development – or Rio+20 – took place in Rio de Janeiro, Brazil on June 20–22, 2012. The General Assembly via resolution 64/236 of 24 December 2009 decided to organize the United Nations Conference on Sustainable Development at the highest possible level in 2012, as well as its resolution 66/197 of 22 December 2011. See United Nations, *Report of the United Nations Conference on Sustainable Development*, June 20–22, 2012, A/CONF.216/16.

[53] The outcome document of the United Nations Conference on Sustainable Development is: UN General Assembly, *Resolution Adopted by the General Assembly: The Future We Want*, 27 July 2012, A/RES/66/288, Annex.

[54] See Letter of the President of the General Assembly to Permanent Representatives of Brazil and Italy sent on 18 December 2012, available at www.un.org/en/ga/president/67/letters/pdf/rio_20_18_dec_2012.pdf.

[55] The General Assembly adopted resolution 67/290 on 9 July 2012 on the format and organizational aspects of the high-level political forum on sustainable development, available at www.un.org/ga/search/view_doc.asp?symbol=A/67/L.72&Lang=E.

[56] Ibid, Preamble, para. 3.

created to address the shortcomings of the current system. The HLPF has been designed to operate at the highest political level and therefore will be convened at the level of heads of state and government every four years under the aegis of the UN General Assembly. Its participation will be universal, as opposed to the fifty-three-member CSD. In intervening years, the HLPF will be convened for eight days under the auspices of ECOSOC and include a three-day ministerial segment. Thus, it seems, HLPF also does not have any independent capacity (like the CSD). On the contrary, it has two masters – UNGA and ECOSOC – that will control its agenda. This hybrid organizational structure raises several issues that need to be addressed. There are concerns that this new arrangement could impede efforts to give coherent and focused treatment to the agenda for sustainable development. A universal model of high-level decision-making has the advantage of widespread legitimacy, but has a limited capacity for deliberation and diffuses peer pressure. The limited frequency of high-level meetings makes it more difficult to address new and current issues and to maintain a flexible and dynamic agenda. The HLPF will need to balance its mandate to "provide political leadership" and "agenda-setting" for sustainable development with its close organizational and political relationship to ECOSOC and the UN General Assembly.[57]

The HLPF has been specifically created to integrate, "in a holistic and cross-sectoral manner at all levels," the "three dimensions" of sustainable development – economic, social, and environmental. The scope of the sustainable development agenda is quite broad and the field has grown manifold since the first UN Conference on Human Environment (Stockholm, 1972). Since the UNCED, sustainable development is being pursued at global, regional, and national levels. This quest for sustainable development is guided by explicit commitments that have been adopted by the international community. These commitments include those contained in Agenda 21, the Programme for the Further Implementation of Agenda 21 (PFIA21), the Johannesburg Plan of Implementation (JPOI), and the outcomes of the Millennium Declaration. Southern countries have been concerned that the full and effective translation of these commitments into tangible sustainable development outcomes will require the mobilization of sufficient resources to provide access to adequate means of implementation. The primary means of implementation identified in Agenda 21, PFIA21, and JPOI are financing, technology development and transfer, capacity development, globalization and trade, regional integration, and South–South cooperation. In order to ensure that these resources are provided, the HLPF will need to effectively advance the concerns of the global South at all levels of the UN and beyond.

---

[57] See S. Bernstein, "The Role and the Place of the High-Level Political Forum in Strengthening the Global Institutional Framework for Sustainable Development," (2013), http://sustainabledevelopment.un.org.

164 *Quest for International Environmental Institutions*

At the same time, the institutional challenge that lies before the HLPF is that sustainable development informs the mandate of many of the UN agencies, regional organizations, the World Bank, and the WTO, as well as a wide variety of partnerships and relatively autonomous non-state or hybrid governance systems. In this situation, it is a challenging task for the HLPF to provide leadership, push its mandate at all levels of the UN, and also take visible actions to assuage the growing disenchantment in the global South by, for example, realizing the North's commitments to reach the United Nations target of 0.7 percent of gross national product (GNP) for Overseas Development Assistance (ODA).

Another noteworthy aspect of the new institutional incarnation is the inclusion of "other relevant stakeholders" in the HLPF mandate.[58] It implies that stakeholders other than those mentioned in Agenda 21 could now participate in the meetings of HLPF. The more inclusive language in the HLPF's mandate highlights the challenge of ensuring inclusive and fair access and the need to engage and attract the widest possible range of relevant stakeholders if the HLPF is to attain legitimacy and provide effective leadership in the field.[59] Furthermore, bringing more transparency and clarity, the constitutive General Assembly resolution allows major groups and other stakeholders to: (i) attend all official meetings of the forum, (ii) have access to all official information and documents, (iii) intervene in official meetings, (iv) submit documents and present written and oral contributions; (v) make recommendations, and (vi) organize side events and round tables.[60]

The new forum appears to be sensitive to the needs and concerns of the global South. It envisages providing adequate space and time for discussion of the sustainable development challenges faced by the Southern countries. In order to facilitate the participation of representatives of least developed countries, their travel expenses will be covered by the United Nations' regular budget.[61] Meanwhile, the UNCSD outcome document – *The Future We Want* – has mobilized more than 700 voluntary commitments with an estimated value in excess of US $500 billion.[62] These commitments have now grown to more than 1,400, with a value greater than US$600 billion – or nearly 1 percent of global annual GDP.[63] The financial commitments are particularly important because UNCSD figures

---

[58] UN General Assembly, *Resolution Adopted by the General Assembly: Forum and Organizational Aspects of the High-level Political Forum on Sustainable Development*, 9 July 2013, A/Res/67/290.

[59] The constituent instrument mentions "other relevant stakeholders", ibid, para. 15. However, paragraph 16 indicates that these could include private philanthropic organizations, educational and academic entities, persons with disabilities, volunteer groups and other stakeholders active in areas related to sustainable development.

[60] Ibid, para. 15.

[61] Ibid, para. 25.

[62] See, Rio+20 United Nations Conference on Sustainable Development, "Rio+20 Voluntary Commitments," http://www.uncsd2012.org.

[63] A. Cutter. J. Lingan, J. Cornforth, S. Bonham, J. Scherr, J. Romano, C. Phipps, and S. Reynolds, "Fulfilling the Rio+20 Promises: Reviewing Progress Since the UN Conference

indicate that in the coming years the cost burden on Southern countries for implementing the sustainable development agenda will be enormous.[64] Thus, the HLPF, in order to fulfill its assigned mandate, must provide the impetus on financing for sustainable development.

5. FUTURE ROLE FOR THE GLOBAL SOUTH

As UNGA President John Ashe succinctly put it in his closing remarks at the HLPF inaugural meeting:

> [t]he decision of Rio+20 to establish a high-level political forum is a powerful step in mainstreaming sustainable development in the post-2015 agenda. The Forum will be a home for the international community to address and coordinate the entirety of sustainable development issues. As guardian of sustainability, it can provide a platform for leaders to reflect on today's priorities, not in isolation but holistically.[65]

The inaugural meeting of the HLPF (24 September 2013), under the auspices of the General Assembly, presented an opportunity to open a new chapter in sustainable development governance.[66] With the participation of presidents, prime ministers, and vice presidents, the event became a "high-level" meeting.[67] The fact that environment ministers were not the only ones in the room reflected a significant evolution from the CSD approach. Speakers included ministers of foreign affairs, development cooperation, multilateral affairs, irrigation and water resources management, social development, and trade, leading to more of a balance between the three dimensions of sustainable development.

The presence of the president of the World Bank Group and the managing director of the IMF provided additional gravitas, and demonstrated the importance that the financial institutions will lend to the process. The heads of state and government, ministers and other leaders articulated a number of concrete proposals on the role of the HLPF, as follows: (i) it should include stakeholders, (ii) it should emphasize accountability, (iii) it should review the post–2015 development agenda and the implementation of the sustainable development goals (SDG), and (iv) it should examine issues from scientific and local

---

on Sustainable Development; Stakeholder Forum and Natural Resources Defense Council," www.stakeholderforum.org/fileadmin/files/rio-20-report.pdf

[64] See Rio+20 United Nations Conference on Sustainable Development, note 62.

[65] "Summary of the First Meeting of the High Level Political Forum on Sustainable Development: 24 September 2013," Earth Negotiations Bulletin, 33(1), 27 September 2013, p. 9.

[66] The President of the General Assembly convened the inaugural meeting of HLPF in 2013. See *Summary of the First Meeting of the High Political Forum on Sustainable Development*, UN GAOR 68, 68th Sess., agenda item 19(a), 13 November 2013. See A/68/588.

[67] "Summary of the First Meeting of the High Level Political Forum on Sustainable Development: 24 September 2013," note 65, p. 9.

166 *Quest for International Environmental Institutions*

perspectives. The Group of 77 and China also put forward the expectation of the global South from the new forum that:

> the High-level Political Forum should provide political leadership to further enhance international cooperation on sustainable development. The Forum should address sustainable development challenges from the prism of poverty eradication as its overarching objective. It should comprehensively implement the Rio+20 mandates and follow-up on the fulfilment of commitments, especially those related to the means of implementation: finance, technology and capacity building.[68]

The new forum could be said to reflect a new chapter in the story of sustainable development governance. The HLPF's increased political weight, compared to the CSD, is especially relevant to the extent to which it could present a unified and independent voice for sustainable development. In particular, a clear division of labor between the environment and sustainable development institutions will be important to avoid perpetuating the dynamic that led to the institutional reform in the first place. Without clear roles and responsibilities, there is a danger of overlap, duplication, and turf wars among the new HLPF, a reformed ECOSOC, UNEP with universal membership, and other UN institutions and multilateral environmental agreements.

Meanwhile, it also becomes incumbent upon the global South to effectively use this platform, which ensures universal participation and could be quite high-profile in practice. The global South as a bloc would need to intensify and accelerate the work already done under the auspices of the CSD in the new HLPF. Southern countries need to understand and provide meticulous evidence to persuade the North to take their longstanding demands about technology, finance, and capacity-building seriously. The principle of common but differentiated responsibilities needs to form the heart of any future decisions taken by the new forum. At the same time, Southern countries need to roll up their sleeves and participate in the marathon environmental law-making process – including intense work, calculated ambiguity, continuous law-making, round-the-year meetings, funding, and factoring scientific input and technological feasibility. Southern countries should actively engage in consultation and coordination on major international issues and try to act in unison to safeguard their collective rights and interests. They also need to take an active part in the formulation of international economic, financial, and trade rules, have a greater say in international affairs and in decision-making, and seek better competition conditions and greater space for their development. The HLPF could also launch South–South partnerships and triangular

---

[68] See The Group of 77, "Statement on Behalf of the Group of 77 and China by H. E. J. V. Bainimarma, Prime Minister of Republic of Fiji, Chair of the Group of 77 at the Inaugural meeting of the High-Level Political Forum on Sustainable Development (New York, 24 September 2013)," www.g77.org.

cooperation to achieve shared goals.[69] As developing countries grow in their economic and political strength, they could resort to more and more South–South cooperation on trade, investment, science and technology, infrastructure, health, and education. Thus the Southern countries should, in light of the circumstances and their own needs and in the spirit of equality and mutual benefit, constantly expand the channels of, create new models for, and add new content to their cooperation.[70] When Southern countries engage in triangular cooperation with their Northern counterparts, Northern financial strength should be combined with Southern countries' ability to provide cheaper and more appropriate technology as well as lower-cost consultancy, training, and other services.

The new HLPF should make accountability a hallmark, and employ tools for enhanced multi-stakeholder participation. At the same time, with rights come obligations and an implicit challenge for the stakeholders: The need to help develop and implement sustainable development policies.

6. CONCLUSION

The growth of international environmental institutions is indeed remarkable in the annals of institutionalized intergovernmental cooperation. These institutional structures reflect the interdependence of states in the quest to protect the global environment and achieve sustainable development. HLPF's appearance on the radar of the sustainable development agenda is a largely welcome and timely step that will fill the void left by its predecessor, the CSD. There are genuine expectations that the HLPF will spearhead and promote the internalization of sustainable development at all the levels. However, the way forward for HLPF may not be very easy, as the legacy and experience of the CSD underscores. Only time will provide an answer to the concern that the penchant at UN conferences to create continual new institutional structures leads to "institutional clogging." In view of the complex challenges that are expected to remain for the foreseeable

---

[69] The post-2015 development agenda will require more effective, strengthened, and improved modes of development cooperation to support its implementation. South–South cooperation is not a substitute for but rather a complement to North–South cooperation, which will remain the primary form of cooperation between countries of the North and South. *Triangular Cooperation* (TC) involves two or more developing countries in collaboration with a third party, typically a developed country government or organization, contributing to the exchanges with its own knowledge and resources. South–South and triangular cooperation can vary greatly in approaches and modalities, yet their importance has increased manifold since the year 2000 and are set to be an important auxiliary tool beyond 2015 for catalyzing implementation efforts amongst developing countries. See UN Economic and Social Council, *Report of the Secretary-General: Trends and Progress in International Development Cooperation*, 10 June 2010, E/2010/93.

[70] See United Nations Conference on Technical Cooperation among Developing Countries, *Buenos Aires Plan of Action for Promoting and Implementing Technical Co-operation among Developing Countries*, http://ssc.undp.org.

future, HLPF will have to tread the difficult path to sustainable development with caution and pragmatism. Meanwhile, in the midst of the seventeen-year-long debate (since the 1997 Nairobi Declaration) on international environmental governance (IEG), including the quest for a "specialized agency" for the environment (such as UN Environment Protection Organization),[71] states will need to streamline priorities, provide adequate resources, and define expectations from the new institutions. New institutions will need to be guided by the realities on the ground and by consensus among the sovereign states through a democratic and transparent process. It remains to be seen how the HLPF will meet the challenge of sustainable development governance. The HLPF presents an opportunity for the global South to ensure that the environment and development equilibrium promotes all three pillars of sustainable development, and advances the interests of its citizens.

---

[71] For a detailed discussion and the proposal for a UN "specialized agency" for the environment called the UN Environment Protection Organization (UNEPO) see Desai (2012), note 48. See also B. H. Desai, *International Environmental Governance: Towards UNEPO* (Leiden: Brill Nijhoff, 2014).

PART II

Selected International Environmental Law Examples

8

Human Rights, the Environment, and the Global South

Louis J. Kotzé

1. INTRODUCTION

Reflection on the relationship between human rights and the environment has never been more urgent. Today, the advent of a new, much less stable, less predictable, and less harmonious geological epoch, called the Anthropocene, is signaling the fact that humanity is blindly, but determinedly, venturing into unchartered territory as far as the Earth system is concerned.[1] Rockström et al. refer to this unchartered territory as an "unsafe operating space" for humans in the Earth system.[2] There is a realization that we are crossing those planetary boundaries that represent the dynamic biophysical "space" of the Earth system within which humanity has to date evolved and thrived.[3] This space is made up of humans as ecological agents, of non-human living entities, and of the many interconnected Earth-system processes that interact in complex ways to sustain life on Earth. Within this space, humans assume a decidedly central position. We carry a tremendous responsibility of care for each other and for non-human life, for while humans are undoubtedly destroyers of ecosystems, we are also in a unique position to respond to and change the toxic behaviors that paradoxically make us so powerful and yet at the same time so vulnerable in relation to the biosphere.[4]

One of the responses to counter environmental degradation and safeguard human interests, that encapsulates both our vulnerability and our power in complex social–ecological systems, is human rights. This is because, perhaps more

---

[1] P. J. Crutzen and E. F. Stoermer, 'The "Anthropocene"' (2000) 41 *Global Change Newsletter* 17.
[2] Johan Rockström et al., "Planetary Boundaries: Exploring the Safe Operating Space for Humanity" (2009) 14(2) *Ecology and Society* 1.
[3] Ibid at 5.
[4] A. Grear, "The Vulnerable Living Order: Human Rights and the Environment in a Critical and Philosophical Perspective" (2011) 2(1) *Journal of Human Rights and the Environment* 23.

172   *Human Rights, the Environment, and the Global South*

than any other legal construct, human rights are intimately "close" to us, acting both as an expression of our "humanness" and of our vulnerability, as a justificatory base for our power, and at the same time as limits to that power. The environment–human rights nexus is obvious: "[h]uman rights are grounded in respect for fundamental human attributes such as dignity, equality and liberty. The realization of these attributes depends on an environment that allows them to flourish."[5]

It is amid this interdependence and a culture of economic globalization, exploitation and neoliberal "development" that disparities, differentiation, and injustices in the biosphere come starkly to the fore. Within the biosphere, people are situated differently, and the disparity between the global North and the global South has never been more obvious. A range of terms that has been fashioned around cultural, sociopolitical, economic, and environmental considerations characterize the rich diversity of our kaleidoscopic world. These include the "global South" and the "global North," which denote, among other things, "a world divided by a poverty curtain."[6] While some question the legitimacy and usefulness of such categorizations, which often work toward (mostly Northern) hierarchical conceptions and ideological representations, these terms are routinely common to the discourse, and categorization seems to remain "an endless pursuit."[7] To be sure, the North–South categorization has some political merit to the extent that it is used to mobilize collective responses from the global South on issues such as humanitarian intervention and aid, trade, labor, and the environment (including the human rights aspects of these issues),[8] as well as to emphasize the urgency and the need to refocus the world's attention on the squalor that often besets the global South. It is the global South where "[m]illions of human beings live in crushing impoverishment, ill-health, political disempowerment and under conditions of profound social exclusion and growing risk [where] environmental degradation presently has a direct and disproportionate impact on the rights of the most vulnerable human beings and communities."[9]

Unsurprisingly, these realities forge various connections and overlap between the North–South discourse and the human rights–environment discourse.[10] Notably, the issue of environmental (in)justice (in an intra- and intergenerational as well as

---

[5] UN General Assembly, *Report of the Independent Expert on the issue of Human Rights Obligations Relating to the Enjoyment of a Safe, Clean, Healthy and Sustainable Environment, John H. Knox*, 24 December 2012, A/HRC/22/43, para. 10.

[6] J-P. Thérien, "Beyond the North–South Divide: The Two Tales of World Poverty" (1999) 20 (4) *Third World Quarterly* 723 at 723.

[7] C. McFarlane, "Crossing Borders: Development, Learning and the North: South Divide" (2006) 27(8) *Third World Quarterly* 1413 at 1413.

[8] Ibid at 1414.

[9] A. Grear, "Editorial: Where Discourses Meet" (2010) 1(1) *Journal of Human Rights and the Environment* 1 at 1.

[10] D. Gillies, *Between Principle and Practice: Human Rights in North–South Relations* (Montreal: McGill-Queen's University Press, 1996).

a North–South sense) permeates current global realities.[11] But because the idea of global procedural and substantive justice is abstract and vague, and thus unable to provide clear guidance to bridging the North–South divide, it remains "merely a non-legal (moral) idea,"[12] requiring more concrete legal constructs such as human rights, which themselves are based on the notion of justice, to help bridge this divide.

Against this background, this chapter seeks to discuss human rights and the environment from the perspective of the global South with particular emphasis on Africa, India, and South America. Human rights in the environmental context can take many forms including the right to a healthy or clean environment and the rights of nature, as well as related substantive (e.g. right to life), procedural (e.g. access to justice, information, and administrative justice), socioeconomic (e.g. rights to water and housing), and political rights (e.g. right to freedom of association) that are variously situated in the international, regional, and domestic spheres.[13] In the interest of consistency, unless specifically indicated otherwise, the chapter uses environmental rights as a compilation term for all the foregoing rights, including the rights of nature. The chapter commences with a brief description of the general evolution of environmental rights globally and then turns to focus on the developments of law in the global South. It concludes by highlighting some environmental rights decisions by regional and domestic courts in the global South.

2. EVOLUTION OF ENVIRONMENTAL RIGHTS

The emergence of environmental rights is well-trodden scholarly ground.[14] The 1948 Universal Declaration of Human Rights does not contain an environmental right and, importantly for the North–South discourse, the Declaration was primarily driven by Northern powers, excluding Southern voices to a great extent. The nexus between human rights and the environment was only formally recognized in 1972 at the Stockholm Conference on the Human Environment, which was a decidedly more inclusive process, thus eliciting greater North–South consensus on the relationship between human rights and the environment.[15] Principle 1 of the Stockholm Declaration states:

[11] C. G. Gonzalez, "Environmental Justice and International Environmental Law," in S. Alam, M.J.H. Bhuiyan, T.M.R. Chowdhury, and E. J. Techera (eds.), *Routledge Handbook of International Environmental Law* (London: Routledge, 2013).

[12] U. Beyerlin, "Bridging the North-South Divide in International Environmental Law" (2006) 66 *Zeitschrift für ausländisches öffentliches Recht und Volkerrecht* 259 at 273.

[13] L.H. Leib, *Human Rights and the Environment: Philosophical, Theoretical and Legal Perspectives* (Leiden: Martinus Nijhoff Publishers, 2011), pp. 3–4.

[14] D. Anton and D. Shelton, *Environmental Protection and Human Rights* (Cambridge: Cambridge University Press, 2011), pp. 151–224.

[15] Although the UN General Assembly, in *Problems of the Human Environment*, 3 December 1968, Resolution 2398(XXIII), expressed concern about "the consequent effects [of environmental degradation] on the condition of man, his physical, mental and social well-being, his dignity and his enjoyment of basic human rights, in developing as well as developed countries."

174   *Human Rights, the Environment, and the Global South*

> Man has the fundamental right to freedom, equality and adequate conditions of life, in an environment of a quality that permits a life of dignity and well-being, and he bears a solemn responsibility to protect and improve the environment for present and future generations.[16]

Ten years later, the World Charter for Nature explicitly referred to the right of access to information and the right to participate in environmental decision-making.[17] Although the Stockholm Declaration did not proclaim a substantive right to environment, following this first momentous phase of the global environmental movement, the 1992 Earth Summit in Rio set the scene for more robust development of a comprehensive framework for human and environmental rights (although the Rio Declaration also did not adopt an explicit environmental right), which was no doubt also influenced by the (UN) General Assembly's formal recognition in 1986 of the relationship between the quality of the human environment and the enjoyment of basic human rights.[18]

While no domestic constitution provided for environmental rights in the 1970s (with the exception of Yugoslavia), the trickledown effect of these global markers led to the steady emergence of many constitutional and broader statutory initiatives to entrench environmental rights in domestic legal systems. It has been estimated that at present three quarters of the world's constitutions (the majority of which are situated in the global South) provide for some form of environmental rights and obligations.[19] Regionally, the incorporation of provisions recognizing the right to a healthy environment in national constitutions mirrors this trend: Africa, thirty-two; Asia, fourteen; Europe, twenty-eight; Latin America, sixteen; and the Caribbean, two.[20]

From 1990 to 1994 the UN Special Rapporteur on Human Rights and the Environment issued several reports further reinforcing the growing political importance of human rights in the environmental domain.[21] A set of Draft Principles on Human Rights and the Environment was appended to her final report.[22]

---

[16] *Declaration on the United Nations Conference on the Human Environment*, Stockholm, 16 June 1972, UN Doc. A/Conf.48/14/Rev. 1(1973); 11 ILM 1416 (1972).

[17] *World Charter for Nature*, New York, 28 October 1982, GA Res. 37/7, UN GAOR, 37th Sess., Supp. No. 51, at 17, UN Doc. A/37/51 (1982); 22 ILM 455 (1983) at paras. 15, 16, 23.

[18] UN General Assembly, note 15.

[19] D. Boyd, *The Environmental Rights Revolution: A Global Study of Constitutions, Human Rights, and the Environment* (Vancouver: UBC Press, 2012), p. 47.

[20] Ibid, pp. 45–77.

[21] Earthjustice, "Environmental Rights Report: Human Rights and the Environment," 2005, http://earthjustice.org, pp. 2–3.

[22] Geneva, 16 May 1994, E/CN.4/Sub.2/1994/9, Annex I (1994). Notably, the final report of the Special Rapporteur mentions the North–South divide as a characteristic of environmental problems, thus acknowledging that human rights could play a role in ameliorating some of the North-South divide's problems that arise in the environmental rights context: F. Z. Ksentini, *Review of Further Developments* 6 July 1994, E/CN.4/Sub.2/1994/9, UN ECOSOC, 46th Sess., Agenda Item 4.

Unfortunately, the Human Rights Commission did not adopt or endorse the draft principles. During the World Summit on Sustainable Development in 2002, the relationship between human rights and the environment was again acknowledged,[23] and the outcome document of the UN Conference on Sustainable Development (Rio+20) affirmed the existence of environmental rights.[24] The growing global recognition of environmental rights probably led to the UN Human Rights Council's (UNHRC) decision to appoint an Independent Expert on Human Rights and Environment in 2012. A Preliminary Report[25] and Mapping Report[26] were published by the independent expert, John Knox, detailing the importance of the relationship between human rights and the environment. During its twenty-fifth session in March 2014, the UNHRC recognized the progress and important work that the independent expert has been doing and confirmed "that human rights law sets out certain procedural and substantive obligations on States in relation to the enjoyment of a safe, clean, healthy and sustainable environment."[27] This could be the single most important step to cement the foundations for the formalization of environmental rights in the global environmental law and governance architecture.

However, to date there is no universally applicable hard law instrument that explicitly provides for an environmental right,[28] nor has such a right been accepted into the corpus of customary international law.[29] It is only regionally that treaties provide for environmental and related rights. While the European Convention for the Protection of Human Rights and Fundamental Freedoms of 1950[30] does not

---

[23] UN, *Report of the World Summit on Sustainable Development*, August 26–September 4, 2002, A/CONF.199/20, resolution 2, Annex (Plan of Implementation of the World Summit on Sustainable Development).

[24] UN Rio+20 Conference on Sustainable Development, *The Future We Want*, 20–22 June 2012, A/CONF/.216/L.1, para. 39.

[25] UN General Assembly, note 5.

[26] United Nations Mandate on Human Rights and the Environment, "Annual Report to the Human Rights Council," 6 March 2014, http://ieenvironment.org.

[27] UN Human Rights Council, *Resolution on Human Rights and the Environment*, 24 March 2014, A/HRC/25/L.31.

[28] S. J. Turner, *A Global Environmental Right* (New York: Routledge, 2013).

[29] At most, environmental entitlements are inferred indirectly from the provisions of other human-focused but environment-related treaties, such as the *International Covenant on Economic, Social and Cultural Rights*, New York, 16 December 1966, in force 3 January 1976, 993 UNTS 3; [1976] ATS 5; 6 ILM 360 (1967), arts. 7(b), 10(3), 12; the *Convention on the Rights of the Child*, New York, 20 November 1989, in force 2 September 1990, 1577 UNTS 3; [1991] ATS 4; 28 ILM 1456 (1989), art. 24; and the *Convention concerning Indigenous and Tribal Peoples in Independent Countries*, Geneva, 27 June 1989, in force 5 September 1991, 72 ILO Official Bull. 59; 28 ILM 1382 (1989), arts. 2, 6, 7, 15. See D. Shelton, "Human Rights and the Environment: Substantive Rights," in M. Fitzmaurice, D. Ong, and P. Merkouris (eds.), *Research Handbook on International Environmental Law* (Cheltenham: Edward Elgar, 2010), pp. 266–267.

[30] Rome, 4 November 1950, in force 3 September 1953, ETS 5; 213 UNTS 221.

176   *Human Rights, the Environment, and the Global South*

provide for an explicit environmental right,[31] environmental entitlements are raised and protected through the assertion of other protected rights.[32] Also, the United Nations Economic Commission for Europe (UNECE) Convention on Access to Information, Public Participation in Decision-making and Access to Justice in Environmental Matters, 1998[33] embodies the right "to live in an environment adequate to … health and well-being."[34] In doing so, the Convention significantly strengthened procedural environmental rights, as it also did by allowing communications to be brought before its Compliance Committee by one or more members of the public concerning any party's compliance with the Convention.[35] Additionally, the European Court of Human Rights is very active in protecting environmental rights through related rights such as the right to privacy (Article 8), as can be seen through its rich jurisprudence on human rights in the environmental context and the recent publication of a manual on human rights and the environment by the Council of Europe.[36] Other regional instruments include the American Convention on Human Rights with its San Salvador Protocol of 1988, which states that "[e]veryone shall have the right to live in a healthy environment and to have access to basic public services,"[37] and Article 3(2) of the *Asian Human Rights Charter* of 1998, providing for the right to a "clean and healthy environment."[38] The Arab Charter on Human Rights of 2004 also includes a right to a healthy environment as part of the right to an adequate standard of living that ensures well-being and a decent life.[39] Article 24 of the African (Banjul) Charter on Human and Peoples' Rights (African Charter) states: "[a]ll peoples

[31] Council of Europe, *Manual on Human Rights and the Environment*, 2nd ed. (Council of Europe Publishing, 2012).

[32] O. Pedersen, "European Environmental Human Rights and Environmental Rights: A Long Time Coming?" (2008) 21 *The Georgetown International Environmental Law Review* 73.

[33] Aarhus, 28 June 1998, in force 30 October 2001, 2161 UNTS 447; 38 ILM 517 (1999) [hereinafter Aarhus Convention].

[34] The Aarhus Convention is applicable to EU and non-EU states (if the latter countries ratify it) and its impact could thus be much broader than the EU region. See, among the many publications on the Aarhus Convention, S. Kravchenko, "The Aarhus Convention and Innovations in Compliance with Multilateral Environmental Agreements" (2007) 18(1) *Colorado Journal of International Environmental Law and Policy* 1.

[35] United Nations Economic Commission for Europe, "Communications from the Public," www.unece.org.

[36] O. Pederson, note 32. For a summary of environment-related cases, see European Court of Human Rights, "Environment-Related Cases in the Court's Case Law," December 2012, www.echr.coe.int.

[37] Additional Protocol to the American Convention on Human Rights in the Area of Economic, Social and Cultural Rights, San Salvador, 17 November 1988, in force 16 November 1999, OAS Treaty Series No 69; 28 ILM 156 (1989), art. 11(1).

[38] *Our Common Humanity: Asian Human Rights Charter, a People's Charter* (Hong Kong: Asian Human Rights Commission and Asian Legal Resource Centre, 1998).

[39] League of Arab States, *Arab Charter on Human Rights*, 22 May 2004, in force 15 March 2008, reprinted in (2005) 12 *International Human Rights Report* 893, art. 38. Notably, neither the Asian Human Rights Charter nor the Arab Charter on Human Rights has enforcement mechanisms.

shall have the right to a general satisfactory environment, favorable to their development."[40] The Charter is the first regional instrument to explicitly recognize an environmental right.

In sum, then, while the UN has been slow to adopt an explicit environmental right globally, this right is included in soft law instruments, and more explicitly in regional treaties. Some are less optimistic about the influence of these developments, stating that it "hardly amounts to a strong momentum towards a new legal framework."[41] While that may be true, one should not discount the political currency that these supranational developments have created for efforts to recognize environmental rights globally. in addition, these developments are providing the legal and justificatory basis for the all-important entrenchment of environmental rights where it really matters: in a large number of (especially the global South's) domestic legal systems. They are also having a profound effect through a process of transnational law-making, including nationalization of international environmental law, the interjurisdictional transplantation of laws, the regionalization of national environmental laws, and the nationalization of regional environmental laws.[42] For example, Boyd indicates that the 1976 Portuguese formulation of a "right to a healthy and ecologically balanced environment" is now found in twenty-one other constitutions and that the Supreme Court of India's decisions on environmental rights have significantly influenced courts in Bangladesh, Pakistan, Sri Lanka, Uganda, and Kenya.[43]

3. PERSPECTIVES ON ENVIRONMENTAL RIGHTS IN THE GLOBAL SOUTH

The rise of the environmental rights movement in the global South must be understood in a very specific context that can be sketched with reference to interlinked political and socioeconomic events, economic globalization practices, and their consequent environmental impacts. What are some of these aspects within which the emergence of environmental rights could be usefully framed?

---

[40] Organization of African Unity, *African Charter on Human and Peoples' Rights (Banjul Charter)*, 27 June 1981, in force 21 October 1986, CAB/LEG/67/3 rev. 5, 21 ILM 58 (1981) [hereinafter African Charter]. In addition, the *Protocol to the African Charter on Human and Peoples' Rights on the Rights of Women in Africa*, Addis Adaba, 11 July 2003, in force 25 November 2005, CAB/LEG/66.6 (13 September 2000) states that women "shall have the right to live in a healthy and sustainable environment" (Article 18), including "the right to fully enjoy their right to sustainable development" (Article 19).

[41] C. Gearty, "Do Human Rights Help or Hinder Environmental Protection?," (2010) 1(1) *Journal of Human Rights and the Environment* 7 at 19.

[42] L. J. Kotzé, *Global Environmental Governance: Law and Regulation for the 21st Century* (Cheltenham: Edward Elgar, 2012), pp. 278–292.

[43] Boyd, note 19, p. 108.

3.1 Colonialism

It starts with the familiar story of colonization. While this has also been prevalent in Latin America and Asia, Africa has been subject to the most widespread colonization practices by Northern powers.[44] Many years of colonial oppression have left their mark on most African countries, in some instances inflicting wounds that will not heal and leaving scars that are all but impossible to conceal. "Drain of wealth" colonial policies coupled with distorted educational practices negatively impacted on human capital accumulation, and societies have been generated that, to this day, are characterized by dysfunctional institutions, rent-seeking elites, and ethnic conflict, often leading to grave human rights abuses and unsustainable developmental practices.[45] In the absence of solid democratic systems, the rule of law, independent judiciaries, fully competent administrative and institutional structures, and human capital to develop and enforce environmental laws, governments are prone to corruption and collusion, leaving colonized countries exposed to exploitation.[46] During colonial reign, colonized countries' abundant oil and mineral resources have been exploited to fill the coffers of the colonizers and, more recently, to bankroll the wars raging on the African continent.[47] For many countries, political independence following the postcolonial era did not necessarily mean economic independence, and some countries in the global South remain in the grip of poverty, isolation, and marginalization.[48]

A subtle form of neocolonialism today exacerbates these conditions. With richer nations increasingly driving the expansion of resource extraction in the world's peripheral nations as their own resources deplete or become economically unviable to exploit,[49] countries such as China invest heavily in the global South to gain access to scarce resources in an effort to ensure human, and especially energy, security in their home territories. While Northern governments drive these neocolonialist practices, it is foreign extraction–based corporations that act

---

[44] G. Bertocchi and F. Canova, "Did Colonization Matter for Growth? An Empirical Exploration into the Historical Causes of Africa's Underdevelopment" (2002) 46 *European Economic Review* 1851.

[45] Ibid at 1853.

[46] M. Faure and W. du Plessis, "Introduction," in M. Faure and W. du Plessis (eds.), *The Balancing of Interests in Environmental Law in Africa* (Pretoria: Pretoria University Law Press, 2011), p. xxi.

[47] UN Security Council, "Letter Dated 12 November 2012 from the Chair of the Security Council Committee Established Pursuant to Resolution 1533 (2004) Concerning the Democratic Republic of the Congo Addressed to the President of the Security Council," 15 November 2012, S/2012/843.

[48] See e.g. N. Nunn, "Historical Legacies: A Model Linking Africa's Past to its Current Underdevelopment" (2007) 83 *Journal of Development Economics* 157.

[49] J. T. Roberts, "Globalizing Environmental Justice," in R. Sandler and C. P. Pezzullo (eds.), *Environmental Justice and Environmentalism: The Social Justice Challenge to the Environmental Movement* (Cambridge: MIT Press, 2007), pp. 285–286.

as conduits to channel benefits back to the home territories, often leaving grave environmental destruction, socioeconomic decay and human rights abuses in their wake, while managing to escape liability.[50] The cumulative result is that dispossessed societies are forced to use the few resources they have in an unsustainable way; an explosive situation which, as the eastern part of the Democratic Republic of the Congo suggests, often leads to armed conflict.[51] In the global South the environment–human rights interface is arguably more closely intertwined with core issues of equity, survival, peace and security, human capital development, and defunct governance practices. These issues render environmental rights particularly pertinent in the global South because they revolve around the need to survive in poor socioeconomic conditions with limited access to life-sustaining resources that must ensure dignity and personal integrity; they point to the prevalence of environmental injustices in societies that are rife with discrimination, exclusion, and marginalization (pre-1994 South Africa being the most notorious example); and they relate to the need to ensure good governance (as the counterpoint to corruption and exclusionary decision-making).[52]

3.2 Orientation of Rights

The conflict between ecocentrism and anthropocentrism is very evident in the environmental rights arena.[53] Most formulations of environmental rights are decidedly anthropocentric.[54] As a result, so too are the central tenets of the environmental rights frameworks focused on humans. For example, Article 24 of the African Charter sets a "general satisfactory environment" as a condition for human development. Reiterating the wording of Article 24 of the African Charter, Article 53 of the Constitution of the Democratic Republic of the Congo, 2006 states: "[e]very person has the right to a healthy environment, one which is favorable to their integral development."[55] While the general trend in the global South is toward anthropocentricism, there are some exceptions. It is particularly

[50] Ibid, p. 286; Human Rights Council, *Report of the Special Representative of the Secretary-General on the Issue of Human Rights and Transnational Corporations and Other Business Enterprises, John Ruggie; Guiding Principles on Business and Human Rights: Implementing the United Nations "Protect, Respect and Remedy" Framework*, 21 March 2011, A/HRC/17/31. See chapter 16, S. H. Baker, "Project Finance and Sustainable Development in the Global South."

[51] Human Rights Council, note 50, Annex.

[52] International Environment House, *Human Rights and the Environment: Proceedings of a Geneva Environment Network Roundtable* (United Nations Environment Programme, 2004), p. 5.

[53] L. Feris, "Constitutional Environmental Rights: An Under-Utilised Resource" (2008) 24 *South African Journal on Human Rights* 29 at 30–33.

[54] See generally Faure and du Plessis (eds.), note 46.

[55] K. B. Kennedy, "The Environmental Law Framework of the Democratic Republic of the Congo and the Balancing of Interests," in Faure and Du Plessis (eds.), note 46, pp. 97–98.

180 *Human Rights, the Environment, and the Global South*

noteworthy that Ecuador's constitutional experiment incorporates a more eco-centric objective by granting nature a "right to exist, persist, maintain and regenerate its vital cycles, structure, functions and its processes in evolution."[56] This right-formulation is the first of its kind at the constitutional level and is exemplary of one of the possible manifestations that an ecocentric right might take.[57] Its application in practice and interpretation by courts, however, remains to be tested.

3.3 *Customary/Indigenous Laws*

Elements of traditional customary/indigenous laws related to environmental rights are sometimes adopted in countries in the global South. For example, many African countries have rich experience in traditional conservation practices, ecological and human adaptive capacity, land-use practices, and biodiversity conservation.[58] Mostly derived from local and indigenous communities,[59] these experiences could enrich national laws in a bottom-up way, create specific obligations on the state in respect of protecting environmental rights, or at the very least guide judicial interpretation of environmental rights that also takes cognizance of indigenous practices and laws. One example is the environmental right in the Kenyan Constitution of 2010 which provides that the state, in giving effect to the environmental right, must "protect and enhance intellectual property in, and indigenous knowledge of, biodiversity and the genetic resources of the communities."[60]

Perhaps more illustrative of the customary law influence on environmental rights in Africa is the belief held by some commentators that "culture" is a consideration (possibly even a central pillar) of sustainable development, and consequently also a part of environmental rights.[61] For Church,[62] culture reflects the "total way of life of a community" and as such it cannot be separated from environmental rights; this is an idea that is reinforced by the UN Educational Scientific and Cultural Organization's (UNESCO) Universal Declaration on

---

[56] Constitution of Ecuador, art. 71.

[57] Boyd, note 19, p. 70. Other examples include the recent Ecuadorean court decision protecting the Vilcabamba River (2011) (see The Rights of Nature, "The First Successful Case of the Rights of Nature Implementation in Ecuador," http://therightsofnature.org) and the recent recognition in New Zealand of the rights of the Whanganui River (2012) (see News Watch National Geographic, "A River in New Zealand Gets a Legal Voice," September 4, 2012, http://newswatch.nationalgeographic.com).

[58] A. du Plessis, "South Africa's Constitutional Environmental Right (Generously) Interpreted: What is in it for Poverty?" (2011) 27(2) *South African Journal of Human Rights* 279 at 288.

[59] J. P. Brosius, A. L. Tsing, and C. Zerner, "Representing Communities: Histories and Politics of Community-based Natural Resource Management" (1998) 11(2) *Society and Natural Resources: An International Journal* 157.

[60] Art. 69(1)(c).

[61] A. du Plessis and C. Rautenbach, "Legal Perspectives on the Role of Culture in Sustainable Development" (2010) 13(1) *Potchefstroom Electronic Law Journal* 26.

[62] J. Church, "Sustainable Development and the Culture of Ubuntu" (2012) 45(3) *De Iure* 511 at 521.

Cultural Diversity, 2001.[63] In the South African context, the cultural identity and practices of communities are merged into the environmental right by the phrase "[e]veryone has the right to an environment that is not harmful to their health or *well-being*."[64] Well-being is considered as including a spiritual and psychological meaning; it also incorporates into the protective realm of the environmental right the idea embedded in African tradition that "personal identity cannot be separated from the environment as a whole which encompass [sic] the natural, socio-cultural, physical and spiritual environment."[65] This idea is expressed by the South African concept of Ubuntu (or *Umuntu ngumuntu ngabantuu*), which means "a person is a person through other persons," thus reflecting a holistic rather than a narrow perspective of (human) relationships. It is also a social ethic that "prescribes that members of a community should care for one another and where one suffers all suffer."[66] In this way Ubuntu reinforces the idea that the South African environmental right applies collectively, and not individually, to "everyone" for the sake of fostering harmony in any collective reality such as the Earth system.

3.4 *Unique Environmental Conditions and Problems*

Every country has a distinctive set of environmental conditions that could lead to differing visions and formulations of environmental rights. For example, Africa is a continent that is prone to severe droughts. Thus, Article 44 of the Constitution of Ethiopia, 1995 provides that "[e]veryone has the right to a clean and healthy environment" and that "[e]veryone who is uprooted from the place of his residence by virtue of programmes undertaken by the Government, or one whose livelihood has been affected shall have the right to receive adequate monetary or other alternative compensation, including transfer, with assistance, to another locality."[67] While it may seem peculiar to include the latter provision as part of an environmental right, it recognizes that Ethiopia is particularly prone to droughts and ecological disasters, thus creating a constitutional avenue to resettle and compensate people in the event of crop failures or other environmental disasters.[68] Thus, environmental rights are formulated to be much more responsive to prevailing

---

[63] 2 November 2001, www.unesco.org, art 1. Annex 11(14), read with the United Nations Declaration on the Rights of Indigenous Peoples, New York, 13 September 2007, GA Res. 61/295, UN Doc. A/RES/61/295 (Sept. 13, 2007); 46 I.L.M. 1013 (2007).

[64] Constitution of the Republic of South Africa, 1996, s. 24 [emphasis added].

[65] Church, note 62 at 524. See also S v *Makwanyane* 1995 6 BCLR 665 (CC) at par 308. In this case, Ubuntu was used by the Constitutional Court to interpret the Western-oriented human right to dignity (section 10 of the SA Constitution). In doing so, the Constitutional Court abolished the death penalty. Ubuntu has not yet been applied in the environmental context by the courts.

[66] Church, note 62 at 528.

[67] M. B. Tekle, "The Scope of Citizens' Environmental Rights Protection under Ethiopian Law" in Faure and Du Plessis (eds.), note 46, pp. 116–117.

[68] Ibid, p. 117.

182 *Human Rights, the Environment, and the Global South*

conditions and problems in the country. Another example is the environmental right entrenched in the Constitution of Kenya of 2010. Article 42 provides that "[e]very person has the right to a clean and healthy environment which includes the right to have the environment protected for the benefit of present and future generations through legislative and other measures."[69] These measures are detailed in Article 69, including the obligation on the state to "work to achieve and maintain a tree cover of at least ten per cent of the land area of Kenya."[70] This novel provision is indicative of the fact that in many African countries industrial pollution is not the main concern; rather, deforestation and desertification is.[71] A final example is Article 95(1) of the Constitution of the Republic of Namibia, 1990. While it is not formulated as an environmental right, this principle of state policy, recognizing that Namibia is often used as a dumping ground for waste by governments and corporations in the global North, provides that the State shall actively promote and maintain the welfare of the people by adopting policies aimed at, among other things:

> [M]aintenance of ecosystems, essential ecological processes and biological diversity of Namibia and utilization of living natural resources on a sustainable basis for the benefit of all Namibians, both present and future; in particular, the Government shall provide measures against the dumping or recycling of foreign nuclear and toxic waste on Namibian territory.[72]

4. JUDICIAL INTERPRETATION AND ENFORCEMENT

Judicial interpretation of environmental rights is particularly helpful to elucidate these rights. The following section discusses how the African Commission of Human Rights (ACHR) has interpreted the environmental and associated rights of the Charter. It also discusses some of the decisions of the Inter-American Commission on Human Rights (IACommHR) and the Inter-American Court of Human Rights (IACHR) that relate to countries in the global South. Finally, important domestic decisions on environmental rights in the global South are discussed briefly.

4.1 The ACHR

The SERAC communication[73] of 2001 before the ACHR is the first ever to pronounce on a supranational environmental right, and it exemplifies the complex

---

[69] R. Kibugi, "Development and the Balancing of Interests in Kenya," in Faure and Du Plessis (eds.), note 46, p. 173.
[70] Ibid, pp. 171–174.
[71] Faure and Du Plessis (eds.), note 46, p. xxi.
[72] A. Louw, "The Balancing of Interests in Environmental Law in Namibia," in Faure and Du Plessis (eds.), note 46, pp. 349–353.
[73] *The Social and Economic Rights Action Center and the Center for Economic and Social Rights v Nigeria*, ACHPR, No. 155/96 [hereinafter Communication] (accessed 27 November 2013).

set of interlinked issues that prevail in the global South's environmental rights paradigm.[74] The communication was brought to the ACHR as an *actio popularis* by SERAC and the Centre for Economic and Social Rights (CESR). According to the communication, the military government of Nigeria had been directly involved in oil production through the state-owned Nigerian National Petroleum Company (NNPC), and these operations caused environmental degradation and health problems among the Ogoni people resulting from environmental contamination.[75] In its decision, the ACHR held that the African Charter imposes on African governments positive (working toward purposive obligations to realize) and negative (working protectively against infringements and toward the limitation of government power) obligations to respect, protect, promote, and fulfill the entire range of human rights contained in the Charter.[76] The communication alleged the violation of, among others, Articles 16 (right to health),[77] 21 (right to free disposal of wealth and resources),[78] and 24 (environmental right) of the African Charter.[79] Recognizing the close linkage between the environmental right and other related rights such as health, the ACHR found that, collectively viewed, the rights in question are closely linked to other economic and social rights in so far as the environment affects the quality of life and safety of the individual.[80] The environmental right, more specifically, "imposes clear obligations upon a government. It requires the state to take reasonable [sic] and other measures to prevent pollution and ecological degradation, to promote conservation, and to secure an ecologically sustainable development and use of natural resources."[81] But in addition to these positive obligations, the environmental right also obliges governments to desist from directly threatening the health and environment of their citizens, and it asks governments to respect the environmental right through non-interventionist conduct. It further obliges governments not to condone practices, policies, or legal measures that violate individual integrity.[82] All the foregoing obligations relate to the substantive components of the environmental right.

[74] See the discussion in section 3.
[75] Communication, note 73, para. 10.
[76] Ibid, paras. 43–48.
[77] Article 16 states, inter alia, "[e]very individual shall have the right to enjoy the best attainable state of physical and mental health [...] States Parties [...] shall take the necessary measures to protect the health of their people."
[78] Article 21 provides: "[a]ll peoples shall freely dispose of their wealth and natural resources [...] States parties [...] shall undertake to eliminate all forms of foreign economic exploitation particularly that practiced by international monopolies so as to enable their peoples to fully benefit from the advantages derived from their national resources."
[79] The others were Articles 2 (non-discrimination), 4 (respect of life and personal integrity), 14 (property right), and 18 (rights of the family).
[80] Communication, note 73, para. 51.
[81] Ibid, para. 52. Arguably, the ACHR meant to use the phrase "reasonable *legislative* and other measures:" a more common formulation as is exemplified by s. 24 of the Constitution of the Republic of South Africa, 1996.
[82] Ibid, para. 52.

184   *Human Rights, the Environment, and the Global South*

The ACHR further stated that in order for governments to comply with Articles 16 and 24, they must facilitate independent scientific monitoring of threatened environments; require and publish environmental and social impact studies prior to any major industrial development; undertake appropriate monitoring; provide information to those communities exposed to hazardous materials and activities; and provide meaningful opportunities for individuals to be heard and to participate in the development decisions affecting their communities.[83] These obligations relate to the procedural obligations required to fulfill the foregoing substantive elements of the environmental right.

Recognizing that Article 21 was adopted in the Charter as a reaction to the "aftermath of colonial exploitation [that] has left Africa's precious resources and people still vulnerable to foreign misappropriation,"[84] the ACHR, relying on European Court of Human Rights and IACHR jurisprudence,[85] confirmed that governments have a duty to protect their citizens not only through appropriate legislation and effective enforcement, but also by protecting them from damaging acts that may be perpetrated by private parties, including foreign oil companies.[86] The ACHR concluded that the "Nigerian Government has given the green light to private actors, and the oil companies in particular, to devastatingly affect the well-being of the Ogonis. By any measure of standards, its practice falls short of the minimum conduct expected of governments, and therefore, is in violation of Article 21."[87] The Commission subsequently found the Nigerian government liable for violation of all the alleged human rights provisions and appealed to the government "to ensure protection of the environment, health and livelihood of the people of Ogoniland," by stopping all attacks on Ogoni communities; conducting an investigation into human rights violations; ensuring adequate compensation to victims of the human rights violations; ensuring that appropriate environmental and social impact assessments are prepared for any future oil development; and providing information on health and environmental risks.[88]

Unfortunately, because the ACHR's decisions are neither binding nor enforceable, very little has changed on the ground – a reality that deeply questions the practical utility of enforcement mechanisms in human rights instruments, especially in Africa.[89] On a more positive note, judging by its decision in the SERAC communication, the ACHR as the regional protector of human rights in Africa clearly indicates that the environmental right is justiciable and that its

---

[83] Ibid, para. 53.

[84] Ibid, para. 56.

[85] Ibid, para. 57 and Inter-American Court of Human Rights, *Velàsquez Rodríguez* v *Honduras* 19 July 1988, Series C, No. 4.14; and European Court on Human Rights *X and Y* v *Netherlands* 91 ECHR (1985) (Ser. A).

[86] Communication, note 73, para. 57.

[87] Ibid, para. 58.

[88] Ibid, para. 69.

[89] Boyd, note 19, p. 104.

realization hinges on governments' responsibilities to fulfill, protect, promote, and respect the substantive and procedural obligations stemming from the right; its deduction of positive state obligations is remarkable.[90] Importantly, these obligations stem from both substantive and procedural environmental rights-related entitlements and guarantees, which suggests the importance of a mutually supportive approach where the substantive component is reinforced by the procedural and *vice versa*.[91] Moreover, the willingness of the ACHR to "borrow" Northern jurisprudence (from Europe and the Americas) exemplifies an encouraging trend where historically isolated African governance and judicial institutions are now becoming more open to external influences through emerging transnational legal processes.

4.2 *The IACHR and IACommHR*

The IACommHR's general approach to environmental protection has been one recognizing that "conditions of severe environmental pollution, which may cause serious physical illness, impairment, and suffering on the part of the local populace, are inconsistent with the right to be respected as a human being."[92] Also, the Commission's recommendations that have been issued relate to the protection of indigenous peoples' rights. For example, in 1985 the IACommHR recognized the link between environmental quality and the right to life by determining that a highway and authorization for the exploitation of natural resources in Brazil violated the rights of the Yanomani Indians to health, life, liberty, personal security, and free movement.[93] More recently in *Maya Indigenous Community of the Toledo District v Belize*, in 2004, the IACommHR determined that:

> [...] the State's failure to respect the communal right of the Maya people to property in the lands that they have traditionally used and occupied has been exacerbated by environmental damage occasioned by certain logging concessions granted in respect to those lands, which in turn has affected the members of those communities.[94]

---

[90] U. Beyerlin and T. Marauhn, *International Environmental Law* (Oxford: Hart Publishing, 2011), p. 396.

[91] A. du Plessis, "The Balance of Sustainability Interests from the Perspective of the African Charter on Human and Peoples' Rights," in Faure and du Plessis (eds.), note 46, p. 43.

[92] Inter American Commission of Human Rights, *Report on the Situation of Human Rights in Ecuador*, OEA/Ser.L/V/II.96, doc. 10 rev. 1, 92 (1997); D. Shelton, "Environmental Rights and Brazil's Obligations in the Inter American Human Rights System" (2009) 40 *The George Washington International Law Review* 733 at 750.

[93] *Yanomami Case*, Case 7615, Inter-Am. C.H.R. Res. No. 12/85, OEA/Ser.L/V/II.66, doc. 10, rev. 1, 24 (1985).

[94] IACommHR, Case 12.053, Report No. 40/04, OEA/SerL/V/II 122 Doc 5 rev 1 (2004) 727, para. 148.

186 *Human Rights, the Environment, and the Global South*

As with the Commission, the IACHR's decisions mostly revolved around indigenous peoples' rights and none of its decisions directly involved environmental rights. The most recent example is the case of *Saramaka People* v *Suriname*.[95] The case involved the government of Suriname's decision to grant mining and logging concessions in the territory of the Saramaka people.[96] The Court had to determine, inter alia, which natural resources found on the traditional territory were essential for the survival of the Saramaka way of life and thereby protected under Article 21 (the right to property) of the American Convention on Human Rights. In doing so, it proposed three safeguards which it deemed essential: (1) the state must ensure the effective participation of the members of the Saramaka people with respect to any development, investment, exploration, or extraction plan within Saramaka territory; (2) the state must guarantee that the Saramakas will receive a reasonable benefit from any such plan within their territory; and (3) the state must ensure that no concession will be issued within Saramaka territory unless a prior environmental and social impact assessment is performed.[97] The IACHR found that the concessions granted by the state failed to comply with the necessary safeguards and hence violated the right to property of the Saramaka people.[98] It awarded US$600,000 as compensation for environmental damage and destruction of lands and resources traditionally used by the Saramakas.

4.3 *Country Examples*

Boyd[99] estimates that of the thirty-two African nations that have entrenched an environmental right in their constitutions, very few have used the judiciary to enforce this right. South Africa – with its revered post–apartheid Constitution – on the other hand has an impressive and growing body of environmental rights jurisprudence.[100] In *BP Southern Africa (Pty) Ltd* v *MEC for Agriculture, Conservation and Land Affairs*,[101] the High Court stated that:

> [...] environmental rights requirements should be part and parcel of the factors to be considered [when assessing whether to permit construction of a fuel station] without any *a priori* grading of the rights. It will require a balancing of rights where competing interests and norms are concerned ... The balancing of environmental interests with justifiable economic and social development is to be conceptualised

[95] *Case of the Saramaka People* v *Suriname*, 2007 Inter-Am. C.H.R. (ser. C) No. 172 (Nov. 28, 2007) [hereinafter *Case of the Saramaka People* v *Suriname*].
[96] Shelton, above note 92 at 764–768.
[97] *Case of the Saramaka People* v *Suriname*, para. 129.
[98] Ibid, para. 158.
[99] Boyd, above note 19, p. 149.
[100] L. J. Kotzé, "The Judiciary, the Environmental Right and the Quest for Sustainability in South Africa: A Critical Reflection" (2007) 16(3) *Review of European Community and International Environmental Law* 298.
[101] 2004 (5) SA 124 (WLD).

well beyond the interests of the present living generation. This must be correct since [the environmental right] requires the environment to be protected for the benefit of 'present and future generations'.[102]

The Court added:

> By elevating the environment to a fundamental justiciable human right, South Africa has irreversibly embarked on a road, which will lead to the goal of attaining a protected environment by an integrated approach, which takes into consideration, *inter alia*, socio-economic concerns and principles.[103]

The contribution that the Court has made in relation to an understanding of Section 24 lies in: its confirmation of socioeconomic factors in the relationship between people and the environment; its view that the entire environmental right must be interpreted in the context of intergenerational equity and within the context of sustainable development; its emphasis on the positive duties that the state incurs in terms of the environmental right; its recognition that constitutional environmental protection requires the balancing of different rights and interests; and its confirmation that the environmental right elevates the status of sustainable development to the constitutional level.[104] This is significant to the extent that it sends an important signal to government and non-governmental entities that environmental considerations must as a matter of constitutional injunction be afforded equal recognition in any development decisions.

The Constitution of the Republic of Cameroon, 1996, provides as a constitutional principle that "every person shall have a right to a healthy environment. The protection of the environment shall be the duty of every citizen. The State shall ensure the protection and improvement of the environment." This constitutional principle, which does not form part of any bill of rights, incorporates the notion of shared responsibility by placing a duty on the state and "every citizen" to protect the environment. The right therefore applies in favor of, but can also be raised against, natural persons; legal persons, including companies; and the state; and even though it is "only" a constitutional principle, all preambular commitments of

---

[102] Ibid, paras. C–D, p. 143. While the balancing of interests test has not been explicitly applied in the SERAC Communication, it has been done to some extent in the *Maya Indigenous Community* case, where the IACommHR stated: "development activities must be accompanied by appropriate and effective measures to ensure that they do not proceed at the expense of the fundamental rights of persons who may be particularly and negatively affected, including indigenous communities and the environment upon which they depend for their physical, cultural and spiritual well-being." *Maya Indigenous Community of the Toledo District v Belize*, IACommHR, Case 12.053, Report No. 40/04, OEA/SerL/V/II 122 Doc 5 rev 1 (2004) 727, para. 150.

[103] Paras B–D, p. 144.

[104] L. J. Kotzé and A. du Plessis, "Some Brief Observations on Fifteen Years of Environmental Rights Jurisprudence in South Africa" (2011) 3(1) *Journal of Court Innovation* 101 at 115.

188   *Human Rights, the Environment, and the Global South*

the Constitution are enforceable and justiciable by virtue of Article 65.[105] This feature has been used successfully in *FEDEV* v *China Road and Bridge Corporation*[106] by a non-governmental organization to bring a public interest suit to compel the China Road and Bridge Corporation to comply with the country's environmental impact assessment procedures. While courts did not pronounce on the environmental right in the Constitution of the Republic of Ghana, 1992, the Constitution extends the State's duty to protect the environment to outside state borders, by providing "[t]he State shall take appropriate measures needed to protect and safeguard the national environment for posterity; and shall seek co-operation with other states and bodies for purposes of protecting the wider international environment for mankind."[107]

Compared to Africa, the judiciary in other countries in the global South has been far more active and creative. For example, while Article 21 of the Indian Constitution only states that "[n]o person shall be deprived of his life or personal liberty except according to procedures established by law," the Supreme Court has recognized that there are some unarticulated liberties implied by this provision. Thus, despite the absence of an explicit constitutional environmental right, the Supreme Court has read the right to life and personal liberty to include the right to a clean environment.[108] This innovative approach has been further strengthened by the Constitution (Forty Second Amendment) Act 1976, which provides in Article 48A that "[t]he State shall endeavor to protect and improve the environment and safeguard the forests and wildlife of the country," with Article 51A of the same Act extending this obligation to private citizens. In 1991, the Supreme Court ruled:

> The right to live [sic] is a fundamental right under Article 21 of the Constitution and it includes the right to enjoyment of pollution-free water and air for full enjoyment of life. If anything endangers or impairs the quality of life in derogation of laws, a citizen has the right to have recourse ... for removing the pollution of water or air which may be detrimental to the quality of life.[109]

This approach was confirmed by the Supreme Court four years later when it stated that the right to life:

> [...] encompasses within its ambit the protection and preservation of the environment, ecological balance, freedom from pollution of air and water, and sanitation,

---

[105] O. N. Fuo and S. M. Semie, "Cameroon's Environmental Framework: Law and the Balancing of Interests in Socio-Economic Development," in Faure and Du Plessis (eds.), note 46, p. 82.
[106] Unreported decision number CFIB/004M/09.
[107] Art. 36(9).
[108] J. Razzaque, "Human Rights and the Environment: The National Experience in South Asia and Africa" in Joint UNEP-OHCHR Expert Seminar on Human Rights and the Environment, Background Paper No. 4 (14–16 January 2002).
[109] *Subhash Kumar* v *State of Bihar* (1991), quoted in Boyd, note 19, p. 176.

without which life cannot be enjoyed. Any contract or action which would cause environmental pollution ... should be regarded as amounting to [a] violation of article 21 ... Therefore, there is a constitutional imperative on the state government and the municipalities, not only to ensure and safeguard proper environment [sic] but also an imperative duty to take adequate measures to promote, protect, and improve both the manmade and the natural environment.[110]

There have been hundreds of cases decided by the Indian courts based on this approach, and it has been estimated that approximately 80 percent of all cases were resolved in favor of the environment.[111] Moreover, the Indian courts have successfully relied upon their "environmental" interpretation of Article 21 to justify the domestic application of the principles of international environmental law, including intergenerational equity, the public trust doctrine, absolute liability for harm caused by hazardous industries, the polluter pays principle, strict liability and the reversal of the onus of proof, sustainable development, and the precautionary principle.[112]

5. CONCLUSION

While the global South has been and will continue to be disproportionately affected by global environmental degradation, it has also been a site of innovation with respect to the human rights–environment interface. Compared to their Northern counterparts, countries of the global South have been the most active in incorporating environmental rights into their constitutions and their courts have been very active in enforcing environmental obligations even where no legal instrument provides for explicit environmental rights, such as in India. Regional bodies such as the ACHR have also been doing pioneering work, even though its directives have had little effect at the grassroots level. It is also noteworthy that the human rights frameworks in many global South countries are specifically aimed at the protection of the environment-related rights and interests of minorities which are in special need of protection, such as the indigenous communities in South America.

Some of the reasons for this general support for environmental rights could be: the potential rights have to elevate environmental concerns above a mere policy choice that may be modified or discarded at will; rights are inherent attributes that must be respected in any well-ordered society and thus offer a compliance pull; environmental rights as constitutional guarantees will trump any conflicting norms of lesser value, giving them precedence over other legal norms; and, at the international level, enforcement of human rights law is more developed than the

---

[110] *Virender Gaur v State of Haryana* (1995) quoted in Boyd, note 19, pp. 176–177.
[111] Boyd, note 19, p. 177.
[112] Ibid, p. 178.

enforcement of international environmental law, thereby significantly extending the scope of regulatory and legal protection of the environment and concomitant socioeconomic entitlements of especially the disenfranchised and marginalized sectors of society particularly in the global South.[113] Also, environmental rights articulate state obligations corresponding to regional and international instruments, thus compelling governments to legislate and regulate to prevent environmental harm that would infringe on human rights.[114] In this way, along with their general international law obligations, the almost absolute discretion of governments to freely decide on the level of environmental protection in a country is significantly diluted. Rights further provide procedural guarantees to ensure as far as possible that environmental concerns are respected in day-to-day governance.

But environmental rights are not a panacea to all governance ills, as the following counterpoints to their positive attributes illustrate. For example, human rights in the environmental context have been criticized for being vague (or "troublingly indeterminate operationally"),[115] absolute, redundant, undemocratic, non-enforceable, and non-justiciable; for being too culturally imperialist and too focused on individuals, and for being disingenuous by creating false hope.[116] More generally, rights are also seen to be couched in a masculinist ontology because they are based on the male as the basis for their normativity; because of their predominant western characteristics, human rights sometimes exclude indigenous non-western cultures and concerns especially in the global South; and the promotion and protection of human dignity through material well-being is seen as the core of human rights, which is mostly achieved through increased economic security and, hence, increased consumption activities at great costs to the environment.[117] Because the origins of human rights have religious roots, they could be used in a perverse way to justify unjustifiable encroachments on the rights and interests of others.[118] Most importantly, human rights provide a basis for complete human mastery over the world that lies outside the human being, by creating entitlements instead of duties. Finally, human rights are individualistic, thus countering efforts that seek to foster harmonious interdependence that instills respect for ecological integrity.[119]

---

[113] Shelton, note 92, at 775–776.

[114] Ibid at 776.

[115] B. Weston and D. Bollier, "Toward a Recalibrated Human Right to a Clean and Healthy Environment: Making the Conceptual Transition" (2013) 4(2) *Journal of Human Rights and the Environment* 116.

[116] Boyd, above note 19, pp. 33–44.

[117] S. Peterson, "Whose Rights? A Critique of the 'Givens' in Human Rights Discourse" (1990) XV *Alternatives* 303 at 305, 308, 310.

[118] J. Shestack, "The Philosophical Foundations of Human Rights" (1998) 20(2) *Human Rights Quarterly* 201 at 205–206.

[119] C. Gearty, "Do Human Rights Help or Hinder Environmental Protection?" (2010) 1(1) *Journal of Human Rights and the Environment* 7 at 8.

Yet human rights instill dialogue where it is most needed; they create and further facilitate a culture of greater care for people and their environment, and provide a broad, paradigmatic framework wherein to situate issues related to environmental justice, protection of indigenous and minority rights and ecological integrity by individuals, government departments, legislatures, and courts. These benefits make human rights particularly relevant and suitable for environmental protection in the global South where greater care needs to be exercised due to the prevalence of corruption, generally "bad" governance practices, and severe environmental injustices.

9

Access and Benefit-Sharing: North–South Challenges in Implementing the Convention on Biological Diversity and Its Nagoya Protocol

Jorge Cabrera Medaglia

This chapter examines the North–South divide in the implementation of the access and benefit-sharing (ABS) component of the Convention on Biological Diversity[1] (CBD) and its Nagoya Protocol[2] (NP or Protocol) on ABS. It presents the legal foundations of ABS in international and domestic law regimes, with a focus on the implementation of the Nagoya Protocol, and investigates some of the key North–South challenges in the context of the legal obligations created by the Protocol.

1. INTRODUCTION

The conclusion of the CBD in 1992 represented a fundamental shift in both international law and the approach taken to conserve biological diversity. Whereas genetic resources had previously been the common heritage of humanity, the Convention changed this approach and granted states sovereignty over the genetic resources found within their borders. The thinking was that this would allow states to control access to genetic resources, setting terms that would allow them to profit from the potential value of these genetic resources and their diversity, thus creating incentives to conserve and sustainably use the resources.

The Convention recognizes the sovereign rights of states over their natural resources in areas under their jurisdiction.[3] Its objectives are:

1. The conservation of biological diversity.
2. Sustainable use of the components of biological diversity.

---

[1] *Convention on Biological Diversity*, Rio de Janeiro, 5 June 1992, in force 29 December 1993, 760 UNTS 79; 31 ILM 818 (1992).

[2] *Nagoya Protocol on Access to Genetic Resources and the Fair and Equitable Sharing of Benefits Arising from Their Utilization to the 1992 Convention on biological Diversity*, Nagoya, 29 October 2010, www.cbd.int [hereinafter Nagoya Protocol].

[3] Convention on Biological Diversity, above note 1, art. 15(1).

3. Fair and equitable sharing of the benefits arising out of the utilization of genetic resources.[4]

According to the Convention, states have the authority to determine access to genetic resources in areas within their jurisdiction. Parties also have the obligation to take appropriate measures with the aim of sharing in a fair and equitable way the benefits arising from the utilization of genetic resources.[5] Two further principles established under Article 15 of the CBD are that "access [to genetic resources], where granted, shall be on mutually agreed terms" and "shall be subject to prior informed consent of the Contracting Party providing such resources, unless otherwise determined by that Party."[6] This provides the basic legal framework under the Convention for access and benefit-sharing arising from the utilization of genetic resources.

Furthermore, the protection of traditional knowledge (TK), innovations, and practices of indigenous and local communities (ILC) plays an important role. TK often provides a lead to genetic resources with beneficial properties and can thus form the basis for ABS mechanisms or entitlements. To this effect, Article 8(j) states that:

> each contracting Party shall, as far as possible and as appropriate, subject to national legislation, respect, preserve and maintain knowledge, innovations and practices of indigenous and local communities embodying traditional lifestyles relevant for the conservation and sustainable use of biological diversity and promote their wider application with the approval and involvement of the holders of such knowledge, innovations and practices and encourage the equitable sharing of the benefits arising from the utilization of such knowledge innovations and practices.[7]

ABS activities should be based on the Bonn Guidelines on Access to Genetic Resources and Fair and Equitable Sharing of the Benefits Arising out of their Utilization (Bonn Guidelines).[8] The Bonn Guidelines were adopted in 2002 at the Sixth Conference of the Parties (COP) to the CBD,[9] but were shortly thereafter

---

[4] Ibid, art. 1.

[5] Ibid, art. 15(7).

[6] Ibid, art. 15(4), (5).

[7] Ibid, art. 8(j).

[8] Sixth Ordinary Meeting of the Conference of the Parties to the Convention on Biological Diversity, The Hague, 7–9 April 2002, *Access and Benefit-Sharing as Related to Genetic Resources*, UN Doc. UNEP/CBD/COP/DEC/VI/24. See also, Secretariat of the Convention on Biological Diversity, *Bonn Guidelines on Access to Genetic Resources and Fair and Equitable Sharing of the Benefits Arising out of their Utilization*, www.cbd.int [hereinafter Bonn Guidelines].

[9] Adopted to assist parties in establishing administrative, legislative, or policy measures on access and benefit-sharing and/or when negotiating contractual arrangements for access to genetic resources and benefit-sharing.

followed by a call for the negotiation of an international regime on ABS, later that year at the World Summit on Sustainable Development (WSSD).[10]

Although these guidelines were welcomed by the Northern countries and companies that use these resources, some Southern countries believed that this effort was fundamentally lacking for two reasons: First, these guidelines are of a voluntary nature; second, they pay little attention to the measures to be taken by the countries in which users are located (Northern countries with companies that use genetic resources) in order to fulfill their obligations under the Convention, especially those related to taking administrative measures and establishing policies and laws on benefit-sharing.[11]

In 2002 the WSSD agreed to the establishment of an international regime to effectively promote and safeguard fair and equitable benefit-sharing. On 20 December 2002, Resolution 57/260 of the UN General Assembly invited the COP to take the necessary measures regarding the commitment established at the Summit to negotiate this regime.[12] This international regime became the Nagoya Protocol.[13]

After six years of negotiations, the tenth COP adopted the Nagoya Protocol.[14] The Protocol provides a transparent legal framework for the effective implementation of its benefit-sharing objective. It covers genetic resources and TK associated with genetic resources, as well as the benefits arising from their utilization, by setting out core obligations for its contracting parties in relation to access, benefit-sharing, and compliance. The Protocol is based on the fundamental principles of access and benefit-sharing enshrined in the CBD. It supports the implementation

[10] World Summit on Sustainable Development, *Johannesburg Declaration on Sustainable Development and Plan of Implementation of the World Summit* (New York: United Nations Department of Public Information, 2003), para. 42.

[11] J. Cabrera Medaglia, *The International Regime on Access to Genetic Resources and Benefit-Sharing: Progress, Elements and Recommendations* (Quito: IUCN, 2006).

[12] UN General Assembly, *Resolution Adopted by the General Assembly: Convention on Biological Diversity*, 20 December 2002, A/RES/57/260.

[13] A significant amount of literature is now being written about the NP. See M. Buck and C. Hamilton, "The Nagoya Protocol on Access to Genetic Resources and the Fair and Equitable Sharing of Benefits Arising from Their Utilization to the Convention on Biological Diversity" (2011) 20 *Review of European Community and International Law* 47; Union for Ethical Biotrade, "Nagoya Protocol on Access and Benefit Sharing," http://ethicalbiotrade.org; G. Nijar, "The Nagoya Protocol on Access and Benefit-Sharing of Genetic Resources: Analysis and Implementation Options for Developing Countries," The South Centre, Research Paper No. 36 (2011); S. Oberthur and R. Kristin (eds.), *Global Governance of Genetic Resources: Access and Benefit Sharing after the Nagoya Protocol* (Abingdon: Routledge, 2014); T. Greiber et al., "Explanatory Guide on the Nagoya Protocol," IUCN Environmental Policy and Law Paper No. 32 (2012); E. Kamau et al., "The Nagoya Protocol on Access to Genetic Resources and Benefit Sharing: What is New and What are the Implications for Provider and User Countries and the Scientific Community" (2011) 6(3) *Journal of Environment and Development* 246; E. Morgera, M. Buick, and E. Tsiomani, *The 2010 Nagoya Protocol on Access and Benefit-Sharing in Perspective: Implications for International Law and Implementation Challenges* (Leiden: Martinus Nijhoff, 2013).

[14] Convention on Biological Diversity, "CBD COP Decision X/1," www.cbd.int.

of the third objective of the CBD by providing greater legal certainty and transparency for both providers and users of genetic resources. It helps to ensure benefit-sharing, in particular when genetic resources leave the providing country, and it establishes more predictable conditions for those wanting to access genetic resources. By enhancing legal certainty and promoting benefit-sharing, the Protocol encourages the advancement of research on genetic resources which could lead to new discoveries for the benefit of all. The Protocol creates incentives to conserve and sustainably use genetic resources, and thereby enhances the contribution of biodiversity to development and human well-being.

As of 22 September 2014, fifty-three countries have ratified the Protocol, which will enter into force on 12 October 2014. The key challenge is the operationalization of the Protocol in a manner that addresses the North–South challenges to be discussed.

2. SETTING THE STAGE FOR ABS: LEGAL AND INSTITUTIONAL CHALLENGES

The roots of ABS can be traced to colonialism and efforts by colonial powers to gain control of the trade in key commodities such as rubber, tea, and cinchona for their own benefit, with little regard for the communities and economies from which these resources originated.[15] More recently, over the course of the twentieth century, the scope of intellectual property protection – including patents and plant breeders' rights – has been extended to cover living organisms and parts thereof, making biodiversity and genes a potentially lucrative resource. Biodiversity-rich countries, primarily from the global South, became increasingly frustrated with the one-way flow of resources. Genetic diversity from the South was being used in research in the North, where it was often patented, but with no returns to the country of origin.[16] The solution to this problem, as adopted in the CBD, is to grant states sovereignty over genetic resources, thus allowing states to control access to genetic resources and negotiate terms for benefit-sharing.

In addition to the CBD, negotiations at the Food and Agriculture Organization have resulted in the International Treaty on Plant Genetic Resources for Food and Agriculture (IT).[17] The IT creates a Multilateral System of Access and Benefit-Sharing for a set of thirty-five food crops and twenty-nine forages. In contrast to the bilateral, contract-negotiation approach of the CBD, access to the varieties in the Multilateral System of the IT is based on uniform rules of access and benefit-sharing set out in the Treaty.

---

[15] K. Gatforth and J. Cabrera Medaglia, "Factors Contributing to Legal Reform for the Development and Implementation of Measures on Access and Benefit-Sharing" in T. McInerney (ed.), *Searching for Success: Narrative Accounts of Legal Reform in Developing and Transition Countries* (Rome: International Development Law Organization, 2006) pp. 139–150.

[16] Ibid.

[17] *International Treaty on Plant Genetic Resources for Food and Agriculture*, in force 29 June 2004, 3 November 2001, FAO Res. 3/2003.

Some of the key issues behind the negotiation of the NP (on which different views and positions exist between Southern and Northern countries) are:[18]

1. Economic expectations of ABS. There is a sense of frustration among Southern countries due to the limited economic and non-economic benefits (monetary and non-monetary) that have been derived to date from the different bioprospecting projects and, in general, from the application of ABS frameworks.[19]

2. Cases of "biopiracy" or misappropriation of GR and associated TK. Cases of illegal access, misappropriation, or "biopiracy" have occurred in various countries and communities, especially in Latin America, Asia, and Africa, and it has been difficult to find cost-effective legal solutions within the framework of national ABS legislation or of industrial property law.[20]

3. Lack of user measures to support national legislation and avoid misappropriation. Although the CBD requires the parties to take measures to ensure fair and equitable benefit-sharing (see particularly the provisions of Article 15.7), it has mostly been Southern countries (the providers of genetic resources) that have issued regulations on ABS.[21] Thus, the countries where pharmaceutical, biotechnological, and agricultural companies have their headquarters (mostly Northern countries) have not implemented the corresponding regulations to ensure benefit-sharing and comply with their legally binding international obligations.

4. Lack of legal certainty and functionality of the ABS regimes existing mostly in Southern countries. Users of genetic resources (primarily Northern countries) contend that there is a need to provide legal certainty in the ABS process for users and providers of genetic resources and associated TK. A concern expressed by these users is the lack of clear regulations regarding ABS in the country of origin of these resources and associated TK; that is, in Southern countries.

---

[18] See Cabrera Medaglia, note 12.

[19] J. Cabrera Medaglia, "Biodiversity Prospecting in Practice," IP Strategy Today No. 11 (2004).

[20] On the topic of biopiracy and the difficulties of judging whether certain activities constitute misappropriation, *cf.* G. Dutfield, "What is Biopiracy?," Expert Workshop on Access and Benefit-sharing (2004); T. Young, "Analysis of Claims of Unauthorized Access and Misappropriation of Genetic Resources and Associated Traditional Knowledge," report prepared for IUCN-Canada and distributed at the Fourth Meeting of the Working Group on ABS, Granada, Document UNEP/CBD/WG-ABS/4/INF/6 (2006).

[21] *cf.* the study by J. Cabrera Medaglia, F. Perron Welch, and F. Kai Philipps, *An Overview of National and Regional Legislation in the Light of the Nagoya Protocol*, 3rd ed. (Montreal: Centre for International Sustainable Development Law, 2014); J. Cabrera Medaglia, *A Comparative Analysis on the Legislation and Practices on Access to Genetic Resources and Benefit-Sharing (ABS)* (Bonn: IUCN ABS Project, 2004).

Finally, the lack of capacity to negotiate ABS agreements persists. The legal and practical process for obtaining PIC and mutually agreed terms (MAT) for certain stakeholders, especially indigenous and local communities in Southern countries, also remains a critical aspect for a functional ABS system. Several capacity-building initiatives have been implemented, such as the recent ABS capacity-building project funded by the Global Environment Fund,[22] aimed at increasing the capacity to develop and implement ABS measures and to negotiate ABS contracts and arrangements.

3. IMPLEMENTATION OF THE NAGOYA PROTOCOL: THE NORTH–SOUTH DIMENSION

This section will provide a brief overview of the NP, emphasizing its key components and significant North–South implementation issues.

3.1 *Objective*

The Protocol objective is very concrete and mirrors the CBD objective: fair and equitable sharing of the benefits arising from the utilization of genetic resources.[23] The concept of fair and equitable benefit-sharing arises mainly under Article 15(7) of the CBD, which regulates access to genetic resources. Although the Protocol does not expressly include the protection of TK associated with genetic resources among its objectives, the text of the Protocol makes it clear that fair and equitable benefit-sharing also pertains to the TK of indigenous and local communities relating to genetic resources.

Achieving this objective requires appropriate access to genetic resources by "users" as well as appropriate transfer of relevant technologies to "providers." Recognition must be given to all rights over genetic resources and technologies. Funding from the public and private sector must be provided in ways that are again "appropriate."

The linkages among ABS, conservation, and sustainable use are novel to the Protocol.[24] The Protocol is innovative in that it spells out these linkages, and promotes this nexus through Articles 9 and 10 of the Protocol.[25] However, this connection, especially between fair and equitable benefit-sharing and conservation, is not clear in all the ABS measures enacted to implement the CBD ABS provisions.[26]

---

[22] For instance the Global Environment Facility project entitled "Strengthening the Implementation of ABS regimes in Latin America and the Caribbean" started in April 2011.

[23] Nagoya Protocol, art. 1.

[24] *cf.* Cabrera Medaglia et al., note 21; Greiber et al., note 14.

[25] See Bonn Guidelines, note 8, para. 48.

[26] The link between ABS and conservation is tenuous or non-existent in several ABS measures in force: see J. Cabrera Medaglia et al., note 21; *Analysis of Existing National, Regional and International Legal Instruments Relating to Access and Benefit-Sharing and Experience Gained in their Implementation, Including Identification of Gaps*, 10 November 2004, UNEP/CBD/WG-ABS/3/2.

Article 9 (contribution to the conservation and sustainable use) requires parties to encourage users and providers to direct benefits arising from the utilization of genetic resources toward the conservation of biological diversity and the sustainable use of its components. Article 10 refers to the Global Multilateral Mechanism. It requests parties to consider the need for and modalities of global multilateral benefit-sharing mechanisms to address the fair and equitable sharing of benefits derived from the utilization of genetic resources and associated TK that occur in transboundary situations or for which it is not possible to grant or obtain prior informed consent. The benefits shared by users of genetic resources and associated TK through these mechanisms shall be used to support the conservation of biological diversity and the sustainable use of its components globally.[27] This Global Multilateral Mechanism was strongly supported by some Southern countries (especially the African Group) and its inclusion was accepted at the final stages in the negotiation of the Protocol in Nagoya as a compromise between some key countries (Norway, EU and Brazil). Because Article 10 only requires parties to consider the need and modalities of the instrument, it did not raise any particular controversy at the time of adoption of the Protocol. However, during the COP/MOP, the discussions on the need and modalities were linked to other controversial issues, such as the materials collected prior to the Nagoya Protocol (but after the CBD).

Finally, the NP does not include the protection of associated TK among its objectives.

3.2 Definitions, the Concepts of "Utilization" and "Derivatives", and Regulatory Implications

The Protocol includes several definitions: Conference of the Parties; Convention; Utilization of Genetic Resources; Biotechnology; and derivatives.[28] Some of the definitions were discussed throughout the Protocol negotiations. They were central to the development of the Protocol and were intended to address one of the most controversial issues at stake: the inclusion of "derivatives" (biochemicals derived from genetic resources that do not contain functional units of heredity). This was a clear North–South issue. Most of the Northern countries were against the inclusion of the term "derivative," considering the lack of clarity around the concept and the fact that its inclusion in the scope of the Protocol could constrain research and development, or the commercialization of products derived from genetic resources. Southern countries fought for the inclusion of derivatives in the NP in order to increase their opportunities for fair and equitable sharing of benefits arising from

---

[27] The exact content and implications of the Global Multilateral Mechanisms were not fully negotiated in Nagoya.

[28] Art. 2.

the utilization of the biochemical components of genetic resources that do not contain functional units of heredity.

In addition, the lack of definitional clarity among biological resources, genetic resources, and genetic material in the CBD (Article 2) prompted discussion regarding the scope of the Protocol. In many laws and regulations on ABS, the terms "genetic resources," "genetic material," and "biological resources" are used in accordance with the CBD's definition, without any further clarification regarding their intended scope. This makes it difficult to clearly determine the reach of access systems, and therefore which activities or resources are covered when referring to "utilization."[29] Furthermore, the term "utilization of genetic resources" is used in Articles 1 and 15(7) of the CBD, but is not defined in that agreement. Prior to the NP, experts and national legislation offered different interpretations of the types of activities that constituted utilization of genetic resources.[30] In this context, the definition of utilization of genetic resources is an innovation of the Protocol. It seeks to resolve, at least in part, the parties' disagreement with respect to the inclusion of derivatives within the scope of the Protocol.

The debate on utilization of genetic resources centered on whether research and development based on naturally occurring material, rather than simply the genetic material itself, was also subject to the Protocol. During negotiations, Northern countries consistently argued that the focus of Article 15 is on access to genetic resources (material containing functional heredity units such as DNA). Southern countries, on the other hand, argued that the actual or potential value of genetic resources rests in the naturally occurring compounds that result from the activity of genes.[31] The Protocol resolved this dispute by defining the term "utilization" to encompass research and development on the biochemical composition of genetic resources.[32] This means that, for example, drugs based on the extraction of chemicals are included and benefit-sharing is supported by the Protocol. The Protocol's use of the term "derivative" lends further support to this interpretation.

---

[29] COP 5 Decision V/26 had indicated the need to gather more information on definitions. The Executive Secretary formed an Expert Group on the Use of Terms, which limited its work to exchange information about national practices. COP 6 Decision VI/ 24 requests that the ABS Working Group study, among other things, the use of terms and definitions. Finally, COP 7 Decision VII/19 B invited parties, organizations, and stakeholders to submit information on the following terms: access to genetic resources, commercialization, derivatives, etc., and also requested the Working Group to continue working on the use of terms not defined by the CBD.

[30] See Fridtjof Nansen Institute, *The Concept of "Genetic Resources" in the Convention on Biological Diversity and How it Related to a Functional International Regime on Access and Benefit-Sharing*, 19 March 2010, UNEP/CBD/WG-ABS/9/Inf/1.

[31] Buck and Hamilton, above note 14, pp. 47–61.

[32] "Utilization of genetic resources means to conduct research and development on the genetic and/or biochemical composition of genetic resources, including through the application of biotechnology as defined in Article 2 of the Convention", Nagoya Protocol, note 2, art. 2(c).

During the negotiating process, a controversial and difficult issue was whether "derivatives" would be included in the scope of the Protocol in addition to the genetic resources/material per se (i.e. material containing functional units of heredity), and if so to what extent. Many Southern countries pushed for the inclusion of "derivatives" in the scope of the Protocol because biochemicals with no functional units of heredity are of great value to industry.[33] In practice, most case studies and examples of successful ABS agreements and relationships involve research and development on the biochemical components of the genetic or biological resources, especially in the case of the pharmaceutical industry. The reference to derivatives in the definition of biotechnology[34] and the inclusion of biochemical components in the definition of utilization represent a significant victory for Southern countries.

However, there remain different interpretations regarding the Protocol's coverage of utilization of "isolated derivatives" that have not been accessed simultaneously with accessing the genetic resources. Despite this uncertainty, it seems clear that in cases where MAT exists for an isolated derivative, its terms would be supported by the Protocol provisions safeguarding MAT. Access and utilization should take place in accordance with the specific conditions of the MAT in place.

The definitions contained in the Protocol clarify that derivatives (biochemicals) can be addressed in national ABS legislation (most likely in Southern countries). If a country decides to do so, its legal framework will be supported by the provisions of the Protocol. While using different definitions (and techniques), several national ABS laws have already incorporated derivatives (or biochemicals), including the Biodiversity Law of Costa Rica (biochemicals); the Philippines Executive Order (by-product and derivatives); The Andean Community Decision 391 (derivatives); the Bhutan Biodiversity Law (biochemicals); and Australia's ABS legislation (biochemicals).[35] However, none or few ABS measures have yet defined the term "utilization," despite its legal relevance for building a functional ABS regime.[36]

From a national perspective, the incorporation of the term "utilization" in ABS measures may provide more clarity on the scope of the measures and improve their implementation. Therefore, the concept of utilization adopted in the Protocol

---

[33] On the value of the "derivatives" for industry see K. ten Kate and S. Laird, *The Commercial Use of Biodiversity: Access to Genetic Resources and Benefit-Sharing* (London: Earthscan, 1999).

[34] "Biotechnology" as defined in Article 2 of the Convention means "any technological application that uses biological systems, living organisms, or derivatives thereof to make or modify products or processes for specific use", Nagoya Protocol, note 2, art. 2(d).

[35] See Cabrera, note 21.

[36] On the issue of the role of "utilization" in the drafting and implementation of functional ABS regimes, see M. W. Tvedt and T. Young, *Beyond Access: Exploring Implementing the Fair and Equitable Sharing Commitments in the CBD* (Gland: IUCN, 2007); J. Cabrera Medaglia and C. López Silva, *Addressing the Problems of Access: Protecting Sources While Giving Users Certainty* (Gland: IUCN, 2007).

can serve as the basis for a functional ABS system.[37] This approach could increase legal certainty by providing concrete indicators to determine whether a particular activity is covered or governed by the Protocol (or Article 15 of the CBD) and when the obligation to share benefits is triggered.[38]

3.3 Scope

Although the scope of the Protocol appears uncontroversial, this was one of the most hotly contested aspects of the negotiations.[39]

Article 3 establishes the scope of application of the Protocol over genetic resources and TK. Many Southern countries aimed for an ambitious and comprehensive Protocol with a broad range of application to biological resources, including ex-situ collections established before the entry into force of the CBD, and TK. On the other hand, many Northern countries sought to limit the breadth of application of the Protocol by excluding TK, pathogens, non-commercial research and emergency situations, and materials within the mandate of other bodies or organizations.[40]

Article 3 limits the scope of the Protocol to those genetic resources that are encompassed by the terms of CBD Article 15, and clarifies two aspects of the Protocol:

- Temporal scope (when the Protocol applies, and what implications this may have on the activities or genetic resources covered, the case of ex-situ collections established before the entry into force of the Protocol, the issue of non-retroactivity, and new utilization of genetic resources).
- Geographical scope (especially for areas beyond national jurisdiction and the Antarctic System).

From the North–South perspective, the most controversial issue was the temporal scope (and the connected issues of ex-situ collections of materials established in the past). Southern countries (especially from Africa) argued that the Protocol should apply to new uses (or utilizations) of genetic resources regardless of whether they were collected before the NP or even before the CBD. These countries sought to address unresolved issues of ex-situ collections or materials stored in foreign countries and their legal status vis-a-vis the rights of the country of origin of these resources. Northern countries opposed the application of the Protocol to materials collected before the NP, much of which is stored in their territories. This issue

---

[37] M. W. Tvedt and O. Rukundo, *The Functionality of an ABS Protocol* (Lysaker: Fridtjof Nansen Institute, 2010).
[38] Ibid.
[39] Greiber et al., note 14.
[40] C. Chiarolla, "Making Sense of the Draft Protocol on Access and Benefit-Sharing for COP 10" (2010) 7 *Idées pour le Debat* 12.

202 Access and Benefit-Sharing

remains unresolved. The regulatory frameworks of Southern countries seem to follow the first interpretation, while those of Northern countries (especially the European Union) seem to restrict the temporal scope of the instrument only to genetic resources acquired after the NP. The controversy will likely be resolved through further negotiations among the parties to the NP.

3.4 Access to Genetic Resources and Benefit-Sharing

There was agreement among the Northern and Southern countries in the late stages of the negotiations that NP must be based on three main components: Access, benefit-sharing, and compliance (the "ABC" of the ABS). Articles 5 and 6 play a relevant role in addressing the first two issues. Article 5.1 of the Protocol confirms the benefit-sharing obligations of the parties under Articles 15.3 and 15.7 of the CBD. Article 5.1 also reiterates (in accordance with Article 15.7 of the CBD) that specific benefit-sharing terms for concrete ABS transactions will be included in the MAT (contracts or other type of material transfer agreements). Benefit-sharing includes benefits arising from the utilization of genetic resources, as well as subsequent applications and commercialization. Article 5.4 includes a list (annexed to the Protocol) of potential monetary and non-monetary benefits that is taken essentially from the Bonn Guidelines Appendix II. In this regard it should be pointed out that "[t]he Nagoya Protocol neither attempts to specify what is meant by 'fair and equitable' in a substantive manner nor does it establish any procedural standards to this effect. The reference to mutually agreed terms (MAT) thus makes the acceptable level of benefit sharing completely relative to any level to which the provider and user agree."[41]

Possibly the main innovation of this provision is the parties' obligation to share benefits from the use of genetic resources that are held by indigenous and local communities with the communities concerned. This obligation is also related to the implementation of Article 6 of the NP, which regulates access to genetic resources. The obligations of the providing country under Article 6 are far more detailed than the obligations of user countries to ensure that benefits are actually shared in an equitable manner. The level of detail in these rules is impressive, requiring providing countries to take very concrete steps in their implementation of the NP.[42]

Article 6 is part of the Protocol's effort to balance the rights and obligations of producers and users of genetic resources. In exchange for the establishment of user measures (in Northern countries) to facilitate compliance with the domestic ABS legislation of Southern countries and avoid biopiracy, several Northern countries requested that provisions be included in the Protocol to increase the legal certainty and functionality of the access regimes (especially in the design of measures and

---

[41] See M. Tvedt, "Beyond Nagoya: Towards a Legally Functional System of Access and Benefit-Sharing," in S. Oberthur and K. Rosendal (eds.), *Global Governance of Genetic Resources: Access and Benefit-Sharing after the Nagoya Protocol* (Abingdon: Routledge, 2014).

[42] Ibid.

procedures to require PIC and negotiate MAT). These "access standards"[43] address the concerns of Northern countries regarding the difficulty of complying with the ABS legislation of some Southern countries and the possibility of being accused of biopiracy. Northern countries (and their companies) have indicated repeatedly that there are legal uncertainties in the ABS regulations of the providers (Southern countries) due to the lack of transparency and clarity in the ABS domestic regimes. Southern countries resisted these access standards and argued that the establishment and design of the ABS regulatory framework should be the sovereign prerogative of each state and should not be prescribed by treaty. The NP resolved this controversy in favor of Northern countries by including specific requirements or standards that a country must follow if it chooses to create a legal regime requiring PIC before access to genetic resources takes place.[44] Southern countries accepted the inclusion of access standards in the Protocol, but sought to link them with strong compliance measures to avoid putting the regulatory burden only on provider countries. These compliance measures are included in Articles 15 to 18 of the NP, as explained later in the chapter.

In sum, Article 6 of the NP sets forth minimum standards for access to genetic resources. These standards are very general and not particularly difficult to fulfill. However, access to genetic resources is also regulated in other articles of the Protocol, particularly Article 8, which requires each party to:

- A) Promote and encourage scientific research, including simplified measures on access for non-commercial research purposes, taking into account the potential for change of intent.[45] Countries have generally recognized and provided for differing permit tracks for commercial versus non-commercial access to genetic resources and TK.[46]
- B) Pay due regard to cases of present or imminent emergencies that threaten human, animal or plant health (the case of the pathogens).
- C) Consider the importance of genetic resources for food and agriculture and their special role for food security.[47]

---

[43] See M. Buck and C. Hamilton, "The Nagoya Protocol on Access to Genetic Resources and the Fair and Equitable Sharing of Benefits Arising from Their Utilization to the Convention on Biological Diversity" (2011) 20 *Review of European Community and International Law* 47.

[44] See *Nagoya Protocol*, above note 2, art. 6.

[45] Ibid, art. 8(a).

[46] See G. R. Nemogá Soto et al., *La Investigación sobre Biodiversidad en Colombia: Propuesta de ajustes al Régimen de Acceso a Recursos Genéticos y Productos Derivados y a la Decisión Andina 391 de 1996* (Bogota: Universidad Nacional de Colombia, 2010); S. Biber-Klem et al., "Access and Benefit Sharing in Latin America and the Caribbean: A Science-Policy Dialogue for Academic Non-Commercial Research," Background document at the twelfth meeting of the Conference of the Parties (2013).

[47] See Decision II/15 and Decision V/ 5 of the Conference of the Parties of the Convention on Biological Diversity adopted at the second and fifth meetings on the special features and characteristics of PGRFA.

These access commitments are also relevant from a North–South perspective. Northern countries insisted on specific provisions for non-commercial research and for access to pathogens. Northern countries feared that the ABS regulations of provider countries might negatively affect basic research (carried out in many cases by Northern research institutions) and that access to pathogens might be denied,[48] thereby hindering public health-related research. Conversely, given the difficulty of distinguishing between commercial and non-commercial uses (especially in the field of biotechnology), Southern countries demanded and obtained language that takes into account changes in intent with respect to non-commercial uses. Southern countries also demanded and obtained language requiring appropriate benefit-sharing measures in cases of expedited or facilitated access to pathogens, including access to vaccines.

3.5 Protection of TK[49]

Some commentators have considered the provisions related to TK among the Protocol's major achievements.[50] Until the very end of the negotiations on the NP, opinions differed between countries (this was not however a North–South split) on whether the Protocol's provisions on TK associated with genetic resources should be confined to one article or dealt with as a cross-cutting issue.[51] Finally, TK issues were integrated in several articles of the Protocol (including Articles 5, 6, 7, and 12).

Fair and equitable sharing of benefits arising from the utilization of TK is derived from Article 5(5) of the NP. Implementing Article 8(j) of the CBD, Article 5(5) covers the utilization of TK associated with genetic resources and recognizes that the use of such knowledge should lead to the equitable sharing of benefits based on MAT.

---

[48] Regarding the pathogens, the decision of Indonesia to withhold samples of the virus (HN51) from WHO researchers under the principle of sovereignty, because samples might be used to produce vaccines that they themselves would not be able to afford, led to the EU's position (backed by private sector representatives) supporting the exclusion of pathogens from the scope of the Protocol. Southern countries argued that exclusion would weaken the Protocol's provisions and spirit. A middle ground was reached, in the sense that the pathogens will remain in the scope of the treaty but special considerations for their access were introduced as an alternative. See L. Wallbott, F. Wolff, and J. Pozarowska, "The Negotiations of the Nagoya Protocol: Issues, Coalitions and Process," in S. Oberthur and K. Rosendal (eds.), *Global Governance of Genetic Resources: Access and Benefit-Sharing After the Nagoya Protocol* (Abingdon: Routledge, 2014).

[49] See G. S. Nijar, "Incorporating Traditional Knowledge in an International Regime on Access to Genetic Resources and Benefit Sharing: Problems and Prospects" (2010) 21(2) *European Journal of International Law* 457.

[50] K. Koutouki and K. R. von Bieberstein, "The Nagoya Protocol: Sustainable Benefits-Sharing for Indigenous and Local Communities" (2012) 13 *Vermont Journal of Environmental Law* 513.

[51] Greiber et al., note 14.

The protections afforded to TK in Article 5(5), read together with Article 7, make up the bedrock provisions of the NP in relation to genetic resources.[52] Pursuant to Article 7, parties are obliged to establish measures to ensure TK associated with genetic resources held by indigenous and local communities (ILC) are only accessed with PIC or the approval and involvement of the community, and with MAT.[53] By making PIC or approval and involvement the key requirement, aside from acknowledging that the TK in question is vested with the indigenous community, the NP underscores the need for genuine understanding on the part of the providing community of the rationale and goals underlying access to TK.[54] While the NP obliges parties to take measures in relation to the protection of TK, it does provide flexibility in domestic implementation in terms of whether a formal PIC is required or if the approval and involvement of the indigenous community is sufficient. This distinction allows Southern and Northern countries to determine if they will design a mechanism based on PIC as a term of art, requiring a particular standard, or simply via approval and involvement of ILC in the process, notwithstanding the distinction between PIC and approval and involvement. In addition, indigenous farmers, as holders of TK relevant to the discovery, extraction, use, or application of genetic resources, are granted the right to engage in the process under MAT, thereby ensuring that their TK is preserved and only accessed based on their approval. These new international obligations need to be taken into account in the process of drafting and implementing ABS (PIC) requirements.

In contrast to the general requirements of Articles 5 and 7, Article 12 of the NP imposes unique procedural obligations.[55] First, Article 12(1) requires the parties, in the execution of their obligations under the Protocol, to take into account the customary norms and community protocols and procedures of indigenous communities. Parties must consult both non-codified and codified indigenous practices when creating their domestic measures to protect TK, thus giving indigenous communities exceptional influence over the method and design of the mechanism of choice. Second, pursuant to Article 12(2), consultation and participation of indigenous communities are both explicitly required in designing mechanisms to inform potential users of TK about their obligations under the Protocol. Again, this places increased influence in the hands of indigenous communities, as the impacted or concerned party, in determining the measures which are to be taken. Third, parties are to support indigenous communities in developing community protocols relating to TK and fair and equitable benefit-sharing, establishing minimum requirements for MAT, and forging model contractual clauses for benefit-sharing agreements relating to the use of TK associated with genetic resources.[56]

[52] Ibid.
[53] Ibid.
[54] Ibid.
[55] Ibid.
[56] Nagoya Protocol, note 2, art. 12(3)(a)–(c).

206   *Access and Benefit-Sharing*

Last, and arguably most importantly, Article 12(4) provides that the customary use and exchange of genetic resources and associated TK among indigenous communities are to be minimally impacted by the NP. This requirement protects the traditional uses and exchanges undertaken by indigenous communities for generations to preserve the intercommunity transfer of genetic material for the conservation of biological diversity and for food security.

The protection of TK is not only a North–South issue. Within Southern countries and also in some Northern countries (such as Canada, Australia, and the Nordic nations), ILC territorial rights, participatory rights, and rights to give or withhold PIC are also matters of tension and disagreement between national authorities and the ILC.

3.6 Compliance and Monitoring

One of the key factors that led to the negotiation of the NP was the absence or inadequacy of measures in countries that use genetic resources (especially Northern countries) to comply with the PIC and MAT requirements of countries and communities that provide these genetic resources and their associated TK (especially those in the South).

User country measures are necessary to guarantee compliance with the provider country's legislative provisions or with the provisions in access contracts. The ability of the provider countries to enforce their legal requirements will largely depend on mechanisms for access to justice (including administrative and judicial remedies) in foreign jurisdictions. Thus, user country measures are essential to support compliance with access conditions given the transnational nature of most ABS agreements. The adoption of effective user country measures would permit regulation of the full spectrum of ABS activities. While provider country measures make it possible to control the access phase, user country measures would permit control of the phases of use, research and development, patenting of products and processes, etc. These measures would help close the gap that exists between the resource-acquisition phase (access permits or contracts) and the development phase. They would also reduce the burden imposed on Southern countries as a result of monitoring and compliance procedures in their national ABS regulations.[57]

The Protocol addresses compliance with ABS requirements in Articles 15 to 17. These provisions show that the Protocol did not adopt the compliance mechanisms advocated by Southern countries. It is also clear that, for the purpose of these provisions, every country can act as a possible user and provider of genetic resources. Articles 15 and 16 of the NP require user countries to:

---

[57] J. C. Fernandez, "The Feasibility, Practicality and Cost of a Certificate of Origin System for Genetic Resources: Economic Considerations," Yokohama Round Table, Towards Fair and Equitable Benefit Sharing: Instruments for the Effective Implementation of the Bonn Guidelines under the Convention on Biological Diversity, UNU-IAS and JBA (2005).

1. adopt user measures against misappropriation;
2. address the situations of non-compliance with these measures; and
3. cooperate in cases of alleged misappropriation "as far as possible and as appropriate."

So far, only a few examples exist of measures developed under Articles 15 and 16, including the European Union's due diligence requirements,[58] Switzerland's due diligence measure approved in 2014,[59] and Norway's compliance requirements.[60]

3.6.1 Monitoring the Utilization of Genetic Resources (Article 17)

Countries are obliged to establish measures to monitor and enhance transparency regarding the utilization of genetic resources. This includes the designation checkpoints to collect or receive relevant information on PIC, the source of genetic resources, the establishment of MAT, and/or the utilization of genetic resources.[61] Users of genetic resources are required to provide the information specified at designated checkpoints, allowing domestic authorities to address situations of non-compliance.[62] This information, including internationally recognized certificates of compliance (IRCC) where available, must be provided to relevant national authorities, to the party providing PIC, and to the ABS–Clearing House Mechanism, without prejudice to the protection of confidential information.[63]

3.6.2 Compliance with Mutually Agreed Terms (Article 18)

Article 18 completes the set of user measures. However, it addresses a different situation: the compliance (or non-compliance) with the MAT (contract) between the user and the provider of genetic resources and associated TK.[64]

3.6.3 Disclosure of Origin and Certificate of Compliance: The CBD and Intellectual Property Rights

One of the first measures suggested in order to achieve mutual supportiveness between the CBD and intellectual property systems (in particular, the WTO

---

[58] "Regulation of the European Parliament and of the Council on Access to Genetic Resources and the Fair and Equitable Sharing of Benefits Arising from their Utilization in the Union" (2014) 150 *Official Journal of the European Union* 59.

[59] Swiss Confederation, *Federal Act on the Protection of Nature and Cultural Heritage*, arts. 23 n (1)(a)–(b), 23p.

[60] Norway, Act relating to the management of biological, geological and landscape diversity: Nature Diversity Act No. 100 of 19 June 2009.

[61] Nagoya Protocol, note 2, art. 17.1(a)(i).

[62] Ibid, art. 17.1(a)(ii).

[63] Ibid, art. 17.1(a)(iii).

[64] Ibid, art. 18.

TRIPS) was the disclosure of the origin of genetic resources or associated TK in intellectual property rights (IPR) applications, particularly in patents. Some countries (mainly Southern countries) proposed that the TRIPS Agreement be amended so as to require that patent applicants disclose, as a condition to patentability, one or more of the following: the source and origin of any genetic material used in a claimed invention and/or any related TK used in the invention; evidence of PIC from the competent authority in the country of origin of the genetic material; and evidence of fair and equitable benefit-sharing. Proponents of disclosure requirements argued that this stipulation would help to support compliance with the CBD provisions on access to genetic resources and benefit-sharing.[65] Opponents of this proposal (primarily Northern countries, especially the United States, Canada, New Zealand, Australia, and Korea, and with a middle ground of Norway, Switzerland, and the EU) argued that such a modification is not necessary to implement the CBD requirements, as they should be implemented through corresponding contracts at the national level, and that the TRIPS Agreement is not the appropriate instrument to regulate ABS.

This debate was originally wide-ranging,[66] and now focuses on how the TRIPS Agreement relates to the CBD and particularly whether the agreement should be amended to require disclosure in IPR applications, or whether alternative approaches, including contractual-based systems or databases of genetic resources and TK, could be more effective in ensuring mutual supportiveness between the TRIPS and the CBD.

This issue was debated during the NP negotiations. Southern countries argued that the inclusion of disclosure requirements and the use of certificates of compliance in patent applications would strengthen the mutual supportiveness between the WTO's IPR system and the CBD and NP. However, some Northern countries and private sector representatives opposed these measures and favored alternative mechanisms to address concerns regarding misappropriation. In their view, new patent disclosure requirements would be ineffective in promoting compliance with ABS requirements and would introduce uncertainties into the patent system.

The NP did not adopt the compliance mechanisms advocated by Southern countries. Instead, the Protocol addresses compliance with ABS requirements in Articles 15 to 17. These articles seek to prevent misappropriation of genetic resources or associated TK by requiring user countries to comply with the domestic legislation and regulation of provider countries. It is clear that every country can act

---

[65] For a detailed analysis see T. Henninger, "Disclosure Requirements in Patent Law and Related Measures: A Comparative Overview of Existing National and Regional Legislation on IP and Biodiversity," Diálogo Andino sobre Medidas relacionadas con la Biodiversidad y el sistema de propiedad intelectual (2009).

[66] See the minutes of the meetings of the TRIPS Council (IP/C/M) which can be found on the WTO website: www.wto.org. See Convention on Biological Diversity, *The Relationship between the TRIPS Agreement and the Convention on Biological Diversity – Summary of Issues Raised and Points Made – Submission by the WTO Secretariat*, 20 February 2006, UNEP/CBD/COP/8/Inf/37.

as a possible user and provider of genetic resources and be obliged by these provisions of the Protocol to enact appropriate user measures.

The above discussion highlights that, in lieu of mandating compliance through the IPR regime, the NP gives user countries the flexibility to design compliance measures. These provisions do not mention any specific checkpoints including IPR applications (patent or plant varieties), leaving to each country the determination of the checkpoints as well as the sanctions for failure to submit (or false submission of) the information requested. This resolution presents a sharp contrast with the strong proposal of Southern countries to list specifically the IPR offices as one of the mandatory checkpoints and to provide more guidance on the content and type of user measures to be adopted under Articles 15 to 17.

4. CHALLENGES AND OPPORTUNITIES IN IMPLEMENTING THE NP AND THE CBD ABS FOR THE NORTH AND THE SOUTH

The NP contains various components that must be operationalized in a manner consistent with existing national legislation. What emerges is a series of implementation challenges – but also opportunities and lessons learned – for countries (both Northern and Southern) in operationalizing the NP.

4.1 Challenges

4.1.1 Defining Ownership

Ownership of genetic resources will have to be fleshed out in order to meet the Protocol's obligations related to genetic resources owned by ILC.[67] Users of genetic resources need to be sure that a provider has the authority to provide such resources. Such authority does not, in many cases, rest only with the government; it also rests with those who have private or other rights or tenure over the land or resources. Therefore, questions of ownership and tenure invariably have an important bearing on the practicalities of ABS and are important elements of national legislation on the basis of which competent national authorities "determine access" to resources. The definition of property rights over genetic resources will then have implications for the right to participate in the decision-making processes on ABS and to be the recipient of potential benefits.

4.1.2 Understanding the Term "Utilization"

The NP contains a somewhat broad definition of utilization of genetic resources, capturing major types of utilization of genetic resources.[68] On the basis of its

[67] Cabrera Medaglia, note 12.
[68] Nagoya Protocol, note 2, art. 2(c).

210 *Access and Benefit-Sharing*

wording alone, the Protocol does not clarify which uses fall under its scope, nor does it provide an operational definition of the term "derivative."[69] The operative provisions of the Protocol, in addition, do not create clear obligations upon user countries, especially from the North, to implement national laws requiring private companies using genetic resources from other countries to share a fair and equitable part of the benefits arising out of such utilization. Despite the adoption of the NP, therefore, the problem of establishing a functional system imposing clear obligations upon private parties persists. National regulation is essential, and will likely yield useful information about the challenges encountered during the NP's implementation phase. The experience of those countries regulating "derivatives" or biochemicals may be particularly relevant.

4.1.3 Making Operative PIC Requirements

With regard to PIC,[70] there appear to be difficulties in making relevant requirements operative and ensuring legal certainty. This is one of the most complex and difficult aspects of obtaining access to genetic resources, particularly because of practical difficulties in obtaining PIC in specific instances.[71] More clarity on PIC and MAT requirements, especially with respect to indigenous and local communities is necessary to create functional domestic ABS systems. In particular, implementation challenges may be likely to arise with regard to the interaction between community protocols and customary law on the one hand,[72] and national legal instruments on the other, even when the role of communities' customary laws is recognized in the constitutions of some countries, such as Ecuador.[73]

4.1.4 Dealing with Special Considerations

Implementing the provisions of the NP on special considerations[74] will require legal and institutional development. In light of the NP provisions on basic research,[75] it can be noted that not all countries differentiate between commercial and non-commercial research, and when they do, determining whether an application is for basic research or for commercial purposes has proven difficult. Accordingly, one of the criticisms of ABS legal frameworks from sectors involved

---

[69] Ibid, art. 2(e).
[70] Ibid, art. 6.2.
[71] See L. Lange, "CBD: Status, Pitfalls, Actions Needed and Perspectives," paper presented at JBA-UNU/IAS Symposium on Access to and Benefit-Sharing of Genetic Resources (2005); and J. Rosenthal, "Politics, Culture and Governance in the Development of Prior Informed Consent and Negotiated Agreements with Indigenous Communities," unpublished paper on file with the author.
[72] Nagoya Protocol, note 2, art. 12(t).
[73] See Constitution of the Republic of Ecuador 2008, art. 171.
[74] Nagoya Protocol, note 2, art. 8(c).
[75] Ibid, art. 8(a).

in basic research (universities and other research centers) concerns the lack of, or insufficient recognition of, the intrinsic advantages of basic research and its contribution to the conservation and sustainable use of biodiversity.[76] Countries (especially Southern countries which have clearly indicated that they will create PIC requirements for access to the genetic resources and associated TK located within their jurisdiction) will thus face several challenges from a legal certainty perspective; they may want to consider providing for flexibility for basic research, while establishing a clear differentiation for access for commercial purposes.[77] They should consider guaranteeing protection of the rights of the provider when a commercially valuable result is obtained from an activity initially considered basic research. Similarly, they should consider how to provide certainty to users when changes of intent result in the pursuit of commercial applications for research that was initially deemed non-commercial. As explained previously, special treatment for non-commercial research and expedited access to pathogens were supported by Northern countries and opposed by Southern countries who were reluctant to accept compromises that could undermine the benefit-sharing and compliance obligations of the NP. However, the design and implementation of strong user measures for Northern countries may provide enough assurance to Southern countries and result in the establishment of special regulations for non-commercial research and access to pathogens. Finally, expedited access to pathogens[78] is a completely new issue for most countries both in the South and in the North; currently there are no examples of specific domestic measures (such as exemptions, facilitative procedures, or quicker response times) developed in the context of domestic ABS systems. However, more general legislation regarding emergencies may apply, or at least be instructive.

4.1.5 Drafting and Implementing "Compliance Measures"

Few of the national ABS measures contain clear compliance-related provisions. As stated above, the Protocol leaves a great degree of latitude to the parties as to the types of measures they may adopt to meet their compliance obligations. It will be incumbent on countries to put in place adequate compliance mechanisms within their national ABS frameworks. So far, most of the draft proposals dealing with compliance measures under Articles 15 to 17 of the Protocol come from Northern countries. As previously explained, this was one of the most contentious issues between Northern and Southern countries. If Northern countries move

---

[76] See A. Grajal, "Biodiversity and the Nation State: Regulating Access to Genetic Resources Limits Biodiversity Research in Developing Countries" (1999) 13(1) *Conservation Biology* 6.

[77] S. Carrizosa, S. Brush, B. Wright, and P. Maguire (eds.), *Accessing Biodiversity and Sharing the Benefits: Lessons from Implementing the Convention on Biological Diversity* (Gland: IUCN, 2004).

[78] Nagoya Protocol, above note 2, art. 8(c).

212 — Access and Benefit-Sharing

quickly to adopt robust compliance measures, considering the flexibility of the NP on this matter, this may send a strong signal to Southern countries of good faith in the implementation of one of the key components of the NP: the compliance component. Evidence of Northern compliance may, in turn, motivate Southern countries to create more transparent, clear, reasonable, and enforceable ABS (PIC) regimes.

4.2 *Opportunities*

The NP also presents some interesting opportunities. It could, for instance, provide the basis for strengthening national competent authorities and for using information technologies to track permits and/or internationally recognized certificates of compliance. It may also create new opportunities for strengthening research and development on genetic and biochemical resources in the provider countries, most likely through partnerships with users.

The need to clarify the subject matter scope of national ABS frameworks,[79] including the definitions of "utilization" and "derivatives," may have a positive impact on legal certainty, leading to a more coherent and consistent interpretation and implementation of ABS measures by national authorities. In addition, the need to appropriately address non-commercial research in national ABS frameworks should take into account the fact that most of the ABS permits/ contracts in some countries are for basic research and mostly concern nationals. Thus, the design of a proper system to facilitate basic research and effectively differentiate between commercial and non-commercial access, while factoring in the potential change of use and intent, may lead to increased acceptance of domestic ABS frameworks by the research community, particularly at the national level.

Furthermore, the adoption of the NP provides new impetus for the adoption of national ABS laws in countries where these are still missing, and for the updating of laws that do not reflect the innovative provisions of the Protocol. Finally, capacity-building and cooperation between national competent authorities and other relevant stakeholders may take place as a result of the process of developing new measures required to implement the Protocol.

Both Northern and Southern countries can also benefit from the growing jurisprudence regarding the human rights of indigenous peoples, especially rights over their lands and territories and the right to participate in any decision-making affecting them. Accordingly, relevant cases of the Inter-American Court of Human Rights[80] can shed light on implementation options concerning key provisions

---

[79] Carrizosa et al. (eds), note 77.

[80] *Case of the Yakye Axa Indigenous Community* v *Paraguay*, Inter-American Court of Human Rights, Judgment of 17 June 2005, Series C No. 125.

of the NP related to the rights of indigenous and local communities,[81] including the right to grant PIC for genetic resources located within their lands.

The conservation obligations of the states must respect indigenous peoples' relationship with their ancestral lands, which constitute "the fundamental basis of their cultures, their spiritual life, their integrity, and their economic survival."[82] In addition, the Court has ruled that indigenous lands must be delimited and titled with the full participation of the community concerned, taking into account the community's customary laws, values, and customs.[83] Finally, the Court also held that states must put in place three safeguards vis-à-vis indigenous peoples: mechanisms for their effective participation in decision-making; benefit-sharing; and environmental and social impact assessments.[84] In this context, the Court pointed out that the duty to actively consult indigenous peoples requires the state to develop and disseminate information, ensure constant communication between the parties, and ensure that consultations are held in good faith, through culturally appropriate procedures, with the objective of reaching agreement.[85]

---

[81] *Nagoya Protocol*, note 2, arts. 5, 7 and 9.

[82] *Case of the Mayagna (Sumo) Awas Tingni Community v Nicaragua*, Inter-American Court of Human Rights, Judgment of 31 August 2001, Series C No. 79.

[83] Ibid.

[84] *Case of the Saramaka People v Suriname*, Inter-American Court of Human Rights, Judgment of 28 November 2007, Series C No. 172.

[85] Ibid.

10

Emerging Powerful Southern Voices: Role of BASIC Nations in Shaping Climate Change Mitigation Commitments

Rowena Maguire and Xiaoyi Jiang

1. INTRODUCTION

Climate change presents significant challenges for the global community. These challenges include increasing severity and occurrence of severe weather events; changes in food production/supply cycles; and the associated impacts of these occurrences on society and the economy.[1] The international community thus has a common goal and a need to work together to limit dangerous anthropogenic greenhouse gas (GHG) emissions. There is, however, no global consensus on who will undertake obligations to reduce GHG emissions beyond 2020. Not only are there tensions between the global North and the global South on the issue of mitigation responsibility, but there are also North/North and South/South tensions. The Durban Platform for Enhanced Action is the process under which a new legally binding climate instrument is being created. The Ad Hoc Working Group on the Durban Platform for Enhanced Action (ADP) was launched to develop "a protocol, another legal instrument or an agreed outcome with legal force under the Convention applicable to all Parties."[2] This new agreement must be drafted by 2015 and will enter into force in 2020.[3] This instrument will aim to prevent warming beyond two degrees Celsius and will require action from the global community.

Climate change has traditionally been perceived as involving a conflict between Northern and Southern interests. Northern nations have historically contributed

[1] See generally Intergovernmental Panel on Climate Change, *Climate Change 2014: Mitigation of Climate Change (Summary for Policymakers)* (New York: Cambridge University Press 2014), p. 9.

[2] UN Framework Convention on Climate Change, *Report of the Conference of the Parties on its Seventeenth Session, Held in Durban from 28 November to 11 December 2011*, 15 March 2012, FCCC/CP/2011/9/Add.1, Decision 2/CP.17 at para. 2. For a detailed interpretation of Parties submissions on the meaning of this provision see R. Maguire, "The Role of Common but Differentiated Responsibility in the 2020 Climate Regime" (2013) 4 *Carbon and Climate Law Review* 1.

[3] Ibid at 4.

much higher levels of emissions compared with Southern nations and have stronger economic and technological capacity to mitigate GHG emissions.[4] However, the impacts of climate change are projected to affect Southern nations disproportionately, particularly small island developing states (SIDS) and other states prone to natural disasters or extreme weather events. Climate change has, therefore, been seen as raising significant equity considerations, given that those least responsible for climate change are the ones most likely to be affected by it.[5] One of the most significant issues in the climate change negotiations has been the failure of the United States to ratify the Kyoto Protocol to the United Nations Framework Convention on Climate Change[6] (Kyoto Protocol) and the lack of obligations for China under it.

Climate change has given rise to considerable North–North tensions. The European Union (EU) is advocating for a new climate instrument to be negotiated at the international level (a top-down approach)[7] while other Northern nations, such as the United States[8] and Japan,[9] favor targets to be set at the domestic level according to national priorities (a bottom-up approach). The EU seeks to strengthen climate commitments by requiring inclusion of the following five principles: transparency, quantifiability, comparability, verifiability, and ambition. By contrast, the United States approach seeks to ensure full flexibility for parties based on national circumstances and capabilities.[10]

The general Southern position advanced by the G77 and China has been to push for an instrument that requires developed countries to take unconditional leadership in the areas of mitigation, adaptation, finance, and technology development and transfer.[11] The South/South tensions have arisen between the interests

[4] J. Brunnee, "Climate Change, Global Environmental Justice and International Environmental Law," in J. Ebbesson and P. Okowa (eds.), *Environmental Law and Justice in Context* (New York: Cambridge University Press, 2009), p. 317.

[5] R. Maguire and B. Lewis, "The Influences of Justice Theories on International Climate Policies and Measures" (2012) 8(1) *Macquarie Journal of International and Environmental Law* 16.

[6] Kyoto, 11 December 1997, in force 16 February 2005, UN Doc FCCC/CP/1997/7/Add.1, Dec. 10, 1997; 37 ILM 22 (1998) [hereinafter Kyoto Protocl].

[7] D. Bodansky, *The Durban Platform: Issues and Options for a 2015 Agreement*, December 2012, www.c2es.org.

[8] U.S. Government, "US Submission on Elements of 2015 Agreement," February 12, 2014, http://unfccc.int.

[9] Japanese Government, "Submission by Japan – Information, Views and Proposals on Matters Related to the Work of Ad Hoc Working Group on the DURBAN Platform for Enhanced Action," May 14, 2013, http://unfccc.int.

[10] A. Herold and A. Siemons, "Up-Front Information for Emission Reduction Contributions in the 2015 Agreements under the UNFCCC," Background paper, OKO-Institut e.V, April 30, 2014, pp. 20–21.

[11] UN Climate Change Newsroom, "Statement on Behalf of Group 77 and China by Mr. Amena Yauvioli, Ambassador, UNFCCC Chair of the G77 and China, at the opening plenary of the 2–3 Session of the Ad Hoc Working Group on the Durban Platform for Enhanced Action (ADP 2–3) Poland, Warsaw, 12 November, 2013," http://unfccc.int.

of Southern nations that are rapidly developing versus other vulnerable or least developed countries, such as SIDS and least developed countries (LDCs). The BASIC acronym refers to Brazil, South Africa, India, and China as a negotiating bloc of rapidly emerging Southern economies. In 2007 BASIC countries accounted for nearly 60 percent of total annual emissions from non-Annex I countries and around 29 percent of total global emissions,[12] hence the need to commit these nations to reduce their emissions in the future.

Statements by the BASIC bloc at the climate negotiations emphasize the continued application of the Convention's method of differentiation between developed and developing countries,[13] seeking to ensure that in future agreements, BASIC nations will not have the same level of mitigation commitments as developed countries. China has worked hard to retain its position as a developing country through the G77 alliance and has embraced its Southern nation status by advocating as the voice of the South within international climate negotiations. Atapattu has argued that the time has surely come to differentiate within the broad categories of developing countries,[14] and this chapter argues that any future mitigation obligations should be based upon differential obligations for at least three categories – developed countries, emerging economies (such as BASIC nations), and vulnerable developing countries – to ensure an equitable and fair approach to mitigation.

Other Southern perspectives are voiced through statements of the Alliance for Small Island States (AOSIS) and submissions of the LDCs. AOSIS seeks to ensure that temperature increases are limited to 1.5 degrees Celsius,[15] while also calling for scaled-up, predictable, new and additional finance and the development of a loss and damage mechanism.[16] This position differs from the broader temperature goal, which seeks to prevent warming beyond two degrees Celsius. Following the Doha Conference of the Parties (COP) negotiations in 2012, where the second commitment period of the Kyoto Protocol was formally adopted, AOSIS lamented: "[w]e see the package before us as deeply deficient in mitigation (carbon cuts) and

---

[12] K. Hallding et al., *Together Alone: BASIC Countries and the Climate Change Conundrum* (Copenhagen: Nordic Council of Ministers, 2011), p. 32.

[13] UN Climate Change Newsroom, "Statement by China on Behalf of Brazil, India, South Africa and China at the Opening Plenary of the Durban Platform, 12 November 2013, Warsaw, Poland," http://unfccc.int.

[14] S. Atapattu, "Climate Change, Differentiated Responsibilities and State Responsibility: Devising Novel Legal Strategies for Damage Caused by Climate Change," in B. Richardson et al. (eds.) *Climate Law and Developing Countries* (Cheltenham: Edward Elgar Publishing, 2009), p. 38.

[15] UN Climate Change Newsroom, "Statement by Nauru on behalf of the AOSIS at the Opening of the Ad Hoc Working Group on the Durban Platform for Enhanced Action, 12 November, Warsaw, Poland," http://unfccc.int.

[16] UN Climate Change Newsroom, "Statement by Nauru on behalf of the AOSIS at the Closing of the Ad Hoc Working Group on the Durban Platform for Enhanced Action, 14 March, Bonn, Germany," http://unfccc.int.

finance. It's likely to lock us on the trajectory to a 3, 4, 5 C rise in global temperatures, even though we agreed to the keep the global average rise of 1.5 C to ensure the survival of all islands."[17]

While it is not uncommon to see AOSIS dissatisfaction featured in media following the annual COP meetings, most AOSIS members continue to participate in G77 submissions to the climate regime despite the significant differences in economic status and GHG emissions within the group. This chapter explores these North/South, North/North and South/South tensions in respect of legally binding mitigation obligations under the United Nations Framework Convention on Climate Change[18] (UNFCCC). The reinterpretation of the principle of common but differentiated responsibility (CBDR) will play a key role in defining the roles of Northern and Southern nations under the ADP. This chapter examines the formation and influence of the BASIC nations in international climate negotiations. BASIC nations hold significant power in the UN climate talks and will play a key role in shaping Southern country emission reduction commitments in the 2020 instrument. The chapter then explores the negotiating positions of Southern and Northern nations in the run-up to the 2020 climate instrument, and explores the parties' positions on how differential treatment should be interpreted under this instrument.

2. NORTH/SOUTH TENSIONS: CLIMATE NORM OF COMMON BUT DIFFERENTIATED RESPONSIBILITY

The climate change legal regime adopts the principle of CBDR, which has had significant influence in shaping the obligations of parties. Article 3(1) of the UNFCCC requires parties to "protect the climate system for the benefit of present and future generations of human kind on the basis of equity and in accordance with their common but differentiated responsibilities and respective capabilities. Accordingly, the developed country parties should take the lead in combating climate change and the adverse effects thereof."

Article 3(3) recognizes that climate policies and measures must take into account different socioeconomic contexts, while Article 3(4) recognizes that policies and measures should be appropriate for the specific conditions of each party. These should be integrated with national development programs taking into account that economic development is essential for adopting measures to address climate change. Some Northern nations, most notably the United States, tried to resist such a strong commitment to differential treatment in both the founding principles and obligations of the UNFCCC, fearing that the principle could be used to create or infer

---

[17] R. Harrabin, "UN Climate Talks Extend Kyoto Protocol, Promise Compensation," BBC, December 8, 2012.

[18] New York, 9 May 1992, in force 21 March 1994, 1771 UNTS 107; S. Treaty Doc No. 102–38; UN Doc. A/AC.237/18 (Part II)/Add.1; 31 ILM 849 (1992).

obligations beyond the scope of the existing agreement.[19] Southern nations were, however, insistent that the UNFCCC must recognize that Northern nations were historically responsible for the cumulative levels of greenhouse gas emissions, and as such were required to take the lead in mitigating climate change.[20]

The Kyoto Protocol was adopted in 1997 with the objective of committing Northern parties to legally binding emission reduction targets. It changed the face of differential treatment within international environmental law by limiting its scope to industrialized nations (Annex I Parties). Earlier interpretations of CBDR, for example under the Montreal Protocol on Substances that Deplete the Ozone Layer[21] (Montreal Protocol), allowed for differentiation based on the implementation obligations of developed and developing countries through the creation of: delayed compliance schedules;[22] different baseline requirements;[23] and obligations to provide financial and technological assistance to developing nations.[24] Thus the differential obligations under the Montreal Protocol *were designed to assist developing countries in meeting their commitments under the relevant treaty, not to exclude or protect them from particular commitments.*[25] This can be contrasted with the Kyoto Protocol model.[26] As Rajamani states: "[t]he Kyoto Protocol bears tremendous significance for developing countries as it endorses a unique form of differentiation in their favour, and captures a model of developed country leadership yet to be seen elsewhere. But it is precisely this form of differential treatment and this model of developed country leadership that have proven contentious."[27]

The lack of emission reduction obligations for all parties to the UNFCCC under the Kyoto Protocol has remained one of the most controversial issues causing divisions among Northern parties – among those who are willing to abide by this model of differentiation (EU) and those unwilling to accept it (United States). The Protocol provides for two types of differential treatment: differential obligations based on industrialized or non-industrialized status and individual emission

---

[19] D. Bodansky, "The United Nations Framework Convention on Climate Change: A Commentary" (1993) 18 *Yale Journal of International Law* 451 at 501.

[20] R. Maguire, "Foundations of International Climate Law: Objectives, Principles and Methods," in E. Hollo et al. (eds.), *Climate Change and the Law* (Berlin: Springer, 2013), p. 83.

[21] Montreal, 16 September 1987, in force 1 January 1989, 1522 UNTS 3; 26 ILM 1550 (1987), Preamble.

[22] Ibid, art. 5.

[23] Ibid, art. 5(3).

[24] Ibid, art. 10(a).

[25] L. Rajamani, "The Changing Fortunes of Differential Treatment in the Evolution of International Environmental Law" (2012) 88 *International Affairs* 605 at 608.

[26] Article 10 of the Protocol seeks to reinforce the obligations created under the UNFCCC and requires both industrialized and non-industrialized parties to take mitigation steps in accordance with the principle of CBDR and their specific national and regional development priorities. However, Article 10 does not require non-industrialized parties to report on these mitigation efforts. For further background on CBDR, see Atapattu, note 14.

[27] Rajamani, note 25 at 612.

reduction pledges for Annex I Parties. The first type means that industrial/Northern states have emission reduction obligations (Annex I Parties) and non-industrial/ Southern parties hold no binding obligations (Non-Annex I Parties) for the first commitment period (2008–2012), which has now been extended to a second commitment period (2013–2020).[28] The second type of differential treatment relates to the emission reduction pledges of Annex I Parties under the Kyoto Protocol. There is a great deal of differentiation in terms of the stringency of these commitments undertaken by the thirty-seven industrialized nations and the European Community. During the first commitment period the European Community pledged an 8 percent reduction, while other countries such as Australia and Iceland were able to increase their emissions from 1990 levels by 8 percent and 10 percent respectively.[29] The Protocol also acknowledged the need for flexibility for those parties undergoing the process of transitioning to a market economy.[30] The obligations of Annex I parties are:

- The first commitment period tasked thirty-seven industrial nations to reduce their overall emissions by at least 5 percent below 1990 levels (2008–2012).[31]
- The second commitment period requires the thirty-eight parties[32] to reduce their overall emissions by at least 18 percent below 1990 levels in the commitment period (2013–2020).[33]

Not all parties to the UNFCCC are parties to the Kyoto Protocol. The United States withdrew before ratification of the first commitment period; Canada withdrew after it ratified the Kyoto Protocol but before the second commitment period; and Japan, Russia, and New Zealand have communicated that they are not planning to ratify the Doha Amendment.[34] The second commitment period now

---

[28] UN Framework Convention on Climate Change, *Report of the Conference of the Parties Serving as the Meeting of the Parties to the Kyoto Protocol on its Eight Session, Held in Doha from 26 November to 8 December 2012*, 28 February 2013, FCCC/KP/CMP/2012/13/Add.1, Decision 1/CMP.8.

[29] Australia won concessions on its target by threatening to withdraw if its 8 per cent increase target was not accepted. The Australian Institute, "A Poisoned Chalice: Australia and the Kyoto Protocol," Background Paper No. 13, 1998.

[30] Kyoto Protocol, note 6, art. 3(6).

[31] Ibid, art. 3(1).

[32] Australia, Austria, Belarus, Belgium, Croatia, Cyprus, Czech Republic, Denmark, Estonia, European Union, Finland, France, Germany, Greece, Hungary, Iceland, Ireland, Italy, Kazakhstan, Latvia, Liechtenstein, Lithuania, Luxembourg, Malta, Monaco, Netherlands, Norway, Poland, Portugal, Romania, Slovakia, Slovenia, Spain, Sweden, Switzerland, Ukraine, and the United Kingdom of Great Britain and Northern Ireland.

[33] *Doha Amendment to the Kyoto Protocol*, Reference C.N.718.2012.TREATIES –XXVII.7.C (Depositary Notification), para. C.

[34] D. Streimikiene, "The 18th Session of the Conference of the Parties to the United Nations Convention on Climate Change (UNFCCC)" (2013) 7(2) *Intellectual Economics* 254 at 256.

covers only 15 percent of global emissions,[35] and as such there is a real need for a new mitigation instrument to be negotiated. BASIC nations do not hold legally binding commitments under either commitment period, despite the significant increase in their emissions. All BASIC nations support the current interpretation of differentiation under the Protocol, and have banded together to ensure that the industrialized/non-industrialized distinction is retained in the 2015 instrument. This is unacceptable to the United States, which insists that emerging economies such as China accept legally binding emission reduction obligations in any future climate instrument.

3. FORMATION AND INFLUENCE OF THE BASIC CLIMATE NEGOTIATING BLOC

The EU has historically been considered a leader within the international climate regime due to its goal of seeking to prevent warming beyond two degrees Celsius and its advocacy of a top-down legally binding instrument applicable to all parties.[36] The EU funded a research program titled "BASIC" from January 2005 to January 2007 to support key developing countries' institutional capacity to undertake analytical work to determine what kind of national and international climate change actions best fit within their circumstances and priorities, in recognition of the importance of gaining buy-in from Southern nations with current and projected high emission growth.[37] "BASIC" here stood for *Building and Strengthening Institutional Capacities on Climate Change in Brazil, India, China and South Africa*. These four countries were chosen because of their environmental, economic, social, and political importance.[38] This project was responsible for creating the BASIC acronym and identity within the international climate arena, which differs from the BRICS acronym used to describe Brazil, Russia, India, China, and South Africa. Russia was not included within the BASIC group as it already had commitments under the Kyoto Protocol.[39]

---

[35] The top ten nations in terms of total carbon dioxide emissions are China, USA, India, Russia, Japan, Germany, Canada, South Korea, Iran, and the United Kingdom. See S. Banerjee, "A Climate for Change? Critical Reflections on the Durban United Nations Climate Change Conference" (2012) 33(12) *Organisation Studies* 1761 at 1772–1773.

[36] C. F. Parker et al., "Fragmented Climate Change Leadership: Making Sense of the Ambiguous Outcomes of COP 15" (2012) 21(2) *Environmental Politics* 268 at 277.

[37] Q. Xinran, "The Rise of BASIC in UN Climate Change Negotiations" (2011) 18(3) *South African Journal of International Affairs* 295 at 301.

[38] F. Yamin, "Strengthening the Capacity of Developing Countries to Prepare For and Participate In Negotiations on Future Actions under the UNFCCC and its Kyoto Protocol," The BASIC Project Final Report, Institute of Development Studies, September 2007.

[39] A-S. Tabau and M. Lemoine, "Willing Power, Fearing Responsibilities: BASIC in the Climate Negotiations" (2012) 3 *Carbon and Climate Law Review* 197 at 199.

At the completion of the project, the Sao Paulo Proposal for an Agreement on Future International Climate Policy[40] was adopted. This instrument outlines twenty elements that the BASIC countries would like to see in an amended Kyoto Protocol. Some of the elements from the Proposal that may influence the shape of the future regime include:

- Parties agree on medium and long-term goals which are used to assess progress (goals should include setting the maximum temperature increase, maximum atmospheric concentrations, maximum loss of natural ecosystems).
- Inclusion of land use, land-use change, and forestry activities within emission limitation commitments.
- Non-Annex I Parties are expected to become Annex I Parties and adopt national emissions limitation commitments when their cumulative transfers of certified emission reduction units and voluntary emission reduction units reach their share of the global transfer limit (the global limit is based on population and an index that reflects the country's responsibility, capability, and potential to mitigate).
- Development of a Convention Fund with contributions of $10 billion in order to enable COP to better raise and manage financial resources needed to address climate change.

The BASIC project has now evolved into a political alliance, and government representatives meet four times a year to find common ground on international climate policy.[41] At the conclusion of each BASIC ministerial meeting a joint statement is released which summarizes the position of the BASIC governments on key issues under negotiation within the UNFCCC.[42]

The rise of the BASIC group has resulted in three power blocs within the UNFCCC negotiations – the EU, the United States, and the BASIC group.[43] Studies, however, show that most stakeholders see China as holding power within the

---

[40] Erik Haites et al., "The Sao Paulo Proposal for an Agreement on Future International Climate Policy," Discussion Paper 09–31, Harvard Project on International Climate Agreements, Belfer Center for Science and International Affairs, Harvard Kennedy School, October 2009.

[41] The thirteenth BASIC Meeting was held in Beijing, China in November 2012; the fourteenth meeting in Chennai, India, in February 2013; the fifteenth meeting in Cape Town, South Africa, in June 2013; and the sixteenth meeting in Foz do Iguaçu, Brazil, September 2013.

[42] See e.g. "Joint Statement on BASIC from 16th Ministerial Meeting on Climate Change in Brazil," September 15, 2013, https://www.environment.gov.za/mediarelease/16thbasic_minister ialmeeting_climatechange.

[43] R. Maguire, "The Rise of the BASIC Nations within the International Climate Regime: The Challenge of Ensuring Equitable Mitigation Obligations," in R. Maguire et al. (eds.), *Shifting Global Powers: Challenges and Opportunities for International Law* (London: Routledge, 2013), p. 116.

222   *Emerging Powerful Southern Voices*

TABLE 10.1 *Actors perceived as leaders on climate change by geographical region (percentages)*

	EU as Leader		US as Leader		China as Leader	
	COP 14	COP 15	COP 14	COP 15	COP 14	COP 15
Africa	38	36	24	47	62	36
Asia	63	31	14	35	35	39
Europe	75	65	42	68	52	54
North America	54	53	38	63	46	47
South/Latin America	57	47	14	29	64	47
Oceania	50	16	17	40	17	36
All respondents	**63**	**46**	**27**	**54**	**47**	**48**

BASIC negotiating bloc.[44] Parker's findings (see note 44) are based on a survey distributed to delegates at the Poznan and Copenhagen UNFCCC negotiations for the purpose of tracking views on leadership perceptions within the UNFCCC negotiations.

These results provide evidence of the growing influence of China within the UNFCCC negotiations, although both the EU and United States are still perceived as holding significant power. These results also suggest that there is no global leader and that power is shared between Northern and powerful Southern voices. This is a positive development as it prevents any one bloc from completely controlling the negotiations. This is a significant power shift within international environmental law and its ramifications are yet to be fully understood.

The rise of China provides an opportunity for Southern voices to shape the international climate regime. However, there are concerns that powerful Southern nations such as China do not represent the interests of vulnerable nations such as SIDS or LDCs.[45] China and the other BASIC nations have sought to retain their position as Southern nations within the international legal order. Such positioning provides huge strategic advantage to BASIC nations when negotiating on issues such as development, equity, financing, technology transfer, and historical responsibility. Given the huge diversity within the Southern bloc and their increasing emissions, it is inequitable for BASIC nations to hold the same level of obligations as SIDS or LDCs. Despite this, the BASIC bloc has used its position to present *the unified voice of developing countries in the climate change negotiations.*[46]

---

[44] C. F. Parker et al., "Fragmented Climate Change Leadership: Making Sense of the Ambiguous Outcomes of COP 15" (2012) 21(2) *Environmental Politics* 268.

[45] K. A. Hochstetler, "The G77, BASIC, and Global Climate Governance: A New Era in Multilateral Environmental Negotiations" (2012) 55 *Revista Brasileira de Política Internacional* 53 at 58.

[46] "Joint Statement on BASIC from 10th Ministerial Meeting on Climate Change in New Delhi, India," February 13–14, 2012, http://www.cseindia.org/userfiles/10th-BASIC-Meeting-Delhi-Joint-Statement.pdf.

The BASIC group is thus seeking to represent the wide diversity of Southern interests, including the interests of the BASIC bloc, for continued rapid development and the need of vulnerable nations for survival.

4. UNLIKELY PARTNERSHIP: EXPLORING BASIC INDIVIDUAL INTERESTS AND POSITIONS

Hallding et al. note that while BASIC nations sometimes work together at the UNFCCC, these countries must be understood as "four separate entities with their own policy priorities and strategies. Different norms and ideas, material concerns and relationships affect the stance that each country brings to the negotiation table and these in turn shape the substance of BASIC cooperation, explaining why they partner on some issues, but not on others."[47]

In order to understand the dynamics of the BASIC group at the international level it is necessary to understand each member's domestic profile and climate politics and policies.

4.1 *China*

China's emissions have rapidly increased, and it has overtaken the United States as the world's largest CO^2 emitter.[48] China has been actively participating in the UN post–Kyoto negotiations as well as other fora, including the G8 + 5 Summit, the APEC Economic Leaders' Meeting and the Asia-Pacific Partnership on Clean Development and Climate. There are three central issues that China has been advocating at every forum:

1. UNFCCC is the central place for the international climate regime and the principle of CBDR is at the heart of this regime.
2. Northern countries must honor commitments relating to technology transfer and to providing financial support to Southern countries.
3. China is aware of the urgent need to address climate change and is willing to take on a range of domestic commitments provided that real action is taken by Northern and other growing Southern countries. China has not made any firm promises regarding any binding commitments at the international level.

China is viewed as a recalcitrant actor within the UNFCCC negotiations.[49] Northern nations see China as only being interested in national issues and not

---

[47] Hallding et al., note 12, p. 14.
[48] Xinran, above note 37 at 299.
[49] S. V. Valentin, "Enhancing Climate Change Mitigation Efforts through Sino-American Collaboration" (2013) 6 *The Chinese Journal of International Politics* 159.

interested in reaching a point of common understanding.[50] China's involvement in all international negotiations is guided by the following three considerations: concern that international cooperation may lead to dependency and instability; a preference for staying out of situations where core economic interests are compromised; and wishing to come across as a responsible player that takes active leadership in the global South.[51] These considerations help explain China's interest in participating in the BASIC bloc and G77 forum at the UNFCCC negotiations. Alignment with the BASIC group is very strategic for China as it means that it can share the blame for growing emission trajectories with other emerging economies, while involvement with the G77 means that China can claim Southern country status and hold Northern states responsible for climate change. China has thus been a master of political maneuvering within the UNFCCC negotiations and has been somewhat successful in distracting attention from its failure to commit to legally binding emission reduction obligations.

At the domestic level, rising public concern over poor air and water quality is driving significant environmental reforms. A 2013 study based on a national sample of the population found that 47 percent of respondents viewed air pollution as a huge concern while 40 percent viewed water pollution as a major issue.[52] Controlling air pollution is seen to bring multiple benefits for both human and environmental health and the 2013 amendments to the National Air Pollution Prevention and Control Laws, which seek to control emissions of six heavy polluting industries (thermal power, iron/steel, petrochemicals, cement, non-ferrous metals, and chemicals) to comply with international standards, have been welcomed by Chinese citizens.[53] In addition to reforming air quality standards, the Chinese government is also developing carbon pricing mechanisms at the domestic level, with the National Development and Reform Commission selecting seven provinces to a pilot emission-trading scheme between 2011 and 2013.[54] This emission-trading pilot scheme has been viewed as a mechanism that will assist China in implementing the commitment made by Premier Wen Jianbao at Copenhagen to reduce national emission intensity by 40–45 percent by 2020, compared to 2005 levels.[55]

---

[50] Hallding et al., note 12, p. 72.

[51] Ibid, p. 73.

[52] A. Kohut and R. Wike, "Environmental Concerns on the Rise in China," Pew Research Center's Global Attitudes Project, September 19, 2013, p. 2.

[53] B. Finamore, "Air Pollution Crisis Gives New Momentum to Environmental Regulation in China," February 22, 2013, http://switchboard.nrdc.org.

[54] The seven provinces are Beijing, Tianjin, Shanghai, Chongqing, Hubei, Guangdong, and Shenzhen. National Development and Reform Commission, "Notice on Launching Pilots for Emissions Trading System" (2011).

[55] D. Zhang et al., "Emissions Trading in China: Progress and Prospects" *Energy Policy* (2014) (in press).

4.2 *India*

India's per capita emissions are very low compared with other BASIC countries and India has strongly advocated for the interpretation of CBDR to be based on a formula that considers emissions per capita.[56] India is home to around 17 percent of the world's population, but is plagued by deep inequality, with around 42 percent of the population living below the national poverty line.[57] It is predicted that India's emissions will rise substantially in the future due to its heavy reliance on fossil fuels. India is now the third largest emitter of CO^2 after China and the US.[58] Given the huge inequality and development needs of the country, India has been staunchly against accepting any type of legally binding cap on emissions within the UNFCCC negotiations. This stance changed during the Copenhagen negotiations, when the Minister for Environment and Forests announced that India would reduce emission intensity of its GDP by 20–25 percent by 2020 in comparison to the 2005 levels. There has been strong opposition to this pledge from all political parties domestically.[59]

Some have questioned India's involvement with the BASIC bloc.[60] It has been suggested that the main benefits for India in being involved in the BASIC bloc is to improve the Sino–Indian relationship, as climate change is one of the rare areas where India and China have a good relationship.[61] Their shared views on the importance of CBDR in shaping future mitigation commitments have created an area of consensus, which has provided a basis upon which to extend dialogue concerning international climate negotiations.[62]

4.3 *Brazil*

The Brazilian position is based around three issues: preservation of the sovereign right to development; opposition to any legally binding initiatives to regulate the Amazon rainforest; and emphasis on the historic responsibility of industrialized countries to compensate for their emissions to date.[63] Of all the BASIC nations, Brazil has one of the cleanest development trajectories, with more than 45 percent

---

[56] P. Shukla and S. Dhar, "Climate Agreements and India: Aligning Options and Opportunities on a New Track" (2011) 11 *International Environmental Agreements* 229 at 232.

[57] Hallding et al., note 12, p.57.

[58] Xinran, note 37 at 299.

[59] Hallding et al., note 12, p. 64.

[60] M. Levi, "International Perspectives on India's Climate Positions," in N. Dubash (ed.), *A Handbook on Climate Change and India: Development, Politics and Governance* (New York: Earthscan, 2011), p. 192.

[61] Hallding et al., note 12, p. 65.

[62] S. Walsh et al., "China and India's Participation in Global Climate Negotiations" (2011) 11 *International Environmental Agreements* 261.

[63] Hallding et al., note 12, p. 38.

of energy being sourced from renewables (31.5 percent biomass and 13.8 percent hydropower),[64] and is the lowest ranked BASIC nation in terms of global emissions.[65] This, coupled with Brazil's natural advantage in the land-use sector (emission reductions from improved forest management), means that Brazil will be able to achieve its Copenhagen pledge of a 36.1–38.9 percent reduction of projected 2020 emissions with relative ease.

The push for climate action in Brazil is driven by growing support for the domestic Green political party, along with Brazil's desire to be viewed as a rising responsible global power. Climate change was an important issue in the 2010 presidential election and Green Party candidate Marina Silva received 19 percent of the total popular vote.[66] The popularity of the green vote pushed both the government and opposition parties to develop climate policies, which then played into Brazil's preparation and participation at the Copenhagen negotiations. Leadership in the UNFCCC is also strategic for Brazil, which seeks to establish itself as a responsible rising power with a history of hosting significant environmental events.[67]

4.4 South Africa

South Africa's economy relies upon its natural mineral and fossil fuel resources, and the country is the world's thirteenth highest emitter of GHGs.[68] Climate change does not feature as a political issue domestically. The main drive for South Africa's Copenhagen pledge of a 34 percent reduction below business-as-usual levels of 2020 and 42 percent below business-as-usual levels by 2020 was the political leadership of President Jacob Zuma.[69] The South African UNFCCC position is normally formed by the Department of Environmental Affairs independent of international political alliances, meaning that Zuma's Copenhagen pledge was met with dismay domestically.[70] Zuma's motivation for involvement in the BASIC bloc is thought to be based upon a desire to be a moral leader within the UNFCCC and to leverage this leadership power in other international fora. A complicating factor for South Africa's involvement with the BASIC bloc is its position within the African Group. The Copenhagen negotiations brought the conflict between BASIC and Africa to the surface, with the African group feeling betrayed by South Africa when it joined other BASIC nations to prevent the adoption of a legally binding instrument.[71] South Africa has significant economic

---

[64] Ibid, p. 40.
[65] Xinran, above note 37 at 299.
[66] K. Hochstetler and E. Viola, "Brazil and the Politics of Climate Change: Beyond the Global Commons" (2012) 21(5) *Environmental Politics* 753 at 764.
[67] Hallding et al., note 12, p. 47.
[68] Xinran, note 37 at 299.
[69] Hallding et al., note 12, p. 54.
[70] Ibid.
[71] Xinran, note 37 at 309.

and security ties within the African region and its continued involvement with the BASIC bloc generates ongoing tensions within the African region.[72]

5. BASIC AT COP 15 COPENHAGEN NEGOTIATIONS 2009

The BASIC bloc has been playing a leadership role in the UNFCCC negotiations since the Copenhagen COP negotiations in 2009, which were meant to produce a new legally binding instrument as a successor to the Kyoto Protocol. Conflicting North/South, North/North and South/South tensions resulted in a non-legally binding instrument being created outside the official negotiations. The Copenhagen Accord[73] has been viewed as a face-saving compromise. It has been heavily criticized for bypassing the main negotiating forum and is perceived as a side deal struck between the United States and BASIC nations that wanted an agreement which avoided any reference to a future legally binding instrument.[74] In addition, these groups wanted monitoring, reporting, and verification standards that were self-assessed rather than subject to international evaluation. These factors meant the Copenhagen Accord was an extremely watered-down instrument which required very little commitment from Northern nations and the BASIC group.

What brought the members of the BASIC group together at Copenhagen was their opposition to the "Danish text" (a draft text made by the UK, United States, and Denmark in preparation for COP15).[75] BASIC felt ambushed by this text,[76] and decided to collectively "peel off the United States from the EU" in order to prevent this document from shaping the negotiations.[77] A leaked cable from the U.S. Deputy National Security Advisor warned his EU counterpart about the increasing influence of BASIC countries:

> It is remarkable how closely coordinated the BASIC group has become in international forums, taking turns to impede US/EU initiatives and playing the US and EU off against each other. BASIC countries have widely differing interests, but have subordinated these to their common short-term goals. The US and EU need to learn from this co-ordination and work much more closely and effectively

[72] Hallding et al., note 12, p. 55.
[73] UN Framework Convention on Climate Change, *Report of the Conference of the Parties on its Fifteenth Session, Held in Copenhagen from 7 to 19 December 2009*, 30 March 2010, FCCC/CP/2009/AA/Add.1, Decision 2/cp.15.
[74] Tabau and Lemoine, note 39 at 202.
[75] Hallding et al., note 12, p. 20.
[76] Details of the "Danish text" were leaked by the *Guardian* newspaper. BASIC nations were opposed to this text as it reinforced unequal limits on per capita emissions (i.e. individuals in Northern nations would continue to have higher emission contributions than individuals in Southern nations): J. Vidal, "Copenhagen Climate Summit in disarray after 'Danish Text' Leak," *The Guardian*, December 9, 2009.
[77] Ibid.

228   *Emerging Powerful Southern Voices*

together ourselves, to better handle third country obstructionism and avoid future train wrecks on climate, Doha or financial regulatory reform.[78]

The Copenhagen Accord is described as "bottom-up" regulation, as parties submitted voluntary emission reduction targets, as opposed to a "top-down" approach negotiated at the international level specifying the commitments needed to prevent anthropogenic climate change.[79] This "bottom-up" approach produced a variety of Annex I emission reduction targets with varying baseline years (while most countries used 1990 per the Convention, other baselines were also submitted), which complicates the development of harmonized rules on monitoring, reporting and verification. Some Non-Annex I Parties submitted Nationally Appropriate Mitigation Action (NAMAs) pledges. There is a lack of consistency within the NAMA pledges; for example, some included an emission reduction commitment (all BASIC nations included an emission reduction target), while others provided a summary of the sectors and policies that will be used to generate emission reductions. Furthermore, some pledges included a base year, while others, such as those from Indonesia and Papua New Guinea, did not.

Table 10.2 summarizes the submissions made after Copenhagen. Some significant pledges came from Southern states that are particularly vulnerable to climate change and whose interests are best advanced by avoiding significant consequences of climate change. Particularly noteworthy pledges came from the Marshall Islands (40 percent below 2009 levels by 2020), and Papua New Guinea (50 percent levels by 2030, no baseline specified), with Bhutan and the Maldives aiming for carbon neutral status.[80] The BASIC nations all pledged emission reduction targets or (in the case of India) reductions in emission intensity by 2020: Brazil 36–38 percent, China 40–45 percent, India 20–25 percent and South Africa 34 percent. Shortly afterwards, the United Nations Environment Program released *The Emission Gaps Report 2010*, which found that there was a significant gap between the Copenhagen emission reduction pledges and the action necessary to limit temperature rise to two degrees Celsius. According to this report, global emissions must not exceed forty-four gigatons of carbon dioxide by 2020 in order to limit the temperature increase to two degrees Celsius. If the lowest-ambition Copenhagen pledges were implemented, it is likely fifty-three gigatons of carbon dioxide would be released by 2020, producing a significant increase of nine gigatons of carbon dioxide.[81]

The failure to reach a legally binding agreement in Copenhagen brought South/South tensions to the surface. The Male' Declaration on the Human Dimension of Global Climate Change emphasized that "small island, low-lying coastal and atoll

---

[78] Banerjee, note 35 at 1779.

[79] D. Bodansky, "The Copenhagen Climate Change Conference—A Post Mortem" (2010) 104 *American Journal of International Law* 230.

[80] Bhutan is already carbon-neutral and the Maldives proposes to be carbon-neutral by 2020.

[81] United Nations Environment Program, "The Emissions Gap Report: Are the Copenhagen Accord Pledges Sufficient to Limit Global Warming to 2 C or 1.5 C?," 2010, www.unep.org.

TABLE 10.2 *Summary of Mitigation Targets and Actions from Copenhagen and Cancun*

Annex I Countries		Non-Annex I Countries		
Country	Economy-Wide Emission Target	Country	NAMA Target	NAMA (no target)
Australia	25% reduction compared with 2000 levels by 2020	Antigua and Barbuda	25% reduction compared with 1990 levels by 2020	Afghanistan; Algeria; Argentina; Armenia; Benin; Cambodia;
		Bhutan	Already carbon neutral	
Belarus	5–10% reduction compared with 1990 levels by 2020	Brazil	Mitigation actions resulting in 36.1%–38.9% below projected 2020 emissions	Cameroon; Central African Republic; Chad; Columbia;
Canada	17% reduction compared with 2005 levels by 2020	Chile	20% reduction below business-as-usual emissions growth trajectory in 2020, as projected 2007	Congo; Costa Rica; Cote d'Ivoire; Ethiopia; Eritrea; Gabon; Georgia;
Croatia	5% reduction compared with 1990 levels by 2020	China	Lower emissions intensity by 40–45% by 2020 compared with 2005	Ghana; Jordan, Madagascar Mauritius;
European Union	20% reduction compared with 1990 levels by 2020	India	Reduce emission intensity of GDP by 20–25% by 2020 compared with 2005	Mauritania; Mongolia; Morocco; Peru; San Marino;
Iceland	30% reduction compared with 1990 levels by 2020	Indonesia	26% reduction by 2020	Sierra Leone Tajikistan; The former Yugoslav Republic of Macedonia; Togo; Tunisia.
Japan	25% reduction compared with 1990 levels by 2020	Israel	20% reduction below business-as-usual levels in 2020	
Kazakhstan	15% reduction compared with 1992 levels by 2020	Maldives	Carbon neutral by 2020	
Liechtenstein	20% reduction compared with 1990 levels by 2020	Marshall Islands	40% reduction below 2009 by 2020	

(continued)

230 *Emerging Powerful Southern Voices*

Table 10.2 (*continued*)

Annex I Countries		Non-Annex I Countries	
Monaco	30% reduction compared with 1990 levels by 2020	Mexico	30% reduction below business-as-usual levels in 2020
New Zealand	10–20% reduction compared with 1990 levels by 2020	Papua New Guinea	50% reduction by 2030 and carbon neutral by 2050
Norway	30–40% reduction compared with 1990 levels by 2020	Republic of Korea	30% below business-as-usual levels in 2020
Russia Federation	15–25% reduction compared with 1990 levels by 2020	Republic of Moldova	At least 25% compared with 1990 levels by 2020
Switzerland	20–30% reduction compared with 1990 levels by 2020	Singapore	16% below business-as-usual levels in 2020
Ukraine	20% reduction compared with 1990 levels by 2020	South Africa	34% below business-as-usual levels of 2020 and 42% below business-as-usual levels by 2025.
United States of America	17% reduction compared with 2005 levels by 2020		

states are particularly vulnerable to even small changes in the global climate and are already adversely affected by alteration in ecosystems, changes in precipitation, rising sea-levels and increased incidence of natural disasters."[82]

The 2007 Declaration wanted to ensure that the parties to the UNFCCC reached "a post-2012 consensus to protect people, planet and prosperity by taking urgent action to stabilise the global climate."[83] The failure of Copenhagen to

---

[82] *Male' Declaration on Human Dimensions of Global Climate Change*, Male, November 14, 2007, available at www.ciel.org/Publications/Male_Declaration_Nov07.pdf.
[83] Ibid, art. 1.

produce a legally binding instrument was viewed by AOSIS as a major disappointment and, in the words of the Chair of AOSIS, "despite agreement on how negotiations should proceed through the year, there were still hurdles to cross in terms of what a new global deal might look like."[84] While the former president of the Maldives was also very critical of the Accord, his opposition was reversed once a US$50 million aid package from the United States was negotiated.[85]

Sudan, on behalf of the African Group, strongly resisted the Accord on procedural grounds, given that it had been negotiated outside the main negotiation sessions.[86] Sudan (as a country) then joined with Bolivia, Cuba, Nicaragua, Pakistan, Tuvalu, and Venezuela to prevent the meeting from formally adopting the Accord on both procedural and substantive grounds.[87] Most other developing countries and the spokespersons for AOSIS, LDCs, and the Africa Group recognized the legitimacy of the negotiation process and urged COP to adopt the Accord. Ultimately, the UN Secretary-General decided to "take note" of the Accord and requested parties to register their targets by 31 January 2010 (a process without precedent within the UNFCCC). The Copenhagen pledges were then formally recognized in the Cancun COP decision.[88]

6. ENHANCING ACTION TO ESTABLISH LEGALLY BINDING MITIGATION TARGETS

6.1 BASIC Relationship Repair

Following Copenhagen, the BASIC group needed to mend relationships with the G77, AOSIS, and the African Group and sought to mould its leadership to be more inclusive at future COP negotiations.[89] During the Cancun negotiations, BASIC sought to retain its position as the voice of the South but was much more diligent in consulting with other Southern nations. The BASIC group also displayed some flexibility with respect to monitoring, reporting, and verification standards by accepting that a top-down approach could be appropriate.[90] It also decided to invite representatives from the G77, AOSIS, and African Group to act as rotating chairs of the BASIC fora. This initiative, referred to as the BASIC+ Approach,

---

[84] "Slim Prospects for Climate Deal This Year, Says UN Climate Change Chief," Sify News, April 12, 2010.

[85] Banerjee, note 35 at 1779.

[86] Hochstetler, note 45 at 58.

[87] Sudan called the Accord a "suicide note for Africa." IISD, "A Brief Analysis of the Copenhagen Climate Change Conference," excerpted from Earth Negotiations Bulletin, vol. 12, No. 459, December 2009, p. 4.

[88] UN Framework Convention on Climate Change, *Report of the Conference of the Parties on its Sixteenth Session Held in Cancun from 29 November to 10 December 2010*, 15 March 2011, FCCC/KP/CMP/2010/12.Add.1, Decision 1/CP.16 at para. 3.

[89] Xinran, note 37 at 312.

[90] Ibid.

was launched at the tenth BASIC ministerial meeting held in February 2012. Tabau and Lemonie comment that this chair status has improved "the transparency and inclusiveness dynamic valorised by the BASIC group" and demonstrates that the group is willing to include other Southern positions beyond BASIC interests.[91] South Africa in particular needed to repair relationships with the African Group following Copenhagen, and did so by going against the BASIC group at the Cancun negotiations to call for a legally binding outcome.[92] South Africa has since used its position within the BASIC group to advocate for a legally binding outcome, which was finally accepted by all BASIC members at the Durban negotiations.[93]

6.2 The Durban Platform for Enhanced Action

The Durban Platform for Enhanced Action[94] is the process that has been established to create emission reduction commitments for all nations in the future. The Durban COP decision notes

> with grave concern the significant gap between the aggregate effect of parties' mitigation pledges in terms of global annual emissions of greenhouse gases by 2020 and aggregate emission pathways consistent with having a likely chance of holding the increase in global average temperature below 2 degrees Celsius or 1.5 degrees Celsius above pre-industrial levels.[95]

UNEP's Emission Gap Report 2012[96] suggests that it is possible to limit the temperature increase to two degrees Celsius by 2020, but meeting this target will require parties to implement ambitious conditional pledges (the higher end of the spectrum commitments) under the Cancun Agreement.[97]

An Ad Hoc Working Group on the Durban Platform for Enhanced Action (ADP) was launched to develop *a protocol, another legal instrument or an agreed*

---

[91] Tabau and Lemoine, note 39 at 199.

[92] Hallding et al., note 12, p. 56.

[93] Banerjee, note 35 at 1780.

[94] UN Framework Convention on Climate Change, *Report of the Conference of the Parties on Its Seventeenth Session, Held in Durban from 28 November to 11 December 2011*, 15 March 2012, FCCC/CP/2011/9/Add.1, Decision 1/CP.17.

[95] Ibid.

[96] United Nations Environment Program, "Emissions Gap Report 2012," November 2012, www.unep.org.

[97] The Climate Action Tracker website tracks progress on meeting these targets (available at http://climateactiontracker.org/methodology.html). Countries currently considered to be making inadequate progress include Northern nations such as Australia, Canada, European Union states, and the United States. China is the only BASIC nation in the inadequate category, while Brazil, India, and South Africa are classified as making medium progress. Maldives is a role model country and sufficient progress is also being made by Norway, South Korea, Bhutan, Costa Rica, Japan, and Papua New Guinea.

outcome with legal force under Convention application to all parties.[98] The new agreement must be drafted by 2015 and will enter into force in 2020.[99] Rajamani states:

> [...] this timeline, with a lengthy gap between the end of the negotiating phase, 2015, and the beginning of the implementing phase, 2020, is a product of compromise between the short timeline the Alliance of Small Island States, Least Developed Countries and the EU sought, and the lengthy timeline some of the major economies, in particular, China and the United States favoured. China had made it clear in the lead up to Durban that it would not participate in a legally binding climate agreement by 2020. The United States has long held the position that it would not participate in any instrument to which other major economies, in particular China, were not party.[100]

This shows a change from the dynamic of North/South tensions to now include North/North and South/South tensions. Two work streams were developed by the ADP:[101]

1. To take steps to negotiate an agreement that will be adopted by 2015 and enter into force in 2020.
2. To explore how to raise global ambition before 2020 to accelerate the response to climate change.

Southern nations accepted the deadlines set by work stream 1 on the condition that Northern nations improve their mitigation efforts between now and 2020. The Durban Platform made no mention of the CBDR principle, which led to speculation that the post–2020 climate agreement would be based on symmetrical emission reduction commitments for developed and developing countries.[102] The Doha COP decision responded to this speculation by *acknowledging that the work of the Ad Hoc Working Group on the Durban Platform for Enhanced Action shall be guided by the principles of the Convention.*[103] This suggests that the new agreement will be adopted under the UNFCCC and will benefit from the existing climate architecture. A more controversial issue will be the new interpretation and application of the CBDR principle. Not only are there differences between Northern

---

[98] UN Framework Convention on Climate Change, *Report of the Conference of the Parties on Its Seventeenth Session, Held in Durban from 28 November to 11 December 2011*, 15 March 2012, FCCC/CP/2011/9/Add.1 at para. 2.

[99] Ibid, para. 4.

[100] Rajamani, note 25 at 511.

[101] UN Framework Convention on Climate Change, *Report of the Conference of the Parties on Its Eighteenth Session Held in Doha from 26 November to 8 December 2012*, 28 February 2013, FCCC/CP/2012/8/Add.1. Decision 2/CP.18 at para. 3.

[102] D. Bodansky, "The Durban Platform Negotiations: Goals and Options," Policy Brief, Harvard Project on International Climate Agreements, Belfer Center for Science and International Affairs, Harvard Kennedy School, July 2012, pp. 1–3.

[103] UN Framework Convention on Climate Change, note 101.

234   *Emerging Powerful Southern Voices*

6.3 *Reinterpreting Differentiation*

At the Doha COP negotiations, states parties and accredited observer organizations were invited to submit information, views, and proposals on matters relating to the work of the ADP, including the application of the principles of the Convention.[104] Parties made individual and group submissions that included a diverse range of perspectives as to the appropriate method of differentiation that should apply in the 2020 climate regime. [105] China, India, Brazil, the African Group, and AOSIS advocated for the existing method of differentiation to remain in place. China argued that it is necessary to retain this distinction when full consideration is given to the development stages and respective capabilities of developing countries, bearing in mind that socioeconomic development and poverty eradication are the first and overriding priorities for developing countries.[106] Brazil focused on the historical responsibilities of developed nations, while India stated that any other approach to differentiation will involve a reinterpretation of the Convention which is beyond the scope of the ADP.[107] India also advocated for differentiation in enforcement, with Annex I Parties being subject to compliance monitoring and penalties for breach, while Non-Annex I are encouraged to remain in compliance through a set of incentives.[108]

A number of Southern nations supported differentiation based on the type or form of emission reduction adopted. For example, the LDC submission classified the parties as vulnerable or non-vulnerable, and advocated economy-wide emission reductions for non-vulnerable nations (regardless of their level of development) and sector-wide emission reduction measures for vulnerable nations.[109] India's submission proposed that Annex I Parties adopt quantified emission limitation and reduction objectives (QELRO) and that Non-Annex I Parties implement NAMAs. Japan agreed that QELROs should be adopted by all major economies. "Major economies" is not defined in the submission, but presumably refers to

---

[104] UN Framework Convention on Climate Change, *Report of the Ad Hoc Working Group on the Durban Platform for Enhanced Action on the Second Part of its First Session, Held in Doha from 27 November to 7 December 2012*, 7 February 2013, FCCC/ADP/2012/3 at para. 29.

[105] List of states parties' submissions available at: United Nations Framework Convention on Climate Change, "Submissions from Parties to the ADP," 2013, http://unfccc.int.

[106] Chinese Government, "China's Submission on the Work of the Ad Hoc Working Group on Durban Platform for Enhanced Action," March 6, 2014, http://unfccc.int, p. 3.

[107] Indian Government, "Submission by India on the work of the Ad Hoc Working Group on Durban Platform for Enhanced Action: Workstream 1," September 13, 2013, http://unfccc.int, para. 5.14.

[108] Ibid, para. 5.21.

[109] Nepal on behalf of the Least Developed Countries Group, "Nepal Submission to the ADP," March 17, 2013, http://unfccc.int/bodies, p. 3.

developed countries and BASIC countries. In short, each country submission took a different approach to defining how differentiation should occur.

The submissions by the United States, Japan and Brazil advocated the establishment of emission reduction obligations at the domestic level, which will feed into an international monitoring, verifying and reporting system. The United States submission argues that this bottom-up approach will result in self-differentiation, with parties determining their contributions based on national circumstances and priorities. Japan's submission suggests that establishing a framework applicable to all parties will require the development of a flexible hybrid system in which each party submits its nationally determined commitments under international common accounting rules. Brazil believes that each party should contribute to global overall emission reductions defined domestically, taking into account historical responsibilities, national circumstances, and capacities.[110] Vulnerable developing nations such as LDCs and SIDS, however, prefer internationally determined obligations on the basis that such targets will ensure environmental stringency and integrity.

The Australian submission recommended that differentiation move beyond the "two room system" of Annex I and Non-Annex I, which does not in reality reflect the wide range of country circumstances and capabilities.[111] The LDC submission states that the 2015 agreement should consider a diversity of contributions from developing countries based on their various capabilities.[112] Many of the submissions state that differentiation should be made on the basis of capacity and responsibility, including the submissions of Brazil,[113] Canada,[114] New Zealand,[115] China,[116] India,[117] LDCs,[118] and the Environmental Integrity Group (EIG).[119]

Most submissions support QELROs for developed and major economies, and sector-based targets or targets based on NAMAs for developing countries. The more controversial issue is determining which parties will require QELROs. The solution may lie in parties defining how capacity and historic responsibility should be assessed. These criteria would likely include economic and emission

---

[110] Brazilian Government, "Overall Views of the ADP Workstream 1 Process and Outcome," September 12, 2013, http://unfccc.int, para. 6.

[111] Australian Government, "The 2015 Climate Change Agreement," March 26, 2013, http://unfccc.int/bodies, p. 3.

[112] Nepal, note 109, p. 4.

[113] Brazil, note 110, para. 3.

[114] Canadian Government, "Submission by Canada – Views on Advancing the Work of the Durban Platform," April 12, 2013, http://unfccc.int/bodies, p. 1.

[115] New Zealand Government, "New Zealand Submission to the Ad Hoc Working Group on the Durban Platform for Enhanced Action," October 11, 2013, http://unfccc.int, p. 3.

[116] China, note 106, para. 6.

[117] India, note 107, para. 5.27.

[118] Nepal, note 109, p. 2.

[119] For a variety of perspectives on the implementation of all elements of Decision 1/cp.17, 20 September 2013 (relating to the work of the ADP), see UNFCCC, "Submissions from Parties to the ADP in 2014," http://unfccc.int/bodies/awg/items/7398.php.

236   *Emerging Powerful Southern Voices*

considerations and would require more nuanced membership categories reflecting the wide diversity of parties. This will involve going beyond a simple two-tier system and establishing differential commitments for at least Northern nations, Southern nations considered to be major economies (such as BASIC nations), and vulnerable Southern nations.

7. CONCLUSION

The BASIC group has been described as a bloc willing to take power but fearing to take responsibility.[120] The CBDR highlights an area of South/South tension where the interests of powerful Southern nations are best served by avoiding deep emission cuts, while vulnerable Southern nations require deep emission cuts to prevent destruction of their homelands. BASIC countries should act as a model for other Southern countries in relation to mitigation. They should use their power within the UNFCCC responsibly and take the lead in committing Southern nations to reduce emissions. If BASIC nations do not adopt significant cuts, this will suggest to other Southern nations that their model of rapid economic development and emission output is the best path to follow to achieve development goals. Moreover, it will be hard to get the United States on board if China refuses binding emission reduction obligations.

This chapter highlighted that the deadlock in international mitigation action can no longer be attributed to North/South tensions. The lines have become increasingly blurred, as nations have formed various blocs and alliances and several Southern countries have become major emitters. There is no one unified voice of the South, and equity requires that the different circumstances of the BASIC bloc versus other Southern nations such as LDCs or AOSIS be factored into future mitigation commitments.

The analysis of CBDR shows that emission contributions (historic, current, and projected) and capacity should be the factors that determine responsibility for reducing emissions. This would mean that China's obligations to reduce emissions should be higher than those of many other Southern nations. It is essential to get all UNFCCC parties to commit to emission reductions. The United States' position will influence other Northern nations, just as China sets up a model for other Southern countries.

---

[120] Tabau and Lemoine, note 39 at 197.

11

Sustainable Development in the Era of Bioenergy and Agricultural Land Grab

Chidi Oguamanam

1. INTRODUCTION

Sourcing energy from diverse renewable biological resources (bioenergy) is a controversial venture, riddled with contradictions on multiple fronts as industrialized countries of the global North look to the global South for solutions to their food and energy needs. The bioenergy drive is linked to intense interest in offshore agricultural land in poor regions of the South. The intersection of energy, food, and agriculture raises tensions over the geopolitics of food security[1] and reinforces asymmetrical North–South power relations.[2]

Bioenergy, and various other reasons for offshore agricultural interests in the South, are anchored on two dubious premises. The first premise is the notion of surplus land in the South. The second is that bioenergy is a viable alternative to fossil fuels. The extent to which bioenergy promotes environmental sustainability through the reduction of greenhouse gas for mitigation of climate change remains contested.[3] Similarly, whether for bioenergy or food crops, large-scale acquisitions of rural agricultural lands in the global South (land grabs) fuel controversy in regard to the distortion of complex land-based social relations in target communities.[4]

Foreign encroachments on poor peoples' agricultural land reveal a discernible shift from the North–South traffic of biophysical resources toward a new

[1] L. R. Brown, "Food, Fuel, and the Global Land Grab," *The Futurist*, January–February 2013, www.wfs.org/futurist/january-february-2013-vol-47-no-1/food-fuel-and-global-land-grab

[2] P. McMichael, "Agrofuels in the Food Regime" (2010) 37 *Journal of Peasant Studies* 609 at 609–610. See generally S. M. Borras et al. (eds.), *The Politics of Biofuels, Land and Agrarian Change* (New York: Routledge, 2011).

[3] McMichael, note 2 at 622: "agrofuels release more than they reduce in substituting for fossil fuel energy."

[4] S. M. Borras and J. Franco, "Towards a Broader View of the Politics of Global Land Grab: Rethinking Land Issues, Reframing Resistance," ICAS Working Paper Series # 001 1-39 (2010), p. 1920.

238 *Sustainable Development in the Era of Bioenergy*

South–South pattern. Overall, the convergence of bioenergy, food security, and land-grabbing raises myriad questions, not the least of which are those around sustainable development. In addition, current attempts to legitimize land-grabbing through codes of conduct warrant careful scrutiny. These trends and their consequences are explored in this chapter.

2. FROM ENERGY SECURITY TO ENVIRONMENTAL GREENING

From the outset, a confluence of factors including pressure from the corporate agribusiness lobby and the ostensible need for energy independence or energy security, more than environmental considerations, accounts for the drive for bioenergy in the United States and other industrialized countries.[5] In their seminal article, Runge and Senauer[6] argue that the oil embargo imposed by the Organization of Petroleum Exporting Countries (OPEC) in the 1970s served as a convenient catalyst for the United States to promote corn-based ethanol as an alternative to fossil fuel. Since the 1970s, the United States has promoted bioenergy through multiple incentive strategies, such as tax credits, subsidies, grants, loans, and a panoply of shields, including a range of exceptions against competition and other tenets of the market economy.[7]

The privileging of bioenergy and, indeed, agricultural production in general in the United States follows a similar pattern in the European Union (EU), which supports various legislative measures and directives[8] aimed at promoting biodiesel from a diversity of crops, including rapeseed, soy, and sunflower. Directive 2009/28/EC of the European Parliament and of the Council focuses on various sustainability strategies, most notably energy-saving and energy-efficiency approaches and the expansion of renewable energy sources.[9] Also, in the EU, combinations of various forms of direct and indirect subsidies are aimed at supporting the production of ethanol from sources other than corn, such as sugar beets, wheat, and so on.[10]

The United States and EU's interest in bioenergy purports to be a push for energy security designed to reduce dependence on volatile regions of the world,

---

[5] M. C. Tiraldo, M.J. Cohen, N. Aberman, J. Meerman, and B. Thompson, "Addressing the Challenges of Climate Change and Biofuel Production for Food and Nutrition Security" (2010) 43 *Food Research International* 1737. See also F. C. Runge and B. Senauer, "How Biofuels Could Starve the Poor" (2007) 86 *Foreign Affairs* 41 at 41 (on the influence of corporate industrial lobby over the U.S. biofuels policy).

[6] Ibid.

[7] Ibid. See also Renewable Energy Policy Network for the 21st Century, www.ren21.net.

[8] European Commission, "Renewable Energy: Targets by 2020," http://ec.europa.eu: "EU renewable energy policy projects that 10% of transport energy be sourced from renewable sourced by 2020." See also Brown, note 1.

[9] See e.g. Articles 17, 18, and 19 of Directive 2009/28/EC of the European Parliament and of the Council of 23 April 2009 on the promotion of the use of energy from renewable sources and amending and subsequently repealing Directives 2001/77/ED and 2003/30/EC, OJ L 140, 05/06/2009.

[10] Runge and Senauer, note 5 at 44.

especially the Middle East and parts of Africa, for energy. The energy security mantra is an alibi for the preferential treatment of the bioenergy sector as a consistent target of unflinching protectionism, especially in the United States For example, while corn-based ethanol is expensive to produce in terms of energy consumption and other environmental and socioeconomic considerations in contrast to sugarcane-based ethanol, until recently the United States used a discriminatory tariffication system to undermine importation of cheaper Brazilian sugarcane-based ethanol into the U.S. market.[11] Ironically, there is no tariff on imported fossil fuel in the United States.[12]

Despite the influence of economic and political considerations, environmental justifications have been used to provide moral high ground for bioenergy. The environmental argument is often associated with the interrelated tripartite notions of "green economy, green growth, and low carbon-development."[13] These concepts, which are the subject of contentious negotiations under the climate change regime(s),[14] refer to a bundle of market solutions to environmental and ecological crises aimed at mitigating unsustainable consumption and production through various sustainable development measures that integrate environment and development. According to the United Nations Environment Programme (UNEP), "green economy" refers to an economic system that "results in improved human well-being and social equity, while significantly reducing environmental risks and ecological scarcities. In its simplest expression a green economy is low carbon, resource efficient, and socially inclusive."[15]

The moral appeal of "greening" finds favor among some environmental actors, and stakeholders, and even among more critical civil society organizations.[16] However, in other constituencies, especially NGOs in the South, greening evokes much criticism and skepticism.[17] In the United States and elsewhere, the notion of

---

[11]   Ibid. See P. Bertrand, "Goodbye to U.S. Ethanol Tax Breaks and Tariffs," *International Business Times*, December 30, 2011, www.ibtimes.com/say-goodbye-us-ethanol-tax-breaks-tariffs-389406

[12]   Runge and Senauer, note 5 at 44.

[13]   For a detailed exploration of the notion of green economy and its evolution in international environmental law and policy, see C. Allen and S. Clouth, "A Guidebook to the Green Economy, Issue 1: Green Economy, Green Growth, and Low-Carbon Development – History, Definitions and a Guide to Recent Publications," Division for Sustainable Development, UNDESA, August 2012.

[14]   *United Nations Framework Convention on Climate Change*, Brazil, 9 May 1992, in force 21 March 1994, 1771 UNTS 107, UN Doc. A/AC.237/18 (Part II)/Add.1; 31 ILM 849 (1992); *Kyoto Protocol to the United Nations Framework Convention on Climate Change*, Japan, 11 December 1997, in force 16 February 2005, UN Doc. FCCC/CP/1997/7/Add.1, Dec. 10, 1997; 37 ILM 22 (1998).

[15]   UNEP, *Towards a Green Economy: Pathways to Sustainable Development and Poverty Eradication* (United Nations Environment Programme, 2011), p. 16.

[16]   Greenpeace, "A Just and Fair Green Economy," www.greenpeace.org.

[17]   See e.g. C. Y. Ling and S. Lyer, "The 'Green Economy Debate' Unfolds in the UN," www.twnside.org.sg.

240 *Sustainable Development in the Era of Bioenergy*

greening has often been used by politicians to legitimize the use of public funds to support industrial lobbying around bioenergy and to fund related research and development.[18]

The bioenergy drive exposes "the extent to which capitalism externalizes its costs" through market-based environmental policies in which biophysical resources, including cropland and forests, are converted into "a new profit frontier" and disguised as "market environmentalism."[19] A crucial aspect of this cost externalization is the quest for feasible sites or available land for production of biofuels.[20] With the possible exception of the United States and a few others, the natural conditions in the countries or regions possessing requisite investment capital constrain the ability to increase the domestic production of biofuel feedstocks. Consequently, so-called "surplus," "degraded," "idle," "waste," "abandoned," "underutilized" lands in countries of the global South become ideal targets for bioenergy.[21] This focus on the global South is consistent with the neoliberal capitalist development model in which agriculture is a constant site for exploitation and plunder. This model reinforces the economically disadvantageous international division of labor that for centuries has relegated the South to the production of primary commodities.[22]

Since 2006, there has been an unprecedented spate of offshore agricultural land acquisitions in the global South.[23] Marking a shift from the bioenergy gold rush, land is now being acquired for speculative investment opportunities.[24] Africa is hosting what is now termed the "Green OPEC" because its vast land reserves

[18] Runge and Senaeur, note 5 at 46.

[19] McMichael, note 2 at 608.

[20] M. Kutchler and B-O. Linnér, "Challenging the Food vs. Fuel Dilemma: Genealogical Analysis of the Biofuel Discourse Pursued by International Organizations" (2012) 37 *Food Policy* 581 at 583.

[21] McMichael, above note 2 at 619; Borras and Franco, note 4, pp. 7, 19. See also S. M. Borras Jr., R. Hall, I. Scoones, W. W. White, and W. Wolford, "Towards a Better Understanding of Global Land Grabbing: An Editorial Introduction" (2011) 38 *Journal of Peasant Studies* 209 at 212; S. Vermeulen and L. Cotula, "Over the Heads of Local People: Consultation, Consent and Recompense in Large-scale Land Deals for Biofuels Projects in Africa" (2010) 37 *Journal of Peasant Studies* 899 at 896.

[22] C. G. Gonzalez, "Trade Liberalization, Food Security, and the Environment: The Neoliberal Threat to Sustainable Rural Development" (2004) 14 *Transnational Law and Contemporary Problems* 419 at 433–438; McMichael, note 2 at 612.

[23] GRAIN, "The Great Food Robbery: How Corporations Control Food, Grab Land and Destroy the Climate," May 4, 2012, www.grain.org, p. 33. See also GRAIN, "Slideshow: Who's Behind the Land Grabs: A Look at Some of the People Pursuing or Supporting Large Farmland Grabs Around the World," October 16, 2012, www.grain.org, p. 2; K. W. Deininger, D. Byerlee, J. Lindsay, A. Norton, H. Selod, and M. Stickler, *Rising Global Interest in Farmland: Can it Yield Sustainable and Equitable Benefits?* (Washington: The World Bank, 2011); J. von Braun and R. Meinzen-Dick, "'Land Grabbing' by Foreign Investors in Developing Countries: Risks and Opportunities," July 14, 2009, www.ifpri.org, pp. 1–2; and Borras et al., note 21 at 209.

[24] Borras and Franco, note 4, p. 4. See also Borras et al., note 21 at 209.

are being targeted for food and bioenergy production by Brazil, Saudi Arabia, China, the World Bank, the United States, the European Commission, and a vast range of private corporate interests.[25] But the social and environmental costs of these new land transactions in target regions, countries, and communities have yet to be addressed.[26]

These large-scale international agricultural land acquisitions are often referred to as "global land grabs." According to Borras and Franco, the phrase is a catch-all reference to "the explosion of (trans)national commercial land transactions (and land speculation) that has been occurring in recent years around large-scale production, sale, and export of food and biofuels."[27] Large-scale land acquisitions morph into land grabs when they disregard human rights, free prior informed consent, social and environmental impacts, transparency, and democracy.[28]

The legitimacy of the emergent international land-use dynamic depends in part on the extent to which such large-scale acquisitions mitigate the asymmetrical power relations between actors; preserve the socioecological functions of land among the world's poor; and promote the principles of sustainable development and, by extension, equity and human rights. Before focusing on the land-grab–sustainable development interface, the next section maps the land-grab phenomenon in order to identify some trends and to examine the bioenergy imperative over other competing considerations.

3. LAND GRAB: BEYOND NORTH–SOUTH AND BIOENERGY

International development and economic organizations do not always agree on the framing of policy questions or the proffered solutions. However, on the twin issue of sourcing liquid biofuel from biomass and strategic responses to global food crisis, they agree that the solution lies in tapping the agro-ecological and land resources of the world's poorest countries. The World Bank,[29] the United Nations Food and Agriculture Organization (FAO), the International Energy Agency (IEA), and the Intergovernmental Panel on Climate Change (IPCC),[30] to name a few, now support public and private initiatives that look to the global South for inexpensive and secure supplies of biofuel feedstocks and food as a means of

---

[25] McMichael, note 2 at 614.
[26] generally Tiraldo et al., note 5 at 1729–1744.
[27] S. M. Borras and J. Franco, note 4, p. 2. See also Borras et al., note 21 at 210.
[28] K. Geary, "Our Land, Our Lives: Time Out on the Global Land Rush," Oxfam Briefing Note (October 2012), pp. 14–15.
[29] McMichael, note 2 at 615: "assisted by the Word Bank policy, the land grab is represented as a form of development insofar as indebted governments in the global South stand to receive foreign investment and hard currency from the conversion of their land and forests into agro-export platforms."
[30] On the combined role of these institutions in promoting land grab, see generally Kutchler and Linnér, note 20.

242   *Sustainable Development in the Era of Bioenergy*

tackling the challenges posed by climate change and food insecurity.[31] The costs of sourcing land and labor, which are critical to the eventual export or, more appropriately, repatriation of biofuels and food, are cheapest in the tropical and subtropical countries of the global South.[32] Consequently, dating back to the early 2000s, sub-Saharan Africa, Latin America, South and Southeast Asia, and to some degree Eastern Europe and Oceania have become the targets of large-scale transnational agricultural land acquisitions.[33]

Reliable details, including credible statistics, on large-scale agricultural land acquisitions in target regions and countries are hard to come by for a number of reasons.[34] First, most of the transactions are not transparent and are conducted in countries with poor democratic credentials.[35] Acquisitions often happen for speculative purpose, with no intention to immediately possess or use the land and without the free prior informed consent of legitimate stakeholders.[36] Second, large-scale agricultural land acquisitions take a long time to conclude. Third, controversies have often trailed these acquisitions, resulting in the reversal or revocation of some of them.[37] However, a number of organizations, including the World Bank, Genetic Resources Action International (GRAIN), Oxfam, the International Food Policy Research Institute (IFPRI), the Brookings Institution, the Wilson Center, and the International Institute for Environmental and Development provide helpful data that reveal the magnitude and trend of large-scale agricultural land acquisitions.[38]

Land and water-challenged countries of the Middle East, including Saudi Arabia, Qatar, Kuwait, Abu Dhabi, Bahrain, the UAE, Libya, Jordan, and Egypt

---

[31] ibid at 585.

[32] E. Aryeety and Z. Lewis, "African Land Grabbing: Whose Interests are Served," June 25, 2010, www.brookings.edu.

[33] Kutchler and Linnér, note 20 at 586; Borras and Franco, note 4, p. 5; Kate Geary, note 28; GRAIN, "The Great Food Robbery: How Corporations Control Food, Grab Land and Destroy the Climate," May 4, 2012, www.grain.org, p. 70; GRAIN, "Slideshow: Who's Behind the Land Grabs: A Look at Some of the People Pursing or Supporting Large Farmland Grabs Around the World," October 16, 2012, www.grain.org, p. 29; and von Braun and Meinzen-Dick, note 23, pp. 5–9.

[34] Aryeety and Lewis, note 32. See also Brown, note 1.

[35] Ibid.

[36] Ibid. See also Brown, note 1.

[37] For example, land transactions in Uganda, Madagascar, Mozambique, and Ethiopia were reversed in response to popular opposition.

[38] Below are examples of the above listed organizations' contributions to auditing of land-grab activities: GRAIN, "New Data Sets on Land Grabbing," February 23, 2012, www.grain.org; Oxfam International, "Land Grabs Q&A," www.oxfam.org. See also GRAIN, "Slideshow: Who's Behind the Land Grabs: A Look at Some of the People Pursing or Supporting Large Farmland Grabs Around the World," October 16, 2012, www.grain.org; GRAIN, "The Great Food Robbery: How Corporations Control Food, Grab Land and Destroy the Climate," May 4, 2012, www.grain.org; Geary, note 28; Aryeety and Lewis, note 34; Brown, note 1. See also Borras and Franco, note 4, p. 4; Borras et al., note 21 at 209–216. See generally Deininger et al., note 23.

are among the major actors in offshore agricultural land acquisitions.[39] Ironically, nearly all of these countries are global players in fossil fuel production and are not in the land-grab business for bioenergy purposes. EU countries, the United States (mainly through transnational corporations), China, India, South Korea, Malaysia, and South Africa are also in the league of regions and countries that are involved in agricultural land acquisitions, with increasingly more interest in food production than in bioenergy, either through government entities or through home-based agribusiness corporations.[40]

Available information shows that more than twenty African countries are prime targets of transnational land acquisitions,[41] among them Congo, Ethiopia, Ghana, Kenya, Liberia, Madagascar, Malawi, Mali, Mozambique, Nigeria, Sierra Leone, Somalia, South Sudan, Sudan, Tanzania, Uganda, Zambia, and Zimbabwe.[42] Other countries prominently reported to be involved in the land grab, either as land-grabbers or as targets of land-grabbing, include the Philippines, Burma, Cambodia, Thailand, Vietnam, Laos, Indonesia, Colombia, Brazil, Paraguay, Argentina, and Australia.[43]

Random first impressions of the land-grab traffic show a convoluted pattern with little rhyme but substantive reason. For example, Brazil is an active participant in the land grab in Africa. The same is true of India and China. Yet China is also grabbing land in Brazil, India, Cuba, and Mexico, whereas Japan is acquiring land in China and Brazil. South Africa is a player in the land grab within Africa. Egypt is grabbing land in Sudan and South Sudan. Saudi Arabia is in Egypt, Sudan, and South Sudan for the same reasons, as is India in Burma. The United Arab Emirates (UAE) is a new player in the agricultural land grab in Sudan. South Korea is in Africa, especially in Madagascar; it is also active in Cambodia, Indonesia, and Ukraine. Malaysia is in Liberia developing plantations for oil palm and rubber. Many Gulf states have significant land-grab footprints in Cambodia, Turkey, Kazakhstan, Uzbekistan, Ukraine, and Georgia. Even though there is a paucity of systematic data aggregation on land-grabbing, information from a variety of sources indicate that, in the past few years alone, more than 50 million hectares of agricultural land have changed hands between farmers and private corporations.[44]

---

[39] See generally Tiraldo et al., note 5. See also Aryeety and Lewis, note 34; Brown, note 1; Geary, note 28, p. 3.

[40] McMichael, note 2 at 614.

[41] J. Vidal, "How Food and Water are Driving a 21st-Century African Land Grab," *The Guardian*, March 7, 2010.

[42] Ibid. See also Aryeety and Lewis, note 34.

[43] Geary, note 28, p. 11; von Braun and Meinzen-Dick, note 23, p. 2. See generally Borras and Franco, note 4; McMichael, note 2; M. S. Kimenyi and Z. Lewis, "The BRICS and the New Scramble for Africa," January 11, 2011, www.brookings.edu; Deininger et al., note 23.

[44] GRAIN, "The Great Food Robbery: How Corporations Control Food, Grab Land and Destroy the Climate," May 4, 2012, www.grain.org. See also GRAIN, "Slideshow: Who's Behind the Land Grabs: A Look at Some of the People Pursuing or Supporting Large Farmland Grabs Around the World," October 16, 2012, www.grain.org.

244 *Sustainable Development in the Era of Bioenergy*

Between 2004 and 2009, the IFPRI reports that at least five African countries transferred 2.5 million hectares in land-grab deals.[45] In one country, 84,000 hectares, which amounts to 2.2 percent of the country's total land surface, was the subject of a single but controversial land-grab negotiation.[46] In another, more than 30 percent of the country's land surface was ceded in a large-scale concession within five years.[47] Oxfam claims that an area eight times the size of the UK has been sold off or leased in the past decade while offshore investors acquired land area the size of London every six days between 2000 and 2010.[48] Countries with serious hunger problems contribute two thirds of foreign land acquisitions.[49] A recent report by the Open African Innovation Research Network (Open AIR) confirms that "[a]n area estimated as almost the size of Western Europe was transferred in land allocation deals from the mid-2000s to 2010s. Deals reported as approved or under negotiation worldwide amounted to a total of 303 million hectares – 134 million of this total (44 percent) is in Africa; 43 million (14 percent) in Asia; and 19 million (6 percent) in Latin America."[50]

As discussed later in the chapter, the escalating interest in land-grabbing has provoked the quest for a regulatory framework by virtually all stakeholders: the FAO, the World Bank, NGOs, corporations, and countries interested in leasing or transferring large-scale offshore agricultural land.[51] But such frameworks are untested and there remains suspicion regarding the extent to which they could mitigate myriad sustainable development and human rights challenges posed by land-grabbing. Among their many weaknesses, these frameworks are based on the contested premise that current trends in food and energy resource consumption in mainly the global North and new emergent economic powers in the global South are inexorable[52] and must be supported at the expense of the world's most vulnerable.

A careful look at the mosaic of actors and patterns in the global land grab helps to piece together the real features of the phenomenon as well as to determine how much influence the bioenergy quest wields as the rationale for large-scale agricultural land acquisition.

---

[45] Aryeety and Zenia, note 34. See also von Braun and Meinzen-Dick, note 23, pp. 2–3.
[46] The reference country is Uganda. See GRAIN, "Seized: The 2008 Landgrab for Food and Financial Security," October 1, 2008, www.grain.org, p. 6. See also Geary, note 28, p. 9.
[47] The country in question is Liberia; see Geary, note 28, p. 2.
[48] Ibid.
[49] Ibid.
[50] S. Elahi, J. de Beer, D. Kawooya, C. Oguamanam, and N. Rizk *Knowledge and Innovation in Africa: Scenarios for the Future* (Cape Town: Open African Innovation Research Network, 2013), p. 113.
[51] M. C. Tiraldo et al., note 5; see generally McMichael, note 2.
[52] Borras and Franco, note 4, p. 7; and S. Borras and J. Franco, "From Threat to Opportunity? Problems with the Idea of 'Code of Conduct' for Land Grabbing" (2010) 13 *Yale Human Rights and Development Law Journal* 507.

First, in contrast to the urgency felt by the United States and the EU in the 1970s for energy independence, the more recent pattern of land-grabbing is a response to the global food crisis as evident in high food prices of the late 2000s.[53] There is an irrefutable corollary between high food prices and the cost of agricultural land. The cost of land is, in turn, partly linked to the use of land for bioenergy production – a practice recognized as a climate change mitigation strategy.[54] Overall, bioenergy production and offshore food production are driving the agricultural land grabs (with negative consequences for food security and social justice among the vulnerable segments of the global South), but offshore food production is quickly becoming the primary driver.[55]

On account of rising food prices, many Gulf states, who are largely food-insecure, and a number of other countries (with different food insecurity and population dynamics),[56] such as China, India, and South Korea, have become the most active actors in recent agricultural land grabs.[57] Of a representative number of 405 land-grab projects between 2008 and 2009 where there is infor-mation on end use, it was found that while an equal percentage (21 percent) of land was slated for biofuel production and for industrial cash crops, 37 percent of land was earmarked for food crops.[58] The declining significance of biofuel production and growing importance of food and cash crops in the competing uses for offshore agricultural land is indicative of the priority that food security has assumed as the key driver of land grabs.

Second, in addition to food security, another propelling, albeit interrelated, factor fueling offshore land grabs is the investment imperative. Partly provoked by the recent global financial crisis, investors have looked to offshore agricultural land for security.[59] The price of agricultural land has been tied to the price of food and, since 2007, has continued to rise in a fairly predictable manner with no volatility.[60] While South–South land grabs are mostly a factor of food insecurity, the global

[53] McMichael, note 2 at 610; Tiraldo et al., note 5 at 1740–1741. See also Runge and Senauer, note 5.

[54] Tiraldo et al., note 5 at 1729. See also Borras and Franco, note 4, p. 7; Borras and Franco, note 52 at 507–523.

[55] C. G. Gonzalez, "The Global Food Crisis: Law, Policy, and the Elusive Quest for Justice" (2010) 13 *Yale Human Rights and Development Law Journal* 462 at 472.

[56] Borras and Franco, above note 4, p. 5. For example, in China, India, and other middle-income economic powers, there is increasingly limited agricultural land as a result of rising population, a new prosperous middle class, and climate change dynamics. This state of affairs contrasts with the food security situation in the Gulf region, which is historically and fundamentally a factor of ecological challenges before any other.

[57] Ibid, p. 14.

[58] Brown, note 1. See generally Deininger et al., note 23.

[59] See generally GRAIN, "Slideshow: Who's Behind the Land Grabs: A Look at Some of the People Pursuing or Supporting Large Farmland Grabs Around the World," October 16, 2012, www.grain.org; GRAIN, "Seized: The 2008 Landgrab for Food and Financial Security," October 24, 2008, www.grain.org, pp. 1–2; Vidal, note 41.

[60] von Braun and Meinzen-Dick, note 23, p. 4.

North, led by corporations and by financial and investments entities in the United States, Europe, and even Japan, appears more active in the acquisition of land for speculative purposes.[61] Various studies illustrate the interest of investment banks, pension funds, university endowments, hedge funds, miscellaneous equity funds, and divergent investment portfolios in offshore agricultural land. Investors are confident that such investment is a cast-iron buffer against recession and volatile global financial markets.[62] The rate of return is estimated by some account at upward of 400 percent per annum![63]

Third, another discernible feature of land-grabbing that discredits the energy security argument and its suspect environmental protection subtext is the active involvement of energy-secure countries. Perhaps more importantly, the political instability of fossil fuel-exporting countries as a reason for Northern countries to seek energy security elsewhere does not seem to support the trend in land-grabbing. Most of the target countries that have featured prominently in the land grabs, especially in Africa, Southeast Asia, and Eastern Europe, do not have strong credentials either in democracy and rule of law or in overall political stability.[64] For example, Somalia and Eritrea, and even the Democratic Republic of the Congo (not to mention Sudan),[65] which rank at the bottom of the African (good) governance index,[66] are not spared from land grabs.[67]

Furthermore, energy-hungry countries of the global North have continued their insatiable quest for energy with only half-hearted commitments to climate change mitigation. Since 2010, expedited technological progress has resulted in the mining of energy using the relatively new and environmentally precarious method of hydraulic fracturing, especially in the United States and Canada.[68] Also known as fracking, this method involves underground injection of pressurized liquid

[61] GRAIN, "Seized: The 2008 Landgrab for Food and Financial Security," October 24, 2008, www.grain.org, p. 9; Brown, note 1.

[62] GRAIN, "Slideshow: Who's Behind the Land Grabs: A Look at Some of the People Pursing or Supporting Large Farmland Grabs Around the World," October 16, 2012, www.grain.org, pp. 7–9.

[63] GRAIN reports a projected annual return of 10 to 40 per cent in Europe and up to 400 per cent in Africa. See GRAIN, "Seized: The 2008 Landgrab for Food and Financial Security," October 24, 2008, www.grain.org, p. 9.

[64] Aryeety and Zenia, note 32. See also E. T. Gonzales and M. L. Mendoza, "Governance in Southeast Asia: Issues and Options" (2004) 31 *Philippine Journal of Development* 135. See generally World Bank, "World Governance Indicators," http://data.worldbank.org.

[65] Ibrahim Index of African Governance (IIAG), it is one of the lowest performing countries in the good governance index.

[66] See generally Mo Ibrahim Foundation, "Ibrahim Index of African Governance: Summary," www.moibrahimfoundation.org.

[67] However, it is noted that the land-grabbers in these countries are mainly the Gulf States, China, and India, which do not put a high premium on good governance in target countries, as opposed to the countries of the global North.

[68] J. Nelson, "Frack Attack: New Dirty Gas Drilling Methods Threaten Drinking Water," December 1, 2009, www.policyalternatives.ca; See also M. A. Sergie, "Hydraulic Fracturing (Fracking)," www.cfr.org.

(oxygenated water combined with various chemicals) as a device to access and extract otherwise inaccessible large deposits of energy resources such as uranium and hydrocarbons. The range of environmental concerns regarding this practice includes noise pollution, uncontrolled escape of dangerous gases to the surface and associated hazards to human health, ground water contamination, and fresh water depletion.[69]

In sum, the recent transnational acquisitions of agricultural land in the global South are driven less by bioenergy or energy security than by the food security challenges of Southern land-grabbers and the opportunistic investment strategies of Northern land-grabbers. Nonetheless, irrespective of what constitutes the dominant driver, the impacts of land-grabbing must be evaluated from various perspectives, including its impact on sustainable development.

4. LAND GRAB WITHOUT SUSTAINABLE DEVELOPMENT

Sustainable development is now an integral aspect of international environmental law. It is most commonly defined as a development model that strives to meet "the needs of the present without compromising the ability of the future generation to meet their own needs."[70] Sustainable development is an attempt to subject the world's economic development ambitions to the limits of the Earth's carrying capacity. However, sustainable development has become a site for mutual suspicion between the global North and South. The latter sees sustainable development as a justification for imposing unfair burdens on its development aspirations, as well as a strategy of protectionism by the global North to ward off competition from the South.[71]

Land-grabbing and some of its underlying rationales unravel the nebulous nature of the sustainable development concept, and how it can readily be evoked to serve conflicting outcomes. For example, whether offshore agricultural land is grabbed for bioenergy, for food security, or for strictly investment (speculative) objectives, there is no dearth of justification or criticism for such initiatives within a sustainable development analysis. First, a key, albeit doubtful, justification for bioenergy production is that it is better than fossil fuel in regard to greenhouse gas emissions.[72] Second, use of offshore agricultural land for food and investment purposes is premised on the doubtful notion of surplus, waste, or underutilized

---

[69] R. W. Howarth, A. Ingraffea and T. Engelder, "Should Fracking Stop? Extracting Gas from Shale Increases the Availability of this Resource, but the Health and Environmental Risks May Be Too High" (2011) 477 Nature 271.

[70] World Commission on Environment and Development, Our Common Future (Oxford: Oxford University Press, 1987), p. 43.

[71] See chapter 3, R. Gordon, "Unsustainable Development." See generally P. Shabecoff, A New Name for Peace: International Environmentalism, Sustainable Development, and Democracy (Hanover: University Press of New England, 1996).

[72] Runge and Senauer, note 5 at 51–52.

248   *Sustainable Development in the Era of Bioenergy*

land in target regions.[73] As such, land-grabbing is a strategy that frees agro-intensification pressures on environmentally or ecologically constrained territories of the world like the Gulf region. Thus, on the foregoing grounds, land-grabbing can be aligned with a development pattern that is sensitive to the Earth's carrying capacity.

On the first point, the theory of bioenergy being environmentally preferable to fossil fuel is not one that enjoys credibility among analysts. For example, the United States' biofuel of choice – corn-based ethanol – has life cycle greenhouse gas (GHG) emissions greater than fossil fuel. According to Runge and Senauer, row crops such as corn and soybean aggravate water pollution as they require large amounts of energy, agro-chemical inputs such as fertilizer, and pesticides to grow and process. Ethanol-producing row crops are the major cause of nitrogen run-off, which accounts for the "dead zone in the Gulf of Mexico, an ocean area the size of New Jersey that has [so] little oxygen that it can barely support life."[74]

In regard to the second point, the devaluation and appropriation of poor peoples' land by labeling it surplus or underutilized does not reflect the actual value of land within the traditional knowledge and ecological ethics of many indigenous and local communities whose land is targeted. In these communities, land is used for different purposes, such as foraging, grazing, and shifting cultivation, which requires leaving agricultural lands fallow over a period of time for ecological replenishing. Land is essential for the preservation of subsistence lifestyles, cultural diversity, and healthy agro-ecosystems and for the exercise of self-determination. Furthermore, the rate of population growth in most regions targeted for land-grabbing suggests that the idea of surplus or idle land is questionable.[75] For example, Africa has the world's youngest and fastest growing population, contributing to more than half of expected global population growth between now and 2050.[76] Population growth in Southern countries and the stakes of future generations in sustainable development call into serious question the idea of surplus land.

Sustainable development has been elaborated as a tripartite but elastic, interdependent framework of environmental protection, economic development, and social development.[77] It is well accepted that "attaining all three of these pillars concurrently is essential to achieve genuine sustainable development."[78]

[73] McMichael, note 2 at 619.

[74] Runge and Senauer, note 5 at 51 (observing that "even if the entire corn crop in the United States were used to make ethanol, that fuel would replace only 12 percent of current U.S. gasoline use").

[75] McMichael, note 2 at 619.

[76] Within that period, for example, a country like Nigeria would have more people than the United States. See "Major Populations in 2100," http://image.guardian.co.uk.

[77] See generally J. Benidickson, B. Boer, A. Herman Benjamin, and K. Morrow (eds.), *Environmental Law and Sustainability After Rio* (Cheltenham: Edward Elgar, 2011).

[78] K. Garforth, W. Damena Yifru, and M. Fujii, "Biosafety, the Cartagena Protocol, and Sustainable Development," in M-C. C. Segger et al. (eds.), *Legal Aspects of Implementing the Cartagena Protocol on Biosafety* (Oxford: Oxford University Press, 2013), p. 23.

The underlying logic of land-grabbing is inconsistent with sustainable development.[79] First, land-grabbing is premised on a market economic valorization of land for industrial and large-scale commercial agricultural production, essentially for export or repatriation purposes.[80] Consequently, land grabs are not sensitive to the socioecological agency of land in rural communities in developing countries that are targets of land-grabbing. In Madagascar, Mozambique, Ethiopia, Uganda, Cambodia, Indonesia, Colombia, Brazil, and elsewhere, land grabs have resulted in the displacement or forced relocation of millions of culturally diverse indigenous and local[81] communities from their ancestral lands. These displacements violate communities' subsistence and self-determination rights and disrupt their environmentally sustainable land stewardship practices. [82]

Second, land-grabbing promotes monoculture or plantation agriculture on an industrial scale,[83] focusing on both cash crops and bioenergy feedstock (biomass) such as wheat, palm trees, rubber, sugar cane, corn, jatropha, canola, soy, millet, sorghum, rapeseed, and sugar beet. This pattern of land-grab–sponsored agriculture undermines the complex relations of indigenous and local communities with their land.[84] This relationship is both spiritually and ecologically grounded and constitutes an important framework for the development and stewardship of transgenerational traditional ecological knowledge.[85] Mixed farming, multiple cropping, and crop rotation are the hallmarks of agro-biodiversity, which has as its corollary cultural diversity.[86] The land-use practices associated with land-grabbing threaten the biological and cultural diversity that represent integral aspects of sustainable agriculture and, by extension, sustainable development.

Third, water-challenged Gulf states (Bahrain, Kuwait, Oman, Qatar, Saudi Arabia, and the United Arab Emirates) perceive land-grabbing as an opportunity to gain access to water resources, which are critical for growing crops offshore.[87]

---

[79] *Rio Declaration on Environment and Development*, Brazil, 13 June 1992, in force 12 August 1992, A/CONF.151/26 (Vol. I); 31 ILM 874 (1992), Principle 4 [hereinafter Rio Declaration].

[80] See generally Geary, note 28.

[81] Aryeety and Zenia, note 32. See also Kutchler and Linnér, note 20. See generally Borras et al., note 21; McMichael, note 2 at 617; Borras and Franco, note 4, p. 29; and von Braun and Meinzen-Dick, note 23.

[82] See generally R. C. Dudgeon and F. Berkes, "Local Understandings of the Land: Traditional Ecological Knowledge and Indigenous Knowledge," in H. Selin (ed.), *Nature across Cultures: Views and the Environment of Non-Western Cultures* (Netherlands: Springer, 2003), pp. 75–96. See also McMichael, note 2 at 616.

[83] Tiraldo et al., note 5 at 1738. See also McMichael, note 2 at 616–617.

[84] See generally Dudgeon and Berkes, above note 82.

[85] Ibid.

[86] S. Brush, *Farmer's Bounty: Locating Crop Diversity in the Contemporary World* (New Haven: Yale University Press, 2004), p. 259; A. Phillips, "The Nature of Cultural Landscapes – A Nature Conservation Perspective" (1998) 23 *Landscape Research* 21. See also, T. Blomley, D. Roe, F. Nelson, and F. Flintan, "Land Grabbing: Is Conservation Part of the Problem or the Solution," September 2013, http://pubs.iied.org, pp. 1–2.

[87] Brown, note 1 ("that a claim on land is a claim on host country's water resources").

250   *Sustainable Development in the Era of Bioenergy*

Agricultural intensification through land-grabbing may produce water crises in vulnerable regions and countries.[88]

Finally, these land grabs are inconsistent with the procedural requirements of sustainable development,[89] including public participation, access to information, and environmental and social impact assessments.[90] In many countries, especially in Africa, these land transactions are noteworthy for their lack of transparency. Governments frequently cede traditional and communal land to foreign entities under opaque and questionable circumstances,[91] with little regard for stakeholder consultation and participation.[92] Indeed, the lack of credible data on most land-grab deals discussed earlier is evidence of the governance deficits that characterize these transactions. While there is no guarantee that negative social or environmental impact assessments could stop land-grabbers from going forward, only few, if any, of these land transactions could pass these tests, especially the social impact assessments.[93] Collectively, public participation, access to information, and impact assessments constitute ingredients of good governance necessary for sustainable development.[94] Clearly, most land-grab practices, irrespective of the underlying motives and resulting land uses, have failed to comply with these good governance requirements.

Regrettably, many Southern countries are complicit in these land grabs through offers of favorable incentives in their drive for foreign direct investment and all its promised attractions.[95] Many countries exploit the convoluted nature of traditional land tenure in their domains to support these land deals.[96] This accumulation by dispossession privileges transnational capital at the expense of some of the world's

---

[88] For example, the savannah regions cover an estimated 40 percent of the world's landmass (see Tiraldo et al., note 5 at 1732) and countries such as Mauritania, Senegal, Kenya, Somalia, and Ethiopia are sites of tensions at the intersection of water crisis and land grab.

[89] Rio Declaration, note 79, Principle 17.

[90] Ibid.

[91] Vermeulen and Cotula, note 21 at 911. See also Brown, above note 1.

[92] This practice is contrary to: Principles 10, 20, and 22 of the Rio Declaration, above note 79; chapter 26 of *Agenda 21: Programme of Action for Sustainable Development*, Rio de Janeiro, 14 June 1992, U.N. GAOR, 46th Sess., Agenda Item 21, UN Doc. A/Conf.151/26 (1992); Articles 10 and 32 of the *United Nations Declaration on the Rights of Indigenous Peoples*, 29 June 2006, in force 2 October 2007, A/RES/61/295, (A/61/L.67 and Add.1) that forbid forceful relocation and emphasize consultation and participation of indigenous peoples, local communities, and all stakeholders.

[93] Villagers in Mozambique were frustrated when their attempt to grow *jatropha* for bioenergy failed for lack of support. See Borras and Franco, note 4, p. 19.

[94] M-C. C. Segger, F. Perron-Welch, and C. Frison (eds.), *Legal Aspects of Implementing the Cartagena Protocol on Biosafety* (Oxford: Oxford University Press, 2013), p. 26.

[95] Vermeulen and Cotula, note 21 at 905. See also GRAIN, "Slideshow: Who's Behind the Land Grabs: A Look at Some of the People Pursing or Supporting Large Farmland Grabs around the World," October 16, 2012, www.grain.org; McMichael, note 2 at 41; and Borras and Franco, note 4, p. 22.

[96] McMichael, note 2 at 617–619.

poorest and most vulnerable communities.[97] It represents the continuation of a broader historical trend whereby technological innovation, intellectual property, and trade liberalization shepherd a new regime of "agriculture without farmers."[98]

Proponents of these agricultural land transactions often associate them with positive social impacts, such as improved rural employment, infrastructure, and economic development.[99] However, the mechanized and industrial orientation of large-scale agriculture generally seeks to minimize labor through the deployment of more efficient production processes.[100] Also, costs are reduced through eliminating middlemen and fostering shorter value chains.[101] Even where local interests are enlisted through contract farming, the beneficiaries are typically the politically privileged who can afford to hold the significant quantities of land required for viable contract agriculture.[102]

There is little doubt that offshore farming is boosting the food, energy, and investment security of the countries and private entities involved in land-grabbing. However, land-grabbing commodifies poor peoples' biophysical resources to satiate rich peoples' often rabid appetites. Land-grabbing fuels rather than curtails these appetites, and, as such, it does not lend significant support to sustainable development. The convergence of agriculture and energy production through the agency of industrial agriculture has triggered an unprecedented rise in the price of staple food, high costs of land in poor countries, and progressive displacement of small-scale farmers, culminating in escalating food insecurity and what analysts call "bio-fueling poverty"[103] among the world's most vulnerable.[104]

The environmental, social, and economic ramifications of land-grabbing represent the perpetuation of exploitation of the world's poor and vulnerable. Despite the arguments associating land grabs with employment, rural development, and infrastructural improvement, there is no evidence that the industrial

---

[97] Ibid at 612; see also Borras and Franco, note 4, p. 23.

[98] McMichael, note 2 at 612; see also Gonzalez, note 55 at 464 (canvassing the historical trajectory of contemporary global food crisis and the role of ill-advised lopsided geopolitical trade and economic policies that privileged the North at the expense of the South). Agriculture without farmers is the notion of global agricultural production and trade under the control of technology-driven transnational corporate agribusiness within a neoliberal trade framework in which smallholder local indigenous community farmers have a radically limited role in agriculture production, food security, and sustainability.

[99] Borras and Franco, note 4, p. 7. See generally World Bank, "World Development Report 2008," http://web.worldbank.org.

[100] In most African country hosts, there is little infrastructural development as a result of its cost intensive ramifications. See Brown, note 1.

[101] Ibid.

[102] Tiraldo et al., note 5 at 1738. See also Borras and Franco, note 4, pp. 12, 22.

[103] See generally, Oxfam, "Bio-Fuelling Poverty: Why the EU Renewable-Fuel Target May Be Disastrous for Poor People," November 1, 2007, www.oxfam.org. See also McMichael, note 2 at 615.

[104] HLPE, "Biofuels and Food Security: A Report by the High Level Panel of Experts on Food Security and Nutrition," June 2013, www.fao.org, pp. 57–59.

252 *Sustainable Development in the Era of Bioenergy*

pattern of agricultural production and embedded investment opportunism in land-grabbing caters to the needs of the world's poor. According to the *Brundtland Report*, the basic needs of the world's poor are an overriding priority of sustainable development.[105] In most regions that are targets of agricultural land grabs, the environmental, socioeconomic, and good governance impacts of land-grabbing suggest that the world's vulnerable are once again being made to bear the brunt of the excesses of the world's strongest.[106]

5. LEGITIMIZING POVERTY AND INEQUITY: IS LAND-GRABBING INEVITABLE?

Most interested international organizations and their critics take the position that the land-grab genie is out of the bottle. As such, their priority is to develop a global framework to make it a fair and just process.[107] In a manner reminiscent of certification or sustainability schemes for bioenergy production,[108] there is hardly a dearth of propositions as to how to regulate land-grabbing and what objectives such regulatory intervention ought to accomplish.[109] Most of the schemes are championed by mainstream development organizations and are gradually coalescing around the idea of a common code of conduct (CoC) for transnational large-scale agricultural land acquisition. For example, the IFPRI argues that risks associated with land-grabbing have embedded opportunities which can be harnessed through "making a virtue of [land grab] necessity" in order to create "win-win [land grab] policies."[110] It articulates key elements of a land-grabbing CoC to include transparency in negotiations, respect for existing land rights, sharing of benefits,[111] environmental sustainability,[112] and prioritizing of host domestic supply in national food trade policies, especially in situations of emergency.

So far, the most prominent CoC framework for land-grabbing is the 2010 joint initiative by the FAO, IFAD, UNCTAD, and World Bank, entitled Principles for

[105] UN Secretary-General, Report of the World Commission on Environment and Development: Our Common Future, 4 August 1987, A/42/427.

[106] Even in some African countries such as Ghana, Mozambique, and Tanzania, which have comparatively better land transfer protocols, that does not guarantee a resolution of land-grab problems. See L. Cotula, S. Vermeulen, R. Leonard, and J. Keeley, *Land Grab or Development Opportunity? Agricultural Investment and International Land Deals in Africa* (London: IIED/IFAD/FAO, 2009), p. 15.

[107] Tiraldo et al., note 5 at 1739.

[108] See generally L. Goovaerts et al., "Strategic Inter-Task Study: Monitoring Sustainability Certificate of Bioenergy," February 2013, www.bioenergytrade.org. See also WWF, "Searching for Sustainability: Comparative Analysis of Certification Scheme for Biomass Used for the Production of Biofuels," November 28, 2013, http://awsassets.panda.org.

[109] Borras and Franco, note 4, p. 7.

[110] von Braun and Meinzen-Dick, note 23, p. 3.

[111] E.g. through lease model to ensure ongoing revenue stream, contract farming, or out-grower schemes that enable smallholder farmers to retain control of their land.

[112] Borras and Franco, note 4, p. 8.

Responsible Agricultural Investment (PRAI).[113] Despite concerns over the lack of transparency in the process leading to development of the PRAI, strikingly, the EU, United States, Japan, G-8, G-20, and Switzerland have given their support to the PRAI.[114] Uncompromising opposition to the PRAI comes from a coalition of civil society organizations.[115] The institutional strength and influence of the sponsors of the PRAI seem to pale in comparison to the groundswell of opposition from a diverse range of stakeholders, including farmers' movements and human rights, social justice, and environmental organizations, not to mention indigenous and local community groups directly affected by land grabs. They challenge the legitimacy of the PRAI and most importantly of land-grabbing.

The seven principles of the PRAI framework, which overlap with the IFRI's policy framework, are: 1) respect for existing rights to land and natural resources; 2) sanctity of food security; 3) transparency in land-acquisition processes; 4) consultation with and participation of people affected in land grabs; 5) economic viability of agro-enterprise investment that respects the rule of law, follows industry best practices, and advances the suspect notion of shared value; 6) social sustainability of investment through positive distributional social impact; and 7) quantifiable environmental impact and sustainability of resource use.

There are two arguments in opposition to the PRAI that unmask the ideological tension within the land-grab phenomenon. The first argument is that the PRAI framework supports an ideology of "successful capitalist economic development [whereby] large-scale investments are seen as the main solution to (rural) poverty."[116] According to Borras and Franco, this narrative emphasizes employment creation, increase in smallholder incomes and food production, new export opportunities, technology transfer, infrastructural development, and access to basic amenities as several key benefits of these land transactions.[117] In other words, high-tech intervention is the magic wand that puts untapped global agricultural lands to *optimal* use. Consequently, the claimed benefits of this techno-economic fix are considered adequate to balance a host of negative consequences that amount to land acquisition by dispossession. These concerns are framed as "mere side effect[s] of an essentially beneficial cure,"[118] which the CoCs can fix.

The second argument is a step-by-step deconstruction of the PRAI principles, which are perceived as serving the interests of its proponents at the expense of local

[113] See generally United Nations Conference on Trade and Development, "The Principles for Responsible Agricultural Investment (PRAI)," http://unctad.org.

[114] See generally GRAIN, "The Great Food Robbery: How Corporations Control Food, Grab Land and Destroy the Climate," May 4, 2012, www.grain.org.

[115] Notably, the Global Campaign for Agrarian Reform, Land Research Action Network, FIAN International, Focus on the Global South, La Via Campesina, Social Network for Justice and Human Rights.

[116] Borras and Franco, note 4, p. 7.

[117] Ibid.

[118] Ibid.

254 *Sustainable Development in the Era of Bioenergy*

and indigenous communities.[119] This second approach demonstrates that full compliance with the PRAI principles is unlikely to produce positive outcomes for the poor and will, at best, entrench the preexisting inequitable status quo. For example, securing "existing" land rights does not benefit landless peasants and future generations. Ensuring participatory and transparent land acquisition processes will make no difference if power relations remain asymmetrical.[120] The same is true of social and environmental impact assessments, regardless of their outcomes.

Industry best practices and economic viability are pro-industry value-laden concepts that do not accommodate the reality and values of agricultural production in indigenous and local communities. Furthermore, it is unlikely that efforts to quantify the environmental impacts of land grabs will adequately account for the holistic "environmental costs of industrial mono-crop agriculture,"[121] including loss of ecosystem services, deforestation, loss of biodiversity, depletion of water supplies, and chemical contamination of lakes and rivers. Simply stated, the PRAI reflects an attempt to preserve the interests of capital, facilitate land acquisition, and sustain an agro-industrial model with marginal regard to complex environmental, economic, and social relations that sustain the livelihoods and culture of local and indigenous farming communities.

Finally, not only does the PRAI not address the question of excessive consumption, the twin issues of energy and food waste, and overall per capita ecological footprint in many land-grabbing countries, it proceeds on the premise that land-grabbing is inevitable. The PRAI framework fails to engage with the issue of unrealistic biofuel and biodiesel targets set by countries of the global North.[122] Even as the advantages of the second generation of biofuels remain unverified,[123] Northern countries have yet to come to terms with the fact that bioenergy is a supplementary energy strategy requiring a more modest approach. In addition to these fundamental weaknesses, the PRAI is essentially a voluntary industry self-regulation initiative with no sanctions for non-compliance.

Both the institutional and country proponents of the PRAI do not seem to attach importance to the counternarratives of the negative impacts of land-grabbing.

---

[119] S. Guttal, "Why We Oppose the Principles for Responsible Agricultural Investment (RAI)," October 12, 2010, http://focusweb.org.

[120] Community participation is not a guarantee that the rural poor will not be displaced or dispossessed of their land. See Borras and Franco, note 4, p. 31.

[121] S. Guttal, note 119.

[122] Oxfam, "Bio-Fuelling Poverty: Why the EU Renewable-Fuel Target may be Disastrous for Poor People," www.oxfam.org, November 1, 2007, pp. 1–2. See generally Tiraldo et al., note 5.

[123] Runge and Senauer, note 5; see also Tiraldo et al., note 5 at 1738. Second-generation biofuels are non-food crop biomass from diverse sources, including wood, organic waste, cellulose, and plants/grasses (e.g. jatropha). While second-generation bioenergy is a proffered solution to the food energy conflict that undermines the first generation, the sustainability and overall viability of the biomass categories of the second generation bioenergy sources remains inconclusive in terms of land use, energy consumption for their production, diversion of resources for food crop production, and their greenhouse gas life cycle.

This gap in the PRAI perhaps explains its failure to integrate human rights impact assessment pursuant to the International Covenant on Economic, Social, and Cultural Rights' (ICESCR) right-to-food framework.[124] Human rights are important considerations for land grabs – a phenomenon now driving unprecedented agrarian system and land distribution changes at local, national, and global levels. The PRAI framework is an attempt at legitimating land-grabbing; an imposition of a development model that perpetuates unsustainable natural resource exploitation on the back of the most vulnerable.[125] There can be no win–win in such a system; neither for the poor nor for the environment, and not even for the temporary custodians of today's financial capital in the global North.

[124] *International Covenant on Economic, Social and Cultural Rights*, New York, 16 December 1966, in force 3 January 1976, 21 UN GAOR Supp. (No. 16) at 49, UN Doc. A/6316 (1966); 993 UNTS 3; 6 ILM 368 (1967), art. 1 (states' obligation to respect, protect and fulfil the right to food). See also *United Nations of Indigenous Peoples*, 29 June 2006, in force 2 October 2007, UN Doc. A/RES/61/295, (A/61/L.67 and Add.1), art. 8 (eschewing actions capable of dispossessing indigenous peoples of their land).

[125] The PRAI fuels the race to turn the rest of the global South, especially Africa, into the "carbon dump" for the North and the new power blocks of the South, an approach that was sanctioned by the Kyoto Protocol when it paved the way for the South to serve as a carbon sink for the North. See generally J. M. Alier, "Socially Sustainable Economic De-Growth" (2009) 40 *Development and Change* 1099.

12

Trade in Hazardous Waste

Zada Lipman

1. INTRODUCTION

Since the 1980s, the management and disposal of hazardous waste has been an ongoing and escalating global problem. While Northern countries generate most of this waste, a large quantity is exported to the global South. This places a disproportionate burden on countries that frequently lack the capacity to deal with such waste safely. It has serious impacts on human health and the environment in these countries and violates the principles of environmental justice. A number of highly publicized incidents of dumping in Africa led to the adoption of the Basel Convention in 1989.[1] To protect developing countries, the Convention first regulated and then attempted to ban North–South movements of hazardous waste. Regrettably, the Convention has failed to achieve its objective. In the twenty-odd years that the Convention has been in force, the trade in hazardous waste has continued, often under the guise of recycling. Dumping incidents such as the Abidjan disaster[2] are still occurring in Southern countries.[3]

This chapter will examine the reasons for the hazardous waste trade and the efficacy of the measures that have been taken to address it. The first section discusses the incidence of and motivation for North–South movements of hazardous waste as an example of toxic colonialism. This is followed by an analysis of the relationship between the hazardous waste trade and environmental justice. The next section considers the international regulation of hazardous waste transfers under the Basel Convention, including the decision to adopt a total ban

---

[1] *Basel Convention on the Control of Transboundary Movements of Hazardous Wastes and their Disposal*, Basel, 22 March 1989, in force 5 May 1992, 1673 UNTS 126; 28 ILM 657.

[2] Hazardous waste dumping in Abidjan, Cote d'Ivoire, on August 19, 2006 resulted in a number of deaths. See section 5 of this chapter and Amnesty International and Greenpeace Netherlands, "The Toxic Truth," September 25, 2012, www.greenpeace.org.

[3] See UNEP, "National Rapid Environmental Desk Assessment – Somalia," 2005, www.unep.org, para. 8.4.

on North–South trade, and the Basel Protocol.[4] Reference is also made to agreements under Article 11 of the Convention and how they can be used to circumvent the obligations imposed. This is followed by a brief evaluation of the Bamako Convention[5] and how it interacts with the Basel Convention, after which the chapter considers a dumping incident in 2006 in Abidjan and argues that the failure of international measures to address the hazardous waste trade is due to a combination of factors, including the weakness of the measures adopted, the illegal waste trade, and a lack of will on the part of some of the more cash-strapped Southern countries. The final section offers some recommendations as to how these factors can be addressed.

2. THE INCIDENCE AND MOTIVATION FOR HAZARDOUS WASTE EXPORTS

The past seventy years has seen an unprecedented increase in the production of new products that generate hazardous waste. In 1945, the global generation of hazardous waste was estimated to be approximately five million metric tons. By 2000, it had increased to an estimated 400 million metric tons, with at least 75 percent of this waste originating in developed countries.[6] Since then there has been no reliable data. This is largely due to the lack of a uniform definition of hazardous waste, a failure to report by many countries, and inconsistencies in how they report.[7] E-waste is currently the most rapidly growing waste stream. It encompasses all end-of-life electronic and electrical equipment that are likely to enter the waste stream, including mobile phones, refrigerators, televisions, and computers. Its global generation was estimated at more than 48 million tons in 2013 and is predicted to rise to 65.4 million tons annually by 2017.[8]

Increased waste generation inevitably leads to disposal problems. If hazardous waste is disposed in landfills, it leaches into the ground and water over time, or is released into the atmosphere. Incineration can also lead to the release of heavy metals, such as lead, or persistent organic pollutants, such as dioxins and furans. Without safeguards, recycling can be even more hazardous because of worker

---

[4] *Basel Protocol on Liability and Compensation for Damage Resulting from Transboundary Movements of Hazardous Wastes and their Disposal*, Basel, 10 December 1999, UN Doc. UNEP/CHW.1/WG/1/9/2 [hereinafter Basel Protocol].

[5] *Bamako Convention on the Ban of the Import into Africa and the Control of Transboundary Movement and Management of Hazardous Wastes within Africa*, Bamako, 30 January 1991, in force 22 April 1998, 2101 UNTS 177; 30 ILM 773 [hereinafter Bamako Convention].

[6] D. Hunter, J. Salzman, and D. Zaelke, *International Environmental Law and Policy*, 3rd ed (New York: Foundation Press, 2007), p. 947.

[7] E. Baker, E. Bournay, A Harayama, and P. Rekacewicz, "Vital Waste Graphics" (Basel Convention, Grid-Arendal, UNEP and DEWA Europe 2004), http://www.grida.no.

[8] Solving the E-Waste Problem, "World E-Waste Map Reveals National Volumes, International Flows," www.step-initiative.org.

exposure to dangerous materials.[9] hazardous waste disposal is often economically unviable in the global North because of high labor costs and environmental restrictions on the disposal of components and residues.[10] These factors have resulted in waste brokers in the North transferring their responsibilities to the South, a classic example of "not in my backyard" syndrome.[11] The dumping of hazardous wastes from the North in countries in the South has been termed "toxic colonialism" because it exhibits many characteristics of colonialism, such as "economic dependence, exploitation, and cultural inequality."[12]

The South provides a disposal option at prices that are often a mere fraction of the equivalent cost in the North. According to one study in the late 1980s, the average disposal costs for one ton of hazardous waste in Africa was US$2.50–$50, while costs in industrialized countries ranged from US$100 to $2,000.[13] In 2006, the cost of disposal of hazardous waste in Africa had risen to US$30 per ton, in comparison with US$600 in the European Union (EU).[14] Recyclers of e-waste in China are currently reported to earn US$1.50 per day.[15] These economic realities have resulted in the South being increasingly targeted as a dumping ground for hazardous waste generated in the North, a practice widely condemned as "environmental injustice."[16]

Hazardous waste imports are a major dilemma for Southern countries that generally do not have the facilities to manage these wastes safely. Many Southern countries accept hazardous waste either through ignorance of the risk it poses to human health and the environment or through necessity in order to support their failing economies.

3. THE RELATIONSHIP BETWEEN THE HAZARDOUS WASTE TRADE AND ENVIRONMENTAL JUSTICE

Environmental justice is a very broad-based concept that has at its heart the inequities between the North and the South. It has been defined as containing

[9] O. Schram Stokke and O. B. Thommessen (eds), *Yearbook of International Cooperation on Environment and Development 2001–2* (London: Earthscan, 2009), p. 43.

[10] L. A. Pratt, "Decreasing Dirty Dumping? A Reevaluation of Toxic Waste Colonialism and the Global Management of Transboundary Hazardous Waste" (2011) 35 *William and Mary Environmental Law and Policy Review* 581 at 590–592.

[11] T. G. Puthucherril, "Two Decades of the Basel Convention," in S. Alam, M. J. H. Bhuiyan, T. M. R. Chowdhury, and E. J. Techera (eds.) *Routledge Handbook of International Environmental Law* (Oxford: Routledge, 2013), p. 296.

[12] Pratt, note 10 at 587.

[13] K. Kummer, *International Management of Hazardous Wastes* (Oxford: Clarendon Press, 1995), pp. 6–7.

[14] L. Widawsky, "In My Backyard: How Enabling Hazardous Waste Trade to Developing Nations Can Improve the Basel Convention's Ability to Achieve Environmental Justice" (2008) 38 *Environmental Law* 577.

[15] K. Lundgren, *The Global Impact of E-Waste: Addressing the Challenge* (Geneva: International Labour Organization, 2012), p. 31.

[16] Widawsky, note 14.

four elements: Distributive justice, procedural justice, corrective justice, and social justice.[17] Distributive justice requires equitable treatment in environmental decision-making; procedural justice involves the right to be consulted and informed; corrective justice requires redress for past inequities; and social justice recognizes the links between environmental and social injustices, such as poverty and disparate exposure to environmental degradation.[18]

The environmental justice movement originated in the United States It first received national attention in 1982 when more than 500 protestors were jailed for demonstrating against the siting of a landfill in North Carolina that was to receive approximately 330,000 cubic yards of polychlorinated biphenyl contaminated soil. Since then, several studies in the United States have identified a correlation between race, socioeconomic status, and the location of hazardous waste facilities.[19] The U.S. Environmental Protection Agency describes environmental justice as the "fair treatment and meaningful involvement of all people regardless of race, color, national origin, or income with respect to the development, implementation and enforcement of environmental laws, regulations and policies."[20]

The siting of hazardous waste facilities in disadvantaged communities has been described as a microcosm of the problem of the practice of exporting hazardous waste to the global South.[21] Under both of these practices, poor communities are required to shoulder the burden of industrialization without having received any of its advantages. Frequently, no prior consultation takes place, or there is no awareness of the dangers associated with the wastes. Where harm occurs to human beings or the environment, compensation is rarely available. When a proliferation of dumping incidents were reported in Africa in the 1980s, the international community condemned this practice and called for a comprehensive legal regime to address the issue.[22]

4. INTERNATIONAL REGULATION OF HAZARDOUS WASTE UNDER THE BASEL CONVENTION

The first step toward an international convention was the development of the Cairo Guidelines for the Environmentally Sound Management of Hazardous Wastes.

---

[17] C. G. Gonzalez, "Environmental Justice in International Environmental Law," in S. Alam, M. J. H. Bhuiyan, T. M.R. Chowdhury, and E. J. Techera (eds.), *Routledge Handbook of International Environmental Law* (Oxford: Routledge, 2013), p. 78.

[18] Ibid.

[19] H. J. Marbug, "Hazardous Waste Exploration: The Global Manifestation of Environmental Racism" (1995) 28 *Vanderbilt Journal of Transnational Law* 251 at 292.

[20] U.S. Environmental Protection Agency, "Environmental Justice," www.epa.gov/environmentaljustice.

[21] Marbug, note 19 at 291.

[22] T. Dalyell, "Thistle Diary: Toxic Wastes and Other Ethical Issues," *New Scientist*, July 2, 1992, p. 50.

These Guidelines were approved by UNEP in 1987 and laid out a number of broad principles for hazardous waste management. A working group was then established to develop a global convention. During negotiations, most Southern countries expressed a preference for a total ban on the transboundary movements of hazardous waste. African countries, in particular, were concerned that any regulation short of a total ban would result in a continuation of hazardous waste shipments to Southern countries.[23] However, some Southern countries with developed recycling industries, such as India, Pakistan, and the Philippines, were less supportive of a ban because of the potential impact on their domestic economy.[24] A total ban on North–South trade was also resisted by the global North because of the economic value of the hazardous waste trade. The outcome was a compromise between both viewpoints. The original text of the Basel Convention did not ban transboundary movements of hazardous wastes,[25] but restricted them in accordance with the principles of environmentally sound management (ESM). As of 2015, there are 181 parties to the Convention. The world's largest producer of hazardous waste, the United States, has yet to ratify.

The Convention does not expressly invoke the principle of environmental justice; however, it is the first multilateral agreement to integrate environmental justice principles into international trade. Its overarching objective to protect human health and the environment from the adverse effects of hazardous waste and its recognition of the limited capabilities of developing countries to manage this waste is in keeping with this principle. This is reinforced by the prior informed consent (PIC) procedure and recognition of the need for technology transfer for the sound management of hazardous waste, particularly to developing countries. However, as was apparent during the negotiation of the Convention, many Southern countries, particularly those in Africa, believed that these commitments did not go far enough. These countries regarded regulation as legitimization of what they regarded as a criminal practice and yet another example of exploitation by the North.[26]

4.1 Overview of the Basel Convention

4.1.1 Definition of Hazardous Wastes

The Convention extends to hazardous wastes that are subject to transboundary movements. The determination of which "wastes" are "hazardous" is therefore critical to the implementation of the Convention. Wastes listed in Annex 1 are

---

[23] Stokke and Thommessen, note 9, pp. 45–46.
[24] Ibid.
[25] With the exception of Antarctica: Article 4.6.
[26] M. K. Tesi (ed.), *The Environment and Development in Africa* (Maryland: Lexington Books, 2000), p. 108.

regarded as "hazardous" if they have defined characteristics, such as flammability or explosivity,[27] or are regarded as hazardous in the domestic legislation of an exporting, importing, or transit party.[28] "Other wastes" listed in Annex II, namely household wastes and residues from the incineration of household wastes, are also treated as hazardous and subject to the Convention. Radioactive wastes and wastes discharged from ships are excluded from the Convention.[29]

The Convention is intended to regulate hazardous waste shipments for recycling as well as waste sent for disposal.[30] The Convention also affirms the sovereign right of parties to exclude imports of waste by respecting their national definitions as to what waste is hazardous. Southern countries can then introduce import bans for these wastes in addition to those listed as hazardous under the Convention. Any import ban introduced and notified to the Secretariat is binding on other parties.[31] However, in practice these bans are often ignored by the North.[32]

The very general definition of "hazardous" in the Convention has created uncertainty as to which wastes fall into this category. Further clarification has been provided by the adoption of two new lists of wastes as Annexes to the Convention. Wastes listed in Annex VIII are presumed hazardous, while those in Annex IX are not.[33] However, this has not resolved all of the definitional issues, as discussed later in the chapter.

4.1.2 Key Obligations Imposed by the Convention

The Convention imposes certain key obligations on parties:

- To minimize the generation of hazardous wastes and ensure the availability of adequate disposal facilities in their territory for their environmentally sound management (ESM).[34]
- To ensure that the transboundary movement of hazardous waste is reduced to the minimum consistent with its ESM.[35]
- To regulate hazardous waste movements in accordance with ESM principles.

In each case, the overarching principle in carrying out these obligations is to ensure the ESM of the wastes. This concept is defined in the Convention as "taking all

---

[27] Annex III.
[28] Art. 1.1(b).
[29] Art. 1.3, 4.
[30] "Wastes" are substances or objects which are intended to be disposed of: Article 2.1; "Disposal operations" are defined in Annex IV to include recycling processes.
[31] Art. 4.1.
[32] E.g. the Abidjan dumping incident, discussed in section 5.
[33] Decision IV/9.
[34] Art. 4.2(a), (b).
[35] Art. 4.2(d).

262   *Trade in Hazardous Waste*

practicable steps to ensure that hazardous wastes and other wastes are managed in a manner which will protect human health and the environment against the adverse effects which may result from such wastes."[36] This wording is very vague and does not clarify what ESM involves or who bears the responsibility for ensuring it. From a Southern perspective, ESM requires Northern countries to take responsibility for their hazardous waste by minimizing its generation through clean production and disposal at the source. The Northern focus, on the other hand, has been more on the capacity of Southern countries to deal with it safely. While the Basel parties have adopted a number of guidelines on ESM that recognize the importance of waste minimization and prevention, the overall focus remains on setting ESM standards for recycling and technical capacity implementation.[37] This does not address Southern concerns regarding their technical and financial capacity to implement import bans and monitor imports of illegal waste. Externally imposed guidelines for ESM also infringe upon the right of the global South to set its own standards.

4.1.3 Regulation of Hazardous Waste Shipments

Generally, hazardous waste movements are restricted, both for final disposal and recycling. However, these are subject to an exception where the state in question does not have the technical capacity to dispose of the waste safely, or where it is needed as a raw material for recycling operations.[38]

The Convention also prohibits the export or import of hazardous waste to, or from, non-parties.[39]

4.1.4 The Prior Informed Consent Procedure

Where transboundary movements of hazardous waste are permitted under the Convention, they are subject to a Prior Informed Consent (PIC) procedure. The waste generator or originating state must provide full information about a proposed shipment of hazardous waste to the state concerned and clearly state the effects on human health and the environment.[40] The shipment will not be permitted until the exporting state receives written consent from the importing state, as well as confirmation that the waste exporter and the disposer have entered into a legal contract that includes procedures for ESM of the waste.[41] The importing state has a duty to prevent

---

[36] Art. 2.8.
[37] E.g. UNEP, *Basel Declaration on ESM*, UNEP/CHW.5/CRP.10 (COP5); UNEP, *Annex: Framework for the ESM of Hazardous Wastes and Other Wastes*, UNEP/CHW.11/3/ADD.1/ Rev.1 (adopted at COP 11).
[38] Art. 4.9(a), (b).
[39] Art. 4.5.
[40] Art. 4.2(f). See also Article 6.1 which states that information in Annex VA must be provided.
[41] Art. 6.3.

the import if it has reason to believe the waste will not be managed in an environmentally sound manner.[42] The PIC procedure also applies to transit states that can refuse to permit the passage of waste through their territory. No shipment can commence until the consent of the transit state has been obtained.[43]

While theoretically these requirements are intended to provide the machinery for the protection of Southern countries, they do not always work in practice. Key issues for Southern countries, as identified by Krueger, are the lack of administrative, technical, and financial resources to monitor the PIC procedure.[44] A major problem with the PIC procedure is whether the importing country has the technical knowledge to assess the risks of the waste involved and to make an informed decision as to whether import consent should be granted.[45] As Kreuger points out, this requires "a sophisticated national infrastructure as well as resources and expertise."[46] Krueger also queries the validity of consent by poor countries in need of money.[47] Moreover, the PIC procedure fails where reporting documents are falsified by the exporter and the true nature of the wastes are not detected by the importing country, or if the authority is in collusion with the exporter.[48]

4.1.5 Illegal Traffic

Illegal trafficking in hazardous waste is criminal under the Convention, and parties are required to introduce domestic legislation to punish illegal trade.[49] The definition of illegal trafficking in the Convention is very broad and extends not only to clandestine shipments and deliberate dumping, but also to any shipments carried out in contravention of the provisions of the Convention.[50] Any shipment of hazardous waste is illegal if carried out without prior notification and consent; or if the consent has been obtained through falsification, misrepresentation, or fraud; or when it does not conform to the documents or results in deliberate disposal of hazardous waste in contravention of the Convention and general principles of international law.[51] Parties are required to cooperate in providing information on the movement of hazardous waste in order to ensure ESM and to prevent illegal traffic.[52]

---

[42] Art. 4.2(g).

[43] Art. 6.4.

[44] J. Kreuger, "Prior Informed Consent and the Basel Convention: The Hazards of What Isn't Known" (1998) 7 *Journal of Environment and Development* 115 at 123.

[45] Ibid at 122.

[46] Ibid at 121.

[47] Ibid.

[48] Ibid. For example, this occurred in the Abidjan dumping case.

[49] Art. 4.3, 4.

[50] Art. 9.1.

[51] Ibid.

[52] Art. 4.2(h).

264 *Trade in Hazardous Waste*

These provisions have not been successful in stopping the trade in illegal waste. The Convention does not have any effective compliance and enforcement mechanism, so detection of illegal shipments is left to the parties. This requires continual and sophisticated monitoring which Southern countries are not always equipped to undertake. There is also no liability mechanism to address any damage that occurs. The only responsibility of state parties is a duty to re-import any waste that cannot be dealt with in accordance with the contract or which was shipped illegally.[53]

4.1.6 Key Concerns of Southern Countries

From a Southern perspective, there are a number of problems with the Basel Convention. The South regards the Basel procedures as a legalization of waste colonialism affording little protection for poorer countries. Ambiguities in the definition of hazardous waste make it difficult to know what wastes are hazardous and subject to the Convention. This is exacerbated by the exclusion of radioactive waste. The greatest drawback of the Convention for most Southern countries is the failure to impose a complete ban on hazardous transfers to developing countries. The South considers that these responsibilities are being unfairly shifted onto the South, instead of the North being required to take responsibility for its own waste. Moreover, Southern countries have long been concerned that the PIC procedure would result in "sham recycling" and illegal exports.[54] They also doubt their capacity to enforce import bans.[55] These views have been borne out by subsequent events, such as the dumping incident in Abidjan[56] and the intractable problem of trade in e-waste.[57] These issues are compounded by the failure of the Convention to include a compensation mechanism.

4.1.7 Bamako Convention

Prior to the adoption of the Basel Convention, the Organization for African Unity (OAU) passed a resolution declaring the dumping of nuclear and hazardous waste into Africa a crime against Africa and the African people.[58] A particular concern was that cash-strapped countries might be persuaded to accept hazardous waste to bolster their economies and that Africa would become a global dumping

---

[53] Arts. 8, 9.
[54] J. Krueger, "The Basel Convention and the International Trade in Hazardous Wastes" [2001/2] *Yearbook of International Co-operation on Environment and Development* 43 at 45.
[55] Ibid.
[56] Discussed in Part 5.
[57] Lundgren, note 15, pp. 14–17.
[58] OAU Council of Ministers Resolution, *Dumping of Nuclear and Industrial Waste in Africa*, 23 May 1988, 28 ILM 567 (1989).

ground.[59] A number of incidents of this type had already occurred. For example, Guinea-Bissau was offered a $600 million contract – four times its gross national product – to dispose of fifteen million tons of toxic waste over five years.[60] The OAU initially refused to participate in the Basel Convention, and instead negotiated the Bamako Convention. The Bamako Convention is regarded as a regional agreement under Article 11 of the Basel Convention.[61]

The Bamako Convention addresses most of the perceived deficiencies of the Basel Convention. It imposes a total ban on nuclear and hazardous waste imports into Africa for final disposal and recycling, and provides criminal sanctions for importers.[62] Hazardous waste movements within Africa are permitted, but subject to regulation. The Convention also imposes a total ban on sea dumping of hazardous wastes.[63] Unlike the Basel Convention, the Bamako Convention imposes unlimited liability, as well as joint and several liability on hazardous waste operators, with the exception of accidents during transboundary shipments.[64] This would enable a country that had suffered damage to recover compensation and clean-up costs from any party to the transaction, regardless of their role.[65]

Although the Bamako Convention was instituted by African countries, it has had very limited success in reducing hazardous waste exports to Africa. Puthucherril attributes this failure to the "lack of an effective monitoring and enforcement operation, an underdeveloped funding mechanism and the lack of solid commitment among the African states."[66] To date, the Convention has been ratified by less than half of African states. Generally, it is supported by poorer, less developed countries, rather than by those with established industries and recycling programs. This is probably due to concerns about the impact of a total ban on the recycling industry and the loss of much needed materials and revenue.

4.2 Weaknesses of the Basel Convention and Measures Taken to Address Them

Although the Convention is an important first step in ensuring environmental justice for Southern countries, it has a number of weaknesses that undermine its effectiveness. Some of these weaknesses will now be discussed, along with the limited success of efforts to address them.

---

[59] A. Ogunlade, "Can the Bamako Convention Adequately Safeguard Africa's Environment in the Context of Transboundary Movement of Hazardous Wastes?" (2009/10) 14 *Centre for Energy, Petroleum, Mineral Law and Policy Annual Review* 5.

[60] A. Vir, "Toxic Trade with Africa" (1989) 23 *Environment, Science and Technology Journal* 23 at 25.

[61] UNEP, "First Conference of Parties to the Bamako Convention," www.unep.org.

[62] *Bamako Convention*, note 5, art. 4.1.

[63] Art. 4.2.

[64] Art. 4.3(b).

[65] Art. 12.

[66] Puthucherril, note 11, p. 304.

4.2.1 The Recycling Loophole

The initial focus of the Basel Convention was on exports of hazardous waste for final disposal rather than recycling. Ironically, the Convention was the trigger for the hazardous waste trade in recycling, for example, ships containing hazardous materials, because of the loophole that permits these exports. Although the scope of the Convention does extend to recycling operations, this is subject to an exception where the waste in question is required as a raw material for recycling or recovery in the importing state.[67] Waste exporters have been quick to exploit this situation. Hazardous waste shipments to the global South are no longer labeled as exports for dumping or final disposal, but rather as commodities for recycling in the country of import. In some cases this is a "sham" operation and the waste ended up being burned or dumped. Where recycling does take place, it is often not managed safely and results in harm to human health and the environment.[68] According to current estimates, approximately 80 percent of e-waste sent for recycling ends up in Southern countries, particularly Asia and Africa.[69]

Shipbreaking is yet another example of the recycling loophole. Shipbreakers have consistently argued that ships are not waste, but entities sent for recycling. These problems have proved so intractable that a separate convention has been adopted to address them: the Hong Kong International Convention for the Safe and Environmentally Sound Recycling of Ships 2009.[70] To encourage its early entry into force, the EU has adopted a Regulation on Ship Recycling that implements the provisions of the Convention.[71] Ship owners have to notify their intention to scrap a ship, provide details of hazardous materials, minimize cargo residues and fuel, and provide a "ready for recycling" certificate.[72] The Regulation restricts ship recycling of EU-flagged ships to facilities on a "European List." States that meet certain requirements, regardless of their location, may apply for inclusion on the list.[73]

4.2.2 Non-Ratification of the Basel Ban

Continuation of the North–South hazardous waste trade under the guise of recycling gave impetus to calls by the global South and environmental NGOs for a total ban on the transboundary movement of hazardous wastes to the global South. At the Second Conference of the Parties to the Basel Convention in 1994,

---

[67] Art. 4.9(b).
[68] Basel Action Network, "Turn Back the Toxic Tide," 2011, www.ban.org, pp. 1–2.
[69] Lundgren, note 15, p. 11.
[70] Hong Kong, 15 May 2009, not yet in force, IMO/SR/CONF/45.
[71] Regulation (EU) No 1257/2013 of the European Parliament and Council of 20 November 2013 on ship recycling and amending Regulation (EC) No 1013/2006 and Directive 2009/16/EC.
[72] Ibid; European Commission, "Environment: Ship Recycling," http://ec.europa.eu.
[73] Ibid.

a decision was passed by consensus banning all exports of hazardous waste from OECD to non-OECD countries.[74] A formal amendment to the Convention incorporating the ban was adopted at the Third Conference of the Parties in 1995, prohibiting all transboundary movements of hazardous wastes for final disposal and recycling from states listed in Annex VII (the OECD, the European Community, and Liechtenstein) to other parties not in the Annex.[75]

The ban was intended to ensure environmental justice by protecting the global South from dangers associated with hazardous wastes. In particular, it sought to "plug the 'recycling' loophole through which more than 90 per cent of exported wastes continues to flow."[76] However, As of March 2015, it had not yet received the requisite number of ratifications to come into effect.[77] Many Northern industrialized countries have failed to ratify the amendment because of the economic implications. It has been cited as a major reason for the United States' continual refusal to ratify the Convention.[78] Although initially the ban was unanimously supported by the South, some Southern countries, such as Bangladesh, the Philippines, India, and Pakistan, have been reluctant to ratify it. These countries rely on the hazardous waste trade in recyclables to support their domestic industries. A complete ban would deprive them of an inexpensive source of raw materials, such as steel, zinc, and lead, and impact their domestic economies.

4.2.3 Article 11 Agreements

Article 11 permits parties to enter into bilateral, multilateral, or regional agreements regarding the transboundary movement of hazardous waste provided that the ESM requirements are at least as rigorous as those required by the Convention, taking into account the interests of developing countries. This loophole permits the United States to trade in hazardous waste with other OECD countries, including Canada, Mexico, and Korea, under an Article 11 agreement, although it is not a party to the Convention.[79] It has also been suggested as a possible means of circumventing the Ban Amendment when it comes into force.[80] This interpretation

---

[74] Decision II/12 (1994).

[75] Decision III/1 (1995).

[76] Greenpeace International, "Toxics Reloaded: Revisiting the Impacts of Lead Battery Waste Trade and Recycling in the Philippines," June 2003, www.greenpeace.org, p 2.

[77] As of March 2015, seventy-eight parties have ratified the Ban Amendment.

[78] Loss to U.S. estimated as $2.2 billion p.a.. See "Chamber of Commerce Withdraws Support for Treaty on Waste Movement, Disposal" (1994) 25 *Environmental Report* 165.

[79] OECD, *Decision of the Council C (02)93/FINAL: Concerning the Control of Transboundary Movements of Wastes Destined for Recovery Operations* (OECD countries). Pre-existing Agreements between the United States, Canada, and Mexico are also recognized under Article 11.

[80] Statements by Canada and Australia following the adoption of the Amendment Decision by Consensus, 22 September 1995, in Secretariat Basel Convention, *Decisions and Report Adopted by the Third Meeting of the Conference to the Parties*, 1995, SBC No. 95/003, paras. 99–101, elaborated in K. Breitmeyer, "Australia's Opposition to the Basel Ban Amendment on

268 Trade in Hazardous Waste

would result in a loss of protection for Southern countries and be counter to the principles of environmental justice, which the ban was intended to uphold.

4.2.4 Lack of a Liability and Compensation Mechanism

The Basel Convention does not provide a mechanism for liability and compensation, which means that there is no mandatory mechanism to compel waste brokers to pay compensation for harm caused by their hazardous shipments. Instead, the Convention requires parties to develop a protocol to address these issues.[81] After protracted negotiations, a Protocol on Liability and Compensation was adopted at the Fifth Conference of the Parties in 1999.[82] However, sixteen years later, the Protocol has not come into force, as only eleven of the twenty required ratifications have been obtained. All ratifications to date are by Southern countries.

The objective of the Protocol is "to provide a comprehensive regime for liability and adequate and prompt compensation for damage resulting from the transboundary movement of hazardous wastes and other wastes and their disposal, including illegal traffic."[83] The Protocol imposes strict liability for "damage" on the person who "notifies" the proposed shipment, who, depending on the circumstances, could be the state of export, generator, or exporter.[84] These persons are required to carry insurance, bonds, or other financial guarantees to cover their liability.[85] Damage for which compensation is available is confined to loss of life, personal injury, or damage to property. Pure environmental damage is not covered unless it results in loss of income or from measures taken to reinstate the environment.[86] The Protocol provides for both fault-based and strict liability.[87] There are no financial limits for fault-based liability, but financial limits are specified for strict liability depending on the tonnage involved.[88] Parties have the option to exclude liability for incidents in their territory.[89]

There are a number of problems with the Protocol that limit its effectiveness. First, it provides for liability to cease when disposal operations are completed. This is a particular concern for Southern countries as it is after the conclusion of disposal operations that significant problems are likely to arise. For example, most damage from dumping incidents results from leakages from inadequate containers

---

the Export of Hazardous Wastes: When will Australia Stop Stalling and Ratify the Amendment?" (1999) 9 *Indiana International and Comparative Law Review* 537 at 539.

[81] Art. 12.

[82] Basel Protocol, note 4.

[83] Ibid, art. 1.

[84] "Notifier" is the person who notifies under Article 6 of the Convention: see Basel Protocol, note 4, art. 4.

[85] Basel Protocol, note 4, art. 14.1.

[86] Ibid, art. 2.2(c).

[87] Ibid, art. 5.

[88] Ibid, Annex B.

[89] Ibid, art. 3.

after disposal, as was the case in the Abidjan disaster. Similarly, damage from recycling operations generally results from inadequate management of residues and emissions, which manifests itself after the process has been completed. Second, a party can exclude liability by concluding an agreement under Article 11 to the Convention, which meets or exceeds the provisions of the Protocol. Third, the Protocol does not apply if another liability and compensation regime covers the incident.[90]

5. DUMPING OF WASTE IN ABIDJAN

Despite the international measures that have been taken to regulate the North–South trade in hazardous wastes, dumping incidents in the South are still being reported. One of the most serious incidents in recent years occurred in Abidjan in the Cote d'Ivoire.

In 2005 Trafigura Ltd, a subsidiary of Trafigura Beheer BV, a Dutch commodities trading company controlled from London, undertook ship-based refining operations of heavy residual fuel oil (coker naptha). This was done by an industrial process called caustic washing.[91] After the process was completed, a disposal site was sought for the hazardous residues. Disposal arrangements fell through when the Amsterdam Port Services found the waste to be severely contaminated and raised the price for treatment to US$600 per ton.[92] The waste was reloaded and taken to Abidjan, where it arrived in August 2006. Trafigura contracted with a local waste company to dispose of the waste for US$30 per ton.[93] Some of the waste was offloaded at a dump site that did not have the capacity to treat hazardous waste and the remainder was dumped at several sites throughout Abidjan.[94] The exact composition of the waste is unknown; however, it is believed to have contained large quantities of hydrocarbons, contaminated with phenols, hydrogen sulphide, mercaptans, and caustic soda.[95] Fifteen people are reported to have died from exposure to the waste, sixty-nine were hospitalized, and more than 107,000 sought medical treatment.[96] Symptoms reported included headaches, vomiting, nose bleeding, gastric problems, nausea, dizziness, and skin irritation.[97]

At the time of the incident, the Cote d'Ivoire had ratified the Basel Convention but not the Ban Amendment.[98] Since it had also ratified the Bamako Convention

[90] Basel Protocol, note 4, art. 11.
[91] Amnesty International and Greenpeace Netherlands, note 2.
[92] Widawsky, note 14 at 577.
[93] Ibid.
[94] Amnesty International and Greenpeace Netherlands, note 2, p. 9.
[95] B. Ziriyo, "Report of the International Investigation Committee on Toxic Waste in the District of Abidjan," February 19, 2007, www.courdescomptesci.com.
[96] Ibid.
[97] Ibid.
[98] The Cote d'Ivoire ratified the Ban Amendment in 2013.

270 *Trade in Hazardous Waste*

it was therefore obliged to take all appropriate measures to prohibit and impose criminal sanctions for any import of hazardous waste from outside Africa.[99] This was reinforced by national legislation in the Cote d'Ivoire banning the import of toxic and hazardous waste and punishing violations as criminal conduct.[100] The Ivorian authorities did not take any measures to prevent the entry of the wastes or to ensure that it could be managed in an environmentally sound manner.[101]

The EU had ratified the Basel Convention and the Basel Ban. Both the Cote d'Ivoire and the Netherlands were parties to the Basel Convention, and were therefore duty-bound to implement and comply with its provisions.[102] The EU had transposed the Basel Convention and Ban into its legislation;[103] thus any EU countries involved had an obligation not to allow hazardous waste exports to non-Annex VII States. The EU was aware of the Cote d'Ivoire's ratification of the Bamako Convention and its stance against hazardous waste exports, and arguably should have been more vigilant in halting the shipment.[104] However, the status of the EU as an exporter was questionable and complicated by the fact that the waste originated on a ship.[105]

Civil proceedings brought by the Cote d'Ivoire government against Trafigura were settled with Trafigura making a payment of approximately US$200m for compensation and clean-up costs in return for immunity from prosecution.[106] A civil action brought by 30,000 Ivorian citizens in the United Kingdom against Trafigura was settled for £45,000.[107]

Criminal proceedings were brought against the head of the waste company and the importing agent in the Cote d'Ivoire and sentences of twenty years' and five years' imprisonment, respectively, were imposed.[108] Criminal proceedings brought against Trafigura in the Netherlands resulted in a conviction for failure to disclose the harmful character of the waste and for illegally exporting it from the Netherlands, and a fine of €1 million.[109] To avoid a drawn-out appeal process,

---

[99] Bamako Convention, note 5, art. 4.1.

[100] Act No 88-651 of 7 July 1988 on the Protection of Public Health and the Environment Against the Effects of Toxic and Nuclear Wastes and Harmful Substances; Act No 96-766 of 3 October 1996 on the Protection of the Environment (Code of the Environment).

[101] Ziriyo, note 95.

[102] UN General Assembly, *Report of the Special Rapporteur on the Adverse Effects of the Movement and Dumping of Toxic and Dangerous Products and Wastes on the Enjoyment of Human Rights, Okechukwa Ibeanu*, 3 September 2009, A/HRC/12/26/Add.2.

[103] Regulation (EC) No 1013/2006 of the European Parliament and of the Council of 14 June 2006 on shipments of waste; see also Europa, "Summaries of EU Legislation: Shipments of Waste," http://europa.eu.

[104] Amnesty International and Greenpeace Netherlands, note 2.

[105] K. Morrow, "The Trafigura Litigation and Liability for Unlawful Trade in Hazardous Waste: Time for a Rethink?" (2010) 18(6) *Environmental Liability* 219 at 224.

[106] Ibid at 133.

[107] *Motto & Ors v Trafigura Ltd and Trafigura Beheer BV* [2009] EWHC 1246 (QB).

[108] Amnesty International and Greenpeace Netherlands, note 2, p. 142.

[109] Ibid, p. 157.

the matter has now been settled out of court, with Trafigura agreeing to pay an additional €300,000 as compensation for its earnings from the illegal export. As part of the settlement, charges were dropped against a Trafigura director and employee in return for the payment of fines of €67,000 and €25,000, respectively.[110]

6. RECOMMENDATIONS ON STRENGTHENING HAZARDOUS WASTE CONTROLS

The case study of toxic waste dumping in Abidjan highlights the failure of international and national measures to manage the hazardous waste trade. Of particular concern is that these events occurred despite the Basel Convention and Ban, the Bamako Convention, and domestic legislation to prohibit the waste trade. Hence, there is a need to strengthen and supplement these measures.

6.1 Clarify the Definition of Hazardous Waste

Definitions of hazardous waste should be standardized. The Basel Convention affirms the sovereign right of parties to ban imports of hazardous waste using their own definitions. This creates uncertainty and ambiguity regarding which wastes are hazardous. A further complication is that under the Basel Convention, the definition of hazardous waste largely depends on the view of its generator.[111] The Convention's failure to adequately distinguish between wastes and products and its vague criteria regarding what is "hazardous" has allowed the continuation of the North–South trade in hazardous waste, enabling waste traders to claim that they are trading in commodities and raw materials for recycling, not in waste. For example, the Basel Convention lacks any test to distinguish between e-waste shipments and used electronics intended for reuse, other than the definitions in Annexes VIII and IX.[112] Companies exporting e-waste from European countries regularly exploit this loophole.[113] This argument has also been used to justify ship recycling on the basis that ships proceeding to scrap yards are entities, not waste, and therefore not covered by the Convention. Thus, since these exports are not labeled as waste, the PIC procedure and national hazardous waste import bans are very difficult to enforce.[114] The result has been that these wastes are frequently

---

[110] Dutch News.nl, "Dutch Probo Koala Toxic Waste Cases Finally Settled out of Court," November 16, 2012, www.dutchnews.nl.

[111] Morrow, note 105 at 224.

[112] K. Wendell, "Improving Enforcement of Hazardous Waste Laws: A Regional Look at E-Waste Shipment Control in Asia," *Ninth International Conference on Environmental Compliance and Enforcement* (2011), p. 632.

[113] S. Laha, "Transboundary Toxic E-Waste Flow: Environmental Injustice through Neo-ecological Imperialism," 2011, www.iss.nl.

[114] J. Clapp, *Toxic Exports: The Transfer of Hazardous Wastes from Rich to Poor Countries* (New York: Cornell University Press, 2001), p. 58.

272   *Trade in Hazardous Waste*

recycled in unsuitable facilities and in unsafe conditions, causing harm to humans and the environment in Southern countries.[115]

A further difficulty is that the Convention excludes wastes that arise from ships from the definition of hazardous wastes, which are instead dealt with under the International Convention for the Prevention of Pollution from Ships (MARPOL).[116] MARPOL regulates discharges from ships and requires the establishment of land-based reception facilities. It has no PIC procedure or ESM requirements in relation to land disposal. The Abidjan dumping incident illustrates the problems than can arise where these two conventions overlap. Effectively it gave Trafigura the option of claiming to follow the Convention that imposed the least onerous procedure.[117] This highlights the necessity to clearly delineate the relationship between these Conventions.

6.2 *Strengthen the PIC Procedure*

The PIC procedure needs to be reformed to ensure that parties comply with their obligations on exchange of information. Under the Convention, the obligation for observing the PIC procedure rests with the generator of the hazardous waste, namely the exporter of the waste (charterer Trafigura) or the country of export. Exporters must provide accurate information about the constitution and hazards of the waste so that the importing state can make an informed judgment as to whether it can be disposed of safely. Clearly, Trafigura misrepresented the nature of the waste in the Abidjan incident: It was described as "routine slops," dirty water from washing naval tanks, when it was in fact a mixture of highly toxic substances.[118]

A further aspect that needs reform is the self-verification procedure, which relieves the exporter of further investigation once assurances have been given by the country of import that the waste can be managed safely. This procedure may not always be appropriate where North–South transactions are concerned. In this regard, Andrews identifies three problems that can arise:[119] First, Southern countries may not have the administrative capacity and technology to assess the potential risks to human health and the environment, which makes it difficult for them to assess whether the disposal facilities are suitable. Second, corrupt officials can also abuse the process. The Commission of Inquiry into the Abidjan disaster

---

[115] Ibid.

[116] *International Convention on the Control of Pollution from Ships*, 2 November 1973, in force 2 October 1983, 12 ILM 1319 (1973); TIAS No. 10,561; 34 UST 3407;1340 UNTS 184.

[117] See Morrow, note 105 at 229.

[118] S. Alam and A. Faruque, "Legal Regulation of the Shipbreaking Industry in Bangladesh: The International Regulatory Framework and Domestic Implementation Challenges" (2014) 47 *Marine Policy* 46 at 50–51.

[119] A. Andrews, "Beyond the Ban—Can the Basel Convention Adequately Safeguard the World's Poor in the International Trade of Hazardous Waste?" (2009) 5(2) *Law, Environment and Development Journal* 167 at 173.

found that corrupt officials played a major role in the incident. Third, it also does not take account of economic conditions that can influence decisions in Southern countries.[120]

A possible solution may be to introduce an international certification system for hazardous waste recycling facilities along the lines of ISO 14000. Waste transfers would then only be permitted to facilities that had been accredited under this system. Southern countries must be involved in this process so that it is not regarded as an invasion of sovereignty. Alternatively, since Southern countries frequently do not have the capacity to develop new standards, the Basel parties could follow the lead of other regimes, such as the WTO Agreement on Sanitary and Phytosanitary Measures (SPM), in placing a stronger emphasis on equivalency as a potential solution.[121] This would require the state of export to accept the measures of an importing Southern country as equivalent to the Basel requirements if these measures can be objectively demonstrated to achieve the same level of protection. To facilitate the evaluation of equivalence, the importing state should provide reasonable access for inspection and testing. Multilateral equivalence agreements could be negotiated between parties to the Convention.

6.3 *Improve Enforcement and Address the Illegal Waste Trade*

The Abidjan incident has demonstrated a total lack of enforcement of international and national measures. Regrettably, the Basel Convention does not have any effective compliance or enforcement mechanisms, relying instead on the transcription of its obligations into national law. Enforcement procedures in the Convention must be strengthened so that states can be penalized for non-compliance. This could be done by restructuring the Convention's Compliance Committee to include an enforcement branch.[122] Penalties imposed could be used to fund additional enforcement measures.

Stronger procedures should be adopted globally to detect and monitor illegal trafficking in hazardous wastes. This should be a multilateral initiative along the lines of the recent operation supported by the Secretariat of the Basel Convention and UNEP, in which customs officers from forty-four countries confiscated more than 7,000 metric tons of illegal waste awaiting export.[123] These bodies could consider establishing a permanent global customs task force to conduct regular inspections and monitoring. An important recent development is the establishment of the Environmental Network for Optimizing Regulatory Compliance on Illegal

---

[120] Ibid.

[121] World Trade Organization, *Agreement on the Application of Sanitary and Phytosanitary Measures*, 15 April 1994, 1867 UNTS 493, art. 4.

[122] Andrews, note 119 at 182.

[123] World Customs Organization, "Tons of Illegal Waste Seized under Operation Demeter III," January 20, 2014, www.wcoomd.org.

274 *Trade in Hazardous Waste*

Traffic, which will deliver capacity-building activities and tools to prevent and combat illegal traffic.[124]

To avoid e-waste being exported in the guise of products for reuse in the South, Northern countries should follow the approach of the EU in laying down minimum reporting requirements for shipments of used electric and electronic products, and pre–shipment clearance should be required.[125] The recent EU Regulation on ship recycling is also a useful model for ensuring that ships are stripped of hazardous materials and sent to approved facilities for recycling.[126]

6.4 *Update the Basel Ban*

It is now twenty years since the Basel Ban was adopted, although it has not yet come into effect. There have been enormous changes during this period. Many relatively sophisticated Eastern Bloc countries with established industries, such as Russia, are now included in the Basel Ban. The appropriateness of a ban that is effectively based on OECD member status is questionable, since it does not recognize that not all Southern countries are at the same level of development. While some Southern countries, such as those in sub-Saharan Africa, may still not have achieved their development potential and need protection, other countries in Asia are rapidly industrializing and have established recycling facilities. Countries like India, the Philippines, and Pakistan require more raw materials than can be supplied domestically and are reliant on the hazardous waste trade to obtain them. Often entire industries in these countries have developed and have long been supported by the hazardous waste trade. For cash-strapped economies, hazardous waste imports offer an important source of revenue and provide employment for thousands of workers. However, a major problem in a number of these countries, such as China and India, is the growth of an illegal "informal" waste-recycling sector which operates without regard to environmental and human health safety factors.[127] A possible solution is to amend the Ban in Annex VII to prohibit exports to Southern countries who have import bans and allow exports to other Southern countries on the basis of the equivalency approach, as provided in the WTO–SPM Agreement. This would allow Southern countries with established recycling facilities to continue to import hazardous waste for recycling provided their facilities have been found to be of equivalence to the Basel standards. A list of accredited facilities could then be added to Annex VII.

[124] UNEP, "Over 30 Nations Meet to Tackle the Illegal Traffic of Hazardous Wastes," November 19, 2013, www.unep.org.
[125] For example, the EU WEEE Directive 2012/19/EU.
[126] Regulation (EU) No 1257/2013 of the European Parliament and Council of November 20, 2013 on ship recycling, note 71.
[127] See Lundgren, note 15, pp. 25–31.

6.5 Address Technology and Funding Issues

Northern countries must require manufacturers to produce products that are easier to repair and recycle. Hazardous materials in products should be replaced with safer alternatives.[128] Extended producer liability schemes which impose cradle-to-grave liability on manufacturers should be introduced. If the Basel Convention is to achieve its ultimate goal of reducing hazardous waste generation through waste minimization and clean production, these technologies must be passed on to Southern countries.[129]

As Southern countries continue to industrialize, they will require additional funding and technology from the North to develop their own industries and build environmentally safe recycling and disposal plants for any waste they create. The Convention encourages the transfer of technology and capacity-building and has established a "synergies" approach with the Rotterdam[130] and Stockholm Conventions.[131] [132] A number of Basel Regional and Coordinating Centres for Capacity Building and Technology Transfer have been established to provide training, information awareness, and technology training on a range of matters.[133] While these are important initiatives, their success is undermined by lack of funding, as only voluntary contributions are required by the Convention. Indeed, while the North regards technology transfer and capacity-building as a panacea for the hazardous waste issues in the South, the issue is more likely to be a lack of resources. As one commentator has observed: "[t]he primary difference in capacity between OECD and non-OECD is one of resources, not know-how. Converting industry to non-toxic methods requires an initial outlay of capital which many developing countries cannot afford."[134]

7. CONCLUSION

Environmental justice for the South has been elusive. Although the Basel Convention has been in force for over twenty years it has not succeeded in protecting

---

[128] For example, Directive 2011/65/EU on the Restriction of the Use of Certain Hazardous Substances in Electrical and Electronic Equipment.

[129] See Conference of the Parties to the Basel Convention, *Cartagena Declaration on the Prevention, Minimization and Recovery of Hazardous Wastes and Other Wastes*, October 10, 2011, www.uncsd2012.org.

[130] *Rotterdam Convention on the Prior Informed Consent Procedure for Certain Hazardous Chemicals and Pesticides in International Trade*, Rotterdam, 10 September 1998, in force 24 February 2004, 224 UNTS 337; [2004] ATS 22; 38 ILM 1 (1999).

[131] *Stockholm Convention on Persistent Organic Pollutants*, 22 April 2001, in force 17 April 2004, 2256 UNTS 119; 40 ILM 532 (2001).

[132] UNEP, "Enhancing Synergies among the Basel, Rotterdam and Stockholm Conventions," http://excops.unep.ch.

[133] UNEP, "The Basel Convention Regional and Coordinating Centres at a Glance," http://archive.basel.int.

[134] Basel Action Network, "BAN Report and Analysis of the Fifth Conference of the Parties to the Basel Convention," December 6–10, 1999, http://ban.org/COP5/cop5rep.html.

human health and the environment in the global South from the hazardous waste trade. The Convention has a number of weaknesses, including a failure to impose a total ban on North–South transfers of hazardous waste, the recycling loophole, and the lack of a liability and compensation mechanism. Amendments to the Convention to incorporate these measures have not yet been ratified. However, even where these measures have been implemented, they are not a panacea for waste trafficking, as illustrated by the case study of dumping in Abidjan. This incident occurred despite the fact that most of the states concerned had ratified the Basel Convention and Ban and enacted national legislation banning waste imports and exports. The Cote d'Ivoire had also ratified the Bamako Convention. The dumping was facilitated by the ambiguity in the Conventions' definition of hazardous waste, the ineffectiveness of the PIC procedure, and a total disregard of national laws. There is a need to ensure that appropriate compensation is available in such instances, and priority should be given to revision and ratification of the Protocol on Liability and Compensation for Damage Resulting from Transboundary Movements of Hazardous Wastes and their Disposal.[135]

Northern countries must take responsibility for their own waste. Toxic colonialism must cease and the North must respect Southern countries' import bans. For those countries that are in need of raw materials for their industries, the Basel Ban should be amended to apply the equivalency approach so that accredited facilities in Southern countries can continue to receive material for recycling. This would remove the OECD/non-OECD political divide which has polarized North–South relations since the inception of the Convention.

[135] 10 December 1992, UN Doc. UNEP/CHW.1/WG/1/9/2.

13

The Right to Water: Constitutional Perspectives from the Global South

Carlos Bernal

1. THE CONSTITUTIONALIZATION AND INTERPRETATION OF THE RIGHT TO WATER

Water is necessary for human life. However, due to poverty and inequality, not all human beings have continuous access to sufficient clean water. According to the 2006 UNDP Human Development Report, in 2006, "1.1 billion people in the developing world [did] not have access to a minimal amount of clean water."[1] This figure does not include the number of people who cannot afford water and who do not receive a continuous supply. This fact explains why one of the goals set in the United Nations Millennium Declaration was to "halve, by the year 2015, [...] the proportion of people who are unable to reach or to afford safe drinking water."[2] This has become one of the Millennium Development Goals (Target 7c). According to the WHO/UNICEF Joint Monitoring Programme (JMP) for Water Supply and Sanitation, the target was met in 2012.[3] However, according to another report, approximately 768 million people still do not use an improved source of drinking water.[4] Furthermore, UNDP's Human Development

---

The author thanks Shawkat Alam and Sumudu Anopama Atapattu for helpful comments to early drafts of this chapter.

[1] UNDP Human Development Report, "Beyond Scarcity: Power, Poverty and the Global Water Crisis," 2006, http://hdr.undp.org, p. 5.

[2] UN General Assembly, *United Nations Millennium Declaration, Resolution Adopted by the General Assembly*, 18 September 2000, A/RES/55/2.

[3] World Health Organization and UNICEF Joint Monitoring Programme, "Progress on Sanitation and Drinking-Water: 2013 Update," 2013, www.wssinfo.org.

[4] According to the JMP, an improved drinking water source is "one that, by nature of its construction or through active intervention, is protected from outside contamination, in particular from contamination with fecal matter." Sources of this kind are: piped water into dwelling; piped water to yard/plot; public tap or standpipe; tubewell or borehole; protected dug well; protected spring; rainwater. See World Health Organization and UNICEF Joint Monitoring Programme, "Improved and Unimproved Water and Sanitation Facilities," www.wssinfo.org.

278   *The Right to Water*

Report 2013 highlights that poverty results in insufficient access to water for less privileged segments of society, particularly in rural areas.[5]

In capitalist economies, water is an economic good.[6] Continuous access to sufficient clean water depends on the existence of a water market and on the fact that individuals have sufficient purchasing power. Poor and vulnerable people encounter a barrier to access this good. To eliminate this barrier, continuous access to sufficient clean water has become the subject matter of a human right guaranteed under international law, and of a fundamental right explicitly or implicitly protected by several constitutions.

The constitutionalization of the right to water has been a remarkable development in the global South. There are only few guarantees of this right in constitutional law of the North. A noteworthy example can be found in the Judgments 9/96 and 36/98, in which the Belgian Constitutional Court acknowledged that Article 23 of the 1994 Belgian Constitution – which states that everyone has the right to lead a life with dignity, with access to health care, and in a healthy environment[7] – includes the right of every individual to have access to drinking water.[8] In the global South, the constitutionalization of the right to water has benefited from the recognition and enforcement of socioeconomic rights. The constitutional entrenchment of socioeconomic rights has become a widespread strategy to address issues of poverty, unsatisfied basic needs, lack of resources to secure a life with dignity, and unequal distribution of opportunities and wealth. Furthermore, international human rights institutions and the constitutional and supreme courts of countries such as South Africa, Colombia, Costa Rica, Argentina, Mexico, Brazil, and India have enforced these rights by using highly creative techniques of judicial reasoning and adopting resourceful remedies.

Within this context, the constitutionalization of the right to water in the global South contributes to bridging the North–South divide concerning various dimensions of environmental justice. As Gonzalez has theorized, environmental justice has a distributive, procedural, corrective, and social justice dimension.[9] Entrenching a constitutional right to access and enjoyment of clean water that cannot be defeated on the basis of a routine cost–benefit calculation institutionalizes these

---

[5] UNPD Human Development Report, "The Rise of the South: Human Progress in a Diverse World," 2013, www.undp.org, p. 13.

[6] International human rights law regulations concerning access to and enjoyment of clean water are not contrary to the nature of water as an economic good. Nevertheless, sources such as the UN Committee on Economic, Social and Cultural Rights (CESCR), *General Comment No. 15: The Right to Water (Arts. 11 and 12 of the Covenant)*, 20 January 2003, E/C.12/2002/1, requires states to guarantee economic accessibility to water, water facilities, and services.

[7] See the text of this provision at www.dekamer.be/kvvcr/pdf_sections/publications/constitution/grondwetEN.pdf.

[8] These judgments are available online at www.const-court.be/en/common/home.html.

[9] C. G. Gonzalez, "Environmental Justice and International Environmental Law," in S. Alam, M.J.H. Bhuiyan, T.M.R. Chowdhury, and E.J. Techera (ed.), *Routledge Handbook of International Environmental Law* (Oxford: Routledge, 2013), p. 78.

dimensions of environmental justice.[10] Such a right reinforces the strength of distributive justice claims to development of water infrastructure, prevention of water pollution, and increased transnational aid. Moreover, that right justifies procedural justice claims of the poor against economic freedoms of multinational companies, and corrective justice claims to redress contamination. All these claims are raised in international, domestic, political, and judicial fora by countries of the global South against governments and private stakeholders of Northern countries.

The constitutionalization and interpretation of the right to water gives rise to many questions, including:

- What is the normative structure of this right?
- Who are the right-holders and the duty-bearers?
- What are their specific rights and obligations?
- How should dilemmas between the right to water and competing rights, such as economic freedoms of water companies, be resolved?

National judges enforcing the constitutional right to water have to answer these questions and justify their answers. For that purpose, it is common for them to use the standards of reasonableness and the minimum core that have developed under international and comparative constitutional law.

The jurisprudence developed by the South African Constitutional Court in the adjudication of cases under sections 26.2 and 27.2 of the 1996 South African Constitution is a paradigmatic use of reasonableness. These sections require the state to "take reasonable legislative and other measures, within its available resources, to achieve the progressive realization" of the rights to housing, health care, food, water, and social security.[11] Consistent with these provisions, the Constitutional Court has held that the scope of the positive duties of political authorities to achieve satisfaction of socioeconomic rights is "defined and limited" by the standard of reasonableness.[12] Scholars and judges have contended that the standard of reasonableness does not suffice for an adequate protection of socioeconomic rights.[13] Moreover, after an analysis of the key right to water case in South Africa,

---

[10] On the significance of constitutional rights see R. Dworkin, *Taking Rights Seriously* (London: Duckworth, 1977), pp. 193–195.

[11] With regard to the right to water, section 27 of the Constitution prescribes: "[e]veryone has the right to have access to [...] sufficient food and water [...]. The state must take reasonable legislative and other measures, within its available resources, to achieve the progressive realization of each of these rights."

[12] *Minister of Health* v *Treatment Action Campaign* (No. 2) 2002 5 SA 721 (CC), paras. 30–39.

[13] For an analysis of the objections against the use of reasonableness, see S. Woolman and M. Bishop, *Constitutional Law of South Africa*, 2nd ed, vol. 5 (Cape Town: Juta, 2013), pp. 56A–12; A. Pillay, "Economic and Social Rights Adjudication: Developing Principles of Judicial Restraint in South African and the United Kingdom" (2013) *Public Law* 599; A. Pillay, "Reviewing Reasonableness: An Appropriate Standard for Evaluating State Action and Inaction?" (2005) 122 *South African Law Journal* 420; C. Steinberg, "Can Reasonableness Protect the Poor? A Review of South Africa's Socio-Economic Rights Jurisprudence" (2006)

Mazibuko, one commentator proclaimed that the use of reasonableness had led to the death of socioeconomic rights.[14]

For this reason, some authors claim that the right to water should be judicially interpreted by means of the identification of a minimum core.[15] Within this context, the minimum core is a bundle of specific rights that should be satisfied under any circumstance. The case law of the Colombian Constitutional Court offers a variety of examples concerning the use of this standard. The Court adopted a doctrine of a vital minimum, under which each citizen has a constitutional right to enjoy the necessary means for a basic level of subsistence.[16] When applied to enforce the constitutional right to water, the minimum core requires the state to ensure that every citizen receives a minimum amount of clean water daily.[17] Furthermore, the Constitutional Court has interpreted the "social state principle" embodied in Section 1 of the Colombian Constitution[18] as requiring the state to build, maintain, and expand a network of social benefits capable of guaranteeing the vital minimum to every person.[19] Nonetheless, opponents consider the use of the minimum core as undemocratic and incompatible with the principles of the rule of law and the separation of powers, because it empowers judges to make decisions about budget allocations for social services and to require the performance of specific administrative actions.[20]

It has been suggested that the principle of proportionality[21] can be beneficial for the adjudication of socioeconomic rights.[22] Through analysis of three case studies,

---

123 *South African Law Journal* 264. A prominent analysis and defense of reasonableness can be found in S. Liebenberg, *Socio-Economic Rights: Adjudication under a Transformative Constitution* (Cape Town: Juta, 2010), p. 132.

[14] P. O'Connell, "The Death of Socio-Economic Rights" (2011) 74(4) *Modern Law Review* 532.

[15] D. Bilchitz, *Poverty and Fundamental Rights: The Justification and Enforcement of Socio-Economic Rights* (Oxford: Oxford University Press, 2007), p. 187.

[16] The most remarkable Constitutional Court judgments that have applied this doctrine are: SU-559/1997, T-068/1998, T-153/1998, SU-090/2000, T-068/2010, T-025/2004 and T-760/2008. All the judgments of the Colombian Constitutional Court are available online at www.constitucional.gov.co.

[17] In this respect, the minimum core is different from reasonableness. The former requires courts to determine the minimum amount of water and political authorities to make the necessary arrangements in order to guarantee the appropriate delivery. The latter empowers the legislature and the executive to determine what the minimum amount should be. Judges should be deferential to this determination unless it is unreasonable.

[18] According to this section, "Colombia is a legal social state [...] based on respect of human dignity."

[19] D. Landau, "The Promise of a Minimum Core Approach: The Colombian Model for Judicial Review of Austerity Measures," in A. Nolan (ed.), *Economic and Social Rights after the Global Financial Crisis* (Cambridge: Cambridge University Press, 2014).

[20] K. Young, *Constituting Economic and Social Rights* (Oxford: Oxford University Press, 2012), p. 91.

[21] On the concept of proportionality, see section 6.

[22] See X. Contiades and A. Fotiadou, "Social Rights in the Age of Proportionality: Global Economic Crisis and Constitutional Litigation" (2010) 10 *International Journal of Constitutional Law* 660.

this chapter proposes that proportionality is a more appropriate standard for judicial interpretation of the right to water than reasonableness or the minimum core. It compares and assesses the use of the three standards and shows that proportionality offers more advantages, in particular concerning the realization of the distributive and procedural dimensions of environmental justice at the constitutional level in the global South.

This chapter proceeds in six parts. It begins with an explanation of the recognition of access to water as a human right in international law and as a constitutional right in various jurisdictions. Then it discusses the normative structure of the positive rights drawn from the constitutional right to water and the interpretive issues that this structure generates. It then evaluates relevant South African and Colombian case law that uses the standards of reasonableness and the minimum core and appraises a paradigmatic employment of proportionality in a right to water judgment by the Israeli Supreme Court. Finally, it discusses why enforcing the constitutional right to water by means of proportionality improves distributive and procedural environmental justice outcomes in the global South.

2. THE HUMAN RIGHT TO WATER UNDER INTERNATIONAL LAW

The Universal Declaration of Human Rights,[23] the International Covenant on Civil and Political Rights,[24] and the International Covenant on Economic, Social and Cultural Rights[25] (ICESCR) do not include a specific guarantee of a human right to water. Nevertheless, there are references to this right in several treaties that protect specific groups: Article 14.2.h of the Convention on the Elimination of All Forms of Discrimination against Women;[26] Article 24.2.c. of the Convention on the Rights of the Child;[27] and Article 28.2 of the Convention on the Rights of Persons with Disabilities.[28] These documents recognize the right to water because

[23] Paris, 10 December 1948, GA Res. 217A (III), UN Doc. A/8810 at 71 (1948).
[24] New York, 16 December 1966, in force 23 March 1976, GA Res. 2200A (XXI), 21 UN GAOR Supp. (No. 16) at 52, UN Doc. A/6316 (1966); 999 UNTS 171; 6 ILM 368 (1967).
[25] New York, 16 December 1966, in force 3 January 1976, 993 UNTS 3; [1976] ATS 5; 6 ILM 360 (1967).
[26] New York, 18 December 1979, in force 3 December 1981, 1249 UNTS 13; [1983] ATS 9/19; 19 ILM 33 (1980), art. 14.2: "States Parties [...] in particular, shall ensure to such women the right: [...] (h) To enjoy adequate living conditions, particularly in relation to [...] water supply."
[27] New York, 20 November 1989, in force 2 September 1990, 1577 UNTS 3; [1991] ATS 4; 28 ILM 1456 (1989), art. 24.2: "'States Parties [...] shall take appropriate measures: [...] (c) To combat disease and malnutrition [...] through the provision of adequate [...] clean drinking-water."
[28] New York, 13 December 2006, in force 3 May 2008, UN Doc. A/61/611, art. 28.2: "States Parties recognize the right of persons with disabilities to social protection [...], and shall take appropriate steps to safeguard and promote the realization of this right, including measures: To ensure equal access by persons with disabilities to clean water services."

282   *The Right to Water*

of its connection to the human rights to equality and health, rather than as a stand-alone right.

A human right to water was recognized for the first time by the Committee on Economic, Social and Cultural Rights in General Comment No. 15 of 2002, in which the Committee declared that "the human right to water is indispensable for leading a life in human dignity." This human right entitles everyone to "sufficient, safe, acceptable, physically accessible and affordable water for personal and domestic uses."[29] This entitlement can be drawn from the human rights to "an adequate standard of living" and to "the enjoyment of the highest attainable standard of physical and mental health" guaranteed under Articles 11 and 12 of the ICESCR.

After General Comment No. 15, the Right to Water was recognized as a self-standing human right by the UN General Assembly in resolution 64/292 of 28 July 2010,[30] and by the Human Rights Council in September 2010.[31] These resolutions were adopted amid a North–South controversy. The General Assembly resolution was adopted by a vote of 122 in favor and none against, with 41 abstentions. While Southern countries such as Bolivia (a country that introduced the text in part as a reaction to a famous calamitous experiment of privatization of water services in Cochabamba)[32] endorsed the acknowledgment of a self-standing human right to water, the U.S. and Canada were not supportive of it. These Northern countries formally invoked that the resolution of the General Assembly "described the right to water and sanitation in a way not reflected in existing international law"[33] and "had not been drafted in a transparent manner."[34] Nevertheless, there is evidence that political debates around privatization may have influenced the positions of these abstaining countries.[35] Despite the fact that there is no conceptual connection between the recognition of a human right to water and the prohibition of privatizing water services, some political and social movements in Southern countries sought that recognition as a means to keep water as a public good that would be accessible to everyone.[36]

---

[29] CESCR, note 6.

[30] UN General Assembly, *Resolution Adopted by the General Assembly: The Human Right to Water and Sanitation*, 28 July 2010, A/Res/64/292.

[31] United Nations, *Report of the Human Rights Council*, 13 September–1 October 2013, A/65/53/Add.1.

[32] On this issue, see K. Bakker, *Privatizing Water Governance Failure and the World's Urban Water Crisis* (Ithaca: Cornell University Press, 2010), p. 165.

[33] United Nations Department of Public Information, "General Assembly Adopts Resolution Recognizing Access to Clean Water, Sanitation as Human Right, by Recorded Vote of 122 in Favour, None Against, 41 Abstentions," 28 July 2010, www.un.org.

[34] Ibid.

[35] S. L. Murthy, "Human Right(s) to Water and Sanitation: History, Meaning, and the Controversy over Privatization" (2013) 31 *Berkeley Journal of International Law* 90.

[36] J. Davis, "Private-Sector Participation in the Water and Sanitation Sector" (2005) 30 *Annual Review of Environmental Resources* 145.

3. THE CONSTITUTIONAL RIGHT TO WATER IN COMPARATIVE LAW

The recognition of a human right to water under international law has influenced the proclamation of a right to water in several constitutions. In Latin America, Article 47.2 of the 1967 Constitution of Uruguay (after the 2004 amendment) declares that "water is a natural resource essential for life" and that "access to clean water is [...] a fundamental human right." Article 12 of the 2008 Constitution of Ecuador states that "the human right to water is essential and cannot be waived. Water constitutes a national strategic asset for use by the public and it is unalienable, not subject to the statute of limitations, immune from seizure and essential for life." Article 16 of the 2009 Bolivian Constitution provides that "each person has a right to water and food." Moreover, Article 20 acknowledges that "each person has a right to universal access to the services of clean water [...]" and that access to water is a "human right" that cannot be privatized.

Similar developments can be seen in Africa, too. Section 27.1 of the 1996 South African Constitution proclaims that "[e]veryone has the right to have access to [...] sufficient food and water." Section 43.1 of the 2010 Constitution of Kenya provides that "[e]very person has the right [...] to clean and safe water in adequate quantities." Article 48 of the 2005 Constitution of the Democratic Republic of the Congo states that "[t]he right to decent housing, the right of access to drinking water and to electric energy are guaranteed." Finally, Section XIV of the 1995 Constitution of Uganda provides that "the State shall endeavor to fulfill the fundamental rights of all Ugandans to social justice and economic development and shall, in particular, ensure that [...] all Ugandans enjoy rights and opportunities and access to [...] safe water."

Moreover, several countries have adopted the right to water as an implicit constitutional right. In Colombia, the Constitutional Court has acknowledged that the constitutional nature of the right to water can be drawn from its connections to the right to life and to the principle of human dignity.[37] A similar connection has been made by the Israeli Supreme Court acknowledging that the right to water is an implicit right to the 1992 Basic Law: Human Dignity and Freedom. According to the Supreme Court, "[a]ccessibility to water sources for basic human use falls within the realms of the right for minimal existence with dignity."[38] Finally, the Indian Supreme Court has ruled that access to clean water is part of the constitutional right to life guaranteed by Article 21 of the Indian Constitution.[39]

---

[37] Colombian Constitutional Court, Judgments T-244/1994, T-523/1994, T-578/1992, T-539/1993, T-140/1994, T-092/1995, T-207/1995, T-379/1995, T-413/1995, T-410/2003, T-1104/2005, T-270/2007, T-022/2008, T-888/2008, T-381/2009, T-616/2010 and T-740/2011.

[38] See CA 9535/06, *Abadallah Abu Massad and Others* v *Water Commissioner and Israel Lands Administration*. Adalah, *Israeli Supreme Court: Arab Bedouin in the Unrecognized Villages in the Negev Have the Right to "Minimal Access to Water,"* para. 23. I thank Aharon Barak for providing me with access to the English version of the judgment.

[39] See *A. P. Pollution Control Board II* v *Prof. M.V. Naidu and Others*, 2000 (3) SCALE 354, [2000] Supp 5 SCR 249.

4. THE NORMATIVE STRUCTURE OF THE CONSTITUTIONAL RIGHT TO WATER

General Comment No. 15 explains the normative structure of the human right to water as a set of claim-rights. In addition to non-discrimination claims,[40] this right attributes to its right-holders both freedoms and entitlements. The freedoms include the right to be free from interference in the access to water and "the right to be free from arbitrary disconnections or contamination of water supplies."[41] Entitlements include "the right to a system of water supply and management that provides equality of opportunity for people to enjoy the right to water."[42] States parties have three kinds of obligations for the fulfillment of the right to water: obligations to respect, protect, and fulfill.[43] The obligation to respect requires that states parties "refrain from interfering directly or indirectly with the enjoyment of the right to water."[44] The obligation to protect requires states "to prevent third parties from interfering [...] with the enjoyment of the right to water."[45] Finally, the obligation to fulfill can be disaggregated into the obligations to "facilitate, promote and provide."[46] The obligation to facilitate requires states to "take positive measures to assist individuals and communities to enjoy the right."[47] The obligation to promote requires states to "take steps to ensure that there is appropriate education" concerning the use and conservation of water. Finally, the obligation to fulfill requires states to "'provide the right when individuals or a group are unable, for reasons beyond their control, to realize that right themselves by the means at their disposal."[48] In addition to these generic obligations, there is a basic core obligation for states to "ensure access to the minimum essential amount of water that is sufficient and safe for personal and domestic uses to prevent disease."[49] The quantity of water that ought to be available for each person should correspond to World Health Organization (WHO) guidelines of "50 liters daily per person."[50]

---

[40] These claims are explicit in the references to the human right to water by the *Convention on the Elimination of All Forms of Discrimination against Women*, New York, 18 December 1979, in force 3 September 1981, GA Res. 34/180, 34 UN GAOR Supp. (No. 46) at 193, UN Doc. A/34/46; 1249 UNTS 13; 19 ILM 33 (1980) and in the *Convention on the Rights of Persons with Disabilities*, New York, 13 December 2006, in force 3 May 2008, A/RES/61/106, Annex I.

[41] CESCR, note 6, para. 10.

[42] Ibid.

[43] Ibid, para. 20.

[44] Ibid, para. 21.

[45] Ibid, para. 23.

[46] Ibid, para. 25.

[47] Ibid.

[48] Ibid.

[49] Ibid, para. 37. On this point, see also the United Nations Department of Public Information, note 33.

[50] World Health Organization, "Report: Domestic Water Quantity, Service Level and Health," www.who.int.

This chapter focuses on the entitlements drawn from the constitutional right to water. Adjudicating those entitlements is the most challenging task for judges. Entitlements belong to triadic legal positions in which a right-holder has a claim-right against a duty-bearer, who, correlatively, has an obligation. The subject matter of the claim-right and, at the same time, of the obligation is a course of action that the duty-bearer ought to perform in favor of the right-holder.[51] The performance of the action will cause the satisfaction of the claim-right at a certain level. Concerning the constitutional right to water, it is possible to represent this relationship in the following way:

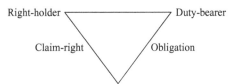

Subject matter (an action that leads to a certain level of satisfaction of the claim-right)

The adjudication of entitlements to water would not be different from the one of ordinary private law obligations, such as the obligation to repay a loan, if the right-holder, the duty-bearer, and the subject matter were determined. However, this does not always occur. Cases involving those entitlements are normally hard cases, in Dworkin's sense. They are cases in which the decision is not clearly directed by the constitution.[52] At first glance, the state could be considered as a universal duty-bearer of the right to water. However, in neoliberal societies private corporations also deliver water to individuals. It is questionable whether these corporations, too, can be considered as duty-bearers of the constitutional right to water.[53] Furthermore, constitutional provisions do not determine the appropriate level of satisfaction of the right. Last, even if the level of satisfaction were clear, there could be several alternative courses of action, policies, and programs that could be implemented to achieve that level. Constitutional provisions do not spell out the details of the concrete water policies that states ought to enact for honoring claim-rights to water. Consequently, it is not evident in all cases when the duty-bearers of the right to water have breached their obligations.

---

[51] On this structure, see R. Alexy, "On Constitutional Rights to Protection" (2009) 3 *Legisprudence* 1.

[52] R. Dworkin, "Hard Cases" (1975) 88 *Harvard Law Review* 1057.

[53] On private individuals and corporations as duty-bearers of socioeconomic rights, see A. Nolan, "Holding Non-State Actors to Account for Constitutional Economic and Social Rights Violations: Experiences and Lessons from South Africa and Ireland" (2014) 12 *International Journal of Constitutional Law* 61.

286 *The Right to Water*

5. IN SEARCH OF A STANDARD FOR THE JUDICIAL ENFORCEMENT OF CONSTITUTIONAL ENTITLEMENTS TO WATER

Judges enforcing the constitutional right to water are expected to determine the content of this right. For the sake of rationality, they should employ a standard for that purpose. The South African Constitutional Court employed the standard of reasonableness in *Mazibuko*.[54] In that case, citizens of Phiri, a suburb of Soweto, challenged a water policy of the City of Johannesburg. Instead of a flat rate, as was formerly used, the policy offered a provision of six kiloliters of water per household, per month, free of charge. Beyond this amount, citizens had to pre-pay for water. The City planned to install pre-paid meters for implementing the system.

In the High Court, Tsoka J held that the installation of pre-paid water meters violated the Constitution,[55] and that the free basic water allowance was inadequate. Six kiloliters monthly per household equates to an average of twenty-five liters per person, per day. This was considered unreasonable. There was evidence that a household would exhaust six kiloliters in about two weeks.[56] Judge Tsoka found that the residents of Phiri ought to be provided with fifty liters of free water per person, per day. However, this decision did not at all address the problem of the costs for the City associated with increasing the amount of free water. Judge Tsoka only assumed "the ability of the respondents to provide more water than 25 liters per day." [57]

Following an appeal, the Supreme Court of Appeal held that in Phiri, forty-two liters per person per day would be a sufficient amount of water. Notwithstanding, the Court of Appeal did not change the policy, but referred back to the City so that a revised policy could be drafted. Thereafter, the Constitutional Court heard the case and held that the policy did not violate Section 27 of the Constitution. Judge O'Regan held that it was "institutionally inappropriate for a court to determine precisely what the achievement of any particular social and economic right entails."[58] The Court refused to adjudicate between the many answers to the question of what amount of water was sufficient. It deferred to the answer provided by political authorities[59] that a monthly quota of six kiloliters per household was enough.[60]

---

[54] *Mazibuko v City of Johannesburg* 2009 (39) BCLR 239 (CC) (S. Afr). See also chapter 22, J. Dugard and E. Koek, "Water Wars: Anti-Privatization Struggles in the Global South."

[55] *Mazibuko et al. v City of Johannesburg et al.*, 2008 (4) SA 471 (W).

[56] *cf.* M. Langford and A. Russell, "Global Precedent or Reasonable No More? The *Mazibuko* Case" (2008) 19 *Water Law* 73.

[57] *Mazibuko et al v City of Johannesburg et al*, 2008 (4) SA 471 (W), para. 181.

[58] *Mazibuko v City of Johannesburg* 2009 (39) BCLR 239 (CC) (S. Afr), para. 61.

[59] An analysis of the extended arguments concerning the application of the standard of reasonableness, at paragraph 71, shows that the Court was highly deferential to the explanations given by the City as justification for the water policy. See *Mazibuko v City of Johannesburg* 2009 (39) BCLR 239 (CC) (S. Afr), para. 71.

[60] Moreover, O'Regan J noted that according to the 2001 census data, on average 3.2 persons lived in a household. On the basis of this estimate, six monthly kiloliters per household equates approximately to sixty liters per person per day. See *Mazibuko v City of Johannesburg*

This outcome is not inconsistent with the theoretical underpinnings of reasonableness as a weak and deferential standard for the judicial interpretation of rights. The minimum core is a standard that could overcome the problems associated with this weakness. Judgment T-740/2011 of the Colombian Constitutional Court provides an example of the use of the minimum core. This case involved a request for an injunction in which the applicant, who lacked financial capacity to pay the water bill, claimed that the suspension of the service by the provider, a private water company, violated her fundamental right to water. On the basis of poverty, the applicant requested a waiver concerning the payment of the bills. Based on the 2003 WHO report,[61] the Court held that the minimum core of the fundamental right to water entitles each person to receive a daily amount of fifty liters. The Court ordered the defendant to provide to the applicant and each member of her family this amount of water free of charge for an unlimited period of time, and held that the company is entitled to seek reimbursement of 50 percent of the price of that water from the state.

The adjudication of a positive right to water by means of a minimum core offers some advantages. In a concrete situation either the minimum core is satisfied, or it is not – for example, in cases of urgency, protection of survival,[62] or extreme economic deprivation.[63] Thus, judicial review conducted by means of this standard is regarded as easy, clear, and predictable. However, the clarity and the limited character of this kind of adjudication are only apparent. As Tushnet explains, the use of the minimum core requires courts to exercise intensive scrutiny of the policies and programs adopted by political authorities.[64] The minimum core attributes a position of supremacy to the courts. They end up determining what the minimum core is, and thereby make decisions about the adequate level and mode of satisfaction of socioeconomic rights. This is at odds with the principles of representative democracy. Provisions establishing socioeconomic rights do not actually determine the minimum core by themselves. Consequently, when courts make reference to this concept, they adopt a determinacy that does not actually exist. Thus, the use of this standard requires courts and not the democratically elected political authorities to

---

2009 (39) BCLR 239 (CC) (S. Afr), para. 88. However, as Murray Wesson highlights, "according to the 2001 census data there [was] an average of 8.8 people per stand in Phiri. In these circumstances, the free basic water allowance provides approximately 23 liters per person per day." M. Wesson, "Reasonableness in Retreat? The Judgment of the South African Constitutional Court in Mazibuko v City of Johannesburg" (2011) 11 *Human Rights Law Review* 390.

[61] World Health Organisation, "Domestic Water Quantity, Service Level and Health," 2003, www.who.int.

[62] Bilchitz, note 15, pp. 187–191.

[63] K. Young, *Constituting Economic and Social Rights* (Oxford: Oxford University Press, 2012), p. 81.

[64] M. Tushnet, "Social Welfare Rights and the Forms of Judicial Review" (2004) 82 *Texas Law Review* 1895 at 1903–1905.

288 *The Right to Water*

determine the core. Courts are not politically accountable for these decisions. This severely undermines the realization of democratic values in society.

Moreover, there are no unique reliable criteria for determining the minimum core. [65] The Colombian case illustrates this point. Even if it is accepted that fifty liters of water per person per day is the minimum core of the right to water, it is not clear why the Constitutional Court considers itself entitled to order a private company to satisfy this right. Furthermore, the minimum core, at least in theory, is not context-sensitive. Consequently, it leads courts to relinquish any assessment of the concrete possibilities to satisfy socioeconomic rights within a specific macro-economic framework of the state. In the Colombian case T-740/2011, for instance, the Constitutional Court did not even take into account the systemic financial impact of its decision for public and private water companies. That decision has become a precedent, the enforcement of which can be claimed by any citizen in identical or analogous circumstances. So, each citizen in circumstances of vulnerability is constitutionally entitled to claim fifty liters of free water daily. Thus, public and private water companies are now responsible for financing half of the free water that citizens in circumstances of vulnerability are entitled to receive.

6. PROPORTIONALITY AND THE RIGHT TO WATER

The principle of proportionality is a legal standard, alternative to reasonableness and the minimum core, which is used around the world for the adjudication of constitutional rights. From its German origins,[66] proportionality has migrated from one jurisdiction to another.[67] Most courts and scholars understand proportionality as a set of three interlinked sub-principles: suitability, necessity, and balancing or proportionality in the narrow sense.[68] Each sub-principle establishes a requirement that any limitation on a constitutional right should meet. The sub-principle of suitability requires that limitations contribute to the achievement of a legitimate end.[69] The sub-principle of necessity requires them to be the least restrictive of all means that are at least equally suitable to achieve the pursued end. Finally, the principle of proportionality in the narrow sense requires that any limitation on a

---

[65] On this objection, see K. Young, "The Minimum Core of Economic and Social Rights: A Concept in Search of Content" (2008) 33 *The Yale Journal of International Law* 112.

[66] M. Cohen-Eliya and I. Porat, "American Balancing and German Proportionality: The Historical Origins" (2010) 8(2) *International Journal of Constitutional Law* 263.

[67] C. Bernal, "The Migration of Proportionality Across Europe" (2013) 11(3) *New Zealand Journal of Public and International Law* 483.

[68] B. Schlink, "Proportionality," in M. Rosenfeld and A. Sajó (eds.), *The Oxford Handbook of Comparative Constitutional Law* (Oxford: Oxford University Press, 2012), p. 721.

[69] See A. S. Sweet and J. Mathews, "Proportionality, Balancing and Global Constitutionalism" (2008) 47 *Columbia Journal of Transnational Law* 68; A. Barak, *Proportionality. Constitutional Rights and their Limitations* (Cambridge: Cambridge University Press, 2012), p. 3.

constitutional right achieves the pursued end to a degree that justifies the degree to which that right is being constrained.

The test of proportionality has given rise to many conflicting views. On the one hand, influential authors embrace this principle with considerable enthusiasm. David Beatty claims that proportionality is law's golden rule[70] because it possesses the ability to make "the legal concept of rights the best it can possibly be."[71] According to Aharon Barak, the constitutionality of every limitation on constitutional rights can only be determined by means of a proportionality analysis;[72] there is no better alternative.[73] Robert Alexy maintains that proportionality provides the only rational way to make a judgment that takes into account the reasons for the existence of rights and for imposing limitations upon them.[74] Finally, Stephen Gardbaum argues that the mechanism of balancing "appropriately bolsters the role of majoritarian decision-making about rights within a system of constitutional democracy."[75] On the other hand, proportionality has also been the target of scorn. [76] Stavros Tsakyrakis holds that this principle is "an assault on human rights" and "a misguided quest for precision and objectivity."[77] Grégoire Webber laments that proportionality has created an unjustified "cult of constitutional rights scholarship."[78] Jürgen Habermas condemns the use of proportionality as deteriorating the priority or "firmness" of constitutional rights as constraints against the exercise of political power.[79] Finally, a common concern is that proportionality allows the judiciary to interfere illegitimately in the competences of parliament and the public administration. Lord Ackner, for example, argued in the *Brind* case that by employing proportionality, judges and courts cannot avoid performing an "inquiry into and a decision upon merits." In a democracy, decisions upon merits ought to be made only by political authorities.[80]

---

[70] D. Beatty, "Law's Golden Rule," in G. Palombella and N. Walker (eds.), *Relocating the Rule of Law* (Oxford: Hart Publishing, 2009), p. 103.

[71] D. Beatty, *The Ultimate Rule of Law* (Oxford: Oxford University Press, 2004), p. 171.

[72] Barak, note 69, p. 3.

[73] Ibid, p. 8.

[74] R. Alexy, *A Theory of Constitutional Rights* (Oxford: Oxford University Press, 2002), p. 74.

[75] S. Gardbaum, "A Democratic Defense of Constitutional Balancing" (2010) 4 *Law and Ethics of Human Rights* 79.

[76] On familiar objections to the balancing tests in American constitutional law, see T. A. Aleinikoff, "Constitutional Law in the Age of Balancing" (1987) 96 *The Yale Law Journal* 943.

[77] S. Tsakyrakis, "Proportionality: An Assault on Human Rights" (2009) 7 *International Journal of Constitutional Law* 468.

[78] G. Webber, "Proportionality, Balancing, and the Cult of Constitutional Rights Scholarship" (2010) 23 *Canadian Journal of Law and Jurisprudence* 180 at 190–191.

[79] J. Habermas, *Between Facts and Norms: Contributions to Discourse Theory of Law and Democracy* (Cambridge: MIT Press, 1996), p. 254. For a thoughtful analysis of this concern, see M. Kumm, "What Do You Have in Virtue of Having A Constitutional Right? On the Place and Limits of Proportionality Requirements," in G. Pavlakos (ed.), *Law, Rights and Discourse: The Legal Philosophy of Robert Alexy* (Oxford: Hart Publishing, 2007), p. 131.

[80] *Regina v Secretary of State for the Home Department ex parte Brind* [1991] 1 AC 696.

290 *The Right to Water*

Despite these criticisms, proportionality has been widely accepted as an appropriate standard for the adjudication of constitutional rights. In the above-mentioned case of *Abu Massad*, the Supreme Court of Israel employed the principle of proportionality for enforcing the right to water.[81] The core legal issue at stake was whether certain Bedouin Israeli citizens, who lived in villages in the region of Negev, were entitled to claim from the state the installation of private connection points to water in their illegal places of accommodation. Without these private connections, Bedouins had to purchase water from water centers located several kilometers away from their villages and transport the water to their homes.

The Supreme Court of Israel acknowledged that the right to water was a right implicit in Section 2 of the 1992 Basic Law: Human Dignity and Freedom, but held that it was not an absolute right. In cases such as *Abu Massad* this right should be balanced against competing legal interests by means of a proportionality analysis. The Supreme Court held that the governmental policy refusing the installation of private connections of water to the illegal Bedouin villages met the requirement of suitability. This policy was an appropriate means to achieve a legitimate end, namely creating an incentive for Bedouins to relocate to recognized cities and settlements. The policy also met the necessity requirement. The existence of water centers enabled the transportation of water to reserves in the villages. Thus, the policy was the least restrictive means for the state to motivate the relocation of the Bedouins to recognized villages. Finally, the policy met the balancing requirements because it only involved inconveniences and the bearing of certain monetary costs related to the transportation of water from the water centers. Although the distribution by means of water centers was not "an optimal system for water consumption," it certainly was a "minimal arrangement, which intends to uphold the basic right to water."[82] The realization of the "full right to water" required the relocation of the Bedouins. This was contingent on their "choice, and open to their decision."[83]

7. PROPORTIONALITY AS THE MOST APPROPRIATE STANDARD FOR THE JUDICIAL ENFORCEMENT OF CONSTITUTIONAL ENTITLEMENTS TO WATER

Proportionality is a better standard for the judicial enforcement of constitutional entitlements to water than reasonableness and the minimum core, although none of

---

[81] CA 9535/06, *Abdullah Abu Massad and Others v Water Commissioner and Israel Lands Administration*; Adalah, note 38. On this case, see S. L. Murthy et al., "The Human Right to Water in Israel: A Case Study of the Unrecognised Bedouin Villages in the Negev" (2013) 46 *Israel Law Review* 25.

[82] CA 9535/06, *Abdullah Abu Massad and Others v Water Commissioner and Israel Lands Administration*. Adalah, note 38, para. 54.

[83] Ibid, para. 54.

these standards are objective. The lack of objectivity does not imply, however, that all that is left is arbitrariness. The entrenchment of enforceable rights in the constitution hangs together with the acceptance of constitutionalism, deliberative democracy, and the rule of law. These principles imply some values that judges should pursue in the adjudication of constitutional rights. Among those values are impartiality and respect for the separation of powers and for the priority of constitutional rights.

Deliberative democracy implies impartiality.[84] In a deliberative democracy, political and judicial decisions aiming to solve social coordination and moral problems should be made through an impartial procedure. [85] A discursive procedure is impartial when it takes into account all relevant arguments offered by those affected by the decision.[86] The rule of law implies respect for the separation of powers. This means that authorities should observe the integrity of the competence of other political powers. In particular, judicial decisions should respect the margin of appreciation of political representatives of the people to make political choices.[87] In a democracy, based on the rule of law, the legitimacy associated with political representation mitigates the uncertainty about what the most appropriate political choices are and about normative and empirical appreciations relevant to them. Finally, aligned with the ideology of constitutionalism, the adjudication of constitutional rights should observe the priority that these rights have over other political common and individual goods and interests. In constitutionalism rights are allocated a special weight when competing with policy goals. As Rawls put it, they are a priority "over the good."[88]

Compared to the standards of reasonableness and the minimum core, proportionality analysis enables judges to achieve these values to a higher degree. Proportionality prioritizes constitutional rights over other policy considerations to a higher degree than reasonableness. While proportionality requires judges to allocate a prima facie priority to rights over other competing interests, reasonableness leads judges to be deferential to decisions by political authorities. Furthermore, proportionality has a more impartial argumentative structure than reasonableness and the minimum core. It displays a standard that openly takes into account all relevant legal, methodological, moral, and empirical reasons for and against the constitutionality of a right's limitation.[89] By using proportionality, the judge must

---

[84] J. Elster, "Introduction," in J. Elster (ed.), *Deliberative Democracy* (Cambridge: Cambridge University Press, 1998), p. 8.

[85] A. Gutman and D. Thompson, *Why Deliberative Democracy* (Princeton: Princeton University Press, 2004), p. 3.

[86] T. Jollimore, "Impartiality" [2011] *Stanford Encyclopedia of Philosophy*.

[87] T. R. S. Allan, *Constitutional Justice: A Liberal Theory of the Rule of Law* (Oxford: Oxford University Press, 2003), chapter 2.

[88] J. Rawls, *Political Liberalism* (New York: Columbia University Press, 1993), p. 173.

[89] K. Möller, "Proportionality: Challenging the Critics" (2012) 3 *I-CON* 726; C-M. Panaccio, "In Defence of Two-Step Balancing and Proportionality in Rights Adjudication" (2011) 24 *Canadian Journal of Law and Jurisprudence* 109.

evaluate the reasons given by both parties (the right-holder and the political authority limiting the right) concerning the relevant aspects of the analysis; that is, the legitimacy of the end, the appropriateness and necessity of the limitation, and the weight that should be allocated to the pursued end and to the constitutional right in the analysis of proportionality in the narrow sense.[90] By contrast, the minimum core focuses only on the discovery of a predetermined, definitive, and minimum core of rights.[91] The use of this standard does not encourage judicial deliberation about the specific normative and empirical aspects relevant to the procedure and linked to the claims of all the relevant parties. Furthermore, proportionality is more respectful of separation of powers and representative democracy than the minimum core. The minimum core presupposes the allocation to the judge of the final power to decide in only one step whether a legislative or administrative limitation violated the core of a right. By contrast, the structure of proportionality encompasses an analysis of the margins of discretion of political authorities.[92] This structure makes it clear that, while political authorities are bound by constitutional rights, they have a scope of deliberation in which they can choose between proportional regulations of competing rights. In this way, proportionality also encourages dialogue instead of dialog between courts, the legislature, and the executive.[93]

The judgment of the Israeli Supreme Court in *Abu Massad* reveals the impartial nature of proportionality analysis and the way it prioritizes rights. The Court took seriously the right to water of the Bedouins, and allocated to it prima facie priority over the legitimate goal of the government concerning incentivizing the resettlement of Bedouins. The decision attempts to make the right and the goal compatible. From this perspective, proportionality is superior to reasonableness and the minimum core. Had Tsoka J of the High Court employed proportionality in *Mazibuko*, he would not have overlooked the costs of providing fifty daily liters of water free of charge to Johannesburg citizens. Similarly, had the South African Constitutional Court employed proportionality in the same case, it would have attributed priority to the constitutional right to water in the light of the fact that six kiloliters per household covered only two weeks' water needs for the residents of Phiri. Finally, had the Colombian Constitutional Court used proportionality, it would have taken into account the constitutional economic rights of the private water company that, in Judgment T-740/2011, is required to fund 50 percent of the free water for the claimant. Certainly, the employment of proportionality would

---

[90] Sweet and Mathews, note 69 at 77.

[91] M. Tushnet, "Comparative Constitutional Law," in M. Reimann and R. Zimmermann (eds.), *The Oxford Handbook of Comparative Law* (Oxford: Oxford University Press, 2006), p. 1251.

[92] J. Rivers, "Proportionality and Discretion in International and European Law," in N. Tsagourias (ed.), *Transnational Constitutionalism: International and European Perspectives* (Cambridge: Cambridge University Press, 2007), p. 108; M. Klatt and J. Schmidt, "Epistemic Discretion in Constitutional Law" (2012) 1 *I·CON* 69.

[93] Barak, note 69, p. 465.

have led the court to assert the right of poor and vulnerable people to receive a sufficient amount of free water for their basic needs. The lack of access to this sufficient amount is a disproportionate infringement of their constitutional right to water. However, it is also disproportionate to judicially attribute to a private company the duty to fund 50 percent of this amount of water. This judicial attribution breaches constitutional, legal, and contractual economic freedoms of the private companies participating in the water market. In a "social state" the political community represented by the state should be considered as the main duty-bearer of the right to water. Thus, the state is ultimately responsible to ensure that each citizen has continuous access to a sufficient amount of clean water, regardless of their ability to pay for it. As mentioned above, the state has clear international and constitutional duties to respect, protect, and fulfill the human right to water. In a holistic evaluation of public finances, honoring this duty ought to have priority over other goals that are less relevant to enable life with dignity to all human beings. In this manner, at least at the domestic level, the use of proportionality fulfills, better than reasonableness and the minimum core, environmental justice claims in the global South.

PART III

Trade, Investment, and Sustainable Development

14

Trade and the Environment: Perspectives from the Global South

Shawkat Alam

1. INTRODUCTION

As a concept, sustainable development has pervaded much of the international legal discourse regarding the world environment over the past thirty years. A confluence of vocal movements in the 1970s paved the way for this paradigm shift, which spotlighted environmental issues on an international scale. *Limits to Growth*[1] warned that unabated economic growth, wasteful consumption, and environmentally unsound practices were untenable, given the earth's finite and non-renewable resources and escalating degradation. However, the environmental focus was on localized disasters, such as Chernobyl and Bhopal, and many environmental norms and regulations were developed to respond to specific environmental concerns.[2] Worsening pollution and climate change cuts across national boundaries and affects all nations. Sustainable development requires concerted efforts, sometimes undermining state "sovereignty," to address environmental problems that are both local and global in scale.

An articulation of the linkage between the natural environment and economic growth was unprecedented until the *Brundtland Report*,[3] which stated that:

> We have in the more recent past been forced to face up to a sharp increase in economic interdependence among nations. We are now forced to accustom ourselves to an accelerating ecological interdependence among nations. Ecology and economy are becoming ever more interwoven locally, regionally, nationally, and globally into a seamless net of causes and effects.[4]

---

[1] Published by the Club of Rome in 1972. D. Meadows et al., *Limits to Growth – The 30-Year Update* (White River Junction: Chelsea Green Publishing, 2004).

[2] M. Jeffery QC, "Environmental Imperatives in a Globalised World: The Ecological Impact of Liberalising Trade" (2007) 7(32) *Macquarie Law Journal* 25.

[3] World Commission on Environment and Development, *Our Common Future* (London: Oxford University Press, 1987), annex (A/42/427, "Development and International Co-operation: Environment") [hereinafter Brundtland Report].

[4] Ibid, p. 9.

Another milestone was the *Rio Declaration on Environment and Development*, which recognized environmental protection as an integral part of sustainable development.[5] It highlighted intergenerational equity, urging development to meet the needs of present and future generations,[6] and shared responsibilities. The iconic Agenda 21[7] emphasized the interdependent and mutually reinforcing components of economic, environmental, and social development. The 2002 World Summit for Sustainable Development in Johannesburg called for capacity-building on trade and environment and for the promotion of cooperation on trade, environment, and development.[8] However, since its popularization in the seminal *Brundtland Report*,[9] sustainable development has been predominantly examined from the viewpoint of Northern countries. Indeed, sustainable development has become synonymous with environmental protection or a "green agenda", without due consideration for the mutually supportive relationship among economic, social, and environmental objectives.

Northern countries have largely shaped the sustainable development agenda.[10] Because the North has already achieved an acceptable standard of living and has, historically, been the site of large-scale pollution,[11] sustainable development has taken on a green hue. Meanwhile, the South is set to become the next area of global economic growth and population expansion,[12] while remaining highly vulnerable to anthropogenic climate change.[13] The need to re-invigorate the concept of sustainable development is a pressing concern.

This chapter will examine the nexus between international trade and environmental sustainability from a Southern perspective. The principle of sustainable

---

[5] Organized under the UNCED framework. *Rio Declaration on Environment and Development*, Rio de Janeiro, 13 June 1992, UN Doc. A/CONF.151/5/Rev.1 (1992), Principle 4 [hereinafter Rio Declaration].

[6] Ibid, Principle 3.

[7] *Agenda 21: Programme of Action for Sustainable Development*, Rio de Janeiro, 14 June 1992, U.N. GAOR, 46th Sess., Agenda Item 21, UN Doc. A/Conf.151/26 (1992) [hereinafter Agenda 21].

[8] UN, *Report of the World Summit on Sustainable Development*, 26 August–4 September 2002, A/CONF.199/20, resolution 2, annex (Plan of Implementation of the World Summit on Sustainable Development), art. 47(e). [hereinafter Johannesburg Plan of Implementation (JPOI)].

[9] *Brundtland Report*, note 3.

[10] See e.g. limited participation in the SPS Agreement and standard setting: K. Mustafa and S. Ahmad, "Barriers Against Agricultural Exports from Pakistan: The Role of WTO Sanitary and Phytosanitary Agreement" (2003) 42(4) *Pakistan Development Review* 487 at 494.

[11] See e.g. time series data and baseline levels of greenhouse gas emissions compared with developing countries: United Nations Framework Convention on Climate Change, "GHG Total Excluding LULUCF," http://unfccc.int.

[12] United Nations, "Population Facts No. 2010/5, August 2010 – Accelerating Achievement of the MDGs by Lowering Fertility: Overcoming the Challenges of High Population Growth in the Least Developed Countries," www.un.org.

[13] O. Mertz et al., "Adaption to Climate Change in Developing Countries" (2009) 43(5) *Environmental Management* 435; P. Ward and G. Shively, "Vulnerability, Income Growth and Climate Change" (2012) 40(5) *World Development* 916.

development advocates a mutually supportive approach between international trade and environmental protection. However, *how* these obligations are interpreted by the World Trade Organization (WTO) and acted upon by the North reveals the extent to which the concerns of the South remain overlooked, thereby perpetuating underdevelopment.

Section 2 will briefly highlight the emergence of the trade and environment nexus and the mutually supportive approach advocated by sustainable development. Section 3 will then examine how this trade and environment nexus has been interpreted by the WTO. Particular reference will be made to the scope of the General Agreement on Tariffs and Trade (GATT) Article XX exceptions and the application of Articles I and III.[14]

Section 4 will examine the "second generation" of sustainable development concerns held by the global South: inter alia, how a range of environmental requirements can now create new non-tariff barriers (NTB) to trade and economic development. This includes NTBs in the form of standards, labeling, packaging, and certification barriers. These NTBs are often imposed by the North, which sets unrealistic standards for Southern countries and inhibits their capacity to achieve sustainable development. Insofar as the GATT/WTO regime enables Northern countries to implement protectionist measures, it has the effect of decreasing market access and/or decreasing export prices, both of which will result in declining trade for the global South.

2. EMERGENCE OF A TRADE AND ENVIRONMENT NEXUS

When the current international trade regime first emerged, there was limited interaction with environmental concerns. Early negotiations to develop the GATT were centered on ensuring that there was an adequate rules-based trade system that promoted comparative advantage and trade liberalization. To facilitate this goal, the GATT required its members to treat imported goods the same as domestically produced goods (the "national treatment principle"),[15] limit quantitative restrictions,[16] and ensure that any trade advantages are shared among all GATT members (the "most favored nation principle," or MFN).[17]

Conversely, international environmental law initially concerned itself with regulating environmental catastrophes and developing a system that allowed the fair allocation of resources that were located beyond sovereign borders, such as fisheries. As Sands points out, "nations began to understand that the process of

---

[14] *General Agreement on Tariffs and Trade (GATT 1947)*, in force 1 January 1948, 55 UNTS 194; 61 Stat. pt. 5; TIAS 1700 arts. I, III, XX [hereinafter GATT].
[15] Ibid, art. I.
[16] Ibid, art. XI.
[17] Ibid, art. III.

300

Trade and the Environment

industrialisation and development required limitations on the exploitation of natural resources and the adoption of appropriate legal instruments."[18]

Previously, both international trade and environmental regimes possessed different objectives and were treated as fundamentally distinct policy areas. However, the concept of sustainable development produced a paradigm shift in development policy. As the *Brundtland Report* explains, sustainable development consists of:

> [...] development that meets the needs of the present without compromising the ability of future generations to meet their own needs. It contains two key concepts: the concept of needs, in particular the essential needs of the world's poor, to which overriding priority should be given and; the idea of limitations imposed by the state of technology and social organization on the environment's ability to meet present and future needs.[19]

The reconciliation of economic development with environmental protection challenged the separation between trade and environmental issues. Agenda 21 reinforced the linkages between trade and environment and sustainable development by recognizing that "the (sustainable) development process will not gain momentum [...] if barriers restrict access to markets."[20] Furthermore, in order to achieve economic growth and sustainable development, states should "promote a supportive and open international economic system."[21] Both the Rio Declaration and Agenda 21 highlighted the need to explore the trade and environment nexus with a mutually supportive approach, which has resonated in later trade and environmental agreements.[22]

Since the emergence of the trade and environment nexus, the North has displayed reluctance in promoting mutually supportive approaches. During the early stages of the Doha Development Round, the South has maintained its call to reform unsupportive trade arrangements in areas such as agriculture. This is reflected in numerous sections of the fourth Doha Declaration, including technical assistance in trade and investment[23] and the environment.[24] However, despite recent gains toward trade facilitation during the Bali Round, the South still faces a number of hurdles in achieving a mutually supportive approach toward trade and the environment.

In recognition of the potential of trade as a means of growth and sustainable development,[25] many Northern nations offer preferential market access to the

---

[18] P. Sands, *Principles of International Environmental Law*, 3rd ed. (Cambridge: Cambridge University Press, 2012), p. 22.

[19] *Brundtland Report*, note 3, p. 43.

[20] Agenda 21, note 7, Principle 1.2.

[21] Rio Declaration, note 5, Principle 12.

[22] JPOI, note 8, para. 2. See also G. P. Sampson, *The WTO and Sustainable Development* (New Delhi: TERI Press, 2005), p. 35.

[23] World Trade Organization, *Doha WTO Ministerial Declaration*, Doha, 14 November 2001, WTO Doc WT/MIN(01)/DEC/1, para. 21.

[24] Ibid, para. 33.

[25] See e.g., Oxfam, "Scaling Up Aid for Trade: How to Support Poor Countries to Trade Their Way out of Poverty," Oxfam Briefing Note (November 2005).

South, particularly to least developed countries (LDCs). Trade preferences have become a common feature of the modern international trading system, and are a means by which the North can cast itself in the role of a charitable benefactor that furthers the cause of intragenerational equity. However, the reality is that trade preferences provide only limited benefits to the South, and the costs of preferential treatment can vastly outweigh the benefits. Furthermore, rather than the benevolent rhetoric of equitable trade, trade preferences are commonly pursued as protectionist measures, consolidating the power and economic interests of the North.

In order to achieve intragenerational equity, Northern countries should provide special and differential treatment in ways that genuinely benefit their Southern trading partners and ensure that Southern nations have the capacity to develop, both sustainably and holistically.

Sustainable development is a responsibility that is shared by the North and the South. However, the obligations of Northern and Southern countries vary in accordance with the principle of common but differentiated responsibility (CBDR). CBDR dictates that responsibility for the realization of sustainable development should be shared according to the resources which states command and the pressures their societies place on the environment.[26] In light of their disparate contribution to global environmental degradation and their abundant financial and technical resources, Northern countries play a vital role in the transition to sustainable development and must, at the very least, provide financing and capacity-building to enable Southern countries to achieve the three pillars of sustainable development: Environmental protection, economic development, and social development. The failure to achieve sustainable development outcomes that are agreed upon in various international trade agreements and environmental agreements is a poignant indication that CBDR is not being meaningfully applied.

3. IMPACT OF THE TRADE AND ENVIRONMENT NEXUS ON INTERNATIONAL TRADE LAW

3.1 *GATT Articles I and III*

Under GATT Articles I and III, MFN and national treatment – core values of the WTO regime – only extend to "like products." Yet, with products being increasingly differentiated on the basis of how they are made, including if a product was made in an environmentally friendly way, the trade and environment nexus has called into question the scope of GATT's core protections.

---

[26] Rio Declaration, note 5, Principle 7.

In the seminal case of *Tuna-Dolphin*, the United States introduced measures through the Marine Mammal Protection Act 1972,[27] which restricted the importation of tuna products that exceeded U.S. standards in incidental marine mammal kill or injury rates. In particular, the Act prohibited the importation of yellowfin tuna in the Eastern Tropical Pacific Ocean, with immediate ramifications for the Mexican tuna industry.

The GATT Panel determined that "like products" refers to the "nature of the product itself" and not its Process and Production Methods (PPMs).[28] Critically, the Panel concluded that a "contracting party may not restrict imports of a product merely because they originate in a country with environmental policies different from its own."[29] The Panel considered that tuna imported from Mexico was a "like product" of U.S. tuna and, as a result, the Marine Mammal Protection Act was inconsistent with the obligations under GATT Article III.

The findings made by the Panel reflect determinations made in other GATT/WTO trade disputes, including the *Thai Cigarettes* case[30] and the *Canadian Fisheries* case.[31] In *Reformulated Gasoline*,[32] Venezuela and Brazil took issue with the United States' implementation of the Clean Air Act 1990.[33] Under the Clean Air Act, the U.S. mandated specific requirements in the composition and emission effects of gasoline by foreign producers. The Panel determined that domestic producers were required to meet less stringent requirements, and that the U.S. requirements under the Clean Air Act constituted an unjustifiable discrimination and were inconsistent with GATT Article III(4).[34]

As these cases demonstrate, GATT Panels have adopted an expansive interpretation of what constitutes a "like product," which increases the scope of MFN and national treatment obligations between trading partners. Yet despite this expansive interpretation, recent WTO jurisprudence suggests that a shift in the interpretation of "like products" under Articles I and III could authorize environmental requirements that restrict Southern access to Northern markets.

In *Shrimp/Turtle*, the Appellate Body allowed trading members to use some measure of flexibility when adopting protective protocols for endangered species. Despite the United States losing on the ground that it had applied environmental protection policy discriminatorily, the Appellate Body accepted that shrimp could

[27] *Marine Mammal Protection Act 1972* 16 USC 1361.
[28] *United States – Restrictions on Imports of Tuna*, GATT Panel Report GATT Doc. DS 21/R: GATT, 30 ILM 1594 (1991).
[29] Ibid.
[30] *Thailand – Restrictions on Importation of And Internal Taxes on Cigarettes*, GATT Doc. DS10/R: GATT BISD 38 Supp. 200,201 (1990).
[31] *Panel Report on Prohibition of Imports of Tuna Fish and Tuna Products from Canada*, GATT BISD 29 Supp. 91 (1983).
[32] *United States Standards for Reformulated and Conventional Gasoline*, 35 ILM 274 (1996) 280.
[33] *Clean Air Act 1990* (U.S.).
[34] *United States Standards for Reformulated and Conventional Gasoline*, note 32.

be differentiated by whether a Turtle Excluder Device (TED) had been used during harvest or not.[35] Although the case was decided in favor of the South, this shift foreshadows how the interpretation of Articles I and III could sway the balance of the trade and environment nexus in favor of allowing environmental non-tariff barriers (NTBs).

Although some environmentalists condemned the result in cases such as *Tuna-Dolphin* for failing to improve environmental outcomes, it must be remembered that sustainable development is not equivalent to environmental protection. Instead, sustainable development advocates a mutually supportive approach between economic, social, and environmental outcomes. The North's reliance on restrictive trade measures as the sole means to improve environmental outcomes is not consistent with fundamental principles of sustainable development, such as common but differentiated responsibilities and intragenerational equity. This is not to say that other fundamental principles, such as intergenerational equity, must be sacrificed in order to facilitate economic growth. Rather, a more nuanced approach is necessary to promote capacity-building, knowledge transfer, and the development of a fair international trade system,[36] which encourages a "race to the top" for long-term environmental and social outcomes instead of structural inequality.

Unfortunately, the South, given its capacity constraints, faces an increased threat of exclusion from Northern markets unless Northern countries provide adequate capacity-building and technical support. This is further complicated by the fact that trade liberalization has also not been reciprocal. While the South has removed many NTBs as part of its macroeconomic reform, the North still maintains relatively high trade barriers, with subsidies in agriculture by members of the Organization for Economic Co-operation and Development (OECD) having doubled since the Uruguay Round.[37]

In addition, as explained in the next section, GATT Article XX provides further avenues for environmental requirements that may disrupt the balance in the trade and environment nexus and impede the South's pursuit of sustainable development.

3.2 *GATT Article XX*

One of the few GATT provisions that explicitly refers to environmental concerns, Article XX allows members to impose requirements "necessary for human, animal or plant life or health"[38] or "related to the conservation of exhaustible natural

---

[35] Indian Ocean – South-East Asian Marine Turtle Memorandum of Understanding, "Projects Database," www.ioseaturtles.org.

[36] GATT, note 14, art. XVIII, which recognizes capacity building for the global South through government assistance; or art. XXXVIII, which aims to reduce barriers to trade to the South.

[37] WTO, "Trade Liberalisation Statistics," www.gatt.org/trastat_e.html.

[38] GATT, note 14, art. XX(b).

304 *Trade and the Environment*

resources if such measures are made effective in conjunction with restrictions on domestic production or consumption."[39]

When applying these NTBs, the chapeau to Article XX further stipulates that "any trade measure cannot be applied to discriminate arbitrarily between countries where the same conditions prevail," as these measures are "necessary" and not a "disguised restriction on international trade."[40]

The purpose of GATT Article XX, and paragraphs (b) and (g) in particular, is to legitimize certain NTBs where they address genuine environmental concerns. However, one of the most contentious issues is finding the appropriate balance between trade and environmental objectives, especially within the North–South dynamic. There has been a significant push by the North to impose environmental NTBs, as evidenced by the increasing number of WTO Panel disputes involving environmental NTBs.[41] Conversely, the South asserts that these trade barriers constitute disguised protectionism and block them from accessing Northern markets. In interpreting Article XX, the WTO has displayed reluctance to expand the scope and extensive use of environmental NTBs. A finding of disguised protectionism depends on the circumstances of each case,[42] with indicia including inflexibility in the application of the trade measure.[43]

In applying the test of "necessity" under Article XX chapeau, Panels have steered away from questioning the policy goals set by WTO members and have focused instead on how the trade measure is used to serve these goals.[44] WTO jurisprudence has demonstrated that the bar to legitimate use of NTBs is set high, with NTBs normally needing to be the last resort available before they are deemed necessary.[45] Only one successful environmental NTB has been allowed in recent WTO disputes: an NTB that prohibits the sale of asbestos within the EU.[46]

---

[39] GATT, note 14, art. XX(g).

[40] GATT, note 14, art. XX.

[41] All recent cases concerning environmental NTBs under Article XX(b) or (g) are either OECD or BRIC countries. See, e.g. (*Brazil – Retreaded Tyres*) Appellate Body Report, *Brazil – Measures Affecting Imports of Retreaded Tyres*, WT/DS332/AB/R, adopted 17 December 2007, DSR 2007:IV, p. 1527; (*China – Raw Materials*) Appellate Body Reports, *China – Measures Related to the Exportation of Various Raw Materials*, T/DS394/AB/R/WT/DS395/AB/R/WT/DS398/AB/R, adopted 22 February 2012; (*EC – Asbestos*) Appellate Body Report, *European Communities – Measures Affecting Asbestos and Asbestos Containing Products*, WT/DS135/AB/R, adopted 5 April 2001, DSR 2001:VII, p. 3243; (*US – Gasoline*) Appellate Body Report, *United States – Standards for Reformulated and Conventional Gasoline*, WT/DS2/AB/R, adopted 20 May 1996, DSR 1996:I, p. 3; (*US – Shrimp*) Appellate Body Report, *United States – Import Prohibition of Certain Shrimp and Shrimp Products*, WT/DS58/AB/R, adopted 6 November 1998, DSR 1998: VII, p. 2755.

[42] (*US – Gasoline*) Appellate Body Report, note 41, p. 23.

[43] (*US – Shrimp*) Appellate Body Report, note 41, para. 164.

[44] (*US – Gasoline*) Appellate Body Report, note 41, p. 16; (*Brazil – Retreaded Tyres*) Appellate Body Report, note 41.

[45] (*EC – Asbestos*) Appellate Body Report, note 41, para. 172.

[46] Ibid.

Conservation of exhaustible natural resources under GATT Article XX(g) has also been subject to a restrictive interpretation by the WTO. The WTO has determined that: a) the NTB must be "primarily aimed at" the conservation of the exhaustible natural resource and b) the NTB must be made effective in "conjunction with domestic production or consumption restrictions."[47] Furthermore, there are Article XX chapeau conditions that prevent arbitrary discrimination or a disguised restriction to trade.[48] In *Canadian Herring and Salmon*, the Panel determined that Canada's ban on herring and salmon was inconsistent with GATT Article XX(g) as it was not equally applied to domestic producers.[49] In terms of the "primarily aimed" test, the Panel in *United States – Tuna* further asserted that an objective standard must be used, such as an ISO standard, unless the use of that standard is ineffective in achieving the conservation of natural resources.[50]

As with Articles I and III, the WTO is reluctant to allow environmental requirements on the basis of Article XX. This provides credence to the South's claim that the use of environmental requirements lends itself to disguised protectionism, which shields domestic producers rather than achieving actual environmental outcomes. This is of great concern, as excluding the South hinders its future capacity for sustainable development.

4. LEAVING THE SOUTH BEHIND: ENVIRONMENTAL REQUIREMENTS AND THE WTO SPS AGREEMENT

Beyond Northern countries' use of environmental NTBs under Article XX, the South faces additional hurdles in achieving sustainable development. While technical and intellectual property barriers faced by the South have been well documented,[51] there are hidden environmental requirements in the form of sanitary and phytosanitary (SPS) measures. These present one of the greatest hurdles for Southern countries, given their position of comparative advantage in industries such as agriculture.[52]

---

[47] GATT, note 14, art. XX(g).

[48] GATT, note 14, art. XX.

[49] *Canada – Measures Affecting Exports of Unprocessed Herring and Salmon*, Panel Report, GATT, BISD 35 Supp. 98 (1988), para. 6.08.

[50] *United States – Restrictions on Import of Tuna (Tuna-Dolphin II)*, 1994, GATT Doc DS29/R, Geneva: GATT 1994.

[51] See e.g. G. Mayeda, "Developing Disharmony? The SPS and TBT Agreements and the Impact of Harmonisation on Developing Countries' (2004) 7(4) *Journal of International Economic Law* 737; A. Disdier et al., "The Impact of Regulations on Agricultural Trade: Evidence from SBS and TBT Agreements' (2008) 90(2) *American Journal of Agricultural Economics* 336.

[52] OECD, "Key Issues for Policy Coherence for Development: Agriculture," www.oecd.org.

4.1 *The WTO Agreement on the Application of Sanitary and Phytosanitary Measures (SPS Agreement)*

SPS measures are regulated by the WTO Agreement on the Application of Sanitary and Phytosanitary Measures (SPS Agreement). SPS measures include stipulations concerning food safety, animal and plant health, packaging and labeling requirements, and the harmonization of safety standards between trading partners.[53]

The SPS Agreement regulates SPS measures by requiring members to identify their appropriate level of protection (ALOP) with respect to risks to human, animal, and plant life or health. This ALOP is ascertained through a risk assessment that is based on scientific evidence.[54] Once a member designates their ALOP, the SPS Agreement authorizes the achievement of this ALOP through international standards or through domestic standards that are based on scientific evidence,[55] so long as they are not protectionist, inconsistent, or discriminatory in nature.[56]

SPS measures are increasing in prominence within international trade, with 635 SPS notifications and fifty emergency notifications recorded in 2009–2010.[57] However, this is complicated by the fact that many SPS measures are becoming "privatized," with more non-government and commercial stakeholders becoming certifiers within food supply chains. Private organizations such as supermarket retailers are becoming significant certifying forces and are using their own standards to determine what may constitute "organic" or "eco-friendly" products.[58] Examples include Tesco's "Nature's Choice" and private industry groups, including EurepGAP.

Yet, despite the growing prominence of SPS measures, several aspects of the SPS Agreement fail to support a mutually supportive trade and environment nexus. This is particularly evident in the undertaking of risk assessments, the standard of review used by the WTO, and traceability requirements.

4.1.1 Risk Assessments and Scientific Evidence

Domestic standards may be more stringent than international standards if justified by sufficient scientific evidence.[59] However, the South possesses limited scientific

---

[53] *WTO Agreement on the Application of Sanitary and Phytosanitary Measures*, 15 April 1994, 1867 UNTS 493, art. 1.1 [hereinafter SPS Agreement].

[54] Ibid, art. 5.2.

[55] Ibid, art. 2.3.

[56] Ibid, art. 5.5.

[57] C. Viju and W. Kerr, "The EU's Global Role and International Institutions," in J. De Bardeleben and C. Viju, *Economic Crisis in Europe: What it Means for the EU and Russia* (New York: Palgrave Macmillan, 2013), p. 119.

[58] G. Chia-Hui Lee, "Private Food Standards and Their Impacts on Developing Countries," http://trade.ec.europa.eu, p. 8.

[59] SPS Agreement, note 53, art. 2.3.

capacity to comply with Northern standards or to challenge Northern standards that constitute disguised protectionism. Northern SPS standards may thereby limit access by Southern producers to Northern markets and deprive Southern nations of the resources necessary to promote sustainable development.

To illustrate, the implementation of a higher aflatoxin standard by the European Union has cost African exports approximately US$670 million, or a 64 percent decrease of trade.[60] This transpired because African nations lacked the capacity to test for aflatoxin in accordance with the higher EU standard. The EU measure reduces the health risk by 1.4 deaths per billion, when compared to the international standard with which the African nations were in compliance. Because of a lack of testing capacity, the African cereals, dried fruits, and nut industries suffered disproportionately.

Furthermore, Southern countries are particularly disadvantaged when there is a lack of scientific consensus regarding the extent of a risk to human, animal, or plant life. In *EC – Hormones*, the EU banned beef imports that used animal hormones in their production.[61] The United States complained that the trade ban was not based on sufficient scientific evidence, as it deviated from accepted international standards produced by the Codex Alimentarius Commission. On appeal, the Appellate Body determined that the EU did not offend the SPS Agreement by having a different ALOP toward the use of hormones. However, the EU's trade ban was not based on sufficient scientific evidence at the time it was adopted.[62] *EC – Hormones* highlights that scientific certainty is difficult to achieve, especially in fields such as agriculture, which are susceptible to technological change.

For the South, it is a challenge to stay up to date with scientific developments in order to scrutinize environmental requirements. As *EC – Hormones* demonstrates, even Northern countries have difficulty contesting the environmental requirements of their fellow trading partners. Southern countries with limited resources may be entirely locked out of Northern markets by these environmental requirements.

In addition, the use of the precautionary principle presents additional challenges for Southern nations. Under the SPS Agreement, a precautionary SPS measure can be adopted in the face of scientific uncertainty. However, it may be difficult for Southern countries to scrutinize the SPS measures adopted by their Northern trading partners to assess whether there is scientific uncertainty or whether the precautionary principle is being abused for protectionist purposes. Southern

---

[60] T. Otsuki, "Saving Two in a Billion: Quantifying the Trade Effect of European Food Safety Standards on African Exports' (2001) 26(5) *Food Policy* 495 at 496.

[61] European Communities – Measures Concerning Meat and Meat Products (Hormones) (*EC – Hormones*), Appellate Body Report, WT/DS26/AB/R; WT/DS48/AB/R (16 January 1998).

[62] Ibid.

308 *Trade and the Environment*

countries lack the resources to continually monitor temporary SPS measures premised on a precautionary approach. To date, only Northern countries have been able to challenge temporary precautionary SPS measures before the WTO.[63] The point here is not that adoption of the precautionary principle is inherently damaging to the South's interests, but that there is potential for it to be deployed in strategic protectionist ways that do not promote environmental objectives. Regrettably, Southern countries often lack the resources to evaluate and contest abuses of the precautionary principle. As Sumudu Atapattu's contribution to this volume demonstrates, this is not the only principle of international environmental law to reveal deep divisions between North and South.[64]

4.1.2 Changing Standard of Review

The SPS Agreement does not specify the risk assessment methodology for determining ALOPs. This allows a degree of flexibility for members to appropriately respond to a wide range of potential risks to life and health. However, recent WTO jurisprudence suggests that the way the Appellate Body (AB) scrutinizes risk assessment has changed, which presents additional hurdles for the South.

Under the Understanding on Rules and Procedures Governing the Settlement of Disputes (DSU) Article 11, the WTO Panel and AB are required to undertake an objective assessment of environmental requirements that is neither purely *de novo* nor deferential.[65] A *de novo* assessment allows a judicial authority to re-question the merits or facts of the case, whereas a deferential assessment only questions the application of the law by the original decision-maker implementing the SPS measure.

When considering the application of a SPS measure, the WTO AB can consider the original risk assessment and gauge expert witness testimony to determine if the decision was based on available scientific evidence. In practice, critiquing the risk assessment itself results in a quasi-*de novo* review by the WTO AB as it reconsiders the merits that were open to the original decision-maker.[66] This occurred in *Japan – Apples* where the AB rejected Japan's use of historical data in its risk assessment that purported to demonstrate its statistical risk to a threat to Japanese apples.[67]

However, in *EC – Hormones II* the AB displayed reluctance in critiquing EU ALOP against hormone use in beef. Instead, the AB centered its attention on

---

[63] Japan – Measures Affecting Agricultural Testing *(Japan – Varieties)*, Appellate Body Report, WT/DS76 (22 February 1999), para. 181.

[64] See chapter 4, S. Atapattu, "The Significance of International Environmental Law Principles in Reinforcing or Dismantling the North–South Divide."

[65] *Understanding on Rules and Procedures Governing the Settlement of Disputes* (DSU), 1869 UNTS 401; 33 ILM 1226 (1994), art. 11.

[66] M. Du, "Standard of Review under the SPS Agreement after EC – Hormones II" (2010) 59(2) *International and Comparative Law Quarterly* 441 at 451-452.

[67] Japan – Measures Affecting the Importation of Apples *(Japan-Apples)*, Appellate Body Report, WT/DS245/AB/R (10 December 2003), para. 161.

whether the risk assessment was supported with an objective, scientific process, and not on whether it reflected the orthodox view of the scientific community.[68] This response, in part, was driven by the fact that this potential risk was newly emerging, and the WTO AB was in no position to adjudicate on whether the use of hormones actually risked human health.

The increased ability to identify new threats to human, plant, and animal health has made the WTO AB rely more on whether the SPS measure was based on an objective process, and less on a substantive examination of the risk assessment itself. This approach tends to favor the North, which possesses greater capacity to regulate on the frontiers of science and to challenge the SPS measures of other countries.

4.1.3 Specificity and Traceability

Specificity requires a member employing an SPS measure to show sufficient connection between the damage to human, animal, or plant health and the product that is being controlled. While specificity previously required a direct correlation (for example, in *Japan – Apples*), the AB in *US – Continued Suspensions* determined that an indirect correlation is sufficient to allow an SPS measure to continue.[69] In other words, a controlled substance need only constitute a contributory factor to adverse human, animal, or plant life or health to justify an SPS measure.

For the South, this opens up a whole suite of products that can be subject to a SPS measure from the North. While it is vital to regulate substances that may have an adverse cumulative impact on human health, the trouble for the South is the absence of technical infrastructure needed to trace all the sources within the supply chain, which produce a final product.

For example, the lack of traceability devastated the shrimp industry of Bangladesh when the EU banned the country's shrimp exports for non-compliance with the hazard analysis critical control point (HACCP), costing approximately US$14.65 million in lost export revenue.[70] The problem is compounded by the North's failure to recognize any equivalent measures that may ensure the same level of quality assurance, which is an approach recognized by the SPS Agreement.[71] While the EU ultimately assisted Bangladesh by implementing technical assistance to ensure HACCP compliance, the North has generally

---

[68] European Communities – Measures Concerning Meat and Meat Products (Hormones) *(EC-Hormones II)*, para. 614. See also, United States – Continued Suspension of Obligations in the EC – Hormones Dispute *(US – Continued Suspension)*, Appellate Body Report, WT/DS320/AB/R (16 October 2008), para. 590.

[69] *US-Continued Suspension*, note 68, para. 562.

[70] J. C. Cato and C. A. Lima Dos Santos, "European Union 1997 Seafood-Safety Ban: the Economic Impact on Bangladesh Shrimp Processing" (1998) 13 *Marine Resource Economics* 215 at 226. HACCP programs are aimed at ensuring food safety through a preventive, hazard-reduction approach that identifies critical control points for managing food safety hazards.

[71] SPS Agreement, note 53, art. 4.1.

310   *Trade and the Environment*

failed to undertake such initiatives. This will remain a continuing problem for the South as new scientific and technological advances unlock discoveries on how products may have adverse cumulative effects on life and health.

4.2 *Avenues for Recourse and Trade Facilitation*

4.2.1 Technical Assistance

The SPS Agreement does recognize that the South requires assistance in order to overcome any trade barriers imposed by the North. Under Article 9.2 of the SPS Agreement, the North can provide technical assistance by engaging in capacity-building projects with exporters to ensure trade compliance.[72] Article 10 also allows the South to receive differential treatment in the development of its standards to reflect their lack of analytical capacity that would result in a loss of a trading opportunity. These key provisions are clear restatements of the common but differentiated responsibility (CBDR) principle, which is enshrined in international environmental law. CBDR recognizes the differences in economic development between states in achieving sustainable development, both in terms of their historical contribution to global environmental problems and their economic and technical capacity to address these problems.[73] Consequently, different states may be assigned different responsibilities for environmental protection.

Yet, much of the South is reporting that the North is simply not engaging in these activities, or that the assistance provided does not meet the specialized needs of the Southern members.[74] This results not only in a delay in trading opportunities, but also in the development of potentially higher standards as the South builds upon its capacity to sustainably develop. While Article 14 of the SPS Agreement allows LDCs to delay the application of the SPS Agreement, it does not grant a substantial reprieve, given the institutional weaknesses of LDCs.

4.2.2 Equivalency and MRAs

Problematic trading practices are also being experienced in relation to obligations imposed by Article 4.1. Under this provision, an importing member must accept an exporter's standard where it is objectively demonstrated that its measures achieve the same level of sanitary or phytosanitary protection as those of the importing country.[75] Equivalency is important as it allows the South to access

---

[72] Reference to Article 9.2.

[73] CISDL Legal Brief, "The Principle of Common but Differentiated Responsibilities: Origin and Scope," 2002, http://cisdl.org. See also chapter 4, S. Atapattu, "The Significance of International Environmental Law Principles in Reinforcing or Dismantling the North–South Divide'.

[74] S. Henson et al., "The Impact of Sanitary and Phytosanitary Measures on Developing Country Exports of Agricultural and Food Products," 2000, www.cid.harvard.edu.

[75] SPS Agreement, note 53, art. 4.1.

Northern markets, and allows the continued production of goods that effectively meet a member's ALOP.

In an era where sustainable practices are becoming increasingly important for improving environmental outcomes, it is vital to recognize the different ways in which the South can produce "like products" and yet still reach an ALOP. This allows production that is suitable to the South's local environment, incorporates local knowledge, and sustains cultural practices associated with production. However, as Donahue reports, the North often mandates compliance with its own standards, rather than accepting the exporting country's equivalent standard.[76] The rejection of equivalency raises considerable concern as it simultaneously offends CBDR and the purpose of Article 4, and places a burden on the South to comply with standards that may not reflect its social and economic realities.

Mutual recognition agreements (MRAs) are another important avenue for individual countries to establish certification and inspection systems with their trading partners in order to ensure ALOP compliance. There are several advantages to MRAs, including eliminating delay points of entry,[77] reduced dependence on routine inspection, the establishment of a consultative mechanism when there are disputes, and assurance of ALOP for the importing country.[78] But MRAs themselves also present challenges. Southern countries can be bullied into accepting less favorable terms in order to give their small producers access to lucrative Northern markets. Furthermore, even when the terms of MRAs are mutually beneficial, Southern countries may not possess the necessary regulatory frameworks to ensure compliance with MRAs, nor the technical infrastructure to undertake scientific assessments. There is huge pressure on Southern countries to develop these regulatory frameworks, which can be facilitated by promoting good manufacturing practices (GMPs)[79] within industries, establishing a suitable administrative base with qualified staff and scientific laboratories, and appointing advisory bodies to provide insight regarding constantly changing industry practices and technologies.

4.3 Future Challenges for Southern Countries in the Trade and Environment Nexus

4.3.1 Participation

The *EC – Hormones* case highlighted the importance of institutions such as the Codex Alimentarius Commission in creating international standards. Soft law

---

[76] A. M. Donahue, "Comment: Not Quite Close Enough for the International Harmonization of Environmental Standards" (2005) 6 *Environmental Law* 363 at 365.

[77] "Delay points of entry" refers to times when goods are held up due to procedural requirements (such as customs) between production and consumption.

[78] R. K. Malik, "Mutual Recognition Agreements in International Food Trade," www.fao.org.

[79] Ibid.

standards[80] are based on the Codex Alimentarius (established by the Food and Agriculture Organization and the World Health Organization), the World Organization for Animal Health (OIE), and the International Plant Protection Convention. The SPS Agreement is seeking to harmonize SPS measures with international standards by recognizing three international standard-setting bodies – the Codex Alimentarius Commission, the Office Internationale des Epizooties, and the Secretariat of the International Plant Protection Convention – in order to make them authoritative.

While SPS measures are based mainly on scientific evidence and standards,[81] the Codex is shaped by the relative political clout of the parties concerned. A major issue for the South is a lack of adequate participation in the creation of these standards, as these institutions often fail to recognize the importance of special and differential treatment. They require entry standards and processes that can only be conducted by highly developed Northern states which possess the necessary scientific and analytical capacity. For some observers, this "techno-imperialism"[82] presents an impediment for the South to actively participate in standard creation or, at the very least, to have their own standards that reflect the economic and social realities recognized by the international trading community.

Southern countries do not possess the governance structures or processes to effectively participate in standard creation. The South has often failed to nominate a contact point to facilitate SPS communication. Furthermore, the South often nominates contact points who may not possess the adequate capacity to undertake the considerable demands required to comply with SPS Agreement obligations. The South's low participation rate in WTO committees means its countries are not consulted on major decisions.[83] Theoretically, the South could be given "differential and favorable treatment" under the SPS Agreement,[84] but it has limited leverage given that 80 percent of agricultural trade is conducted mainly between Northern countries.[85]

---

[80] WTO, "Work of other Relevant Organizations," www.wto.org.

[81] But theoretically, institutions such as the Codex Alimentarius can use principles to develop standards such as the precautionary principle. See also, A. Laowonsiri, "Application of the Precautionary Principle in the SPS Agreement," Thesis, University of Heidelberg (2009), p. 582.

[82] U. Ofodile, "Import (Toy) Safety, Consumer Protection and the WTO Agreement on Technical Barriers to Trade: Prospects, Progress and Problems" (2009) 2(2) *International Journal of Private Law* 163 at 163. See also M. Issacs, "The World Trade Organization (WTO) Agreement on Sanitary and Phytosanitary Measures and the Bahamas," October 18, 2009, www.iica.int.

[83] D. A. French, "Change for Sustainable Development: Technology, Community and Multi-lateral Environmental Agreements" (2007) 7 *International Environmental Agreements* 218.

[84] SPS Agreement, note 53, art. 10.

[85] C. Thomas and J. P. Trachtman, *Developing Countries in the WTO Legal System* (New York: Oxford University Press, 2009), p. 342.

4.3.2 Expansion of PPMs to Include Life Cycle Analysis and Transparency Issues

Another key dynamic that Southern countries must respond to is the growing use of eco-labeling. This may have a significant impact on a product's demand, especially in increasingly eco-conscious markets in the North. The International Organization for Standardization (ISO) has attempted to create a system to categorize different forms of eco-labeling, including Type 1 (life cycle-based), Type 2 (self-declared claims), and Type 3 (environmental performance declarations).[86]

Eco-labels have made important contributions to the education of consumers and have improved environmental outcomes. The current stance of the WTO is that these labels do not alter the final form of the product, so products with eco-labels are "like" the products without these labels.[87] Eco-labeling schemes are allowed in accordance with the Technical Barriers to Trade (TBT) Committee's Code of Good Practice, but are prohibited from becoming disguised restrictions on trade. The TBT Agreement has stronger control over mandatory labels than voluntary eco-labels.

However, these eco-labels may impede the achievement of intragenerational equity. Eco-labels strongly influence consumer preferences, with many eco-labels increasing the consumers' willingness to pay.[88] Creating opportunities that can link this increased willingness to pay with capacity-building, rather than condemning the South to continued underdevelopment, may present new ways to bridge the North–South divide. The equity issues associated with eco-labeling schemes, such as the associated cost burden imposed on Southern countries with respect to verification and certification costs, have been well noted.[89] As Charnovitz, explains, environmental PPMs are almost always employed by the North, often at the expense of the South.[90] Consequently, policy-makers would do well to be sensitive to how much of the financial burden for ecological protection is being shifted to the South.[91] Beyond these more ethical considerations, Article 12.3 of the WTO Technical Barriers to Trade Agreement (TBTA) requires that members,

---

[86] ISO, "Standards Catalogue: 13.020.50," www.iso.org.

[87] WTO, "Labelling," www.wto.org.

[88] I. Olsen et al., "Eliciting Consumers' Willingness to Pay for Organic and Welfare Labelled Salmon in a Non-Hypothetical Choice Experiment" (2010) 127(2) *Livestock Science* 218.

[89] H. Ward, "Trade and Environment Issues in Voluntary Eco-Labelling and Life Cycle Analysis" (1997) 6(2) *RECIEL* 139 see also, "Eco-Labels: Trade Barriers or Trade Facilitators?," Discussion Paper 1, CUTS Centre for International Trade, Economics and the Environment (2009), p. 2.; M. Joshi, "Are Eco-Labels Consistent with WTO Agreements?" (2004) 38 (1) *Journal of World Trade Law* 69.

[90] S. Charnovitz, "The Law of Environmental 'PPMs' in the WTO: Debunking the Myth of Illegality" (2002) 27 *Yale Journal of International Law* 59 at 62; see also F. Biermann, "The Rising Tide of Green Unilateralism in World Trade Law: Options for Reconciling the Emerging North-South Conflict" (2001) 35(3) *Journal of World Trade* 421 at 422.

[91] Charnovitz, note 90 at 74.

"in the preparation and application of technical regulations [...] take account of the special development, financial and trade needs of developing country Members [...] with a view to ensuring that such technical regulations [...] do not create unnecessary obstacles to exports from developing country Members." In this respect, additional measures that enable the transfer of technology or assistance of either a technical or financial nature would seem an attractive means of ensuring the scheme's commensurability with objectives of the global trading system, particularly that of sustainable development.[92] Moreover, as the WTO case law in this area makes clear, evidence of "serious good faith efforts [...] to negotiate an international agreement,"[93] combined with sensitivity to the needs of Southern countries with regard to transparency and procedural fairness,[94] have been critical to the legality of environmental requirements under the GATT.[95]

A further complicating factor is that private certifiers are increasingly being used to create such labels, rather than governments. Private boards, rather than a panel of state actors, control popular eco-labels that Southern countries resent as an additional barrier to trade.[96] This is coupled with companies becoming stronger players along food supply chains. Increasingly, as noted above, supermarket chains are undertaking their own certification requirements for producers, with significant implications for market access. The privatization of certification raises accountability and transparency issues, as these stakeholders possess powerful sway over final demand for a product rather than imposing delay points in Northern markets. While in some circumstances private certifiers may have greater independence than public certifiers (which can, in certain situations, have close ties to the sector they are trying to regulate, or an interest in its economic performance),[97] private certifiers can also pose an issue for Southern countries if their certification standards exceed domestic capacity to meet them.[98]

---

[92] *Marrakesh Agreement Establishing the World Trade Organization*, Marrakesh, 15 April 1994, in force 1 January 1995, 1867 UNTS 3, Preamble.

[93] Appellate Body Report, *United States – Import Prohibition of Shrimp and Certain Shrimp Products*, WT/DS58/AB/RW (22 October 2001) ('*US – Shrimp II*') [134].

[94] Charnovitz, note 90 at 95–96.

[95] See generally ibid at 99; Biermann, note 90 at 432.

[96] J. Wouters and D. Gerates, "Private Food Standards and the World Trade Organization: Some Legal Considerations" (2012) 11(3) *World Trade Review* 479.

[97] P. Moye, "Private Certification versus Public Certification in the International Environmental Arena: The Marine Stewardship Council and Marine Eco-Label Japan Fisheries Certification Schemes as Case Studies" (2010) 43(2) *Vanderbilt Journal of Transnational Law* 533 at 561–562.

[98] There are some suggestions that multi-stakeholder initiatives regulating responsible business behavior may facilitate greater involvement in outcomes by social stakeholders: see L. W. Fransen and A. Kolk, "Global Rule-Setting for Business: a Critical Analysis of Multi-Stakeholder Standards" (2007) 14 *Organization* 667 at 679. WWF Germany has recently found, in a comparison of biofuel certification initiatives, that multi-stakeholder schemes tend to have a better environmental and social performance: WWF, "Searching for

4.3.3 Expansion of the Trade and Environment Nexus Beyond the Trade in Goods

Finally, a key future challenge remains in translating the trade and environment nexus to hold greater meaning than trade in goods. While this chapter has examined SPS issues, there is the potential for environmental requirements to present NTBs for Southern countries in industries within the service sector[99] as well as with respect to intellectual property. For example, seeds that have been developed by local and indigenous communities based on traditional knowledge may be appropriated by Northern corporations, patented, and commercialized.[100] Similarly, there is a long history of pharmaceutical companies appropriating, patenting, and commercializing applications of plant materials developed by local or indigenous groups.[101] This presents a huge hurdle for Southern countries that wish to diversify their economies beyond their reliance on primary industries.

5. CONCLUSION

The SPS Agreement contains numerous opportunities for the imposition of environmental NTBs. Some SPS measures may unbalance the trade and environment nexus by creating unnecessarily high requirements that lock Southern countries out of Northern markets and serve as obstacles to economic development. Although the SPS Agreement does allow some flexibility for countries to identify their ALOP and develop their own standards, this must be supplemented by sufficient scientific analysis and risk assessment. Unfortunately, most Southern countries do not possess adequate scientific and analytical capacity to challenge Northern SPS measures that constitute disguised protectionism.

The trade and environment nexus is subject to a wide variety of influences. This includes: the growing role of private stakeholders as certifiers along the supply chain; emerging developments in science and technology; and the interpretive approach of the WTO toward key provisions. These drivers have significantly altered the development opportunities for Southern countries.

Sustainability: Comparative Analysis of Certification Schemes for Biomass Used for the Production of Biofuels," November 28, 2013, http://wwf.panda.org.

[99] For detail see S. J. Tania and S. Alam, "Liberalisation of Sewerage and Waste Management Services and the GATS: Implications and Challenges for Developing Countries' (2011) 12(4) *Journal of World Investment and Trade* 519; S. Alam et al., "The WTO Agreement on Trade in Services, Water Services, and Human Rights from the Perspective of Developing Countries' (2011) 58(1) *Netherlands International Law Review* 43.

[100] See e.g. J. K. Plahe, "The Implications of India's Amended Patent Regime: Stripping Away Food Security and Farmer's Rights?" (2009) 30(6) *Third World Quarterly* 1197.

[101] N. Roht-Arriaza, "Of Seeds and Shamans: The Appropriation of the Scientific and Technical Knowledge of Indigenous and Local Communities" (1996) 17 *Michigan Journal of International Law* 919.

One of the principal issues is that the SPS Agreement contains provisions that *could* promote intra-generational equity and a mutually supportive approach between trade and the environment. Yet these provisions remain largely rhetorical, given their discretionary nature and non-support by Northern countries through trade practice. The South does not require aid in order to achieve a sustainable future; rather, the onus lies on the North to facilitate sustainable development and trade for Southern countries. This allows the South to increase its capacity for economic, social, and environmental outcomes, while recognizing that its decision-makers possess a vital role in creating appropriate regulatory frameworks. The concerns of the South in the trade–environment interface can best be assuaged by greater market access and appropriate technology transfer and financing. The use of trade policy measures to enforce environmental policies should be non-discriminatory and transparent, and should consider the special conditions and developmental requirements of the South.

15

From a Divided Heritage to a Common Future? International Investment Law, Human Rights, and Sustainable Development

Shyami Puvimanasinghe

1. INTRODUCTION: A DIVIDED HERITAGE

On 24 April 2013, an eight-story building housing several garment factories collapsed in Savar, near Dhaka, Bangladesh, killing over a thousand workers and injuring thousands more. The building, Rana Plaza, housed Phantom Apparels, New Wave Style, and New Wave Brothers, garment factories supplying major global brands including Benetton, Dress Barn, KiK, Mango, The Children's Place, Primark, and Wal-Mart.[1] Reports made a connection between alleged substandard construction of the building and the collapse.[2] Trade unions and labor rights organizations such as Clean Clothes Campaign, IndustriALL Global Union, and International Labour Rights Forum called for immediate action on health and safety from the international brands that used suppliers in the building,[3] and for the government to allow workers' freedom of association and increase the minimum wage.[4] 27 December 2013 saw the signing of a landmark agreement to deliver US$40 million in compensation to the families of those killed in the Rana Plaza collapse.[5] Signatories of this "Arrangement," facilitated by the International Labour Organization, included El Corte Ingles, Bon Marche, Primark, Loblaw, and others, included trade unions, employer associations, and the government of Bangladesh.[6] The key issue for victims and their families will be whether fair compensation will be paid out, which in turn depends on whether all parties

---

The views expressed herein are those of the author and do not necessarily reflect the views of the United Nations.

[1] Business and Human Rights Resource Centre, "Rana Plaza Building Collapse," April 2013, www.business-humanrights.org.

[2] Ibid.

[3] Ibid.

[4] Ibid.

[5] IndustriALL Global Union, "Action on Bangladesh," www.industriall-union.org.

[6] Ibid.

deliver on their commitments. Moreover, issues of regulation and accountability will be raised for years to come. This catastrophe is reminiscent of the world's worst industrial disaster, also located in South Asia. 3 December 2014 marked three decades since the people of Bhopal in India were exposed to forty tons of methyl isocyanate, which escaped from a pesticide plant of Union Carbide India Limited (UCIL), a subsidiary of the U.S.-based Union Carbide Corporation (UCC). In 1989, UCC negotiated a settlement with the Indian Government for US$470 million. Dow Chemical Company, following a merger with Union Carbide,[7] refused to assume these liabilities.[8] The disaster, which has claimed over 22,000 lives, still affects over 500,000 people,[9] and chronic health problems from exposure and soil and groundwater contamination still plague survivors. The intergenerational impacts have resulted in developmental disabilities and congenital malformations among children of persons exposed to the gas. In 2010, seven ex-employees, including the former UCIL chairman, were convicted for causing death by negligence, fined, and sentenced to imprisonment.[10] The struggle for justice in Bhopal continues,[11] and civil and criminal cases are still pending. On 30 July 2014, District Judge John Keenan of the U.S. Southern District of New York dismissed the second of a long-running set of suits aimed at holding UCC and its owner, Dow, responsible for faulty design of the Bhopal pesticide plant and pollution of the site and surrounding area.[12] On 1 August 2014, India's Supreme Court announced that it would hear a "curative petition" for compensation of those injured or killed by the Bhopal gas explosion and the ongoing disaster caused by persistent contamination of soil and water.[13] And on August 4, the Bhopal District Court summoned Dow to appear in the ongoing criminal case over responsibility for the 1984 disaster.[14]

These are only two of many examples of adverse impacts of investment projects involving multinational corporations based in the global North, doing business in the global South. They reflect how economic, social, and environmental interests can conflict, particularly in Southern host states which often have weaker institutions and less regulation in place in the areas of health, safety, labor, anticorruption, human rights, and the environment, as compared with Northern home states.[15] The rising complexities of international business and global value chains,

[7] Wikipedia, "Bhopal Disaster," 37 July 2014, http://en.wikipedia.org.
[8] Greenpeace, "Bhopal Disaster," www.greenpeace.org.
[9] Popular Resistance, "On 30th Anniversary, Campaign for Justice in Bhopal N.A. Calls for Solidarity," 17 June 2013, www.popularresistance.org.
[10] Wikipedia, note 7.
[11] Live Wire, "Ray of Hope for Survivors of the Bhopal Disaster," 7 August 2013, http://livewire.amnesty.org.
[12] Pesticide Action Network, "30 Years Later, Justice Still Delayed for Bhopal," 7 August 2014, www.panna.org.
[13] Ibid.
[14] Ibid.
[15] See e.g. Business and Human Rights Resource Centre, Lawsuits and Regulatory Action, www.business-humanrights.org.

including through outsourcing and international supply chains, makes the regulation of these activities increasingly challenging.[16]

Foreign direct investment (FDI) involves the transfer of tangible or intangible assets from one country to another for use in that country to generate wealth under the total or partial control of the owner of the assets.[17] Human rights entail obligations that states have committed to, and must uphold. "Sustainable development,"[18] the guiding concept for the Post-2015 Development Agenda and Sustainable Development Goals, mandates a holistic approach, integrating environment and development,[19] economy, society, and the environment.[20] This chapter explores paths to sustainable development by: addressing interlinkages of international investment law, human rights, and sustainable development; considering interventions which can bridge divides; and reflecting on the quest for a common future.

2. INTERNATIONAL INVESTMENT LAW, HUMAN RIGHTS, AND SUSTAINABLE DEVELOPMENT

While there are different views on what constitutes the purpose of investment, to the majority its primary aim should be development, in its conventional sense, through economic growth from incoming capital, tax revenues, and increased productivity. What constitutes "development" is likewise open to diverse perspectives. Traditionally defined as economic growth and industrialization, economic aggregates continue to be the barometer of progress, as represented by gross domestic product (GDP) in the dominant development paradigm.[21] Even according to this narrow approach, many investments are not necessarily motivated by development. Not all investment inevitably leads to development. Therefore, policies defining the investment landscape are critical in ensuring investment for development. For capital-exporting countries, motivations of investment include maximizing profits and expanding overseas trade. Competition from new companies may lead to productivity gains and greater efficiency in the host country, and the application of a foreign corporation's policies to a domestic subsidiary may

[16] S. Puvimanasinghe, *Foreign Investment, Human Rights and the Environment: A Perspective from South Asia on the Role of Public International Law for Development* (Leiden: Martinus Nijhoff Publishers, 2007).

[17] M. Sornarajah, *The International Law on Foreign Investment* (Cambridge: Cambridge University Press, 2004), p. 7.

[18] World Commission on Environment and Development, *Our Common Future* (London: Oxford University Press, 1987) [hereinafter Brundtland Report].

[19] *Rio Declaration on Environment and Development*, Rio de Janeiro, 14 June 1992, UN Doc. A/CONF.151/26 (vol. 1); 31 ILM 874 (1992), Principle 4 [hereinafter Rio Declaration].

[20] *Johannesburg Declaration on Sustainable Development: Report of the World Summit on Sustainable Development*, Johannesburg, 4 September 2002, UN Doc. A/CONF. 199/20), Resolution 1, Annex [hereinafter Johannesburg Declaration].

[21] Sornarajah, note 17, p. 27.

improve local corporate governance standards. Investment can promote exports and infrastructure development, as well as the transfer of knowledge, skills, and technology.

The model for investment agreements was developed in the political context of the 1950s and 1960s,[22] characterized by concern for the impacts of decolonization on business interests in newly independent countries of the South. Foreign investment law evolved primarily to serve the North's interests, and its history was determined by the political and economic environment and underlying power relationships and structures.[23] Initial agreements focused on one aspect: The protection of foreign capital and investments,[24] through attracting foreign investment, protecting property interests, enhancing investor rights, and giving them legal standing in trade and investment disputes. Regulating in the public interest was extrinsic to the international law of foreign investment.[25]

In the realm of trade, the Agreement on Trade-Related Aspects of Investment Measures (TRIMS),[26] General Agreement on Trade in Services (GATS),[27] Agreement on Trade Related Aspects of Intellectual Property Rights (TRIPS),[28] and Agreement on Agriculture[29] constitute the Final Act of the Uruguay Round and the Marrakesh Agreement establishing the World Trade Organization (WTO Agreement).[30] They comprise a legally binding framework for liberalizing trade and investment for goods, services, and property, further to globalization's agenda of liberalization, privatization, and deregulation. By incorporating TRIMs and GATS, investment issues come within the General Agreement on Tariffs and Trade (GATT).[31]

For over three decades, attempts to negotiate legally binding multilateral regulation of investment failed – in the United Nations, the Organization for Economic Co-operation and Development (OECD), and the WTO. The North, motivated by maintaining its economic prosperity, supported a minimalist approach, while the South, motivated by achieving development, advocated a binding code. The most far-reaching effort was the 1990 Draft Code of Conduct for Transnational

---

[22] H. Mann, K. von Moltke, L. E. Peterson, and A. Cosbey, *IISD Model International Agreement on Investment for Sustainable Development: Negotiator's Handbook* (International Institute for Sustainable Development, 2006).

[23] Sornarajah, note 17, pp. 18–30.

[24] Ibid.

[25] M. Sornarajah, "The Clash of Globalizations and the International Law of Foreign Investment," Simon Reisman Lecture in International Trade Policy, Norman Paterson School of International Affairs, Ottawa (12 September 2002).

[26] *Marrakesh Agreement Establishing the World Trade Organization*, Marrakesh, in force 1 January 1995, 1867 UNTS 3, Annex 1A, 1868 UNTS 186 [hereinafter Marrakesh Agreement].

[27] Ibid, 186 UNTS 183; 33 ILM 1167 (1994), Annex 1B.

[28] Ibid, 1869 UNTS 299; 33 ILM 1197 (1994), Annex 1C.

[29] Ibid, 1867 UNTS 410, Annex 1A.

[30] Ibid.

[31] Ibid, 1867 UNTS 187; 33 ILM 1153 (1994), Annex 1.

Corporations[32] of the United Nations Centre for Transnational Corporations (UNCTC), with comprehensive articles for maximizing the contributions of transnational corporations (TNC) to economic development and minimizing adverse effects, including through national sovereignty of host states and their permanent sovereignty over natural resources, human rights, and environmental protection. Inability to reach consensus due to North–South divides, opposition by TNCs and their home states, and an acute shortfall of investment in developing countries in the post–Cold War era led to the abortion of the Draft Code and the closure of UNCTC, which subsequently merged into the United Nations Conference on Trade and Development (UNCTAD).[33]

With the rise of environmental and social consciousness, the North endeavored to include broader concerns in trade and investment arrangements but faced resistance from the South, which saw these as protectionism and non-trade barriers.[34] In the 1990s, the draft Multilateral Agreement on Investment (MAI)[35] saw another attempt at binding multilateral regulation. A revised version of the 1976 OECD Guidelines on Multinational Enterprises,[36] the MAI was not conducive to sustainable development and was opposed by Southern states, student activists, NGOs, and others, for various reasons. France and Canada claimed a broad cultural exception, opposed by the U.S. and Japan,[37] signaling fragmentation within the North. France finally withdrew support, preventing its adoption. In the WTO framework, investment and its regulation were included in the Doha Development Agenda (DDA).[38] The Doha Declaration envisaged negotiations on a balanced and comprehensive multilateral investment agreement taking due account of the development objectives of host countries and their right to regulate in the public interest, and the special needs of developing and least developed countries. There has been no substantial progress on the DDA to date.

These failures are not cause to abandon the search for multilateral rules, but rather an indication of their importance.[39] In the absence of multilateral arrangements, bilateral investment treaties (BITs) and international investment agreements (IIAs)[40] predominate the international investment landscape and

---

[32] UN Commission on Transnational Corporations, *Proposed Text of the Draft Code of Conduct on Transnational Corporations*, 12 June 1990, E/1990/94, Annex.
[33] Puvimanasinghe, note 16, p. 148.
[34] Ibid.
[35] 31 ILM 1992, p. 1363.
[36] OECD *Declaration and Guidelines on International Investment and Multinational Enterprises*, adopted 21 June 1976, 15 ILM (1976) 967, as revised and adopted in the OECD *Guidelines for Multinational Enterprises*, adopted 27 June 2000, 40 ILM 237 (2000).
[37] Puvimanasinghe, note 16, pp. 148–149.
[38] *Doha Ministerial Declaration*, Doha, 4 November 2001, WT/MIN (01) dec/1, 20 November 2001.
[39] Mann et al., note 22.
[40] See UNCTAD database of BITs and other IIAs, http://investmentpolicyhub.unctad.org.

largely operate outside any regulatory framework. Starting with the BIT of the Federal Republic of Germany and Pakistan in 1959,[41] the IIA regime now consists of more than 3,000 BITs and "other IIAs"[42] in the form of free trade agreements (FTAs) with investment provisions. Their proliferation advances the deregulation of investment, and along with similar trends in trade and finance, fuels ascendant neoclassical, neoliberal globalization. Consequently, significant issues arise, including regulating in the public interest and safeguarding global public goods vis-à-vis the seminal goal of corporate profit-making. In a global environment of economic and financial crises and dwindling resources, especially in the North, regulation in the public interest could mean a decline in investment. The "race to the bottom" through lowering regulatory standards in competition for FDI leaves Southern countries with a dilemma, given their imperative need for development.

The UN Guiding Principles on Business and Human Rights[43] support policy coherence between economic activities including trade and investment and human rights. Produced by John Ruggie, former Special Representative of the UN Secretary-General on Business and Human Rights, the Guiding Principles were endorsed by consensus by the UN Human Rights Council on 16 June 2011. The non-binding principles rest on a framework of three pillars: The State's duty to protect against human rights abuses by third parties, including business; the corporate responsibility to respect human rights, requiring business to act with due diligence;[44] and the need for greater access to effective remedies. Some principles have been road-tested, with stakeholder consultation held in preparation, involving governments, businesses, and associations; individuals and communities; civil society; and experts. The workability of the human rights due diligence provisions was tested internally by ten companies and discussed with corporate law professionals from over twenty countries with expertise in more than forty jurisdictions.[45] Efforts have been made for inclusivity, although Southern stakeholders do not always have optimum representation due to various limiting factors.

The Guiding Principles on Human Rights Impact Assessments of Trade and Investment Agreements[46] developed by the former UN Special Rapporteur on the

---

[41] *Treaty for the Promotion and Protection of Investments*, Bonn, in force 28 April 1962, 457 UNTS 23.

[42] United Nations Conference on Trade and Development, *World Investment Report 2011: Non-Equity Modes of International Production and Development* (Geneva: United Nations, 2011).

[43] UN General Assembly, *Report of the Special Representative of the Secretary-General on the Issue of Human Rights and Transnational Corporations and Other Business Enterprises, John Ruggie*, 21 March 2011, A/HRC/17/31, Annex.

[44] The term "due diligence" was used in the *Guiding Principles on Business and Human Rights* to mean the steps and processes by which a company understands, monitors and mitigates its human rights impacts, including Human Rights Impact Assessments.

[45] UN General Assembly, note 43.

[46] UN General Assembly, *Report of the Special Rapporteur on the Right to Food, Olivier de Schutter*, 19 December 2011, A/HRC/19/59/Add.5, Addendum.

Right to Food, Olivier de Schutter, also offer guidance. Thereunder, impact assessments must be conducted before approving an investment or trade agreement and continue throughout its implementation.[47] Specific measures must be taken to mitigate negative human rights impacts. The principles guide states in ensuring that their trade and investment agreements are consistent with their obligations under international human rights instruments.[48] Impact assessments can help to ensure that states will not make demands or concessions that make it more difficult for them, or for others, to comply with their human rights obligations.[49] They can support companies carrying out human rights due diligence to identify, prevent, mitigate, and account for the human rights impacts of their activities, particularly in the negotiation and conclusion of investment agreements. The principles were made in consultation with international experts, human rights special procedures mandate-holders, treaty bodies, and the Human Rights Council Advisory Committee. A public consultation invited comments from multiple stakeholders, including states.[50] The implementation of both sets of guiding principles in resource-constrained settings is limited by lack of capacity, and this issue must be addressed.

The core labor conventions of the International Labor Organization (ILO),[51] the ILO Tripartite Declaration of Principles Concerning Multinational Enterprises and Social Policy,[52] and the OECD Guidelines for Multinational Enterprises are among other relevant instruments. The Global Compact[53] stresses the need for business to observe environmental standards, transparency standards, and human rights in the Universal Declaration of Human Rights (UDHR),[54] and core labor standards in the 1998 ILO Declaration on Fundamental Principles and Rights at Work.[55] The UN World Tourism Organization's Global Code of Ethics for Tourism states: "multinational enterprises of the tourism industry [...] should

---

[47] Ibid.

[48] Ibid, Principle 1.1.

[49] Ibid, Principle 3.

[50] Ibid.

[51] Eight ILO Conventions are considered fundamental to workers' rights, irrespective of levels of development of member states: *Forced Labour Convention*, Geneva, 28 June 1930, in force 1 May 1932, 39 UNTS 55; *Freedom of Association and Protection of the Right to Organise Convention*, San Francisco, 9 July 1948, in force 4 July 1950, 68 UNTS 17; *Equal Remuneration Convention*, Geneva, 29 June 1951, in force 23 May 1953, 165 UNTS 303; *Abolition of Forced Labour Convention*, Geneva, 25 June 1957, in force 17 January 1959, 320 UNTS 291; *Discrimination (Employment and Occupation)* Convention, Geneva, 25 June 1958, in force 15 June 1960, 362 UNTS 31; *Minimum Age Convention*, Geneva, 26 June 1973, in force 19 June 1976, 1015 UNTS 297; *Elimination of the Worst Forms of Child Labour*, Geneva, 17 June 1999, in force 19 November 2000, 38 ILM 1207.

[52] Geneva, 16 November 1977, 17 ILM 422.

[53] K. Annan, "World Economic Forum," Davos, 31 January 1999.

[54] 10 December 1948, GA Res. 217A(III); UN Doc. A/810 at 71(1948).

[55] Geneva, 19 June 1998, 37 ILM 1233 (1998); CIT /1998/PR20A.

involve themselves in local development, avoiding, by the excessive repatriation of their profits or their induced imports, a reduction of their contribution to the economies in which they are established."[56] The 2006 Principles for Responsible Investment[57] embody voluntary principles by institutional investors under the aegis of the UN Secretary-General to link investment with environmental, social, and corporate governance and anti-corruption. UN initiatives involve substantial participation by the South, given their multilateral character. However, resource constraints hamper the level of participation and limit implementation capabilities.

The UN Declaration on the Right to Development[58] defines development as "an inalienable human right by virtue of which every human person and all peoples are entitled to participate in, contribute to, and enjoy economic, social, cultural and political development, in which all human rights and fundamental freedoms can be fully realized."[59] The Declaration provides a normative framework for holistic development aimed at the improvement of human well-being and calls on states to cooperate to create an enabling environment for development. It upholds self-determination and sovereignty over natural wealth and resources; and requires free, active, and meaningful participation in development and fair distribution of its benefits. The Declaration followed from decolonization of Asian and African countries and their quest for a New International Economic Order. It supports fairness, equity, democracy, and redress of asymmetries, for a social and international order in which all rights and freedoms can be fully realized by everyone, under Article 28 of the UDHR. Despite the South's consistent advocacy and repeated reaffirmation by the UN General Assembly, geopolitical debates around the operationalization of this right prevail to date – among them the resolve of the South to progress toward a binding legal instrument and resistance to this from the North, and the objections of the North regarding its international dimension.[60]

The right to development is integral to sustainable development, as reflected in the Rio Declaration and the Vienna Declaration and Programme of Action: "[t]he right to development should be fulfilled so as to meet equitably the developmental and

---

[56] Santiago, 27 September–1 October 1999, GA A/RES/406(XIII), art. 9(5).

[57] UN Department of Public Information, "Secretary-General Launches, 'Principles for Responsible Investment' Backed by World's Largest Investors," 27 April 2006, www.un.org.

[58] 4 December 1986, GA res. 41/128, annex, 41 UN GAOR Supp. (No. 53) at 186, UN Doc. A/41/53 (1986), adopted by a recorded vote of 146 in favour, one against, and eight abstentions, all the latter being Northern states. See chapter 4, S. Atapattu, "The Significance of International Environmental Law Principles in Reinforcing or Dismantling the North–South Divide."

[59] Art. 1(1).

[60] See UN General Assembly, *Report of the Working Group on the Right to Development on its fifteenth session (Geneva, 12–16 May 2014)*, 7 July 2014, A/HRC/27/45.

environmental needs of present and future generations."[61] This right requires policy space, and would entail that investment agreements allow states to regulate in the public interest. This is essential to maximizing the positive and minimizing the negative effects of investment,[62] and addressing new and emerging challenges such as land-grabs in the South, especially in Africa.[63] In the progressive development of international law, an evolutionary interpretation aligned with subsequent developments implies that development, under the Right to Development Declaration, must be sustainable. Equality, non-discrimination, and all human rights principles apply to development and warrant safeguards for the vulnerable and marginalized, including the poor, women, youth, children, the disabled, the elderly, minorities, migrants, refugees, and indigenous peoples. Likewise, they guarantee equality and non-discrimination to peoples of all countries, including developing countries, least developed countries (LDCs), landlocked developing countries (LLDCs), and small island developing states (SIDS) of the South.[64]

Defined as "development that meets the needs of the present without compromising the ability of future generations to meet their own needs,"[65] sustainable development presents an alternative paradigm for development in a climate-constrained world. Its principles as articulated in the Rio Declaration include justice and equity for present and future generations (inter- and intragenerational equity),[66] and state that "[h]uman beings are at the centre of concerns for sustainable development. They are entitled to a healthy and productive life in harmony with nature."[67] "Shared responsibilities" are further developed in the Rio Declaration to recognize common but differentiated responsibilities[68] as embodied in the UN Framework Convention on Climate Change.[69]

---

[61] Rio Declaration, note 19, Principle 3; and *Vienna Declaration and Programme of Action*, Vienna, 25 June 1993, UN Doc. A/CONF.157/23; 32 ILM 1661 (1993), para. 11.

[62] W. Alschner and E. Tuerk, "The Role of International Investment Agreements in Fostering Sustainable Development," in F. Baetens (ed.), *Investment Law within International Law: Integrationist Perspectives* (New York: Cambridge University Press, 2013), p. 218.

[63] See chapter 11, C. Oguanaman, "Sustainable Development in the Era of Bioenergy and Agricultural Land Grab."

[64] LDCs are particularly vulnerable to external economic shocks and volatilities, as are SIDS to to climate change. These states, and developing countries in general, still lack equality in global governance. They do not enjoy equal participation in international financial institutions and face unfair trade and investment arrangements.

[65] Brundtland Report, note 18, chapter 2, para. 1. See also chapter 3, R. Gordon, "Unsustainable Development'.

[66] Rio Declaration, note 19, Principle 15.

[67] Rio Declaration, note 19, Principle 1.

[68] Rio Declaration, note 19, Principle 7.

[69] New York, 9 May 1992, in force 21 March 1994, 1771 UNTS 107; S. Treaty Doc No. 102-38; UN Doc. A/AC.237/18 (Part II)/Add.1; 31 ILM 849 (1992), Article 3.

326   *From a Divided Heritage to a Common Future?*

The Future We Want, following the UN Conference on Sustainable Development (Rio+20) in June 2012,[70] reaffirms the Stockholm Declaration,[71] all the principles of the Rio Declaration, and the commitment to fully implement the Rio Declaration, and calls for the full implementation of commitments under the Rio Conventions.[72] It refers to investment for sustainable development, science, innovation, and transfer of environmentally sound technologies, and responsible agricultural investment.[73] Investments, especially those straddling the borders of states at fundamentally unequal levels of development, cannot operate in a vacuum. International investment law is a branch of international law which includes human rights and sustainable development.[74] Sovereignty over natural resources; economic, social, and cultural rights;[75] and participatory rights[76] are particularly relevant to investment for sustainable development. Corporate social responsibility (CSR)[77] can support sustainable investment.

3. REINFORCING OR BRIDGING THE DIVIDES

The divides in this context are complex and interconnected. They are geopolitical and substantive; old and new. This section focuses on four key interventions which bridge or, conversely, reinforce them: namely, the Settlement of International Investment Disputes, the IISD Model International Agreement for Sustainable

---

[70] UN General Assembly, *Resolution Adopted by the General Assembly: The Future We Want*, 27 July 2012, A/RES/66/288, Annex [hereinafter *The Future We Want*].

[71] *Declaration of the United Nations Conference on the Human Environment*, Stockholm, 16 June 1972, UN Doc. A/CONF.48/14.

[72] *The Future We Want*, note 70, paras. 14–18.

[73] Ibid, para. 271. See C. Smaller and H. Mann, A *Thirst for Distant Lands: Foreign Investment in Agricultural Land and Water* (Winnipeg: IISD, 2009). See also Committee on World Food Security, "Principles on Responsible Agricultural Investment and Food Systems," www.fao.org. These draft principles, which are being negotiated in the UN, are grounded in the human rights framework and put small-scale producers and workers at the center of global efforts to increase investment in the agriculture sector.

[74] See M-C. Cordonier Segger, M. W. Gehring, and A. Newcombe (eds.), *Sustainable Development in World Investment Law* (The Netherlands: Kluwer Law International, 2011); J. E. Viñuales, *Foreign Investment and the Environment in International Law* (New York: Cambridge University Press, 2012).

[75] See *International Covenant on Economic, Social and Cultural Rights*, 16 December 1966, in force 3 January 1976, GA Res. 2200A (XXI), 21 UN GAOR Supp. (No. 16) at 49, UN Doc. A/6316 (1966); 993 UNTS 3; 6 ILM 368 (1967).

[76] See *Convention on Access to Information, Public Participation in Decision-Making and Access to Justice in Environmental Matters*, Aarhus, 28 June 1998, in force 30 October 2001, 2161 UNTS 447; 38 ILM 517 (1999) [hereinafter Aarhus Convention].

[77] CSR denotes that companies should adhere to shared or universal values in social and sustainable development and that rights of companies must be balanced with responsibilities, for corporate citizenship and sustainability. It guides the ethical behavior of companies towards various stakeholders and involves codes of conduct, social and environmental reporting, and improvements in occupational health, safety, and environmental management systems. See *Research for Social Change* (Geneva: UNRISD, 2003), p. 109.

Development, the UNCTAD Investment Policy Framework for Sustainable Development, and Public Interest Litigation in South Asia.

3.1 Settlement of International Investment Disputes[78]

There are different avenues for investment tribunals to consider non-investment obligations such as labor, human rights, and the environment in deciding investor–state disputes.[79] The latitude of investment tribunals in both legal rules and treaty interpretation appears to allow consideration of the broader normative environment without exceeding jurisdictional limits.[80]

Investment law evolved in investors' interests, excluding the broader public interest. Under the national treatment principle, foreign investors can allege discrimination if locals are given preference or other advantage. Under the fair and equitable treatment rule, investors can sue on grounds of non-renewal or change in terms of contract and changes in policies or regulations, which will allegedly reduce future profits. Investors can claim and sue for "indirect expropriation." Seen differently, this circumscribes the domestic policy space of states. In order to increase investment for sustainable development, IIAs must involve more actors, cover more issues, and balance the interests of all parties, including investors, host states, and home states.[81]

Arbitration under the investor–state dispute settlement system (ISDS) has come under strong criticism.[82] Recent claims have reached billions of U.S. dollars.[83] Paying such amounts, and related exorbitant legal fees, drains scarce resources, especially from countries of the South. Arbitration takes place primarily in the tribunals of the International Centre for the Settlement of Investment Disputes (ICSID), an affiliate of the World Bank; the International Chamber of Commerce; and the United Nations Commission on International Trade Law (UNCITRAL). Allegations include: that the tribunal decisions are arbitrary; that a few lawyers monopolize the arbitration business; and that there is a pro-investor bias and unfairness to governments sued. There is no right of appeal and the awards are high, with strong enforcement measures, including seizure of assets. In *Chevron* v

---

[78] See chapter 28, J. Razzaque, "Access to Remedies in Environmental Matters and the North–South Divide."

[79] V. Prislan, "Non-Investment Obligations in Investment Treaty Arbitration: Towards a Greater Role for States?," in F. Baetens (ed.), *Investment Law within International Law: Integrationist Perspectives* (New York: Cambridge University Press, 2013), pp. 450–481.

[80] Ibid, p. 480.

[81] H. Mann and K. von Moltke, *A Southern Agenda on Investment? Promoting Development with Balanced Rights and Obligations for Investors, Host States and Home States* (Winnipeg: IISD, 2005), p. 5.

[82] M. Khor, "When Foreign Investors Sue the State," *South Bulletin*, 21 November 2013.

[83] Ibid.

328 *From a Divided Heritage to a Common Future?*

Ecuador,[84] ICSID awarded to Chevron, a U.S. oil company, US$2.3 billion against Ecuador. Chevron's drilling activities had caused devastating environmental and human consequences, especially to indigenous peoples of the Amazon. The company failed to compensate the victims as ordered by the Court, and instead brought a defamation suit against the plaintiffs in another jurisdiction. Other cases include a suit against South Africa by a European mining company claiming losses from the government's black empowerment program[85] and a US$2 billion claim against Indonesia by a UK-based oil company[86] after its contract was cancelled because it was not in line with the law. Australia has also been sued for billions of dollars by the tobacco company Philip Morris because of its regulation that cigarette boxes cannot promote logos and brand names.[87] American company Renco sued Peru[88] for US$800 million because its contract was not extended after the company's operations caused massive environmental and health damage.

In other examples, foreign investors have invoked or threatened to invoke international arbitration in the ISDS provisions under BITs, comprehensive economic cooperation agreements, or FTAs to which India is a party.[89] Recently the world's largest mobile phone service provider, Vodafone Plc, a UK-based company, notified the Indian government of its impending action against a proposal for retrospective application of capital gains tax contained in the Finance Bill 2012, pending before parliament. It alleged that the proposed amendment violates the international legal protections granted to Vodafone and other international investors and that the proposals amount to a denial of justice and a breach of the government's obligations under the BIT to accord fair and equitable treatment to investors.

Arbitration tends to reinforce North–South divides rather than bridge them. ISDS typically takes place against the backdrop of highly unequal North–South dynamics of wealth and power, and systemic asymmetries. Most often, the investor is from an industrialized, capital-exporting state in the North and the host government a developing country in the South. Most FDI flows covered by BITs tend to be in one direction.[90] The total number of known treaty-based cases reached

---

[84] *Chevron Corporation and Texaco Petroleum Corporation v The Republic of Ecuador*, UNCITRAL, PCA Case No. 2009-23.

[85] *Piero Foresti, Laura de Carli and others v Republic of South Africa*, ICSID Case No. ARB(AF)/07/1.

[86] *Churchill Mining PLC and Planet Mining Pty Ltd v Republic of Indonesia*, ICSID Case No. ARB/12/14 and 12/40.

[87] *Philip Morris Asia Limited v The Commonwealth of Australia*, UNCITRAL, PCA Case No. 2012-12.

[88] *The Renco Group, Inc. v The Republic of Peru*, ICSID Case No. UNCT/13/1.

[89] K. M. Gopakumar, "India: Investment Treaties Stifle Public Policy Objectives," *South-North Development Monitor*, 26 April 2012.

[90] M. Hallward-Driemeier, in *Do Bilateral Investment Treaties Attract FDI? Only a Bit . . . and They Could Bite* (Washington: World Bank, 2003), p. 8, states that the OECD was the source of over 85 percent of FDI flows to developing countries between 1980 and 2000. The study of

568 in 2013;[91] 85 percent were by investors from developed countries, with claimants from the EU and the U.S. accounting for 75 percent of all disputes.[92] International arbitration is likely to be increasingly challenged in coming decades as the current format does not provide sufficient space to regulate in the public interest, especially in the South. According to some commentators:

> "Despite a pressing need for (r)evolution, conservatism firmly holds the international investment legal regime, especially on the part of capital-exporting countries, as their corporations value highly the possibility of resorting to arbitration. One would hope that, in the absence of a sea-change, small tides of reform will, in the course of the twenty-first century, progressively shape a fairer and more open dispute settlement system that is more concerned with the general interest."[93]

3.2 IISD Model International Agreement for Sustainable Development

In 2005 the International Institute for Sustainable Development (IISD)[94] proposed a model aimed at being consistent with sustainable development and a contemporary global economy.[95] It presented a negotiating agenda to: ensure that investor rights and public goods are protected in a legitimate, transparent, and accountable manner; establish the aspirations of Southern countries and promote sustainable development; balance investor rights with responsibilities and host and home state rights and obligations; and propose a credible dispute settlement process. IISD supported a multilateral approach with advantages over further proliferation of bilateral and regional agreements. Under Article 12, environmental and social impact assessments must be carried out and made public and accessible to the local community and affected interests in the host state before an investment is established.

Under the IISD Model, investors must adopt certain human rights instruments and uphold rights in the workplace, state, and community, and must not be complicit with the violation of human rights by others in the host state, including by public authorities or during civil strife. They must not circumvent international environmental, labor, and human rights obligations to which the host state and/or home state are parties. Investors are required to meet national and international

---

    bilateral FDI flows from the OECD to developing countries found little evidence that BITs stimulated additional investment.

[91] "Recent Developments in Investor–State Dispute Settlement (ISDS)," UNCTAD Issues Note No. 1, April 2014.

[92] Ibid.

[93] N. Hachez and J. Wouters, "International Investment Dispute Settlement in the Twenty-First Century: Does the Preservation of the Public Interest Require an Alternative to the Arbitral Model?," in F. Baetens (ed.), *Investment Law within International Law: Integrationist Perspectives* (New York: Cambridge University Press, 2013), pp. 448–449.

[94] Mann et al., note 22.

[95] Ibid.

standards of corporate governance for the relevant sector. They should maximize their contributions to the sustainable development of the host state and local community through socially responsible practices. Furthermore, they must apply the ILO Tripartite Declaration on Multinational Enterprises and Social Policy and the OECD Guidelines for Multinational Enterprises, as well as specific or sectoral standards of responsible practice.

The Model Agreement envisages civil actions for liability of investors in the judicial process of their home state for significant damage, personal injury, or loss of life in the host state. Parties cannot circumvent domestic labor, public health, safety, or environmental measures. Article 21 encourages high levels of protection with regard to labor, human rights, and the environment. The Model Agreement recognizes the inherent right of host states to pursue their own development objectives and priorities and to take regulatory and other measures.

More recently, the Southern African Development Community (SADC) published the SADC Model Bilateral Investment Treaty Template with Commentary[96] and the Commonwealth Secretariat launched 'Integrating Sustainable Development into International Investment Agreements: A Guide for Developing Countries'.[97] The International Bar Association's (IBA) Model Mine Development Agreement contains provisions supporting economic and social development.[98] The SADC and Commonwealth initiatives reflect largely Southern perspectives. These initiatives and their implementation can help to bridge North–South divides and inherent unfairness in IIAs. Southern states face constraints in implementing model agreements due to inequality in bargaining power in making IIAs, limited expertise in investment and legal and policy frameworks for sustainable development, inadequately developed negotiating skills, and constrained financial resources.

3.3 Investment Policy Framework for Sustainable Development (IPFSD)

UNCTAD's Investment Policy Framework for Sustainable Development (IPFSD)[99] presents an approach that promotes sustainable development including human rights in international investment agreements and regional integration initiatives. The IPFSD aims to ensure that the development benefits of FDI are realized and respond to major trends, including: the changing global investment landscape; the imperative of mainstreaming sustainable development;

---

[96] "SADC Model Bilateral Investment Treaty Template with Commentary," South African Development Community, July 2012.

[97] J. A. Van Duzer, P. Simmons, and G. Mayeda, "Integrating Sustainable Development into International Investment Agreements: A Guide for Developing Countries," *Commonwealth Secretariat*, August 2012.

[98] "Model Mine Development Agreement," International Bar Association, 4 April 2011.

[99] 2012, http://unctad.org.

the fact that national investment policy-making is at a crossroads, given the growing dichotomy between liberalization and regulatory measures; and systemic flaws and the need for policy coherence.

The IPFSD addresses the different dimensions of investment policy and fosters interaction with relevant national and international policies.[100] Its main elements are the core principles, the guidelines for national investment policy-making, and the policy options for IIAs. The principles comprise investment for sustainable development, policy coherence, and governance. The framework emphasizes the right to regulate and balance investors' rights and obligations.[101] In its policy options for IIAs, the IPFSD includes special and differential treatment for developing countries and/or LDCs. The toolkit provides policy options for all, to guide and inform the making of sustainable, development-friendly investment policy at the national and international levels.[102]

The IPFSD's core principles are derived in part from the Universal Declaration of Human Rights and the Guiding Principles on Business and Human Rights. Some instruments mentioned in the principles are soft law and non-binding, but can have persuasive value. Under Principle 9, investment promotion and facilitation policies should be aligned with sustainable development goals. Several proposals for guidelines for national investment policy-making and policy options for IIAs incorporate human rights and call for policy space and public policy exceptions in IIAs. The IPFSD has entry points for human rights, which may be extended to include further obligations in future revisions. They may also be extended through interpretation and implementation, where rights frameworks can be an aid. In the South, however, implementation of the framework requires capacity-building.

3.4 Public Interest Litigation in South Asia

Foreign investors use IIAs and BITs to bypass domestic legal processes and take host governments to international arbitration. However, local judicial processes might be more suitable for several reasons, including the context-specific nature of sustainable development. This section gives an insight into public interest litigation (PIL) in South Asia. The cases provide guidance on how courts can address interactions between economic and broader interests for sustainable development, including investment cases. Jurisprudence from this region was selected because of its groundbreaking developments. South Asia spans the Indian subcontinent and includes Afghanistan, Bangladesh, Bhutan, India, Maldives, Nepal, Pakistan,

---

[100] Alschner and Tuerk, note 62.
[101] Ibid.
[102] Ibid.

332 *From a Divided Heritage to a Common Future?*

and Sri Lanka. From the mid-1980s, PIL evolved as a popular tool[103] in cases involving economic development, including investment.

Several constitutions in the region recognize an obligation of the state and citizens to protect the environment. The right to life (and liberty) enshrined in some constitutions has been interpreted to include the right to a clean and healthy environment.[104] Following the Bhopal case,[105] the superior courts in India became catalysts for judicial activism and innovation, closely followed by the lower courts. In *Subash Kumar* v *State of Bihar*,[106] the petitioner pleaded infringement of the right to life due to pollution of the Bokaro River by sludge from the Tata Iron and Steel Company, making the water unfit for drinking or irrigation. The court held that the right to life includes the right to enjoyment of pollution-free water and air. It recognized that any affected person or genuinely interested person can bring a public interest suit in legal proceedings to vindicate or enforce the fundamental rights of a group or community unable to do so due to incapacity, poverty, or ignorance of the law.

In Pakistan, in *Shehla Zia and Others* v WAPDA,[107] an adequate standard of living was construed to include an environment adequate for the health and well-being of the people and the right to life, to encompass a healthy environment. Residents near a grid station under construction alleged that the electromagnetic field created by high-voltage transmission lines would pose a serious health hazard. Noting that energy is essential for life, commerce, and industry, and in the interest of balanced, sustainable development, the court appointed a Commissioner to examine the scheme. In *Surya Prasad Sharma Dhungel* v *Godavari Marble Industries et al.*[108] the Supreme Court of Nepal held that a clean and healthy environment is part of the right to life. In *Bangladesh Environmental Lawyers Association* v *Secretary, Ministry of Shipping*,[109] the Supreme Court of Bangladesh ordered the closure of shipbreaking yards operating without environmental clearance.

In Sri Lanka, the case of *Tikiri Banda Bulankulama et al.* v *Secretary, Ministry of Industrial Development et al.*[110] concerned a joint venture agreement between the government and the local subsidiary of a transnational corporation for mining phosphate. The terms of the agreement, which were not made public, were highly beneficial to the company and had little regard for human rights and the environment; indigenous culture; history, religion, and value systems; and sustainable development. Local villagers brought a public interest suit.

---

[103] This section is based on S. Puvimanasinghe, "Towards a Jurisprudence of Sustainable Development in South Asia: Litigation in the Public Interest" (2009) 10 *Sustainable Development Law and Policy* 41.

[104] Ibid.

[105] Wikipedia, note 7.

[106] AIR 1991 SC 420 (1991) (India).

[107] PLD 1994 SC 693.

[108] No. 35 (Nepal SC 1995).

[109] (Bangl SC 2009).

[110] 3 Sri LR 243 (decided 2 June 2000).

The project was to displace over 2,600 families – a total of around 12,000 persons. The Supreme Court found that at previous rates of extraction, there were sufficient deposits to last 1,000 years, but that the proposed agreement would lead to complete exhaustion of phosphate in thirty years. Stating that fairness to all, including the people of Sri Lanka, was the basic yardstick in doing justice, the Court held that there was an imminent infringement of the fundamental rights of the petitioners, in particular the right to equality and equal protection of the law; the freedom to engage in any lawful occupation, trade, business, or enterprise; and freedom of movement and to choose a residence.

The Court disallowed the project from proceeding until legal requirements of rational planning including an environmental impact assessment (EIA) were done. It found that the proposal would harm health, safety, livelihoods, and cultural heritage. Noting that economic growth is not the sole criterion for measuring human welfare, the court placed value on heritage, historical and archaeological site preservation, and ancient irrigation tanks which were non-renewable. It drew inspiration from international environmental law, intergenerational equity, and sustainable development (including as articulated by Judge Weeramantry in the *Hungary* v *Slovakia case*),[111] and the ancient wisdom and local history of conservation, sustainability, and human rights. The company's exemption from submitting to an EIA was held to be an imminent violation of the equal protection clause. Although the constitution provides only for justiciability of civil and political rights, the court allowed for a broader interpretation to include social and economic rights. Natural resources were found to be held by the government in guardianship and trust for the people, both present and future generations. Moreover, safeguarding nature and the environment were held to be a shared responsibility of the state and the people.

In other cases,[112] judicial measures placed a public trust obligation on states over natural resources,[113] imposed absolute liability for accidents in ultra-hazardous activities,[114] applied the polluter pays and precautionary principles,[115] and promoted sustainable development and good governance.[116] Public interest suits have also been filed against governmental authorities to enforce implementation of statutory duties.[117]

---

[111] *Case Concerning the Gabcikovo Nagymaros Project* (Hungary v Slovakia) [1997] ICJ Reports 228.

[112] See, e.g., *Mundy v Central Environmental Authority and others* (SC Appeal 58/2003) (decided 20 January 2004) and *Environmental Foundation Ltd. v Urban Development Authority et al.* (Case No. 47/2004) (decided 28 November 2005).

[113] *M.C. Mehta v Kamal Nath & others*, (1997) 1 SCC 388.

[114] *M.C. Mehta v Union of India and others*, AIR 1988 SC 1086.

[115] *Vellore Citizens' Welfare v Union of India* (1996) 5 SCC 647.

[116] *Gunaratne v Homagama Pradeshiya Sabha & others* (1998) 2 Sri LR 11 (decided 3 April 1998).

[117] *Withanage v Director Coast Conservation*, CA Application No. 551/2005 (decided 7 April 2005).

334 *From a Divided Heritage to a Common Future?*

4. CONCLUSION: A COMMON FUTURE?

International investment law, human rights, and sustainable development reveal a divided heritage, against the backdrop of a complex legal landscape. The quest of a common future would require the rebalancing of their interactions, in a nuanced and contexualized manner. Regulating in the public interest is at the core of rebalancing for sustainable development.

That "neither the MNEs themselves nor their activities abroad or the activities of any foreign investor, is regulated by a binding and comprehensive international instrument"[118] holds true to date. The model for IIAs does not meet the needs of the contemporary global economy.[119] Many consider the international investment regime to be so inherently flawed as to be beyond reform[120] and advocate an alternative based on the obligations of transnational actors.[121] These actors straddle a gray area between global and national regimes. The fragmented nature of international law underlines the need for policy coherence between economic progress, often driven by private interests and the global public interest.[122] International law must reflect the evolving body of global public values,[123] which are increasingly defined by emerging actors, including global civil society. Arguments are made for the reunification of the divided legal communities, identification of overlapping roles, and eliminating incompatibilities.[124]

The current scope of IIAs is insufficient to reflect the fuller relationship between investment and sustainable development.[125] Some scholars regard sustainable development as decisive in the applicability of IIAs.[126] A better understanding of investments and applicable laws could contribute to their de-mystification by examining how they interact with other priorities such as sustainable development.[127] Some countries have begun to include sustainable development

---

[118] F. Weiss, E. M. G. Denters and P. J. I. M. de Waart, *International Economic Law with a Human Face* (The Hague: Kluwer Law International, 1998), p. 414.

[119] Mann et al., note 22.

[120] Ibid.

[121] Ibid.

[122] Puvimanasinghe, note 16, pp. 254–260.

[123] Ibid.

[124] R. A. Lorz, "Fragmentation, Consolidation and the Future Relationship between International Investment Law and General International Law," in F. Baetens (ed.), *Investment Law within International Law: Integrationist Perspectives* (New York: Cambridge University Press, 2013), pp. 482–493.

[125] H. Mann, "Reconceptualizing International Investment Law: Its Role in Sustainable Development" (2013) 17 *Lewis and Clark Law Review* 521.

[126] D. A. Desierto, "Deciding International Investment Agreement Applicability: The Development Argument in Investment," in F. Baetens (ed.), *Investment Law within International Law: Integrationist Perspectives* (New York: Cambridge University Press, 2013), pp. 240–256.

[127] M. W. Gehring and A. Kent, "International Investment Agreements and the Emerging Green Economy: Rising to the Challenge," in F. Baetens (ed.), *Investment Law within International Law: Integrationist Perspectives* (New York: Cambridge University Press, 2013), pp. 187–216.

in their model BITs, notably Canada, in its Model Foreign Investment Promotion and Protection Agreement (FIPA).[128] Others have resorted to exception clauses in their model BITs[129] and still others have introduced sustainable development into IIAs by aligning dispute settlement provisions with sustainable development practices.[130] While host states' development goals are increasingly addressed in IIAs, this has been done in an indirect manner. Allowing for exceptions and reservations may be seen as shielding contracting parties from assuming the full scope of obligations under the IIA.[131]

By and large, the South continues to advocate development, sustainability, finance, technology transfer, and investors' duties, while the North, often with little regard for these concerns, still emphasizes investors' rights, good governance, anti-corruption, and the rule of law. However, both groups and the issues they advance are not homogenous and human rights and the environment are increasingly common concerns, especially among civil society in the North. As most of the FDI stock is still from the North, the continued maintenance of a rights-based regime for investors with no, or limited, obligations is likely seen to reflect their interests. However, as Southern states, and especially the resource-rich ones among them, increasingly withdraw from the current regime, the more recalcitrant Northern states may find greater motivation for rethinking current approaches.[132] Southern states are renegotiating, amending, and denouncing their BITs to rebalance the international investment regime,[133] and to some extent to illustrate trends of recalibration of sovereignty by the South. Brazil has rejected ratifying any of the fourteen BITs it has signed; South Africa has started withdrawing from existing BITs and has not ratified some signed agreements. Ecuador continues to review its options, Venezuela has withdrawn from ICSID, and many Southern countries have refrained from entering into Economic Partnership Agreements.

The Rio Declaration sets the goal of establishing a new and equitable global partnership through new levels of cooperation among states, key sectors of society, and people.[134] Renewed collaboration for the greater good of humanity and the

---

[128] Foreign Affairs, Trade and Development Canada, "Foreign Investment Promotion and Protection," www.international.gc.ca.

[129] Mann, note 125.

[130] Ibid.

[131] Ibid.

[132] Ibid.

[133] United Nations Conference on Trade and Development, *World Investment Report 2011: Non-Equity Modes of International Production and Development* (Geneva: United Nations, 2011).

[134] Principle 5 states that: "[a]ll States and all people shall cooperate in the essential task of eradicating poverty as an indispensable requirement for sustainable development, in order to decrease the disparities in standards of living and better meet the needs of the majority of the people of the world."

environment requires a new approach to international relations[135] based on compromise, common interests, and long-term perspectives.[136] To realize inter- and intragenerational equity for present and future generations, there is a need to reconcile the conflicting interests. The investment regime needs to take into account the profound changes in the international investment law and policy landscape.[137] Multiple stakeholders are calling for a new regulatory framework,[138] along with calls for North–South trade and investment agreements to permit policy space for development and for redress of the democratic deficit in global economic governance.[139] There is a need to redress systemic limitations, including through educating and sensitizing international commercial arbitrators on human rights, environment, and development.

In renewed efforts, the UN Human Rights Council recently resolved to establish a working group to draft an international legally binding instrument on trans- national corporations.[140] Twenty members of the Council, all from the South, voted for the resolution, which was co-sponsored by Ecuador and South Africa, and supported by Bolivia, Cuba, and Venezuela. Thirteen abstained and fourteen voted against it. In presenting the resolution, Ecuador noted that victims of disas- ters, such as Union Carbide in India, Shell in Nigeria, and Chevron in Ecuador, are still without remedy. In increasingly fragmented trends blurring distinctions between North and South and amplifying the voice of global civil society, this initiative has the support of over 500 civil society organizations.[141]

The need to understand investment law as a component of international law relating to globalization calls for integration of the public interest through systemic and institutional reforms, including regulation. Writers[142] cite signs of change, and the search for options continues.[143] Domestic measures such as public interest

---

[135] K. Hussein, "Sustainable Development: A Normative Framework for Evolving a More Just and Humane International Economic Order?," in S. R. Chowdhury et al. (eds.), *The Right to Development in International Law* (Dordrecht: Martinus Nijhoff, 1992), p. 259.

[136] I. M. Porras, "The Rio Declaration: A New Basis for International Cooperation," in P. Sands (ed.), *Greening International Law* (London: Earthscan, 1993), pp. 20–33.

[137] K. P. Sauvant and F. Ortino, *Improving the International Investment Law and Policy Regime: Options for the Future* (Helsinki: Ministry for Foreign Affairs of Finland, 2013).

[138] M. Sornarajah advocates (substantial) improvement of the regime in "Toward Normlessness: The Ravage and Retreat of Neo-Liberalism in International Investment Law," in K. P. Sauvant (ed.), *Yearbook on International Investment Law and Policy* (New York: Oxford University Press, 2010), pp. 595–642.

[139] The South Centre, "G-77 Extraordinary Summit Declaration," 15 June 2014, www.southcentre. int.

[140] UN General Assembly, *Elaboration of an International Legally Binding Instrument on Trans- national Corporations and Other Business Enterprises with Respect to Human Rights*, 20 June 2014, A/HRC/RES/26/9.

[141] K. Mohamadieh, "Human Rights Council: Historic Resolution Adopted for a Legally Binding Instrument on TNCs," 30 June 2014, www.twnside.org.sg.

[142] Alschner and Tuerk, note 62.

[143] Sauvant and Ortino, note 137.

litigation and *ex ante* human rights, environmental, social, sustainability, and strategic impact assessments can provide tools and alternatives to rebalance. Going forward, as the international community deliberates on a new development agenda and goals, parallel trade negotiations[144] are revealing trends in shrinking domestic policy space in public and private services regulation[145] and circumscribing the industrial, macroeconomic, financial, social, and environmental policies of Southern states.[146] In this climate of mixed trends, which both bridge and reinforce divides, a note on the reform of the regime[147] remarked on the contemporary concerns of states, including the development dimension of IIAs, the balance of rights and obligations between investors and states, and the complexity of the regime. Ongoing efforts to address challenges include the quest for systemic reform to comprehensively address them in a holistic manner. Meanwhile, small tides of reform may progressively pave the way to "our common future."

[144] B. Stokes and P. S. Mehta, "The Transatlantic Trade and Investment Partnership (TTIP) and Emerging Economies," Friedrich Ebert Foundation and Just Jobs Network Roundtable, 9 April 2014.

[145] "Threats to the Post-2015 Agenda from Trade Agreements," Public Symposium Side Event, United Nations Conference on Trade and Development, 19 June 2014.

[146] S. R. Smith and R. Sengupta, "Exploring Elements of a Global Development Agenda for International Trade and Investment," 2 May 2014, www.un-ngls.org.

[147] United Nations Conference on Trade and Development, *World Investment Report 2014: Investing in the SDGs* (Geneva: United Nations, 2014).

16

Project Finance and Sustainable Development in the Global South

Shalanda H. Baker

1. INTRODUCTION

The pervasive use of private law in modern international development projects situates it as a background element of development, where the activity itself may be critiqued, but the mechanism utilized for the development is itself nearly invisible and resistant to critique. Indeed, it appears that private law is an integral part of the development narrative, ubiquitous and benign. This makes it difficult for Southern states to question whether private law should continue to be used to achieve sustainable development. Private law is therefore a constitutive element of development, including development deemed "sustainable."[1]

This chapter examines the primary mechanism used to finance large energy and infrastructure projects all over the world – project finance. It argues that the key risk mitigation methods used by private developers engaged in project finance make it the wrong financing mechanism for sustainable development, given that the principal actors are shielded from the consequences of their risky behavior. Although the structure of project finance may lead to unacceptable risk-taking in other areas of development, this chapter argues that with respect to sustainability, reliance on project finance for renewable energy projects could actually undermine the goals of sustainable development, lead to greater inequality and subordination, and diminish opportunities for participation by affected communities.

---

[1] In 1983, the United Nations convened the World Commission on Environment and Development (WCED) to find ways to reconcile economic development with environmental protection. In its report the Commission stated that, "[h]umanity has the ability to make development sustainable to ensure that it meets the needs of the present without compromising the ability of future generations to meet their own needs," World Commission on Environment and Development, *Our Common Future* (London: Oxford University Press, 1987) [hereinafter *Our Common Future*], Part I.3. See also chapter 3, R. Gordon, 'Unsustainable Development'.

Acknowledging that the term "sustainable development" is itself a contested concept, this chapter accepts, without critiquing, the dominant narrative of sustainable development.[2] Particular attention is paid to the intragenerational aspect of sustainable development, which emphasizes economic and social justice for the current generation.[3] With this lens, the chapter explores the relationship among sustainable development, project finance, and risk-taking in the global South.

Section 2 defines project finance, its theoretical rationales, and the ways it is deployed by Northern entities. Section 3 looks to the South and describes the extraordinary effects of the current development of "clean" or "green" energy projects on indigenous farming communities in the El Istmo de Tehuantepec region of Oaxaca, Mexico (the "Isthmus").[4] This section also provides stark insight into the moral hazard that arises when development is conducted by private actors who proliferate behind a cloak of contractual opacity that encourages extraordinary risk-taking. Section 4 provides a framework for questioning the utility of project finance to meet the goals of sustainable development.

2. AN EXPLICATION – PROJECT FINANCE IS RISK MITIGATION

2.1 A Brief History

Project finance refers to the contractual framework that allows a project developer to pay for the cost of the project through its revenues. Quite simply, the "project *finances* itself."[5] Project finance first presents itself as a benign collection of contracts. It gained prominence as the Washington Consensus model of development, or neoliberalism, encouraged Southern states to adopt law reforms that protected the primacy of contract and private property rights.[6] The Washington Consensus is rooted in the idea that the market is the best vehicle for economic development, and thus private actors are more appropriate than states for such activity.[7] Indeed, in the

---

[2] Sustainable development as a concept is particularly vulnerable to critique, as it implicitly incorporates an imperative to "develop" along a linear arc of modernity, which itself could be antithetical to any notion of sustainability.

[3] In *Our Common Future* the WCED takes a similar view, noting that "[e]ven the narrow notion of physical sustainability implies a concern for social equity between generations, a concern that must logically be extended to equity within each generation": note 1, chapter 2.

[4] International Finance Corporation, "Eurus: Summary of Proposed Investment," http://ifcext. ifc.org (noting that the state of Oaxaca in Mexico has "one of the best wind resources in the world").

[5] S. H. Baker, "Unmasking Project Finance: Risk Mitigation, Risk Inducement, and an Invitation to Development Disaster?" (2011) 6 *Texas Journal of Oil, Gas, and Energy Law* 273 at 308.

[6] Ibid at 295.

[7] J. W. Dellapenna, "Climate Disruption, The Washington Consensus, and Water Law Reform" (2008) 81 *Temple Law Review* 383 at 386.

340 *Project Finance and Sustainable Development in the Global South*

post–debt crisis years of the 1980s and 1990s, Southern states were often forced to adopt such reforms in order to receive much needed aid.[8]

In this move to emphasize the private sector, project finance emerged: a transplant from the North to the South; a purportedly neutral way for private project developers to test their newly obtained contractual and property rights; and a way to bring efficiency to developing nations.[9] Moreover, the structure of project finance allowed developers to incur minimal financial risk, a crucial "carrot" to entice them to engage in risky development in the global South. The assumed neutrality and efficiency of project finance are rarely questioned,[10] but a brief discussion of its key features raises questions. In particular, the diminished accountability of private developers and lack of opportunities for affected third parties to participate meaningfully in the project development process undermine the potential of project finance to be used for sustainable development by communities in the global South.

2.2 *Key Features*

Project finance is seen as one of the most complex ways to engage in deal-making.[11] It is noted for its high transaction costs.[12] Indeed, the legions of costly lawyers required for project finance transactions and the very few standardized contracts involved make project finance a cumbersome method of developing projects.[13] This complex network of contracts and experts work together to offer the key benefit associated with project finance: risk mitigation. The following section describes many of the common features of transactions structured using project finance, with the caveat that no two project finance transactions look alike.[14]

Most energy projects begin with an equity investment (an investment of capital) by two to five investors into a special purpose entity (SPE) or special purpose

---

[8] A. Anghie, "Time Present and Time Past: Globalization, International Financial Institutions, and the Third World" (2000) 32 *New York University Journal of International Law and Policy* 243 at 256 (critiquing International Monetary Fund and World Bank structural adjustment programs as enhancing the power of capital flowing from the global North through multinational enterprises while also diminishing the power of the regulatory state).

[9] Baker, note 5 at 295 (noting that the assumed neutrality of private law has a subordinating effect on indigenous populations).

[10] Among the few exceptions are M. B. Likosky, *Law, Infrastructure and Human Rights* (Cambridge: Cambridge University Press, 2006); Baker, note 5; and S. Leader and D. Ong (eds.), *Global Project Finance, Human Rights and Sustainable Development* (Cambridge: Cambridge University Press, 2011).

[11] Baker, note 5 at 276.

[12] Ibid.

[13] M. B. Likosky, "Mitigating Human Rights Risks Under State-Financed and Privatized Infrastructure Projects" (2003) 10 *Indiana Journal of Global Legal Studies* 65 at 67.

[14] E. R. Yescombe, *Principles of Project Finance* (San Diego: Academic Press, 2002), p. 7; S. L. Hoffman, *The Law and Business of International Project Finance* (Cambridge: Cambridge University Press, 2008), p. 78.

vehicle (SPV).[15] This entity becomes the face of the project. It contracts with: the banks, which supply the debt financing for the project; the purchaser of energy or refined product, which is often a utility or other public entity; suppliers and contractors, who provide the raw material; and a number of other entities essential to the successful operation of the project.[16]

The SPE is also the project's risk-taker and engages in the riskiest activity of all: starting the project. The banks, which provide anywhere from 70 to 90 percent of the overall financing, accept as security the project's assets; in the event of failure or losses at the project, the equity investors' assets are not placed at risk.[17] This type of liability shielding is a common feature of corporations, but in the development context, where private development activity has the potential to cause extensive social and environmental harm, it should raise renewed concerns.[18]

Affected members of the community, particularly those who lack the sophistication of project experts, must seek recovery through the SPE. In the event of extensive damage to the community or environment, the chances of recovery by the community are minimal, as they must compete with the project's creditors to recover from an insolvent SPE. Further, the SPE's limited liability prevents any additional recovery from the project's equity investors, who would have additional assets.[19]

2.3 Underlying Assumptions

Despite the foregoing concerns for third-party stakeholders, proponents of project finance endorse it because of its ability to mitigate or "neutralize" a developer's economic and political risk.[20] Another rationale for project finance is efficiency. Its structure effectively shields developers from financial liability arising from the project. The political risk insurance available to developers also allows developers to minimize their exposure to risks due to political instability. Moreover, the use of subsidiaries to conduct project business adds a layer of political cover between developers and affected communities. These protections result from the complex contracts that comprise project finance transactions. Such contracts neutralize potential risks of the project for developers, but externalize harm. As a result, despite the dizzying array of contracts that comprise project finance transactions,

---

[15] Baker, note 5 at 300.

[16] Ibid at 300–305.

[17] Ibid at 304.

[18] Indeed, the commonly cited rationale for limited liability specifically relates to risk-taking, which has become a normative backdrop for commerce and business development, and even the most critical agree that a certain amount of risk allows societies to move forward. But how much risk-taking is too much? Where sensitive ecosystems and cultures often bear the brunt of developers' activities, this question is critical.

[19] Baker, note 5 at 321.

[20] Baker, note 5 at 314 (describing developer risk as fitting into two categories: "(1) commercial, or economic, risks and (2) political risks, such as government expropriation, currency inconvertibility, and war").

342 *Project Finance and Sustainable Development in the Global South*

it is deemed "efficient."[21] The resultant effect of this "efficient" development financing mechanism is far from neutral.

Affected communities often lack meaningful opportunities for representation. Despite the recent adoption by the World Bank's International Finance Corporation (IFC)[22] and major multinational banks[23] of the principle of Free, Prior, and Informed Consent (FPIC), in projects where indigenous communities may be affected, representational concerns persist.[24] One reason for this is that the meaning of "consent" is not clear.[25] Further, the difficulty in identifying leaders who speak for affected populations makes FPIC difficult to operationalize.[26] Affected communities are effectively shut out of meaningful opportunities to engage developers. They either become passive recipients of the many negative externalities that accompany large projects or active voices against the projects.[27] When this one-sided development is coupled with limited opportunities for recovery embedded in the project finance structure, the rationales supporting the use of project finance collapse.

The following case study of wind energy development in Oaxaca supports the above assertions. It illustrates the key concerns of relying on project finance to advance the ideals of sustainable development.

3. GREEN ENERGY DEVELOPMENT CASE STUDY

Rows of windmills dot the landscape throughout the Isthmus of Tehuantepec in Oaxaca, Mexico. The people in this region are a mix of more than fourteen indigenous communities who own the land collectively, speak more than fourteen distinct and separate indigenous languages, and have relied on the earth for generations for

---

[21] Ibid at 305.

[22] International Finance Corporation, "Performance Standards on Environmental and Social Sustainability," 1 January 2012, www.ifc.org (an objective of Performance Standard 7 is to "ensure the Free, Prior, and Informed Consent (FPIC) of the Affected Communities of Indigenous Peoples" under certain development circumstances).

[23] The Equator Principles is a set of ten principles intended to provide a non-binding framework to guide the financing of projects by international financial institutions. Currently seventy-nine financial institutions in thirty-five countries have adopted them, reflecting "70 percent of international Project Finance debt in emerging markets", Equator Principles, "About the Equator Principles," www.equator-principles.com.

[24] The *United Nations Declaration on the Rights of Indigenous Peoples*, New York, 12 September 2012, A/61/L.67/Annex also incorporates the concept of free, prior, and informed consent, in several instances.

[25] B. McGee, "The Community Referendum: Participatory Democracy and the Right to Free, Prior, and Informed Consent" (2009) 27 *Berkeley Journal of International Law* 570 at 591 (noting disputes regarding the meaning of consent).

[26] See generally S. H. Baker, "Why the IFC's Free, Prior, and Informed Consent Policy Does Not Matter (Yet) to Indigenous Communities Affected by Development Projects" (2012) 30 *Wisconsin International Law Journal* 668.

[27] McGee, note 25 at 573.

subsistence farming and fishing.[28] They are poor, among the poorest in the state of Oaxaca.[29] Yet they are sitting on a veritable gold mine. The Isthmus of Oaxaca, the 120-mile wide strip of land that separates the Pacific and Atlantic oceans, is one of the windiest places on Earth. It is also ground zero of a pitched, sometimes violent,[30] battle between residents and wind farm developers.[31]

Mexico has adopted a neoliberal development model, including comprehensive reform of its energy law to permit the private development of the Isthmus into a sea of wind farms.[32] The energy will power some of the largest corporate entities in the world, including Walmart, FEMSA (a Mexican beverage company), Coca-Cola, Heineken, and Cemex (a Mexican cement manufacturer).[33] The following section highlights a few of these projects.

3.1 Wind Development in Oaxaca

A 2003 report by the United States National Renewable Energy Laboratory indicates that approximately 7 percent of the state of Oaxaca, an area of approximately 6,600 square kilometers, is land with "good-to-excellent wind resource potential."[34] There are currently fourteen individual wind projects underway in the Isthmus.[35] The extensive development is a part of the Mexican government's attempt to "go green" through the adoption of neoliberal reforms.[36]

---

[28] The Zapotec and Huave indigenous people reside in the areas subject to the current wind development. See D. LaGesse, "Mexico's Robust Wind Energy Prospects Ruffle Nearby Villages," 7 February 2013, http://news.nationalgeographic.com (discussing Zapotec and Huave indigenous groups living in the area of development); L. Stephen, "Negotiating Global, National, and Local 'Rights' in a Zapotec Community" (2005) 28 *The Political and Legal Anthropology Review* 133.

[29] World Bank, "Supporting the Reform Agenda for Inclusive Growth in Oaxaca, Mexico," 4 September 2013, www.worldbank.org.

[30] E. Vance, "The 'Wind Rush': Green Energy Blows Trouble into Mexico," January 26, 2012, www.csmonitor.com (noting wind farm-related protests and the death of a contractor at a wind farm).

[31] Ibid.

[32] International Finance Corporation, "Clean Technology Fund, Project Proposal for Mexico: Private Sector Wind Development (Current Information Document)," 29 June 2009, www.climateinvestmentfunds.org (describing, in paragraph 22 of the document, the Inter-American Development Bank's efforts to assist Mexico with the implementation of its Renewable Energy Law, which will help to "remove existing barriers which impede the increased use of non-conventional forms of renewable energy which include wind").

[33] LaGesse, note 28 (noting the Mexican cement company Cemex and Walmart de Mexico as beneficiaries of certain wind projects); Reuters, "Vestas Winds Order for Biggest Latam Wind Project," 12 March 2012, http://mobile.reuters.com (discussing the Marena Renovables project, slated to be the largest wind energy project in Latin America, which will provide power to Coca-Cola FEMSA, OXXO (FEMSA's convenience store chain), and Heineken NV in Mexico).

[34] D. Elliot et al., "Wind Energy Resource Atlas of Oaxaca," www.nrel.gov, p. vi.

[35] Baker, note 5 at 281.

[36] "UN Says Renewable Energy Investment Down in 2009," Reuters, 7 October 2009 (noting Mexico's goal to have 25 percent of its energy generated by renewable sources by the year

344   *Project Finance and Sustainable Development in the Global South*

In 1992, the Mexican government adopted extensive legal reforms to allow for private investment and allow indigenous communities to lease previously inalienable land to private developers.[37] In the realm of energy, which was an area of development previously restricted to the state, the country enacted two major reforms: (1) the Electric Energy Public Service Law, which was amended in 1992 to allow private participation in the generation of energy[38] and (2) the self-generation law, which allows private parties to develop projects that sell energy to private entities so long as the private entity also has a nominal ownership interest in the project.[39] Mexico's adoption of its 2008 Renewable Energy Law[40] further eased the way for private investment.[41]

Development banks have also been heavily involved in the advancement of the neoliberal project in Mexico. The World Bank provided seed money for a government-led "test" pilot project[42] and worked with the government on issues arising from the *ejido* structure, or communal form of land ownership.[43] The IFC also has deep roots in the Oaxaca wind industry. A 2009 document of the Bank noted that "Mexico is one of the most promising yet untapped areas for wind energy development in Latin America."[44] Finally, the Inter-American Development Bank (IADB), a regular funder of Oaxaca wind projects, has provided technical assistance to the Mexican government in connection with the 2008 Renewable Energy Law. This includes assisting with the removal of barriers to expansion of renewable energy and evaluating the potential financial feasibility of such projects.[45]

All of the foregoing legal reforms and assistance efforts created a framework for the extensive energy development currently underway in Oaxaca.[46] Notably absent from these efforts are the communities who will be impacted by the development.

2012). See also C. Hawley, "Clean-Energy Windmills A 'Dirty Business' For Farmers in Mexico," 16 June 2009, http://usatoday30.usatoday.com.

[37] Baker, note 5 at 286, note 73 (discussing the extensive changes to the *ejido* system of communal land ownership in Mexico, which made previously owned communal land alienable).

[38] A. Laguna-Estopier, "Wind Energy in Mexico: Regulation and Project Development," 28 February 2014, www.eprg.group.cam.ac.uk.

[39] R. Bierzwinsky, "Renewables Opportunities in Mexico; Mexico Sets Ambitious Goal of Having 35% of All Energy Production Derive from Renewable Energy Sources by 2024," June 2011, www.chadbourne.com.

[40] Ibid.

[41] Baker, note 5 at 297.

[42] Ibid.

[43] Ibid.

[44] International Finance Corporation, note 32, para. 7.

[45] Ibid, para. 48.

[46] A key component of the reform is the Plan Mesoamerica, formerly known as Plan Puebla-Panama. The plan involves extensive infrastructure projects throughout Central America, including a railway in the Isthmus of Tehuantepec: M. E. Padua, "Mexico's Part in the Neoliberal Project" (2002) 8 *University of California Davis Journal of International Law and Policy* 30. See also J. Martinez and J. L. Davila, "Windmills, the Face of Dispossession," LDPI Working Paper 55, 2014, p. 1, note 1.

3.2 A Sampling of Projects

With the exception of the first "test" wind farms run by the state,[47] the projects are initiated by private actors using project finance.[48] Developers can also expect ample support from the IFC and IADB. This section briefly describes three projects in various stages of development and sheds light on the range of problems that have arisen.

3.2.1 Eurus Wind Project

The Eurus wind farm, a US$525 million project,[49] is the largest wind development in Latin America and the Caribbean.[50] The project developer, Acciona Energía México, is a wholly owned subsidiary of the Spanish company, Acciona Energía. The project borrower is Eurus SAPI de CV, a special purpose limited liability company.[51] The energy created by the project's 167 turbines is sufficient to power a city of 500,000 people.[52] Instead, however, the project will generate and sell power to Cemex, a multinational cement company that netted almost US$14 billion in sales in 2012.[53] Construction on the project was halted on at least six separate occasions due to conflicts regarding adequate compensation for utilizing indigenous land.[54] During the disruptions, community members posted signs stating that the region belongs to the *ejido*.[55]

3.2.2 Mareña Renovables Wind Project

The Mareña Renovables wind project, also known as Parque Eolico San Dionisio, is a 132-turbine wind farm that was initially slated for completion in July 2013,[56] to be the largest wind project in Latin America.[57] The turbines will be placed in the ocean along the beach outside of the town of San Dionisio del Mar, the home of

---

[47] For a discussion of these test projects, see Baker, note 5 at 281.

[48] Ibid at 297–298.

[49] Inter-American Development Bank, "ME-L1068 : Eurus Wind Project," www.iadb.org.

[50] Inter-American Development Bank, "IDB to Finance Historic Expansion of Wind Power in Mexico," 15 December 2009, www.iadb.org.

[51] International Finance Corporation, "Eurus, Summary of Proposed Investment," http://ifcext.ifc.org.

[52] Z. Dyer, "Clean Energy Plays Dirty in Oaxaca," http://nacla.org.

[53] Cemex, "Financial Highlights," www.cemex.com.

[54] Hawley, note 36.

[55] Ibid.

[56] "Mitsubishi to Acquire 345 Stake in Marena Renovables Wind Power Project," Datamonitor Financial Deals Tracker, 27 February 2012.

[57] "When the Wind Blows, PF Follows," Project Finance International, 18 December 2012, available at 2012 WLNR 27209430.

346   *Project Finance and Sustainable Development in the Global South*

approximately 5,000 residents, and Santa Maria del Mar.[58] The project is located on land that has been inhabited by the Ikoots people of Oaxaca for more than 3,000 years.[59] The Ikoots rely on fishing to support a subsistence way of life.[60] Activists argue that the project will deeply impact the society, culture, and environment, which consists of twenty-seven kilometers of coastline.[61] They also argue that the wind farm will desecrate sacred Ikoots (Huave) land.[62]

The investors are Macquarie Mexican Infrastructure Fund, Macquarie Asset Finance Limited, and FEMSA (the largest beverage company in Latin America and the largest convenience store operator in Mexico).[63] The project will cost an estimated US$1.2 billion, and will be financed through a group of commercial and international development banks.[64] The borrower is Mareña Renovables Capital, SAPI De CV SOFOM ENR,[65] presumably a subsidiary of the project developers. Under thirty-three power supply agreements, the project will supply energy to subsidiaries of FEMSA and Cerveceria Cuauhtémoc Moctezuma (Heineken).[66]

Parque Eolico San Dionisio has been a source of great distress for the local community. Fishermen worry that the wind turbines will affect the abundance of fish in the area.[67] Activists point to a larger trend in the Isthmus, where wind farm developers pressure rural farmers to sign long-term leases for communally owned land.[68] In an interview with a leading industry publication regarding the project, a representative of Mareña Renovables stated that the developers are relying on the Inter-American Development Bank to "deal with" local indigenous communities who have lived in the development area for thousands of years, and that the developer is relying on the Bank's protocol for consultation.[69]

---

[58] "Indigenous Communities in Oaxaca, Mexico Fight Corporate Wind Farms," 1 November 2012, http://earthfirst.org.uk.

[59] Ibid.

[60] Ibid.

[61] Ibid.

[62] Ibid.

[63] Inter-American Development Bank, "Eolica del Sur to Build Biggest Wind Farm in Mexico with IDB Support," 24 November 2011, www.iadb.org.

[64] Infrastructure Journal, "396 MW Marena Renovables Wind Farm," 1 March 2013, www.ijonline.com.

[65] Ibid. See also Inter-American Development Bank, "Document of the Independent Consultation and Investigation Mechanism," http://idbdocs.iadb.org, p. 2 (investigating the Mareña Renovables Wind Project and stating that the borrower is owned in whole or part by one or more of the project developers, Fomento Economico Mexicano, SAB de CV (FEMSA), Macquarie Mexican Infrastructure Fund, and Macquarie Asset Finance Limited (a subsidiary of Macquarie Capital Group Limited).

[66] Inter-American Development Bank, note 63.

[67] Earth First, note 58 (as one resident, Laura Celaya Altamirano, notes, "[t]his is the life of the poor: we fish so we can eat and have something to sell, to have a bit of money. They say that now that the wind project is here, they'll give us money for our land and sea, but the money won't last forever. We don't agree with this. How are we going to live?").

[68] Ibid.

[69] 'When the Wind Blows, PF Follows," note 57.

The developers' website also provides some information regarding this process. The page states that the project was developed through open and transparent communication with the community. Further, Mareña Renovables "organizes informative meetings in the various communities" and aims "to consult the communities on social projects they wish to implement, and how the economic benefits obtained from rent and the generation of electricity [to FEMSA and Heineken] can be invested for the good of the community."[70] The site further notes that the project consulted extensively with local communities potentially affected by the project, and the desires of "those communities that decided not to participate in the installation of the turbines" were respected.[71] Unfortunately, obtaining records of this extensive consultation would prove to be difficult, as the "contact us" page of the developer's web site contains the following generic information:

John Doe, Inc.
1234 Main Street Anywhere, USA
Phone: 123 456 7890
Fax: +49 123 456 7891
e-mail: hello@example.com[72]

Activists in the region have a different take on the developers' consultative efforts, and state that the Ikoots community was not informed and did not provide consent for the project, in contravention of law.[73] According to the groups, access to the project territory was granted to the developers by the top official in the land collective in exchange for approximately US$2 million and without a community process for obtaining consent.[74] The group also states that additional access to the territory was granted by public officials in the absence of a community process.[75] Residents have initiated legal action against the developers, saying that the developers did not receive their consent for the project.[76] Opponents have also engaged in acts of civil disobedience.[77] Currently, the project is suspended due to the work of opposition groups barring access to the site.[78] These protests increase the

---

[70] Mareña Renovables, originally available at http://marena-renovables.com.mx/en/marena-renovables/dialogue-and-transparency/, subsequently removed.

[71] Ibid.

[72] Ibid.

[73] Earth First, note 58 (noting that the International Labor Organization Convention 169, to which Mexico is a signatory, provides that the rights of indigenous peoples should be respected).

[74] Ibid.

[75] Ibid.

[76] O. Bellani, "Mexico: Communities Oppose Wind Projects," 14 November 2013, http://lapress.org (stating that a court in Salina Cruz ruled to suspend construction after receiving a request from the governing body of San Dionisio del Mar).

[77] Earth First, note 58.

[78] S. Nielsen, "Vestas Says Mexican Marena Wind Farm Project Delayed Further," 4 December 2013, www.businessweek.com.

348 *Project Finance and Sustainable Development in the Global South*

economic risks to developers. In the absence of a formal process of FPIC, however, they may provide the only leveraging mechanism for affected communities.

3.2.3 La Mata–La Ventosa Wind Project

With only twenty-seven turbines, the La Mata–La Ventosa project is the smallest of the three projects, but it is one of the World Bank's "flagship" Clean Technology Fund[79] projects in Mexico.[80] This project *could* also generate enough energy to power approximately 160,000 homes.[81] However, the US$200 million project will generate power for four Walmart de México subsidiaries.[82] La Mata-La Ventosa is being developed by a special purpose limited liability company, namely Eléctrica del Valle de México S de RL de CV, a subsidiary of the dominant French power company, EDF Energies Nouvelles.[83]

According to the project developer, the project will generate 150 unskilled jobs during construction and ten permanent jobs.[84] The World Bank further claims that the project will provide a monthly income for those who lease their land to developers. Based on prior bad experiences with developers, these claims have been challenged by local residents and activists.[85]

For example, according to the developer, it paid "an annual fixed compensation fee for the land permanently affected" in the construction process.[86] Further, the company promises to compensate residents in the "area of influence" for harm suffered as a result of the project.[87] According to the company, over fifty-seven thirty-year contracts have been entered into that involve *ejido* land and the property of individual residents. Residents counter these promises, pointing to other situations in which "poor, largely non-Spanish speaking indigenous people" were manipulated into "signing tenancy contracts that in practice meant giving up their lands for up to 30 years for a ridiculously low amount of money."[88] Moreover, given the misunderstandings related to the transactions, several farmers had the impression that they could continue to cultivate the land. However, their common crops, such as sorghum and corn, often exceeded the two-meter height limitations for crops imposed by the project contract.[89] These misunderstandings, local activists

---

[79] International Finance Corporation, note 32, para. 31.
[80] O. Reyes, "Power to the People? How World Bank Financed Wind Farms Fail Communities in Mexico," November 2011, www.wdm.org.uk, p. 4.
[81] Ibid.
[82] Ibid.
[83] "EDF Energies Nouvelles Closes Long-Term Financing for La Mata La Ventosa Wind Park in Mexico," Reuters, 14 December 2010.
[84] International Finance Corporation, note 32, para. 13.
[85] Reyes, note 80, p. 13.
[86] Ibid.
[87] Ibid.
[88] Ibid.
[89] Ibid.

say, point to a lack of free, prior, and informed consent.[90] Unfortunately, with respect to La Mata–La Ventosa, there is no record of pre-project consultations with the community that would refute this claim.[91]

All of these projects sit squarely at the heart of indigenous land that bears environmental, cultural, and social significance.[92] Moreover, these projects are all funded in some way by leading development banks. This designation should theoretically provide added protection to communities who disagree with the pro-wind development stance of the Mexican government. Thus far, however, even the development banks have taken the position that only good results can be reaped from the pervasive development occurring in La Ventosa.

3.3 Development Narrative

These projects follow the script of neoliberal development. The private actors receive great deference from the state and development banks due to their expertise within the industry, while the state has taken a minor, even damaging, supporting role by opening the country up to unfettered development. The supposed benefits arising from this arrangement are numerous. They include jobs within the community, economic growth, and above all clean energy.

A video from the Inter-American Development Bank regarding the wind development underway in Oaxaca shows a light-skinned Latina standing in front of a field of wind turbines. With her hair blowing in the wind, she states, "the winds of change are blowing in Oaxaca."[93] The video describes the unexpectedly rich wind resource in Oaxaca and, through an interview with a native Oaxaqueño, how this resource may be an avenue to economic empowerment and jobs.[94] The reality is very different.

Developers who have staked claims in Oaxaca's wind rush have largely brought in their own workers from the United States.[95] Those who have been tapped to work on projects from the community engage primarily in manual labor with no hope of upward mobility. According to one report, the Mareña Renovables project "would generate about 300 construction jobs but only 30 positions for the life of the wind farm, which is projected to be 30 years."[96] Given the amount of disruption to the local community's way of life, including their ability to fish for subsistence, this level of economic development seems untenable. Although the developer also points to compensation of the local community as "rent" for the turbines and a

[90] Ibid.
[91] Ibid.
[92] La Mata-La Ventosa is located in *ejidal* lands of the villages of La Mata and La Ventosa: ibid, p. 9.
[93] Inter-American Development Bank, "Winds of Change in Oaxaca," www.iadb.org.
[94] Ibid.
[95] Reyes, note 80, p. 10.
[96] LaGesse, note 28.

percentage of the overall energy revenue, the specific payment amounts have not been disclosed.[97] In any event, the community has raised concerns that the costs of the project may outweigh its purported benefits, and the project is on hold.

Localized prosperity has yet to materialize, due in part to the structure of the projects. With the exception of payments to the Mexican government and development banks, all benefits flow exclusively to corporate actors. Indeed, the energy produced is sold to corporations such as Walmart, Cemex, Heineken, and Coca-Cola. Debt payments are made to private banks. Once the debt payments are made, profit flows up to the private developers who are the initial investors in the projects. The structure of the projects themselves impedes any hope of authentic community benefits. Proponents of the projects point to one public good: a net positive reduction in greenhouse gas emissions.[98]

The buyers of the energy produced on what was formerly indigenous land are large corporate entities that make money by producing consumer goods. The presumably low costs associated with the wind projects will affect the pricing of energy sold, which ironically could allow them to produce even more consumer products at a cheaper rate. Such products are not necessarily "clean" or "green."

Thus, the so-called green energy projects in the South ultimately benefit large corporate entities in the North while the poor communities in the South derive no direct benefit from them. Not only do they receive few tangible benefits, they also stand to lose their traditional lands and way of life. This seems to reinforce a colonial system of domination. Moreover, this outcome is incompatible with the social pillar of sustainable development.

It could be argued that many of the problematic features of the wind projects themselves may be inherent within the projects, regardless of the way they are financed. The next section contests this assertion and points out how some of the ways in which project finance is conducted may destabilize communities, make it difficult for citizens to have a say in how development occurs, and ultimately undermine sustainable development goals.

4. PROJECT FINANCE AND SUSTAINABLE DEVELOPMENT

If sustainability is to have real meaning, the long-term effects of projects financed utilizing project finance must be evaluated. Preliminary data from La Ventosa reveals that the affected communities are suffering in real ways. Their indigenous way of life has been disrupted or permanently changed. Their ability to engage in subsistence farming or fishing has been impacted. Overall, the region is facing a

---

[97] "When the Wind Blows, PF Follows," note 57.
[98] The press surrounding the financing of the Mareña Renovables project provides one example. See "IDB Approves $72 mn Loan for Wind Farm in Mexico," EVE World News Service (via COMTEX), 25 November 2011 (noting that the project is "aimed at expanding the supply of renewable energy in Mexico and reducing greenhouse gas emissions").

socioecological transformation that could leave its residents in even deeper poverty. Project finance plays a role in this disruption. In particular, the structure of the transactions gives rise to a moral hazard that allows key players to avoid and externalize the risks associated with their activities. For subsistence communities in the global South like the Isthmus, this results in a bad bargain. For society at large, relying on a mechanism like project finance to usher in a new era of "green" energy reflects a gamble.

4.1 High Risk to Communities

One of the most consistent concerns raised by communities in the Isthmus relates to land leases.[99] Many residents who are non-Spanish speakers entered into contracts with subsidiaries of wind developers. These contracts, written in Spanish, allowed for the building of wind turbines or some other wind farm-related activity. In some cases, the contracts were not provided to the lessor. In others, the terms of the contracts were themselves unfair. For example, one lease provides for $120 per year per hectare, for twenty-five years, renewable at the lessee's option.[100] This example comports with other accounts of the leases reported in the popular press.[101] This essentially provides a lease in perpetuity; even after the expiration of the lease, the windmills will remain. The land used will be gone forever. Taking this long-term view, the loss to the farmer far outweighs the minimal compensation he receives.[102] He has been permanently dispossessed of his ancestral territory.

Project finance contributes to this dispossession. The use of the SPE further limits the farmer's ability to seek redress for potential harm arising from the lease. In this regard, project finance is unique. Although a standard corporate financing transaction involving a major project developer would involve the same sophisticated parties, the structure of project finance increases the overall opacity of the transaction, which decreases an affected farmer's ability to recover.

By design, developers remove themselves from the locus of risky activity in the project. This means that the primary parties through which developers act are subsidiaries, which themselves are often difficult to identify. This makes meaningful negotiation a challenging task for local, unsophisticated – and often unrepresented – residents.

The dispossession of rural indigenous farmers in Oaxaca through the myriad, complex contractual arrangements from these projects should give us pause. The

---

[99] See e.g. "Oaxaca: Rural Mexican Communities Protest Wind Farms," Indigenous Peoples Issues & Resources (Blog) available at 2013 WLNR 14999742 (noting that the contracts involving land are one-sided and have been rented "for next to nothing," and that the "land produces more than what the companies are offering").

[100] Baker, note 5 at 286.

[101] Ibid, note 71.

[102] See note 99.

352   *Project Finance and Sustainable Development in the Global South*

gradual displacement of residents of the Isthmus into urban areas will disrupt their way of life, but it could affect the North in less obvious ways. Indigenous communities are the keepers of traditional knowledge. This knowledge will become increasingly valuable as the extremes of climate change place strain on global ecosystems.

4.2 *Unsustainable for the Environment*

In addition to the loss of traditional knowledge, these wind projects have the potential to create significant environmental damage.[103] The density of the wind farm development could affect the water table and the flight path of migratory birds.[104] The Isthmus is a dry region, but local farmers have adopted techniques over time to best utilize the limited water available. Residents and engineers argue that the more than 200 tons of concrete poured for each wind turbine could reduce the overall permeability of the soil, leading to crop flooding and the gradual depletion of the water table.[105]

The Isthmus also serves as a key location for migratory birds. Nearly six million birds, including thirty-two endangered and nine indigenous species, fly through the region on an annual basis.[106] The impact from the pervasive development in the area is unknown, but the IFC fails to recognize the cumulative impact of these projects. It categorized the La Mata–La Ventosa project as a Category B project. Such projects have "limited adverse social or environmental impacts that are few in number, generally site-specific, largely reversible and readily addressed through mitigation measures."[107] While each project, standing alone, may have a minimal environmental impact, cumulatively their impact may prove devastating.

Actors engaged in activity that affects an ecosystem should be made to pay for any damage they cause. The nature of project finance makes this type of accountability difficult and may make cumulative impacts difficult to register. As discussed in the next section, these structural issues also limit avenues for legal remedies.

4.3 *Lack of Domestic Accountability*

The structure of project finance transactions makes it difficult for individuals or communities to hold actors accountable for the harm they cause. The use of SPEs contributes to these difficulties, and the lack of a mechanism for redress exacerbates this problem.

The nature of the wind energy development in Oaxaca leaves residents with no particular unified party against whom to lodge complaints. It is pervasive and

---

[103] See note 99.
[104] Baker, note 5 at 287.
[105] Ibid.
[106] Ibid.
[107] Ibid at 288 (citing IFC and discussing water and impact on birds).

conducted by multiple private actors. The widespread development, coupled with the lack of transparency, creates genuine confusion with respect to accountability. One developer may have several projects underway, each operated by a different SPE.[108] Residents seeking to negotiate are left to negotiate individually with each entity, rather than the parent company responsible for the overall development. Often residents are unable to obtain detailed information regarding the development, which is considered not subject to public disclosure.

Moreover, from a community perspective, there are inefficiencies built into the project finance structure. Although the individuals engaged in high-level management at one SPE are also engaged in management at other projects, residents are forced to negotiate separately and with multiple entities. The structure of project finance-backed projects requires this type of complexity and redundancy, whereas a project financed by a developer without the use of a SPE would reduce complexity and give affected community members more direct access to the developer.

Even if the correct actors are identified for negotiation, the project finance transaction structure allows SPEs to slip through the gaps of accountability. Struggling or failing projects may be managed in two primary ways. First, the SPE may declare bankruptcy and the project may be turned over to the banks. The banks could sell off the project assets to minimize loss to the banks. Second, the banks could also sell the entire project as a going concern to another entity. In either case, the original SPE would no longer be accountable to the community.

In the first case, the creditors of the bankrupt SPE would line up for payment, often receiving pennies on their original loan to the entity. Victims of tort, as unsecured creditors, are unlikely to receive anything, which exposes another problematic aspect of project finance. It leaves victims very little by way of recovery. In the second scenario, the original creditors would aim to negotiate with the new project entity regarding debt service and other obligations entered into by the prior project SPE. Victims of tort, particularly in a place like Oaxaca, are unlikely to have the bargaining power needed to negotiate with the new company. Their claims would thus likely go unresolved.

This discussion highlighted the structural aspects of project finance that render it difficult for community members to access justice. Project finance also lacks legibility within the international legal system.

4.4 *International Accountability: Tension at the Public–Private Border*

The privileging of private actors within the neoliberal development framework obscures the particularly damaging effects of their activities. Although the field of

---

[108] Acciona, for example, is the developer of at least three different wind projects in Oaxaca: "ACCIONA Completes the Assembly of Three Wind Parks in Mexico Totaling 306 MW," Acciona, 27 September 2011.

corporate social responsibility has adopted voluntary frameworks to limit negative impacts of private activity, the limitations of international human rights law and international law generally leave private actors unaccountable for the harm they cause. This section discusses the Equator Principles, and the difficulties of reaching project finance actors within international law.

The Equator Principles are a voluntary set of principles developed in 2003 to respond to the rampant risks that accompany project finance transactions. Developed by a group of banks, the principles attempt to address social and environmental risks through monitoring and reporting. The banks that sign on to the principles thereby agree to hold their financed projects accountable under the Equator Principles framework. Several early critiques of the principles focused on the ambiguity and non-binding nature of the principles.[109] Subsequent empirical examination of the principles has revealed that they have limited impact on stemming the harm experienced by communities.[110] The principles reflect an implicit acknowledgment that project finance transactions are risky, but the architects of the voluntary framework failed to change the incentives for risk-taking.

Project finance exists in a gray area where private actors who are engaged in development elude the types of legal accountability mechanisms that would bind a state. Under international human rights law, states are the primary duty-holders,[111] and can be held accountable to citizens in international legal fora.[112] The UN has made efforts to close this gap through the development of the protect, respect and remedy framework reflected in the Guiding Principles on Business and Human Rights. The Guiding Principles recognize the duty of the host state to protect the human rights of its citizens by third parties, including private enterprises; the obligation of private enterprises to respect the human rights of local citizens within a host country; and the need for affected communities and individuals to have effective remedies.[113]

Despite these developments and the effort to place a voluntary burden on private actors to "respect" human rights, contemporary international law still only recognizes states as its principal subjects. Indeed, the most progressive of frameworks developed to address the existing gaps in international law – the Guiding Principles – explicitly states that it creates no new rights or obligations under

[109] See R. F. Lawrence and W. L. Thomas, "The Equator Principles and Project Finance: Sustainability in Practice?" (2004) 19 *Natural Resources and Environment* 20.

[110] Baker, note 5 at 318.

[111] S. R. Ratner, "Corporations and Human Rights: A Theory of Legal Responsibility" (2001) 111 *Yale Law Journal* 443 at 462 (noting that states and individuals are the actors contemplated as duty holders under international human rights law).

[112] *cf.* ibid at 470 (noting that in some cases the Inter-American Court of Human Rights has found that private activity can give rise to international human rights violations when the state tolerates abuse by the private actor, but that the responsibility remains with the state).

[113] UN General Assembly, *Report of the Special Representative of the Secretary-General on the Issue of Human Rights and Transnational Corporations and Other Business Enterprises*, John Ruggie, 21 March 2011, A/HRC/17/31, Annex.

international law.[114] Corporate actors thus lack true visibility – and accountability – beyond state borders. This lack of accountability makes the use of project finance by private actors as a means for financing "sustainable" renewable energy projects particularly problematic.

5. CONCLUSION

When using project finance, renewable energy projects contain many of the inherent structural flaws of more traditional projects. Developers are incentivized to increase their return on investment by taking risks; community voices with local knowledge are shut out; and, when concerns arise, the key actors escape visibility and liability under both domestic and international law.

The structure of project finance also invites risk-taking by private actors. Further, it undermines sustainability by disenfranchising affected third parties and limiting accountability for social and environmental harm. True sustainable development will incorporate the meaningful participation of all affected parties, and preserve the ecological and cultural heritage of communities. Project finance, with its complexity, built-in incentives, and primary features, appears ill suited for this role. The imperative of sustainability requires more.

[114] Ibid, p. 1.

17

International Environmental Law and Sovereign Wealth Funds

Benjamin J. Richardson

1. INTRODUCTION

The lightly regulated global economy, catering to business corporations, financiers, and other entrepreneurs of the private sector, is increasingly home to another actor, but from the public realm. In recent decades, sovereign wealth funds (SWFs) have become a salient actor in the global marketplace, especially in the global South. SWFs are state-owned funds that invest financial assets to achieve governments' macroeconomic objectives. Recent commentary on SWFs locates their global power and legitimacy largely within their adoption of Western investment models and market orthodoxy, rather than seeking to usurp it with a radically different economic agenda based on social justice or environmental sustainability.[1] The success of SWFs in emerging economies such as those proliferating in the Gulf states and East Asia is similarly tied to their embrace of Western economic doctrines. SWFs' growing presence in financial markets and resulting influence on economic development, coupled with their institutional status as public entities, make SWFs increasingly relevant to international environmental governance.

While international environmental law has yet to discipline SWFs or be considered a material factor in their governance, some scrutiny of the environmental and social performance of SWFs is coming from the merging global movement for socially responsible investing (SRI), which seeks to align investing with social and environmental considerations. SRI, which is gaining momentum in a number of developing countries, is a phenomenon that draws attention to both the impacts of investing on the environment and the impacts of the environment on investing. The salience of these connections has been recognized by some SWFs, several of which have legal mandates to practice SRI. These include the Norwegian Government Pension Fund – Global, the French Pension Reserve Funds, and

---

[1] G. L. Clark, A. D. Dixon, and A. Monk, *Sovereign Wealth Funds: Legitimacy, Governance and Global Power* (Princeton: Princeton University Press, 2013).

the New Zealand Superannuation Fund. Several others, such as the Canada Pension Plan, have adopted policies to stimulate action in the realm of SRI. Many SWFs have also been established in developing countries, especially in the Gulf States and East Asia, with 40 percent of global SWFs' assets from Asia and 35 per cent from the Middle East.[2] With these trends, some observers envision SWFs bringing a greater public interest perspective to financial investing, including to further sustainable development.[3] For now, this trend is most likely to arise with those Northern SWFs subject to SRI legal mandates. Many of these SWFs have created positive economic impacts in developing countries by "injecting capital into local companies and emerging countries' projects."[4] But, unlike the trend toward SRI found in some Northern SWFs, those of the global South have so far largely ignored SRI. One can only speculate as to the reasons for this disparity, but they are likely due to the more established SRI markets in the North from which pressures developed on SWFs in these regions to consider SRI.

While in theory financial returns should, over the long term, be dependent on environmentally responsible development, in practice many SWFs (and other financial institutions) have tended to treat environmental issues as only tangentially relevant to investment performance. Furthermore, the recent natural resources commodities boom has fueled the riches of many SWFs, especially those in developing countries.[5] This bias against or indifference to sustainability owes to a variety of factors, including the underlying short-term orientation of financial markets, the paucity of quantifiable data on the financial salience of environmental issues, and the continuing business case for investment in many environmentally dubious ventures such as fossil fuel industries.[6] Consequently, any legal mandate to practice SRI may be implemented perfunctorily, rather than treated as an integral cog in a SWF's operations.

The application of international environmental law to SWFs is thus important to ensure that their investing supports environmentally prudent activities. This chapter investigates how such law may influence SWFs and the scope for holding them accountable to it. Given the number of SWFs, the chapter is necessarily highly selective, and only examines the two SWFs with the most emphatic legal mandates to practice SRI – the Norwegian Government Pension Fund – Global (NGPF-G) and the New Zealand Superannuation Fund (NZSF). In assessing the

---

[2] V. Shunmugam, "Sovereign Wealth Funds and Emerging Economies: Reap the Good; Leave the Bad" (2012) 5(2) *Macroeconomics and Finance in Emerging Market Economies* 281 at 285.

[3] United Nations Environment Programme Finance Initiative (UNEP-FI) and UK Social Investment Forum (UKSIF), *Responsible Investment in Focus: How Leading Public Pension Funds are Meeting the Challenge* (UNEP-FI, 2007); Clark et al., note 1.

[4] J. Santiso, "Sovereign Development Funds: Key Financial Actors of the Shifting Wealth of Nations," OECD Emerging Markets Network Working Paper, 2008, p. 13.

[5] "Sovereign Wealth Funds Growing 24% Annually," Dow Jones Newswires, April 29, 2008.

[6] See B. J. Richardson, "Being Virtuous and Prosperous: SRI's Conflicting Goals" (2010) 92(1) *Journal of Business Ethics* 21.

influence of international environmental law on these SWFs, the chapter addresses three questions: (i) to what extent and how do the SWFs' investment decisions acknowledge international environmental law and related soft law standards; (ii) are SWFs accountable under international law for their environmental performance; and (iii) what scope is there under national law, including international laws implemented domestically, to hold SWFs accountable for their environmental performance? The answers to these questions can help us understand the role that SWFs can play in promoting sustainable development in the global South through their economic investments.

The ensuing argument is that although international environmental law can cast a normative shadow over the investment decisions of SWFs by providing guidance to fund managers on societal expectations about desirable environmental practices, there is meager scope to hold SWFs formally accountable under international environmental law, whether directly or via domestic law. The highly discretionary and perceived expert nature of SWFs' decision-making renders their decisions on consideration of environmental issues largely beyond the purview of courts. Ultimately, the best route to hold SWFs accountable is through elaboration of a more exacting legislative framework and greater public oversight. At an international level, corresponding changes could also be made through an agreement that goes beyond the rather parsimonious and non-binding Santiago Principles.

The remainder of this chapter focuses on two examples – the Norwegian and New Zealand SWFs – in order to highlight how international environmental law may influence the SRI practices of SWFs. At the time of writing this analysis, none of the SWFs established in the global South have adopted formal legal mandates for SRI, and none appear to practice SRI in any significant manner. After considering these two case studies, the chapter canvasses the scope for legal accountability of these SWFs' environmental performance, first under international law and then under domestic law. The following section introduces a bit of background on SWFs and SRI before turning to the case examples.

2. BACKGROUND TO SWFS AND SOCIAL INVESTING

States have been establishing SWFs since the 1950s, and approximately seventy-five are found throughout the world today. The Sovereign Wealth Fund Institute (SWFI) defines a SWF as "a state-owned investment fund or entity that is commonly established from balance of payments surpluses, official foreign currency operations, the proceeds of privatizations, governmental transfer payments, fiscal surpluses, and/or receipts resulting from resource exports."[7] SWFs are usually created as separate legal entities with plenary investment and financial management powers

---

[7] Sovereign Wealth Fund Institute (SWFI), "What is an SWF?," www.swfinstitute.org.

enumerated by a specific constitutive law.[8] Over the past half-century, SWFs have surged in both number and size, seemingly defying a supposed era in which many governments have deregulated or minimized their presence in the market (at least before the 2008 global financial crisis).[9] The SWFI's data calculate SWFs' collective assets at about US$6.8 trillion as of October 2014.[10] As a proportion of global financial securities, SWFs' share in 2012 was approximately 2 percent (holding some US$5 trillion of $225 trillion in global financial assets).[11]

This financial clout has made some observers wary that SWFs could surreptitiously insinuate state political interests through foreign investment in nationally sensitive and strategic economic sectors.[12] For the global South, which has suffered from a history of colonial and neocolonial despotism, this concern is not academic. As Drenzer explains, "[t]here are several means through which [SWFs] could, theoretically, influence the policies and capabilities of recipient countries. The most direct means could take place through direct ownership and control of strategic sectors or critical infrastructure. SWFs could sabotage the firms they purchase, crippling the recipient country's capabilities. Leverage could also be exercised through the threat of investment withdrawal."[13] Alternatively, "[l]everage can also be exercised more subtly, through the cooptation of domestic interests within recipient countries."[14] But as Drenzer explains, much of this concern is directed to SWFs owned by developing countries, such as China, that tend to govern less transparently.

These concerns extend to the potential adulteration of SWFs' financial goals with SRI practices.[15] The funds' financial performance might consequently suffer,[16]

---

[8] E. L. van der Zee, "In between Two Societal Actors: The Responsibilities of SWFs towards Human Rights and Climate Change," Masters thesis, Utrecht University (2012), p. 12.

[9] A. H. B. Monk, "Sovereignty in the Era of Global Capitalism: The Rise of Sovereign Wealth Funds and the Power of Finance" (2011) 43(8) *Environment and Planning A* 1813; R. Beck and M. Fidora, "The Impact of Sovereign Wealth Funds on Global Financial Markets" (2008) 43 (6) *Intereconomics* 349.

[10] SWFI, "Sovereign Wealth Fund Rankings," www.swfinstitute.org.

[11] McKinsey and Company, "Financial Globalization: Retreat or Reset?," March 2013, www. mckinsey.com.

[12] L. C. Backer, "Sovereign Investing in Times of Crisis" (2010–11) 19 *Transnational Law and Contemporary Problems* 3 at 11; E. M. Truman, *Sovereign Wealth Funds: The Need for Greater Transparency and Accountability* (Peterson Institute for International Economics, 2007).

[13] D. W. Drezner, "Sovereign Wealth Funds and the (in)Security of Global Finance" (2008) 62 (1) *Journal of International Affairs* 115 at 118.

[14] Ibid at 119.

[15] G. L. Clark and A. Monk, "The Norwegian Government Pension Fund: Ethics Over Efficiency" (2010) 3(1) *Rotman International Journal of Pension Management* 14 at 17; L. C. Backer, "Sovereign Wealth Funds as Regulatory Chameleons: The Norwegian Sovereign Wealth Funds and Public Global Governance through Private Global Investment" (2010) 41 (2) *Georgetown Journal of International Law* 425 at 453.

[16] G. L Clark and A. Monk, "Partisan Politics and Bureaucratic Encroachment: The Principles and Policies of Pension Reserve Fund Design and Governance" (2004) 3(2) *Journal of Pension Economics and Finance* 233 at 233.

and a dual, potentially conflicting mandate might make it difficult to hold SWF managers accountable. To illustrate, a 2009 survey of 146 fund managers having routine dealings with SWFs reported that most "did not think governments should have any influence over investment decisions despite the fact that SWFs are managing governments' money."[17]

Such concerns perhaps misunderstand SRI's changing purpose as a financial due diligence strategy to ensure that financially material social and environmental concerns are managed in order to achieve optimal investment returns. Historically, SRI meant virtuous investing predicated on maximizing ethical concerns.[18] The fair trade movement and green consumerism are other variants of the same phenomenon, whereby people seek to align their economic decisions with their moral compasses. Social investors draw upon a variety of methods, the mainstay of which has been screening investments in certain industries or companies because of the characteristics of their products or operations, or engaging with businesses to encourage them to improve their behavior.

The SRI movement has surged to prominence since the early 2000s in a world troubled by economic and environmental concerns. The trend is reflected in the throng of signatories to the United Nations Principles for Responsible Investment (UNPRI), the world's premier voluntary code for SRI, as endorsed by several SWFs and some 1,350 signatories as of March 2015. But this "surge" has come about by shifting the rationale of SRI from ethical to financial considerations. As mainstream institutional investors such as pension plans have begun to embrace SRI for pragmatic reasons, they have distanced themselves from the overtly ethical stance championed by some social investors, primarily because such conduct is perceived to be financially imprudent and incongruous with their fiduciary responsibility to their beneficiaries. This "business case" mode of SRI is increasingly coming to be known as "ESG analysis," referring to the potential financial salience of "environmental, social and governance" (ESG) issues.[19]

At present, SRI has gained a strong market niche in Western Europe, North America and Oceania, with some industry-sponsored research boasting that between 10 and 20 percent of investment portfolios are now managed for SRI purposes.[20] These surveys almost certainly exaggerate the market's size, due to

---

[17] G. L. Clark and A. Monk, "The Oxford Survey of Sovereign Wealth Funds' Asset Managers," Working Paper, July 1, 2009, p. 1.

[18] A. Domini and P. Kinder, *Ethical Investing* (Reading: Addison Wesley, 1984); R. Sparkes, *The Ethical Investor* (London: HarperCollins, 1995).

[19] H. Jemel-Fornetty, C. Louche, and D. Bourghelle, "Changing the Dominant Convention: The Role of Emerging Initiatives in Mainstreaming ESG," in W. Sun, C. Louche, and R. Perez (eds.), *Finance and Sustainability: Towards a New Paradigm? A Post-Crisis Agenda* (Bingley: Emerald Books, 2011), p. 87.

[20] European Social Investment Forum (Eurosif), *European SRI Study 2012* (Eurosif, 2013); U.S. Social Investment Forum (US-SIF), *2010 Report on Socially Responsible Investing Trends in the United States* (US-SIF, 2010).

rather broad and indiscriminate definitions of SRI that include much financial activity that resembles conventional investment. Nonetheless, the SRI market niche has grown considerably from its fringe status before 2000. Part of this growth is attributable to the practices of some SWFs. Geographically, the SRI industry has also spread and diversified, taking root in a number of emerging economies, including India and South Africa.[21]

The growth of SRI in the latter regions, which builds on the older microfinance movement, has been accompanied by growing appreciation of its potential to help alleviate poverty and promote enduring social and economic development, and the possibility that SWFs can play a facilitatory role.[22] Yet commentators have cautioned that:

> SWFs are not donors, they are not pursuing MDGs (Millennium Development Goals) and are not held to development rhetoric or practice [...] They require returns, risk adjusted diversification and, above all, good investments. But through their investing in developing and emerging countries, they contribute to development: generating employment, providing capital for infrastructure and supplying long term money for diverse industries from telecoms to banking services.[23]

The following case examples from Norway and New Zealand illustrate the potential and limitations of SWFs to be vehicles for financing sustainable development in the global South and other regions.

3. NORWEGIAN GOVERNMENT PENSION FUND – GLOBAL (NGPF-G)

The NGPF-G has been a pioneer of SRI among the SWF community, and has been governed since 2004 by a statutory framework that directs it to consider specific social and environmental criteria.[24] These criteria provide a framework for the incorporation of international environmental law standards into its financial investing decisions. The use of international standards for its SRI decisions can help mitigate the potential concern of some developing countries that the Norwegian SWF imposes its own, Western environmental values.

The Norwegian SWF's experience with SRI began in 2001, when a trial environment fund within its portfolio was established for investing in companies in emerging economies in the global South that met environmental performance criteria. In 2004, regulations to formalize and structure the SRI activities of the NGPF-G were adopted. These regulations did not aim to make the NGPF-G an

---

[21] S. Giamporcaro, "Sustainable and Responsible Investment in Emerging Markets: Integrating Environmental Risks in the South African Investment Industry" (2011) 1(2) *Journal of Sustainable Finance and Investment* 121.

[22] C. Ochoa and P. Keenan, "The Human Rights Potential of Sovereign Wealth Funds" (2009) 40 *Georgetown Journal of International Law* 1151.

[23] Santiso, note 4, p. 14.

[24] *Act of the Government Pension Fund (Lov om Statens pensjonsfond)*, 123/2005.

362   *International Environmental Law and Sovereign Wealth Funds*

agent of sustainable development, but rather to avoid its *complicity* in gross or systematic breaches of ethical norms relating to human rights and the environment. The Graver Committee, which drafted the regulations, relied on international agreements on environmental protection and human rights that Norway supports as the source of such ethical precepts.[25]

That the NGPF-G may implicate Norway in any investments contrary to international law is reinforced by how the governance of the fund is closely enmeshed within the Norwegian state. The Ministry of Finance handles overall management of the fund, including SRI decisions to divest from any entity. Norges Bank, Norway's central bank, has operational control, and through its shareholding it undertakes any SRI-focused engagement and dialogue with companies. The Bank has devolved many of its responsibilities to Norges Bank Investment Management (NBIM).[26] A government-appointed Council on Ethics advises on possible SRI decisions, particularly those relating to the exclusion of companies.

The Council on Ethics plays a pivotal role in the administration of the SRI regulations, and provides a forum to consider international legal norms in evaluating the behavior of companies and other entities considered for investment.[27] The five members of the advisory council make recommendations to the Ministry of Finance on divestments, with wide discretion in passing judgment on serious human rights violations, gross corruption, severe environmental damage, and general violations of fundamental ethical norms.[28] The council relies not only on international treaties ratified by Norway, but also on soft law standards approved by Norway such as the UN Global Compact. In November 2013, a government-appointed commission recommended the abolition of the Council on Ethics, and the transfer of some of its functions to the Norges Bank.[29] The rationale for this advice, which has not been implemented at the time of writing, seemed to be: "[o]ther large sovereign wealth funds [...] do not have such an approach to responsible investing. Yet, even within our sample of funds, it is clear that responsible investment has no singular motivation and that there is no single strategy or set of approaches that is followed universally."[30]

The SRI regulations governing the NGPF-G, which were revised in 2010, comprise the *Guidelines for Observation and Exclusion from the Government*

---

[25] Ministry of Finance, "The Report from the Graver Committee," July 11, 2003, www.regjerin gen.no.

[26] Norges Bank Investment Management (NBIM), www.nbim.no.

[27] *Regulations on the Management of the Government Pension Fund – Global* (2006), s. 8(1).

[28] G. Nystuen, A. Follesdal, and O. Mestad, "Introduction," in G. Nystuen, A. Follesdal, and O. Mestad (eds.), *Human Rights Corporate Complicity and Disinvestment* (Cambridge: Cambridge University Press, 2011), p. 8.

[29] E. Dimson, I. Kreutzer, R. Lake, H. Sjo, and L. Starks, *Responsible Investment and the Norwegian Government Pension Fund Global* (Oslo: Strategy Council, November 2013).

[30] Ibid, p. 6.

Pension Fund Global's Investment Universe[31] (Guidelines I) and the *Guidelines for Norges Bank's Work on Responsible Management and Active Ownership* (Guidelines II).[32] The terminology of "guidelines" is misleading, as the regulations are legally binding. Guidelines I require the NGPF-G, on the advice of the Council, to exclude producers of specified harmful products, including tobacco and weapons, deemed to violate fundamental humanitarian principles.[33] Exclusion is also contemplated where "there is an unacceptable risk that the company contributes to or is responsible for" itemized concerns including "serious or systematic human rights violations" and "severe environmental damage."[34] Within these categories, which already pitch a high threshold of harm, the Council's "aim is to target [the] worst case[s]."[35] Consequently, some unethical behavior will be overlooked. The Guidelines' threshold of "severe environmental damage" is too high to capture much environmental degradation such as ongoing greenhouse gas emissions, whose effect is piecemeal and only significant cumulatively.

Whereas international environmental law focuses on the behavior of states, the SRI regulations ultimately address mainly non-state actors, particularly business corporations. They also depart from international environmental law by taking into account possible future harmful behavior rather than past misconduct. Guidelines I elaborate that the Ministry may take into consideration "the probability of future violations of ethical norms, the severity and extent of the norm violations, the connection between the norm violations and the company in which the Fund is invested, and whether the company does what may reasonably be expected to reduce the risk of future violations of norms within a reasonable time frame."[36] Positive actions taken by a company to safeguard the environment may also be taken into account,[37] and companies excluded may be readmitted to the NGPF-G if their behavior improves.

Guidelines II, supervised by Norges Bank, reflect the assumption held by many in the SRI industry that long-term financial returns depend on an environmentally sustainable economy.[38] While Guidelines II require the Bank to achieve the "highest possible return" from the NGPF-G,[39] this objective is "dependent on

---

[31] Council on Ethics, "Guidelines for the Observation and Exclusion of Companies from the Government Pension Fund Global's Investment Universe," www.regjeringen.no (hereinafter Guidelines I).

[32] Norges Bank Investment Management (NBIM), "Management Mandate for the Government Pension Fund Global," www.nbim.no (hereinafter Guidelines II).

[33] Guidelines I, note 31, ss. 2(1)-(2).

[34] Ibid, s. 2(3).

[35] Nystuen et al., note 28, p. 9.

[36] Guidelines I, note 31, s. 2(4).

[37] Ibid, s. 2(5).

[38] The Norwegian Ministry of Finance has explicitly endorsed this thesis: *The Management of the Government Pension Fund in 2009* (Report No. 10 (2009–2010) to the Storting, 2010), 133–136.

[39] Guidelines II, note 32, s. 1–2(3).

364   *International Environmental Law and Sovereign Wealth Funds*

sustainable development in economic, environmental and social terms [and] well-functioning, legitimate and effective markets."[40] Relatedly, Guidelines II oblige it to integrate good corporate governance and environmental and social issues in its investments,[41] and to foster robust international standards in responsible management and active ownership.[42] These standards dovetail with the ethos of corporate social responsibility and sustainable development found in numerous international codes and agreements that emphasize the connections between business success and stewardship of the natural environment.[43]

The foregoing provisions suggest the NGPF-G has some ability to be a tool of international environmental governance through divestments and engagement with companies, which may be particularly useful within developing countries where local environmental controls can be relatively weak. The NGPF-G has divested from companies producing cluster bombs (e.g. Lockheed Martin) and nuclear weapons components (e.g. Boeing), those breaching human rights and labor standards (e.g. Walmart), and those causing severe environmental damage (e.g. Freeport-McMoRan). The latter divestment was triggered by concerns about Freeport's mining activities in Indonesia. As of October 2014, the NGPF-G had excluded sixty-four companies, a tiny fraction of the some 8,300 companies it holds.[44] Other businesses may also be divested from the portfolio as a result of the actions of the NBIM; in 2012 it divested from twenty-three palm oil producers, mainly in Southeast Asia, because of concerns of tropical deforestation.[45] Even if a business is not specifically targeted by the NGPF-G, the fund's often well-publicized SRI interventions actions may have a deterrent effect. The fund's ostracism of Walmart, for example, precipitated a visit from the U.S. ambassador to Norway.[46] A difficulty the fund faces in scrutinizing all NGPF-G investments is that the Council on Ethics has a support staff of eight and an annual budget of NOK11.6 million (as of 2012).[47] The use of external consultants to monitor companies on behalf of the Council improves its capacity to be a kind of environmental "watchdog," though there will invariably remain gaps in its knowledge and understanding of corporate behavior.

The NGPF-G can also communicate international environmental and human rights norms to companies through its engagement with firms' management, and

---

[40] Ibid, s. 2–1(1).

[41] Ibid, s. 2–1(2).

[42] Ibid, s. 2–3.

[43] B. Horrigan, *Corporate Social Responsibility in the 21st Century* (Northampton: Edward Elgar Publishing, 2011); V. Nanda and G. Pring (eds.), *International Environmental Law and Policy for the 21st Century*, 2nd ed. (Leiden: Martinus Nijhoff, 2013).

[44] Norwegian Ministry of Finance, "Companies Excluded from Investment Universe," www.regjeringen.no.

[45] NBIM, *Government Pension Fund Global: Annual Report 2012* (Oslo: NBIM, 2013), p. 35.

[46] M. Landler, "Norway Backs Its Ethics with Cash," *New York Times*, May 4, 2007.

[47] Council on Ethics for the Government Pension Fund Global, *Annual Report 2011* (Oslo: Council on Ethics, 2012), p. 10.

by channeling investment to businesses demonstrating best practices. The NBIM is responsible for sponsoring and supporting shareholder resolutions, proxy voting, and informal corporate engagement on SRI and other issues of concern to the NGPF-G.[48] The NBIM's normative compass for such engagement is based on the UN Global Compact and the OECD's Principles of Corporate Governance and Guidelines for Multinational Enterprises.[49] These voluntary codes incorporate an expectation that businesses will abide by national and international legal standards. The OECD's Guidelines for Multinational Enterprises, for example, declares: "[e]nterprises should, within the framework of laws [...] in the countries in which they operate, and in consideration of relevant international agreements [...] take due account of the need to protect the environment."[50] The reference to international agreements can be important when local environmental laws are insufficient or not enforced – an endemic problem in some developing countries. A further way that the NGPF-G can leverage change is through its program of *positive* environmental investment, which presently targets firms pioneering climate-friendly energy efficiency, carbon capture and storage, water technology, and waste management.[51] The program is worth about NOK20 billion to be invested mainly in developing countries between 2010 and 2015 (equivalent to less than 1 percent of the NGPF-G's portfolio).[52] For example, protection of tropical forests from deforestation is an important part of this investment program.

The NGPF-G's capacity to internalize international environmental norms systematically across its portfolio is constrained by its imperative to generate investment returns in a global economy that contains too few investment opportunities that are truly ecologically sustainable. Consequently, the NGPF-G sometimes faces trade-offs between maximizing financial returns and investing in environmentally dubious businesses. Its investment regulations do not guide how to resolve any trade-offs between such considerations.[53] The Ministry of Finance believes "[s]olid financial returns over time depend on sustainable development in economic, environmental and social terms."[54] Nonetheless, the Ministry of Finance also acknowledges: "[i]n some cases, the concerns of ensuring long-term financial returns and taking widely shared values into account will coincide, but not always.

---

[48] See A. M. Halvorssen, "Using The Norwegian Sovereign Wealth Fund's Ethical Guidelines as a Model for Investors" (2011) 8(2–3) *European Company Law* 88.

[49] NBIM, note 45, p. 32.

[50] OECD, *Guidelines for Multinational Enterprises* (Paris: OECD, 2008), p. 19.

[51] T. Myklebust, "The Norwegian Government Pension Fund: Moving Forward on Responsible Investing and Governance" (2010) 3(1) *Rotman Journal of International Pension Management* 20 at 21.

[52] Ministry of Finance, *On the Management of the Government Pension Fund in 2008* (Report No. 20 (2008–2009) to the Storting, 2009), p. 11.

[53] Ibid, pp. 11, 16; see also Secretary General T. Eriksen, *The Norwegian Petroleum Sector and the Government Pension Fund-Global* (Oslo: Ministry of Finance, 2006), p. 23.

[54] Norwegian Ministry of Finance, *The Management of the Government Pension Fund in 2010* (Report No. 15 (2010–2011) to the Storting, 2011), p. 3.

366   *International Environmental Law and Sovereign Wealth Funds*

For example, the Fund will not invest in companies that are in gross breach of fundamental ethical norms, regardless of the effect this will have on returns."[55]

Overall, the SRI practices of the NGPF-G reflect a delicate balance between the need to avoid the most unethical and problematic companies and participating in global financial markets in the pursuit of profitable returns. The NGPF-G's governance framework has so far left largely unquestioned the structure of finance capitalism, yet it creates a space for critical reflection through the Council on Ethics and the corporate engagement practices of Norges Bank that could potentially question that economic system's impact on long-term sustainability. International environmental law informs the work of these institutions by setting normative parameters for acceptable investments. But only the most environmentally problematic companies face close scrutiny.

4. NEW ZEALAND SUPERANNUATION FUND (NZSF)

The environmental performance of companies and other entities in the global South and other parts of the world has also been of relevance to the SRI policies of New Zealand's SWF. It differs from the Norwegian SWF in a number of crucial ways – it is a much smaller fund, it has a less prescriptive regulatory framework, and it has relatively greater independence from the sitting government. Created by the New Zealand Superannuation and Retirement Income Act 2001 to invest government financial contributions to address this demographic trend, the fund began operations in September 2003 and invests principally in corporate securities, commodities, and fixed interest in both local and global markets including in emerging economies. The NZSF statutory framework seeks to insulate the management of the fund – handled by the Guardians of New Zealand Superannuation – from political interference. The Guardians possess a broad plenary power to invest, subject only to specified statutory restrictions.[56] While the Minister of Finance can issue directions to the Guardians regarding the government's expectations to the NZSF's performance, the Minister cannot give any direction that is "inconsistent with the duty to invest the Fund on a prudent, commercial basis."[57]

The Guardians' governing board consists of up to seven members appointed by the Cabinet on the recommendation of the Minister of Finance.[58] Only persons with "substantial experience, training, and expertise in the management of financial investments" may be board members.[59] While the Guardians exercise

---

[55] Ibid, p. 15.
[56] *New Zealand Superannuation and Retirement Income Act 2001*, 2001/84, s. 49(4), with specified restrictions in ss. 58, 59 and 64.
[57] Ibid, s. 64(1).
[58] Ibid, ss. 54(1), 56.
[59] Ibid, s. 55(1)(a).

overall control over the Fund, they have, like other SWFs, outsourced much work to external fund managers who can offer expertise on investment and development issues in other jurisdictions, including in emerging economies.[60]

The NZSF legal mandate to practice SRI is much less prescriptive than that of the NGPF. The Guardians' primary duty is to "invest the Fund on a prudent, commercial basis [...] in a manner consistent with (a) best-practice portfolio management, and (b) maximizing return without undue risk to the Fund as a whole, and (c) avoiding prejudice to New Zealand's reputation as a responsible member of the world community."[61]

While the Guardians have ample discretion to determine how to implement these goals, they must prepare a statement of investment standards and procedures that include "ethical investment, including policies, standards, or procedures for avoiding prejudice to New Zealand's reputation as a responsible member of the world community."[62] The Fund must also report annually to the government on its performance.[63]

There are several important features of the NZSF's mandate for SRI that reflect the influence of international environmental law. First, by linking the obligation to invest ethically to New Zealand's "reputation as a responsible member of the world community," the legislation nods at international norms. A "responsible" member of the global community is presumably one who respects legal standards to protect and sustainably utilize the natural environment. However, there can be significant differences of opinion between countries of the North and South, and within each of these categories, about what is "responsible" social or environmental behavior. Second, the NZSF legislation neither defines key terminology nor offers guidance on reconciling any conflicts between the stipulated social and financial goals. Its SRI duty is comingled with other legislative goals relating to financial considerations, which is quite unlike the Norwegian SWF's regime, in which an institutionally separate Council on Ethics provides advice exclusively on SRI. Third, the NZSF's duty to invest ethically is framed negatively as "avoiding prejudice," which implies an obligation to eschew only the most socially and environmentally problematic activities. Thus, active consideration of positive, sustainable development, which is a particularly pressing issue in the global South, is not expected of the NZSF. In 2006 and 2010, the New Zealand parliament debated a Private Member's Bill that sought to remedy this deficiency in the SRI framework of the NZSF.[64] The unsuccessful proposal would have obliged

---

[60] Controller and Auditor-General, *Guardians of New Zealand Superannuation: Governance and Management of the New Zealand Superannuation Fund* (Wellington: New Zealand Government, May 2008), para. 5.8.
[61] *New Zealand Superannuation and Retirement Income Act 2001*, s. 58(2)(c).
[62] Ibid, s. 61(d).
[63] Ibid, s. 68(e)–(f).
[64] *Ethical Investment (Crown Financial Institutions) Bill*, 2006.

NZSF Guardians "to promote socially responsible and environmentally sustainable development"[65] and to implement investment policies that take into account international norms and conventions supported by the New Zealand government.[66]

The Guardians have established a range of processes and policies for SRI that perhaps seeks to demonstrate that such legal intervention is unnecessary.[67] Its published SRI policies evince attentiveness to social and environmental issues as a financial due diligence concern,[68] and to this end exclude a limited number of problematic sectors and activities, such as whaling, the manufacture of tobacco and some weaponry.[69] The Guardians rationalize such exclusion decisions on the basis of international law and New Zealand law and policy. For instance, the Guardians' exclusion of producers of cluster mines was triggered by the government's pending ratification of the Convention on Cluster Munitions.[70] In April 2009, the Guardians released a separate environmental policy statement and action plan that prioritizes four issues of global relevance, including to developing countries: minimizing waste, using energy efficiently, green procurement, and reducing greenhouse gas emissions.[71] However, much of this effort centers on reducing the direct eco-footprint of the NZSF's in-house operations (e.g. use of office spaces and staff travel). While the NZSF has made great strides in its SRI policy and practices since 2006, it still tends to trail its Norwegian counterpart and has been dogged by criticisms for alleged complicity in some unethical or unsustainable businesses.[72]

International environmental norms evidently guide some of the NZSF's ethical investment policies and procedures, though none specifically reflect issues pertaining to the global South. The fund, like the NGPF-G, is a signatory to the UNPRI and the Carbon Disclosure Project (CDP), both of which facilitate global collaboration among institutional investors on ESG issues. Through the CDP, the NZSF is able to cooperate with institutional investors, including other SWFs, to advocate corporate disclosure of climate-related impacts and policies.[73] In 2008, the Guardians wrote to every company in the NZX 50 Index (New Zealand's

---

[65] Ibid, cl. 9.

[66] Ibid, cl. 10.

[67] Guardians of New Zealand Superannuation, *Annual Report 2010* (Auckland: Guardians of New Zealand Superannuation, 2010), p. 133.

[68] NZSF, *Statement of Responsible Investment Policies, Standards and Procedures* (Auckland: Guardians of New Zealand Superannuation, October 2009).

[69] See the Guardians' Responsible Investment in Practice Reports, available at www.nzsuper fund.co.nz/index.asp?pageID=2145855970.

[70] NZSF, *Responsible Investment in Practice Report* (Auckland: Guardians of New Zealand Superannuation, 2009), p. 10. The text of the convention is at ILM (2009) 48: 354.

[71] Ibid, p. 12.

[72] R. Norman, *Betting the Bank on the Bomb* (Green Party of Aotearoa, 2007); Investment Watch, "NZ NGOs Call for Superfund Divestment from Israeli War Crimes," December 3, 2009, http://investmentwatch.wordpress.com.

[73] CDP, www.cdproject.net.

premier stock market index) to encourage replies to CDP disclosure requests. According to the Guardians, the response rate increased to 50 percent from 38 percent in the previous year, partly as a result of the Fund's presence.[74]

5. STATE RESPONSIBILITY UNDER PUBLIC INTERNATIONAL LAW

Having thus examined the SRI policies, practices, and governance of the Norwegian and New Zealand SWFs, and their relevance to investments in the global South, we must now consider whether and how each is legally accountable. Given the conflicted mandates of each SWF, and the market pressure to prioritize financial returns, what opportunities exist for individuals or groups in Norway and New Zealand, or governments of other states, to challenge the SWFs' decisions? Both SWFs have occasionally been mired in controversy over alleged "dodgy investments," which have mainly occurred in developing countries, where relatively lax environmental controls can exist. EarthRights International, an environmental NGO, has censured the NGPF-G for its investments in the problematic Burmese oil and gas sector.[75] The NZSF has been targeted by Investment Watch Aotearoa,[76] which has accused the NZSF of "invest[ing] large amounts of our taxpayer money in companies who [...] commit mass environmental destruction."[77] While such allegations may be dismissed as extremist views that do not accurately reflect the general character of these SWFs' investments, such allegations can damage their reputations.

But investing in companies or regimes that do violate human rights or damage the environment could make the investor seem complicit in such conduct. The public nature of SWFs further raises the question of whether any such complicity could be attributable to the state. When the conduct violates international law, and the conduct is attributable to that state, the state incurs legal responsibility. In these circumstances, states might wish to ensure that their SWFs take SRI more seriously.

The leading statement on state responsibility is the International Law Commission's (ILC) Draft Articles on the Responsibility of States for Internationally Wrongful Acts (Draft Articles).[78] Most commentators doubt that an SWF's investments could make a state to which it belongs responsible under international law.[79]

---

[74] NZSF, note 70, p. 9.

[75] EarthRights International (ERI), *Broken Ethics: The Norwegian Government's Investments in Oil and Gas Companies Operating in Burma (Myanmar)* (Washington, DC: ERI, 2010).

[76] Investment Watch, http://investmentwatch.wordpress.com.

[77] Investment Watch, "NZ Super Fund Invests Our Money in Mass Murder," March 18, 2007, www.indymedia.org.nz.

[78] UN General Assembly, *Resolution Adopted by the General Assembly: Responsibility of States for Internationally Wrongful Acts*, 28 January 2002, A/RES/56/83.

[79] R. McCorquodale and P. Simons, "Responsibility Beyond Borders: State Responsibility for Extraterritorial Violations by Corporations of International Human Rights Law" (2007) 70 *Modern Law Review* 599.

370   *International Environmental Law and Sovereign Wealth Funds*

The default position under the ILC's Draft Articles is that a non-state entity's conduct cannot be attributable to a state, unless one of the exceptions outlined in Articles 5, 8, and 11 – which set high thresholds – are met. There is little doubt that an SWF is an organ of the state, according to Article 4 of the Draft Articles;[80] but the SWF is not ipso facto the entity actually undertaking the imputed activity merely because it purchases the shares or bonds of such an entity. The conceptual bridge is to attribute the behavior of a non-state, foreign corporation to the state to which the investing SWF belongs.

Article 5 of the Draft Articles delineates the scope for attribution to the state of acts of entities that are not considered to be state organs, but which are nevertheless authorized to exercise governmental authority. The acts of public corporations, parastatal enterprises, and even privatized state companies, for instance, may be attributable to the state where the entity is linked to it through law and by its public functions. However, this provision does not apply to investment by an SWF, as no such organization in which an SWF invests would be "empowered by the law of the state to exercise [...] elements of governmental authority." While the SWF may exercise governmental authority, the entity it invests in would not.

Article 8, which deals with entities acting on the "instructions of, or under the direction or control of" a state, would not apply to a typical investment portfolio of an SWF. This would only arise in the unlikely situation that an SWF were a controlling shareholder, and able to dictate operational decisions to the company's management. That scenario is improbable; SWFs typically seek highly diversified portfolios, owning only a tiny fraction of the securities issued by a corporation. The International Court of Justice (ICJ) established a test for control over non-state actors acting extraterritorially in *Nicaragua v United States of America*, where the U.S. government funded and trained paramilitary groups in Nicaragua who committed atrocities. The ICJ held that, despite the U.S. government's actions, there was "no clear evidence of the United States having actually exercised such a degree of control in all fields as to justify treating the contras as acting on its behalf."[81] Such a high threshold for the "effective control" test means that it is practically impossible to attribute acts of private entities to the state under Article 8.

Under Article 11 of the Draft Articles, internationally wrongful conduct can also be attributed to the state "if and to the extent that the state acknowledges and adopts the conduct in question as its own." This is a far-fetched scenario given the nature of SWFs' investing; not only do they not seek to claim responsibility for the conduct of corporations in which they hold securities, they would certainly

---

[80] In the case of the NGPF-G and the NZSF, their institutional structure and governance strongly suggest that they are organs of the state – the funds of each SWF are owned by the state and each is subject to specific legislation that serves to align the activities of the SWF with the interests of the state.

[81] *Military and Paramilitary Activities in and Against Nicaragua* (Nicaragua v United States), ICJ (27 June 1986), para. 109.

not seek to adopt such conduct as their own if it involved environmentally controversial impacts. Article 11 does not apply when the state merely acknowledges or endorses that the non-state actor violates human rights or unacceptable environmental damage. Rather, the state must intentionally accept responsibility for the otherwise non-attributable behavior.

Apart from the situations covered in the ILC Draft Articles, a SWF's investments might still be rendered illegal under international public law by virtue of the state's treaty obligations. They might prohibit investments in companies that act in conflict with the treaty's provision, irrespective of whether the conduct might be attributable to the state. Although there are no treaties that explicitly prohibit investments in companies that violate human rights or damage the environment, there are some treaties that might have this ensuing effect. One example is the 2008 Convention on Cluster Munitions, which obliges the presently 110 state parties to not assist, encourage, or induce anyone to engage in using, developing, producing, or otherwise acquiring cluster munitions.[82] Due to the wide scope of the foregoing provision, it can be argued that it includes a prohibition on investments in cluster munitions producers. Many parties to this convention, such as Belgium, Ireland, Luxembourg, and New Zealand, have adopted legislation that prohibits investing in producers or traders in cluster munitions.[83] The NGPF-G and NZSF have excluded investments in these and some other weapons producers in order to align their behavior with the treaty commitments of their governments.

Finally, a further potential basis for international legal accountability of a SWF relates to a failure to exercise due diligence. Van der Zee suggests that "[w]hen the conduct of a private actor [...] violate[s] human rights, and the response of the state is non-existent or clearly inadequate, states might be held responsible, because they failed to exercise 'due diligence'."[84] The "due diligence" standard in international law behooves states – including organs of the state such as an SWF – to employ all possible means and measures to prevent violations committed by private actors. The due diligence doctrine was elaborated in the *Velásquez-Rodriguez* v *Honduras* case, where the Inter-American Court of Human Rights (IACHR) examined disappearances in Honduras. The Court determined that the Honduran government could be held liable under the American Convention on Human Rights if it failed to take appropriate steps to prevent or punish private individuals who caused others to disappear. In examining the emerging case law and academic commentaries, Rosenberg concludes that the due diligence "duty arises when the state has significant influence over the actor committing the infringement or is under a duty of care in relation to the victim."[85]

---

[82] *Convention on Cluster Munitions*, Oslo, 30 May 2008, CCM/77, 48 ILM 357, art. 1(c).
[83] Examples of such legislation are detailed in the "Stop Explosive Investments" campaign website, www.stopexplosiveinvestments.org/legislation.
[84] Van der Zee, note 8, p. 43.
[85] S. P. Rosenberg, "The Duty to Protect: A Framework for Prevention" (2009) 1 *Global Responsibility to Protect* 442 at 458.

372   *International Environmental Law and Sovereign Wealth Funds*

The concept of due diligence also underpins the framework John Ruggie developed for the social responsibility of transnational corporations. His 2008 report to the UN Human Rights Council explains that due diligence describes "the steps a company must take to become aware of, prevent and address adverse human rights impacts," in order to "discharge their responsibility to respect human rights."[86] Arguably, the same should be expected of SWFs, not only because they are state actors but because they also function like private investors.

While the duty of due diligence is becoming well recognized for conduct in a state's own territory, whether states have a similar obligation under international law to prevent human rights abuses or severe environmental damage extraterritorially or by other states is less established. Sornarajah argues that such a duty exists, and he further contends that because the home states of the foreign investor benefits from its investments (e.g. by taxing the company's earnings), a duty arises on the home state to ensure that the company's profits "are not secured through means that violate international norms."[87] This argument would apply even more forcefully to SWFs, which are owned by the state and investing for its benefit. The due diligence standard can excuse states from responsibility when they have taken reasonable measures to prevent and react to those violations; perhaps, in the case of SWFs, by establishing procedures and policies for SRI.

In conclusion, we should remember that regardless of the consequences of the scope for state responsibility for SWF investments, it would be difficult to establish at the outset that the activities they invest in are contrary to international law. Much environmental damage worldwide, especially in developing countries, occurs with the imprimatur of law, and most international environmental law seeks to promote interstate cooperation, sharing of information, and exchange of best practices rather than to prohibit or limit specific economic activities. Without robust and stringent underlying environmental standards, any state responsibility under international law is likely to be limited to narrow circumstances such as severe, deliberate pollution damage.

6. SANTIAGO PRINCIPLES

Before turning to the legal accountability of SWFs under the domestic law of the states to which they belong, a few remarks about the Santiago Principles should be made. The Principles constitute the only international standards specifically

---

[86] UN General Assembly, *Promotion and Protection of all Human Rights, Civil, Political, Economic, Social, and Cultural Rights, Including the Right to Development: Protect, Respect and Remedy: A Framework for Business and Human Rights*, 7 April 2008, A/HRC/8/5, para. 56.

[87] M. Sornarajah, *The International Law on Foreign Investment*, 3rd ed. (Cambridge: Cambridge University Press, 2010), p. 166.

governing SWFs.[88] Drafted in 2008, the Principles have been adopted by twenty-six countries with SWFs, including a number from the global South, who are members of the International Working Group on Sovereign Wealth Funds (IWG). The Principles aim "to avoid political interference by SWFs"[89] and declare three general purposes: (i) "to identify a framework of generally accepted principles and practices that properly reflect appropriate governance and accountability arrangements as well as the conduct of investment practices by SWFs on a prudent and sound basis," (ii) "increase understanding of SWFs to home and recipient countries and the international financial markets," and (iii) "ensure that [...] SWFs continue to bring economic and financial benefits to home countries, recipient countries, and the international financial system."[90]

The Santiago Principles emphasize transparency, clarity, and equivalent treatment to private funds, and stress that an SWF's priority should be to "maximize risk-adjusted financial returns in a manner consistent with its investment policy, and based on economic and financial grounds."[91] Such a philosophy dovetails closely with the practices of SWFs from developing countries without SRI mandates. Principle 19.1 concedes that SWFs may exclude certain investments on other non-economic grounds, including social, environmental, or ethical reasons, so long as such considerations are clearly explained and publicly disclosed. However, there is certainly no expectation or encouragement that SWFs practice SRI. Also relevant is Principle 21, which describes the nature of shareholder activism and engagement that will be acceptable: "[i]f an SWF chooses to exercise its ownership rights, it should do so in a manner that is consistent with its investment policy and protects the financial value of its investments." Taking climate change and other environmental degradation into consideration can arguably help protect the long-term value of investments. Also relevant is Principle 22, which stipulates that SWFs "should have a framework that identifies, assesses, and manages the risks of its operations." Those risks are classified into four broad categories: Financial, operational, regulatory, and reputational risks. Thus, ESG issues could be integrated in the investment policy as a means of enhancing due diligence. Human rights harm or environmental damage caused by businesses in which an SWF has invested could directly affect the fund and its parent state's reputation.

In July 2011, the International Forum of Sovereign Wealth Funds (IFSWF) – which was established in 2009 "to meet, exchange views on issues of common interests, and facilitate an understanding of the Santiago Principles and SWF

---

[88] "Sovereign Wealth Funds: Generally Accepted Principles and Practices – "Santiago Principles," International Working Group of Sovereign Wealth Funds (IWG), October 2008.

[89] Nystuen et al., note 28, p. 5.

[90] IWG, note 88, p. 4.

[91] Ibid, p. 8.

374 *International Environmental Law and Sovereign Wealth Funds*

activities"[92] – released a report about the experiences of its members in implementing the Santiago Principles.[93] The report elaborated on SRI and commented on the activities of the NZSF and NGPF-G. The survey states that both SWFs believe that long-term financial performance can be affected by ESG issues and have, for that reason, adopted SRI considerations in their investment policies. The survey is silent on whether such practices are allowed under the Santiago Principles.

The Santiago Principles have been analyzed by Anita Halvorssen, an environmental law scholar, who argues that "sustainable development needs to be incorporated into the[m]."[94] Although her proposal would presently lack the support of nearly all SWFs, especially those from the global South, Halvorssen recommends that the Principles should explicitly require SWFs to take climate change into account as a key investment variable. Such a reform would render the Santiago Principles ahead of most SRI codes such as the UNPRI. However, as a voluntary regime, the Principles are structurally limited in their means of ensuring accountability of SWFs. In sum, the Santiago Principles offer limited scope for international environmental accountability of SWFs, though the Principles and the IFSWF offer a forum to foster dialogue about the role and practices on SRI for SWFs.

7. HOLDING SWFS ACCOUNTABLE UNDER DOMESTIC LAW

The scope for holding SWFs legally accountable for their investment decisions is similarly rather limited under domestic law. The countries that host SWFs' investments can certainly use their own laws to control and discipline economic development and companies funded by SWFs. But many such countries, especially in the global South, may be reluctant to assert such control if it could trigger capital flight to more benign investment environments. Such countries could for similar reasons be reluctant to use international legal channels, which in any event, as the previous discussion suggests, are not particularly effective.

The legislative regimes governing the SWFs considered in this chapter provide no opportunities for courts to review the substantive merits of SWF investment decisions.

New Zealand has an enviable record of engagement in international law, acting as a party to numerous treaties along with being a signatory to many declarations and other soft law instruments that touch on environmental and natural resources

---

[92] International Working Group of Sovereign Wealth Funds (IWG), "'Kuwait Declaration': Establishment of the International Forum of Sovereign Wealth Fund," April 6, 2009, www.iwg-swf.org.

[93] International Forum of Sovereign Wealth Funds (IFSWF), *IFSWF Members' Experiences in the Application of the Santiago Principles* (IFSWS, 2011).

[94] Halvorssen, note 48 at 90.

issues.[95] This record still stands despite a few anomalies, such as the country's controversial withdrawal from the Kyoto Protocol in 2012. While many of New Zealand's international environmental obligations are fulfilled through dedicated national legislation, some are not. A treaty may be ratified but not yet incorporated into domestic law, and rules of customary international law may not be formally recognized in regulations. An important question, then, is to what extent the decisions of the Guardians of the NZSF are answerable to international environmental rules and standards that apply to New Zealand. The NZSF legislation itself is silent on this question, apart from the vague stipulation that the NZSF investments must not prejudice the country's world reputation.

The basic constitutional principle in New Zealand that the executive cannot change the law by entering into a treaty, does not disallow the courts from having regard to treaties, unless parliament has already acted to incorporate their provisions into law. According to the New Zealand Law Commission, courts might take treaties into account when relevant to the determination of the common law or the interpretation of a statute, and as evidence of public policy.[96] Customary international law is also a seminal source of New Zealand's international obligations, and courts can apply it directly unless there is legislation to the contrary. According to the government's Legislative Advisory Committee, "The courts will not hesitate to look beyond the words embodied in legislation to the relevant international obligations, both to aid interpretation (if necessary and appropriate) and, in the context of judicial review of administrative action, to examine whether decision-makers have taken the relevant considerations into account."[97]

Although the substantive merits of the NSZF's decisions probably could not be challenged in the courts, decision-making may be reviewable for errors of law, such as failure to consider relevant considerations (such as potentially an international law consideration). In such cases, courts have remedies available in the nature of mandamus, prohibition, or certiorari, or for a declaration or injunction. For example, a court might restrain a proposed investment decision or order by mandamus that the Guardians undertake a specific course of action. The NZSF is subject to judicial review by virtue of the Crown Entities Act 2004,[98] which provides that acts of the fund may be rendered invalid if "contrary to, or outside of, an Act" or "done otherwise than for the purpose of performing its functions."[99]

---

[95] As of March 2015, it is a party to about 900 multilateral and 1,400 bilateral treaties on all subjects: see the Ministry of Foreign Affairs and Trade, "New Zealand Consolidated Treaty List," www.mfat.govt.nz.

[96] New Zealand Law Commission (NZLC), *International Law and the Law of New Zealand*, report 34 (Wellington: NZLC, 1996), para. 65.

[97] Legislative Advisory Committee, "Guidelines on Process and Content of Legislation," www.pco.parliament.govt.nz, s.6.12,

[98] *Crown Entities Act 2004*, 2004/115, s. 4(1).

[99] Ibid, s. 19(1).

However, reviewability of NZSF decisions would still depend heavily on whether the particular imputed decision is an exercise of a public or commercial function. Although the NZSF is a public institution, and thus ostensibly within the court's purview, it may be construed as exercising private, commercial functions that are not generally justiciable unless there are allegations of bad faith or corruption.[100] In *Napier City* v *Healthcare Hawke's Bay*, Justice Ellis noted: "many commercial transactions cannot be reviewed, but the difficulty has arisen in some cases where the importance or significance of the decision takes it out of the realm of purely commercial and into the realm of quasi governmental administrative decisions which is reviewable."[101]

There is no known case law on the NZSF itself, but decisions on other state economic institutions suggest only limited scope to hold the NZSF judicially accountable. In the *Mercury Energy* case, the Privy Council declined to review a contract between Electricity Corporation of New Zealand and Mercury Energy to supply bulk electricity at agreed prices, but acknowledged that commercial decisions may be reviewed where they "may adversely affect the rights and liabilities of private individuals without affording them any redress."[102] However, the investment decisions of the NZSF do not affect individuals' rights and liabilities. In *Major Electricity Users' Group Inc* v *Electricity Commission and Transpower New Zealand Ltd*, the Court of Appeal declined to review a decision of the Commission regarding a proposal by state-owned enterprise to upgrade a power substation because of "the Commission's position as an expert body, the process and consultation requirements imposed on it and the nature of the investment decision involved."[103]

A further obstacle to challenging an NZSF decision relates to standing to bring proceedings. The Guardians do not owe a duty of procedural fairness to any putative beneficiary of the NZSF, as no individual citizen has any financial entitlement to the fund. Foreign citizens would also lack standing. Thus, without any personal economic grievance, it is unlikely that any individual person would have standing to challenge NZSF investment decisions. On the other hand, New Zealand courts have increasingly taken a broad view of standing for public interest organizations wishing to challenge administrative decisions that relate to their mandate.[104] The Council on Socially Responsible Investment[105] is one New Zealand organization that could potentially have standing to challenge a decision relating to the NZSF.

[100] J. Cassie and D. Knight, "The Scope of Judicial Review: Who and What may be Reviewed," in *NZLS Administrative Law Intensive* (Wellington: New Zealand Law Society, 2009), p. 89.
[101] HC Napier, CP 29/94, 15 December 1994.
[102] *Mercury Energy Ltd* v *Electricity Corporation of New Zealand* [1994] 2 NZLR 385, 388.
[103] [2008] NZCA 536, para. 56.
[104] See e.g. *Environmental Defence Society (Inc)* v *South Pacific Aluminium Ltd (No 3)* [1981] 1 NZLR 216.
[105] See Council for Socially Responsible Investment, www.csri.org.nz.

The picture in Norway offers similarly sparse opportunities for the public to legally challenge the investments of the NGPF-G, such as on the grounds that it failed to properly consider international environmental or human rights standards in managing its investment portfolio. Like New Zealand, Norway follows the "dualist" tradition that international law is not directly applicable domestically, but must first be translated or transformed into national legislation before it can be applied by its courts.[106] However, as in New Zealand, Norwegian courts follow the principle that in cases of ambiguity, domestic legislation should be interpreted, where possible, in conformity with international law that Norway is bound by. This chapter has already noted how international environmental and human rights law informs the decision-making of the NGPF-G, particularly in the deliberations of the Council on Ethics.

In Norway the principle of judicial review of executive action is regarded as "an unwritten constitutional principle."[107] Standing for review of administrative decisions is accorded to individuals directly affected, as well as to public interest organizations whose philosophical or policy interests are involved.[108] In the seminal *Alta* case, the Norwegian Supreme Court affirmed the right of public interest environmental organizations to challenge administrative actions and compliance with legislation.[109] Nevertheless, there are formidable obstacles for either individuals or organizations who aim to challenge NGPF-G investment decisions. First, it invests only in foreign assets, and therefore no Norwegian corporation or other entity is involved. Second, the fund's capital does not belong to any individual or group; no person has any individual legal entitlement to a portion of the fund – a situation like that of the NZSF. The absence of any direct stake in the fund effectively denies any individual standing in a court. While a public environmental organization or group interested in SRI is better placed to seek judicial review, the discretionary and expert nature of decision-making by the entities that administer the NGPF-G, such as Norges Bank, would insulate the fund from judicial scrutiny absent a gross legal violation.

8. CONCLUSIONS

A proper understanding of international environmental law's role and impact in the global South would not be complete without reflection on the growing role of

---

[106] A. Kierulf, "Er internasjonale menneskerettigheter en relevant rettskilde ved grunnlovstolking?" (2011) 34(1) *Retfærd Årgang* 23–48.

[107] O. Mestad, "Rights to Public Participation in Norwegian Mining, Energy, and Resource Development," in D. M. Zillman, A. Lucas, and G. Pring (eds.), *Human Rights in Natural Resource Development: Public Participation in the Sustainable Development of Mining and Energy Resources* (Oxford: Oxford University Press, 2002), p. 393.

[108] Ibid.

[109] Norsk Retstidende [1980], 569 (case concerned a challenge to a large dam and hydropower project).

SWFs (especially SWFs in developed countries) as engines of economic development and investment in emerging economies and other regions. This chapter has investigated how international environmental law influences SWFs. Through case studies on the Norwegian and New Zealand SWFs, the chapter has illuminated how their legal mandates to practice SRI provide space to incorporate international standards on environmental issues and human rights. The fact that the funds invest primarily in foreign markets, especially in the global South, makes such international standards particularly relevant, especially when investing in jurisdictions where local environmental regulations may be lax or incomplete. On the other hand, these SWFs tend to practice SRI in a limited manner in which only the most controversial and problematic companies are excluded from investment, and only a relatively small number are targeted for engagement and dialogue with the aim of improving corporate behavior. As in the SRI industry generally, social and environmental issues garner attention primarily because they may be financially material to investment performance rather than because they are ethical imperatives. To the extent that there are shortcomings in the SRI practices of SWFs and their investments in developing countries, there is little scope to hold them accountable under international or domestic law.

Strengthening the legal accountability of these and other SWFs could be undertaken through other routes. One option is statutory reform to enshrine more robust and comprehensive legal obligations to have regard to international environmental law when investing in global financial markets. Already, however, attempts in 2006 and 2010 to amend the SRI mandate of the NZSF to oblige it to promote sustainable development failed to secure sufficient parliamentary support. The political climate for such reform in New Zealand (and Norway too) may improve if the SRI movement gains greater market strength to the point where the "social license" of any fund requires that it respect fundamental human rights and environmental norms of the international community.

Another option would be to create an international agreement or code on SRI specifically for SWFs. This route is also fraught with difficulties. A formal intergovernmental agreement is highly unlikely at this stage, given that most SWFs do not practice SRI and many states would be hostile to non-financial obligations being imposed on their funds (which were created with different macroeconomic objectives). Perhaps, more realistically, as an interim measure a voluntary code of conduct could be drafted to promote SRI among SWFs. As already noted in this chapter, a few SWFs, including those from Norway and New Zealand, are signatories to the UNPRI. The latter code has attracted wide-ranging support from many private and public investors, and in the near term will likely provide the main vehicle for promoting dialogue, transparency, and accountability on SRI practices in the SWF sector. But the UNPRI has significant limitations that inhere in its rather broad and discretionary principles. The Santiago Principles, as already noted in this chapter, have the advantage of specifically catering to SWFs. But presently they do not acknowledge SRI, let alone encourage SWFs to invest in sustainable development. However, if SWFs were to attract more international criticism for unethical or environmentally problematic investments, states might be motivated to introduce some SRI standards through revised Santiago Principles. In the foreseeable future, such support would likely only come from Northern SWFs, which are ahead of their Southern counterparts in embracing SRI.

18

Transnational Corporations and Extractive Industries

Sara L. Seck

1. INTRODUCTION

Transnational corporations in the extractive industries frequently reference international sustainable mineral development law as evidence of a global consensus that mining, minerals, and metals are important for economic development and essential for modern living.[1] At the same time, there is a clear understanding that this consensus also requires resource extraction to be undertaken in a sustainable manner. However, the sustainable mineral development consensus does not in fact reflect the views of many in the global South, in particular historically marginalized communities, who struggle with local environmental and social impacts that undermine their ability to choose to live without embracing the ecologically destructive overconsumption patterns of the North.

This chapter will first describe the history of international sustainable mineral development law from Stockholm to Rio +20 as the story is traditionally told, then contrast this narrative with views from the global South. Yet, as this chapter will illustrate, a complexity emerges when attempting to understand international sustainable mineral development law from the perspective of the global South, due to the diversity of voices that express concern over mining development. Among highlighted features of the perceived global consensus on sustainable mineral development is the understanding that international law accords host states the sovereign right to develop natural resources in accordance with their own internal environmental and developmental policies. By contrast, mining-affected communities of the global South embrace understandings of environment and human rights as inextricably intertwined, and call out for participation, if not consent, in decision-making over resource extraction and environmental justice in the event of harm. Importantly, these views are expressed by communities within states of the

---

[1] This chapter will focus primarily on mineral extraction rather than oil and gas, although both create common problems from the perspective of local communities of the "South."

South (the so-called developing world or Third World states)[2] as well as within states of the North (the so-called developed world or First World states).[3] Moreover, sometimes these views are expressed by communities that identify as indigenous peoples,[4] and sometimes by those that do not.[5] Yet a commonality emerges as strategies of peaceful resistance too often lead to repression of environmental human rights defenders expressing opposition to mining development.[6]

The chapter will then illustrate how the structures of global and transnational governance have begun to respond to local community resistance to extractive sector development by integrating community demands into existing frameworks. However, due both to the nature of the frameworks and the diversity of states – both "North" and "South" – that are home to members of the transnational mining industry, this integration has, to date, proven ineffective in addressing the environmental justice concerns of mining-affected communities of the global South. In conclusion, the chapter will explore the challenges faced by these governance structures and international law in bridging the gap between South and North.

2. A BRIEF HISTORY OF INTERNATIONAL SUSTAINABLE MINERAL DEVELOPMENT LAW

Mining involves the exploitation of non-renewable and finite natural resources, often located in remote areas. This reality, combined with the significant environmental impacts associated with mining, makes it intuitively difficult to reconcile mining with notions of sustainability. Yet, sustainable development has become the mantra of the global mining industry, and a focus on sustainable development has

[2] L. North, T.D. Clark, and V. Patroni, (eds.), *Community Rights and Corporate Responsibility: Canadian Mining and Oil Companies in Latin America* (Toronto: Between the Lines, 2006); B. K. Campbell (ed.), *Mining in Africa: Regulation and Development* (Ontario: International Development Research Centre, 2009); D. Zillman, A. Lucas, and G.R. Pring, (eds.), *Human Rights in Natural Resource Development: Public Participation in the Sustainable Development of Mining and Energy Resources* (Oxford: Oxford University Press, 2002).

[3] "Bearing the Burden: The Effects of Mining on First Nations in British Columbia," International Human Rights Clinic, Harvard Law School, October 2010; S. H. Ali, *Mining, the Environment and Indigenous Development Conflicts* (Tucson: University of Arizona Press, 2009); Zillman et al. (eds.), note 2.

[4] UN General Assembly, *Report of the Special Rapporteur on the Rights of Indigenous Peoples, James Anaya: Extractive Industries and Indigenous Peoples*, 1 July 2013, A/HRC/21/41.

[5] Earthjustice, "United Nations Working Group Concludes U.S. Visit Exploring Human Rights Cost of Mountaintop Removal Mining,' May 1, 2013, http://earthjustice.org. Whether or not a particular community self-identifies and is recognized as indigenous in the mining context is complex. See S. K. Date-Bah, "Rights of Indigenous People in Relation to Natural Resources Development: An African's Perspective" (1998) 16 *Journal of Energy and Natural Resources Law* 394 at 395; D. Szablowski, *Transnational Law and Local Struggles: Mining, Communities and the World Bank* (Oxford: Hart Publishing, 2007), pp. 138–150.

[6] UN General Assembly, *Report of the Special Rapporteur on the Situation of Human Rights Defenders, Margaret Sekaggya*, 21 December 2011, A/HRC/19/55 (21 December 2011), paras. 60–87, 124–126; UN General Assembly, note 4, paras. 19-25.

382   *Transnational Corporations and Extractive Industries*

arguably changed both corporate strategies and the "goals and objectives of mining law reform."[7] This section will explore the recent history of mining and sustainability as the story is traditionally told, and reveal the emergence of the ideal of "achieving sustainable development of local communities in mining regions."[8]

The story of international environmental law usually begins with the 1972 Stockholm Conference on the Human Environment.[9] The Stockholm Declaration provides that non-renewable resources must be employed guardedly so as to ensure against their future exhaustion and to ensure their shared utilization with all humankind.[10] Recommendation 56 of the Action Plan for the Human Environment specifically addresses mining and mineral resources, recommending information exchange on mining and the environment.[11] Furthermore, the Action Plan proposed that appropriate United Nations bodies assist developing countries by providing experts and information on technology that could prevent the adverse effects of mining on the environment.[12] The 1982 World Charter for Nature again called for restraint in the exploitation of non-renewable resources, as well as the need to take account of the compatibility of exploitation with the functioning of natural systems.[13]

The concept of sustainable development was first articulated in 1987 by the World Commission on Environment and Development (WCED) in the *Brundtland Report*[14] and reiterated in the Rio Declaration on Environment and

---

[7] J. P. Williams, "Legal Reform in Mining: Past, Present, and Future," in E. Bastida, T. Wälde, and J. Warden-Fernandez (eds.), *International and Comparative Mineral Law and Policy: Trends and Prospects* (The Hague: Kluwer Law International, 2005), p. 62.

[8] Ibid, p. 67.

[9] *Declaration of the United Nations Conference on the Human Environment*, Stockholm, 16 June 1972, UN Doc. A/CONF.48/14 (hereinafter Stockholm Declaration); K. Mickelson, "South, North, International Environmental Law and International Environmental Lawyers" (2000) 11 *Yearbook of International Environmental Law* 52.

[10] M. C. G. Dalupan, "Mining and sustainable development: Insights from international law," in Bastida et al. (eds.), *International and Comparative Mineral Law and Policy: Trends and Prospects* (The Hague: Kluwer Law International, 2005), p. 160. See *Stockholm Declaration*, note 9, Principle 5.

[11] Dalupan, note 10, p. 160. See *Action Plan of the United Nations Conference on the Human Environment*, Stockholm, 16 June 1972, UN Doc. A/CONF.48/14/Rev.1, Recommendation 56 (hereinafter Action Plan).

[12] Action Plan, note 11, Recommendation 56; Dalupan, note 10, p. 161.

[13] Dalupan, note 10, p. 161; *World Charter for Nature*, New York, 28 October 1982, UNGA Res. 37/7; UN GAOR, 37th Sess., Supp. No. 51, at 17; UN Doc. A/37/51 (1982); 22 ILM 455 (1983), Principle 9(d).

[14] World Commission on Environment and Development, *Our Common Future* (London: Oxford University Press, 1987) (hereinafter *Brundtland Report*). See further on the development of the concept of sustainable development: K. Ginter, E. Denters, and P. J. I. M. de Waart (eds.), *Sustainable Development and Good Governance* (Dordrecht: Martinus Nijhoff, 1995); A. Boyle and D. Freestone, *International Law and Sustainable Development: Past Achievements and Future Challenges* (Oxford: Oxford University Press, 1999); M-C. Cordonier Segger and A. Khalfan, *Sustainable Development Law: Principles, Practices & Prospects* (Oxford: Oxford University Press, 2004); B. J. Richardson and S. Wood (eds.), *Environmental Law for Sustainability* (Oxford: Hart Publishing, 2006).

Development, which sets out twenty-seven principles of sustainable development, together with the program of action in Agenda 21.[15] Agenda 21 does not specifically address mining, although it does treat minerals and metals indirectly under chemicals management and hazardous wastes.[16] Consequently, specific discussion of mining and sustainable development could not take place at the Commission on Sustainable Development (CSD), the United Nations body established to oversee the implementation of Agenda 21. However, at the eighth session of the CSD in 2000, "minerals, metals and rehabilitation in the context of sustainable development" were listed as a priority area for future work, and "governments, the international community and other relevant actors" were urged to "examine the social, economic, and environmental impacts of minerals extraction and metals production" and "encouraged to formulate and implement strategies that provide for the rehabilitation of land degraded by mining."[17]

Industry's response to the call may be found in the report of the Mining, Minerals and Sustainable Development (MMSD) project.[18] Yet the 2002 MMSD report also provides insights into the complexity of the mining industry, for it notes that the majority of junior companies and many intermediate companies believe sustainable development to be a "big company game" that is of no relevance to them, while many of the large multinationals make a "substantial effort to assess, minimize, and mitigate many of the environmental and social impacts, to develop an effective mine closure plan, and to foster constructive and consensual involvement with the local community."[19] However, in practice, larger mining companies

---

[15] *Rio Declaration on Environment and Development*, Rio de Janeiro, 14 June 1992, UN Doc. A/CONF.151/26 (vol. 1); 31 ILM 874 (1992) (hereinafter Rio Declaration); *Agenda 21: Programme of Action for Sustainable Development*, Rio de Janeiro, 14 June 1992, U.N. GAOR, 46th Sess., Agenda Item 21, UN Doc. A/Conf.151/26 (1992) (hereinafter Agenda 21).

[16] Agenda 21, note 15, chapter 19 ("Environmentally Sound Management of Toxic Chemicals, Including Prevention of Illegal International Traffic in Toxic and Dangerous Products") and chapter 20 ("Environmentally Sound Management of Hazardous Wastes, Including Prevention of Illegal International Traffic in Hazardous Wastes"). Other sections of Agenda 21 also apply to mineral development, such as chapter 10 ("Integrated Approach to the Planning and Management of Land Resources") and chapter 30 ("Strengthening the Role of Business and Industry").

[17] Commission on Sustainable Development, *Report on the Eighth Session* (New York: UN Economic and Social Council, 2000), Decision 8/3, paras. 4, 25. Another priority area for future work listed under Integrated Approach to Planning and Management of Land Resources is access to information and stakeholder participation.

[18] The MMSD project was sponsored by nine of the world's largest mining companies as the Global Mining Initiative, and undertaken by the International Institute of Environment and Development. See International Institute for Environment and Development, "Mining, Minerals and Sustainable Development (MMSD), Background and Publications," www.iied.org. See also H. Dashwood, *The Rise of Global Corporate Social Responsibility: Mining and the Spread of Global Norms* (New York: Cambridge University Press, 2012).

[19] Mining, Minerals and Sustainable Development, *Breaking New Ground: The Report of the MMSD Project* (London: Earthscan Publications Ltd., 2002), pp. 62–63 (hereinafter MMSD Report).

384   *Transnational Corporations and Extractive Industries*

may be as likely as smaller mining companies to be implicated in unsustainable practices that violate international norms, including human rights.[20] These issues do not depend upon corporate structure either, which in practice vary widely, with mines operated by wholly owned subsidiaries, through joint ventures, or by state-owned enterprises.[21] A further complexity noted in the MMSD report is the importance of the artisanal and small-scale mining sector.[22] Often illegal or unregulated, and heavily criticized for its environmental and health impacts, artisanal mining and small-scale mining provides a livelihood for many millions of people worldwide.[23]

The *Brundtland Report*'s definition of sustainable development as "development that meets the needs of the present without compromising the ability of future generations to meet their own needs"[24] is commonly cited in discussions of policy options surrounding mineral development.[25] These include: whether to set aside "reserved" mineral deposits for future development; whether to impose production quotas or caps; whether to restrict the number of exploration licenses issued; whether to restrict the number of mines; whether to require a longer mine life by reducing annual capacity; and whether to restrict areas open for exploration.[26] A commonly held mining industry perspective is that sustainable mineral development inevitably involves finding the "right" balance among environmental, economic, and social sustainability.[27]

The Johannesburg Plan of Implementation of the World Summit on Sustainable Development (WSSD) in Johannesburg in 2002 explicitly addressed mining, stating in part that "mining, minerals and metals" are "important to the economic

---

[20] For example, at a UN consultation on human rights and the extractive sector, no difference was noted between large and small companies. See UN Economic and Social Council, *Report of the United Nations High Commissioner for Human Rights on the Sectoral Consultation Entitled "Human Rights and the Extractive Industry"*, 10–11 November 2005, 19 December 2005, E/CN.4/2006/96.

[21] MMSD Report, note 19, pp. 58–64.

[22] MMSD Report, note 19, pp. 313–334.

[23] For a recent initiative, see the website of the Alliance for Responsible Mining, www.commu nitymining.org. See also the work project of the International Council on Mining and Metals (ICMM) on Artisanal and Small-Scale Mining, www.icmm.com.

[24] *Brundtland Report*, note 14, p. 43. For a discussion of the origin of the term, see M. C. W. Pinto, "Reflections on the Term Sustainable Development and Its Institutional Implications" in Ginter et al. (eds.), note 14, p. 72. See also, J. Cordes, "Normative and Philosophical Perspectives on the Concept of Sustainable Development," in J. Otto and J. Cordes (eds.), *Sustainable Development and the Future of Mineral Investment* (Paris: United Nations Environmental Program, 2000), pp. 1–1 to 1–54.

[25] J. Otto and J. Cordes, *The Regulation of Mineral Enterprises: A Global Perspective on Economics, Law and Policy* (Colorado: Rocky Mountain Mineral Law Foundation, 2002), pp. 2–12.

[26] Ibid, pp. 2–12.

[27] R. G. Eggert, "Sustainable Development and the Mineral Industry," in J. Otto and J. Cordes (eds.), *Sustainable Development and the Future of Mineral Investment* (Paris: United Nations Environmental Program, 2000), pp. 2–1 to 2–15.

and social development of many countries," and that "minerals are essential for modern living."[28] The WSSD listed three specific actions designed to enhance the contribution of mining, minerals, and metals to sustainable development: (1) to support efforts to address the environmental, economic, health, and social impacts and benefits of mining, minerals, and metals throughout their life cycle; (2) to enhance the participation of stakeholders, "including local and indigenous communities and women," to play an active role in minerals, metals and mining development; and (3) to foster sustainable mining practices through the provision of financial, technical, and capacity-building support to developing countries, including for small-scale mining.[29] Specific mention was also made in the Johannesburg Plan of Implementation of the need to enhance the contribution of mining to the sustainable development of Africa,[30] and of the need to enhance corporate environmental and social responsibility and accountability[31] by encouraging dialogue between enterprises and communities, as well as by encouraging financial institutions to incorporate sustainable development considerations in decision-making.[32]

The partnership initiative announced at the Johannesburg Summit to create a "Global Dialogue of Governments on Mining/Metals and Sustainable Development" was another important and related development in keeping with the spirit of capacity-building for development.[33] Announced by Canada and South Africa, this initiative led to the formation of the Intergovernmental Forum on Mining, Minerals, Metals and Sustainable Development, in effect in February 2005. The Intergovernmental Forum is designed to function on a consultative and advisory basis and to bring together governments with an interest in policy, governance, and other issues related to sustainable mineral development that would benefit from consideration at a global level.[34] Forty-three member countries from around the world, representing a diverse range of mineral-rich states from both the North

---

[28] UN, *Report of the World Summit on Sustainable Development*, 26 August–4 September 2002, A/CONF.199/20, resolution 2, annex (Plan of Implementation of the World Summit on Sustainable Development), p. 29, para. 46 [hereinafter Johannesburg Plan of Implementation].

[29] Ibid, p. 29, para. 46; p. 6, para. 10(d).

[30] Ibid, p. 37, para. 62(g).

[31] "Accountability" is often associated with corporate legal accountability to victims of human rights and environmental violations, while "responsibility" is often associated with corporate social responsibility (CSR) initiatives. The provision in the Johannesburg Plan of Implementation is focused upon CSR and collaborative responses rather than legal accountability.

[32] Johannesburg Plan of Implementation, note 28, p. 8, para. 18. The implications of these provisions are evident in the development of transnational governance frameworks, as will be discussed later in the chapter.

[33] Intergovernmental Forum on Mining, Minerals, Metals and Sustainable Development, "Introduction," http://globaldialogue.info.

[34] See generally Intergovernmental Forum on Mining, Minerals, Metals and Sustainable Development, "Terms of Reference," http://globaldialogue.info.

386 *Transnational Corporations and Extractive Industries*

and South, participated in the drafting of a Mining Policy Framework in 2010; it was updated in 2013, by which time membership had grown to forty-seven.[35] The Mining Policy Framework describes itself as outlining the "best practices for good environmental, social and economic governance of the mining sector and the generation and equitable sharing of benefits in a manner that will contribute to sustainable development."[36] The Framework, which was submitted to the 2011 meeting of the Commission on Sustainable Development (CSD), claims to represent "the commitment of the IGF members to ensuring that mining activities within their jurisdictions are compatible with the objectives of sustainable development and poverty reduction."[37] It also explicitly called on the "international community, particularly the UN and donor agencies, to enhance support towards capacity building that promotes the good governance of the mining/metals sector and its contribution to sustainability."[38]

One item of interest in the Framework is its reference to the need to address potential security issues and to respect human rights, including those of indigenous peoples.[39] To do this, governments and "mining entities" are encouraged to be "guided in their actions by international norms," including the International Finance Corporation's Performance Standards on Social and Environmental Sustainability and the Voluntary Principles on Security and Human Rights, as well as the Organisation for Economic Cooperation and Development (OECD) Guidelines for Multinational Enterprises.[40] These international normative standards, which will be discussed further in the next part, are often described as voluntary or soft law, although they may be hardened by explicit incorporation in contractual agreements or used to inform the standard of care in tort.[41] Another point of interest is the attention given to artisanal and small-scale mining, described as a "diversified sector that includes poor informal individual miners seeking to eke out

---

[35] Intergovernmental Forum on Mining, Minerals, Metals and Sustainable Development, "A Mining Policy Framework: Mining and Sustainable Development," October 2013, http://globaldialogue.info, p. 3. State members from the North were few, with Canada playing a lead role. State members from the South were many, representing all parts of the world, including several BRIC countries (Brazil, Russia, India, and South Africa, but not China), as well as many economically poor countries (such as Sierra Leone, Bolivia, and Papua New Guinea). All references are to the 2013 text of the Policy Framework.

[36] Intergovernmental Forum on Mining, Minerals, Metals and Sustainable Development, note 35, p. 6.

[37] Ibid, p. 6.

[38] Ibid, p. 5.

[39] Ibid, p. 11.

[40] Ibid, pp. 1, 34–35. See further later in the chapter.

[41] On contractual aspects see M. Torrance (ed.), *IFC Performance Standards on Environmental & Social Sustainability: A Guidebook* (Ontario: LexisNexis Canada, 2012), pp. 18–19; on CSR frameworks and the standard of care in transnational corporate accountability tort litigation, see *Choc v Hudbay Minerals Inc*, 2013 ONSC 1414. See generally E. Morgera, *Corporate Accountability in International Environmental Law* (Oxford: Oxford University Press, 2009).

or supplement a subsistence livelihood."[42] Best practice recommendations here include finding ways to integrate informal artisanal and small-scale mining activities into the legal system and the economic system, as well as finding ways to reduce their social and environmental impacts.[43]

The most recent global statement on mining and sustainable development may be found in the 2012 Rio +20 conference's outcome document, *The Future We Want*.[44] After reiterating support for the principles in the Rio Declaration and Agenda 21, among other "political" commitments,[45] and making proposals for a "green economy,"[46] *The Future We Want* addresses numerous topics, including mining, with "minerals and metals [acknowledged] to make a major contribution to the world economy and modern societies" and to "all countries with mineral resources, in particular developing countries."[47] However, while mining is said to offer "the opportunity" to provide economic development and poverty reduction, this will only happen if "managed effectively and properly" and must at the same time "effectively address negative environmental and social impacts."[48] To do this, "governments need strong capacities to develop, manage, and regulate their mining industries."[49]

Thus, global consensus of resource-rich states together with the mining industry suggests that mining is not only essential for modern living but can also provide a pathway to poverty alleviation through sustainable development. This can only be accomplished, however, if governments take seriously their responsibility to effectively regulate mining so as to prevent and remedy environmental and social harms even while reaping economic benefits. In practice, this is a challenging proposition, and negative impacts often fall upon mining-affected communities of the global South.

3. THE ALTERNATE CONSENSUS OF THE GLOBAL SOUTH: GLOBAL ENVIRONMENTAL JUSTICE AND MINING-AFFECTED COMMUNITIES

The traditional history of international sustainable mineral development law, as evident from the previous section, is one of state consensus over the important

---

[42] Intergovernmental Forum on Mining, Minerals, Metals and Sustainable Development, note 35, p. 15.

[43] Ibid, pp. 15–16.

[44] UN General Assembly, *Resolution Adopted by the General Assembly: The Future We Want*, 27 July 2012, A/RES/66/288 [hereinafter *The Future We Want*].

[45] Ibid, pp. 3–10 (Part II).

[46] Ibid, pp. 10–14 (Part III). On green economy and natural resources see especially paras. 60–61.

[47] Ibid, p. 44, para. 227.

[48] Ibid.

[49] Ibid, p. 44, para. 228. In addition, both governments *and* businesses need "to promote the continuous improvement of accountability and transparency, as well as the effectiveness of the relevant existing mechanisms to prevent the illicit financial flows from mining activities."

388   *Transnational Corporations and Extractive Industries*

benefits of mining for sustainable development. Yet the concept of sustainable development is not accepted by all as the key to solving problems of environmental degradation and poverty. For example, the development discourse is described by Wolfgang Sachs as being "deeply imbued with western certainties like progress, growth, market integration, consumption, and universal needs" which are all "part of the problem, not of the solution."[50] Accordingly, these notions "cannot but distract attention from the urgency of public debate on our relationship with nature, for they preclude the search for societies which live graciously within their means."[51] Indeed, the entire process of defining sustainable development at the Rio Conference has been described as having "trapped" environmental NGOs in a "farce," for, having "lent support to governments in return for some small concessions on language," they have "thus legitimized the process of increased industrial development."[52] Furthermore, the price of placing environment on the global agenda has been the "reduction of environmentalism to managerialism,"[53] with claims of global management coming inevitably into "conflict with the aspirations for cultural rights, democracy and self-determination."[54] The Third World critique is even more severe, with the discourse of sustainable development accused of providing "a new, more intrusive set of reasons for managing the 'dark, poor and hungry masses' of the Third World."[55]

It is clearly evident that many mining-affected communities in both the South and the North do not endorse the sustainable development consensus, and often frame their opposition to mining in the language of environmental human rights. Indeed, evidence suggests that an alternate consensus may be found in many mining-affected communities – a consensus that is allied with the global

---

[50] W. Sachs, "Global Ecology and the Shadow of "Development," in W. Sachs (ed.), *Global Ecology: A New Arena of Political Conflict* (London: Zed Books, 2003), p. 4. See generally W. Sachs (ed.), *The Development Dictionary: A Guide to Knowledge as Power* (London: Zed Books, 1999); G. Rist, *The History of Development: From Western Origins to Global Faith* (London: Zed Books, 1997); F. Fischer and M. A. Hajer (eds.), *Living with Nature: Environmental Politics as Cultural Discourse* (Oxford: Oxford University Press, 1999).

[51] Sachs, note 50, p. 4.

[52] M. Finger, "Politics of the UNCED Process," in W. Sachs (ed.), *Global Ecology: A New Arena of Political Conflict* (London: Zed Books, 2003), p. 36.

[53] Sachs, note 50, p. 11.

[54] Sachs, note 50, p. 19.

[55] B. Rajagopal, *International Law from Below: Development, Social Movements and Third World Resistance* (Cambridge: Cambridge University Press, 2003), p. 117. He continues:

> "The logic of the discourse was the following: (a) the poor, not the rich alone, can damage the environment due to their unsustainable practices; (b) for this reason, they need to be managed to ensure that their practices are sustainable; (c) since the ultimate way to reduce the unsustainable practices of the poor is to make the poor richer, the heart of the strategy must be economic growth. Thus, the development rhetoric completed a full cycle, and practices that had been discredited became resuscitated under the new banner of "sustainable development'."

environmental justice movement.[56] For example, the agreed-upon text that "minerals are essential for modern living" from the 2002 World Summit on Sustainable Development was condemned by both environmentalists and affected community representatives, who boycotted the WSSD process several days into PrepCom IV, in Bali, Indonesia, in protest.[57] Among the complaints were the sense that the statement that "minerals are essential for modern living" was "skewed towards the satisfaction of the consumption patterns of the north,"[58] and that participation in the WSSD process was not furthering their struggles for human rights and ecological justice.[59] On the other hand, others have described the Johannesburg Plan of Implementation as a whole as noteworthy for its incorporation of a separate section on globalization, and for treating poverty and unsustainable production and consumption patterns as crosscutting issues.[60] According to this view, poverty is a "running theme" in the Johannesburg Plan of Implementation, and treated in a "multidimensional approach that embraces a vision of 'sustainable livelihoods'."[61] In this light, it is therefore important to acknowledge that there are communities in both South and North that do indeed choose mining as a path to economic development, whether by pursuing "their own initiatives for resource extraction" or by pursuing opportunities advanced by states and "third party business enterprises."[62]

The final text on mining in *The Future We Want* reinforces the fundamental international law principle of sovereignty over natural resources, as found in Principle 2 of the Rio Declaration: "States have, in accordance with the Charter of the United Nations and the principles of international law, the sovereign right to exploit their own resources pursuant to their own environmental and

---

[56] On the global environmental justice movement, see Environmental Justice Organisations, Liabilities and Trade (Ejolt), www.ejolt.org. See also J. Martinez-Alier, *The Environmentalism of the Poor: A Study of Ecological Conflicts and Valuation* (Cheltenham: Edward Elgar Publishing, 2002).

[57] Project Underground, "Affected Communities and Non-Governmental Organizations Boycott the WSSD" (2002) 7(5) *Drillbits and Tailings*; Statement of the Participants of the International Mining Workshop, Bali, News Release, No Tears for the WSSD, June 4, 2002 as cited in S. L. Seck, "Home State Responsibility and Local Communities: The Case of Global Mining" (2008) 11 *Yale Human Rights and Development Law Journal* 177 at 197. According to members of the Africa Initiative on Mining, Environment and Society (AIMES), the Canadian delegation at the Bali PrepCom were "among the architects of the mining section": Third World Network Africa, "Statement by AIMES on Mining," June 5, 2002, http://twnafrica.org. For a general critique, see G. Pring, "The 2002 Johannesburg World Summit on Sustainable Development: International Environmental Law Collides with Reality, Turning Jo'Burg into 'Joke'Burg'" (2002) 30 *Denver Journal of International Law and Policy* 410.

[58] Third World Network Africa, note 57.

[59] Statement of the Participants of the International Mining Workshop, note 57.

[60] Cordonier Segger and Khalfan, note 14, p. 29.

[61] Ibid, p. 29.

[62] UN General Assembly, note 4, paras. 9–11, 18; Ali, note 3.

developmental policies."[63] Principle 2 goes on to speak to the responsibility of states to avoid transboundary harm and harm to areas beyond the jurisdiction of any state. Yet, the local impacts of environmental harms experienced by mining-affected communities of the global South are beyond the realm of Principle 2, for they are matters of intraterritorial local harm subject to host state jurisdiction only.[64] While it is true that under Principle 11 of the Rio Declaration all states "shall enact effective environmental legislation," Principle 11 then explicitly qualifies this claim by noting that the "[e]nvironmental standards, management objectives and priorities should reflect the environmental and development context to which they apply. Standards applied by some countries may be inappropriate and of unwarranted economic and social cost to other countries, in particular developing countries." Thus a double standard of environmental protection, with implications for local ecology and health, is embedded within international environmental law. Yet it is not evident that this double standard is one that mining-impacted local communities of the global South want. Indeed, claims against transnational corporate actors for environmental harm are often informed by the claim that the harm violates environmental standards of the TNC home state.[65]

Importantly, however, environmental human rights defenders, whether indigenous or not, choose to resist extractive industry development not only within states of the South but also within those of the North, although the consequences are often more severe for those within the South.[66] Transnational civil society organizations have responded to the call, offering assistance to mining-affected communities seeking to learn lessons of resistance from others in a position to share their experiences.[67] Confronted with resistance, states and corporate actors respond by engaging security forces to remove protestors from contested lands. Resistance is

---

[63] Rio Declaration, note 15, Principle 2; *The Future We Want*, note 44, para. 227: "We acknowledge that countries have the sovereign right to develop their mineral resources according to their national priorities, and responsibility regarding the exploitation of resources described in the Rio Principles."

[64] S. L. Seck, "Transnational Business and Environmental Harm: A TWAIL Analysis of Home State Obligations" (2011) 3(1) *Trade, Law and Development* 164 at 173–181.

[65] See e.g. G. Eweje, "Environmental Costs and Responsibilities Resulting from Oil Exploitation in Developing Countries: The Case of the Niger Delta of Nigeria" (2006) 69 *Journal of Business Ethics* 27.

[66] UN General Assembly, note 6, paras. 60–87, 124–126; UN General Assembly, note 4. See also UN General Assembly, *Report of the Special Rapporteur on the Rights of Indigenous Peoples, James Anaya: Extractive Industries Operating Within or Near Indigenous Territories*, 11 July 2011, A/HRC/18/35; UN General Assembly, *Report of the Special Rapporteur on the Rights of Indigenous Peoples, James Anaya*, 6 July 2012, A/HRC/21/47. See also UN General Assembly, *Note by the Secretary-General, Situation of Human Rights Defenders*, 5 August 2013, A/68/262.

[67] Mines and Communities, www.minesandcommunities.org; North-South Institute, "Through Indigenous Eyes: Toward Appropriate Decision-Making Processes Regarding Mining On or Near Ancestral Lands," Final Synthesis Report of the North-South Institute (Canada), Amerindian Peoples Association (Guyana) and Institute of Regional Studies of the University of Antioquia (Colombia), September 2002.

too often met, particularly in states of the South, with violence in the form of physical and sexual assaults, killings, or imprisonment of environmental human rights defenders and their families.[68] Where state governments choose to listen, withdrawing permits or approvals held by mining industry players, the result is troubling. Foreign investors, protected by the terms of bilateral investment treaties or mining investment agreements and principles of international law, respond by suing host state governments for regulatory expropriation or equivalent doctrines in expensive binding international arbitration proceedings that lack legitimacy and transparency.[69] The resulting regulatory chill inhibits host states from regulating in the public interest, particularly in countries heavily dependent upon the returns of mineral revenue.

International law has responded to local community resistance through recognition of human rights to consultation or consent where development is proposed on indigenous lands, or where ecologically concerned local communities seek to participate in decision-making.[70] An international normative framework has developed, consisting of multilateral instruments explicitly or implicitly recognizing indigenous rights.[71] Much has been written about the right of indigenous peoples to free, prior, and informed consent (FPIC) before the exploitation of mineral and other resources affecting indigenous lands.[72] Yet the implementation

[68] UN General Assembly, note 6, paras. 60–87, 124–126; UN General Assembly, note 4, paras. 19–25. See also *Choc v Hudbay Minerals Inc*, 2013 ONSC 1414; *Guerrero and others v Monterrico Metals plc and another* [2009] EWHC 2475 (QB).

[69] S. Anderson and M. Perez-Rocha, "Mining for Profits in International Tribunals: Lessons for the Trans-Pacific Partnership," Institute for Policy Studies, April 2013, pp. 9–14; see generally K. Tienhaara, *The Expropriation of Environmental Governance: Protecting Foreign Investors at the Expense of Public Policy* (Cambridge: Cambridge University Press, 2009).

[70] Zillman (eds.), note 2; Seck, note 57.

[71] *Convention Concerning Indigenous and Tribal Peoples in Independent Countries*, Geneva, 27 June 1989, in force 5 September 1991, 72 ILO Official Bull. 59; 28 ILM 1382 (1989) [hereinafter ILO Convention 169]; *United Nations Declaration on the Rights of Indigenous Peoples*, New York, 12 September 2012, UNGA Res 61/295; A/61/L.67/Annex; *Convention on the Elimination of All Forms of Racial Discrimination*, New York, 21 December 1965, in force 4 January 1969, 660 UNTS 195; GA Res. 2106 (XX), Annex, 20 UN GAOR Supp. (No. 14) at 47; UN Doc. A/6014 (1966) [hereinafter CERD]; *International Covenant on Civil and Political Rights*, New York, 16 December 1966, in force 23 March 1976, GA Res. 2200A (XXI), 21 UN GAOR Supp. (No. 16) at 52; UN Doc. A/6316 (1966); 999 UNTS 171; 6 ILM 368 (1967) [hereinafter ICCPR]: rights to self-determination (Art. 1) and minorities' right to culture (Art. 27); *International Covenant on Economic, Social and Cultural Rights*, New York, 16 December 1966, in force 3 January 1976, GA Res. 2200A (XXI), 21 UN GAOR Supp. (No. 16) at 49; UN Doc. A/6316 (1966); 993 UNTS 3; 6 ILM 368 (1967) [hereinafter ICESCR]: rights to self-determination (Art. 1). In 2000, the United Nations established the UN Permanent Forum on Indigenous Issues.

[72] J. Cariño, "Indigenous Peoples' Right to Free, Prior, Informed Consent: Reflections on Concepts and Practice" (2005) **22** *Arizona Journal of International and Comparative Law* 19; B. McGee, "The Community Referendum: Participatory Democracy and the Right to Free, Prior and Informed Consent to Development" (2009) **27** *Berkley Journal of International Law* 570; T. Ward, "The Right to Free, Prior and Informed Consent: Indigenous Peoples'

of this right in practice has proven difficult, particularly in the resource extraction context. This has led to further studies and reports by various United Nations human rights mechanisms, including the UN Expert Mechanism on the Rights of Indigenous Peoples[73] and the Special Rapporteur on the Rights of Indigenous Peoples.[74] According to former Special Rapporteur James Anaya, the reasons for this difficulty in implementation relate in part to challenges associated with ensuring consultations are conducted in good faith.[75] These include: the fact that states "in effect delegat[e] to companies the execution of the State's duty to consult;" the existence of "significant imbalances of power" between indigenous peoples and both states and companies; a lack of access by indigenous peoples to technical information about proposed projects; a problem with timing, as exploration activities are often conducted before consultation; and the need to ensure that participation by indigenous peoples happens through representative institutions and decision-making structures.[76] There is also increasing evidence of the emergence of a normative framework of rights of ecologically concerned non-indigenous local communities. Many sources of international law identify both procedural and substantive environmental rights for individuals and groups.[77] These participatory rights include the right to information, the right to participate in decision-making, and rights of access to justice.[78] Substantive environmental rights include the right

---

Participation Rights within International Law" (2011) 10 *Northwestern Journal of International Human Rights Law* 54.

[73] UN General Assembly, *Final Report of the Study on Indigenous Peoples and the Right to Participate in Decision-Making*, 17 August 2011, A/HRC/18/42.

[74] UN General Assembly, note 4. According to Anaya in UN General Assembly, *Report of the Special Rapporteur on the Rights of Indigenous Peoples, James Anaya*, 6 July 2012, A/HRC/21/47, paras. 50 and 79, the content of FPIC will be determined in part by the nature of the substantive rights at issue, such as "rights to property, culture, religion, and non-discrimination in relation to lands, territories and natural resources, including sacred places and objects; rights to health and physical well-being in relation to a clean and healthy environment; and rights to set and pursue their own priorities for development, including development of natural resources, as part of their fundamental right to self-determination."

[75] UN General Assembly, note 4, paras. 58–60.

[76] Ibid, paras. 61–71.

[77] Rio Declaration, note 15, Principle 10; D. K. Anton and D. L. Shelton, *Environmental Protection and Human Rights* (New York: Cambridge University Press, 2011); UN General Assembly, *Report of the Independent Expert on the Issue of Human Rights Obligations Relating to the Enjoyment of a Safe, Clean, Healthy and Sustainable Environment, John. H. Knox*, 24 December 2012, A/HRC/22/43; UN General Assembly, *Report of the Independent Expert on the Issue of Human Rights Obligations Relating to the Enjoyment of a Safe, Clean, Healthy and Sustainable Environment, John H. Knox*, 30 December 2013, A/HRC/25/53.

[78] *Convention on Access to Information, Public Participation in Decision-Making and Access to Justice in Environmental Matters*, Aarhus, 28 June 1998, in force 30 October 2001, 2161 UNTS 447; 38 ILM 517 (1999) [hereinafter Aarhus Convention]; B. Richardson and J. Razzaque, "Public Participation in Environmental Decision-Making," in B. J. Richardson and S. Wood (eds.), *Environmental Law for Sustainability* (Oxford: Hart Publishing, 2006), p. 165; UN General Assembly (2013), note 77, paras. 29–43.

to water, the right to health, and the right to a healthy environment.[79] Increasingly, domestic constitutions are incorporating protections of environmental rights, although enforcement of these rights at times proves challenging.[80] Recognition of environmental rights is clearly evident in the resource extraction context.[81] Moreover, recent evidence of the application of these norms to the extractive industries can be found in the reports of special procedures mandate-holders at the UN Human Rights Council, including on the topic of the environmentally sound management and disposal of hazardous wastes[82] and the enjoyment of a safe, clean, healthy, and sustainable environment.[83]

The holder of international law duties under a state-centric analysis of international law would be the state, and indeed, much international law can be found holding states in violation of rights of indigenous and sometimes other local communities in the resource extraction context.[84] Yet many United Nations reports increasingly also identify the responsibility of corporations to respect human rights, including those of indigenous peoples, irrespective of host state compliance with international law.[85] The need for businesses to better understand environmental rights is also increasingly evident from UN identification of the problematic

---

[79] S. Atapattu, "The Right to Life or the Right to Die Polluted: The Emergence of a Human Right to a Healthy Environment Under International Law" (2002) 16 *Tulane Environmental Law Journal* 65; M. Fitzmaurice, "The Human Right to Water" (2007) XVIII *Fordham Environmental Law Review* 537; D. Shelton, "Human Rights and the Environment: Substantive Rights," in M. Fitzmaurice, D. Ong, and P. Merkouris (eds.), *Research Handbook on International Environmental Law* (Cheltenham: Edward Elgar Publishing, 2010), p. 265.

[80] D. R. Boyd, *The Environmental Rights Revolution: A Global Study of Constitutions, Human Rights, and the Environment* (Toronto: UBC Press, 2012); R. Tempitope, "The Judicial Recognition and Enforcement of the Right to Environment: Differing Perspectives from Nigeria to India" (2010) 3 *NUJS Law Review* 423.

[81] Seck, note 57; G. Pring and S. Y. Noe, "The Emerging International Law of Public Participation Affecting Global Mining, Energy and Resources Development," in Zillman et al. (eds.), note 2, pp. 11–52.

[82] UN General Assembly, *Report of the Special Rapporteur on the Human Rights Obligations Related to Environmentally Sound Management and Disposal of Hazardous Substances and Waste, Calin Georgescu*, 2 July 2012, A/HRC/21/48.

[83] UN General Assembly (2012), note 77, para. 28; UN General Assembly (2013), note 77, paras. 18, 61, 78.

[84] *The Case of the Mayagna (Sumo) Awas Tingni Community v Nicaragua*, Inter-Am Ct HR(Ser C) o 79 (31 August 2001), reprinted in (2002) 19 *Arizona Journal of International and Comparative Law* 395; L. Brunner, "The Rise of Peoples' Rights in the Americas: The Saramaka People Decision of the Inter-American Court of Human Rights" (2008) 7 *Chinese Journal of International Law* 699; J. Gilbert, "Indigenous Peoples' Human Rights in Africa: The Pragmatic Revolution of the African Commission on Human and Peoples' Rights" (2011) 60 *International and Comparative Law Quarterly* 245.

[85] Human Rights Council, *Guiding Principles on Business and Human Rights: Implementing the United Nations "Protect, Respect and Remedy" Framework, John Ruggie*, 21 March 2011, A/HRC/17/31; Human Rights Council, *Report of the Working Group on the Issue of Human Rights and Transnational Corporations and Other Business Enterprises*, 6 August 2013, A/HRC/68/279; UN General Assembly (2013), note 77, paras. 58–61.

394 *Transnational Corporations and Extractive Industries*

suppression of environmental human rights defenders.[86] As will be seen below, the idea that mining companies have a responsibility to respect rights when encountering local community resistance is permeating corporate social responsibility frameworks, although the ability of affected communities to seek environmental justice remains limited.

4. THE RESPONSE OF GLOBAL AND TRANSNATIONAL MINING GOVERNANCE FRAMEWORKS

Corporate social responsibility governance frameworks in the transnational mining context are increasingly responding to international law's recognition of the rights of indigenous and ecologically concerned local communities by integrating these rights into applicable frameworks. This should not be surprising if Rajagopal's analysis of "resistance-renewal" is accepted, according to which international law and institutions "renew and grow more" as "social movements resist more."[87] Indeed, according to Rajagopal, the Bretton Woods institutions "acquired their present agenda of sustainable human development, with its focus on poverty alleviation and environmental protection, as a result of their attempts to come to grips with grassroots resistance from the Third World in the 1960s and 1970s."[88] The call for increased industry support for company–community dialogue identified above in the 2002 Johannesburg Plan of Implementation provides additional evidence of this "resistance-renewal."

Transnational mining governance frameworks can be found at many levels. Industry association codes of conduct increasingly include express reference not only to the importance of environment and sustainable development, but also to indigenous rights and human rights.[89] In addition, a growing body of international corporate social responsibility guidelines recognize indigenous and environmental rights to participation, consultation, and even at times consent in resource extraction decision-making. Two notable examples are the Sustainability Framework of the World Bank's International Finance Corporation (IFC), which articulates the IFC's commitment to sustainable development as part of risk management

---

[86] UN General Assembly (2012), note 77, paras. 28, 61; General Assembly (2013), note 77, para. 83.

[87] B. Rajagopal, "From Modernization to Democratization: The Political Economy of the "New" International Law," in R. Falk, L. E. J. Ruiz, and R. B. J. Walker (eds.), *Reframing the International: Law, Culture, Politics* (New York: Routledge, 2002), pp. 136, 155; Rajagopal, note 55, pp. 133–134, 161. See further S. L. Seck, "Unilateral Home State Regulation: Imperialism or Tool for Subaltern Resistance?" (2008) 46 *Osgoode Hall Law Journal* 565.

[88] Rajagopal, note 55, p. 49 (emphasis added).

[89] International Council on Mining and Metals (ICMM), "Sustainable Development Framework," www.icmm.com; related position statements including ICMM, "Indigenous Peoples and Mining, Policy Statement," May 2013, www.icmm.com. See also Dashwood, note 18; United Nations Global Compact, "A Business Reference Guide: United Nations Declaration on the Rights of Indigenous Peoples," http://web.cim.org.

strategy,[90] and the Organisation for Economic Co-operation and Development (OECD) Guidelines for Multinational Enterprises (MNE Guidelines).[91]

The IFC Sustainability Framework comprised of the Policy and Performance Standards on Environmental and Social Sustainability, an Access to Information Policy, and a Policy on Social and Environmental Sustainability. Of note are the Performance Standards, which address the client's responsibilities for managing environmental and social risks.[92] Compliance with the Performance Standards is a condition of IFC financing support,[93] and an independent Compliance Advisor Ombudsman (CAO) is charged with responding to complaints by project-affected communities concerned with environmental and social impacts.[94] The original Performance Standards were released in 1998, updated in 2006, and updated again in 2011 after an eighteen-month review.[95] The 2012 Performance Standards provide guidance on many issues, including notably the Assessment and Management of Environmental and Social Risks (Performance Standard 1); Community Health, Safety and Security (Performance Standard 4); Land Acquisition and Involuntary Resettlement (Performance Standard 5); Biodiversity Management and Sustainable Management of Living Natural Resources (Performance Standard 6); and Indigenous Peoples (Performance Standard 7).[96]

Many problems have been identified with the implementation of the IFC standards and CAO mechanism.[97] Moreover, the coverage of the IFC standards remains limited for communities of the South within the North due to commonly built-in exceptions for high-income OECD countries, where local laws are presumed to be an acceptable substitute.[98] Yet despite the recent update and adoption of IFC standards by other institutions, including the Equator Principles for financial institutions,[99] it remains to be seen whether the IFC standards and implementing mechanisms can evolve to address local community environmental justice concerns.

[90] International Finance Corporation, "IFC's Sustainability Framework," http://www1.ifc.org. See also Torrance (ed.), note 41.

[91] *OECD Guidelines for Multinational Enterprises* (Paris: OECD Publishing, 2011) (hereinafter OECD MNE Guidelines).

[92] IFC, "Performance Standards on Environmental and Social Sustainability," www1.ifc.org.

[93] Morgera, note 41, pp. 209–216.

[94] Ibid, pp. 216–222; Compliance Advisor Ombudsman, "Our Mandate,' www.cao-ombudsman. org

[95] Morgera, note 41, pp. 147–148; IFC, "IFC Sustainability: Events and Milestones," www1.ifc. org.

[96] IFC, note 92; Torrance (ed.), note 41.

[97] Szablowski, note 5; S. Marshall et al., "Access to Justice for Communities Affected by the PT Weda Bay Nickel Mine – Interim Report," October 2, 2013, www.buseco.monash.edu.au

[98] Equator Principles, "Frequently Asked Questions," www.equator-principles.com, p. 3. However, members of the Equator Principles include many emerging market financial institutions: Equator Principles, "Members and Reporting," www.equator-principles.com.

[99] S. L. Seck, "Canadian Mining Internationally and the UN Guiding Principles for Business and Human Rights" (2011) **49** *Canadian Yearbook of International Law* 51 at 104–105; Equator Principles, "About the Equator Principles," www.equator-principles.com.

396 *Transnational Corporations and Extractive Industries*

The OECD initially put forward the OECD MNE Guidelines in 1976 as an Annex to the Declaration on International Investment and Multinational Enterprises.[100] The OECD MNE Guidelines describe themselves as "recommendations addressed by governments to multinational enterprises operating in or from adhering countries" providing non-binding principles and standards for businesses in a global context.[101] In addition to a discussion of general policies,[102] the OECD MNE Guidelines specifically address a number of areas of interest, including human rights[103] and environment.[104] The guidelines have been revised three times since initial adoption in 1976, with the addition of new environmental provisions in 1991 and more wide-ranging changes being made in 2000.[105] The most recent update, in 2011, focused on promoting responsible business conduct, including an updated human rights chapter and guidance on corporate due diligence and responsible supply chain management.[106]

Though the standards are non-binding, the OECD does require supporting countries to implement a mechanism designed to encourage compliance, in the form of National Contact Point (NCP) Agencies, initially proposed in 2000.[107] The NCP mechanisms also offer mediation services in relation to complaints submitted as "specific instances" that allege corporate contravention of the MNE Guidelines, and must contribute to the resolution of the practical issues raised in the implementation of the Guidelines.[108] Yet in practice both the substance of the Guidelines and the structure of NCPs, and thus their effectiveness, have led to many unsatisfactory experiences to date,[109] and a smaller number of claims of success.[110]

---

[100] OECD, *Declaration on International Investment and Multinational Enterprises*, 21 June 1976, 15 ILM 967; OECD Declaration C(76)99/FINAL (1976).

[101] OECD MNE Guidelines, note 91, p. 3.

[102] Ibid, p. 19.

[103] Ibid, p. 31.

[104] Ibid, p. 42.

[105] Morgera, note 41, pp. 102–103.

[106] OECD, "2011 Update of the OECD Guidelines for Multinational Enterprises – Comparative Table of Changes Made to the 2000 Text," 2011, www.oecd.org.

[107] OECD, *Decision of the Council on the OECD Guidelines for Multinational Enterprises*, OECD Decision C(2000)96/FINAL (2000), as amended by OECD Decision C/MIN(2011)11/FINAL (2011) at I(1)-(4).

[108] OECD, "National Contact Points for the OECD Guidelines for Multinational Enterprises," www.oecd.org.

[109] C. Coumans, "Mining and Access to Justice: From Sanction and Remedy to Weak Non-Judicial Grievance Mechanisms" (2012) 45 *University of British Columbia Law Review* 651; see e.g. Canadian National Contact Point for the OECD Guidelines for Multinational Enterprises, "Request for Review – the Operations of Centerra Gold Inc. at the Boroo Mine and the Gatsuurt Gold Deposit in Mongolia," March 14, 2012, http://oecdwatch.org.

[110] See L4BB, "Dongria Kondh Celebrate Victory in Vedanta Case," 2012, www.l4bb.org; L. C. Backer, "Governance Without Government: An Overview and Application of Interactions between Law–State and Governance–Corporate Systems" in G. Handl, J. Zekoll, and P. Zumbansen (eds.), *Beyond Territoriality: Transnational Legal Authority in an Age of Globalization* (Dordrecht: Martinus Nijhoff, 2012), p. 87.

Indeed, "success" may ultimately depend upon the way in which the outcome of NCP mediation influences legal proceedings in the host state.[111] While OECD NCPs are designed to promote mediation to prevent harm, many complainants in the extractive industry context invoke human rights and environmental justice.[112] Interestingly, the potential does exist for an NCP to hear claims brought by both the South within the South and the South within the North, even where the home state is an emerging market like Brazil.[113]

Both the IFC and OECD standards have evolved and broadened their mandates in response to resistance. While this has included providing affected communities with the opportunity (though limited) to bring a non-judicial grievance and seek resolution, the structure of these mechanisms and their ability to respond appears, to date, to be rarely in accordance with the desires of affected communities who either seek to prevent harm in advance or access justice after the fact.[114] Meanwhile, access to transnational legal remedy for local communities seeking remedy for environmental human rights harms arising from transnational resource extraction remains elusive despite increasing acceptance that home states are permitted, if not required, to protect human rights against corporate abuse and provide access to remedy in case of harm.[115] Home state legislatures and courts appear reluctant to embrace their duties as organs of the state.[116] On the other hand, some home states are very committed to providing host state governments with capacity-building support to facilitate mining investment by home state companies, even supporting the CSR efforts of industry.[117] Meanwhile, the voices of affected communities seeking justice are increasingly heard in alternate fora

---

[111] Backer, note 110. See also H. Ward, "The OECD Guidelines for Multinational Enterprises and Non-Adhering Countries: Opportunities and Challenges of Engagement," October 21, 2004, www.oecd.org.

[112] Institute for Human Rights and Business (IHRB), "Update on the Role of OECD National Contact Points with Regard to the Extractive Sectors," March 22, 2013, www.ihrb.org.

[113] OECD, "OECD Guidelines for Multinational Enterprises, National Contact Points," http://www.oecd.org.

[114] Morgera, note 41, pp. 209–246; N. L. Bridgeman and D. Hunter, "Narrowing the Accountability Gap: Toward a New Foreign Investor Accountability Mechanism" (2008) 20 *Georgetown International Environmental Law Review* 188; D. D. Bradlow, "Private Complainants and International Organizations: A Comparative Study of the Independent Inspection Mechanisms in International Financial Institutions" (2005) 36 *Georgetown Journal of International Law* 405; Szablowski, note 5; Seck, note 99 at 65.

[115] Seck, note 99 at 87–105; Human Rights Council, note 85.

[116] Seck, note 99; S. Seck, "Kiobel and the E-word: Reflections on Transnational Environmental Responsibility in an Interconnected World," July 5, 2013, http://lcbackerblog.blogspot.ca.

[117] See e.g. the newly established Canadian International Institute for Extractive Industries and Development (CIIEID) funded by the Canadian International Development Agency, CIDA, as discussed in Beedie School of Business, Simon Fraser University, "UBC, FSU to Further Global Sustainable Mining Practices through $25M Institute," December 5, 2012, http://beedie.sfu.ca.

398 Transnational Corporations and Extractive Industries

such as peoples' tribunals, where industry can be at least symbolically convicted in absentia.[118] Ultimately, the potential for corporate social responsibility governance frameworks to align with the environmental justice concerns of local communities of the global South depends upon the extent to which companies embracing these frameworks understand the importance of community participation and consent processes as driven by communities, with full support for capacity-building.[119]

5. CONCLUSIONS

Despite the emergence of transnational governance frameworks ostensibly designed to prevent and remedy environmental human rights harms arising from resource extraction, the journey is incomplete, with many unanswered questions for South and North. Notably, the "South" in the resource extraction context may be a local community in a Third World state or a local community in a First World state. Local communities affected by mining development may be indigenous, or they may be non-indigenous but equally ecologically concerned – a distinction that appears to matter under international law, but perhaps less so under frameworks of transnational governance. From the perspective of communities of the global South, what matters is access to environmental justice, yet this has so far proved elusive.

Mining companies too are not monolithic. State-owned enterprises may engage in resource extraction as much as domestic enterprises, joint ventures, artisanal and small-scale miners, and transnational or multinational enterprises. Home states of TNCs may also vary, with emerging market multinationals particularly from BRICS countries (Brazil, Russia, India, China, and South Africa) increasingly playing a central role in global mining. Moreover, while the transnational governance frameworks described in this chapter were designed to assist communities in Third World states of the global South, neither fully respond to First World or emerging market multinationals infringing the rights of local communities, including indigenous peoples in First World states. The presumption under the traditional story of international environmental law is that the developed states of the First World have both strong laws and sufficient governance capacity and political will to enforce them. But in the resource extraction context, colonialism runs deep.[120] Indeed, it is embedded within the very structure of international law.[121]

---

[118] Tribunal Popular Internacional de Salud, "Health Tribunal: In the Case of GoldCorp versus Mining Affected Communities," August 4, 2012, http://healthtribunal.org.

[119] See e.g. C. Rees, D. Kemp, and R. Davis, "Conflict Management and Corporate Culture in the Extractive Industries: A Study in Peru," Corporate Social Responsibility Initiative, Mossavar-Rahmani Center for Business and Government, Report No. 50, 2012.

[120] See e.g. S. Freeman, "Canada, Aboriginal Tension Erupting over Resource Development Study Suggests," Huffington Post, October 30, 2013.

[121] A. Anghie, Imperialism, Sovereignty and the Making of International Law (New York: Cambridge University Press, 2007).

PART IV

Environmental Justice and Vulnerable Groups

19

Food Justice: An Environmental Justice Critique of the Global Food System

Carmen G. Gonzalez

1. INTRODUCTION

Environmental justice is an important framework for understanding the North–South divide in many areas of international law and policy, including energy, climate, hazardous wastes, and food. An environmental justice analysis makes visible the ways in which the global North benefits from unsustainable economic activity while imposing the environmental consequences on the global South and on the planet's most vulnerable human beings, including women, racial and ethnic minorities, indigenous peoples, and the poor.[1]

From the colonial era to the present, the North has exploited the fertile lands, forests, and vast mineral resources of Asia, Africa, and Latin America, and wreaked havoc on the livelihoods and ecosystems of the region's inhabitants.[2] In recent decades, Northern countries have also used the global South as a dumping ground for hazardous wastes and a haven for polluting industry, a practice known as "toxic colonialism."[3] Finally, the global North has contributed disproportionately to climate change by utilizing more than its fair share of the atmosphere to deposit its greenhouse gases and by maintaining per capita emissions that continue to dwarf those of the South.[4]

---

[1] C. G. Gonzalez, "Environmental Justice and International Environmental Law," in S. Alam, M. J. H. Bhuiyan, T. M. R. Chowdhury, and E. J. Techera (eds.) *Routledge Handbook of International Environmental Law* (New York: Routledge, 2013), pp. 78–84.

[2] P. Hossay, *Unsustainable: A Primer for Global Environmental and Social Justice* (London: Zed Books, 2006), pp. 52–55; C. Ponting, *A Green History of the World: The Environment and the Collapse of Great Civilizations* (New York: Penguin Books, 1991), pp. 195–223.

[3] See generally J. Clapp, *Toxic Exports: The Transfer of Hazardous Wastes from Rich to Poor Countries* (Ithaca: Cornell University Press, 2010). See also Chapter 12, Z. Lipman, "The Hazardous Waste Trade."

[4] A. Simms, *Ecological Debt: The Health of the Planet & The Wealth of Nations* (London: Pluto Press, 2005), pp. 93–109.

402 Food Justice

While everyone suffers from the effects of environmental pollution, natural resource degradation, and climate change, socially and economically marginalized communities are disparately burdened due to their proximity to environmental hazards, their dependence on natural resources, and their limited access to good nutrition, decent housing, adequate health care, and other means of protecting themselves from environmental ills. In response to these inequities, environmental justice movements have arisen in both the North and the South, and are demanding healthy environments, sustainable livelihoods, and equitable access to natural resources.[5]

The global food system is a paradigmatic example of environmental injustice. Decades of Northern aid, trade, finance, and investment policies have devastated the livelihoods and ecosystems of rural communities in the global South while producing bountiful harvests and hefty profits for the Northern transnational corporations that dominate the global food system.[6] Despite global agricultural yields sufficient to supply every person on the planet with approximately 2,700 calories per day,[7] nearly a billion people, most of whom reside in the global South, experience chronic undernourishment because they lack the resources to purchase food on the market or to grow the food they require.[8]

This chapter applies an environmental justice analysis to the global food system, and identifies the ways in which this system perpetuates food injustice among and within nations. It adopts a tripartite definition of food justice consisting of ecologically sustainable food production, equitable access to food and food-producing resources, and democratic local and national control over food and agricultural policy. Because the concept of food justice originates in the theory and practice of the environmental justice movement,[9] the chapter describes the origins of this movement and explains how environmental justice as an analytical framework applies to North–South relations. The chapter then analyzes the underlying causes of food injustice, and outlines several strategies to create a more equitable and sustainable approach to global food governance.

---

[5] K. Harper and S. R. Rajan, "International Environmental Justice: Building the Natural Assets of the World's Poor," Political Economy Research Institute, University of Massachusetts Amherst, Working Paper Series No. 87 (2004), p. 1.

[6] E. Holt-Gimenez and R. Patel, *Food Rebellions! Crisis and the Hunger for Justice* (Oakland: Food First Books, 2009), pp. 1, 6, 20.

[7] J. Ziegler, C. Golay, C. Mahon, and S. Way, *The Fight For the Right to Food: Lessons Learned* (New York: Palgrave Macmillan, 2011), p. 3.

[8] C. G. Gonzalez, "Institutionalizing Inequality: The WTO, Agriculture and Developing Countries" (2002) 27 *Columbia Journal of Environmental Law* 431 at 468–470 (explaining the causes of chronic undernourishment).

[9] A. H. Alkon and J. Agyeman, "Introduction: The Food Movement as Polyculture," in A. H. Alkon and J. Agyeman (eds.), *Cultivating Food Justice: Race, Class and Sustainability* (Cambridge: MIT Press, 2011), pp. 7–9.

2. FROM ENVIRONMENTAL JUSTICE TO FOOD JUSTICE

The environmental justice movement emerged in the United States in the 1980s as a grassroots response to the concentration of polluting industries and abandoned hazardous waste sites in low-income communities of color.[10] Environmental justice scholars and activists articulated four distinct but interrelated dimensions of environmental injustice. They alleged distributive injustice in the form of disparate exposure to environmental hazards and inadequate access to environmental amenities (such as parks and open space); procedural unfairness due to the exclusion of socially and economically marginalized communities from governmental decision-making; corrective injustice in the form of ineffective enforcement of the environmental laws; and social injustice because environmental degradation is inextricably intertwined with other social ills, such as poverty and racism.[11]

From movements to secure access to clean water and sanitation to popular mobilizations against dams, mining, and petroleum extraction, grassroots environmental movements in the global South have embraced the language of environmental justice and have developed North–South and South–South transnational networks dedicated to specific issues, including water justice, food justice, energy justice, and climate justice.[12] Known collectively as "the environmentalism of the poor,"[13] these grassroots environmental justice movements dispel the myth that environmental protection is a luxury that the South can ill afford and emphasize the rights of local communities to self-determination, democratic participation, and access to the basic necessities of life.[14]

The inequities of the global food system have sparked a variety of movements in both the North and the South, most notably the food justice movement in the United States and the international movement for food sovereignty.[15] Reflecting its

---

[10] L. Cole and S. Foster, *From the Ground Up: Environmental Racism and the Rise of the Environmental Justice Movement* (New York: New York University Press, 2001), pp. 19–33.

[11] R. R. Kuehn, "A Taxonomy of Environmental Justice" (2000) 30 *Environmental Law Reporter* 10681 at 10685, 10689, 10694–10695, 10700–10702.

[12] J. Martinez-Alier et al., "Between Activism and Science: Grassroots Concepts for Sustainability Coined by Environmental Justice Organizations" (2014) 21 *Journal of Political Ecology* 19 at 27–42.

[13] Ibid, at 24–25.

[14] C. G. Gonzalez, "Beyond Eco-Imperialism: An Environmental Justice Critique of Free Trade" (2001) 78 *Denver University Law Review* 979 at 985–986, 999.

[15] For example, La Vía Campesina, one of the most prominent advocates of food sovereignty, is a network of small-scale farmers, farm laborers, fisherfolk, and indigenous communities, composed of more than 164 local and national organizations in seventy-three countries in both the North and the South. La Vía Campesina promotes small-scale sustainable agricultural as an alternative to the globalization of industrial agriculture, and advocates removing food from the purview of the World Trade Organization Agreement on Agriculture. See La Via Campesina, "The International Peasant's Voice," http://viacampesina.org. An example of the US-based food justice movement is the Growing Food and Justice for All Initiative, a network of individuals and organizations working to create healthy and sustainable food

Food Justice

roots in the environmental justice movement, the U.S. food justice movement denounces the social and economic factors that prevent low-income communities of color from purchasing or producing healthy, nutritious, environmentally sustainable, and culturally appropriate food. The movement seeks to empower these communities to create local food systems that meet their needs (through urban gardens, farmworker organizing, and indigenous subsistence–based practices such as hunting and fishing) as a transition to a more equitable and sustainable food system.[16] The international food sovereignty movement seeks to dismantle the corporate-dominated free trade policies that have devastated rural livelihoods and environments in both the North and the South, promotes the redistribution of land and water rights to small-scale farmers, and advocates the right of peoples and nations to define their own food policies and control their food-producing resources.[17] While international aid agencies strive to achieve food security, defined as "physical and economic access to sufficient, safe and nutritious food"[18] regardless of where, how, and by whom such food is produced, the food sovereignty and food justice movements demand a structural transformation of national and global food systems to promote democratized, localized, equitable, and sustainable food production.[19]

This chapter adopts a definition of food justice that reconciles the aims of both movements and emphasizes ecological sustainability, equitable access to food and food-producing resources, and democratic control over food and agricultural policy. For the purposes of this chapter, food justice is the right of communities to grow, sell, and consume healthy, nutritious, affordable, and culturally appropriate food produced through ecologically sustainable methods, and their right to democratically determine their own food and agriculture policies.[20] In other words, food

---

systems in communities of color known as *food deserts* due to the absence of fresh, high-quality foods. This network also advocates on behalf of farmworkers, who produce most of the nation's food but ironically suffer from chronic undernourishment. See Growing Food and Justice for All Initiative, www.growingfoodandjustice.org.

[16] Alkon and Agyeman, note 9, p. 414; E. Holt-Gimenez, "Food Security, Food Justice, or Food Sovereignty? Crises, Food Movements, and Regime Change," in A. H. Alkon and J. Agyeman (eds.), *Cultivating Food Justice: Race, Class and Sustainability* (Cambridge: MIT Press, 2011), p. 323.

[17] Holt-Gimenez, note 16, pp. 124–125; J. Clapp, *Food* (Cambridge: Polity Press, 2012), p. 172.

[18] World Food Summit, "Rome Declaration on World Food Security and World Food Summit Plan of Action," www.fao.org, para. 1.

[19] E. Holt-Gimenez and Y. Wang, "Reform or Transformation? The Pivotal Role of Food Justice in the U.S. Food Movement" (2011) 5 *Race/Ethnicity: Multidisciplinary Global Contexts* 83 at 89–90.

[20] This definition is consistent with food sovereignty: "the right of peoples to healthy and culturally appropriate food produced through ecologically sound and sustainable methods, and their right to define their own food and agriculture systems." R. Patel, "What Does Food Sovereignty Look Like?" (2009) 36(2) *Journal of Peasant Studies* 663 at 666 (quoting the 2007 Nyéléni Declaration on Food Sovereignty). This definition is likewise compatible with one of the definitions of food justice articulated by the U.S. food justice movement: "communities exercising their right to grow, sell, and eat [food that is] fresh, nutritious, affordable, culturally

justice is grounded in the human right to food, and is based on the principles of intergenerational equity, intragenerational equity, public participation in decision-making, and economic self-determination. Like the food sovereignty movement's call for local and national control of food-producing resources, this definition "does not negate trade, but rather it promotes the formulation of trade policies and practices that serve the rights of peoples to safe, healthy and ecologically sustainable production."[21]

Achieving food justice requires careful attention to North–South power imbalances that determine where, how, and by whom food is grown and consumed. Environmental justice is a useful framework for analyzing North–South power asymmetries and for developing legal strategies to promote a more equitable and sustainable global economic order. North–South relations are grounded in *distributive injustice* because the global North consumes a disproportionate share of the planet's resources and also contributes disproportionately to global environmental degradation; Southern countries bear most of the harm due to their vulnerable geographic locations, lack of resources, and limited capacity to grapple with environmental problems.[22] North–South relations raise issues of *procedural injustice* because the North dominates the institutions of global economic governance, including the World Bank, the International Monetary Fund (IMF), and the World Trade Organization (WTO), whose policies have increased economic inequality within and among nations and have accelerated natural resource exploitation.[23] *Corrective injustice* is perhaps most evident in the inability of vulnerable nations to obtain compensation for harms inflicted by powerful states, as exemplified by the small island states facing imminent destruction of their territories due to climate change.[24] Finally, North–South environmental conflicts are grounded in broader *social injustice* because they cannot be studied in isolation from the colonial and postcolonial policies that impoverished the global South and enabled the North to appropriate its natural resources.[25] The remainder of this chapter will examine the global food system through an environmental justice lens, and will explicitly apply this fourfold framework at the conclusion of the analysis.

---

appropriate and grown locally with care for the well-being of land, workers, and animals." Alkon and Agyeman, note 9, p. 5.

[21] Patel, note 20 (quoting the definition of food sovereignty developed in 2002 by the Peoples Food Sovereignty Network).

[22] R. Anand, *International Environmental Justice: A North–South Dimension* (Burlington: Ashgate, 2001), pp. 128–130; Gonzalez, note 14 at 987–1000.

[23] Anand, note 22, pp. 132–133; Hossay, note 2, pp. 191–198; R. Peet, *Unholy Trinity: The IMF, World Bank and WTO* (London: Zed Books, 2003), pp. 200–204.

[24] See Chapter 20, M. Burkett, "Climate Change and Small Island Nations."

[25] C. G. Gonzalez, "Genetically Modified Organisms and Justice: The International Environmental Justice Implications of Biotechnology" (2007) 19 *Georgetown International Environmental Law Review* 583 at 595–602.

3. GLOBAL FOOD INJUSTICE

According to the United Nations Food and Agriculture Organization (FAO), approximately 842 million people do not consume enough calories to satisfy their dietary energy requirements.[26] An additional two billion people suffer from deficiencies of essential micronutrients (such as Vitamin A and iron), and 26 percent of the world's children fail to achieve normal height and weight due to malnourishment.[27]

Chronic undernourishment is a result of poverty rather than food scarcity.[28] Even though the world's population (which stands at over seven billion[29]) is expected to reach 9.6 billion in 2050 and 10.9 million in 2100,[30] the global food system currently produces enough food to feed a global population of 12–14 billion.[31] Thus, efforts to boost food production through technological innovation are unlikely to eradicate world hunger. We will not eliminate chronic undernourishment unless we tackle its underlying causes – poverty and inequality.[32]

Chronic undernourishment is primarily a rural phenomenon. Approximately 80 percent of the world's undernourished people are small farmers, herders, fisherfolk, and landless workers in the rural areas of the global South who produce at least 70 percent of the world's food.[33] The vast majority are small farmers who are net food purchasers because they have been consigned to plots of land that are too small, too hilly, too arid, or inadequately irrigated due, in part, to competition for land and water from large-scale agricultural producers.[34] As explained later in the chapter, the livelihoods of these rural dwellers have been and continue to be undercut by Northern aid, trade, finance, and investment policies that favor large-scale industrial agriculture, accelerate environmental

---

[26] United Nations Food and Agriculture Organization (FAO), *The State of Food Insecurity in the World 2013: The Multiple Dimensions of Food Insecurity* (Rome: FAO, 2013), p. 8.

[27] FAO, *The State of Food and Agriculture 2013: Food Systems for Better Nutrition* (Rome: FAO, 2013), p. ix.

[28] See generally A. Sen, *Poverty and Famines: An Essay on Entitlement and Deprivation* (New York: Oxford University Press, 1990); O. de Schutter, "International Trade in Agriculture and the Right to Food," Friedrich-Ebert-Stiftung Occasional Papers No. 64 (2009), p. 10.

[29] World Population Clock, www.worldometers.info/world-population.

[30] United Nations Department of Social and Economic Affairs, *World Population Prospects: The 2012 Revision, Key Findings and Advance Tables*, 2013, ESA/P/WP.227, p. 1.

[31] UNCTAD, *Trade and Environment Review 2013, Wake Up Before It is Too Late: Make Agriculture Truly Sustainable Now for Food Security in a Changing Climate* (Geneva: United Nations Publication, 2013), p. 2.

[32] R. M. Bratspies, "Food, Technology and Hunger" (2014) 10 *Law, Culture and the Humanities* 212 at 220–224.

[33] O. de Schutter, "How Not to Think of Land-Grabbing: Three Critiques of Large-Scale Investments in Farmland" (2011) 38(2) *Journal of Peasant Studies* 249 at 256–257; IFAD, *Rural Poverty Report 2011* (Rome: IFAD, 2010), p. 6; ETC Group, "Who Will Feed Us? Questions for the Food and Climate Crises," ETC Group Communiqué, November 1, 2009, p. 1.

[34] de Schutter, note 33 at 256.

degradation, enrich local elites or Northern transnational corporations, and increase the gap between the rich and the poor.

3.1 The Global Food System: From Colonialism to the Green Revolution

A useful framework for understanding the evolution of the global food system is the food regime analysis introduced by Harriet Friedman and Philip McMichael.[35] A food regime is a system of production and consumption of food on a global scale that advances the interests of one or more dominant powers.[36]

During the first global food regime (1870–1930s), cheap food and raw materials from the colonies and from independent settler states fueled the industrialization of Europe.[37] European control over a significant part of the planet's natural resources enabled it to achieve a standard of living far beyond the constraints of its own resource base while relegating the South to the production of raw materials and the purchase of manufactured goods.[38] This pattern of trade and production has persisted into contemporary times, and has impoverished the South by subjecting it to the volatility of agricultural commodity prices (including boom and bust cycles) and the declining terms of trade for agricultural products relative to manufactured goods.[39] Nevertheless, the global South was largely food self-sufficient during the first food regime.[40]

During the second food regime (1930s to 1970s), the United States played a pivotal role in the global transition to industrial agriculture, and adopted aid and trade policies that dispossessed small farmers in the global South, undermined Southern food self-sufficiency, and laid the groundwork for the dominance of Northern transnational corporations in the global food system.[41] In the decades following World War II, the United States and Western European nations provided generous subsidies to their agricultural producers, and imposed both tariff and non-tariff import barriers to protect them from foreign competition.[42]

---

[35] H. Friedmann and P. McMichael, "Agriculture and the State System: The Rise and Decline of National Agriculture, 1870 to the Present" (1989) 29(2) *Sociologia Ruralis* 93.

[36] E. Holt-Gimenez and A. Shattuck, "Food Crises, Food Regimes and Food Movements: Rumblings of Reform or Tides of Transformation?" (2011) 38 *Journal of Peasant Studies* 109 at 110.

[37] H. Friedmann and P. McMichael, note 35 at 95–103.

[38] L. Young, *World Hunger* (London: Routledge, 1997), pp. 41–42.

[39] Ibid; Ponting, note 2, pp. 213–214.

[40] H. Friedmann, "From Colonialism to Green Capitalism: Social Movements and Emergence of Food Regimes" (2005) 22 *Research in Rural Sociology and Development* 227 at 238.

[41] Holt-Gimenez and Shattuck, note 36 at 110.

[42] T. P. Stewart (ed.), *The GATT Uruguay Round: A Negotiating History (1986-1992)* (Boston: Kluwer Law and Taxation Publishers, 1993), pp. 125, 141, 155–156; M. A. Aksoy, "Global Agricultural Trade Policies," in M. A. Aksoy and J. C. Beghin (eds.), *Global Agricultural Trade and Developing Countries* (Washington DC: The World Bank, 2005), p. 37.

408   *Food Justice*

By contrast, most Southern countries taxed the agricultural sector in order
to finance industrialization.[43]

The United States and European subsidies and import barriers were permitted
under the 1947 General Agreement on Tariffs and Trade[44] (1947 GATT), which
generally exempted agriculture from the GATT's trade liberalization requirements.[45] Indeed, the 1947 GATT benefited the North at the expense of the South
by mandating the reduction of tariffs on manufactured goods (produced primarily
by the North) while authorizing import barriers that enabled Northern countries to
limit or exclude Southern textiles, clothing, and agricultural products.[46] By the
mid-1950s, Southern countries had organized to demand a variety of measures to
address these inequities, including the phase-out of Northern agricultural subsidies
and import barriers; preferential access to Northern markets; and the right to use
quotas and tariffs to protect infant industries from foreign competition.[47] In
response to sustained Southern pressure, amendments and side agreements to the
1947 GATT incorporated Southern demands for preferential treatment (known
as special and differential treatment).[48] However, these measures were largely
ineffective because they were couched in non-binding language and often
excluded the products of greatest significance to Southern countries, such as
agricultural products, clothing, and textiles.[49]

When Northern agricultural subsidies (as well as agricultural mechanization and
the application of chemical fertilizers and pesticides) resulted in overproduction,
the United States and the European Community exported their surplus food to the
global South as food aid or provided a variety of subsidies and credits to private
grain traders to facilitate the purchase of this food by Southern countries.[50] The
provision of surplus food to Southern countries free of charge or at reduced prices
exacerbated poverty and hunger in the global South by depressing local food prices
and undermining the livelihoods of small farmers.[51] As small farmers lost their
lands and swelled the ranks of landless rural workers, wages for agricultural labor
declined – increasing rural inequality and generating widespread undernourishment.[52] Prime agricultural lands became concentrated in the hands of affluent
farmers, who produced coffee, cocoa, beef, vegetables, bananas, and feed grains for

[43] Stewart, note 42, pp. 154–157; Aksoy, note 42, p. 37.
[44] In force 1 January 1948, 55 UNTS 194; 61 Stat. pt. 5; TIAS 1700.
[45] Gonzalez, note 8 at 440–446.
[46] F. Ismail, "Rediscovering the Role of Developing Countries in GATT Before the Doha
Round" (2008) 1 *Law and Development Review* 49 at 58–59.
[47] Ibid at 59–67.
[48] Ibid at 65–67.
[49] Y-S. Lee, *Reclaiming Development in the World Trading System* (Cambridge: Cambridge
University Press, 2006), pp. 107–110.
[50] Clapp, note 17, pp. 26–33.
[51] J. Wessel, *Trading the Future: Farm Exports and the Concentration of Economic Power in Our
Food System* (San Francisco: Institute for Food and Development Policy, 1983), p. 168.
[52] Ibid, pp. 166–168.

export rather than for domestic consumption.[53] As domestic food production declined, many of the world's poorest countries became dependent on food imports.[54]

In the 1960s and 1970s, during the height of the Cold War, the United States sought to alleviate chronic malnourishment in the global South and forestall communist revolutions by exporting not just food, but the industrial agricultural model, including new high-yielding seeds, fossil fuel–based pesticides, and fertilizers, machinery, irrigation, and monocropping.[55] Known as the Green Revolution, this industrial agricultural model increased global food production, but displaced ecologically sustainable agricultural practices and fostered dependence on agricultural inputs manufactured by Northern transnational corporations.[56] The Green Revolution's impact on undernourishment remains fiercely contested. While some observers contend that the Green Revolution enabled food production to outpace population growth, others point out that the Green Revolution increased rural inequality by benefiting the large farmers who could afford the necessary agricultural machinery, irrigation systems, and other expensive inputs.[57] When rising food production caused prices to plummet, many small farmers were rendered destitute and landless.[58] An influential study analyzing more than 300 published reports on the Green Revolution concluded that the Green Revolution generally exacerbated rural inequality.[59]

The primary beneficiaries of food aid and of the rapid industrialization of Southern agriculture were the Northern industrial farmers, grain traders, and input manufacturers that received generous government subsidies, access to new consumer markets in the global South, and the opportunity to supply Southern farmers with machinery, pesticides, fertilizers, and seeds.[60] Even in the United States, small farmers were squeezed by the rising costs of agricultural inputs and the declining prices of agricultural commodities caused by the global sourcing of agricultural products by transnational corporations.[61] In the course of a few decades, farming operations in the United States became larger, more integrated into corporate supply chains, and more dependent on government export subsidies.[62]

---

[53] Ibid, p. 167.

[54] Clapp, note 17, p. 33; Friedmann, note 40 at 242.

[55] Clapp, note 17, p. 33.

[56] C. Fowler and P. Mooney, *Shattering: Food, Politics, and the Loss of Genetic Diversity* (Tucson: University of Arizona Press, 1990), pp. 54–79.

[57] Clapp, note 17, pp. 38–41; V. Shiva, *The Violence of the Green Revolution* (London: Zed Books, 1991), pp. 176–177.

[58] Shiva, note 57, p. 177; K. Griffin, *The Political Economy of Agrarian Change: An Essay on the Green Revolution* (Cambridge: Harvard University Press, 1974), p. 73.

[59] D. K. Freebairn, "Did the Green Revolution Concentrate Incomes? A Qualitative Study of Research Reports" (1995) 23 *World Development* 265 at 277.

[60] Clapp, note 17, pp. 32–33; Friedmann, note 40 at 243.

[61] Wessel, note 51, pp. 23–25.

[62] Friedmann, note 40 at 243.

410   *Food Justice*

The North's promotion of industrial agriculture also generated a variety of negative environmental consequences that currently threaten food production, including a dramatic worldwide decline in crop genetic diversity, dependence on fossil fuel–based inputs, massive soil erosion, depletion of aquifers, and rising greenhouse gas emissions.[63] Approximately 75 percent of the planet's food crop diversity was lost in the twentieth century as farmers ceased to cultivate an assortment of local crops in favor of the genetically uniform, high-yielding varieties of wheat, rice, maize, and potato introduced by the Green Revolution.[64] This loss of genetic diversity increased the vulnerability of the global food system to pests, drought, floods, and other external shocks, including those associated with climate change.[65] And climate change, although caused primarily by the historic and current greenhouse gas emissions of the global North, is anticipated to disproportionately affect Southern countries, to depress food production (including the productivity of fisheries), and to raise food prices.[66] Ironically, agriculture currently generates more anthropogenic greenhouse gas emissions than any other sector of the economy.[67] While industrial agriculture is a significant contributor to climate change, small-scale sustainable agriculture[68] can play an important role in climate change mitigation and adaptation.[69] Sustainable agriculture mitigates greenhouse gas emissions by minimizing the use of fossil fuel–based pesticides and fertilizers and increasing carbon sequestration in soils.[70] It also promotes climate change

[63] J. N. Pretty, *Regenerating Agriculture: Policies and Practices for Sustainability and Self-Reliance* (Washington DC: Joseph Henry Books, 1995), pp. 58–80; F. Kirschenmann, "Do Increased Energy Costs Offer Opportunities for A New Agriculture," in F. Magdoff and B. Tokar, *Agriculture and Food in Crisis* (New York: Monthly Review Press, 2010), p. 227.

[64] Pretty, note 63, p. 93.

[65] Fowler and Mooney, note 56, pp. 42–46.

[66] IPCC, *Climate Change 2014: Impacts, Adaptation, and Vulnerability, Summary for Policymakers* (Cambridge: Cambridge University Press, 2014), pp. 7–8, 16–18.

[67] K. Hahlbrock, *Feeding the Planet: Environmental Protection through Sustainable Agriculture* (London: Haus Publishing, 2007), p. 217; J. Bellarby, B. Foereid, A. Hastings, and P. Smith, *Cool Farming: Climate Impacts of Agriculture and Mitigation Potential* (Amsterdam: Greenpeace International, 2008), pp. 15–17.

[68] This chapter uses the term "sustainable agriculture" to refer to a goal rather than a rigid set of practices. Sustainable agriculture incorporates natural pest, nutrient, soil, and water management technologies into the production process and seeks to reduce the use of fossil fuel-based fertilizers and pesticides. It strives to conserve and enhance biodiversity, including plant genetic resources, livestock, soil organisms, and insects. Finally, sustainable agriculture combines the traditional knowledge of farmers with the latest scientific innovations to enhance farmer self-reliance and reduce dependence on costly external inputs. See Pretty, note 63, pp. 8–12.

[69] Working Group on Climate Change and Development, *Other Worlds Are Possible: Human Progress in an Age of Climate Change* (International Institute for Environment and Development, 2009), pp. 40–42; International Trade Centre (UNCTAD & WTO) & Research Institute of Organic Agriculture, "Organic Farming and Climate Change," http://intracen. org, p. 7–9, 117–118, 21.

[70] International Trade Centre (UNCTAD & WTO) & Research Institute of Organic Agriculture, note 69, pp. 7–8.

adaptation because it enhances resilience to drought, floods, and pests by diversifying the variety of crops cultivated and by increasing the soil's organic matter and water retention ability.[71]

Thus, the realization of food justice – particularly ecologically sustainable food production and equitable access to food and food-producing resources – will turn on the global food system's ability to enhance the well-being of small farmers and promote environmentally friendly cultivation practices. Unfortunately, the global food system has done precisely the opposite.

3.2 Double Standards in International Agricultural Trade

Prior to the debt crisis of the 1980s, Southern countries could insulate their farmers from unfair competition with highly subsidized United States and EU agricultural producers by imposing tariffs on imported food products. This policy space was quickly eroded during the third food regime, which emerged in the aftermath of the global economic shocks of the 1970s and 1980s, and is characterized by the unprecedented domination of agricultural markets by Northern transnational corporations.[72] Enticed into borrowing money from Northern commercial banks to finance a variety of development projects, many Southern countries were unable to pay their debts when the oil price shocks of 1973 and 1979–1980 increased energy costs and sent interest rates skyrocketing.[73] Many food import-dependent Southern countries were particularly affected because they had borrowed heavily in the early 1970s, when soaring food prices coincided with the first oil price shock.[74] In exchange for loan repayment assistance from the IMF and the World Bank, three quarters of Latin American countries and two thirds of African countries were required to adopt a one-size-fits-all package of economic reforms known as structural adjustment.[75]

The structural adjustment programs mandated by the IMF and the World Bank inaugurated the double standards that plague international agricultural trade to the present day: protectionism for the North and open markets for the South.[76] These structural adjustment programs required Southern countries to adopt a standard package of neoliberal economic reforms, including lowering tariffs, eliminating non-tariff import barriers, and slashing government assistance to the agricultural sector (such as marketing assistance, price guarantees, social safety

---

[71] Ibid.

[72] Holt-Gimenez and Shattuck, note 36, at 111.

[73] Peet, note 23, pp. 71–75; S. George, *A Fate Worse Than Debt: The World Financial Crisis and the Poor* (New York: Grove Press, 1990), pp. 28–29.

[74] Friedmann, note 40, at 244.

[75] Peet, note 23, p. 75.

[76] C. G. Gonzalez, "Markets, Monocultures, and Malnutrition: Agricultural Trade Policy Through an Environmental Justice Lens" (2006) 14 *Michigan State Journal of International Law* 345 at 364.

412   *Food Justice*

nets, and agricultural research and education).[77] However, Northern agricultural producers continued to receive lavish agricultural subsidies from their governments, and benefited handsomely from the opening of additional export markets in the global South.[78]

The reduction of Southern import barriers and diminution of support to small farmers devastated rural livelihoods by placing resource-poor Southern farmers in direct competition with highly subsidized Northern agricultural producers.[79] As cheap food imports flooded Southern markets, food production in the global South declined, and waves of impoverished farmers migrated to urban slums.[80] Unable to find remunerative employment or adequate housing, millions of displaced farmers wound up working in low-wage informal jobs, residing in self-constructed dwellings, and struggling to obtain the basic necessities of life.[81] In India, over 250,000 farmers have committed suicide since the 1990s as a consequence of the economic hardships inflicted by the neoliberal economic reforms mandated by the IMF and the World Bank (including reduction of agricultural import barriers and elimination of domestic agricultural subsidies).[82]

The structural adjustment policies of the IMF and the World Bank diminished food self-sufficiency in the global South by dispossessing small farmers and by requiring Southern countries to dedicate prime agricultural lands to agro-export production in order to service the foreign debt.[83] Many Southern countries curtailed domestic food production in order to grow "non-traditional" agricultural exports such as flowers, fruits, and vegetables in addition to the "traditional" exports introduced during the first food regime, such as sugar, coffee, cocoa, and other tropical commodities.[84] Diversion of fertile agricultural lands from food cultivation to the chemical-intensive production of cash crops increased dependence on food imports and intensified the environmental damage associated with industrial agriculture.[85]

---

[77] M. Chossudovsky, *The Globalisation of Poverty: Impacts of IMF and World Bank Reforms* (London: Zed Books, 1997), pp. 62–63; J. Madeley, *Hungry for Trade: How the Poor Pay for Free Trade* (New York: Zed Books, 2000), p. 77.

[78] C. G. Gonzalez, "The Global Food Crisis: Law, Policy, and the Elusive Quest for Justice" (2010) 13 *Yale Human Rights and Development Law Journal* 462 at 469.

[79] Ibid.

[80] Ibid at 469–470.

[81] V. Prashad, *The Poorer Nations: A Possible History of the Global South* (London: Verso, 2012), pp. 272–273.

[82] Center for Human Rights and Global Justice, *Every Thirty Minutes: Farmer Suicides, Human Rights and the Agrarian Crisis in India* (New York: New York University School of Law, 2011), pp. 5–12.

[83] George, note 73, pp. 28–29; Peet, note 23, p. 71.

[84] Friedmann, note 40 at 251.

[85] A. Mittal, UN Conference on Trade and Development (UNCTAD), *The 2008 Food Price Crisis: Rethinking Food Security Policies*, G-24 Discussion Paper No. 29, June 2009, UNCTAD/GDS/MDP/G24/2009/3, pp. 13–15; Structural Adjustment Participatory Review International Network (SAPRIN), *The Policy Roots of Economic Crisis and Poverty: A Multi-Country Participatory Assessment of Structural Adjustment* (SAPRIN, 2002), pp. 124–126.

The WTO Agreement on Agriculture (AoA), which entered into force in 1995, purported to eliminate the double standards in global agricultural trade and to "establish a fair and market-oriented agricultural trading system."[86] The AoA required WTO members to reduce trade-distorting agricultural subsidies (including both domestic subsidies and export subsidies), convert all import barriers to tariffs (a process known as "tariffication"), and reduce these tariffs over time.[87]

The AoA failed to achieve its subsidy reduction objectives because Northern countries made aggressive use of the ambiguities in the AoA to continue to subsidize their agricultural producers and exporters.[88] Agricultural subsidies in the North actually *increased* in the aftermath of the AoA.[89] Ironically, since most Southern countries had already liberalized their markets pursuant to structural adjustment programs, the primary impact of the AoA was to preclude these countries from adopting export subsidies in the future and from providing domestic subsidies beyond *de minimis* levels.[90]

The AoA tariffication requirements did not open up Northern markets for the benefit of Southern exporters, but did succeed in restricting the ability of Southern countries to raise tariffs when confronted with surges of cheap, subsidized agricultural products.[91] Because the AoA did not specify how to convert non-tariff import barriers into tariffs, most Northern countries adopted tariffs that were far more import-restrictive than the non-tariff barriers they replaced (a phenomenon known as "dirty tariffication").[92] Northern countries maintained high tariffs on many Southern products (particularly those that competed with domestically produced equivalents, such as fruits and vegetables), and also engaged in tariff escalation – the practice of charging higher tariffs as the processing chain advances.[93] Tariff escalation harms Southern countries by discouraging them from diversifying their economies into higher value-added processed goods.[94] By contrast, most Southern countries did not engage in tariffication at all because they had already eliminated their non-tariff barriers (and reduced their tariffs) pursuant to IMF/World

---

[86] WTO *Agreement on Agriculture*, Geneva, 15 April 1994, in force 1 January 1995, 1867 UNTS 410, preamble para. 2.

[87] Gonzalez, note 8 at 450–456.

[88] Ibid at 459–468 (analyzing the ambiguities in the AoA that enabled the United States and the EU to maintain their domestic subsidies and export subsidies); J. A. McMahon and M. G. Desta, "The Agreement on Agriculture: Setting the Scene," in J. A. McMahon and M. G. Desta (eds.), *Research Handbook on the WTO Agriculture Agreement* (Cheltenham: Edward Elgar, 2012), pp. 12–16 (explaining why the AoA's restrictions on domestic subsidies and export subsidies are easy to circumvent).

[89] Gonzalez, note 8 at 366.

[90] Ibid, at 453–454, 479.

[91] Ibid at 458–461, 476–477.

[92] Ibid at 458; M. G. Desta, *The Law of International Trade in Agricultural Products* (The Hague: Kluwer, 2002), pp. 75–76.

[93] Gonzalez, note 8 at 461–462.

[94] Ibid at 462.

414   *Food Justice*

Bank-mandated structural adjustment programs.[95] Southern countries that did not engage in tariffication were particularly vulnerable to Northern agricultural export dumping because the AoA mechanism authorizing tariff increases to protect small farmers from devastating influxes of cheap, imported food (the "special safeguard mechanism") was only available to countries that engaged in tariffication.[96]

In sum, while the AoA did not create the double standards in international agricultural trade that systematically disfavor small farmers in the global South, it did reinforce these inequities by embedding them in a legally binding international agreement. These double standards enabled Northern agricultural producers to destroy the livelihoods of small farmers in the global South by dumping agricultural products on world markets at prices that are below the local cost of production.[97]

Over the course of several decades, Southern countries that were once net food exporters have been transformed into net food importers.[98] Poor harvests, fluctuating demand for these nations' exports, and rising prices for food imports can trigger balance of payments crises, chronic food shortages, and famines.[99] Indeed, both low-income and middle-income Southern countries are now being buffeted by higher food prices.[100] In 2008, 2011, and 2013, soaring food prices sparked food riots in countries as diverse as Argentina, Brazil, China, Turkey, Egypt, Syria, Iraq, Somalia, Yemen, Tunisia, Haiti, Mozambique, Sudan, and Saudi Arabia.[101]

The redirection of food trade from national to global markets has also reinforced the power of transnational corporations that dominate the global food system. Supported by decades of overseas food aid programs, government subsidies, and public sector agricultural research, these transnational grain traders, seed and agrochemical corporations, and retail supermarket chains wield unprecedented market power.[102] This market power enables these companies to pay farmers low prices for their agricultural output, charge high prices for agricultural inputs (such as seeds and fertilizers), and impose product quality standards that may be too onerous for many small farmers to satisfy.[103]

---

[95] Ibid at 476.

[96] Ibid at 477.

[97] S. Murphy, B. Lilliston, and M. B. Lake, *WTO Agreement on Agriculture: A Decade of Dumping* (Minneapolis: IATP, 2005), p. 1; C. Häberli, "The WTO and Food Security: What's Wrong with the Rules?" in R. Rayfuse and N. Weisflet, *The Challenge of Food Security* (Cheltenham: Edward Elgar, 2012), pp. 163–164.

[98] Action Aid, *The Impact of Agro-Exports Surges in Developing Countries* (Johannesburg: ActionAid, 2008), p. 8.

[99] United Nations Food and Agriculture Organization, *The State of Agricultural Commodity Markets 2009* (Rome: FAO, 2009), pp. 32–34.

[100] N. Hossain, R. King, and A. Kelbert, *Squeezed: Highlights from Life in a Time of Food Price Volatility, Year 1 Results* (Oxford: Oxfam GB for Oxfam International, 2013).

[101] N. Ahmed, "Global Riot Epidemic Due to Demise of Cheap Fossil Fuels," *The Guardian*, March 1, 2014.

[102] Clapp, note 17, pp. 96–118.

[103] Ibid.

Carmen G. Gonzalez 415

In addition to dispossessing small farmers in the global South through low-priced exports, transnational corporations have also displaced local food retailers and promoted a worldwide convergence of urban diets on a narrow range of staple foods as well as meat, edible oils, fats, sugars, and cheap, unhealthy processed foods – thereby contributing to a global epidemic of obesity and diet-related diseases.[104] Contrary to popular misconception, two thirds of the planet's overweight and obese people reside in the global South.[105] This means that many of the low- and middle-income Southern countries struggling with chronic malnutrition are also disproportionately burdened with diet-related diseases, including diabetes, cancer, and cardiovascular disease.[106]

Finally, Monsanto and other proponents of biotechnology have unduly influenced public debates over genetically modified (GM) crops by touting this technology as the solution to the problem of world hunger.[107] They argue that genetic engineering will address chronic malnourishment in the global South by boosting food production and generating crops with useful characteristics, such as enhanced nutritional content, insect resistance, and greater tolerance for drought and salinity.[108] Regrettably, the obsessive focus on agricultural production obscures the actual causes of undernourishment (poverty and inequality), the economic and environmental impacts of GM crops, and the propensity of this technology to reinforce corporate domination of the global food system.

The extremely high cost of biotechnological research and development, combined with intellectual property rights in GM crops, has facilitated the rise of a global oligopoly in the seed industry.[109] Currently, six corporations control 66 percent of global seed sales.[110] In addition to the patent protection accorded to GM crops in the global North, the WTO Agreement on Trade-Related Aspects of Intellectual Property Rights (TRIPS) requires WTO member states to protect plant varieties by patents or by an effective *sui generis* system.[111] These intellectual

---

[104] P. McMichael, "Global Development and the Corporate Food Regime" (2005) 11 *Research in Rural Sociology and Development* 269 at 288–289.

[105] U. Friedman, "Two-Thirds of Obese People Now Live in Developing Countries," *The Atlantic*, May 29, 2014.

[106] Ibid; S. E. Clark, C. Hawkes, S. M. Murphy, K. A. Hansen-Kuhn, and D. Wallinga, "Exporting Obesity: U.S. Farm and Trade Policy and the Transformation of the Mexican Consumer Food Environment" (2012) 18 *International Journal of Occupational and Environmental Health* 56 (analyzing the negative impacts of trade liberalization on obesity and declining public health in Mexico).

[107] C. Todhunter, "The GMO Biotech Lobby's Emotional Blackmail and Bogus Claims: GM Crops Will Not Feed the World," www.globalresearch.ca (quoting Monsanto CEO Robert Fraley); N. E. Borlaug, "Farmers Can Feed the World," *Wall Street Journal*, July 30, 2009.

[108] K. Aoki, "Food Forethought: Intergenerational Equity and Global Food Supply – Past, Present, and Future" (2011) *Wisconsin Law Review* 399 at 458.

[109] Ibid at 481.

[110] ETC Group, "Gene Giants Seek Philanthrogopoly," *Communiqué*, 110, March 2013, p. 3.

[111] *WTO Agreement on Trade-Related Aspects of Intellectual Property Rights*, Geneva, 15 April 1994, 1869 UNTS 299; 33 ILM 1197 (1994), art. 27. The relationship between the TRIPS

416 Food Justice

property rights give corporations like Monsanto, Syngenta, and Pioneer the power to require all end-users of their seeds to sign restrictive license agreements.[112] Instead of exercising their traditional rights to improve, market, and save seeds from season to season, farmers who purchase GM seeds must buy new seeds every growing season at prices dictated by the global seed industry.[113] Indeed, these licenses are so restrictive that they even forbid the use of GM seeds for independent research, including research investigating the environmental and human health impacts of GM crops.[114]

Ironically, many of the GM crops marketed by Northern transnational corporations were developed from germplasm and traditional knowledge acquired free of charge from local and indigenous communities in the global South (a phenomenon known as biopiracy).[115] As one observer points out:

> Under the legal regime in place prior to the 1990s, once "primitive" or "raw" plant germplasm was construed legally as the "common heritage of mankind," it could be removed from genetically rich regions for as little as it cost to gather a few samples. These "free" genetic resources then flowed into Northern gene banks and laboratories of agrichemical giants, where their genetic diversity was "worked" to improve and safeguard proprietary, patented varieties. Then, these "stabilized" varieties were sold at a premium in the emerging agricultural markets of the very countries and regions where the genetic resources originated, pushing formerly genetically diverse countries toward industrial agriculture and monoculture.[116]

GM crops replicate the anti-poor bias of the Green Revolution. GM crops favor wealthy farmers because poor farmers generally lack the cash or credit necessary to purchase patented seeds every season as well as the expensive chemical inputs necessary to cultivate these crops.[117] Small farmers who incur debt to purchase this technology risk losing their lands if seed and agrochemical prices rise and/or yields

---

regime, the *Convention on Biological Diversity*, Rio de Janeiro, 5 June 1992, in force 29 December 1993, 1760 UNTS 79; 31 ILM 818 (1992) (hereinafter CBD), and the *International Treaty on Plant Genetic Resources for Food and Agriculture*, 3 November 2001, in force 29 June 2004, www.planttreaty.org, all of which govern the treatment of plant genetic resources, is beyond the scope of this chapter. For an excellent analysis of this topic, see Aoki, note 108. The North–South tensions on access to genetic resources and equitable sharing of the resulting benefits under the CBD and the *Nagoya Protocol on Access to Genetic Resources and the Fair and Equitable Sharing of Benefits Arising from their Utilization to the 1992 Convention on Biological Diversity*, www.cbd.int, are discussed in Chapter 9 of this volume by J. Cabrera, "Access and Benefit Sharing: North–South Challenges in Implementing the Convention on Biological Diversity and its Nagoya Protocol."

[112] Aoki, note 108 at 470.
[113] Ibid at 452–455.
[114] Ibid at 470.
[115] K. Aoki, "Seeds of Dispute: Intellectual Property Rights and Agricultural Biodiversity" (2009) 3 *Golden Gate University Environmental Law Journal* 79 at 133–136.
[116] Ibid at 135–136.
[117] Gonzalez, note 25 at 604–605.

fluctuate or decline.[118] In addition, GM crops (such as herbicide-resistant crops) reduce the demand for manual labor (including weeding) in Southern countries with abundant rural populations and limited capacity to absorb rural migrants into urban employment. By reducing labor costs, GM crops benefit large commercial farms at the expense of landless laborers and small farmers who augment their income through part-time employment on large commercial farms.[119] In so doing, they undermine the livelihoods of the world's most malnourished population while contributing to the displacement of small-scale farming by industrial agriculture.[120]

GM crops also pose significant environmental risks. First, GM crops reinforce monocropping, thereby supplanting the diverse indigenous crops cultivated for millennia in the global South and the traditional knowledge of the subsistence farmers who preserve much of the world's agrobiodiversity.[121] The growing genetic uniformity of the world's food supply increases the likelihood of catastrophic crop failure (akin to the Irish potato famine, but this time on a global scale) in the event of drought, pest infestations, or other environmental disruptions.[122] Genetic erosion in the global South due to monocropping deprives plant breeders of the genetically diverse cultivated and wild species necessary to identify traits that provide resistance to new pests and diseases.[123] As climate change introduces new challenges, GM crops may "be incapable of changing, of evolving, of adapting to new conditions, or stronger pests."[124] Second, insect-resistant crops (such as crops containing the natural microbial pesticide *Bacillus thuringiensis*) and herbicide-tolerant crops (such as crops resistant to Monsanto's Roundup herbicide) may accelerate the evolution of resistance in weeds and pests, thereby requiring the use of more powerful herbicides and pesticides.[125] This has already occurred in the United States, where the appearance of Roundup-resistant weeds has necessitated greater use of herbicides.[126] Third, GM crops may disrupt the mechanisms used by small farmers to maintain soil fertility and control pests by harming non-target organisms, such as beneficial soil organisms and natural predators of insect pests.[127] Fourth, GM crops may transfer transgenes containing herbicide resistance or natural insecticides to other plants, which could then become super-weeds immune to herbicides and insects. The risk of gene transfer is particularly high for crops grown in close proximity to wild or weedy relatives (such as maize in Mexico),

---

[118] Ibid at 604.
[119] Ibid at 604–605.
[120] Aoki, note 108 at 478.
[121] Gonzalez, note 25 at 607–608.
[122] Ibid.
[123] Aoki, note 108 at 125–126.
[124] Fowler and Mooney, note 56, p. 53.
[125] Gonzalez, note 25 at 608–609.
[126] Aoki, note 108 at 459–460.
[127] Gonzalez, note 25 at 609–610.

418 *Food Justice*

and may result in the loss of genetic variability necessary to adapt crops to changing environmental conditions.[128]

In short, the profit-driven biotechnology industry has generally catered to the interests of large-scale commercial farmers while devoting scant resources to the needs of small-scale producers.[129] Genetic engineering has also reinforced the negative environmental consequences of industrial agriculture (such as monocropping) and introduced new risks (such as the transfer of transgenes).[130] While a full discussion of GM crops is beyond the scope of this chapter, it is important to recognize that genetic engineering might be beneficial if the technology were controlled by the public sector with farmer input and participation, priced at affordable rates, available without restrictive licenses, deployed to enhance the livelihoods of small farmers rather than the profits of transnational corporations, and subjected to rigorous assessments of environmental and human health risks.

3.3 *Financial Speculation, Biofuels, and the Global Land Rush*

Small farmers in the global South face additional challenges in the form of financial speculation in agricultural commodity markets, biofuels production, and large-scale acquisitions of agricultural lands. When the U.S. housing market collapsed in 2007, speculative investment flooded into agricultural commodity markets and contributed significantly to the 2008 global food price crisis.[131] This influx of speculative investment commenced with the deregulation of over-the-counter (OTC) derivatives following the passage of the U.S. Commodity Futures Modernization Act in 2000.[132] This statute and the subsequent decisions of the Commodity Futures Trading Commission exempted OTC derivatives (including commodity index funds) from regulatory oversight, including reporting requirements and position limits (restrictions on the number of contracts that non-commercial traders can hold).[133] The failure of governments to curb speculation in agricultural commodity markets increases market volatility and poses particularly serious risks to low-income consumers (including small farmers) and to net food-importing Southern nations.[134]

---

[128] Ibid at 608–609.

[129] Ibid at 603–604; Aoki, note 108 at 476–478.

[130] Gonzalez, note 25 at 607–610.

[131] P. Wahl, "The Role of Speculation in the 2008 Food Price Bubble," in S. Murphy and A. Paasch (eds.), *The Global Food Challenge: Towards a Human Rights Approach to Trade and Investment Policies* (Minneapolis: IATP, 2009), pp. 70–71; F. Kaufman, "How Goldman Sachs Created the Food Crisis," *Foreign Policy*, April 27, 2011.

[132] O. de Schutter, "Food Commodities Speculation and Food Price Crises," United Nations Special Rapporteur on the Right to Food, Briefing Note 02, September 2010.

[133] Ibid, p. 5–6; Clapp, note 17, pp. 139–142; N. Colbran, "The Financialisation of Agricultural Commodity Futures Trading: The 2006–2008 Global Food Crisis," in R. Rayfuse and N. Weisflet, *The Challenge of Food Security* (Cheltenham: Edward Elgar, 2012), pp. 173–174.

[134] Wahl, note 131, pp. 75–76.

Another driver of food price volatility is the growing demand for biofuels. Although most studies question the net carbon benefits of the vast majority of biofuels,[135] the European Union and the United States have encouraged the development of the biofuels industry through their renewable fuels mandates, and through policies that subsidize or protect this industry.[136] Biofuels production competes with food production for land, water, and other productive resources, and has contributed to rising food prices.[137]

The final threat to the livelihoods of small farmers in the global South is the proliferation of large-scale leases or purchases of Southern agricultural lands on terms that may deprive current users and occupiers of food-producing resources.[138] Despite the lack of systemic data regarding these land transactions, a 2012 report by the International Land Coalition (ILC), a collaboration among forty grassroots and civil society organizations, estimated that an area eight times the size of the United Kingdom or nearly the size of western Europe was transferred between January 2000 and November 2011.[139] While the ILC has since revised this figure to approximately fifty-two million hectares transferred or under negotiation, the size of the global land rush is nevertheless significant.[140]

As Chidi Oguamanam explains in his contribution to this volume, these so-called "land grabs" have been driven by transnational corporations eager to exploit the growing demand for biofuels; by foreign investors (including Northern hedge funds, investment banks, and pension funds) speculating on arable land; and by middle-income Southern countries (such as Saudi Arabia, Qatar, China, India, and South Korea) seeking to engage in the offshore production of food to mitigate food price volatility on international markets and domestic shortages of arable land and irrigation water.[141] Africa appears to be the primary target of these

---

[135] R. Sims, M. Taylor, J. Saddler, and W. Mabee, *From 1st to 2nd Generation Biofuel Technologies: An Overview of Current Industry and R&D Activities* (International Energy Agency, Paris, 2008), pp. 6, 18–19.

[136] Committee on World Food Security, "Biofuels and Food Security: A Report by the High Level Panel of Experts on Food Security and Nutrition" (Rome, 2013), www.fao.org, pp. 27–32.

[137] Ibid, pp. 13–15.

[138] W. Answeeuw, L. A. Wiley, L. Cotula, and M. Taylor, *Land Rights and the Rush for Land: Findings of the Global Commercial Pressure on Land Research Project* (Rome: International Land Coalition, 2012); L. Cotula, S. Vermeulen, R. Leonard, and J. Keeley, *Land Grab or Development Opportunity? Agricultural Investment and International Land Deals in Africa* (London: FAO/IIED/IFAD, 2009); A. Spieldoch and S. Murphy, "Agricultural Land Acquisitions: Implications for Food Security and Poverty Alleviation," in M. Kugelman and S. L. Levenstein (eds.), *Land Grab? The Race for the World's Farmland* (Washington DC: Woodrow Wilson International Center for Scholars, 2009).

[139] Answeeuw, note 138, p. 19.

[140] Land Matrix, http://landmatrix.org.

[141] M. Kugelman and S. L. Levenstein (eds.), *Land Grab? The Race for the World's Farmland* (Washington DC: Woodrow Wilson International Center for Scholars, 2009), p. 2; Spieldoch and Murphy, note 138, pp. 41–42; Answeeuw, note 38, p. 21; Clapp, note 17, pp. 150–151. See Chapter 11, C. Oguanaman, "Bioenergy and Land Grabs."

420 *Food Justice*

land acquisitions.[142] While Northern companies account for most of the land transactions, middle-income Southern nations (including India, Brazil, South Africa, and China) have become significant participants in the global land rush.[143] The growing demand for Southern agricultural lands has produced South–South tensions as more affluent Southern nations emulate the resource-grabbing practices of their Northern counterparts at the expense of the planet's poorest communities.[144]

These transactions pose serious risks to small farmers in the targeted Southern countries, including eviction from their lands, depletion or pollution of water resources, and loss of access to forests, fisheries, and other natural resources.[145] For example, small farmers and herders whose ownership or usufruct rights are not recognized by government officials may be dispossessed by foreign investors or by local elites eager to sell or lease these lands to foreign investors.[146] The conversion of labor-intensive subsistence farms to highly mechanized export-oriented industrial agriculture may reduce local food availability, intensify poverty by shrinking rural employment, contaminate the local water supply with pesticide and fertilizer run-off, degrade the land through intensive cultivation, increase greenhouse gas emissions, and deplete water resources needed by local communities.[147]

These land acquisitions are accelerating the South's transition from peasant cultivation to large-scale industrial agriculture at the precise moment when scientists and policy-makers are advocating a shift to small-scale sustainable agriculture in food-insecure countries. In 2013, the United Nations Conference on Trade and Development (UNCTAD) published a major report urging a paradigm shift in agriculture – away from industrial agriculture and toward sustainable, regenerative production systems that enhance the productivity of small-scale farmers.[148] Indeed, sustainable agriculture has produced significant increases in agricultural yields in Asia, Africa, and Latin America while enhancing environmental quality, reducing

---

[142] Answeeuw, note 138, p. 23.

[143] L. Cotula, *The Great African Land Grab? Agricultural Investments and the Global Food System* (London: Zed Books, 2013), pp. 55–67.

[144] T. Ferrando, "Land Grabbing under the Cover of Law: Are BRICS-South Relationships any Different?," September 2014, www.tni.org.

[145] Spieldoch and Murphy, note 138, pp. 43–48.

[146] R. Q. Montemayor, "Overseas Farmland Investments – Boon or Bane for Farmers in Asia?," in M. Kugelman and S. L. Levenstein (eds.), *Land Grab? The Race for the World's Farmland* (Washington DC: Woodrow Wilson International Center for Scholars, 2009), pp. 101–102; O. de Schutter, "The Green Rush: The Global Race for Farmland and the Rights of Land Users' (2011) 52(2) *Harvard International Law Journal* 501 at 537.

[147] R. Meinzen and H. Markelova, "Nuance: Toward a Code of Conduct in Foreign Land Deals," in M. Kugelman and S. L. Levenstein (eds.), *Land Grab? The Race for the World's Farmland* (Washington DC: Woodrow Wilson International Center for Scholars, 2009), p. 74; Montemayor, note 146, pp. 102–105; Spieldoch and Murphy, note 138, pp. 46–47.

[148] UNCTAD, note 31.

dependence on external inputs, and protecting the traditional agroecological knowledge of small farmers and indigenous communities.[149]

International investment law has facilitated the global land rush by enabling foreign investors to obtain more favorable treatment than domestic stakeholders.[150] In Africa, where these land transactions are concentrated, control over land remains largely in the hands of the government or, in some jurisdictions, in the hands of customary chiefs.[151] Far from protecting the rights of local communities, government officials and local elites have often welcomed foreign agricultural investment and collaborated in the dispossession of rural dwellers in order to enrich themselves and enhance their control of the state through political patronage.[152]

Contracts between the foreign investor and the host state typically provide the foreign investor with rights and benefits not guaranteed to the local population, including secure land and water rights, tax incentives, and the right to export the agricultural commodities produced.[153] Because domestic legal protection for local land users is often weak, [154] the rights of the foreign investor will generally trump those of local communities.[155] Many contracts also include "stabilization" clauses that require the host state to compensate the foreign investor for any economic losses attributable to the host state's modification of the regulatory

---

[149] UN General Assembly, *Report Submitted by the Special Rapporteur on the Right to Food*, 20 December 2010, A/HRC/16/49; UNCTAD and UNEP, *Organic Agriculture and Food Security in Africa*, 2008, UNCTAD/DITC/TED/2007/15; C. Badgley, J. Moghtader, E. Quintero, E. Zakem, M. J. Chapell, K. Avilés-Vázquez, A. Samulon, and I. Perfecto, "Organic Agriculture and the Global Food Supply" (2007) 22 *Renewable Agriculture and Food Systems* 86; J. Pretty, A. D. Noble, D. Bossio, J. Dixon, R. E. Hine, F. W. T. Penning de Vries, and J. I. L. Morison, "Resource Conserving Agriculture Increases Yields in Developing Countries" (2006) 40 *Environmental Science and Technology* 1114; IFAD, "The Adoption of Organic Agriculture among Small Farmers in Latin America and the Caribbean," www.ifad.org; N. Parrott and T. Marsden, *The New Green Revolution: Organic and Agroecological Farming in the South* (London: Greenpeace Environmental Trust, 2002); J. N. Pretty, "Reducing Food Poverty by Increasing Sustainability in Developing Countries" (2003) 95 *Agricultural Ecosystems and the Environment* 217; J. N. Pretty and R. Hine, "The Promising Spread of Sustainable Agriculture in Asia" (2000) 24 *Natural Resources Forum* 107; J. N. Pretty, "Can Sustainable Agriculture Feed Africa? New Evidence on Progress, Processes and Impacts" (1999) 1 *Environment, Development and Sustainability* 253.

[150] C. Smaller and H. Mann, *A Thirst for Distant Lands: Foreign Investment in Agricultural Land and Water* (Winnipeg: International Institute for Sustainable Development, 2009), p. 14.

[151] Cotula, note 143, pp. 27, 86–87, 90–100.

[152] L. Cotula, "Land Grabbing in the Shadow of the Law: Legal Frameworks Regulating the Global Land Rush," in R. Rayfuse and N. Weisfelt, *The Challenge of Food Security* (Cheltenham: Edward Elgar, 2012), p. 218.

[153] Smaller and Mann, note 150, p.14.

[154] K. Deininger and D. Byerlee, *Rising Global Interest in Farmland: Can It Yield Sustainable and Equitable Benefits?* (Washington DC: The International Bank for Reconstruction and Development/The World Bank, 2011), pp. 97–98.

[155] United Nations Department of Economic and Social Affairs (UNDESA), "Foreign Land Purchases for Agriculture: What Impact on Sustainable Development?," Sustainable Development Innovation Briefs, January 2010, p. 2.

422   Food Justice

framework applicable to the investment.[156] This provision essentially "freezes" the law applicable to the investment and may deter host states from taking legal action to protect human rights and the environment, such as reallocating water rights to ensure that local communities have sufficient water for drinking, cooking, bathing, sanitation, and irrigation; restricting food exports at times of critical food shortages; and enhancing labor and environmental standards as the country's regulatory framework evolves.[157]

Bilateral investment treaties (BITs) between the host state (mainly Southern countries) and the investor's home state (typically Northern countries) usually provide additional protections to the foreign investor, including national treatment; the prohibition against expropriation without compensation; fair and equitable treatment (also known as international minimum standards of treatment); the right to export the products produced; and the investor–state arbitration mechanism, which authorizes the foreign investor to commence arbitration against the host state in the event of a breach of the BIT.[158] These provisions may limit the ability of the host state to protect the human rights of its citizens. For example, the fair and equitable treatment provision requires the host state to honor the "legitimate expectations" of the investor arising from the contract or other government commitments.[159] If the contract is silent on water rights, an arbitration tribunal might conclude that the investor's "legitimate expectation" of water for irrigation overrides the current or future water needs of the local community for drinking, bathing, sanitation, small-scale farming, and other uses.[160] If the host state reallocates water rights to fulfill the rights of its citizens, the foreign investor may be entitled to compensation.[161] The right to export agricultural products could likewise require the host state to compensate the foreign investor if the host state imposes export restrictions to address domestic food shortages – even if these export restrictions are otherwise permissible under international trade law.[162]

In short, Northern countries have reinforced the structural inequities in the global economic order that produce chronic undernourishment by failing to curb speculation in agricultural commodity markets, adopting policies that foster speculative investment in Southern agricultural lands (such as U.S. and EU biofuels policies), and imposing one-sided investment agreements that benefit foreign investors at the expense of local communities in the global South.

Based on the foregoing account of the global food system, the North–South dimension of food injustice can now be articulated. The global food system is a

---

[156] L. Cotula, "Regulatory Takings, Stabilization Clauses and Sustainable Development," OECD Global Forum on International Investment, March 27–28, 2008.
[157] UNDESA, note 155, pp. 3–4.
[158] Smaller and Mann, note 150, pp. 11–13.
[159] Ibid, p. 12.
[160] UNDESA, note 155, p. 3.
[161] Smaller and Mann, note 150, pp. 16–17.
[162] UNDESA, note 155, p. 4.

Carmen G. Gonzalez

paradigmatic example of North–South *distributive injustice* because Northern grain traders, agrochemical companies, food retailers, and financial speculators reap the benefits of the South's transition to export-oriented industrial agriculture, while the costs are borne disproportionately by net food-importing Southern states and by the planet's poorest rural dwellers, who are displaced, marginalized, and undernourished. *Procedural injustice* is evident in the North's domination of the international economic institutions that determine global patterns of agricultural trade and production, including the IMF, the World Bank, and the WTO. Southern states are generally marginalized, and civil society is often excluded altogether.[163] The global food system is an example of *corrective injustice* because victims of chronic undernourishment may not be able to bring a claim against the Northern states whose economic policies have inflicted unspeakable harm due, in part, to the difficulty of establishing causation. The destruction of Southern ecosystems and livelihoods exacts an enormous toll on marginalized populations, but is often rendered invisible by the distance in space and time between the institutions that govern the global economic order and the local communities that bear the social and environmental costs.[164] Finally, the global food system is an example of *social injustice* because it cannot be analyzed in isolation from the colonial and postcolonial economic policies that impoverished the global South and brought the planet's ecosystems to the brink of collapse.

4. A JUSTICE-CENTERED APPROACH TO GLOBAL FOOD POLICY

A justice-based approach to global food policy must promote the human right to food, curtail the power of transnational corporations, mitigate North–South inequality, and ensure the full and effective participation of Southern nations and peoples in local and global food governance. While a full discussion of these strategies is beyond the scope of this chapter, this section discusses several necessary reforms in order to illustrate the ways in which an environmental justice framework might influence the evolution of international law.

4.1 *Human Right to Food*

Food justice, like environmental justice more broadly, is grounded in human rights. The human right to food is recognized in the Universal Declaration of

[163] McMichael, note 104 at 285.
[164] R. Nixon, *Slow Violence and the Environmentalism of the Poor* (Cambridge: Harvard University Press, 2011), pp. 10–17; C. G. Gonzalez, "An Environmental Justice Critique of Comparative Advantage: Indigenous Peoples, Trade Policy, and the Mexican Neoliberal Economic Reforms" (2011) 32 *University of Pennsylvania Journal of International Law* 723 at 786–789 (discussing the responsibility of Northern countries to ameliorate the human rights violations caused their trade policies and by the structural adjustment programs mandated by the IMF and the World Bank).

424 *Food Justice*

Human Rights (UDHR) and in the International Covenant on Economic, Social and Cultural Rights (ICESCR).[165] The right to food is also protected through Article 6(1) of the International Covenant on Civil and Political Rights (ICCPR), which guarantees the right to life and has been interpreted to require the implementation of affirmative measures to eliminate chronic undernourishment.[166] Additionally, Article 1 of both the ICESCR and the ICCPR prohibits states from interfering with a population's means of subsistence.[167]

In order to provide authoritative guidance on the right to food, the United Nations Committee on Economic Social and Cultural Rights published General Comment 12, which clarifies the obligations of states to respect, protect, and fulfill this right.[168] First, states must *respect* the right to food by "not taking any measures that result in preventing such access."[169] In other words, states must consider the impact of legislation, regulation, and treaties on the right to food, and must refrain from actions that interfere with the ability of communities and individuals to feed themselves.[170] For example, states must respect the subsistence rights of small farmers by protecting them from foreign dumping of subsidized food products. Second, General Comment 12 requires states to *protect* the right to food by implementing measures "to ensure that enterprises or individuals do not deprive individuals of their access to adequate food."[171] For example, states must prevent third parties (such as local elites and foreign corporations) from depriving vulnerable populations of access to land, water, and other inputs necessary to grow food, and must develop and enforce environmental regulations to prevent the degradation of ecosystem services that support agricultural production.[172] Third, states must *fulfill* the right to food by providing food directly "whenever an

---

[165] *Universal Declaration of Human Rights*, Paris, 10 December 1948, GA res. 217A (III), UN Doc A/810 at 71 (1948), art. 25 [hereinafter UDHR]; *International Covenant on Economic, Social and Cultural Rights*, New York, 16 December 1966, in force 3 January 1976 GA res. 2200A (XXI), 21 UN GAOR Supp. (No. 16) at 49, UN Doc. A/6316 (1966); 993 UNTS 3; 6 ILM 368 (1967) [hereinafter ICESCR].

[166] *International Covenant on Civil and Political Rights*, New York, 16 December 1966, in force 23 March 1976, GA res. 2200A (XXI), 21 UN GAOR Supp. (No. 16) at 52, UN Doc. A/6316 (1966); 999 UNTS 171; 6 ILM 368 (1967), art 6(1) [hereinafter ICCPR]; Office of the High Commissioner for Human Rights, *General Comment No. 6: The Right to Life*, 30 April 1982, para. 5 in *Compilation of General Comments and General Recommendations adopted by Human Rights Treaty Bodies*, 8 May 2006, UN Doc. HRI/GEN/REV.8, p. 166.

[167] ICCPR, note 166, art. 1; ICESCR, note 165, art. 1.

[168] UN Committee on Economic Social and Cultural Rights, *General Comment No. 12: The Right to Adequate Food*, 12 May 1999, UN Doc. E/C.12/1999/5 [hereinafter General Comment 12].

[169] Ibid, para. 15.

[170] N. C. S. Lambek, "Respecting and Protecting the Right to Food: When States Must Get Out of the Kitchen," in N. C. S. Lambek , P. Claeys, A. Wong, and L. Brilmayer (eds.), *Rethinking Food Systems: Structural Challenges, New Strategies, and the Law* (Dordrecht: Springer, 2014), p. 108.

[171] General Comment 12, note 168, para. 15.

[172] Lambek, note 170, pp. 109–110.

individual or group is unable, for reasons beyond their control, to enjoy the right to adequate food by the means at their disposal."[173] States must also facilitate the right to food by enhancing the livelihoods of food-insecure populations through social safety nets and other assistance programs.[174]

Some scholars have questioned the usefulness of the human rights framework in light of the "diminished governance capacity of Third World states, which is the result of years of intervention by international law and international institutions."[175] Indeed, as explained earlier in this chapter, the lending practices of the IMF and the World Bank as well as international trade and investment agreements have created an international legal framework that benefits foreign investors and transnational food corporations and constrains the ability of Southern states to comply with their right to food obligations.

In order to secure food justice, international human rights law must hold accountable the Northern states that are complicit in the widespread violation of the right to food. Human rights institutions should recognize and enforce what John Knox, the United Nations Independent Expert on Human Rights and the Environment, calls "diagonal human rights." Diagonal human rights are rights held by individuals against foreign governments for the extraterritorial conse- quences of their aid, trade, finance, and investment policies, including the power they wield in international financial institutions.[176]

Article 56 of the Charter of the United Nations imposes diagonal or extraterritor- ial obligations on all states by requiring all UN members to "take joint and separate action in cooperation with the Organization" to ensure the realization of human rights.[177] In addition, Article 2(1) of the ICESCR obligates states parties to "take steps, individually and through international assistance and cooperation" to progressively realize the rights set forth in the treaty.[178] General Comment 12 explains the extraterritorial aspects of the right to food as follows:

---

[173] General Comment 12, note 168, para. 15.

[174] Lambek, note 170, pp. 110.

[175] P. Simons, "International Law's Invisible Hand and the Future of Corporate Accountability for Violations of Human Rights" (2012) 3 *Journal of Human Rights and the Environment* 5 at 40.

[176] J. Knox, "Diagonal Human Rights," in M. Gibney and S. Skogly (eds.), *Universal Human Rights and Extraterritorial Obligations* (Philadelphia: University of Pennsylvania Press, 2010), p. 83.

[177] *Charter of the United Nations*, San Francisco, 26 June 1945, in force 24 October 1945, 59 Stat. 1031; TS 993; 3 Bevans 1153, art. 56. These obligations are extraterritorial because they require countries to work together toward the realization of human rights in their own countries and in other countries. They create diagonal human rights to the extent that they authorize individuals and communities to bring human rights claims not only against their own states (vertical claims) but also against other states (diagonal claims) whose action or inaction contributed to human rights violations – such as countries that permitted agricultural dumping in foreign markets. See Knox, note 176.

[178] ICESCR, note 165, art. 2(1).

426   *Food Justice*

> In the spirit of article 56 of the Charter of the United Nations [...], States parties should take steps to respect the enjoyment of the right to food in other countries, to protect that right, to facilitate access to food, and to provide necessary aid when required. States parties should, in international agreements whenever relevant, ensure that the right to adequate food is given due attention and consider the development of further international legal instruments to that end.[179]

In order to comply with these extraterritorial obligations, Northern states must *respect* the right to food in the global South by negotiating, interpreting, and applying trade and investment agreements in ways that provide Southern countries with sufficient flexibility to regulate in the public interest and to deploy subsidies, tariffs, and other import barriers to enhance the livelihoods of small farmers and other food-insecure populations. Northern states must *protect* the right to food by ensuring that third parties subject to their jurisdiction and control, such as transnational corporations, do not violate the right to food in other countries. States that are members of the IMF, the World Bank, and regional development banks must take affirmative steps to guarantee that the policies and practices of these institutions are consistent with their right to food obligations. Finally, Northern countries must *fulfill* the right to food by providing food aid in ways that enhance rather than undermine the livelihoods of small farmers in the global South – by, for example, purchasing such food from Southern farmers rather than using food aid as a pretext for Northern export dumping.

A human rights approach is essential to the achievement of food justice because it gives agency to the individuals and communities experiencing chronic undernourishment rather than treating them as objects of "development." Human rights law puts a human face on food injustice, and empowers subordinated communities to speak for themselves in domestic or international tribunals and in the court of public opinion. In so doing, human rights law serves as a powerful tool to educate the public about food injustice, name and shame human rights abusers, foster dialogue about alternatives to the current food system, and create the political mobilization necessary to bring about change.

4.2 *Corporate Accountability*

One of the most daunting obstacles to the realization of food justice is corporate impunity for human rights abuses – including agricultural export dumping and land-grabbing. The governance challenges of Southern states and the unwillingness of Northern states to regulate the extraterritorial conduct of their transnational corporations enable these corporate entities to escape liability for their violations of the right to food. The question of how best to regulate corporations to prevent extraterritorial human rights abuses has been the subject of intense debate and

---

[179] General Comment 12, note 168, para. 36.

remains largely unsettled. While a complete discussion of the legal strategies that might be pursued to achieve corporate accountability is beyond the scope of this chapter, possible approaches include strengthening the human rights enforcement capacity of Southern countries, holding Northern countries liable for failing to regulate the extraterritorial conduct of their corporations, enhancing the mechanisms available in the home state to adjudicate human rights violations abroad, developing treaties that impose human rights obligations directly on corporations, and aggressive antitrust enforcement.

The ICESCR obligates states to ensure that business entities incorporated in their jurisdiction do not violate economic, social, and cultural rights in other countries.[180] In 2011, a distinguished group of human rights experts adopted a series of principles (known as the Maastricht Principles on Extraterritorial Obligations of States in the Area of Economic, Social and Cultural Rights) that reaffirm the duty of states to ensure that non-state actors (such as transnational corporations) do not engage in extraterritorial human rights violations.[181] Some scholars argue that failure to regulate the extraterritorial conduct of corporate nationals renders states liable for the human rights violations of their corporations – particularly if a state has actual or constructive knowledge of potential human rights violations (caused, for example, by food dumping or land-grabbing) and either fails to exercise due diligence to prevent such violations or enters into trade and investment agreements that restrict the ability of the affected states to protect the human rights of their citizens.[182] Alternatively, a home state's failure to regulate or mitigate the human rights violations of corporate nationals' foreign subsidiaries may constitute a violation of the duty to refrain from causing transboundary harm.[183]

As a practical matter, Northern states have not generally regulated the extraterritorial conduct of their corporations. Moreover, Southern states that experience corporate human rights abuses often find their regulatory authority hamstrung by international trade and investment law.[184] In addition, corporate impunity is fostered by the ways that international and domestic law treat parent companies, subsidiaries, and foreign affiliates as separate entities subject to the domestic laws of the state of incorporation. Domestic courts are generally

---

[180] R. McCorquodale and P. Simons, "Responsibility Beyond Borders: State Responsibility for Extraterritorial Violations by Corporations" (2007) 70 *Modern Law Review* 598 at 617–619.

[181] *Maastricht Principles on Extraterritorial Obligations of States in the Area of Economic, Social and Cultural Rights*, Maastricht, September 28, 2011, www.etoconsortium.org, Principle 17; O. de Schutter et al., "Commentary to the Maastricht Principles on Extraterritorial Obligations of States in the Area of Economic, Social and Cultural Rights" (2012) 34 *Human Rights Quarterly* 1084 at 1122–1124.

[182] McCorquodale and Simons, note 180 at 619–623.

[183] Ibid at 624.

[184] P. Simons and A. Macklin, *The Governance Gap: Extractive Industries, Human Rights, and the Home State Advantage* (New York: Routledge, 2014), pp. 7–8.

428   *Food Justice*

reluctant to pierce the corporate veil and impose liability on parent companies for the activities of their subsidiaries.[185]

An alternative solution to corporate impunity is the direct imposition of human rights obligations on corporations. In 2004, the United Nations Human Rights Commission rejected a proposal by the Sub-Commission on the Promotion and Protection of Human Rights to impose international human rights obligations on transnational business entities.[186] Instead, the United Nations Special Representative of the Secretary-General on the Issue of Human Rights and Transnational Corporations and other Business Enterprises, John G. Ruggie, developed a framework consisting of non-binding norms along with measures to enhance the ability of states to regulate transnational corporations.[187] Critics denounced Ruggie's proposal as tantamount to self-regulation.[188] In June 2014, the United Nations Human Rights Council voted to convene a working group to develop a legally binding instrument to impose human rights obligations on corporations.[189] While this represents an audacious move to curb corporate impunity, it is unclear that the Northern countries in which many of these corporations are located would sign or ratify such treaties. Finally, anti-competition law is an important tool to reduce the power of transnational corporations in the global food system. U.S. antitrust law tends to focus on harm to consumers rather than producers, and has generally turned a blind eye to market concentration in the agricultural sector.[190] At the global level, UNCTAD has developed a model law on competition that seeks to "control or eliminate [...] abuse of dominant positions of market power, which limit access to markets or otherwise unduly restrain competition, adversely affecting domestic or international trade or economic development."[191] Regardless of whether anti-competitive activity is addressed at the national or international level, it is essential to develop new approaches that consider harm to producers as well as consumers and to aggressively curb the concentration of market power in the agri-food industry.[192]

---

[185] Ibid, pp. 8–9.

[186] Ibid, p. 3.

[187] *See UN Sub-Commission on the Promotion and Protection of Human Rights, Norms on the Responsibilities of Transnational Corporations and other Business Enterprises with Regard to Human Rights*, 26 August 2003, E/CN.4/Sub.2/2003/12/Rev.2; UN Sub-Commission on the Promotion and Protection of Human Rights, *Commentary on the Norms on the Responsibilities of Transnational Corporations and other Business Enterprises with Regard to Human Rights*, 13 August 2003, E/CN.4/Sub.2/2003/12/38/Rev.2.

[188] Simons and Macklin, note 184, pp. 7–8.

[189] UN Human Rights Council, *Elaboration of an International Legally Binding Instrument on Transnational Corporations and Other Business Enterprises with Respect to Human Rights*, 25 June 2014, A/HRC/L.22/Rev.1.

[190] Aoki, note 108 at 451–452.

[191] UN Conference on Trade and Development, *Model Law on Competition*, 2007, TD/RBP/CONF.5/7/Rev.3, p. 3.

[192] Aoki, note 108 at 451–452.

4.3 Mitigating North–South Economic Inequality

A justice-based approach to global food policy requires redressing the North–South economic disparities arising from the colonial and postcolonial policies and practices described above. A key step toward a more just economic order is the implementation of differential treatment in international economic law.[193] Differential treatment is a means of remedying past inequities by giving Southern countries more favorable treatment in international legal instruments.[194] The 1947 GATT incorporated differential treatment through a series of amendments and side agreements that permitted, but did not require, Northern countries to give preferential treatment to their Southern trading partners (such as greater market access and non-reciprocal tariff concessions). However, because the North's obligations were largely voluntary, Northern governments evaded these commitments.[195] Southern demands for differential treatment were later overridden by the free-market economic reforms imposed through IMF and World Bank structural adjustment policies and through multilateral and regional trade agreements, including the WTO – which imposed similar obligations on all countries, but simply gave Southern countries more time to comply. These reforms required Southern countries to remove the import barriers that protected their industries from more technologically advanced Northern competitors, and also restricted the South's ability to use tariffs and subsidies to protect and promote nascent industries and domestic food producers.[196]

In order to address the structural causes of food injustice, international trade agreements must permit Southern countries to utilize a variety of tariffs, subsidies, and other protectionist measures to diversify and industrialize their economies

---

[193] Differential treatment in international law is a means of reducing the economic disparities between the global North and the global South by giving more advantageous treatment to the latter in both international economic law (special and differential treatment in the GATT/WTO) and international environmental law (common but differentiated responsibility in a variety of environmental treaties). In the decades following World War II, Southern nations came together as the Group of 77 to demand differential treatment in international economic law in order to overcome the legacy of colonialism and facilitate the global South's economic development. Differential norms were initially incorporated into the 1947 GATT, and were known as special and differential treatment. Differential norms were later included in several environmental treaties (including the Montreal Protocol on Substances that Deplete the Ozone Layer, the United Nations Framework Convention on Climate Change, and the Kyoto Protocol) in accordance with the principle of common but differentiated responsibility, which authorizes asymmetrical obligations on Northern and Southern countries based on the North's superior financial and technical resources, the North's disproportionate contribution to global environmental problems, and the South's economic and ecological vulnerability. Gonzalez, note 1, pp. 88–92.

[194] Ibid, p. 88.

[195] Ibid, pp. 88–89; P. Kishore, "Special and Differential Treatment in the Multilateral Trading System" (2014) 13 Chinese Journal of International Law 363 at 369–372, 376–388.

[196] Gonzalez, note 1, p. 89.

430 *Food Justice*

and end their crippling dependence on the export of primary commodities. As economist Ha-Joon Chang and others have observed, Northern countries industrialized and prospered through a broad array of protectionist measures (including subsidies, tariffs, and state financing of major industries) that are now prohibited or restricted by IMF/World Bank loan conditions or by the WTO and other trade agreements.[197] If we are to mitigate North–South economic disparities, then trade agreements must curtail Northern protectionism while giving Southern countries the flexibility to intervene strategically in the economy to foster long-term economic development.

In the agricultural sector, eliminating Northern domestic and export subsidies is an important first step toward addressing the double standards in international agricultural trade that devastate the livelihoods of small farmers in the global South. However, trade agreements and the policies and programs of the IMF and World Bank must also give Southern countries the "policy space" to comply with their right to food obligations. Southern countries should utilize this "policy space" to reinvest in the agricultural sector after decades of neglect and to use an appropriate combination of subsidies and import barriers to protect the livelihoods of small farmers, restore ravaged ecosystems, revitalize domestic food production, and promote environmentally friendly cultivation practices.[198]

In addition to creating "policy space" for development, Northern governments should finance Southern government projects designed to increase food self-sufficiency, enhance the livelihoods of small farmers, and encourage the transition to sustainable agriculture. While skyrocketing food prices in 2008 did trigger Northern investment in Southern agriculture, much of that investment was designed to boost the productivity of conventional fossil fuel-dependent industrial agriculture and to increase Southern countries' integration into global food markets.[199]

---

[197] H-J. Chang, *Kicking Away the Ladder: Development Strategy in Historical Perspective* (London: Anthem Press, 2002), pp. 19–51, 59–66; Y.-S. Lee, *Reclaiming Development in the World Trade System* (Cambridge: Cambridge University Press, 2009), pp. 9–13, 156–165.

[198] Several mechanisms have been proposed in the Doha Round of WTO negotiations to provide Southern countries with greater policy flexibility, including exemptions from tariff cuts for "special products" (SP) essential to food security and rural livelihoods; a special safeguard mechanism (SSM) to allow Southern countries to raise tariffs in response to surges of cheap subsidized imports; and the easing of restrictions on public food reserves as a means of reducing price volatility and ensuring a secure supply of food in the event of shortages or price shocks: Clapp, note 17, p. 79; S. Murphy, *Trade and Food Reserves: What Role Does the WTO Play?* (Minneapolis: Institute for Agriculture and Trade Policy, 2010).

[199] A. Mittal, United Nations Conference on Trade and Development (UNCTAD), *The 2008 Food Price Crisis: Rethinking Food Security Policies*, June 2009, UNCTAD/GDS/MDP/G24/2009/3, pp. 16–17. For example, the Bill and Melinda Gates Foundation, the Rockefeller Foundation, the World Bank and the FAO, with the support of transnational agribusiness firms, launched the Alliance for a Green Revolution in Africa, an effort to boost agricultural productivity among small farmers in the African continent. S. Suppan, "Challenges for Food Sovereignty" (2008) 32 *Fletcher Forum of World Affairs* 111 at 112–113; G. Toenniessen, A. Adesina, and J. De Vries, "Building an Alliance for a Green Revolution

This single-minded emphasis on increasing agricultural production is misguided in light of the fact that one third of the food produced for human consumption is currently lost due to inadequate infrastructure to properly manage and store food between production and consumption (primarily in the global South) or discarded due to stringent quality standards or "best-before dates" (primarily in the global North).[200] Northern investment in rural infrastructure in the global South (such as roads, storage and refrigeration facilities, and processing centers) could improve food availability and reduce pressure on land, water, and biodiversity.[201] However, these investments will not promote food justice unless they enhance the ability of small farmers to grow, sell, and purchase food and encourage the adoption of ecologically sustainable production methods. As Olivier de Schutter, the former UN Special Rapporteur on the Right to Food, observes:

> [I]nvestments that increase food production will not make significant progress in combatting hunger and malnutrition if they do not lead to higher incomes and improved livelihoods for the poorest – particularly small-scale farmers in developing countries. And short-term gains will be offset by longer-term losses if they cause further degradation of ecosystems, thus threatening the ability to maintain current level of production in the future [...]. Pouring money into agriculture will not be sufficient; the imperative today is to take steps that facilitate the transition towards a low-carbon, nature-conserving type of agriculture that benefits the poorest farmers.[202]

Finally, there are several additional steps that Northern countries can take to remedy some of the more egregious examples of food injustice. First, because the growing demand for biofuels is a significant driver of food price volatility and speculative investment in Southern agricultural lands, Northern countries should reduce this demand by phasing out their renewable fuels mandates for first and second generation biofuels that compete with food for land, water, and other agricultural inputs. Second, Northern countries should discourage speculative investment in agricultural commodities by developing internationally coordinated

---

in Africa" (2008) 1136 *Annals of the New York Academy of Sciences* 233. Critics contend that this initiative will replicate the anti-poor bias of the Green Revolution and undermine the livelihoods and agroecological practices of small farmers by emphasizing biotechnology, synthetic fertilizers, and debt-driven, export-oriented commercialization of agricultural products. African Centre for Biosafety, "Alliance for a Green Revolution in Africa (AGRA): Laying the Groundwork for the Commercialisation of African Agriculture," www.acbio.org.za.

[200] J. Gustavsson, C. Cederberg, U. Sonesson, R. van Otterdijk, and A. Meybeck, *Global Food Losses and Food Waste: Extent, Causes and Prevention* (Rome: Food and Agriculture Organization of the United Nations, 2011), pp. 4–15.

[201] Food and Agriculture Organization of the United Nations, *Food Wastage Footprint: Impacts on Natural Resources* (Rome: Food and Agriculture Organization of the United Nations, 2013); A. Telesetsky, "Waste Not, Want Not: The Right to Food, Food Waste and the Sustainable Development Goals" (2014) 42 *Denver Journal of International Law and Policy* 481.

[202] UNCTAD, note 31, p. 34.

432   *Food Justice*

measures to regulate and tax these transactions. Third, Northern countries should
work with their Southern counterparts to develop model investment contracts
and bilateral investment treaties that impose binding human rights obligations on
foreign investors (enforceable in both the home state and the host state), allow host
states to bring counterclaims in arbitral proceedings for violations of these obligations, and contain targeted provisions that address the host state's food security and
sustainable development priorities. Finally, Northern and Southern countries
should collaborate to impose a moratorium on Southern land grabs until such
time as host states, home states, civil society, and international institutions develop
robust and effective mechanisms to oversee and regulate these transactions.

4.4 *Regime Change*

Chronic undernourishment is merely one symptom of a larger problem: a
corporate-dominated food regime that exacerbates North–South inequality, ignores
ecological limits, and dispossesses rural communities in the name of modernization and development. As Philip McMichael observes:

> The development project incorporated post-colonial states into a universal system
> of national accounting methods, standardizing the measurement of material well-
> being (GNP), and the "externalization" of a variety of environmental degradations
> and social catastrophes. Only monetized transactions were counted as productive,
> devaluing subsistence, cooperative labor, indigenous culture, seed saving, and
> managing the commons as unproductive, marginalized and undeveloped activity.
> As a consequence, the world's rural population decreased by some 25 percent
> in the second half of the twentieth century, with the steady displacement of
> peasant cultures.[203]

In recent decades, national and transnational food movements (including
the Northern food justice movement and the international food sovereignty movement) have spearheaded the struggle for food justice and challenged the corporate
food system. These movements have forged alliances across the North–South
divide to demand a more equitable and sustainable food system premised on
democratic community control over food and food-producing resources.[204]
Framing their demands in the language of human rights, these movements call
for the collective right of peoples to food sovereignty.[205] The right to food
sovereignty rejects the individual focus of the Northern human rights canon in
favor of the collective rights of communities, peoples, and nations to freely choose

---

[203] McMichael, note 104 at 279–280.
[204] Holt-Gimenez and Wang, note 19 at 88–90.
[205] Ibid at 90–91; P. Claeys, "The Creation of New Rights by the Food Sovereignty Movement:
The Challenge of Institutionalizing Subversion" (2012) 46 *Sociology* 844 at 849.

their economic, political, and social system.[206] In so doing, the call for food sovereignty echoes the rights of indigenous peoples to self-determination within the confines of the nation-state and reinvigorates the collective human rights invoked by Southern nations during decolonization, including the right to permanent sovereignty over natural resources and the right to development.[207]

In other words, the demand for food justice is ultimately a call for the vesting of the right to development and the right to permanent sovereignty over natural resources in *peoples* rather than states. The peoples would be regarded as the owners of natural resources, and the states would be viewed as trustees responsible for managing them for the collective benefit of the entire population.[208] This reinvigoration of the principle of permanent sovereignty over natural resources responds to the problem of kleptocratic rulers who have "interpreted PSNR as conferring ownership of their nations' resources on themselves" and have "robbed their countries dry, derailing or stunting economic progress in the process." [209] Instead of the traditional focus on the rights of states over their countries' natural resources, this approach would emphasize the duties of states to discharge their fiduciary obligations to their citizens in good faith, the democratization of control over productive resources,[210] and the obligations of states and citizens to promote ecologically sustainable use of these resources.[211]

This interpretation of food justice represents a paradigmatic break with the traditional notion of human rights based on the duty of the liberal democratic state to ameliorate the injustices of the capitalist market economy.[212] While the right to food reinforces the power of the state, the collective right to food sovereignty politicizes the struggle for food justice, promotes the right of peoples to democratically determine their food and agriculture policies, and facilitates the development of transnational alliances to challenge the corporate-dominated food system.

---

[206] Ibid.

[207] Ibid.

[208] E. Duruigbo, "Permanent Sovereignty and Peoples' Ownership of Natural Resources in International Law" (2006) 38 *George Washington International Law Review* 33 at 37. This interpretation of the right to permanent sovereignty over natural resources bears some resemblance to the common law public trust doctrine, which provides that the state holds certain natural resources in trust for the public and may bar the state from selling these resources to private parties. C. Rose, "Joseph Sax and the Idea of the Public Trust" (1998) 25 *Ecology Law Quarterly* 351; M. C. Mehta v Kamal Nath (1997) 1 SCC 388 (India) (holding that the public trust doctrine applies in India); M. I. Builders Private Ltd v Radhey Shyam Sahu (1999) 6 SCC 464 (India) (finding a violation of India's public trust doctrine when a government agency approved the destruction of a public park and market to build a shopping complex).

[209] Duruigbo, note 208 at 35.

[210] Ibid at 67–68.

[211] H. Wittman, "Reconnecting Agriculture and the Environment: Food Sovereignty and the Agrarian Basis of Ecological Citizenship," in H. Wittman et al. (eds.), *Food Sovereignty: Reconnecting Food, Nature and Community* (Oakland: Food First, 2010), p 103.

[212] Claeys, note 205 at 848.

5. CONCLUSION

Solving the problem of chronic undernourishment requires an analysis of the structural causes of food injustice within and among nations. An environmental justice approach to the global food system reveals the ways in which the struggles of marginalized communities for a clean environment, for equitable access to natural resources, and for sustainable livelihoods are embedded in contemporary and historic North–South conflicts – and can produce alliances that transcend the North–South divide. Achieving food justice requires dismantling the corporate-dominated food regime, developing more effective mechanisms to enforce the right to food, and transforming the conventional development discourse by heeding the call for bottom-up approaches based on the knowledge, skills, and values of local communities

20

A Justice Paradox: Climate Change, Small Island Developing States, and the Absence of International Legal Remedy

Maxine Burkett

Despite their clear and significant vulnerability to climate change, small island developing states (SIDS) have not had the opportunity to pursue, in earnest, a just, legal remedy for the impacts of that change. This presents a justice paradox, in which the current international legal regime forecloses any reasonable attempts at a just remedy for the victims of climate change who are the most vulnerable and the least responsible.[1] Worse still, attempts to seek justice in such clear instances of need may yield negative political outcomes for the claimants themselves, namely the loss of aid for other critical functions from wealthy large emitters. Nonetheless, it is still necessary for SIDS to pursue vigorously both aggressive emissions abatement and assistance with adapting to climate impacts. This is true if only for the likely result that climate change losses and any bold action to mitigate or adapt to them will dwarf the costs of retaliation that island states might face from the wealthy nations. This chapter recommends possible pathways for concerted and effective action.

1. INTRODUCTION

All SIDS face dangerous impacts to their economic well-being and the availability of basic resources, including food and water. Some face the loss of all habitable territory. After over two decades of knowledge of these impacts, however, SIDS are unable to have their claims heard in major legal fora – never mind the more

---

I thank Mahina Tuteur for excellent research assistance.

[1] The concept of a "justice paradox" has been employed before. See generally, R. E. Scott, "Chaos Theory and the Justice Paradox" (1993) 35 *William and Mary Law Review* 329. For a full discussion of the relevance of Scott's article to climate change and the global South, see M. Burkett, "A Justice Paradox: On Climate Change, Small Island Developing States, and the Quest for Effective Legal Remedy" (2013) 35 *University of Hawaii Law Review* 633. This chapter is largely adapted from Burkett (2013).

435

436   A Justice Paradox

formidable tasks of identifying and implementing adequate abatement and repara-tive measures. This is not for want of trying. Indeed, there has been extensive research and scholarship on viable claims, as well as abbreviated attempts in international arenas to hold large greenhouse gas emitters accountable.[2] This author's early research attempted to do the same by identifying meaningful avenues of remedy through reconciliation and reparation.[3] These efforts have not been wholly effective to date. Today, there are renewed efforts to invite the International Court of Justice (ICJ) to advise on the legal responsibility of the largest emitters vis-à-vis climate change.[4] This effort by Palau, a particularly vulnerable Pacific island state, however, has been met with threats of reprisal by the largest historical emitter, the United States.[5] This kind of intimidation, coupled with a weak international legal regime at base, delays justice for SIDS. It lays bare the fact that in the face of one of the most poignant instances of grave injustice – the loss of one's land, livelihood, culture, and ancestors as a result of unabated emissions by others – our legal systems at the international, national, and subnational levels are unable to effect a swift, definitive, and just resolution for the victims. The absence of a clear legal pathway, coupled with fears that some countries might retaliate effect-ively stifles legal action.

This chapter discusses the failure of the international legal regime to provide adequate process and substantive remedy for SIDS, either through the lack of viable legal theories or through uneven power dynamics in the international arena. Although SIDS have persistently called for action in international climate negoti-ations and at the ICJ, none of these efforts to date have resulted in significant progress. Despite skepticism about their efficacy in light of present-day exigencies, the costs of pursuing these claims – and other novel approaches the chapter introduces – are dwarfed by the costs to small island communities of unabated climate impacts. By introducing new approaches, the chapter attempts to respond to a striking and persistent (if unsurprising) justice paradox.

The chapter proceeds as follows. Section 2 briefly describes the current science of climate change, including forecast impacts as well as recommendations for

---

[2] These include liability theories based on the *United Nations Convention on the Law of the Sea*, Montego Bay, 10 December 1982, in force 16 November 1994, 1833 UNTS 3; 21 ILM 1261 (1982); the *Alien Tort Claims Act 1789*, 28 USC § 1350 (2000) (hereinafter ATS), international human rights law, tort law, and the principle of state responsibility for transboundary harm. There have been efforts to obtain advisory opinions from the International Court of Justice (ICJ), as well as to bring suit in the ICJ. For an overview of these efforts, see Burkett, note 1. See also section 3 for more in-depth discussion.

[3] See generally M. Burkett, "Climate Reparations" (2009) 10 *Melbourne Journal of International Law* 509.

[4] L. Hurley, "Island Nation Girds for Legal Battle Against Industrial Emissions," *New York Times*, September 28, 2011.

[5] D. Clark, "Which Nations are Most Responsible for Climate Change?," *The Guardian*, April 21, 2011. See also R. Brown, "The Rising Tide of Climate Change Cases," *The Yale Globalist*, March 4, 2013.

emissions abatement. In addition, it looks at the severe current and forecast climate impacts to SIDS. Section 3 describes the geopolitical backdrop of claims against large emitters, which explains in part the uphill battle that SIDS face. Section 4 introduces the possibility of identifying and pursuing claims using unconventional plaintiffs and defendants, and even borrows from proposals in the international economic law realm to consider the possible efficacy of "class action litigation" to empower individual SIDS. Section 5 further notes the political milieu in which SIDS might bring these claims and considers how the value of publicity and notions of interest converge may advance claims beyond their prospects in the courtroom alone.

2. THE IMPACTS OF CLIMATE CHANGE ON SMALL ISLAND DEVELOPING STATES

2.1 Climate Impacts Generally

The international community has been aware of the grave risks of climate change and the imperative of brisk and aggressive attempts to mitigate those risks for decades, but no measurable action to mitigate has been taken. During this time, venerable institutions, such as the National Academy of Sciences, have declared repeatedly that human-caused climate change is a settled fact.[6] Noted climate scientist Dr. James Hansen has stated that the current atmospheric concentration of carbon dioxide, approaching 400 parts per million, "is already in the 'dangerous zone'."[7] This concentration, Hansen states, is too high to maintain "the climate to which humanity, wildlife, and the rest of the biosphere are adapted."[8] Additionally, there is significant warming in the pipeline.[9] In other words, global temperature might rise by two to three degrees Celsius even without additional greenhouse gas emissions. According to Hansen, "[h]umanity's task of moderating human-caused global climate change is urgent."[10]

The impacts are not solely prospective and, for all intents and purposes, are irreversible.[11] Current, and often jarring, signs of climate disruption are legion.[12]

---

[6] U.S. National Academy of Science and Engineering, *America's Climate Choices: Advancing the Science of Climate Change* (Washington: The National Academies Press, 2010), pp. 21–22.

[7] J. Hansen et al., "Target Atmospheric CO_2: Where Should Humanity Aim?" (2008) 2 *The Open Atmospheric Science Journal* 217 at 218.

[8] Ibid at 228.

[9] Ibid at 226.

[10] Ibid at 228.

[11] See generally, S. Solomon, Gian-Kasper Plattner, Reto Knutti, and Pierre Friedlingstein, "Irreversible Climate Change Due to Carbon Dioxide Emissions" (2009) 106(6) *Proceedings of the National Academy of Sciences* 1704: "irreversible" is defined as a time scale exceeding the end of the millennium in the year 3000.

[12] Ibid at 1709. See A. Freedman, "U.S. Dominated Global Disaster Losses in 2012: Swiss Re," Climate Central, April 1, 2013. See also A. Steer, "Listening to Hurricane Sandy: Climate Change is Here," Bloomberg, November 2, 2012.

438 A Justice Paradox

Further, they outpace the modeling of climate phenomenon,[13] producing more significant impacts than predicted. Impacts include changes in rainfall, with adverse effects on water supplies for humans, agriculture, and ecosystems; increased fire frequency; desertification; and irrevocable sea-level rise.[14] The latter might be so severe that sea walls and other measures to adapt will prove inadequate.[15] In short, as atmospheric scientist and key contributor to the Intergovernmental Panel on Climate Change Susan Solomon explains, carbon dioxide emissions might peak to levels that would lead to eventual sea-level rise in the order of meters, "implying unavoidable inundation of many small islands and low-lying coastal areas."[16]

The need to rapidly decrease emissions of carbon dioxide and other greenhouse gases to below current atmospheric concentrations cannot wait until a future date if humanity is to avoid catastrophic changes.[17] Indeed, the period for carbon emissions to peak and then fall dramatically to avoid these changes is rapidly closing, with less than ten years remaining to halt emissions growth in order to have a palpable effect on worsening climate change.[18] For Hansen, prompt policy changes are imperative,[19] and the failure to act suggests to him that "decision-makers do not appreciate the gravity of the situation."[20]

The United Nations Framework Convention on Climate Change (UNFCCC or Framework Convention), to which the global community committed some twenty years ago, specifically speaks of "threats of serious or irreversible damage."[21] In addition, it pays particular attention to the plight of small island states, seen as among the most vulnerable to climate change. If preserving a climate "similar to that on which civilization developed and to which life on Earth is adapted"[22] is desired, the international community must never emit the vast majority of the remaining fossil fuel carbon.[23] This is indeed a Herculean task.[24] Hopes for later and rapid reductions are, however, "risky, expensive and disruptive" and, as such, far less politically feasible.[25] For SIDS, it may herald the "end of their history."[26]

[13] Hansen et al., note 7 at 226.
[14] Solomon et al., note 11 at 1708.
[15] Ibid at 1708.
[16] Ibid at 1704.
[17] Ibid at 1708–1709; Hansen et al., note 7 at 217.
[18] Hansen et al., note 7 at 229.
[19] Ibid at 217.
[20] Ibid at 229.
[21] Solomon et al., note 11 at 1704, citing *United Nations Framework Convention on Climate Change*, Rio de Janeiro, 9 May 1992, in force 21 March 1994, 1771 UNTS 107; S. Treaty Doc No. 102-38; UN Doc. A/AC.237/18 (Part II)/Add.1; 31 ILM 849 (1992), art. 3 [hereinafter UNFCCC].
[22] Hansen et al., note 7 at 217.
[23] Ibid at 226.
[24] Ibid at 229.
[25] M. Allen, D. Frame, K. Frieler, W. Hare, C. Huntingford, C. Jones, R. Knutti, J. Lowe, M. Meinshausen, N. Meinhausen, and S. Raper, "The Exit Strategy" (2009) 3 *Nature Reports: Climate Change* 56.
[26] "Islands Fear 'End of History' Due to Climate Changes," Reuters, November 29, 2010.

2.2 Climate Change and Small Island Developing States

Leaders from the Pacific Islands Forum to the Secretary-General of the United Nations recognize the dire consequences of climate change for SIDS, describing it as the greatest threat to livelihoods, security, and well-being.[27] This echoes the United Nations General Assembly's repeated and unanimous affirmation of the seriousness of climate change and the particular vulnerability of SIDS.[28] Though geographically disparate,[29] SIDS share many preexisting vulnerabilities, such as limited resources and high vulnerability to external economic and geopolitical shocks.[30] These vulnerabilities, exacerbated by climate change and coupled with low adaptive capacity, inspired special recognition of SIDS within the Framework Convention.[31] They have also inspired "persistent and innovative" arrangements between SIDS to facilitate cooperation and regional collaboration,[32] which may bode well for future legal and political actions against large emitters such as those described later in this chapter.

Among the most striking climate change impacts is the acute coastal vulnerability of SIDS, and in some cases the almost certain uninhabitability of islanders' ancestral homes.[33] In the Pacific, for example, SIDS risk many of the more globally widespread climate impacts, including coastal inundation, rising air temperatures, decreased rainfall, increased severe weather events, and rising ocean temperatures.[34] With these climatic changes come increased coral bleaching, increased coastal flooding, and erosion. Threats to traditional lifestyles of indigenous communities and human migration will also occur.[35]

Islanders have long been aware of these impacts.[36] The Joint Statement by Leaders of Pacific Islands Forum and the UN Secretary-General echoes this

[27] UN Secretary-General, *Joint Statement by Leaders of Pacific Islands Forum*, 10 October 2012, SG/2191 (hereinafter Joint Statement).

[28] See A. Korman and G. Barcia, "Rethinking Climate Change: Towards an International Court of Justice Advisory Opinion" (2012) 37 *Yale Journal of International Law Online* 35 at 36.

[29] T. Neroni Slade, "The Making of International Law: The Role of Small Island States" (2003) 17 *Temple International and Comparative Law Journal* 531.

[30] See generally Burkett, note 3 at 533; A. Gillespie, "Small Island States in the Face of Climate Change: The End of the Line in International Environmental Responsibility" (2004) 22 *UCLA Journal of Environmental Law and Policy* 107.

[31] UNFCCC, note 21, art. 4.

[32] Slade, note 29 at 533–534, 540.

[33] See generally M. Burkett, "In Search of Refuge: Pacific Islands, Climate-Induced Migration, and the Legal Frontier" (2011) 98 *Asia Pacific Issues* 1 at 1. It is important to note that coastal erosion and seawater inundation will likely render atoll islets uninhabitable long before the sea level overtops the surfaces. W. R. Dickinson, "Pacific Atoll Living: How Long Already and Until When?" (2009) 19 *GSA Today* 4.

[34] R. K. Pachauri and A. Reisinger (eds.), *Intergovernmental Panel on Climate Change, Climate Change 2007: Synthesis Report* (Geneva: IPCC, 2011), pp. 48–49.

[35] See generally V. W. Keener et al. (eds.), *National Climate Assessment Regional Technical Input Report Series, Climate Change and Pacific Islands: Indicators and Impacts* (Washington: Island Press, 2012).

[36] Slade, note 29 at 540.

440 *A Justice Paradox*

sentiment in its call to the international community to identify threats – such as the violation of territorial integrity and increased natural resource scarcity – and to assist these vulnerable countries.[37] The Joint Statement also stresses the need to address these impacts in "all relevant international forums, including but not limited to the United Nations Framework Convention on Climate Change, the General Assembly and the Security Council."[38] It is not clear, however, that these fora will yield much progress. To date they have not.

3. CREATIVITY, FUTILITY, AND REALPOLITIK

There have been many claims and avenues for remedy posited by academics and practitioners, including those based on international human rights law and tort law.[39] Pioneering individuals and communities from the most vulnerable regions of the world have pressed or attempted to pursue some of these claims in international fora, though without successful resolution. These claims include liability theories based on the United Nations Convention on the Law of the Sea[40] (UNCLOS), the Alien Tort Statute (ATS),[41] international human rights law, tort law, and the principle of state responsibility for transboundary harm.[42] There have also been efforts to obtain advisory opinions from the International Court of Justice (ICJ), as well as to bring suit in the ICJ.[43] In 2002, for example, Tuvalu threatened to bring suit in the ICJ in response to the United States' intransigence regarding emissions reductions.[44] Of course, the ICJ's lack of jurisdiction over the United States would have been the first major jurisdictional hurdle, followed perhaps by several substantive law issues.[45]

Many of the remaining claims are robust in the academic realm alone. This is the case for proposed claims under the UNCLOS,[46] ATS,[47] and advisory opinions of the ICJ, for example. The search for a viable means for remedy demonstrates

---

[37] Joint Statement, note 27.

[38] Ibid.

[39] For a survey of claims posited, see Burkett, note 3. Legal theories posited have also included those based on public nuisance law, the public trust doctrine, and reparations.

[40] Montego Bay, 10 December 1982, in force 16 November 1994, 1833 UNTS 3; 21 ILM 1261 (1982) (hereinafter UNCLOS).

[41] ATS, note 2.

[42] Burkett, note 3.

[43] D. A. Kysar, "Climate Change and the International Court of Justice," Public Law Research Paper No. 135, Yale Law School, 2013.

[44] R. E. Jacobs, "Treading Deep Waters: Substantive Law Issues in Tuvalu's Threat to Sue the United States in The International Court of Justice" (2005) 14 *Pacific Rim Law and Policy Journal* 103 at 112.

[45] Ibid at 105.

[46] Ibid at 116.

[47] See generally R. Reed, "Rising Seas and Disappearing Islands: Can Island Inhabitants Seek Redress Under the Alien Tort Claims Act?" (2002) 11 *Pacific Rim Law & Policy Journal* 399. For further discussion of possible claims, see note 3.

the failure of the UNFCCC to address the absence of enforceable compliance mechanisms to date.[48] Although there is a renewed effort to pursue avenues under the UNFCCC,[49] this chapter examines fundamental geopolitical questions that complicate these kinds of cases at the outset.

SIDS appear to have a viable claim at base: The unabated emissions activity of the highest emitters has resulted in altered atmospheric chemistry which, in turn, has created a climate extremely hostile to small island states in particular.[50] Further, it seems reasonable to allege that the highest emitters were aware of the consequences of their actions since at least 1992, when the Framework Convention was drafted. A compelling case could, in theory, proceed on the merits in domestic or international fora on the basis of tort law,[51] international human rights law,[52] or state responsibility for transboundary harm[53] – although proving causation would undoubtedly be challenging. There are, however, antecedent concerns regarding the geopolitical milieu in which these cases are brought. For example, does the complaining island nation have the financial and human resources and capacity to

---

[48] Jacobs, note 44 at 112.

[49] These include employing an "obscure dispute settlement provision of the U.N. Framework Convention on Climate Change (UNFCCC)," under chapter 14 of the Convention. L. Friedman, "Island States Mull Risks and Benefits of Suing Big Emitters," E&E Reporter, November 16, 2012; see also Jacobs, note 44 at 118.

[50] Friedman, note 49.

[51] Considering complex issues such as causation and multiple actors, it is unclear whether such tort claims would ultimately be successful. D. A. Kysar, "What Climate Change Can Do About Tort Law" (2011) 41 Environmental Law 1 ("diffuse and disparate in origin, lagged and latticed in effect, anthropogenic greenhouse gas emissions represent the paradigmatic anti-tort, a collective action problem so pervasive and so complicated as to render at once both all of us and none of us responsible"). There is, however, a valid argument that a violation of tort law has been committed, and, in theory, that it could be resolved in a court of law. M. Burkett, "Climate Change and the Elusive Climate Tort" (2011) 121 Yale Law Journal Online 115.

[52] Under international human rights law, states are liable to damage to their own citizens. Thus, it would be difficult to bring a claim based on this theory in relation to mitigation. It would perhaps be more successful in relation to adaptation. Academics have debated what human rights obligations a nation may owe to the citizens of another nation. For example, John Knox has advanced the theory of "diagonal responsibility," whereby individuals and groups can enforce their environmental rights against the governments of states other than their own. See J. Knox, "Diagonal Environmental Rights," in M. Gibney and S. Skogly (eds.), Universal Human Rights and Extraterritorial Obligations (Philadelphia: University of Pennsylvania, 2010), p. 148. Human rights law operates along a vertical axis, setting out individuals' rights against their own governments, whereas international environmental law operates along a horizontal axis, regulating duties owed by states to other states, not to private actors. See generally M. Gibney and S. Skogly (eds.), Universal Human Rights and Extraterritorial Obligations (Philadelphia: University of Pennsylvania, 2010). Thus, the challenge is to derive diagonal rights from both. See generally Gibney and Skogly (eds.) (2010).

[53] It is questionable whether state responsibility principles, which are very bilateral in nature, can be applied to climate change, especially because it is so global in nature. For an in-depth discussion on the international campaign to secure an advisory opinion from the ICJ on the question of state responsibility for transboundary harm caused by greenhouse gas emissions see Kysar, note 51.

442

A Justice Paradox

pursue these claims against large emitters? And, on a related note, if a vulnerable nation pursues legal recourse, will the very nation-state(s) from which it seeks remedy retaliate?

There is evidence that both lack of resources and fear of retaliation have stymied efforts to hold large emitters accountable for their actions in the international arena.[54] That may color the proposed legal actions' viability. Backed by wealthy European nations, the Republic of Palau is currently leading a coalition of vulnerable states in a campaign to request an advisory opinion from the ICJ.[55] The request seeks:

> on an urgent basis [. . .] an advisory opinion from the ICJ on the responsibilities of States under international law to ensure that activities carried out under their jurisdiction or control that emit greenhouse gases do not damage other States.[56]

Reports indicate, however, that diplomats and attorneys are "putting on the brakes" for fear of losing billions in aid from China and the United States for non-climate needs, such as education, roads, and HIV–AIDS clinics.[57] The United States, for example, "made its objections known," using threats of worsening "[c]ongressional inaction as a clear warning" against pursuing legal action.[58] Conversations regarding more "confrontational alternatives" are occurring at the "margins" of the negotiations and the largest impediment for poor nations, generally, is their "near-total dependency on big emitters for development, trade and, increasingly, money to adapt to climate change."[59] Former president of Palau Johnson Toribiong insists, however, that the advisory opinion would "complement and not conflict" with international negotiations.[60] This action would perhaps "renew our faith in a system of law that has guided States' actions in the past and gives them legitimacy today," according to President Toribiong.[61]

This kind of stifled voice, as a result of capacity constraints or power differentials, is not unique to climate-related circumstances, though the consequences here are perhaps most dire. In fact, similar capacity and retaliation concerns operate in the World Trade Organization's (WTO) dispute settlement regime. Lack of resources and legal capacity and fear of non-WTO or extralegal retaliation by more powerful trading partners are two among the handful of reasons why southern states might

---

[54] Friedman, note 49.
[55] See generally ibid.
[56] United Nations, "Press Conference on Request for International Court of Justice Advisory Opinion on Climate Change," 3 February 2012, www.un.org (hereinafter Advisory Opinion on Climate Change).
[57] Friedman, note 49.
[58] Ibid.
[59] Ibid.
[60] Advisory Opinion on Climate Change, note 56.
[61] Ibid.

not invoke the relevant dispute settlement mechanisms.[62] The persistent capacity and power differential in the climate context, and in other areas of international law, threatens to compromise confidence in international law's ability to promote and defend legal rights.[63] Indeed, one scholar has questioned if international law is able to provide effective legal mechanisms to protect sovereign interests when other states control the unyielding emissions that accelerate climate change.[64] If international law cannot do this for the most vulnerable, it does not bode well for SIDS, for which the international legal regime is an indispensable piece of their efforts to halt dangerous climate change.

4. WEIGHING AID AGAINST EXTINCTION

The existence of a justice paradox in the climate change context is perhaps unsurprising when set against the backdrop of other international law dynamics. Power disparities in the international community are arguably inherent in the conception and structure of current international organization,[65] with the Security Council serving as a paragon of the imbalance. The paradox is most striking in this instance, however, because the stakes for SIDS are unusually high, completely unprecedented, and likely irreversible in terms of the nature and scope of the impacts.

The prognosis for atoll nations like the Maldives, Tuvalu, and Kiribati is that they will lose all of their territory, a loss that significantly dwarfs the aid money that some countries currently fear losing. In fact, a comparison of the annual aid dollars that the United States gives to the Maldives versus the cost of certain adaptations or the loss of GDP due to the total loss of territory demonstrates the uneven impacts of

[62] P. X. F. Cai, "Making WTO Remedies Work for Developing Nations: The Need for Class Actions" (2011) 25 *Emory International Law Review* 151 at 155–156. The global South may "fear the possibility of unilateral retaliation by the United States, either through a decrease in development or military aid or by revoking access to the Generalized System of Preferences, which grants them preferential trade terms as developing nations." Cai (2011) at 180. But see A. T. Guzman and B. A. Simmons, "Power Plays and Capacity Constraints: The Selection of Defendants in World Trade Organization Disputes" (2005) 34 *Journal of Legal Studies* 557 (finding that although capacity constraints may limit the number of cases the global South may pursue, political hurdles, such as fear of retaliation by the would-be defendant, are less supported). Although the study is useful overall, Guzman and Simmons' methodology is not directly useful for the parallel I wish to draw here. Among several other reasons, Guzman and Simmons' chapter has limited relevance: (i) because of the choice of defendants on whom they focus their study; and (ii) because they do not isolate the particularly resource- and power-constrained SIDS I am concerned with here. Nevertheless, the authors admit, "[a]lthough our results fail to support the power hypothesis, we cannot rule out the possibility that power plays an important role in determining the number of cases filed": at 571.

[63] On this point, see Badrinarayana's trenchant argument in D. Badrinarayana, "Global Warming: A Second Coming for International Law" (2010) 85 *Washington Law Review* 253.

[64] Ibid at 254.

[65] See generally ibid at 253.

444   *A Justice Paradox*

climate change.[66] Indeed, a survey of aid money across similarly situated SIDS reveals the same imbalance.[67] Some countries appreciate this imbalance and are fearless in the face of it.[68] Palau Ambassador to the United Nations Stuart Beck acknowledges the United States' objections and maintains that Palau "'gives far more in strategic value' to the United States than it takes in assistance."[69]

Although the general fear of retaliation may be warranted today, the calamity that some of these nations face requires creativity and courage – and, perhaps, a few other legal and political approaches that might yield results. This section explores the possibility of pursuing second-tier defendants, identifying representative parties or class action litigation to bring claims, and the value of litigation generally in moving the legal and political needle.

4.1 *Second-Tier Defendants*

One way to sidestep concerns of reprisals from major economic powers is to look to the actions of other significant sources of emissions from countries on which SIDS are less dependent. In this "thousand cuts" approach, SIDS can seek to limit the current unabated emissions from other high emitters that provide little if any aid, and at the same time deter other similarly situated countries from continuing or expanding its use of fossil fuel resources.[70] The Federated States of Micronesia modeled this approach in its novel challenge to the Czech upgrade of the Prunerov power plant.[71]

Though ultimately unsuccessful, the claim brought against the Czech Republic arguing transboundary impacts under the 1991 Espoo Convention[72] put

---

[66] The U.S. plans to give between US$2 to $3 million to the Maldives. www.foreignassistance. gov, "Maldives." See also H. H. Shihab, First Secretary of the Permanent Mission of the Maldives to the UN, "Statement to the Chairperson at the General Debate of the Second Committee," 8 October 2012, www.un.org.

[67] For a comparison of aid numbers, see generally AidFlows, www.aidflows.org. The United States has a unique relationship to the freely associated island nations. Additional cash flows go to the Republic of Marshall Islands, the Federated States of Micronesia, and Palau from the United States, beyond the aid numbers given through aid agencies. See F. X. Hezel, "Pacific Island Nations: How Viable Are Their Economies?" (2012) 7 *Pacific Islands Policy* 1 at 21-23. Although this may shift the balance slightly, acting in response to the cost of climate impacts is still preferred. Hezel at 3–4.

[68] Friedman, note 49.

[69] Ibid.

[70] Ibid.

[71] See generally R. Maketo, L. Bacalando, Jr., J. Teulings, K. Casper, Jan Šrytr, and K. Šabová, "Transboundary Climate Challenge to Coal: One Small Step Against Dirty Energy, One Giant Leap for Climate Justice," in M. Gerrard and G. Wannier (eds.), *Threatened Island Nations: Legal Implications of Rising Seas and a Changing Climate* (Cambridge: Cambridge University Press, 2013), p. 589; E. Munk, "Czech Ministry Accepts Micronesian Input in Assessing Impact of Power Plant Upgrade," Daily Environment Report, January 25, 2010.

[72] *Convention on Environmental Impact Assessment in a Transboundary Context,* Espoo, 25 February 1991, in force 10 September 1997, 1989 UNTS 309. The Convention gives states

Maxine Burkett

governments and corporations "on notice."[73] With the upgrade, the power plant is among the highest greenhouse gas-emitting plants in Europe.[74] Micronesia requested inclusion in the transboundary environmental impact assessment prior to project commencement, a request that delayed but did not halt the upgrade.[75] Nonetheless, Micronesia's approach was considered "precedent-setting." Indeed, it provides a skeletal roadmap of how to explore and employ similar provisions to pursue actions against significant yet "second-tier" emitters.

4.2 Representative Parties and Class Action Litigation

Another approach that utilizes existing laws in novel ways would be to rethink the plaintiffs that would bring these claims. Representative parties who will suffer significant impacts and are large in number across disparate communities could make the greatest strides. Similarly, countries might act in concert to deflect some of the specific scrutiny a single country might face if it brings claims on its own. These actions might advance efforts that could assist the most vulnerable small island states.

Representative parties that suffer similar impacts from across a particular region might serve as compelling claimants in an action against large emitters or "second-tier" defendants. Representative parties might bring these claims in relevant international fora or in U.S. district courts, depending on where plaintiffs can sustain jurisdiction over defendants. For example, the plight of Palauan women demonstrates great possibility in the legal arena.[76] During his impassioned analysis of "diplomats dither[ing]" at the climate summits in Copenhagen and Cancun, Palau Ambassador to the United Nations Stuart Beck decried the impotence of the UNFCCC meetings while his island lost land and the capacity to grow taro.[77] This acutely impacts the women of the most vulnerable Pacific islands. Beck explained: "[i]f the ladies can't grow taro, and it's generally a matriarchal task, they're going to move from that island. And that's a slow-moving kind of depopulation, but it's a real one nonetheless. [. . .] It's death by a thousand cuts, and every time somebody leaves the island, that's another cut."[78]

A claim brought by women taro growers against a variety of large emitting entities (under the ATS, for example) might be an effective means of pursuing litigation and galvanizing myriad smaller lawsuits to arrest growing greenhouse gas emissions.

---

that signed the right to enter impacts assessments in other member states. See arts. 3–5. Micronesia is not a signatory, whereas the Czech Republic is a party. See UN Treaty Collection, "Status of Ratification," http://treaties.un.org.

[73] Munk, note 71.
[74] Ibid.
[75] G. Hold, "Prunéřov Expansion Approved," *The Prague Post*, May 5, 2010.
[76] Friedman, note 49.
[77] Ibid.
[78] Ibid.

446

A Justice Paradox

In addition to administrative efficiency, class action suits have been an effective mechanism for pooling resources and leveling the playing field between many similarly situated plaintiffs and powerful defendants in the United States Other countries, such as India, have used public interest litigation as a powerful tool.[79] This is a potentially powerful mechanism in the international arena as well, and has been contemplated – though not tested – by other scholars and practitioners.[80] In her analysis of the feasibility of islanders seeking redress under the ATS, RoseMary Reed suggests that "[w]hile it is possible for a single individual or nation to bring this action, it may be even more powerful if several nations band together to form a class action and litigate this issue once."[81] Professor Phoenix Cai makes a similar suggestion in the context of the World Trade Organization (WTO) and expands on the promise of class actions in the dispute settlement mechanism to pool benefits and risks – including very damaging retaliation or extralegal contraction of aid.[82]

The class action regime proffered for the WTO might be instructive in the international climate litigation context. When a member of the WTO violates a rule or trade term, the affected party may bring a complaint under the WTO's dispute settlement regime.[83] The process and remedy for developing nations, however, suffers from similar concerns of retaliation and parties' uneven resources. In response, Professor Cai proposes a class action-type mechanism that would allow developing nations to pool their complaints in cases against larger or more developed nations.[84] Importantly, the group of nations could also use the class action strategy against emerging developing nations, such as China and India;[85] and it would afford countries of the global South the right to join as a third party in the dispute settlement process.[86] Although there would be burdens and risks to such an approach, particularly to the "lead" developing nation plaintiff,[87] there

---

[79] See e.g. S. Deva, "Public Interest Litigation in India: A Critical Review" (2009) 1 *Civil Justice Quarterly* 19.

[80] Z. Holladay, "Public Interest Litigation in India as a Paradigm for Developing Nations" (2012) 19 *Indiana Journal of Global Legal Studies* 555 at 571–573 (discussing how the India experience can serve as a model for other developing nations).

[81] Reed, note 47 at 423. The author made similar calls in the context of a reparations claim. See generally Burkett, note 3.

[82] See generally Cai, note 62. More than two thirds of the 153 WTO member nations are members of the global South: Cai (2011) at 154. Cai explains, "despite their strength in numbers, developing nations as a group rarely participate in dispute settlement, a core aspect of the WTO. This is problematic because the WTO is essentially a self-enforcing system of reciprocal trade rights that relies on proactive monitoring by all members": at 154.

[83] In fact, it is incumbent on each WTO member to "police its interests." According to Cai, "[w]hen developing nations fail to initiate cases, the result is both under-enforcement of key WTO norms and skewed enforcement in favor of developed nations": at 155.

[84] Ibid at 157 (describing the proposal in a nutshell).

[85] Ibid at 157.

[86] Ibid.

[87] Ibid at 184–185.

would be many systemic benefits to class action litigation, including the ability to engage in litigation without risking extrajudicial threats of retaliation and without the fear of lengthy and costly litigation; the ability to bring suits that advance developing nation agendas and interests; valuable opportunities for coalition-building; and, perhaps most important, the benefits of greater developing nation participation "in the WTO system as a whole, especially in terms of perceived legitimacy."[88]

In the climate context, class action litigation can serve similar functions as proposed in the WTO and remain consistent with what it seeks to achieve in the larger societal context. As Cai explains:

> Class actions serve important societal functions. They are often used as a tool to compensate for small losses and enforce regulations. They enable less powerful groups to act as private attorneys general. They have also been effectively employed as a means for lasting social change, as during the civil rights era. As a result of all these dynamics, class actions more deeply embed social values embodied in laws in the greater society by giving voice to the otherwise voiceless.[89]

Based on the climate impacts forecast for small islands, it is critical for them to acquire that voice rapidly.

4.3 Interest Convergence and the Power of Publicity

The value of all of the proposed claims is perhaps greatest in their ability to spark and sustain a conversation about the disproportionate harms suffered by small island states. Publicity, the airing of injuries, and the shaming of large emitters might spur measurable reparative developments depending on the political moment in which they occur. Perhaps the most common refrain from practitioners, scholars, and vulnerable communities alike is that engaging in the uphill battle of climate litigation, with the accompanying losses and false starts, remains important for its storytelling capacity.[90] This is particularly true in the human rights context.[91] It served that purpose for the claimants in the Inuit action brought before the Inter-American Court of Human Rights and gave a human face to climate change.[92] Whether or not the plaintiffs win, high-profile litigation is likely to

---

[88] Ibid at 182–183, 189.

[89] Ibid at 196.

[90] See the discussion in M. Burkett, "Legal Rights and Remedies," in M. Gerrard and K. Kuh (eds.), *The Law of Adaptation to Climate Change* (Chicago: American Bar Association, 2012). See also Advisory Opinion on Climate Change, note 56.

[91] E. K. Yamamoto and A. K. Obrey, "Reframing Redress: A 'Social Healing Through Justice' Approach to United States-Native Hawaiian and Japan-Ainu Reconciliation Initiatives" (2009) 16 *Asian American Law Journal* 5 at 39 ("Human rights norms remain largely aspirational").

[92] Ibid. See also H. M. Osofsky, "The Inuit Petition as a Bridge? Beyond Dialectics of Climate Change and Indigenous Peoples' Rights," in W. C. G. Burns and H. M. Osofsky (eds.),

448 *A Justice Paradox*

change popular consciousness – moving public perception away from highly technocratic approaches to climate change and toward the human dimension. In fact, many of the leading environmental cases in domestic environmental law actually failed in the courts, but nevertheless had a huge impact on public opinion.[93] As more stories are told, perhaps collectively they will have the power to incite rapid emissions reduction and aggressive and concerted adaptation action from the largest emitters. Indeed, the storytelling value of these claims becomes clear when viewed alongside stories that are not told. Publicizing injustices has the power to catalyze efforts to redress those injustices.[94]

An important complement to the powerful public narrative is a receptive audience, particularly if that audience is a world leader that small island nations seek to influence. Further, the offending party is more likely to remedy the injustice complained of if it is in its interest to do so. In the international context this is the geopolitical parallel to Derrick Bell's interest convergence theory, which Bell employed in the context of American race politics.[95] Further, Eric Yamamoto and Ashley Obrey argue that a country's desire to achieve democratic legitimacy might occur at the same moment that a community or country is seeking redress for harms suffered because of that democracy's unjust actions.[96] The perception of a government's validity in terms of democratic governance and its commitment to civil and human rights determines its "democratic legitimacy."[97]

Through the lens of the interest convergence theory, therefore, a dominant power will "countenance civil and human rights advances only when those gains simultaneously serve its larger political interests."[98] In the climate context, President Obama has repeatedly articulated concern about dangerous climate impacts. In his 2013 inaugural address kicking off his final term in office, President Obama suggested a recommitment to the hard work of reining in U.S. emissions.[99] On November 1, 2013, President Obama issued an Executive Order entitled "Preparing the United States for the Impacts of Climate Change," acknowledging that the "impacts of climate change [...] are already affecting communities, natural resources, ecosystems, economies, and public health across the Nation" and reiterating that

---

Adjudicating Climate Change: State, National, and International Approaches (Cambridge: Cambridge University Press, 2009).

[93] J. L. Sax, "Preface," in C. Rechtschaffen and D. Antolini (eds.), *Creative Common Law Strategies for Protecting the Environment* (Washington: ELI Press, 2007), pp. xvii–xxii.

[94] See e.g. T-U. Baik, "A War Crime Against an Ally's Civilians: The No Gun Ri Massacre" (2001) 15 *Notre Dame Journal of Law, Ethics and Public Policy* 455 at 463.

[95] See generally D. A. Bell, "Brown v. Board of Education and the Interest-Convergence Dilemma" (1980) 93 *Harvard Law Review* 518.

[96] Yamamoto and Obrey, note 91 at 41.

[97] Ibid at 40.

[98] Ibid.

[99] R. W. Stevenson and J. M. Broder, "Speech Gives Climate Goals Center Stage," *New York Times*, January 21, 2013, p. A1.

managing these risks requires deliberate preparation, close cooperation, and coordinated planning by the Federal Government, as well as by stakeholders, to facilitate Federal, State, local, tribal, private-sector, and nonprofit-sector efforts to improve climate preparedness and resilience.[100]

Evidence of the applicability of interest convergence is extensive and militates in favor of a continuous drumbeat of litigation and storytelling. Litigation, according to Yamamoto and Obrey, "serves as a lightning rod for recognition and responsibility and as a bully pulpit for community organizing about the injustice and need for system-wide reconstruction and reparation."[101] Public pressure is essential.[102] Even conservative commentators in the United States acknowledge the important catalyst that litigation can be, remarking:

> [i]f you have sensitive climate change treaty negotiations going on, you have a compliant president and there is some looming international lawsuit pending, it can't help but move the negotiations forward.[103]

Further, it appears convincing that a country's "quest for enhanced international stature can shape that country's evolving responses to redress claims."[104] This kind of interest convergence at the international level is also understood as correcting for the "reputational costs" of an action, or failure to act.[105]

5. CONCLUSION

This chapter attempts to take stock of viable legal avenues posited to date and push the conversation regarding effective legal and political avenues available to small island states. It does so fully cognizant of the formidable challenges of climate litigation in the current geopolitical environment. It also does so fully aware of the bleak climate forecast for islands, and for the rest of the globe. Though litigation is certainly not the only, or even the strongest, weapon available, it is perhaps one of several that SIDS need to employ in their fight to survive.

Critics of public interest litigation have argued that litigation itself cannot change social institutions, that it might divert resources from potentially more effective political strategies, and even that it may disempower the communities it

---

[100] Exec. Order No. 13,653, 78 Fed. Reg. 70,843, 1 November 2013.
[101] Yamamoto and Obrey, note 91 at 40.
[102] Ibid.
[103] Ibid (quoting Steven Groves, a fellow at the Heritage Foundation, a conservative think tank).
[104] Ibid at 52.
[105] Badrinarayana, note 63 at 282; A. T. Guzman, "A Compliance-Based Theory of International Law" (2002) 90 *California Law Review* 1823 at 1827; B. A. Simmons, "The Legalization of International Monetary Affairs" (2000) 54 *International Organization* 573 at 574. See also Cai, note 62 at 183 (arguing that an additional value of class action litigation at the WTO is that the reputation harms of non-compliance or foot-dragging in compliance increases with the number of complainants).

seeks to assist.[106] Although litigation may be expensive, time-consuming, and incredibly complex, it has the potential for far-reaching impacts, not only on the ground in affected communities, but also because the law can shape social meaning and inform both individual and collective action.[107] Legal action may enable "activists to leverage gains by putting specific issues on the public agenda and threatening to impose litigation costs if decision makers fail to find political solutions."[108] Litigation has been described as an "imperfect, but indispensable strategy of social change" and one that "cannot effectively work in isolation from other mobilization efforts."[109] Specifically for SIDS, in addition to all other current strategies utilized in various international fora, litigation provides a unique opportunity for plaintiffs to pool the benefits and risks of such bold action, therefore providing a pathway for vulnerable nations to seek redress despite the risk of retaliation.

On balance, therefore, this chapter hopes to have made clear that litigation is an important option, as the option of allowing climate change to continue on its current path is simply unviable.

---

[106] Scott L. Cummings and Deborah L. Rhode, "Public Interest Litigation: Insights from Theory and Practice" (2008) 36 *Fordham Urban Law Journal* 603 at 604.

[107] Ibid at 610.

[108] Ibid at 610.

[109] Ibid at 604, 605.

21

South of South: Examining the International Climate Regime from an Indigenous Perspective

Elizabeth Ann Kronk Warner

1. INTRODUCTION

When the roof over his home in Amazonas, Brazil, sprung a leak, Antonio Alves ventured into the 1.57 million square kilometers of forest around him to gather wood. Instead of finding material to fix the leak, Alves found the Green Police, a group of local law enforcement officials hired by General Motors, American Electric Power, and Chevron. [...] Hoping forest conservation will allow them to offset their own emissions and make money on the carbon market, the companies created forest reserves and hired the Green Police to protect their investments. [...] After spending eleven days in jail, Alves eventually moved to avoid further harassment by the Green Police.[1]

The foregoing is a poignant example of how international law, and specifically international law related to climate change, potentially negatively impacts indigenous peoples. The irony of the international climate regime is that projects such as the one detailed above, designed to benefit primarily the global North and perhaps even better the global environment, can infringe upon the legal rights of indigenous people.

Focus on the impacts of climate change on the indigenous world is appropriate given that many indigenous communities are situated in ways that make them uniquely vulnerable to climate change. This chapter examines the role (or lack thereof) of indigenous peoples in the development of international law as it applies to climate change. Because international law is largely a product of state power and (until recently) indigenous voices had been marginalized by such state power, indigenous peoples have historically been excluded from the narrative of

---

[1] S. Baez, "The Right REDD Framework: National Laws that Best Protect Indigenous Rights in a Global REDD Regime" (2011) 80 *Fordham Law Review* 821 at 823.

international law.[2] This chapter argues that international law would be improved through fuller incorporation of concerns of indigenous communities. "Having expanded the histories of international law, as well as problematized the professional languages of international law, it seems that both the mainstream and the critical histories can only be improved through acknowledgement of the laws and practices of other political communities, such as indigenous peoples."[3] Accordingly, this chapter begins by examining some of the commonalities of indigenous communities that become important when examining the rights of such communities within the climate regime. This discussion of commonalities explores international law applicable to indigenous peoples, especially highlighting the role of the United Nations (UN) Declaration of the Rights of Indigenous Peoples. Second, the chapter examines two examples, the Inuit Circumpolar petition to the Inter-American Commission of Human Rights and the REDD mechanism, where indigenous communities have called for (or are calling for) the incorporation of their legal rights into the dialogue surrounding climate change. Ultimately, the chapter concludes that the development of climate change law would be improved by mechanisms allowing active participation from indigenous peoples and the protection of indigenous rights.

2. COMMONALITIES AMONG UNIQUE INDIGENOUS COMMUNITIES

This chapter will first examine commonalties that exist among many indigenous communities. It is helpful to first understand the meaning of the term "indigenous peoples." Professor S. James Anaya explains that

> [t]he rubric of indigenous peoples includes the diverse Indian and aboriginal societies of the Western Hemisphere, the Inuit and Aleut of the Arctic, the aboriginal peoples of Australia, the Maori of Aotearoa (New Zealand), Native Hawaiians and other Pacific Islanders, the Sami of the European far North, and at least many of the tribal or culturally distinctive non-dominant people of Asia and Africa. They are *indigenous* because their ancestral roots are embedded in the lands on which they live, or would like to live, much more deeply than the roots of more powerful sectors of society living on the same lands or in close proximity. And they are *peoples* in that they comprise distinct communities with a continuity of existence and identity that links them to the communities, tribes, or nations of their ancestral past.[4]

[2] A. Bhatia, "The South of the North: Building on Critical Approaches to International Law with Lessons from the Fourth World" (2012) 14 *Oregon Review of International Law* 131 at 150 ("postcolonial histories of international law that begin with an initial acknowledgement of indigenous importance, or at least narrative necessity, are largely eclipsed by the focus on the European colonization and then decolonized states of Asia, Africa, or elsewhere").

[3] Ibid at 149.

[4] S. J. Anaya, *International Human Rights and Indigenous Peoples* (New York: Aspen Publishers/Wolters Kluwer, 2009), p. 1.

Elizabeth Ann Kronk Warner 453

With this understanding in place, the chapter explores some commonalities of experience of indigenous peoples. Although each indigenous community is unique, such common threads are important for consideration of indigenous rights as represented in the developing law of climate change.

2.1 *Impacts of Climate Change*

One "common" experience of many indigenous communities today is the negative impact of climate change. Unlike other populations, indigenous peoples tend to reside in vulnerable locations throughout the world.[5] Through the process of colonization, the global North generally moved indigenous communities into less desirable locations that are also more susceptible to damage from climate change. Today, indigenous communities deal with the impacts of climate change in their daily lives.[6]

The Arctic is being particularly hard-hit by the ravages of climate change.[7] Climate change is causing indigenous peoples to lose land and natural resources that are crucial to their subsistence lifestyle. Sea ice and permafrost are melting as a result of increasing temperatures.[8] Consequently, the daily activities of Arctic indigenous peoples, such as whaling, sealing, fishing, and reindeer herding, are fundamentally changing,[9] as hunting, fishing, and travel are becoming increasingly more difficult.[10] Some Arctic species, such as caribou, upon which indigenous peoples rely heavily for their survival, have migrated away from their traditional habitats and ranges due to shifts in weather patterns. Because many indigenous people are legally tied to the land where they reside

---

[5] A. Parker, et al., "Climate Change and Pacific Rim Indigenous Nations, Executive Summary," in A. Parker et al. (eds.), *Climate Change and Pacific Rim Indigenous Nations* (Olympia: Northwest Indian Applied Research Institute, 2006), pp. 1–2, 19; N. G. Maynard (ed.), *Native Peoples – Native Homelands Climate Change Workshop: Final Report* (Albuquerque: U.S. Global Change Research Program, 1998).

[6] UN, *International Expert Group Meeting on Indigenous Peoples and Climate Change: Darwin, Australia, April 2–4, 2008*, 14 April 2008, E/C.19/2008/CRP.9, p. 2.

[7] "Petition to the Inter-American Commission on Human Rights Seeking Relief from Violations Resulting from Global Warming Caused by Acts and Omissions of the United States," April 23, 2013, http://earthjustice.org.

[8] D. Cordalis and D. B. Suagee, "The Effects of Climate Change on American Indian and Alaska Native Tribes" (2008) 22 *Natural Resources and Environment* 45 at 47 (citing "Alaska Villages: Most Are Affected by Flooding and Erosion, but Few Qualify for Federal Assistance," General Accounting Office, December 2003, GAO-04-142); M. Nuttall, F. Berkes, B. Forbes, G. Kofinas, T. Vlassova, and G. Wenzel, "Hunting, Herding, Fishing, and Gathering: Indigenous Peoples and Renewable Resource Use in the Arctic," Arctic Climate Impact Assessment, Scientific Report, 2006 (explaining that the release of greenhouse gases from the melting permafrost is exacerbating the impact of climate change in the Arctic).

[9] Nuttall et al., note 8.

[10] Ibid; A. Ansari, "Climate Change Forces Eskimos to Abandon Village," CNN.com, April 28, 2009.

454 *South of South*

(e.g. through the creation of reservations), they are unable to follow animals when their migration habits change.[11]

The Arctic is only one example of places where indigenous peoples are being impacted by climate change on a daily basis. Indigenous peoples living in low-lying island nations are also facing the negative impacts of climate change disproportionately.[12] As the sea ice at the poles melts due to increased temperatures related to climate change and the world's ocean levels rise, low-lying nations are disappearing. Indigenous peoples living within low-lying island nations are also facing a loss of biodiversity, as climate change threatens coral reefs and fish populations.[13] As in the Arctic, food security of indigenous peoples is threatened because of species loss. Accordingly, although the Arctic and low-lying island indigenous peoples live far from each other, the ultimate impact of climate change on their communities is similar.

Moreover, indigenous communities are not only being displaced by the impacts of climate change on their environments, but also because of measures designed to mitigate such impacts, including hydroelectric dams, forest conservation measures, biofuels cultivation, and carbon offsets.[14] Perhaps ironically, "[i]n this way, many indigenous communities are threatened by initiatives designed to benefit foreign communities."[15]

In sum, although the individual impacts may vary between indigenous communities, in many instances the results are very similar. Indigenous peoples are facing dramatic changes to their environments as a result of climate change that threaten their culture and livelihoods. Given the dramatic impacts and the high-level stakes involved, indigenous peoples must be included in any discussion of an international climate regime.

2.2 *Connection to Land and the Environment*[16]

The fact that many indigenous communities are being negatively impacted by climate change is particularly problematic given the unique connection between

---

[11] 43 USC § 1603 (2006); Cordalis and Suagee, note 8 at 47 (citing "Alaska Villages: Most Are Affected by Flooding and Erosion, but Few Qualify for Federal Assistance," note 8).

[12] Parker et al., note 5, p. 23.

[13] Ibid.

[14] Ibid.

[15] R. S. Abate and E. A. Kronk, "Commonality among Unique Indigenous Communities: An Introduction to Climate Change and Its Impacts on Indigenous People," in R. S. Abate and E. A. Kronk (eds.), *Climate Change and Indigenous Peoples: The Search for Legal Remedies* (Northampton: Edward Elgar Publishing, 2013), pp. 8–9.

[16] In discussing the special relationship between many indigenous communities and their environment, this chapter does not mean to stereotype indigenous peoples as environmental stewards or as persisting in some historical notion of indigenousness.

many indigenous communities and their environment.[17] This connection is both legal and, for many communities, spiritual and/or cultural.[18] From the legal perspective, many indigenous communities were moved to reservations by the colonizers, or in some countries domestic laws were developed to protect the traditional homelands of indigenous communities. Regardless of which scheme was used by the external, foreign nation state, the result has been that many indigenous communities have legal rights to the place where they reside. Although this may be helpful in protecting indigenous rights, it also constrains the ability of indigenous communities to adapt, as they may be unable to move to a different location without risking loss of legal rights. Such limitations are particularly problematic in the face of climate change, where movement may be necessary for climate change adaptation. For example, in the United States, several Native Alaskan villages, such as Kivalina and Newtok, are having to relocate entire communities because their homelands have been destroyed as a result of climate change.[19]

Outside the legal realm, many indigenous peoples are closely connected to their land and environment for cultural and spiritual reasons. For example, in Brazil, many indigenous communities have substantial connections to the forests, which will be impacted by REDD policies discussed later in this chapter.[20] As George Manuel, author of the groundbreaking book *The Fourth World: An Indian Reality*, has explained: "it seems to me that all of our structures and values have developed out of a spiritual relationship with the land on which we have lived. Our customs and practices vary as the different landscapes of the continent, but underlying this forest of legitimate differences is a common soil of social and spiritual experience."[21]

Because of this close connection to the land, indigenous peoples are often well placed to observe and interpret changes to their environment. Such observations and interpretations may be especially important in the development of climate change mitigation and adaptation strategies. This is yet another reason why indigenous environmental knowledge (IEK)[22] should be incorporated into

---

[17] The connection to land and environment varies amongst indigenous communities. However, there is commonality in that many indigenous communities are connected, for cultural and spiritual reasons, legal reasons, or both.

[18] F. Pommersheim, "The Reservation as Place: A South Dakota Essay" (1989) 34 *South Dakota Law Review* 246 at 250.

[19] E. A. Kronk, "Effective Access to Justice: Applying the *Parens Patriae* Standing Doctrine to Climate Change-Related Claims Brought by Native Nations" (2011) 32 *Public Land & Resources Law Review* 1 at 5–10.

[20] See generally A. Long, "REDD+ and Indigenous Peoples in Brazil," in R. S. Abate and E. A. Kronk (eds.), *Climate Change and Indigenous Peoples: The Search for Legal Remedies* (Cheltenham: Edward Elgar Publishing, 2013).

[21] G. Manuel and M. Posluns, *The Fourth World: An Indian Reality* (New York: The Free Press, 1974), p. 7.

[22] Notably, there is no single concept of indigenous environmental knowledge, as each indigenous community's environmental knowledge differs from the next. But commonalities within indigenous environmental knowledge can be found, such as respect for humans and nature, humility, sharing and reciprocity. M. Burkett, "Indigenous Knowledge and Climate Change

456 South of South

international strategies dealing with the impacts of climate change. Because indigenous peoples have the ability to draw on (sometimes) centuries of knowledge related to a particular place, they are well positioned to conceive of unique solutions to the problem of climate change. Also, IEK, which is often premised on notions of communal management, is antithetical to non-indigenous property systems and therefore offers refreshing perspectives on these challenges. These observations are relevant to discussions aimed at increasing indigenous participation in the international legal regime, such as through the REDD mechanism discussed below.

2.3 Fourth World

Although indigenous communities around the world may have much in common with the global South, their concerns and struggles may not always align with those in the global South. These differences are captured and expounded upon in the seminal book, *The Fourth World: An Indian Reality*. Exploration of the concept for the "Fourth World" is helpful toward understanding how the needs of indigenous communities may differ from those of the global South.

To begin, it is helpful to understand how the Fourth World differs from the "Third World." As Vine Deloria, Jr. explained, "[t]he 'Third World' was to be a great coalition of oppressed peoples of the world rising up against the technology and tyranny of the western European peoples."[23] The idea of the Third World arose from Asian and African countries' emergence from colonialism. The Fourth World is distinguished from the Third World for political reasons, as members of the Third World generally possess political recognition by the global community. A common understanding of the universe and a threatened worldview distinguish the Fourth World from the First and Third Worlds. The Fourth World calls on institutions to re-examine their own origins and ensure that they are based on integrity and sound moral principles. There may also be economic and religious differences.

Furthermore, the Fourth World evolves from the connection which many indigenous communities have with their environment. Recent history is defined by the disconnection of humanity – especially the global North – from the environment. "The Fourth World emerges as each people develops customs and practices that wed it to the land as the forest to the soil, and as a people stop expecting that there is some unnamed thing that grows equally well from sea to sea."[24]

Adaptation," in R. S. Abate and E. A. Kronk (eds.), *Climate Change and Indigenous Peoples: The Search for Legal Remedies* (Northampton: Edward Elgar Publishing, 2013).

[23] V. Deloria, Jr., "Foreword," in G. Manuel and M. Posluns (eds.), *The Fourth World: An Indian Reality* (New York: The Free Press, 1974), pp. ix–xii.

[24] G. Manuel and M. Posluns, *The Fourth World: An Indian Reality* (New York: The Free Press, 1974), p. 7. Here, the authors explain that Fourth World communities rely on connections to

It is not necessary for indigenous communities to continue living in the same way in which their ancestors lived.[25] However, it is necessary to "create new forms that will allow the future generations to inherit the values, the strengths, and the basic spiritual beliefs – the way of understanding the world – that is the fruit of a thousand generations' cultivation of North American soil by Indian people."[26]

Development of Fourth World institutions, which includes both institutions of self-government and those necessary to facilitate indigenous participation in state and international fora, is necessary because the political institutions of the global North and, in many instances, those of the global South have failed to adequately represent the general needs of their citizenry and, specifically, indigenous communities contained within. If these institutions cannot meet the needs of their citizens in general, there is little hope that such institutions can protect and promote the needs of indigenous people. Moreover, development of the Fourth World helps to undo the myths created through colonization, as a healthy relationship between the Fourth World and others will emerge. Accordingly, indigenous peoples must develop their own institutions to promote their needs and to reduce reliance on the global North.[27] The ability of indigenous people to design their own governing model is the first step toward the Fourth World. Ultimately, "[t]he fastest way to bring about change among an oppressed people is to put the decision-making authority, and the economic resources that go with it, into their own hands."[28]

There is opportunity to give life to the Fourth World through the international legal regime as it applies to climate change by giving indigenous peoples an opportunity to participate at all levels of climate change decision-making. Furthermore, indigenous peoples must be given space to create their own institutions through which they will participate in decision-making processes.[29]

---

their present environment rather than hoping for support or protection from something foreign or apart from themselves.

[25] "Remaining Indian does not mean wearing a breech-cloth or a buckskin jacket, any more than remaining English means wearing pantaloons, a sword, and a funny hat . . . Remaining Indian means that Indian people gain control of the economic and social development of our own communities, within a framework of legal and constitutional guarantees for our land and our institutions." Ibid, p. 221.

[26] Ibid, p. 4.

[27] Ibid, p. 217.

[28] Ibid, p. 246.

[29] An example of the ability of indigenous peoples to help craft their own institutions to ensure their ability to participate is the United Nations Permanent Forum on Indigenous Issues. "The United Nations Permanent Forum on Indigenous Issues (UNPFII) is an advisory body to the Economic and Social Council (ECOSOC), with a mandate to discuss indigenous issues related to economic and social development, culture, the environment, education, health and human rights." United Nations Permanent Forum on Indigenous Issues, "Indigenous Peoples at the United Nations," http://undesadspd.org.

458　　　　　　　　　　　　　　*South of South*

2.4 *International Law Applicable to Indigenous People*[30]

Furthermore, indigenous peoples possess certain rights under international law that are particularly relevant to the development of the climate change regime. As a starting point, there are some rights under international law applicable to all people, which are helpful when discussing indigenous rights in the climate change context. For example, nation-states have an obligation to respect the human rights of individuals subject to their authority.[31] Moreover, in the Americas, the right to hold property has also been identified as a human right under Article 21 of the American Convention on Human Rights and Article 17 of the Universal Declaration of Human Rights.[32] Furthermore, the right to development was recognized in 1986 by the UN General Assembly.[33] The Declaration on the Right to Development is important for indigenous peoples because it refers to both persons and peoples as rights-holders. Furthermore, the Declaration connects the person's or peoples' right to development with self-determination. Nation states are required to implement their domestic laws in a way that allows individuals to effectuate

---

[30] This portion of the chapter provides merely an overview of international law applicable to indigenous people. A complete discussion of applicable international law is beyond the scope of this chapter.

[31] *American Convention on Human Rights*, San Jose, 21 November 1969, in force 18 August 1978, OAS Treaty Series No. 36; 1144 UNTS 123; 9 ILM 99 (1969), art. 1; *Additional Protocol to the American Convention on Human Rights in the Area of Economic, Social and Cultural Rights*, San Salvador, 17 November 1988, in force 16 November 1999, OAS Treaty Series No. 69; 28 ILM 156 (1989), art. 1; *Charter of the United Nations*, San Francisco, 26 June 1945, in force 24 October 1945, 59 Stat. 1301; TS 993; 3 Bevans 1153, art. 55; Universal *Declaration of Human Rights Preamble*, Paris, 12 December 1948, GA Res. 217A, UN Doc. A/810, 71; *International Covenant on Civil and Political Rights*, New York, 16 December 1966, in force 23 March 1976, GA Res. 2200A (XXI), 21 UN GAOR Supp. (No. 16) at 52, UN Doc. A/6316 (1966); 999 UNTS 171; 6 ILM 368 (1967), arts. 2(1), 2(2); *International Covenant on Economic, Social and Cultural Rights*, New York, 16 December 1966, in force 3 January 1976, GA Res. 2200A (XXI), 21 UN GAOR Supp. (No. 16) at 49, UN Doc. A/6316 (1966); 993 UNTS 3; 6 ILM 368 (1967), art. 2(2); *International Convention on the Protection of the Rights of All Migrant Workers and Members of their Families*, New York, 18 December 1990, in force 1 July 2003, GA res. 45/158, annex, 45 U.N. GAOR Supp. (No. 49A) at 262, UN Doc. A/45/49 (1990), art. 7; *International Convention on the Elimination of All Forms of Racial Discrimination*, New York, 21 December 1965, in force 4 January 1969, 660 UNTS 195; GA Res. 2106 (XX), Annex, 20 U.N. GAOR Supp. (No. 14) at 47, UN Doc. A/6014 (1966), Preamble; *European Convention for the Protection of the Human Rights and Fundamental Freedoms*, 4 November 1950, in force 3 September 1953, ETS 5; 213 UNTS 221, Art. 1; *European Social Charter*, 18 October 1961, in force 26 February 1965, 529 UNTS 89; ETS 35, Preamble; *African Charter of Human and Peoples' Rights*, 27 June 1981, 21 October 1986, OAU Doc. CAB/LEG/67/3 rev. 5; 1520 UNTS 217; 21 ILM 58 (1982), art. 1; Council of the League of Arab States, *Arab Charter of Human Rights*, 15 September 1994, Res. 5437 (102nd Sess.), art. 2.

[32] Baez, note 1 at 843 (citations omitted). Notably, however, the Universal Declaration of Human Rights is not binding, although it is generally accepted as reflecting customary international law.

[33] *Declaration on the Right to Development*, New York, 4 December 1986, GA Res. 41/128, annex, 41 UN GAOR Supp. (No. 53) at 186, UN Doc. A/41/53 (1986).

their right to develop. As seen later in the chapter, the REDD mechanism potentially constrains the ability of indigenous peoples to develop and could, therefore, violate this right.

International law also contains provisions that are specific to indigenous peoples. Adopted in 1989, the International Labour Organization's Convention Concerning Indigenous and Tribal Peoples in Independent Countries (ILO 169) is a foundational document on the rights of indigenous peoples. Notably, ILO 169 recognizes the right of indigenous peoples to "exercise control [...] over their economic, social and cultural development" and participate in development that "may affect them directly."[34] Moreover, Article 14 of the Convention guarantees that indigenous peoples' "rights of ownership and possession [...] over the lands which they traditionally occupy shall be recognized," and Article 16 states that indigenous peoples "shall not be removed from the lands they occupy."[35]

Building on ILO 169, the United Nations Declaration on the Rights of Indigenous Peoples (UNDRIP) was adopted by the United Nations General Assembly in 2007.[36] In notable part, the UNDRIP provides that indigenous peoples have the right to self-determination, to lands and territories that they have traditionally occupied, and to legal redress for claims and land taken without free, prior, and informed consent.[37] Furthermore, UNDRIP provides that indigenous peoples shall not be subject to forced assimilation, nor shall they be forcibly removed from their lands.[38] The free, prior, and informed consent (FPIC) requirement of UNDRIP has come to be an important component of indigenous rights, as indigenous communities must be included early in any discussions potentially affecting indigenous peoples.[39] In terms of indigenous communities, FPIC might mean that such communities have the right to participate in climate change-related decisions, having been given both adequate notice of opportunities to participate and adequate information to allow full participation.[40] Such participation should be absent of "coercion, intimidation

---

[34] *International Labour Organization Indigenous and Tribal Peoples Convention*, Geneva, 27 June 1989, 72 ILO Official Bull. 59; 28 ILM 1382 (1989), art. 7.

[35] Ibid, arts. 14 and 16.

[36] Notably, some of the countries with the largest indigenous populations, such as the United States and Canada, did not originally endorse UNDRIP. However, they have now done so.

[37] UNDRIP, New York, 2 October 2007, A/61/L.67/Annex, arts. 3, 26, 28.

[38] Ibid, arts. 8, 10.

[39] "Both UNDRIP and ILO 169 explicitly recognize that indigenous peoples have a right to 'free, prior and informed consent' (FPIC) regarding activities that directly or indirectly affect them. FPIC is crucial to the protection of indigenous peoples' right to self-determination." Baez, note 1 at 842.

[40] M. Barelli, "Free, Prior and Informed Consent in the Aftermath of the UN Declaration on the Rights of Indigenous Peoples: Developments and Challenges Ahead" (2012) 16 *The International Journal of Human Rights* 3 (citing *Report of the International Workshop on Methodologies Regarding Free, Prior and Informed Consent and Indigenous Peoples*, New York, 17–19 January 2005, 17 February 2005, E/C.19/2005/3, para. 45).

460 *South of South*

or manipulation," and "'consent' should be intended as a process of which consultation and participation represent central pillars."[41]

Although UNDRIP is not legally binding, it does provide evidence of the consolidation of global recognition of indigenous legal rights. Many of the provisions of UNDRIP reflect general human rights law and to that extent they are binding. Some scholars have argued that ILO 169 and UNDRIP taken together should be considered evidence of customary international law.[42]

Although each indigenous community is unique, some commonalities exist which are especially important to any discussion of the role that indigenous people will play (or should play) in the development of the international climate regime. Failure to consider these unique aspects of indigenous communities decreases the likelihood of the climate regime's success and continues to preserve norms of colonialism perpetrated against indigenous peoples.

3. INCORPORATING INDIGENOUS PEOPLES INTO THE INTERNATIONAL CLIMATE REGIME: THE ICC PETITION AND REDD MECHANISM

Recognizing the unique role they play within the global community, indigenous peoples have actively attempted to participate in the development of international law as it applies to climate change, with varying levels of success. This section of the chapter explores two examples of how indigenous communities have attempted to participate in different fora.

3.1 ICC Petition[43]

"Climate change has become the ultimate threat to Inuit culture."

– *Sheila Watt-Cloutier*[44]

The Inuit Circumpolar Council (ICC) represents over 150,000 Inuit residing in Canada, Greenland, Russia, and the United States.[45] The Arctic Inuit are experiencing profound changes to their environment as a result of climate change, which

---

[41] Ibid.

[42] S. J. Anaya, *International Human Rights and Indigenous Peoples* (New York: Aspen Publishers/Wolters Kluwer, 2009) p. 185.

[43] This portion of the chapter is based on E. A. Kronk Warner and R. S. Abate, "International and Domestic Law Dimensions of Climate Justice for Arctic Indigenous Peoples" (2013) 43 *Revue Générale De Droit* 113.

[44] Inuit Circumpolar Conference, "The Climate Change Petition by the Inuit Circumpolar Conference to the Inter-American Commission on Human Rights," December 7, 2005, www.inuitcircumpolar.com.

[45] Inuit Circumpolar Conference, "Presentation by S. Watt-Cloutier," December 7, 2005, www.inuitcircumpolar.com.

has life-altering implications for the Inuit and their culture.[46] Although the Inuit have previously demonstrated the ability to adapt to a changing environment, the extensive and likely permanent changes to the Arctic because of climate change will drastically decrease their adaptive ability.[47]

On December 7, 2005, the ICC filed a petition with the Inter-American Commission on Human Rights (IACHR)[48] against the United States.[49] The ICC argued that as a significant contributor to climate change through its greenhouse gas emissions, the United States was contributing to the negative environmental impacts affecting the Inuit in both Canada and the United States.[50] As a result, the ICC asserted that Inuit rights under the American Declaration of the Organization of American States had been violated.[51] Specifically, the ICC argued that the United States infringed upon the following rights under the American Declaration: the right to enjoy the benefits of their (Inuit) culture; the right to use and enjoy lands they have traditionally used and occupied; the right to use and enjoy their personal property; the right to the preservation of health; the right to life, physical integrity, and security; the right to their own means of subsistence; and the Inuits' rights to residence, movement, and inviolability of the home.[52]

Although the ICC knew it would be exceedingly difficult to succeed before the IACHR, it moved forward with the petition in an effort to open up the dialogue about the link between climate change and human rights, as well as the effects of

---

[46] Ibid.

[47] Ibid.

[48] Although the ICC represents Inuit living in Greenland and Russia as well as in Canada and the United States, the ICC's 2005 petition was limited to those Inuit living in Canada and the United States, as the IACHR's jurisdiction is limited to nation states within the Americas. "Petition to the Inter-American Commission on Human Rights Seeking Relief from Violations Resulting from Global Warming Caused by Acts and Omissions of the United States," December 7, 2009, http://earthjustice.org.

[49] The ICC petition focused on the United States in part because of the American withdrawal from Kyoto, "a decision which the petition argues forms a key part of the U.S. failure to control its greenhouse gas emissions adequately." H. M. Osofsky, "Complexities of Addressing the Impacts of Climate Change on Indigenous Peoples Through International Law Petitions: A Case Study of the Inuit Petition to the Inter-American Commission on Human Rights," in R. S. Abate and E. A. Kronk (eds.), *Climate Change and Indigenous Peoples: The Search for Legal Remedies* (Cheltenham: Edward Elgar, 2013), p. 318.

[50] "Petition to the Inter-American Commission on Human Rights Seeking Relief from Violations Resulting from Global Warming Caused by Acts and Omissions of the United States," December 7, 2009, http://earthjustice.org.

[51] "[T]he petition relied upon rights contained in the regionally-based American Declaration of the Rights and Duties of Man because the United States is not party to the American Convention on Human Rights." Osofsky, note 49, p. 325.

[52] "Petition to the Inter-American Commission on Human Rights Seeking Relief from Violations Resulting from Global Warming Caused by Acts and Omissions of the United States," 7 December 2009, http://earthjustice.org. For a general discussion of each of these claims, see S. Nuffer, "Human Rights Violations and Climate Change" (2007) 37 *Journal of Rutgers School of Law* 189.

climate change on indigenous people.[53] As Sheila Watt-Cloutier noted, the petition had "great moral value" and was a vehicle to "educate and encourage."[54] The petition was a mechanism to engage the United States on the issue of its greenhouse gas emissions and its significant contributions to climate change.[55] Although the IACHR would not have had the authority to compel the United States to reduce its greenhouse gas emissions, the ICC hoped that a favorable outcome would have encouraged the United States to enter into negotiations related to its greenhouse gas emissions.[56]

The IACHR's response to the ICC's petition was exceedingly brief, constituting just two paragraphs.[57] The IACHR determined that "the information provided [in the ICC's petition] does not enable us to determine whether the alleged facts would tend to characterize a violation of the rights protected by the American Declaration."[58] In response to the IACHR's letter and determination of the merits of the ICC's petition, the ICC requested that the IACHR hold a hearing on the link between climate change and human rights.[59] The IACHR granted the ICC's request and held a hearing in March 2007.[60] Since then, the IACHR has indicated that it remains interested in the rights of indigenous peoples within the Americas.[61]

The ICC petition is an example of how indigenous communities may be empowered to participate in the international regime in a manner that is culturally appropriate. The ICC petition is consistent with Inuit tradition and culture, which relies on oral traditions.[62] "The petition provides a telling of the story of the US

---

[53] Osofsky, note 49, p. 315. Interestingly, however, the petition was not a "lost cause." As Professor Osofsky explained, "[t]he Inuit petition builds on the existing jurisprudence in the Inter-American Commission on Human Rights by presenting an environmental rights' harm that is separated in both time and location from the behavior causing it. The previous decisions of the Inter-American Commission and Court on Human Rights demonstrate receptiveness to the interweaving of environmental harm and human rights violations, especially in the context of indigenous peoples." Ibid p. 327.

[54] Nuffer, note 52 at 192 (citing H. M. Osofsky, "The Inuit Petition as a Bridge? Beyond Dialectics of Climate Change and Indigenous Peoples' Rights" (2007) 31 *American Indian Law Review* 675 at 687).

[55] Osofsky, note 49, p. 315. Although it would be difficult to draw a direct connection between the ICC's petition and the United States' subsequent actions, it is notable that the United States' participation in international discussions related to climate change and its domestic regulation of greenhouse gases have all increased since the ICC's petition was filed in 2005. Ibid pp. 318–319.

[56] M. Wagner and D. M. Goldberg, *An Inuit Petition to the Inter-American Commission on Human Rights for Dangerous Impacts of Climate Change* (Washington: CIEL, 2004).

[57] Letter from the Organization of American States to S. Watt-Cloutier et al. regarding Petition No. P-1413-05, November 2006, http://graphics8.nytimes.com/packages/pdf/science/16commissionletter.pdf, p. 16.

[58] Ibid.

[59] Osofsky, note 49, p. 314, note 3.

[60] Ibid, pp. 314.

[61] Ibid.

[62] Although this chapter makes reference to cultures and traditions referenced in the ICC petition, the author recognizes that one should not pigeonhole indigenous peoples into

responsibility for the devastation climate change has wreaked upon them."[63] In this sense, the ICC petition is consistent with George Manuel's call for the development of effective Fourth World institutions. What is missing in these instances, however, is effective enforcement by the international legal regime and the full incorporation of indigenous perspectives and Fourth World institutions in the climate change regime.

Indigenous perspectives and Fourth World institutions allow for the consideration of and possible utilization of indigenous methods of responding to the impacts of climate change. Notably, IEK is based on proven historical adaptations. Moreover, utilization of such worldviews potentially facilitates long-range, multigenerational adaptive governance. Accordingly, in the case of the ICC petition, incorporation of these perspectives and institutions may open up the Commission and other American institutional entities to long-term adaptive governance strategies premised on proven IEK.

3.2 REDD

While the ICC petition is a recent example of indigenous communities asserting their rights at the international level, ongoing efforts are being made to do the same within the Reducing Emissions from Deforestation and Forest Degradation (REDD) regime.[64] REDD, as originally conceived, creates a mechanism whereby those in the global North needing to offset greenhouse gas emissions may establish programs largely in the global South that reduce greenhouse gas emissions from deforestation. Eventually, the mechanism came to also include reducing forest degradation and reforestation efforts. Increasingly, REDD has become an important part of the national policy of tropical forest nations – countries which tend to

---

cultural stereotypes. See J. M. Hohmann, "Igloo as Icon: A Human Rights Approach to Climate Change for the Inuit?" (2009) 18(2) *Transnational Law and Contemporary Problems* 295 at 295 ("Similarly, to emphasize the differences between them and the rest of Canadian society, some Inuit organizations may deem it useful to depict their members as primarily preoccupied with traditional pursuits. In both cases, though, it is wrong to believe and let others believe that Inuit identity is bounded by a narrowly defined series of traditional cultural traits"), citing L-J. Dorais, *Quaqtaq Modernity and Identity in an Inuit Community* (Toledo: University of Toledo Press, 1997). Moreover, it is important not to view culture and tradition as "frozen" and impervious to change: J. Dorais, *Quaqtaq: Modernity and Identity in an Inuit Community* (Toronto: University of Toronto Press, 1997), pp. 313–314, citing J. Borrows, "Frozen Rights in Canada: Constitutional Interpretation and the Trickster" (1997) 22 *American Indian Law Review* 37 at 60.

[63] Osofsky, note 49, p. 333.

[64] Although the REDD mechanism has also been referred to by various names throughout its history, such as REDD+ and REDD plus, for the sake of readability, it will be referred to as REDD in this chapter.

have indigenous populations.[65] For example, REDD is a crucial piece of Brazil's climate change initiatives.[66]

In many instances the activities that lead to deforestation threaten indigenous communities. Even generally, "[p]re-existing deforestation drivers reduce resilience to the extent that climate change may push degraded forest ecosystems beyond tipping points, leading to severe ecological and social impacts."[67] The threat of climate change therefore creates an urgency for indigenous peoples to protect their traditional forests, and, in this case REDD has the potential to assist indigenous communities, assuming that REDD mechanisms do not push indigenous peoples out of their traditional forests, as discussed later in the chapter.

It is important to note, however, that REDD currently does not contain an explicit recognition of indigenous legal rights. Accordingly, despite the potential for REDD to benefit indigenous communities by protecting their traditional forests, many indigenous communities are concerned about the manner in which REDD is being implemented.[68] First, because of the broader, more complicated focus of REDD (i.e. deforestation, degradation, and reforestation, as opposed to a singular focus on deforestation), implementation and enforcement increasingly occurs at the state level, and no international, mandatory requirements for REDD implementation have yet been developed. Thus, voluntary implementation is left to the individual nation states and subnational groups have played a prominent role in the development of legal infrastructure related to REDD. Many of these subnational groups have historically been hostile to indigenous communities leading to concerns about the protection of indigenous rights.[69] These concerns may be compounded by the fact that international actors, such as the World Bank, which provide funding for REDD projects have failed to put legal protections into place related to respecting indigenous rights, despite their own guidelines on indigenous peoples.[70]

---

[65] Given the relatively short length of this chapter, a full discussion of the REDD mechanism is beyond its scope. For a complete discussion of the REDD framework, see A. Wiersema, "Climate Change, Forests, and International Law: REDD's Descent into Irrelevance" (2014) 47 *Vanderbilt Journal of Transnational Law* 1.

[66] It is helpful to look at the manner in which REDD has been implemented in Brazil, as both Brazil and Indonesia have been at the forefront of REDD implementation and both nations have significant indigenous populations.

[67] A. Long, "REDD+ and Indigenous Peoples in Brazil," in R. S. Abate and E. A. Kronk (eds.), *Climate Change and Indigenous Peoples: The Search for Legal Remedies* (Cheltenham: Edward Elgar Publishing, 2013), p. 158.

[68] One can look to Brazil for evidence that indigenous people have been slow to adopt the REDD mechanism: "[a]s of July 2010, only four tribes (of approximately 230 recognized indigenous tribes in Brazil) had adopted REDD+ projects or programs, representing less than two percent of the territory managed by indigenous people." Long, note 67, p. 166.

[69] Long, note 67, p. 161.

[70] See generally L. Crippa, "REDD+: Its Potential to Melt the Glacial Resistance to Recognize Human Rights and Indigenous Peoples' Rights at the World Bank," in R. S. Abate and E. A. Kronk (eds.), *Climate Change and Indigenous Peoples: The Search for Legal Remedies* (Cheltenham: Edward Elgar Publishing, 2013), p. 123.

Next, given that some indigenous communities actually rely on deforestation-related activities for their income, such as through agriculture, logging, and infrastructure development, REDD's environmental goals may be accomplished at the expense of indigenous livelihood. This economic insult is compounded by the fact that REDD projects, in many instances, will allow companies in the global North to continue with "business as usual," as these companies will not have to reduce their existing emissions because of the offsets from the REDD projects. Indigenous communities have argued that this is a fundamental injustice. For example, one scholar explains that "REDD would curb development for indigenous peoples, who have contributed least to climate change, while allowing Annex 1 nations to continue with business as usual. [. . .] Annex 1 nations may be able to benefit economically and environmentally from indigenous groups' loss of livelihood."[71] Notably, such restriction on the ability for indigenous peoples to develop is a violation of the right to development recognized by the UNDRIP.

Furthermore, and perhaps most importantly, significant concerns exist regarding the role indigenous communities will play in planning REDD projects and whether the appropriate decision-makers of the various indigenous communities will be invited to participate. Failure to include the correct indigenous decision-makers in REDD discussions violates the international requirements of FPIC. Moreover, failure to include indigenous communities in such discussions also likely means a failure to incorporate IEK into such decisions. Ultimately, "REDD+ projects taking place in indigenous territories will likely undermine indigenous peoples' collective rights, including full ownership rights to land and natural resources and the right to self-determination."[72]

Finally, concern has been expressed that indigenous people will not be able to fairly participate in negotiations related to REDD development. Indigenous peoples have felt excluded from United Nations Framework Convention on Climate Change negotiations related to REDD, as demonstrated by indigenous protests at the Conference of the Parties.[73] Indigenous exclusion at the international level is directly related to indigenous exclusion at the national level, as nation states play an important role in international negotiations. Indigenous exclusion may result in forest use being restricted in such a way so as to prohibit traditional indigenous uses of the forests, including subsistence needs. Exclusion from participating at both the domestic and international levels violates the principles of self-determination and FPIC. Principles of FPIC may also be implicated, as the ideological foundations of many REDD programs reflect ideologies of the global North – ideologies that may prove incompatible with indigenous ideologies. For instance, as noted earlier in the chapter, incorporation of IEK might facilitate

[71] Baez, note 1, p. 840.
[72] Crippa, note 70, p. 124.
[73] Long, note 67, p. 163.

long-range, multigenerational adaptive governance. Many American Indians, for example, speak of planning for the Seventh Generation, which can mean making decisions that are protective of the seven generations following the decision-maker. Because many non-indigenous institutions consider the ramifications of decisions within relatively short time periods that are often chosen on the basis of politics, indigenous participation premised on long-range, multigenerational governance is excluded.

The foregoing concerns focus on the initial set-up and implementation of REDD projects. Concern also exists on the "back-end" of REDD projects, as questions arise regarding the distribution of monies and other benefits derived from REDD projects. Given that indigenous communities may be the most immediately impacted by restrictions on forest use imposed by REDD projects, it would seem equitable that these communities should have a substantial share of the benefits from such projects. However, in most instances, indigenous communities have not directly benefitted from such projects. Furthermore, for those benefits that do reach indigenous communities, it may also be a challenge to ensure that the entire community (or those most directly impacted by the REDD project) benefits, rather than a few individual members of the indigenous community. In other words, there is no way to ensure distribution to individual members of an indigenous community without interfering with the community's internal governance.[74]

Furthermore, indigenous concerns may conflict with desires of the international environmental community, as projects that some environmentalists deem successful may be seen by indigenous communities as problematic. For example, the Nature Conservancy describes the Guaraquecaba Climate Action Project as a model of environmental protection. However, the project has been cited by anti-REDD activists as the single worst REDD project in the world. This project relies on the branch of the Brazilian military known as the *Force Verde* ("Green Police") to enforce restrictions imposed by carbon projects. Local residents, including members of the indigenous Guarani tribe, complain that enforcement of the Guaraquecaba Climate Action Project's rules has interfered with their traditional activities.[75]

As with the ICC petition, there are positive developments related to the progression of the REDD mechanism. Indigenous communities and scholars are actively pushing for increased indigenous participation and, in some instances, their efforts have borne fruit. However, the REDD mechanism has yet to explicitly protect indigenous rights or incorporate Fourth World mechanisms. Currently, REDD merely makes note of the General Assembly's adoption of UNDRIP. Accordingly, REDD does not explicitly incorporate any rights for indigenous peoples. This is

---

[74] Ibid, p. 173.
[75] Ibid, pp. 169–170.

disappointing given that previous REDD drafts recognized UNDRIP as an affirmative source of rights for indigenous people. Today, even the few safeguards incorporated into REDD to protect the rights of indigenous groups are subject to minimal international oversight.[76] Ultimately, UNDRIP may have to be used to protect indigenous rights under the REDD mechanism, which may be accomplished by either requiring the REDD mechanism to explicitly recognize UNDRIP as an affirmative source of rights or using UNDRIP in combination with ILO 169 as a source of customary law.

4. CONCLUSION

Indigenous communities differ from other communities in the global South. They are particularly vulnerable to the impacts of climate change and therefore deserve special consideration and accommodation within the international legal regime, particularly within the climate change regime. While each indigenous community is unique, commonalities do exist, which can instruct how the international climate regime should respond to indigenous communities. First, the international community must recognize that indigenous people are particularly vulnerable to impacts of climate change. Felix Cohen, a founding father of modern American Federal Indian Law, once equated American Indians to the miner's canary – if indigenous peoples go, so does the rest of the world. Indigenous peoples and their cultures are dying as a result of climate change and the international community must pay heed.

Second, indigenous peoples, in many instances, possess unique legal, cultural, and spiritual connections to their land and environment. These connections allow for the creation of indigenous environmental knowledge that can be beneficial in the development of climate change solutions. Moreover, because of these connections, the international community must create space for indigenous peoples when negotiating the climate regime. The preferred mechanism for creating space is through the recognition and promotion of indigenous institutions. Such recognition is a vehicle for development of the Fourth World. ILO 169 and UNDRIP are particularly helpful in acknowledging and protecting the indigenous right to FPIC, property, and self-determination, and effective recourse for the violation of their rights. Given the broad recognition of these indigenous rights under international law, climate change mechanisms, such as REDD, must explicitly incorporate such rights.

Indigenous communities have attempted to represent their interests within the international legal regime with various degrees of success. The ICC's petition to the IAHRC, although rejected by the Commission, certainly brought climate change's impact on Arctic indigenous peoples to the forefront of the climate

---

[76] Wiersema, note 65.

change debate. Also, the IAHRC remains interested in the connection between climate change and indigenous peoples. Similarly, indigenous protests against the REDD mechanism during Conference of the Parties negotiations highlighted concerns regarding the implementation and protection of indigenous rights. Despite these protests, participation of indigenous communities in REDD development is occurring on an ad hoc, domestic level.

Given that indigenous communities in many instances exist outside the traditional nation-state framework, they exist apart from the global North and the global South. They may be considered south-of-south. Indigenous communities have much to offer the global climate regime in terms of IEK. Moreover, indigenous legal rights exist, as exemplified by ILO 169 and UNDRIP. Continued failure to incorporate indigenous communities into the international climate regime constitutes an extreme moral and legal failure on the part of the international community, which in turn would doom any international climate change regime to illegitimacy and ultimate ruin.

22

Water Wars: Anti-Privatization Struggles in the Global South

Jackie Dugard and Elisabeth Koek

1. INTRODUCTION

Since the 1980s development agencies and international financial institutions in the global North have promoted private sector ownership and management of water services and infrastructure across the global South, assuming this would promote greater investment, transparency, and efficiency in what had previously been an overwhelmingly public sector. The reality over the past thirty years has been that many of these expectations have not been fulfilled, and the push for water privatization is no longer as strong as it used to be.[1] This is due in no small part to strong opposition to the privatization of water services from civil society[2] based on perceived conflicts between privatization and equity.[3] Such opposition, which has been mounted by a wide range of groups, has not been confined to the global

---

[1] See e.g., M. Langford, "Privatisation and the Right to Water," in M. Langford and A. Russell (eds.), *The Right to Water and Sanitation in Theory and Practice: Drawing from a Deeper Well?* (Cambridge: Cambridge University Press, in press). Notwithstanding any retreats from outright privatization, in recent years the privatization revolution has arguably given way to the more insidious commercialization and corporatization of water services across the world, in terms of which water services have begun to be viewed primarily as an economic product rather than a public health-related service, regardless of whether they are privately or publicly controlled: see D. Hemson, "Water for All: From Firm Promises to 'New Realism'," in D. Hemson, K. Kulindwa, H. Lein and A. Mascarenhas, *Poverty and Water: Explorations of the Reciprocal Relationship* (London: Zed Books, 2008), p. 30. Also, it should be noted that the top-down push for outright privatization persists. For example, in 2011 during the financial crisis in the wake of the Wall Street crash of 2008, Greece was forced to privatize its water sector to gain financial relief from the International Monetary Fund and European Union: see D. Hall, "Water in Europe," presentation to Attac ENA, Freibourg (2011), cited in M. Langford, 'Privatisation and the Right to Water'.

[2] It is also due to un-met expectations for large profits and increasing unease in the international development community that water privatization was not delivering the assumed efficiency-related benefits: Langford, note 1.

[3] D. Hall, E. Lobina and R. de la Motte, "Public Resistance to Privatisation in Water and Energy" (2005) 15 *Development in Practice*, pp. 286–301.

470 *Water Wars*

South. Indeed, globally there has been strong resistance to privatization, and not only in respect of water specifically or utilities more generally; however, contestation over the privatized control of water resources and services has certainly been one of the most vibrant spheres of opposition to privatization (and much of this has emanated from the global South). As pointed out by McDonald and Ruiters in their 2012 book on *Alternatives to Privatization*: "[w]ater appears to be the most dynamic [positive example of opposition to privatization]. This is likely due to the fact that it has been one of the services most affected and politicized by privatization, but also because it is the only truly "non-substitutable" service [...] and the easiest to imagine having more community/public control over."[4]

Indeed, the North-led privatization of water "remains widely and increasingly unpopular, largely because of the perception that it is fundamentally unfair, both in conception and execution."[5] Over the past twenty years, opposition to water privatization (or its commercialization and corporatization) has generated a counter-wave of popular resistance in the global South, which has focused as much on opposition to privatization as it has on broader discontent with North-led economic imperialism as entrenched through international financial institutions such as the World Bank and the International Monetary Fund (IMF), international legal instruments such as bilateral investment treaties (BITs), and transnational water corporations such as Suez and Vivendi from France and Bechtel from the United States of America. This opposition has taken many forms, including protests, political campaigns, and terminations of government contracts, with activists at times invoking rights or litigation to reverse private deals and fight for public provision. While the use of traditional struggle tactics such as protests and petitions has a long history in many countries of the global South, and particularly in Latin America, the use of rights and courts to fight water privatization – so-called water rights lawfare[6] – has been more recent and has been strengthened by the longstanding campaign to recognize an international right to water.[7]

This chapter examines the genesis and achievements of anti-privatization-related water struggles (by various means[8]) in four countries from the global South – Argentina, Bolivia, Uruguay, and South Africa. The focus on these countries does

---

[4] D. McDonald and G. Ruiters (eds.), *Alternatives to Privatization: Public Options for Essential Services in the Global South* (New York: Routledge, 2012), p. 10.

[5] N. Birdsall and J. Nellis, "Winners and Losers: Assessing the Distributional Impact of Privatization," Center for Global Development Working Paper No. 6, 2002, p. i.

[6] See e.g. C. Vallejo and S. Gloppen, "Red-Green Lawfare? Climate Change Narratives in Courtrooms," in J. Dugard, A. St. Clair and S. Gloppen, *Climate Talk: Rights, Poverty and Justice* (Cape Town: Juta, 2013), pp. 208–235.

[7] This was finally achieved through the adoption of resolutions in the United Nations General Assembly and Human Rights Council in 2010.

[8] Two of the examples in our chapter – Uruguay and South Africa – involve rights-based tactics, whereas two other examples – Argentina and Bolivia – do not. We have therefore not used a rights-based analysis for the chapter as a whole as we are interested in the tactics as employed by the activists themselves rather than in attempting to force the empirical studies into an overarching normative frame.

not imply that these are the only countries in which there have been anti-privatization struggles over water. Our choice of case studies was informed by two main factors. First is the fact that the initial and strongest wave of water privatizations occurred in Latin America, meaning that Latin America is the site of more privatizations and contested privatizations than any other region of the world. Second, the inclusion of South Africa was informed by the authors' personal knowledge. The chapter does not evaluate the relative strengths and weaknesses of privatized versus public water services per se.[9] Rather, it seeks to document a range of case studies in which there have been popular struggles against privatized control over water services, highlighting the role of North-led neoliberal economic agendas in exacerbating socioeconomic and environmental conditions and focusing on the achievements and challenges of these struggles.

2. CASE STUDIES

As noted by Langford, the move to privatize water "catalyzed enormous reactions in many but not all countries in which it was introduced."[10] Notwithstanding any instances where water privatization did not provoke resistance, it is clear that globally, and especially in the global South,[11] there has been an overwhelming contestation of the commodification of water in its various guises:

> A mighty contest has grown between those (usually powerful) forces and institutions that see water as a commodity and, to be put on the market and sold to the highest bidder, and those who see water as a public trust, a common heritage of people and nature and a fundamental human right. The origins of this movement, generally referred to as the global justice movement, lie in the hundreds of communities around the world where people are fighting to protect their local water supplies.[12]

2.1 Argentina

In the early 1990s, with the backing of the World Bank, Argentina embarked on "one of the most ambitious privatization programs in the world,"[13] targeting large natural monopolies in sectors such as electricity, oil and natural gas,

---

[9] For an examination of alternatives to privatization, see e.g. McDonald and Ruiters (eds.), note 4.

[10] Langford, note 1.

[11] It should be noted that there has also been a significant move against water privatization in the global North. For example, in 2011 Italians voted overwhelmingly to reject a proposed privatization of their water supply, and at the time of writing, a European Citizens' Initiative was underway to oppose any water liberalizations in Europe (the Initiative had gained 1.9 million signatures, almost double the number needed to pass the required quorum).

[12] M. Barlow, *Blue Covenant: The Global Water Crisis and the Coming Battle for the Right to Water* (New York: New Press, 2008), p. 102.

[13] S. Galiani, P. Gertler, and E. Schargrodsky, "Water for Life: The Impact of the Privatization of Water Services on Child Mortality" (2005) 113 *Journal of Political Economy* 90.

472   *Water Wars*

telecommunications, transportations, mail services, and, most importantly, Argentina's public water systems.[14] By the mid-1990s approximately 30 percent of municipal water supply[15] was privatized and by 1999 twenty-two private operators were supplying 71 percent of the urban population.[16] In Argentina, as in many other countries around the world, water privatization was unpopular, and by the 2000s most of the private concessions had been reversed, such as in the case of Tucumán province, where strong public pressure forced the government to rescind the contract with the French multinational water company Vivendi (formerly Compagnie Générale des Eaux).[17] Similarly, resistance against the privatized water supply in Buenos Aires culminated in the government rescinding that contract too. Thus, by 2007, the number of urban residents supplied by private water contractors had fallen to 12.1 percent.[18]

2.1.1 Tucumán

In 1995, Aguas del Aconquija, a subsidiary of Vivendi, was granted a thirty-year concession to supply water services to the Argentine province of Tucumán. On taking over the concession, the company immediately raised water tariffs by 104 percent while failing to implement the planned investment program, allowing the water to turn brown, and igniting "civil disobedience" across the province.[19]

Residents from different cities in Tucumán came together to form La Asociación en Defensa de los Usuarios y Consumidores de Tucumán (ADEUCOT, or "Association for the Defense of Users and Consumers in Tucumán"). ADEUCOT organized marches and demonstrations, initiated a movement to boycott water payments, and ultimately demanded that the provincial government terminate the concession contract.[20] The protest and boycott actions started in seven small towns, and soon water clients were collectively refusing to pay their bills for water and sewage services.[21] Withstanding pressure from Aguas del Aconquija, which threatened to litigate against boycotters, as well as the French government,

---

[14] Ibid at 89–90.

[15] Ibid at 83.

[16] J. Ducci, *Salida de Operadores Privados Internacionales de Agua en América Latina* (Washington: Inter-American Development Bank, 2007), pp. 64–65.

[17] G. Amorebieta, "Campaign to Take Back Jakarta Water from Private Concessionaires," presented at the Campaign to Take Back Jakarta Water from Private Concessionaires seminar, 2006, p. 3.

[18] Langford, note 1.

[19] D. Hall and E. Lobina, "Water Privatization in Latin America, 2002," July 2002, http://psiru.org, p. 14.

[20] T. Coleman, "Who Owns the Water? An Analysis of Water Conflicts in Latin American and Modern Water Law" (2012) 12 *Intersections* 1.

[21] Food and Water Watch, "The Social Protest for Water in Tucuman," November 4, 2009, www.foodandwaterwatch.org.

which tried to get the national government of Argentina to end the boycott,[22] the resistance campaign sought support from the Ombudsman.[23] The Ombudsman filed legal action on behalf of ADEUCOT to challenge key aspects of the company's service delivery performance and also to partially legalize the actions of the payment boycotters in the context of the service delivery failures, thereby offering some protection against providers who actively pursued them.[24] The provincial government responded to the collective resistance by terminating the concession in October 1998. In 2001, the national government decided against a new privatized concession for Tucumán's water system, instead awarding a thirty-year contract to Sapem, a 90 percent provincially owned enterprise.[25]

2.1.2 Buenos Aires

In 1993, following a loan from the World Bank that was conditioned on the privatization of water services,[26] Argentina's public national water services company (Obras Sanitarias de la Nación (OSN)) sold a private concession for Buenos Aires's water supply to the Aguas Argentinas SA consortium, formed by France's two powerful water companies, Vivendi and Suez (formerly known as Lyonnaise des Eaux). As part of the deal, union leaders were offered a 10 percent stake in the new company, thereby effectively neutralizing initial opposition to the privatization by the union – which then acquiesced when half of the OSN's workers, some 7,200 people, lost their jobs as a result of the deal.[27] With the unions at bay, the consortium took over operations, almost immediately implementing a 13.5 percent tariff increase despite commitments not to increase water rates.[28]

Exposure of the false promises regarding tariff increases, as well as the imposition by Aguas Argentinas of a substantial connection fee on new water clients, catalyzed dissent, and civil unrest against the company steadily grew. In April 1996, a protest movement took to the streets in the suburban area of Lomos de Zamora, and the resistance soon spread across Buenos Aires, with thousands of protestors blocking roads into the city and the formation of an umbrella Federation of

---

[22] Coleman, note 20 at 12–13.
[23] The Ombudsman is a national autonomous institution related to the Argentine National Congress with authority to represent the interests of the public by investigating and addressing complaints of maladministration or violation of rights.
[24] B. Morgan, "Building Bridges Between Regulatory and Citizen Space: Civil Society Contributions to Water Service Delivery Frameworks in Cross-National Perspective" (2008) 1 *Law, Social Justice and Global Development* 5.
[25] Hall and Lobina, note 19, pp. 14–15.
[26] Food and Water Watch, "Buenos Aires: Collapse of the Privatization Deal," November 4, 2009, www.foodandwaterwatch.org.
[27] Ibid.
[28] D. Santoro, "The 'Aguas' Tango," February 6, 2003, www.publicintegrity.org.

474   *Water Wars*

Drinking Water Co-operatives of the Province of Buenos Aires (FEDECAP).[29] In response, the company agreed to lower the connection fee, but it later levied a higher fee on water users in order to recoup its financial losses.[30]

By 1997, four years after the concession was granted, Aguas Argentinas had built only a third of the infrastructure it had promised to complete and had only invested a mere US$9.4 million of a promised US$48.9 million in the city's sewage networks. On top of this, the company was delaying construction of the Berazategui wastewater treatment plant, allowing it to save money and to add some US$35 million per year in profits.[31] Despite such clear failings, the water privatization contract was renegotiated following political pressure by the French government. With support from the World Bank, which sent one of its own senior water managers to join the staff of Aguas Argentinas to negotiate rate increases, a new contract was signed in 2000.

Following the collapse of the Argentine economy in 2001, in February 2002 the company threatened to suspend certain water services and all construction plans and demanded a fixed peso–dollar exchange rate for repayment of its external debt of nearly US$700 million. This demand was followed by another rate increase of 42 percent when the government refused the fixed exchange rate. A few months later, Aguas Argentinas defaulted on its loans. Subsequent efforts to renegotiate the contract were overshadowed by the company's constant threat to take the Argentine government to the World Bank's International Center for the Settlement of Investment Disputes (ICSID) for violating the terms of a France–Argentine BIT. In July 2003 this threat was realized when Aguas Argentinas, Suez, and Vivendi instigated proceedings against the Argentine government for alleged breaches of the BIT arising from the three water concessions in Buenos Aires, Cordoba and Santa Fe.[32] The consortium demanded US$1.7 billion in losses caused by currency devaluation as a result of the government's policy to freeze tariffs.[33]

At the time of writing the case is pending before the ICSID, but the proceedings with respect to Aguas Argentinas have been discontinued, and Aguas Argentinas ceased to be a party to the case in 2006.[34] In that same year, the Argentine government terminated the contract with Aguas Argentinas and returned Buenos

---

[29] See further A. D. Muñoz, "Water Co-Operatives in Argentina," in B. Brennan, O. Hoedeman, P. Terhorst, S. Kishimoto, and B. Balanyá, *Reclaiming Public Water: Achievements, Struggles and Visions from around the World* (Amsterdam: Transnational Institute & Corporate Europe Observatory, 2005), pp. 95–101.

[30] Santoro, note 28.

[31] Ibid.

[32] The French multinational Suez acquired not only the concession contract for federal capital Buenos Aires and the seventeen districts, but also for the province of Santa Fe in 1995 and in the city of Cordoba in 1997.

[33] E. Lobina and D. Hall, "Water Privatization and Restructuring in Latin America, 2007," pp. 13–14 September 2007, http://psiru.org.

[34] ICSID ARB/03/19, Procedural Order No. 1 Concerning the Discontinuance of Proceedings with Respect to Aguas Argentinas SA (14 April 2006).

Aires water and sanitation services to public control, with the trade union acting as the technical operator in the public company, Aguas y Saneamientos Argentinos (AYSA). AYSA was owned 90 percent by the Argentine government and 10 percent by the trade union CGT, which held the same equity stake in Aguas Argentinas.[35]

2.2 Bolivia

Perhaps the most famous water wars in the world occurred in Bolivia between the late 1990s and early 2000s, following the privatization of water supplies in the wake of neoliberal economic reforms that began in September 1985 under the Paz Estenssoro center-right government. These reforms, which were aimed at decreasing government involvement in the economy and attracting foreign investment in line with World Bank structural adjustment loans, included the privatization of all state-owned enterprises, with the exception of mines, under the Plan de Todos (Plan for All), which was initiated by President Gonzalo Sánchez de Lozada in 1993.[36]

Strong public resistance against Bolivia's privatization drive was not limited to the water sector, but opposition to the privatization of water services was particularly pronounced and arguably the best known international fight against water privatization unfolded in the late 1990s in the city of Cochabamba, Bolivia's third largest city, with some 800,000 inhabitants.[37]

2.2.1 The First Water War in Cochabamba

In 1999, the Bolivian government granted Aguas del Tunari SA – a subsidiary of the U.S. transnational Bechtel – a forty-year concessional contract for Cochabamba's water services. The concession granted the consortium control over all of Cochabamba's surface and subterranean water resources, aimed at "expanding water services to the poor."[38]

On assuming operations, Aguas del Tunari immediately increased water tariffs – in some cases by 100 to 200 percent[39] – meaning that households were faced with increases of US$20 per month and higher, when the minimum wage in the city of Cochabamba is less than US$100 per month.[40] The concession arrangement also allowed the company to charge people for the water they took from their own wells and to send collection agents to homes to charge for rainwater collected in cisterns

---

[35] Lobina and Hall, note 33, p. 16. See also Food and Water Watch, "Changing the Flow: Water Movement in Latin America," p. 23 1 May 2009, www.foodandwaterwatch.org.

[36] Coleman, note 20 at 9–10.

[37] W. Finnegan, "Letter from Bolivia: Leasing the Rain," *The New Yorker*, April 8, 2002.

[38] See P. Jones, "Bolivia and the Right to Water," PowerPoint slides (on file with the authors).

[39] Lobina and Hall, note 33, p. 15.

[40] J. Shultz, "Bolivians Take to the Streets Over Globalized Water Prices," http://democracyctr.org.

476   *Water Wars*

on roofs.[41] These measures – particularly the charges on household collection of rainwater – sparked immediate civil society opposition and social unrest. Factory workers and engineers formed the Coordinadora Departamental en Defensa del Agua y de la Vida (Coalition in Defense of Water and Life) in November 1999, bringing together community groups, human rights defenders and labor representatives, local businesses and farmers, and water vendors to call for an end to the privatization.

In mid-January 2000, the Coordinadora organized a four-day general strike that brought the city to a complete standstill. According to a commentator present during the strike, "[i]t was the kind of action that could only happen with broad popular support and it culminated in a mass march to the city's central plaza as thousands of angry water users, urban and rural, gathered and chanted just outside the windows of the government's offices where protest leaders and officials were negotiating."[42] In response, the government offered the protestors a rebate on their water rates and a review of the water contract. However, the movement and its leaders dug in and demanded that the government terminate the privatization contract with Aguas del Tunari.[43]

As the four-day strike and further talks between officials and the Coordinadora did not result in a negotiated solution, the coalition announced plans for a massive peaceful march to the city's central plaza, to be held on February 4, 2000. People from all walks of life took part in the march. Peasants from the nearby countryside manned barricades, sealing off all roads to the city. Inside the city, the elderly constructed more roadblocks, while the youth marched up front to the city's central plaza. The government met the protestors with more than 1,000 police officers and soldiers sent in from Oruro and La Paz, imposing a military takeover on the city center. During the February uprisings, nearly 200 protestors were arrested and more than seventy-five people were injured.[44]

The following month, the Coordinadora held a popular referendum in which the preponderance of votes called for the termination of the water concession and the modification of Law 2029,[45] through which the government had retroactively legalized the expropriation of Cochabamba's water resources.[46] Throughout March and April, the siege of Cochabamba's central plaza continued. Meanwhile,

---

[41] M. Barlow and T. Clark, "The Struggle for Latin America's Water," August 14, 2004, http://cadtm.org.

[42] Shultz, note 40.

[43] Public Citizen, "Water Privatization Fiascos: Broken Promises and Social Turmoil," April 4, 2006, p. 5 www.foodandwaterwatch.org. See also Shultz, note 40.

[44] Finnegan, note 37.

[45] For further analysis of Law 2029 and the role of the German development cooperation GTZ, see T. Fritz, *Development Aid and Water Privatisation: The Example of German Development Cooperation in Bolivia* (Berlin: Center for Research and Documentation Chile-Latinamerica, 2006).

[46] Coleman, note 20 at 10.

public outrage about the privatization deal in Cochabamba spread across the country, igniting civil protests against the government's economic policies in La Paz, Oruro, and Potosí, and in many rural communities.[47]

In the face of a massive civic uprising and the killing of a 17-year-old boy in Cochabamba's central plaza during a protest, it became clear to the Bánzer government that Aguas del Tunari had no future in the city.[48] The concession contract with Aguas del Tunari was terminated in April 2000.[49] The company responded by instigating a complaint under a BIT, demanding US$25 million in damages and another US$25 million in compensation for lost future profits from the Bolivia government.[50] The case was settled in 2006 for the symbolic sum of two Bolivianos in the wake of years of international civil society campaigning.[51] The question of whether or not the settlement was the direct result of the amicus intervention endorsed by civil society groups from forty-three different countries in the World Bank's ICSID proceeding remains unanswered, but Cochabamba certainly represents a striking example of a social movement that combined direct action, advocacy and lobbying, traditional representative politics, and action in expert professional fora.[52]

2.2.2 The Second Water War in La Paz/El Alto

Cochabamba was not the only city in Bolivia where water privatization backfired. In 2005, El Alto, one of several poor neighborhoods just outside the city of La Paz, became the scene for Bolivia's second citizen revolt against an earlier water privatization. In 1997, the Bolivian government granted a concession for the city of La Paz's water supply to another Suez subsidiary, Aguas del Illimanai SA. Part of the contract terms were to provide 71,752 additional water connections in El Alto.[53] However, five years into the contract, by 2002 the company had installed significantly less connections in El Alto – just under 45,000 – and the connections made were too expensive for poor households to maintain, leaving thousands of poor families in El Alto with no access to water.[54] As reported in *The Nation* newspaper at the time, "[i]n El Alto the cost of getting a water and sewage hook-up exceeded a half-year's income at the minimum wage."[55]

---

[47] Finnegan, note 37.
[48] Public Citizen, note 43, p. 5. See also Shultz, note 40.
[49] M. Arce and R. Rice, "Societal Protest in Post-Stabilisation Bolivia" (2009) 44 *Latin American Research Review*, pp. 88–101.
[50] Lobina and Hall, note 33, pp. 15–16.
[51] Morgan, note 24 at 7.
[52] Ibid at 6–7.
[53] J. Pérez, "Social Resistance in El Alto – Bolivia: Aguas del Illimani, A Concession Targeting the Poor," 2006, www.tni.org.
[54] J. Shultz, "The Politics of Water in Bolivia," *The Nation*, January 28, 2005.
[55] Ibid.

478 Water Wars

More generally, by the mid-2000s the company had complied with only 62 percent of its contractual obligations,[56] mobilizing opposition that was inspired by the ongoing "water war" in Cochabamba at the start of 2005.[57] The El Alto anti-privatization campaign was spearheaded by El Alto's local neighborhood councils (juntas) – affiliated at the citywide level through the Federación de Juntas Vecinales de El Alto (Federation of Neighborhood Councils). The juntas, with their long tradition of mobilizing residents to demand from municipal authorities what they cannot build or deliver themselves, organized blockades, strikes, and protests. In addition, a number of people filed complaints against Aguas del Illimanai in local courts, claiming irregularities in billing and collection processes.[58] Although neither the protests nor any other actions rose to the level of those of Cochabamba, January 2005 was a turning point for the company and the citizens of El Alto. Massive protests forced then president, Sánchez de Lozada, to promulgate a decree that guaranteed the termination of the contract with Aguas del Illimanai two years later.

2.3 Uruguay

In Uruguay, the four neoliberal governments that followed the harsh dictatorship of the mid-1980s had each promoted the deregulation of public water services.[59] This paved the way for two concession contracts in the water sector – the first in 1993 and the second in 2000 – in the Maldonado province, where the capital city of Montevideo is located. The push toward the privatization of water services was supported by the World Bank, which in March 2003 provided President Jorge Luis Battle Ibáñez (2000–2005) with a US$151.52 million structural adjustment loan of which water privatization was a key component.[60]

The first concession occurred in 1993. Here, the government of Uruguay granted a twenty-five-year concession for a relatively small area (to the east of the Maldonado stream the company supplied water and sanitation services to just over 3,000 consumers in the wealthier areas of La Barra, Manantiales, and José Ignacio, next to the internationally known resort of Punta del Este) to a Uruguayan private water engineering firm, Aguas de la Costa, that later became majority-owned by Aguas de Barcelona (Spain), a subsidiary of Suez.[61]

---

[56] See Jones, note 38.
[57] C. Crespo, "Aguas del Illimani y la Resistencia Social," November 30, 2004, www.bolpress. com (in Spanish).
[58] Ibid.
[59] Food and Water Watch, note 35, p. 4.
[60] P. Bakvis, M. McCoy, and T. Shorrock, "Fighting for Alternatives: Cases of Successful Trade Union resistance to the Policies of the IMF and World Bank," June 3, 2006, http://firgoa.usc.es, p. 16.
[61] F. Borraz, N. Gonzáles-Pampillón, and M. Olarreaga, "Water Nationalization: Network Access, Quality, and Health Outcomes," Research Papers by the Department of Economics, University of Geneva 11051, 2011, p. 7.

The larger and more socioeconomically diverse area west of the Maldonado stream was privatized in the year 2000.

Almost immediately after the private water concessions were granted, the quality of water and sanitation facilities deteriorated. As a result of the exorbitant increases of water rates, in some cases ten times higher than before privatization, many residents were unable to afford the privatized service and were left with no access to water services at all. In addition, the quality of the water dropped below the minimum standards, to the extent that health officials advised residents not to consume the water. Not only did the privatizations impede water access and degrade water quality; they also proved financially burdensome for the government of Uruguay. Throughout the course of the concessions, the companies did not meet their obligations stipulated in the contracts, failing to keep up with their work schedules and refusing to pay the fees that had originally been agreed upon. However, instead of addressing the companies' failures, revisions of the original contracts were embarked upon by which the state covered the companies' financial deficits – effectively making the Uruguayan people pay double the price for the companies' malfunctioning. The companies' environmental record was no more encouraging, with Aguas de la Costa being responsible for the drying up of Laguna Blanca, a lake used as a source of drinking water.[62]

From the time of the first privatization of 1993, but gaining momentum with the second privatization of 2000, the negative impacts of the privatization sparked a range of reactions from civil society. Community-based organization Liga de Manantiales, for instance, demanded "water for a fair price" in response to the deteriorating quality and high pricing of water services in the coastal areas. The struggle in the impoverished neighborhoods of Maldonado rather focused on the defense of "public or popular faucets" (communal water supply posts). These water points had previously been installed across the country to ensure an adequate basic supply of water but, in a move to force people to purchase their water, the companies began to remove the "popular faucets." In response, some households resorted to drilling their own wells or developing rainwater collection systems, but the majority of the residents in the city of Maldonado were left directly suffering the adverse consequences of privatization.[63]

When confronted with the second, much larger, privatization in 2000 (awarded to URAGUA, a subsidiary of Spain's Aguas de Bilbao), local residents began to mobilize and garnered broader popular support for public services. What could have remained a localized issue quickly became national, mainly because of the

---

[62] C. Santos and A. Villarreal, "Uruguay: Victorious Social Struggle for Water," in B. Brennan, O. Hoedeman, P. Terhorst, S. Kishimoto and B. Balanyá (eds.), *Reclaiming Public Water: Achievements, Struggles and Visions from around the World* (Amsterdam: Transnational Institute and Corporate Europe Observatory, 2005), p. 174. See also J. Dugard and K. Drage, "Shields and Swords: Legal Tools for Public Water," Occasional Paper No. 17, 2012, p. 8.

[63] Santos and Villarreal, note 62, pp. 174–175.

480   *Water Wars*

large alliances that were pulled into a coalition.[64] Founded in 2002, the National
Commission for the Defense of Water and Life (Comisión Nacional en Defensa
del Agua y de la Vida, CNDAV) led a two-year grassroots campaign against private
water supply. Similar to Bolivia's Coordinadora, the CNDAV was a broad coalition
representing labor groups, grassroots and local communities, environmental movements, science and engineering students, and the left-wing Frente Amplio
(Broad Front) political party. Friends of the Earth, the Green Ecological Party,
the Centre of Uruguayan Wine Producers, the Sustainable Uruguay Program,
and the Union of Uruguayan Women were just a few of the organizations that
formed the coalition. The coalition was spearheaded by the federated trade unions
representing water and sewerage workers (Federación de Funcionarios de Obras
Sanitarias del Estado, FFOSE) and Uruguay's state-owned water and sanitation
utility, Obras Sanitarias del Estado (OSE).

Between the second Maldonado concession in 2000 and the formation of the
CNDAV in 2002, the FFOSE held numerous assemblies to study the issue of
privatization. Once it understood its implications, it began to educate the public
on the negative impacts of the Maldonado privatizations and to warn against
the risks associated with future planned privatizations. The FFOSE started
coalition-building at the local level by organizing events through union locals in
community centers or other neutral places where communities could gather independently from their political, social, or religious affiliations. The establishment of
these local social fronts, often neighborhood committees that were converted into
local CNDAVs, was the seed that allowed the coalition to organize the nation-wide
CNDAV.[65]

Apart from equity considerations, the CNDAV campaign stressed the need to
preserve and protect the Guaraní Aquifer for the public good.[66] University experts
wrote scientific reports on the question of water resource usage in the country.
Public events, lectures, and demonstrations on key dates contributed to the unified
message of the campaign and raised the profile of the campaign of dissatisfaction
to a national level.[67]

2.3.1 Uruguay's Water Rights Referendum

While the success of Bolivia's broad-based coalition was largely attributable to
popular mobilization and protests, Uruguay's CNDAV chose a more formal
avenue to protect public water by advocating for an amendment to the Constitution that would recognize a right to public water. Once the CNDAV had

---

[64] Dugard and Drage, note 62, p. 8.
[65] P. Bakvis, M. McCoy, and T. Shorrock, note 60, p. 17.
[66] Shared and managed by Paraguay, Uruguay, Brazil, and Argentina, the Guaraní Aquifer is one
of the largest groundwater sources in the Americas.
[67] P. Bakvis, M. McCoy, and T. Shorrock, note 60, p. 18.

demonstrated to the Uruguayan parliament that it had substantial support for constitutional reform,[68] a referendum proposing a constitutional amendment on the right to water and water privatization was initiated in 2004. On October 31, 2004, more than 60 percent of the Uruguayan voters came out in favor of introducing a constitutional clause that puts an end to outright private concessions in the water sector. Rooted in the notion that "[a]ccess to drinking water and sewage system services constitute a fundamental human right," the resultant Article 47 ensured first and foremost that water and sewage services could be provided "exclusively and directly by legal state representatives."[69] The amendment further guaranteed social participation in water services, aimed at protecting the public utility from corruption and the vices that had affected its operations previously, and prioritized sustainability of all water resources over economic considerations. The referendum and the adopted amendment to the Constitution were a powerful example of the use of the right to water and anti-privatization language within the legal framework. Nonetheless, the legal victory did not immediately translate into elimination of the private water concessions – this final step required further popular mobilization.

On accession to power, the newly elected Vázquez government (Frente Amplio) faced intense pressure from the private water companies to uphold their contracts, pitting the right to water against water company profits and economic law as supported in BITs signed between Uruguay on the one hand, and Spain and France on the other. Within a year after the referendum, the government attempted to keep the private concessions in place through an executive resolution stating that the concessions granted prior to the 2004 constitutional amendment could continue until the contractually agreed termination date. Not only was the legal validity of the government decree dubious, it also contravened the popular mandate behind the vote, which had been initiated precisely to reverse the existing privatizations and outlaw future concessions in the water sector.

Responding to renewed opposition from the CNDAV, the government eventually had to take steps to cancel its contract with URAGUA, following which URUAGUA launched proceedings at the ICSID against the Uruguayan government under the terms of the BIT signed with Spain in 1992. The matter was eventually settled through a "friendly" accord which determined that Uruguay would pay the company US$15 million (around the same time, Suez decided to exit Uruguay, securing a financially lucrative exit deal in terms of which the

---

[68] As enshrined in Article 331 of the Constitution of Uruguay, the process for amendment requires the signatures of 10 percent of the electorate and then a 35 percent quorum among those voting in the referendum, which is then voted on by the general electorate during legislative and presidential elections. The CNDAV collected the 283,000 signatures in October 2003, initiating the successful referendum a year later. See Dugard and Drage, note 62, pp. 8–9.

[69] For a translation of Article 47 of the Constitution, see Santos and Villarreal, note 62, p. 6.

482

Water Wars

government of Uruguay paid the company US$3.4 million for its shares in Aguas de la Costa).[70] This meant that the CNDAV could reclaim the water services, which it did by symbolically decorating the exterior of the URAGUA offices with national flags.

Notwithstanding the rocky road to ultimately reversing water privatization, the achievements of Uruguay's popular struggle – particularly the formal recognition of water as a human right in the Constitution – have had a ripple effect on water campaigns throughout Latin America (specifically Colombia, not discussed here)[71] and the world, including South Africa.[72]

2.4 *South Africa*

South Africa has not experienced the same degree of *direct* pressure from Northern financial institutions as experienced by the Latin American countries outlined earlier. Nonetheless, South Africa's re-emergence into the global economy during the transition to democracy[73] brought with it (often contradictory) pressures to open the economy to globalized capital and to guarantee a set of basic rights to everyone in line with the new constitutional legal order.[74] On the economic policy front, hoping to attract foreign investment, in 1993 the transitional government entered into a credit arrangement with the IMF that advanced a fiscally austere approach.[75] On the

---

[70] Santos and Villarreal, note 62, pp. 2–4.

[71] In Colombia as in Uruguay, the privatization agenda initiated in the late 1980s and early 1990s (also dominated by transnational water companies such as Suez repatriating profits to the North) had a devastating impact on access to water for the poorest sections of society and mobilized a popular struggle to entrench a right to water. Although the campaign, mounted under the auspices of ECOFUNDO, an environmental non-governmental organization, has been relatively successful at raising national and international awareness about the issues, the movement's main concrete project – a referendum to recognize the human right to water and guarantee a basic minimum amount of water for every household in the country – was defeated by, first, a compromise to the proposed text as insisted on by strong corporate lobbies, and second, in May 2010, the Colombian Congress dismissing the draft referendum bill as "idealistic and nonviable" and a threat to long-term investment strategies. The failure of the referendum initiative in Colombia has led to ECOFUNDO no longer using legal tools in its ongoing anti-privatization campaign (Dugard and Drage, note 62, p. 11).

[72] Dugard and Drage, note 62, pp. 10–11.

[73] South Africa's transition began in 1990 when the apartheid regime released key liberation movement leaders such as Nelson Mandela. The formal transition ended with the country's first democratically held elections on April 27, 1994. Arguably, the transition is still far from complete given the high degree of racialized socioeconomic inequality that persists.

[74] We do not delve into debates about whether human rights intrinsically support neoliberal economic models. In our view, human rights are tools that can be used to either support or oppose the status quo. For a discussion on the use of law as a tool for social change see for example Dugard and Drage, note 62.

[75] The credit agreement demanded a reduction in deficit of two percentage points of the gross domestic product over two years, an increase in value-added tax, wage restraint, and a postponement of the bracket of adjustments under personal income tax: see M. Horton, "Role

sociopolitical front, the anti-apartheid liberation movements insisted on a Constitution with entrenched rights, including socioeconomic rights.

The result is a mix of essentially neoliberal economic policies (often described as South Africa's self-imposed structural adjustment program) alongside seemingly robust rights-based protections. Thus, macroeconomic policy focuses on inflation targeting, reducing deficits, and cost recovery.[76] At the same time, the Constitution of the Republic of South Africa Act 108 of 1996 (Constitution) enshrines a set of socioeconomic rights, including everyone's right of access to sufficient water,[77] and there is a Free Basic Water (FBW) policy to provide every household with a basic amount of water for free. However, such legal guarantees and limited forms of redistribution have been wholly insufficient to tackle apartheid's socioeconomic legacy and foster a truly inclusionary economy. This reality is evidenced by the fact that inequality is rising rather than falling, and the racialized nature of the inequality has hardly shifted at all since 1994.[78]

Against this backdrop, access to water has been a vexed source of contestation almost from the outset of the democratic era. Campaigns waged in the early 2000s by social movements such as the Anti-Privatization Forum (APF) were largely successful in removing outright privatization from government agendas but did not succeed in defeating broader corporatization and/or commercialization initiatives, which have sparked more recent waves of struggle – first the concerted

---

of Fiscal Policy in Stabilization and Poverty Alleviation," in M. Nowak and L. Ricci (eds.) *Post-Apartheid South Africa – The First Ten Years* (Washington: IMF, 2005), p. 84.

[76] There is no simple answer to why the government has pursued such a (largely self-imposed) neoliberal economic model, including its focus on the commercialization and corporatization of water services. Some commentators point to the fact that the African National Congress (ANC) was always a more elite organization than many have presumed; others highlight the comparative lack of economic expertise within ANC ranks at the time of the formal negotiations (1991–1994), meaning that the old guard, with its entrenched and largely internationalized financial interests, could dominate the negotiations and set the agenda. Still others suggest that post-apartheid South Africa is a classic case of a liberation movement changing its tune once in power and attempting to maximize extraction for its own elites. There is not the space here to resolve these arguments. However, at a structural level, it is clear that, because municipal services are one of the main sources of revenue for municipalities, municipal governments are under financial pressure to commercialize such services, including water services.

[77] Section 27(1)(b) of the Constitution guarantees everyone's right of access to sufficient water.

[78] Although there has been a remarkable decrease in extreme poverty since 1994, mainly as a result of social security grants, these grants are unable to erode a persistent and indeed worsening state of racialized inequality – not only has South Africa's Gini coefficient (which measures income inequality on a ration of 0 to 1, with 0 representing an equal society and 1 representing a completely unequal society) increased since 1994 (see M. Leibbrandt, A. Finn, and I. Woolard, "Describing and Decomposing Post-Apartheid Income Inequality in South Africa" (2012) 29 *Development Southern Africa* 19), but inequality has grown between races so that South Africa has the highest inequality between race groups in the world: see M. Leibbrandt, I. Woolard, A. Finn, and J. Argent, "Trends in South African Income Distribution and Poverty Since the Fall of Apartheid," OECD Social, Employment and Migration Working Papers No. 101, 2010.

484   *Water Wars*

campaign against PrePayment Water Meters (PPMs) during the mid to late 2000s, especially in Soweto; second the ongoing "service delivery" protests that have been gaining momentum in local communities since the mid-2000s.

2.4.1 The Soweto Battle Against PPMs

There have been very few instances of outright privatization of water in post–apartheid South Africa. However, especially in the municipal sphere,[79] there has been a growing thrust since the late 1990s toward the commercialization of water services, highlighting its role mainly as an economic good and a source of revenue for cash-strapped municipalities.

In the main metropolitan municipalities, the commercialization of water services has often also entailed their corporatization. For example, in 2001, the water services of the City of Johannesburg (South Africa's biggest city) were corporatized under the auspices of Johannesburg Water (Pty) Ltd. (Johannesburg Water). This is a public company with the City of Johannesburg as its only shareholder but is otherwise operated largely as a commercial venture, albeit with some regulated minimum subsidies, including the national Free Basic Water policy to supply every household with six kiloliters of water per month, funded by the National Treasury. For its first five years of operation (2001 to 2005), Johannesburg Water's management subsidiary, Jowam, entered into a management support contract with Suez.

One of Johannesburg Water's key projects in this period focused on resolving the issue of "unaccounted-for water losses," including the historical non-payment of water services (linked to the historical rates and services boycotts of the apartheid era), in Soweto (South Africa's largest and most famous township[80]) through the introduction of PPMs. Calling the project Operation Gcin'Amanzi (meaning "to save water" in isiZulu), Johannesburg Water decided that PPMs would both "reduce demand" for water among Soweto residents and improve the "financial positions" of the city by ensuring that – beyond the regulated FBW amount – water would have to be paid for upfront, and when the credit was exhausted the meter would disconnect the water supply, meaning there would be no unpaid-for water losses for the city.[81]

---

[79] The municipal or local sphere was the last sphere of government to be institutionally finalized post-1994. It is responsible for the delivery of basic services, including water, and among its main sources of revenue are municipal services, including water. This means that instead of water being viewed primarily as a public health and human developmental good, it is viewed as a revenue stream for cash-strapped municipalities.

[80] In the South African context, townships are apartheid-inherited, densely populated satellite suburbs on the urban periphery that were designed during apartheid to serve as dormitory settlements of black workers, many of whom worked in white homes and gardens.

[81] *Mazibuko and Others v City of Johannesburg and Others* (CCT 39/09) [2009] ZACC 28; 2010 (3) BCLR 239 (CC); 2010 (4) SA 1 (CC) (8 October 2009) (*Mazibuko* High Court case) First and Second Respondents Heads of Argument, 16 November 2007: para. 17.8, cited in J. Dugard, "Civic Action and Legal Mobilisation: The Phiri Water Meters Case," in J. Handmaker and R. Berkhout (eds.), *Mobilising Social Justice in South Africa: Perspectives from Researchers and Practitioners* (Pretoria: Pretoria University Law Press, 2010), p. 83, note 37.

Selecting Phiri (one of the poorest and most densely populated suburbs of Soweto, with multiple households living on each cramped property, many in makeshift backyard shacks) as the pilot for Operation Gcin'Amanzi, the bulk infrastructure construction work for the installation of PPMs began on August 11, 2003 and the first individual house connections began in February 2004. Phiri residents were not consulted or given a choice regarding the changes to their water supply. Initially, the households that resisted PPMs were left with no water supply at all. Later on in the operation, as resistance mounted, those who refused the PPMs had their in-house supply terminated and were left with an outside cold water tap.

From the outset, PPMs compromised Phiri residents' lives in very tangible ways. With an average number of thirteen people living in each property (in multi-dwelling households), the standard FBW allocation of six kiloliters per month[82] typically ran out within the first two weeks even where residents attempted to conserve water – often in ways that compromised their health and dignity, such as parents having to choose between flushing the toilet and bathing their children before school, and people living with HIV/AIDS having to choose between washing soiled sheets and drinking water.[83] Moreover, in a context of high levels of poverty and unemployment, there was typically no money to purchase water credit for the PPMs once the FBW allocation ran out. In this case, the PPM would automatically disconnect the water supply, meaning that the household had no further water supply until the following month's FBW allocation was loaded and/or unless the household managed to purchase additional water credit. Over and above the mundane violations of residents' rights to water, healthcare, dignity, and due process, there were also tragic consequences such as the deaths of two young children in a shack fire that neighbors could not extinguish because they had insufficient water credit.[84]

Responding to these conditions, opposition against PPMs mounted among the residents of Phiri, who were supported by the APF, a social movement that was formed in Johannesburg in 2000 to oppose all forms of privatization and commercialization of public services. Among the APF's core objectives were "a halt to all privatization of public sector entities and return of public control

---

[82] The FBW allocation is based on a calculation of twenty-five litres of water per person per day in a household of eight persons. This amount is insufficient to meet the basic needs of Phiri households for two reasons. First, the international expert on water sufficiency Peter Gleick has estimated that fifty litres per person per day is the absolute minimum amount necessary to lead a dignified and healthy existence in conditions such as in Phiri, especially given that the only form of sanitation is waterborne toilets (affidavit of Peter Gleick in the *Mazibuko* case, on file with authors). Second, because the average stand in Phiri had thirteen people, each person living on the stand could only access much less than even the relatively low amount of twenty-five litres per person per day.

[83] Dugard, note 81, p. 84.

[84] Ibid, p. 85.

486   *Water Wars*

and ownership; and the co-ordination and intensification of anti-privatization struggles in communities."[85] In the early months of the campaign against PPMs, increasing numbers of residents joined the struggle, embarking on protest marches to Johannesburg Water's offices and engaging in direct resistance, including attempts to stop municipal workers from installing PPMs in Phiri. Under the auspices of the APF, spontaneous protests morphed into mass action, and for a while the residents effectively prevented Johannesburg Water from continuing its work. As described by water activist and APF member, Prishani Naidoo, "[r] esidents came together to physically prevent the work of Johannesburg Water. They were supported in their actions by members of [. . .] and the Anti-Privatization Forum. Several altercations ensued between the police and private security hired by Johannesburg Water, and the residents."[86]

When such altercations threatened to derail the entire project and pre-empt further direct resistance, Johannesburg Water successfully applied to the Johannesburg High Court for an injunction against the activists; this was granted on August 22, 2003, interdicting activists from interfering with the operations of Operation Gcin'Amanzi and preventing members of the APF from coming within 50 meters of any work undertaken by Johannesburg Water in Phiri. The APF responded by forming a new sub-organization, the Coalition Against Water Privatization (CAWP), but within a few months CAWP leaders had been charged with public violence, malicious damage to property, and incitement. These reprisals by the government took a toll on the resistance campaign, with energy and funds having to be diverted to defending activists. Although almost all charges were ultimately dropped, the repression effectively undermined the collective resistance and, despite formidable resistance by individual households, Johannesburg Water was able to continue its project of installing PPMs across Phiri. By 2005, the last remaining households had given in, "choosing" PPMs or outside taps rather than no water at all.

The seeming failure of the direct resistance campaign was perceived by the APF and community alliance to mark a low point in the struggle against PPMs. Yet soon it was apparent that the closing-off of one avenue of activism opened the way for a new line of resistance – that of rights-based litigation against the PPMs. Thus, in July 2006, with the assistance of a public interest litigation organization – the Centre for Applied Legal Studies (CALS) – the residents of Phiri launched a constitutional challenge against PPMs on the basis of the right of access to sufficient water in the Constitution, along with several other laws and regulations safeguarding access to water.

The case of *Mazibuko and Others* v *City of Johannesburg and Others* was won in the Johannesburg High Court (now called South Gauteng High Court) and the

---

[85] Ibid, p. 87, note 51.
[86] P. Naidoo, "Eroding the Commons: Prepaid Water Meters in Phiri, Soweto," www.citizen. org, cited in Dugard, note 81, p. 88, footnote 53.

applicants won on all substantive grounds in the Supreme Court of Appeal. However, to many commentators' surprise and criticism,[87] the applicants lost on all grounds in the Constitutional Court's judgment of October 8, 2009. Nonetheless, as analyzed elsewhere, between 2006 and 2009 the litigation had a positive effect by energizing the APF and CAWP, as well as struggles against the commercialization of basic services more broadly. In the words of APF founder Dale McKinley, *Mazibuko* "provided something to organize around; hope and recognition after having been fucked over by the police – it became the center of mobilization and reinvigorated the struggle, as well as catalyzing political discussions and refining strategy."[88] Other outcomes of the litigation were that, despite losing in the court, by 2009 the case had succeeded in sufficiently politicizing the issues to the extent that the city of Johannesburg took the decision to double the amount of FBW it made available to poverty-stricken households and to replace all PPMs with ones that no longer automatically discontinue the water supply, but rather provide a "lifeline" trickle amount of water following the exhaustion of the FBW allocation.[89]

2.4.2 Mushrooming "Service Delivery" Protests

Alongside the geographically and conceptually focused struggles against PPMs in Phiri, since 2004 there has been a mushrooming movement of local protests, amounting to a rebellion of the poor across the country and earning South Africa the dubious distinction of hosting the highest number of protests in the world.[90] These local community protests, referred to in the media as "service delivery" protests, are as much about being heard as they are about the government's failure to deliver key services.[91] As argued by political analyst Richard Pithouse, the protests are best understood as being about "the material benefits of full social inclusion [. . .] as well as the right to be taken seriously when thinking and speaking through community organizations."[92]

---

[87] There is not the space here to explain the Court's findings against the applicants, many of which have been criticized for being incorrect and/or highly problematic. Indeed, *Mazibuko* remains one of the most criticized judgments of the Constitutional Court: see e.g. S. Liebenberg, *Socio-Economic Rights: Adjudication under a Transformative Constitution* (Cape Town: Juta, 2010), pp. 466–480; S. Wilson and J. Dugard, "Constitutional Jurisprudence: The First and Second Waves," in M. Langford, B. Cousins, J. Dugard, and T. Madlingozi (eds.), *Socio-Economic Rights in South Africa: Symbols or Substance?* (Cambridge: Cambridge University Press, 2013), pp. 35–62.

[88] J. Dugard, "Urban Basic Services: Rights, Reality and Resistance," in M. Langford, B. Cousins, J. Dugard, and T. Madlingozi, *Socio-Economic Rights in South Africa: Symbols or Substance* (Cambridge: Cambridge University Press, 2013), p. 301.

[89] Ibid, pp. 301–302.

[90] P. Bond, "South Africa's Bubble Meets Boiling Urban Protest" (2010) 62 *Monthly Review*, pp. 17–28.

[91] See e.g. Dugard, note 88, pp. 275–309.

[92] R. Pithouse, "The University of Abahlali baseMjondolo," April 6, 2008, https://libcom.org.

488 *Water Wars*

Notwithstanding broader issues of inclusion, at the core the protestors' demands are a common mix of issues, with access to water being the second most commonly expressed concern by protestors (after access to housing).[93] As related to water, the underlying determinants are some of the same issues that sparked the resistance in Phiri – inadequate and unaffordable water services to poor localities as compared with "world class" services in rich areas. Heightening the acuteness of the struggles, in many cases the police have responded with often unlawful and sometimes deadly force. For example, on April 13, 2011, a water rights-related protest by the community of Maqheleng (Ficksburg) was intercepted by police officers who fired rubber bullets directly into the chest of one of the community leaders, Andries Tatane, killing him.[94] Commenting in the aftermath of the protest – which was organized by the community group, Maqheleng Concerned Citizens, in response to inadequate water and sanitation services in Maqheleng township (Setsoto municipality, Ficksburg) – *The Times* newspaper quoted the group's chair, Sam Motseare, as saying:

> Tatane sacrificed his life to free us from the shackles of the Setsoto municipality. If our rights for clean water had been respected we wouldn't be here. If our rights for a clean environment that is free of stinking sewage had been respected, we wouldn't be here. When will this substandard life come to an end, just when? Maybe the day Tatane died marked a turning point in the history of Ficksburg, Maqheleng.[95]

Although so far many of the protests remain locally focused and largely organizationally uncoordinated, there have been signs, especially in the most recent and upcoming elections, that politicians are beginning to take note of the rising discontent over water (and other) services-related failures.[96] Indeed, with images of burning tires and street blockades dominating the run-up to the 2014 national elections, it is undeniable that social tensions are rising and the limits of South Africa's socioeconomic transformation projects are becoming increasingly apparent – forcing the ruling African National Congress party to acknowledge key failings around, for example, the delivery of water services, or risk losing further political support.[97]

---

[93] H. Jain, "Community Protests in South Africa: Trends, Analysis and Explanations," Local Government Working Paper Series No. 1, Community Law Centre, University of the Western Cape, 2010, pp. 29–30.

[94] J. Dugard, note 88, p. 291.

[95] S. Masondo, "ANC Roasts Mayor Over Its Open Toilets," *The Times* (South Africa), May 10, 2011, cited in Dugard, note 88, p. 291.

[96] As mentioned earlier, access to housing is the main stated reason for local protest. Although not technically a "service," access to housing is related to service delivery in the sense that the government has to fulfill its obligations regarding the right of access to housing (section 26 of the Constitution). Moreover, access to housing impacts other service-delivery issues, such as electricity and refuse services – as with water services, neither electricity nor refuse services have been outright privatized, but they too have been commercialized and corporatized.

[97] The ANC lost seats and had a decline in the percentage share of the vote during the national elections of 2009: see Dugard, note 88, p. 293.

3. CONCLUSION

Initiatives since the 1990s to privatize (or commercialize) the water supplies of the global South have been part of a broader North-initiated neoliberal push to open Southern economies to finance and manufacturing capital. In all of the case studies outlined in this chapter, this has involved pressure from the World Bank and/or IMF. It has also involved the direct interests of transnational water corporations, such as Suez (Argentina, Bolivia, Uruguay, and South Africa), Vivendi (Argentina), and Bechtel (Bolivia). In the Latin American cases, these transnational companies have also applied pressure on the host governments in the global South to protect their investments at all costs by instituting complaints at ICSID under the terms of applicable BITs despite the fact that these companies failed to fulfill their obligations under the agreements.

In all of the case studies, the privatization (or commercialization) of water supplies has exacerbated poverty/socioeconomic inequality and has adversely impacted people's access to water, as well as environmental resources, which have been depleted to bolster profits that are commonly repatriated to the North. As highlighted in this chapter, because of these problematic socioeconomic impacts, the privatization of water has often been met with popular resistance that, in many cases, has succeeded in reversing the privatizations. The anti-privatization struggles documented here have been characterized by a range of tactics, including boycotts, protests, petitions, and legal processes. And, while the precise role-players and characteristics of each campaign have been context-specific, all the struggles have shared core concerns about equitable, affordable, and sustainable access to water.

As successful as these struggles have been in weakening the globalized push for water privatization, some notes of caution should be sounded. First, as the Uruguay case study highlighted, securing a right to water and even ousting a private water company does not necessarily easily translate into more equitable and environmentally sustainable water services to the poor. Rather, if social movements want to ensure genuinely democratic and participatory public services, this requires continued mobilization even after key victories have been won. As Spronk and Terhorst warn, it is easier for struggles to "[g]enerate procedural outcomes than it is to enforce substantive change. [...] Social movements are more likely to be successful in a campaign to prevent a 'public bad' (for example, by preventing privatization), than in creating substantive movement outcomes that generate a new 'public good' (for example the reform of an ill-performing public utility)."[98]

Second, one of the unanticipated outcomes of the campaigns against water privatization has been the strategic policy shift away from outright privatization toward more insidious (though by no means less unjust) forms of commodification

---

[98] S. Spronk and P. Terhorst, "Social Movement Struggles for Public Services," in D. McDonald and G. Ruiters (eds.), *Alternatives to Privatization: Public Options for Essential Services in the Global South* (New York: Routledge, 2012), p. 149.

of water, such as the commercialization and/or corporatization of public water. This is illustrated by Johannesburg Water (Pty) Ltd, a wholly publicly owned and operated water service provider that entered into a management support contract with Suez and is largely run on private sector operating principles. Although this represents a significant retreat from outright privatization and provides civil society activists with additional "hooks" for holding the government politically accountable for water services – including the use of water rights, as demonstrated in the struggle against PPMs in Soweto – it poses a new complex ideational reality in which the previously more stark dichotomies of public and private have been broken down and in which struggles can no longer be simply focused against privatization and/or North–South divides per se.

23

Natural Disaster and Climate Change

Paul J. Govind and Robert R.M. Verchick

1. INTRODUCTION

In the twenty-first century, it is nearly impossible to talk about the environment without also talking about climate change, while in turn it is nearly impossible to talk about climate change without also talking about natural disasters. Global warming, rising seas, and recurring drought are all part of the same unfolding story. One can hardly read an Intergovernmental Panel on Climate Change (IPCC) assessment or government white paper without finding themselves browsing through page after glossy page showing swamped fishing villages, collapsed favelas, and withering maize. What saves the photo spreads from fetish is that the hazards they depict are real and ongoing.

Despite this increasing evidence, policy-makers have been slow to align the legal mechanisms confronting climate change and natural disaster. This is especially true at the international level, where attempts to bridge the gap between climate change adaptation (CCA) and disaster risk reduction (DRR) have reopened old debates between the global North and global South, and where ideas hatched in sparkling banquet rooms never make it to the eroding banks of the riverside slum.

In this chapter, we examine the relationship between international adaptation efforts with regard to climate change on the one hand, and disaster management policy on the other. Reviewing the respective United Nations (UN) frameworks for both climate and natural disasters, we find many shared interests and opportunities for collaboration. In particular, we think that notions of causation and group responsibility – both found in international climate policy – can provide a necessary context for imagining disaster resilience on a warming planet. Similarly, we

---

Our discussion of Surat, India, is based on field research that Professor Verchick conducted in 2012, while working as a Fulbright-Nehru Environmental Leadership Scholar and a Visiting Scholar at the Center for Policy Research (CPR) in New Delhi. He is grateful to the Fulbright Scholar Program and to CPR for their generous support.

492   *Natural Disaster and Climate Change*

believe the emphasis on local action and socioeconomic conditions – a trademark of disaster planning – can inspire the next wave of adaptation efforts. We will make these arguments by way of two very different case studies. The first examines the recent international negotiations over "loss and damage" under the United Nations Framework Convention on Climate Change (UNFCCC), which have now erupted into a major debate about the North's responsibility to the South.[1]

The second case study examines a relatively small climate resilience project, funded by a private foundation, in the Indian city of Surat, a global center for textile manufacturing and diamond polishing, which is also prone to enormous coastal floods. The relative success realized here suggests the promise of integrating local organizational methods into a global commitment to climate adaptation. The example suggests how wealthy actors (in this case a foundation) can guide and empower vulnerable communities by tapping into local values and existing networks. Our aim is to begin a conversation about the relationship between CCA and DDR.

2. FRAMING THE DISCUSSION

2.1 *An Introduction to Natural Disasters and Climate Change*

Before turning to the case studies, we will frame the discussion by reviewing some facts about natural disasters, climate change impacts, and the applicable law. A "natural disaster," as the term is generally used, describes a calamitous event that is triggered at least in part by a natural force – an earthquake, a flood, a hurricane, a drought, or something else similar. Many experts dismiss the possibility of any disaster being completely "natural," since human decisions about settlement or planning always play a role.[2] Global warming, which has the potential to influence nearly any weather-related event, challenges the term in even stronger ways – a point we will investigate later. Disaster, of course, implies disruption, or, in language approved by the United Nations, "a serious disruption of the functioning of a community or a society involving widespread human, material, economic or environmental losses and impacts, which exceeds the ability of the affected

---

[1] *United Nations Framework Convention on Climate Change*, New York, 9 May 1992, in force 21 March 1994, 1771 UNTS 107; S. Treaty Doc No. 102–38; UN Doc. A/AC.237/18 (Part II)/ Add.1; 31 ILM 849 (1992).

[2] R. R. M. Verchick, *Facing Catastrophe: Environmental Action for a Post-Katrina World* (Cambridge: Harvard University Press, 2010), describing an increased trend in disasters as driven by growing population, expanded development, and global warming; B. Bolin, "Race, Class, Ethnicity, and Disaster Vulnerability," in H. Rodrìguez et al. (eds.), *Handbook of Disaster Research* (New York: Springer, 2006), pp. 113–114, quoting E. L. Quarantelli, "Disaster Prevention and Mitigation in Planning and Implementing in Composite Country," Colloquium on the Environment and Natural Disaster Management, World Bank, 1990: "there can never be a natural disaster; at most there is a conjuncture of certain physical happenings and certain social happening."

community or society to cope using its own resources."[3] Two points are worth noting. First, an extreme event is only a "disaster" if the affected community is overwhelmed and cannot "cope." Second, a community's ability to cope will necessarily depend on its exposure to a hazard *and* its economic and social capacity to withstand the blow.

Every year natural disasters cause thousands of deaths and cost billions of dollars in disaster aid, disruption of commerce, and destruction of homes and critical infrastructure. In 2013, for instance, Typhoon Haiyan – considered the strongest storm ever to make landfall – tore through the central Philippines, killing more than 6,000 people and costing US$13 billion in economic loss.[4] The same year, Cyclone Phailin raked through the Indian state of Odisha, demolishing hundreds of thousands of homes and affecting nine million people; the storm also destroyed paddy crops worth hundreds of millions of U.S. dollars.[5] Viewed over many years, the losses are almost hard to imagine. Between January 1975 and October 2008, and excluding epidemics, the International Emergency Disasters Database EMDAT recorded 8,866 events killing 2,283,767 people.[6] Of course, natural disasters strike Northern countries too. In the spring of 2013, hammering rains caused massive flooding across Germany, Austria, and East–Central Europe. At least twenty-one lives were lost and economic damage totaled US$22 billion.[7] The year before, Hurricane Sandy swept through the northeastern United States, killing 159 people and causing US$65 billion in economic losses.[8] The data reveal how fatalities in the South dwarf fatalities in the North, and how economic loss in the North so often exceeds, in absolute terms, similar loss in the South. [9] In terms of public safety, the difference in fatalities shows how much higher the stakes are in the developing world. But economic risk is also higher in the South, since even comparatively small losses in a poor country can represent a significant share of its GDP.[10]

---

[3] United Nations International Strategy for Disaster Reduction (UNISDR), 2009 *UNISDR Terminology on Disaster Risk Reduction* (Geneva: United Nations Press, 2009).

[4] "Stress Test: Responding to This Disaster is Essential, But So is Preparing for the Next," *The Economist*, November 16, 2013 (noting fatalities); *Annual Global Climate and Catastrophe Report: Impact Forecasting – 2013* (Impact Forecasting, 2014), p. 4, Exhibit (noting economic impact).

[5] "Cyclone Phailin Hits 90 Lakh People; 23 Dead, Lakhs of Homes Damaged," *Times of India*, October 13, 2013.

[6] United Nations International Strategy for Disaster Reduction Secretariat (UNISDR), "Risk and Poverty in a Changing Climate: Summary and Recommendations," 2009, www.preven tionweb.net.

[7] "Europe Flood Kills at Least 21," CBS News, June 9, 2013 (noting fatalities); *Annual Global Climate and Catastrophe Report: Impact Forecasting – 2013*, above note 4, p. 4, Exhibit 1.

[8] "Hurricane Sandy Rebuilding Strategy: Stronger Communities, A Resilient Region," U.S. Department of Housing and Urban Development, United States of America, 2013.

[9] See generally UNISDR, note 6.

[10] Ibid, p. 7 (concluding "poorer countries have disproportionately higher mortality and economic loss risks, given similar levels of hazard exposure").

494 *Natural Disaster and Climate Change*

In January 2005, government officials from around the globe met in Kobe, Japan, to discuss disaster preparation and response. By an odd coincidence, only days before, an enormous earthquake off the west coast of Sumatra had triggered the devastating Asian tsunami that battered the coasts of eleven countries and killed more than 225,000 people. At that international meeting, called the World Conference on Disaster Reduction, all UN member states agreed to reduce disaster loss by strengthening the resilience of nations and communities at risk. The conference produced an early warning system to identify coastal threats and proposed an ambitious framework to reduce disaster risk throughout the world.[11] Called the Hyogo Framework for Action (HFA) (named after the prefecture in which Kobe is located), the agreement lays out expectations for the world's disaster initiatives through 2015 and charges the United Nations International Strategy for Disaster Reduction (UNISDR) with overseeing its implementation.[12]

Climate change should be discussed against this backdrop. According to the IPCC, the effects of climate change are already occurring "on all continents and across the oceans."[13] Observed "climate-related extremes" include "heat waves, droughts, floods, cyclones, and wildfires."[14] The IPCC finds that "[f]or countries at all levels of development, these impacts are consistent with a significant lack of preparedness for current climate variability in some sectors," adding that the impacts of climate-related hazards on the poor are particularly devastating.[15] The need to adapt to these impacts is crucial. The IPCC defines climate change adaptation as "the adjustment in natural or human systems in response to actual or expected climatic stimuli or their effects."[16] The IPCC recognizes that climate impacts have occurred and are continually occurring; it presumes that many of these trends will inevitably continue to some degree, independent of our efforts to reduce greenhouse gases ("mitigation"). Adaptation aims to lessen the magnitude of these impacts through proactive or previously planned reactive actions. As the IPCC states, "mitigation will always be required to avoid 'dangerous' and irreversible changes to the climate system. Irrespective of the scale of mitigation measures that are implemented in the next 10–20 years, adaptation measures will

---

[11] D. A. Farber et al. (eds.), *Disaster Law and Policy* (Philadelphia: Aspen Publishers, 2015) (forthcoming).

[12] UNISDR, "Hyogo Framework for Action 2005–2015: Building the Resilience of Nations and Communities to Disasters: Extract from Report of the World Conference on Disaster Risk Reduction, January 2005, Kobe, Japan," www.unisdr.org.

[13] C. B. Field et al. (eds.), *IPCC, 2014: Summary for Policymakers. In Climate Change 2014: Impacts, Adaptation, and Vulnerability. Part A: Global and Sectoral Aspects. Contribution of Working Group II to the Fifth Assessment Report of the Intergovernmental Panel on Climate Change* (New York: Cambridge University Press, 2014), p. 6.

[14] Ibid, p. 7.

[15] Ibid, pp. 6–7.

[16] M. Parry et al., *Technical Summary. Climate Change 2007: Impacts, Adaptation and Vulnerability. Contribution of Working Group II to the Fourth Assessment Report of the Intergovernmental Panel on Climate Change* (New York: Cambridge University Press, 2007).

Paul J. Govind and Robert R.M. Verchick

still be required due to inertia in the climate system."[17] Or, as President Obama's science advisor, James Holdren, explains, "[w]e must avoid the climate impacts we can't manage and manage the climate impacts we can't avoid."[18]

2.2 Linking Disaster Policy to Climate Policy

Global law and policy on climate change and disaster management has reached a critical juncture. At the conclusion of 2013, the Warsaw International Mechanism for Loss and Damage (Warsaw International Mechanism or WIM) became part of the international climate change regime, reinforcing the link between DRR and CCA.[19] While nations under the UNFCCC begin work under WIM, negotiations continue within disaster policy circles to realize a successor to the HFA.[20] Recent developments in both the international climate change and disaster regimes suggest increased alignment between DRR and CCA. Indeed, since the adoption of the Bali Action Plan in 2007, there have been attempts within the climate regime to characterize the issue of linkage between DRR and CCA.[21]

The relationship between climate change and disaster management raises themes important to this book. Central to the "North–South divide" is the complaint that increased standards of living in the North derive from environmental destruction in the South. For more than a century, the North has pumped carbon dioxide into the atmosphere beyond its "fair share," but the nations most stressed about famine and flood are in the South. Global development has always been about insulating communities from the vagaries of nature (disease, poor harvests, and, of course, natural disasters), but global warming amplifies the moral and economic dimensions.[22] Climate change also feeds into the tension between global and local action. For understandable reasons, the North's central focus has been

---

[17] H-H. Rogner et al., "Introduction 101," in B. Metz et al. (eds.), *Climate Change 2007: Mitigation of Climate Change* (Cambridge: Cambridge University Press, 2007).

[18] J. Holdren, Assistant to the President for Science and Technology and Director of the White House Office of Science and Technology Policy, "Remarks at the National Climate Adaptation Summit," May 25, 2011 (notes on file with the authors).

[19] UNFCCC, *Report of the Conference of the Parties on Its Nineteenth Session, Held in Warsaw from 11 to 23 November 2013 – Addendum – Part Two: Action Taken by the Conference of the Parties at Its Nineteenth Session*, 31 January 2014, FCCC/CP/2013/10/Add.1, Decision 2/CP.19 (Warsaw International Mechanism).

[20] UNISDR, note 12.

[21] UNFCCC, *Report of the Conference of the Parties on Its Thirteenth Session, Held in Bali from 3 December to 15 December 2007 – Addendum – Part Two: Action Taken by the Conference of the Parties at Its Thirteenth Session*, UN Doc. FCCC/CP/2007/6/Add.1 (14 March 2008) Decision 1/CP.13. For further background see L. Schipper, "Meeting at the Crossroads? Exploring the Linkages Between Climate Change Adaptation and Disaster Risk Reduction" (2009) 1(1) *Climate and Development* 16 at 20; M. K. Van Aalst, "The Impacts of Climate Change on the Risk of Natural Disasters" (2006) 30(1) *Disasters* 5.

[22] R. R. M. Verchick, "Adaptation, Economics, and Justice," in D. M. Driesen (ed.), *Economic Thought and U.S. Climate Change Policy* (Cambridge: The MIT Press, 2010), p. 277.

496 *Natural Disaster and Climate Change*

to reduce carbon emissions on a global scale, while the South emphasizes the more local and immediate needs of energy production and climate resilience. The global perspective highlights the significant inequalities between affluent and poorer countries, but that focus also helps conceal substantial inequalities *within* nations (both rich and poor). Thus, social vulnerability at the regional and local level demands much more attention than it is receiving.

Addressing adaptation and disaster management together offers several advantages. Most obviously, it is more efficient to double up when the risks imposed by climate change and natural disasters take the same form. Governments and civil society groups already have disaster management structures in place, with attendant legal authorities, staff, lines of communication, and channels of distribution.[23] Social and family networks have also developed strategies for reducing and responding to disaster emergencies. Integrating adaptation into this infrastructure is easier than starting from scratch. Much of the conceptual work in modern disaster management, the product of decades of study, also transfers readily to adaptation.

In addition, merging the two fields helps appeal to a wider range of culture-based values. For instance, the importance of better disaster management has always been obvious to those in the monsoon belt or the quake-prone Himalayas, but global efforts to reduce the risks of "ordinary" natural disasters (those not previously associated with climate change) have never matched the need. The focus on "climate" disasters, however, appears to be changing the conversation in the North by tapping into values beyond sympathy. When an earthquake kills thousands in Pakistan, it is hard to say that policies in the North contributed to that misery; when an island sinks in the Bay of Bengal, however, the link is direct. The fact that global warming is also threatening lives and treasure in the North further pulls the South into the North's circle of concern.[24] This gives leverage for Southern countries to demand more in the way of disaster risk reduction.[25]

On the flip side, the traditional disaster management concerns of poorer nations help residents in vulnerable areas to see the value of focusing on climate change. The vegetable farmer in Kerala may know nothing about the "450 ppm" threshold,[26] but she can tell you how late the monsoon was this year and what it

---

[23] See e.g. Farber et al. (eds.), note 11(describing disaster management structures in the United States); see also PreventionWeb, "Countries, Territories and Regions," www.preventionweb. net (offering information about national disaster management structures in countries throughout the world).

[24] Verchick, note 22, pp. 289–290 (describing how the global economy requires participation of the South to meet goals of the North, including the goal of reducing carbon emissions).

[25] Ibid.

[26] An average global carbon dioxide reading of 450 parts per million (ppm) is seen by many climate experts as the maximum level compatible with limiting the damage from climate impacts to a tolerable degree. See J. Gillis, "Heat Trapping Gas Passes Milestone, Raising Fears," *New York Times*, May 10, 2013. In the spring of 2013, the earth's average carbon dioxide reading surpassed 400 ppm: Ibid.

means for her harvest. Social scientists tell us that such "back-loop learning" helps communities understand and address new versions of old threats.[27] Finally, the traditional disaster management perspective emphasizes the importance of localized knowledge, participation, and buy-in. It is said that the earliest "first responders" are affected residents. This insight can help expand the role for local contributions in adaptation policy.

However, there are challenges in linking adaptation to disaster risk reduction. The most obvious is that their circles of concern do not exactly match. Not all natural disasters are linked to climate change (earthquakes being the classic example). And not all climate impacts are natural disasters. Disaster usually implies a sudden change, an outsize scale, and an overwhelming impact. However, many climate effects will unroll slowly and incrementally, such as rising seas or species extinction; they will challenge, but not always overwhelm, existing systems. At a time when much global assistance is flowing toward adaptation, advocates of traditional disaster management will find themselves competing with other non-disaster-related adaptation goals.

A second challenge involves predictability. Before the era of global warming, disasters like storms and floods followed general historical patterns. Assigning probabilities to events of defined magnitudes was something experts became relatively good at. Over time local people developed workable understandings of such risks and prepared for them; with assistance from scientists and engineers, their efforts were further sharpened. But global warming has changed all this. The uncertainties involved in the climate process make many forms of prediction dubious. We know the future will not follow the wheel-ruts of the past. For this reason, experts in climate adaptation warn against using probabilities and predictions. They instead speak of "projections," "multiple scenarios," and "adaptive management." This reflects a different way of thinking that is only now becoming familiar to policy-makers. Modeling scenarios (and scaling them to specific regions) requires technical skill, terabytes of data, and enormous computing power. In the field, it means implementing responses that are monitored, adjustable, and informed by local judgments of acceptable risk. Adaptation projects therefore stress land-use planning and often prefer dynamic "green" infrastructure (such as barrier islands and mangrove forests) to static "gray" infrastructure (such as seawalls and dikes).[28] This sort of resilience requires efforts that are both top-down and bottom-up.

2.3 Two Critical Issues: Group Responsibility and Local Vantage

The frameworks addressing climate change and disaster risk each have strengths potentially beneficial to the other. In particular, we think that notions of causation

---

[27] S. O. Reed et al., "'Shared Learning' for Building Urban Climate Resilience – Experiences from Asian Cities" (2013) 25(2) *Environment and Urbanization* 393.

[28] For a discussion of green infrastructure as a means of reducing disaster risk in the developing world, see Verchick, note 2, pp. 25–37.

498 *Natural Disaster and Climate Change*

and group responsibility found in international climate policy are important for understanding the future of disaster planning in the era of climate change. Similarly, we believe the emphasis in DRR policy upon local action and socio-economic conditions can inspire the next wave of adaptation efforts. We introduce these two critical issues below. After a brief examination, we then turn to the case studies.

2.3.1 Group Responsibility

Global warming is driven by natural forces and by human ones, but there is little doubt we humans are responsible for the lion's share – about 74 percent, by some estimates.[29] And while large developing countries such as China and India are swiftly increasing their carbon output, it remains true that the largest historical contributions to the greenhouse effect have come from the global North.[30] If we make a list of the largest historical contributors *per citizen*, not a single poor country breaks into the top ten.[31]

For this reason, the UNFCCC early on directed industrialized nations to take the lead in reducing emissions and addressing climate impacts. Through the legal framework, developed nations agreed to provide financial and technical support to developing nations to help them reduce carbon emissions and adapt to climate-induced hazards.[32] Legal hooks were carved from the foundational "polluter pays principle" and the doctrine of "transboundary harm," under which a polluting state is held responsible for damage caused to its neighbors.[33] The legal framework is based on the principle of "common but differentiated responsibilities and respective capabilities" (CBDR/RC),[34] a widely accepted notion that a state's duty toward global environmental sustainability should be proportionate to its contribution to a given problem and its capacity to address it. To use a dichotomy associated with political philosopher Judith Shklar, climate disruption, as

---

[29] Q. Schiermeier, "At Least Three-Quarters of Climate Change Is Man-Made," *Nature*, December 4, 2011.

[30] D. Clark, "Which Nations Are Most Responsible for Climate Change?," *The Guardian*, April 22, 2011.

[31] Ibid.

[32] M. J. Mace and M. Schaeffer, "Loss and Damage Under the UNFCCC: What Relationship to the Hyogo Framework," www.lossanddamage.net.

[33] Ibid, p. 2.

[34] For a broader discussion of CBDR/RC in the context of climate change law, see L. Rajamani, *Differential Treatment in International Environmental Law* (Oxford: Oxford University Press, 2006); S. Atapattu, "Climate Change, Differentiated Responsibilities and State Responsibility: Devising Novel Legal Strategies for Damage Caused by Climate Change," in B. J. Richardson et al. (eds.) *Climate Change Law and Developing Countries: Legal and Policy Challenges for the World Economy* (Northampton: Edward Elgar Publishing, 2009), pp. 37–62.

experienced by the global South, is not a blameless "misfortune," but a blameworthy "injustice."[35] And that requires a sincere attempt to make the injured party whole.

In contrast to climate-induced hazards, international law treats natural disasters like garden-variety misfortune. At the root is a desire for charity well spent. As policy analysts Mace and Schaeffer write:

> The motivation for DRR [...] and the Hyogo Framework is to reduce environmental, human and economic losses from natural disasters, and the costs of humanitarian assistance in responding to disasters, by encouraging impacted countries to take greater responsibility for reducing their pre-disaster vulnerability and exposure to hazards – to move to a "prevention culture." These approaches also encourage self-reliance and greater reliance on national resources to facilitate recovery.[36]

Reduced loss, more self-reliance, and a smarter "prevention culture" are terrific goals. But the HFA envisions a world where the worst hazards are traceable either to natural forces or to a state's own failure to plan. Thus, while the HFA strongly encourages international cooperation, the document makes it clear that "each State has the *primary responsibility* for its own sustainable development and for taking effective measures to reduce disaster risk."[37] The HFA focuses mainly on the deployment of a state's own resources, institutions, and existing revenue streams.[38] While the DRR regime contemplates hazards arising from "climate change," its use of that term (in contrast to that of the UNFCCC) includes *both* natural and anthropogenic causes.[39] Otherwise, risks caused by human action beyond national borders are not addressed at all.[40]

Aid from other countries depends on voluntary contributions based on what geographer Mark Pelling calls a "flexible commitment, largely based on self-regulation and trust."[41] While the idea makes sense for at least many kinds of natural disasters, it loses traction in an era in which blameworthy carbon dioxide emissions have been raising the seas, swelling the rivers, and baking the fields in provinces all over the world. As we will see in section 3, it is this

---

[35] J. N. Shklar, *The Faces of Injustice* (New Haven: Yale University Press, 1990), p. 50. For a discussion of Shklar's "misfortune/injustice" thesis in the context of natural disaster, see R. R. M. Verchick, "Disaster Justice: The Geography of Human Capability" (2012) 24 *Duke Environmental Law and Policy Forum* 23 at 27–29.

[36] Mace and Schaeffer, note 32.

[37] UNISDR, note 12, III A(b). [emphasis added].

[38] Mace and Schaeffer, note 32.

[39] Ibid.

[40] Ibid.

[41] M. Pelling, *Adaptation to Climate Change from Resilience to Transformation* (Abingdon: Routledge, 2011), p. 44. See also L. Schipper and M. Pelling, "Disaster Risk, Climate Change, and International Development, Scope for, and Challenges to Integration" (2006) 30(1) *Disasters* 19.

500   *Natural Disaster and Climate Change*

debate over misfortune and injustice that is bogging down current efforts to integrate DRR and CCA.

2.3.2 Local Vantage

The issues of causation and responsibility were highlighted by the global South during the formative stages of climate negotiations, and despite being largely unresolved in the UNFCCC, they remain critical elements of a global resilience strategy. DRR has something to teach CCA advocates as well – namely that effective policy must take the right vantage point. International efforts to curb GHGs understandably began with a global perspective in mind. They came from everywhere; they went everywhere; and each unit of a given gas (carbon dioxide, methane) was fungible. Policy was shaped at the international level then kicked down to the national and local governments. The UNFCCC acknowledged the need for adaptation strategies from the very beginning, but took several years to produce specific programs. Today, there are special assistance funds to help least developed countries draft adaptation plans, support local resilience projects, preserve important ecosystems, and aid coastal zone planning.[42] But the programs, which intersect mainly at the national level, are not very effective at harnessing energy at the local level. They are also severely underfunded.

In contrast, the DRR regime has primarily been driven by a "bottom-up" approach. Disaster is recognized at the point of impact, and in that sense is localized. It follows that disaster policy is an example of bottom-up policy-building that moves in an upward direction from the local to national and then international levels.[43] The arrangement arises partly from the assumption, discussed earlier, that natural disasters are inherently domestic affairs, but the local vantage comes also from the recognition that to be effective, response and recovery demand planning and implementation at the local level. The UNISDR has thus had a hand in incorporating disaster response information in grade school curricula in Kazakhstan, in building risk reduction into regional planning budgets in Nigeria, and in lifting villagers out of poverty in the low-lying river basins of Vietnam.[44]

This last example – lifting villagers out of poverty – points to another aspect of the bottom-up point of view, namely that a community's risk to disasters is a product of *both* physical exposure *and* social vulnerability. Indeed, factors contributing to social vulnerability – poverty, low literacy, racism, sexism, and

---

[42] Verchick, note 22, pp. 280–281.

[43] IPCC, "Climate Change 2014: Impacts, Adaptations, and Vulnerability," 2014, https://ipcc-wg2.gov, p. 427.

[44] Farber et al. (eds.), note 11, chapter 9.

the like – can contribute as much to a community's disaster risk as any geological or hydrological feature.[45] While the UNFCCC does recognize that poverty alleviation is an overriding priority for countries in the global South, it fails to provide any meaningful detail on how to continue economic development in the context of climate vulnerability, risk, and resilience. One reason is that poverty and related ills belong to *other* offices in the UN family. Bureaucracies lend themselves to specialized subdivisions, and integration is hard. A second, more substantive reason is that taking on social vulnerability would involve yet another discussion of causation and responsibility. How, after all, does one decide what share of a developing country's climate vulnerability is attributable to greenhouse gas (GHG) emissions and what share is attributable to indigence? And what responsibility, if any, do countries in the global North have for conditions of poverty in the global South? The line between misfortune and injustice is fading quickly.

To sum up, we have briefly outlined the similarities and differences between disaster risk management and climate resilience, both conceptually and as envisioned in law. Among the many differences between these two regimes, we have emphasized two that we think will play a critical role in the global South: Group responsibility and local vantage. Group responsibility, which derives from the climate regime, stresses the obligation that the global North owes to the global South because of its disproportionate historical contribution to climate change. Local vantage, which derives from the disaster management regime, stresses the viewpoint of communities that experience the direct effects of storms, floods, and droughts. The idea stresses the need for local engagement as well as the broader reality of social vulnerability. Both concepts are important to developing countries eager to move forward on climate resilience. To show the specific role that each concept can play, we turn now to two case studies, one involving the global policy-making stage, the other the diamond-polishing capital of India.

3. "LOSS AND DAMAGE" UNDER THE UNFCCC

The most recent battle on group responsibility is now taking place over the issue of "loss and damage" under the UNFCCC. Under the Warsaw International Mechanism or WIM, established in 2013, parties agreed to integrate DRR and CCA to "address loss and damage associated with climate change[,] adding that loss and damage [...] in some cases involves more than that which can be reduced by adaptation."[46]

---

[45] Verchick, above note 2, pp. 111–116; see generally K. Dow et al., "Commentary: Limits to Adaptation" (2013) 3 *Nature Climate Change* 305; W. N. Adger et al., "Are There Social Limits to Adaptation to Climate Change?" (2009) 93 *Climatic Change* 335.

[46] UNFCCC, *Report of the Conference of the Parties on Its Nineteenth Session, Held in Warsaw from 11 to 23 November 2013 – Addendum – Part Two: Action Taken by the Conference of the Parties at Its Nineteenth Session*, 31 January 2014, FCCC/CP/2013/10/Add.1, Decision 2/CP.19.

502   *Natural Disaster and Climate Change*

The issue of "loss and damage" had long been pursued by the global South. During the negotiations of the UNFCCC, for instance, the Alliance of Small Island States (AOSIS) had proposed an international insurance scheme to "compensate the most vulnerable small-island and low-lying coastal developing countries for loss and damage arising from sea level rise."[47] At the time it was clear that the issue of vulnerability *and* responsibility were at play. Contributions to an assistance fund were to be determined on the basis of nations' contributions to global warming and their relative economic strength. Funding under the insurance scheme was to apply to adverse impacts from sea-level rise that exceeded reasonable adaptation efforts of the "most vulnerable small-island and low level developing countries."[48]

The acknowledgment of DRR has added a significant element of complexity to the overall debate on loss and damage, particularly with regard to the issue of responsibility. It has prompted the global North to discuss loss and damage within the parameters of DRR. The potential to divert the conversation outside the purview of climate change law and policy was evident in the negotiations following the eighteenth Conference of the Parties to the UNFCCC (COP 18)[49] and in the lead-up to the WIM. The global South was adamant that the institutional arrangements mentioned in the COP 18 decision take the form of a new international mechanism that provided support to vulnerable developing countries in minimizing the impacts of loss and damage, especially in the form of more frequent and severe weather events, as well as the progressive loss and damage caused by slow onset events.[50] By contrast, the global North maintained that a new, specific international mechanism was unnecessary and that the concerns of countries vulnerable to adverse impacts and therefore loss and damage could be adequately addressed under the existing disaster risk reduction frameworks, institutions, and processes – namely the UNISDR and HFA – that are located

For further commentary see K. Dow and F. Berkhout, "Climate Change, Limits to Adaptation and the "Loss and Damage" Debate," www.e-ir.info; R. Verheyen, "Tackling Loss and Damage – A New Role for the Climate Regime?," November 16, 2012, www.lossanddamage. net, pp. 6–7.

[47] Intergovernmental Negotiating Committee (INC) for a Framework Convention on Climate Change (FCCC), *Report of the Intergovernmental Negotiating Committee for a Framework Convention on Climate Change on the Work of its Fourth Session, held at Geneva from 9 to 20 December 1991*, 9–20 December 1991, A/AC.237/15/Corr.1, at p. 127.

[48] Mace and Schaeffer, note 32.

[49] UNFCCC, *Report of the Conference of the Parties on Its Eighteenth Session, Held in Doha from 26 November to 8 December 2012 – Addendum – Part Two: Action Taken by the Conference of the Parties at Its Thirteenth Session*, 14 March 2008, FCCC/CP/2007/6/Add.1.

[50] Submission by Nauru on behalf of AOSIS, FCCC/SBI/2012/MISC.14; Submission by Gambia on behalf of the LDCs, FCCC/SBI/2011/MISC.8. More generally, see UNFCCC, Subsidiary Body for Implementation, *Views and Information from Parties and Relevant Organizations on the Possible Elements to be Included in the Recommendation of Loss and Damage in Accordance with Decision 1/CP.16*, 8 October 2012, FCCC/SBI/2012/MISC.14.

outside the UNFCCC.[51] For example, the United States opposed the inclusion of loss and damage in the climate change regime on a number of grounds, including that the issue is adequately represented in DRR instruments and that national response measures were sufficient, thereby negating the need for an international approach.[52] The European Union asserted that the gap between DRR and CCA needed to be bridged and that "assessing the risk of loss and damage associated with the adverse impacts of climate change should be seen in the broader context of disaster risk management, where interventions pertain to reducing the risk, anticipating the risk and responding to it as well as interventions to recover from impacts."[53]

The global South has argued that such submissions reflect the propensity of the global North to continually deflect questions of responsibility.[54] It is claimed that the inclusion of references to DRR in documents dedicated to CCA, such as the Cancun Adaptation Framework, and promotion of the HFA has come at the insistence of the global North and is a deliberate tactic to move the discussion out of the context of climate change and into that of disaster policy.[55] The object is to neutralize the issue of state responsibility that still underlies the relationship between the global North and South in the climate change context. Mace and Schaeffer note that some nations of the global South view the attempt to relocate the discussion of loss and damage into a different international framework as severing "the causal link between emissions and impacts" and thereby placing "responsibility on countries to find ways to reduce their own vulnerabilities, using their own resources."[56]

The South may be right. The HFA, as noted before, has no way of accounting for human causation, pollution spillovers, or group culpability. It anticipates no role for the polluter pays principle, transboundary harm, or CBDR/RC. If climate hazard is a matter of injustice rather than misfortune, it makes more sense to integrate DRR into CCA, and not the other way around. The global discussion of "loss and damage" is an example, in our eyes, of integration between disaster resilience and climate resilience going wrong. That is because influential parties in the North are underestimating (or willfully ignoring) the importance of responsibility and justice that underlies all climate change issues.

However, there is also potential for integration to go right. Adaptation efforts under the UNFCCC have arguably failed to reach their potential in part because

---

[51] UNFCCC, Subsidiary Body for Implementation, *Views and Information on the Thematic Areas in the Implementation of the Work Programme, Item 8 of the Provisional Agenda, Approaches to Address Loss and Damage Associated with Climate Change Impacts in Developing Countries that are Particularly Vulnerable to the Adverse Effects of Climate Change to Enhance Adaptive Capacity*, 14 November 2011, FCCC/SBI/2011/MISC.8/Add.1.

[52] R. Verheyen, note 46, pp. 6–7.

[53] Subsidiary Body for Implementation, note 51.

[54] Mace and Schaeffer, note 32.

[55] Ibid.

[56] Ibid.

504   *Natural Disaster and Climate Change*

they are poorly funded and do not adequately engage the local community. The challenge is immense. Yet some private foundations have begun experimenting with pilot projects across the developing world to see how true climate resilience might take root. Many of these projects are informed by basic teachings in DRR literature, which emphasize local networking and social and economic conditions in the community. Were adaptation efforts under the UNFCCC to integrate these lessons, the result might be a more community-based model such as the one described below.

4. SURAT, INDIA

Perhaps no country in the world is as vulnerable on so many fronts to climate change as India. With 7,000 kilometers of coastline, the vast Himalayan glaciers, and nearly seventy million hectares of forests, India is especially vulnerable to a climate trending toward warmer temperatures, erratic precipitation, higher seas, and swifter storms. Then there are India's megacities (housing nearly a quarter of the population, many of them living in slums), where all of these trends conspire to threaten public health and safety on a grand scale – portending heat waves, drought, thicker smog layers, coastal storms, and blown-out sewer systems. These problems will surely grow as rural populations displaced by negative climate effects migrate into the cities, overwhelming critical services related to health, transportation, housing, energy, and water. When experts rank countries in terms of population centers most exposed to extreme weather events (such as droughts and floods) or the hazards of sea-level rise, India is always at the top of the list.[57] Yet, in the midst of these grim facts, there are glints of hope, as are found in a recent resilience project taking place in Surat.

Surat, a medium-sized Indian city of 4.5 million people, is a global center for textile production and diamond polishing. [58] In total, 80 percent of the diamonds sold in jewelry shops around the world are shaped by Surati hands. Nearly every Indian has something in their wardrobe from Surat – which is what one would expect from a city whose clattering looms churn out thirty million meters of fabric a day.[59] The city lies 250 kilometers north of Mumbai, near the Arabian Sea. Its proximity to the Tapti River delta – a strategic advantage in trade – also makes Surat a flood magnet. In the past twenty years, the city has been drowned by three

---

[57] See e.g. UN Office for the Coordination of Humanitarian Affairs, "Global: Twelve Countries on Climate Change Hit-List," IRIN News, July 8, 2009 (citing a World Bank study that ranks India as among the countries that are most vulnerable to droughts, floods, and agricultural disasters, which are all linked to climate change); see also S. Hallegatte et al., "Future Flood Losses in Major Coastal Cities" (2013) 3 *Nature Climate Change* 802 (ranking Mumbai, India, as the fifth most vulnerable city, in terms of material assets at risk to sea-level rise).

[58] Asian Cities Climate Change Resilience Network, "Surat City Resilience Strategy," April 2011, http://acccrn.org.

[59] Ibid.

major floods caused by emergency releases from an upstream dam. Lesser floods, caused by hard rains, occur more frequently. In 1994, such a flood led to an outbreak of plague.[60] In addition, tidal surges moving up the mouth of the Tapti River threaten the city from the opposite direction. Even on calm days, high tides push saltwater into parts of the river needed for drinking. All of these problems will be aggravated by climate change, due to stronger downpours and rising seas.

For these reasons, Surat has developed an urban "resilience strategy," focused on adapting to climatic change.[61] The initiative is supported by the Asian Cities Climate Change Resilience Network (ACCCRN), an organization funded by the Rockefeller Foundation. With the help of outside experts, the city has assessed the climatic risks in relation to flood management, energy, and public health. The city is implementing a new early warning system for major floods and designing an inflatable dam to protect the river from saltwater intrusion. Much of this work has been accomplished through a flexible and relatively loose network of public officials, business people, and community members organized around one compelling goal: climate resilience. But that goal serves an array of interests. The political and business communities were concerned about trade and economic growth, which were threatened by downtown floods. The public health community, still haunted by its experience with plague, was committed to cleaning the streets and delivering potable water. And everyone, most notably the poor and working classes, wanted housing that would not wash away with the next monsoon. Addressing climate impacts, it must be noted, was not anyone's first priority. But when ACCCRN announced its interest in funding projects pursuing that goal, city managers were savvy enough to jump at the chance. While not without their flaws, Surat's efforts are considered one of the success stories of urban adaptation projects in Asia.

Integrating climate resilience into everyday governance requires effective networking and a solid legal framework – features that have been previously referred to as "rope lines" and "footholds."[62] "Rope lines" describe the formal or informal relationships among public and private actors at various levels of jurisdictional boundaries (national, regional, local) and across given sectors (public health, agriculture, energy, and so on).[63] The relationships can be described as vertical (related to level of jurisdiction) or horizontal (related to sector).[64] "Footholds" describe existing policies or laws that may be used to "anchor" new initiatives related to climate adaptation.[65]

---

[60] A. K. Dutt et al., "Surat Plague of 1994 Re-Examined" (2006) 37 *Southeast Asian Journal of Tropical Medicine and Public Health* 755.

[61] Asian Cities Climate Change Resilience Network, note 58, p. 11.

[62] R. R. M. Verchick and A. Hall, "Adapting to Climate Change While Planning for Disaster: Footholds, Rope Lines, and the Iowa Floods" (2011) 6 *Brigham Young University Law Review* 2203.

[63] Ibid at 2204–2205.

[64] Ibid at 2210–2211.

[65] Ibid.

506   *Natural Disaster and Climate Change*

The climate resiliency initiatives in Surat illustrate the importance of vertical rope lines. Developing a municipal warning system for river-based floods proved challenging because the events were triggered by planned releases from a dam in a neighboring state.[66] Negotiating the plan took years and involved local leaders, state water management offices, and participation from India's central government. Other adaptation efforts also relied on existing land-use authorities ("footholds") to reconfigure street drainage and public health laws to support efforts to protect drinking water from saltwater intrusion. All of this is overseen by a recently created municipal climate adaptation council – a horizontal "rope line," whose participants include representatives from city government, the local chamber of commerce, and public health advocates.[67]

Additional horizontal networking came about through experiences of "shared learning." Shared learning emphasizes the role of local actors in complex adaptive systems. By involving community members early in the process and actively facilitating planning and communication strategies, the method "promote[s] learning and co-production of knowledge; build[s] new formal and informal networks across scales and sectors; build[s] capacities of stakeholders for analysis and self-representation; and spark[s] innovative responses to problems."[68] There is also more of a chance that outcomes will be "socially just."[69] But social learning demands more than an organizational template or policy "tool kit." It requires high levels of involvement not only from residents, but also from sponsors and facilitators.

Techniques in social learning, described earlier, can help communities identify vulnerabilities and develop practical solutions. Some municipalities are also taking advantage of new technological tools, such as GIS mapping. As part of its climate vulnerability assessment, the city of Surat used a combination of household interviews, hydrological data, and GIS mapping to create a "vulnerability and capacity" index for the city's neighborhoods. The index combined data on physical vulnerabilities such as flood risk and sewer backups with social vulnerabilities, measured in terms of income, education, and social cohesion. The highlighted risk in slums and low-income neighborhoods prompted several proposals, including a computer database of vulnerable households, stronger building codes in poor areas, and community banks where flood-prone households can protect valuable goods.[70]

But Surat's experience raises a cautionary note. One of the city's most dramatic efforts to reduce flood risk involves the relocation of slums, many of which are located along tidal creeks, river banks, or drainage lines. Over the past decade,

---

[66] Ibid at 2236–2237.
[67] Ibid at 2235.
[68] Reed et al., note 27 at 393–412.
[69] Ibid.
[70] G. K. Bhat et al., "Addressing Flooding in the City of Surat Beyond its Boundaries," July 23, 2013, http://eau.sagepub.com, p. 11.

Surat moved tens of thousands of families from flood-prone slums to townships in safer parts of the city.[71] Similar efforts are planned for the future. But these townships, sometimes located several kilometers away, lack the work opportunities and city services found in the urban core. Many residents are moving back and re-settling (illegally) in the flood plains, again increasing the city's vulnerability index.

5. CONCLUSION

Natural disasters and global warming compound preexisting risks and present a double menace. Thus far, the international frameworks we use for regulating and combating these issues have lacked alignment. Integration is crucial, but not without deliberation. If integrating CCA into DRR means giving up notions of group responsibility – the leverage the South needs to win aid from the North – the marriage would be a failure. If CCA continued without learning lessons in local networking and social vulnerability from decades of DRR research, much potential good will have been lost. The question is not whether the policies of disaster resilience and climate resilience must align, but how, and in whose interest.

[71] Asian Cities Climate Change Resilience Network, note 58, p. 26.

24

International Law, Cultural Diversity, and the Environment: The Case of the General Forestry Law in Colombia

Daniel Bonilla Maldonado

1. INTRODUCTION

International law has been repeatedly challenged for its exclusionary character[1] and its imperial uses.[2] These critiques, which are widely known, have three key overlapping dimensions. First, it is argued that the countries of the global South have played a very limited role in the processes that create international law, and that the resulting legal regimes reflect North–South power imbalances where Southern interests and perspectives are largely unrepresented.[3] When applied to the environment, this critique emphasizes international environmental law's failure to adequately address the North's historic contribution to environmental degradation in the South by, for example, confronting the thorny issue of reparations.[4] This critique also questions the depiction of Southern countries as reluctant participants in the creation of international environmental law,[5] and condemns the North's indifference to Southern

---

[1] I. Gunning, "Modernizing Customary International Law: The Challenge of Human Rights" (1991) 31 *Virginia Journal of International Law* 211 at 217–218. See generally H. Charlesworth, C. Chinkin, and S. Wright. "Feminist Approaches to International Law" (1991) 81 *American Journal of International Law* 613; "Feminist Inquiries into International Law" (1993) 3 *Transnational Law and Contemporary Problems* 293.

[2] A. Anghie, *Imperialism, Sovereignty and the Making of International Law* (New York: Cambridge University Press, 2005), p. 14. See also K. Mickelson, "South, North, International Environmental Law, and International Environmental Lawyers" (2000) 11 *Yearbook of International Environmental Law* 52.

[3] M. Mutua, "Savages, Victims, and Saviors: The Metaphor of Human Rights" (2001) 42 *Harvard International Law Journal* 201 at 201–245; M. Mutua, "The Ideology of Human Rights" (1996) 36 *Virginia Journal of International Law* 589.

[4] Mickelson, note 2 at 54–60.

[5] Ibid at 60–69.

understandings of environmental protection as inextricably linked to economic development and poverty eradication.[6]

A second critique of international law challenges the liberal character of its norms and dominant justificatory theories.[7] This critique questions the supposed objectivity of international law;[8] makes explicit its ideological character; challenges the separation between law and politics that constitutes one of its pillars; and demonstrates the ways in which its norms have been utilized by the North to subordinate the economically, militarily, and politically weaker states.[9] Three examples highlight the implications of this critique for Southern forests and historically subordinated communities. First, North–South conflicts at the 1992 UN Conference on Environment and Development derailed the negotiation of a treaty on forests.[10] The North's view of Southern forests as part of the common heritage of mankind was perceived by Southern states as a serious threat to national sovereignty, a continuation of the colonial project, and an obstacle to development and poverty reduction. The result was the negotiation of a set of non-binding forest principles[11] rather than a treaty – a serious setback for the protection of forests around the world.[12] Second, international trade and investment law, and institutions such as the International Monetary Fund (IMF) and the World Bank, have exacerbated deforestation and encroachment on indigenous territories in the global South by reinforcing the international division of labor that relegates many countries in the South to the export of timber, minerals, and agricultural products.[13] The 1947 General Agreement on Tariffs and Trade (GATT),[14] for example, was negotiated at a time when most countries of the global South were still controlled by colonial powers. The GATT therefore did not take into account

---

[6] Ibid at 76–81. For an analysis of North–South conflicts in the evolution of international environmental law, see chapter 5, K. Mickelson, "The Stockholm Conference and the Creation of the South–North Divide in International Environmental Law and Policy."

[7] M. Koskenniemi, *From pology to Utopia: The Structure of International Legal Argument* (New York: Cambridge University Press, 1989), pp. 66–67.

[8] N. Purvis, "Critical Legal Studies in Public International Law" (1991) 32 *Harvard International Law Journal* 81.

[9] M. Mutua, "What is Twail?" (2000) 94 *American Society of International Law Proceedings* 31 at 31–39.

[10] G. Palmer, "The Earth Summit: What Went Wrong at Rio?" (1992) 70 *Washington University Law Quarterly* 1005.

[11] UN General Assembly, *Report of the United Nations Conference on Environment and Development: Non-Legally Binding Authoritative Statement of Principles for a Global Consensus on the Management, Conservation and Sustainable Development of All Types of Forests*, 14 August 1992, A/CONF.151/26 (Vol. III) [hereinafter Forest Principles].

[12] World Watch Institute, *State of the World 1998* (New York: W. W. Norton & Company, 1998), p. 39.

[13] See C. G. Gonzalez, "Environmental Justice and International Environmental Law," in S. Alam, M. J. H. Bhuiyan, T. M. R. Chowdhury, and E. J. Techera (eds.), *Routledge Handbook of International Environmental Law* (Oxford: Routledge, 2013), pp. 77–97.

[14] Geneva, in force 1 January 1948, 55 UNTS 194; 61 Stat. pt. 5; TIAS 1700.

510   *International Law, Cultural Diversity, and the Environment*

the South's needs for economic diversification and industrialization.[15] Third, the North's use of the international law concept of *terra nullius* was instrumental in the conquest of indigenous peoples and the appropriation of their lands and natural resources. By arguing that indigenous peoples' territories were in fact "land belonging to no one," European imperial powers were able to "legally" take them.[16]

Finally, the third critique states that liberal international law, focused on the interests of the global North, does not allow for the political, economic, and cultural emancipation of the countries of the global South, or of the vulnerable groups within these countries.[17] These critics contend that international environmental law is anthropocentric and incapable of defending the interests of nature, and that international law generally subordinates and oppresses the most fragile states and historically marginalized groups, including women, racial and ethnic minorities, indigenous peoples, and the poor.[18] Indeed, some critics argue that international environmental law is androcentric, based on the hierarchical superiority of men to both women and nature, and is therefore incapable of defending the interests of women and nature.[19] Some critics also argue that the existing international law on climate change has had very few positive consequences. They claim that this is partially caused by the international community's resistance to including the idea that climate change is, in part, a matter of sustainable development and international equity. Accordingly, critics maintain that until international environmental law includes what has been called a climate justice perspective, it will not achieve the aims that it is supposed to attain and will not address the needs of particularly vulnerable Southern states, such as small island states that could literally disappear if climate change is not controlled.[20]

This chapter argues that these critiques of international law are useful but incomplete and insufficiently nuanced. The critiques that depict international law as exclusionary and as an instrument of imperial domination describe many of its structures and dynamics in a precise manner. However, international law may be a useful instrument for protecting the legitimate interests of the states of the global South in general, and of the distinct social and cultural groups that form

---

[15] Gonzalez, note 13, p. 88.

[16] See J. Gilbert, *Indigenous Peoples' Land Rights Under International Law: From Victims to Actors* (New York: Transnational Publishers, 2006).

[17] D. Otto, "Subalternity and International Law: The Problems of Global Community and the Incommensurability of Difference" (1996) 5 *Social and Legal Studies: An International Journal* 337.

[18] H. Charlesworth, "Feminist Critiques of International Law and Their Critics" (1995) 13 *Third World Legal Studies* 1 at 2.

[19] A. Rochette, "Stop the Rape of the World: An Ecofeminist Critique of Sustainable Development" (2002) 51 *University of New Brunswick Law Journal* 145 at 149. For a feminist critique of the neutrality of international law see H. Charlesworth, C. Chinkin, and S. Wright, "Feminist Approaches to International Law" (1991) 85 *American Journal of International Law* 613.

[20] K. Mickelson, "Beyond a Politics of the Possible? South-North Relations and Climate Justice" (2009) 10 *Melbourne Journal of International Law* 411.

them, in particular. Yet, in order to understand international law's potential for emancipation or social resistance, it is necessary to complement theoretical critiques like those discussed earlier with the examination of concrete forms through which the global South makes use of international law to resist or transform its social reality. It is important to develop theoretical tools that allow us to describe, analyze, and evaluate the counterhegemonic uses that international law may have. This is a subject that is largely unexplored by theorists of international law.[21] However, this theorization must emerge, at least in part, from the particular experiences that social movements and organizations have had with the use of international law for the defense of their communities, lands, and natural resources.

This chapter goes on to explore the ways in which international law may be used as a tool to protect the rights and natural resources of some of the most vulnerable groups in the global South: indigenous peoples and culturally diverse black communities. This analysis proceeds by means of a case study. This chapter examines the strategic litigation project that began when a public action of unconstitutionality (*acción pública de inconstitucionalidad*) was brought before the Colombian Constitutional Court against the General Forestry Law (GFL), which culminated in ruling C-075 of 2008 declaring the law unconstitutional. The analysis of this strategic litigation project is divided into two parts. The first part examines the way in which international law and national law are interwoven for the protection of the rights of Colombian cultural minorities and of the environment, focusing on the right to prior consultation recognized in the Indigenous and Tribal Peoples Convention 1989 (ILO Convention 169)[22] and the concept of the "block of constitutionality" that is part of the Colombian Constitution of 1991. The second part presents the legal and political arguments that explain why, in Colombia as well as in other countries of the global South, international environmental law and the international law on cultural minorities may be (and are) used effectively in national courts. This section examines the historical, political, cognitive, and tactical arguments that have allowed for the use of the institution of the block of constitutionality by national courts, social organizations, and legal academics in the country.

2. THE CASE: ITS BASIC STRUCTURE AND INTERNATIONAL LAW

The GFL articulated the general normative and institutional framework that would govern the exploitation of Colombia's forests.[23] In 2006, the Public Interest Law

---

[21] B. Rajagopal, "International Law and Social Movements: Challenges of Theorizing Resistance" (2003) 41 *Columbia Journal of Transnational Law* 397.

[22] *Convention Concerning Indigenous and Tribal Peoples in Independent Countries*, Geneva, 27 June 1989, in force 5 September 1991, 72 ILO Official Bull. 59; 28 ILM 1382 (1989) [hereinafter ILO Convention 169].

[23] L.1021 of 2006, art. 1.

Group of the University of the Andes (GDIP), in association with the Inter American Association for Environmental Defense, the Colombian Commission of Jurists, the National Indigenous Organization of Colombia, the Process of Black Communities, and Censat Agua Viva,[24] brought an *actio popularis*[25] before the Colombian Constitutional Court challenging the constitutionality of the GFL.[26]

The central argument of the lawsuit was that the national government had violated the right to prior consultation of indigenous and culturally diverse black communities in Colombia. The legal basis for this argument is found in both Colombian constitutional law and the international law on cultural minorities. The claim was based upon Article 93 of the Constitution of 1991, which recognizes the doctrine commonly known as the block of constitutionality.[27] This doctrine expands the concept of "supreme norm" of the legal system to encompass not only the text of the Constitution but also a set of norms derived from heterogeneous legal sources. In order to invoke the block of constitutionality, it is necessary to identify at least one referral clause granting this special legal status to one or more norms that are not part of the Constitution. This referral clause may be part of the text of the Constitution or it may be a creation of case law. For example, the supreme norm of a country may include norms as varied as the preamble of a previous constitution or a group of treaties.[28]

In particular, Article 93 of the Constitution states that all of the international human rights treaties ratified by Colombia and that prohibit their limitation in states of emergency form part of, and prevail in, the internal legal order. It likewise indicates that the rights and responsibilities in the Constitution should be

---

[24] GDIP started the analysis of the GFL by request of the Inter American Association for the Protection of the Environment. This organization also made substantive comments to the lawsuit drafted by GDIP. Other institutions that filed amicus curiae briefs and requested the Court to declare the GFL unconstitutional were Universidad Nacional de Colombia, Universidad del Rosario, Red Latinoamericana Contra los Monocultivos, Asociación de Autoridades Tradicionales del Consejo Regional Indígena del Medio Amazonas, and some individual members of indigenous reservations.

[25] The *action popularis* or public action of unconstitutionality (*acción publica de inconstitucionalidad*) is a legal action that any Colombian can use to challenge the constitutionality of any statute before the Constitutional Court. It puts Colombia's judicial review system into operation.

[26] For more information on the lawsuit and amicus briefs, see D. Bonilla, *Justicia Colectiva, Medio Ambiente y Democracia Participativa* (Bogota: Universidad de los Andes, 2009).

[27] See R. Uprimny, "El bloque de constitucionalidad en Colombia. Un análisis jurisprudencial y un ensayo de sistematización doctrinal," in 1 *Compilación de Jurisprudencia y Doctrina Nacional e Internacional* (Oficina en Colombia del Alto Comisionado de las Naciones Unidas para los Derechos Humanos, 2000); and M. Arango, "El Bloque de Constitucionalidad en la Jurisprudencia de la Corte Constitucional Colombiana," www.icesi.edu.co.

[28] In France, for example, the Constitutionality Council stated that the supreme norm of the French legal order was constituted not only by the 1958 Constitution but also by the preamble of the 1948 Constitution and the Declaration of the Rights of Man and Citizen. See notes 90, 91, and 92.

interpreted in light of these treaties.[29] In any case, international human rights treaties ratified by Colombia are justiciable. The block of constitutionality therefore has two meanings: strict and broad. The first indicates that international human rights treaties have the same status as the Constitution, and therefore that all the inferior norms, laws, and decrees, for example, should recognize and never contradict the mandates of these treaties. The second views international human rights treaties as hermeneutic tools. International human rights law is thus seen as the lens through which specific content should be given to the Constitution. International environmental law is not considered, in principle, as part of the block of constitutionality in Colombia. The Constitution has no referral clause regarding environmental treaties, and these treaties are not considered human rights treaties that include rights that cannot be limited even during states of emergency.[30] However, environmental clauses that are part of human rights treaties ratified by Colombia are considered part of the block of constitutionality and can be judicially enforced. Examples include the right to a healthy environment recognized by Article 11 of the Additional Protocol to the American Convention on Human Rights in the Area of Economic, Social and Cultural Rights[31] and Article 12(b) of the International Covenant on Economic, Social and Cultural Rights.[32]

Making use of the block of constitutionality doctrine, the lawsuit invoked international law to challenge the constitutionality of the GFL. The plaintiffs argued that the GFL violated the ILO Convention 169, ratified by Colombia and perhaps the most important international instrument for protection of the rights of cultural minorities. In particular, the lawsuit asserted that the GFL violated Article 6 of the Convention, which recognizes the right to prior consultation that indigenous and tribal peoples have in the face of legislative and administrative measures that are likely to affect them in a direct manner.

The claim under Article 6 of the Convention is particularly significant because it expands the right to prior consultation that was recognized by the Constitution.[33] Whereas the Constitution recognized the right to prior consultation only for indigenous communities and only in the face of projects that seek to explore or exploit natural resources within their territories, Article 6 of the Convention expanded the subjects that are entitled to prior consultation, as well as the kinds

---

[29] The Constitution includes other referral clauses that expand the block of constitutionality: art. 214 (humanitarian international law); art. 101 (international treaties on borders); art. 94 (innominate rights); art. 53 (ILO treaties and conventions); art. 44 (children's rights); and art. 9 (international relations).

[30] See Constitutional Court, C-988 of 2004, M.P. Humberto Sierra Porto.

[31] *Additional Protocol to the American Convention on Human Rights in the Area of Economic, Social and Cultural Rights*, San Salvador, 17 November 1988, in force 16 November 1999, OAS Treaty Series No 69; 28 ILM 156 (1989) [hereinafter Protocol of San Salvador].

[32] *International Covenant on Economic, Social and Cultural Rights*, New York, 16 December 1966, in force 3 January 1976, 993 UNTS 3; [1976] ATS 5; 6 ILM 360 (1967).

[33] Constitution of 1991, art. 330.

514 *International Law, Cultural Diversity, and the Environment*

of activities that trigger the duty to consult. In this international instrument, prior consultation is a right of both indigenous communities and tribal peoples. This point is important inasmuch as the Colombian Constitutional Court had specified in previous decisions that the culturally diverse black communities should be understood as tribal peoples.[34] In addition, Article 6 requires prior consultation not only when there is the intention to explore or exploit natural resources located in the territories of indigenous or tribal communities, but also when there is the intention to approve a bill or issue an administrative act that may directly affect indigenous communities or tribal peoples.

The invocation of Article 6 of the Convention allowed the claim to proceed under a broader and more ambitious legal and political framework. It achieved the protection of the rights of two of the most vulnerable groups in Colombia: indigenous peoples and culturally diverse black communities.[35] It also allowed for the protection of the country's enormous environmental wealth. Finally, this strategy mandated the protection of all of these rights as part of the duty to bring to fruition the kind of state established in the Constitution, namely a culturally diverse Social State of Law (*Estado Social de Derecho*) committed to participatory democracy. The remainder of this section examines each of these three arguments, accepted by the Constitutional Court in ruling C-030 of 2008, in greater detail.[36]

There are eighty-seven indigenous peoples in the country that speak thirty-four different languages[37] and form 3.4 percent of the population.[38] Some 72.83 percent of the members of the indigenous peoples live on reservations that are collectively owned territories recognized by the Colombian state.[39] Indigenous peoples are owners of approximately 31,207,978 hectares of land in the national territory.[40] The black communities recognized as culturally diverse form 10.4 percent of the population[41] and are divided into three groups: the rural communities that live in the Colombian Pacific corridor extending from the department of Chocó to that

---

[34] See e.g. Sentencia C-169 de 2001, M.P. Carlos Gaviria Díaz.

[35] In Sentencia T-704/2006 M.P.Humberto Sierra Porto, the Colombian Constitutional Court recognized in unequivocal terms the difficult socioeconomic and cultural situation of indigenous communities and the duty to recognize and protect their constitutional rights.

[36] Sentencia O-030 de 2008, M.P. Rodrigo Escobar Gil.

[37] Departamento Nacional de Estadística, "Colombia una Nación Multicultural," www.dane. gov.co.

[38] Departamento Nacional de Estadística, "La Visibilización Estadística de los Grupos Étnicos Colombianos," www.dane.gov.co.

[39] A reservation is a territory over which one or more indigenous groups exert collective ownership and where they can govern their public and private lives through their cultural traditions. See Decreto 2164/95, diciembre 7, 1995, art. 21. See also Departamento Nacional de Estadística, "Colombia una Nación Multicultural," www.dane.gov.co.

[40] Instituto Colombiano de Desarrollo Rural, "Reforma Agrarian y Desarrollo Rural para los Grupos Etnicos en Colombia," www.incoder.gov.co.

[41] Ibid.

of Nariño,[42] the Raizal communities of the department of San Andrés, Providencia, and Santa Catalina,[43] and the Palenque of San Basilio.[44] The culturally diverse black communities possess 149 titles for collective property, corresponding to 5,128,830 hectares. If lands in the process of adjudication are included (approximately 500,000 hectares), the lands possessed by the culturally diverse black communities encompass 5 percent of the national territory.[45] Combined, then, the indigenous and culturally diverse black communities are the owners of 34 percent of Colombian territory.[46] These collective territories are primarily located in forested areas, particularly on the Pacific Coast and in the Amazon, Orinoquía, and Sierra Nevada de Santa Marta regions.[47] Additionally, these territories shelter an important part of the biodiversity that characterizes Colombia. It is important to note that, as indicated in the Convention on Biological Diversity,[48] Colombia is one of the world's "megadiverse" countries, or those that contain 40 percent of the world's species.[49] More precisely, Colombia contains 14 percent of the planet's biodiversity[50] and possesses a large quantity and variety of biomes, including tropical rainforests, dry forests and subtropical rainforests, Andean forests, Amazonian grasslands and Caribbean grasslands, deserts, and mangrove swamps.[51] Colombia has between 45,000 and 55,000 species of plants[52] and 2,890 species of vertebrates. Colombia is also the country with the greatest number of bird species (approximately 1,721), which corresponds to 19 percent of the planet's bird species.[53]

---

[42] Groups of black families of African ancestry that inhabit the rural lowlands of the Pacific Coast. L. 70/93 recognized the collective property of the national territories that these groups inhabit. This law was enacted as a development of Article 55 (transitory) of the Constitution.

[43] Groups of black families of African ancestry that speak Caribbean English or Creole (mixture of English and Spanish) and that, in great majority, belong to the Baptist Church. See N. S. de Friedmann, "Religión y tradición oral en San Andrés y Providencia," in I. Clemente (ed.), *San Andrés y Providencia: Tradiciones Culturales y Coyuntura Política* (Bogota: Ediciones Uniandes, 1989); W. G. Petersen, "Cultura y Tradición de los Habitantes de San Andrés y Providencia" (1999) 86 *Boletín de Historia y Antigüedades*.

[44] Black communities of African descent that speak a mixture of Spanish and various African languages. Slaves who escaped from their masters created the first *Palenques* during the colonial period.

[45] See note 17 at 115.

[46] Departamento Nacional de Estadística, "Colombia una Nación Multicultural," www.dane. gov.co.

[47] Departamento Nacional de Planeacion, "Ordenamiento y Desarrollo Teritorial," www.acnur. org.

[48] Rio de Janeiro, 5 June 1992, in force 29 December 1993, [1993] ATS 32/1760 UNTS 79/31 ILM 818 (1992).

[49] Ministerio del Medio Ambiente, Departamento Nacional de Planeación, Instituto Alexande Von Humboldt, "Política Nacional de Biodiversidad," www.minambiente.gov.co.

[50] Convention on Biological Diversity, "Colombia Overview," www.cbd.int.

[51] Ibid.

[52] Ibid.

[53] Ibid.

516   *International Law, Cultural Diversity, and the Environment*

The strategic litigation process under study tried to protect the rights of cultural minorities as well as the biodiversity that exists in the country through the defense of what may be called the "Multicultural Constitution"[54] and the "Ecological Constitution,"[55] namely the two pillars of the Constitution. The Multicultural Constitution was safeguarded through the protection of the right to prior consultation – an expression of participatory democracy to which the Constitution is particularly committed.[56] For this reason, the lawsuit argued that all Colombian indigenous peoples and culturally diverse black communities have a right to be part of the legal decision-making processes that affect them directly. Under this interpretation, prior consultation does not promote a private interest. Rather, it promotes a collective interest – namely, the consolidation of Colombian democracy. The Multicultural Constitution is also protected by linking the rights of cultural minorities with the Colombian state's interest in the protection of Colombia's cultural diversity. Again, what is defended in the claim and in the ruling is not just the legitimate interests of particular cultural communities but the model of state that the Constitution establishes: a state that recognizes and seeks to duly accommodate the cultural diversity of its citizens.

The Ecological Constitution is defended by the lawsuit in an indirect manner. The country's biodiversity is safeguarded through protection of the right to prior consultation of indigenous peoples and culturally diverse black communities whose religious rites, collective symbolic references, and very material survival are closely connected with the spaces that they have inhabited ancestrally.[57] Additionally, Colombian cultural minorities, especially indigenous peoples, do not have a relationship of domination and exploitation with nature, but one of

---

[54] Some of the components of the Multicultural Constitution are the following: the definition of Colombia as a participative and *pluralist* state (Article 1) and its recognition of the equality and dignity of all cultures (Article 70). Other relevant provisions are: Articles 7, 8, 10, 63, 68, 171, 176, 287–289, 329, and 330.

[55] In case C-595 of 2010, MP Jorge Ivan Palacio Palacio, the Constitutional Court stated that the Environmental Constitution is constituted by thirty-three provisions. Some of the most important provisions in this regard include arts. 58, 67, 79, 80, 58, 282.

[56] Art. 1.

[57] Regarding this point, several Colombian Indian leaders point out that "[t]his right to autonomy, which we the Indian people have over our territories and our resources, must be valued and respected before any kind of action or policy which affects it is undertaken or managed. Only the knowledge that supports this autonomy provides tools and elements necessary to make proposals which will lead to our conservation as peoples and to the possibilities of providing balanced management of our territories, guaranteeing not only our survival but the future of the nation": C. Z. Arregocés and V. T. Danilo, "Autonomía y cultura en los Kággaba, Iky y Wiwa de la Sierra Nevada de Santa Marta," in *Organización Regional Embera Wounaan (OREWA), Autonomía Territorial y Jurisdicción Indígena en Del Olvido Surgimos para Traer Nuevas Esperanzas* (Bogota: Ministerio De Justicia y del Derecho, 1997), p. 141 (hereinafter Autonomía Territorial).

synergy and protection.[58] As a consequence, the defense of the right to prior consultation is a defense of the natural riches that exist in the country.[59]

Thus, the arguments of the claim in particular, and the related strategic litigation project in general, are directly connected with the global movement for environmental justice.[60] Both the litigation and the movement have the normative objectives of the fair distribution of environmental goods, their sovereign administration by all of its owners, and the prevention of environmental damage.[61] The global movement for environmental justice and the strategic litigation project do not see environmental, socioeconomic, and cultural issues as separate, watertight compartments. Promoting social and cultural justice implies promoting environmental justice. The distribution of environmental resources has a direct effect on people's quality of life, particularly for vulnerable or historically discriminated-against groups. In addition, this distribution partially determines people's potential to construct their individual and collective life plans in an autonomous manner. Similarly, the global movement for environmental justice and the strategic litigation project regard the national and international distribution of environmental benefits and burdens as closely intertwined. The national dimension sheds light on the unequal allocation of environmental resources and damages within a state; the international dimension reflects the unequal distribution of environmental resources among states, particularly among countries of the North and South. Yet,

---

[58] This association can be clearly seen in several texts that appear in the memoirs of the IV Latin-American Conference of the Legal Anthropology Network. For example, Iza Rona dos Santos states that "I speak in the name of my Macuxi, Wapichana, Ingarikó, Taurepang, and Patamona relatives. I do it so that others will hear their efforts to defend that which we define as the primordial reason of our existence: TERRITORY, without which life in its fullest does not exist [. . .]. In silence, our main strategy is not to abandon our ancestral territories; to do so is to abandon our life [. . .] the cosmological world of these peoples, the relationship with the land and nature provide full conservation of the environment in an area rich in biological diversity and important springs of water": I. R. dos Santos, "Raposa Sierra del Sol: Thirty Years of Struggle for an Irrevocable Rights," in *Pueblos en Lucha* 10, 17 (IV Latin American Congress of the Legal Anthropologic Network, 2004). See also M. Melo, *El caso Sarayaku y los derechos humanos:¿Por qué Sarayaku constituye un caso emblemático de exigibilidad de derechos a nivel internacional?*, in *Pueblos en Lucha* 10, 17 (IV Latin American Congress of the Legal Anthropologic Network, 2004), pp. 50–51 and J. Serrano, *Conclusiones de la mesa sobre las experiencias de lucha de los pueblos indígenas*, in *Pueblos en Lucha* 10, 17 (IV Latin American Congress of the Legal Anthropologic Network, 2004), pp. 23, 26.

[59] The argument that connects cultural minorities with the environment was strategically useful in this project. Yet it is theoretically problematic in as much as it essentializes and ecologizes cultural minorities. See L. Ariza, *Derecho, Saber e Identidad Indígena* (Bogota: Siglo del Hombre Editores, 2009). See also, D. Bonilla, "Indígenas Urbanos y Derechos Culturales: Los Límites del Multiculturalismo Liberal" (2011) 7 *Revista Direito GV* 569.

[60] C. Crawford, "La protección social y cultural y la justicia ambiental: lecciones del modelo colombiano," in D. Bonilla (ed.), *Justicia Colectiva, Medio Ambiente y Democracia Participativa* (Bogota: Universidad de los Andes, 2009), pp. 30–35.

[61] S. Krakoff, "Tribal Sovereignty and Environmental Justice," in K Mutz, M. Bryner, C. Gary, and Douglas Kennedy (eds.), *Justice and Natural Resources* (California: Island Press, 2002), pp. 161–183.

518   *International Law, Cultural Diversity, and the Environment*

both dimensions are in many cases strongly connected, as illustrated by the fact that 20 percent of the world's population consumes 85 percent of the planet's timber, that these consumers are mostly affluent individuals in the global North and South, and that most timber is harvested in poor rural areas of the global South.[62]

In this case, the objective of the strategic litigation project was to allow indigenous peoples and culturally diverse black communities to be a part of the decision-making processes that affect them directly. More precisely, the objective was to enable these communities to make their voices heard with respect to all of those legal or administrative measures that might affect their territories and therefore the integrity of their cultures. However, the strategic litigation project does not just have the objective of protecting the interests of cultural minorities. The ecologically sensitive way in which these communities have historically managed the natural resources they control also benefits the dominant culture by protecting the country's biodiversity. Protecting the Orinoquía, Amazon, and Sierra Nevada de Santa Marta regions, for example, is in the interests of all of the members of the political community.

International environmental law also supports the connection between environmental justice and the strategic litigation project.[63] Although international environmental law arguments were not explicit in the litigation discussed earlier, the lawsuit is consistent with various key instruments in this area of international law. For example, the Rio Declaration on Environment and Development (Rio Declaration) states that signatory states should promote citizen participation in all of the decisions related to the environment (Principle 10) and the Declaration recognizes the importance that the traditions of indigenous and other "local communities" have in the management of the environment and the achievement of sustainable development (Principle 22).[64] The Rio Declaration also indicates that states should support the identity and culture of these communities, and makes them participants in the decisions to allow for the advancement of sustainable development (Principle 22).[65] The United Nations Framework Convention on Climate Change[66] and the Convention on Biological Diversity also recognize the various obligations that the parties have in the protection of the environment, protecting the principle of participatory democracy, and promoting the participation of vulnerable and historically marginalized groups in the processes of making

---

[62] W. Sachs, *Planet Dialectics: Explorations in Environment and Development* (London: Zed Books, 1999), p. 171.

[63] See notes 61, 62, and 63.

[64] *Rio Declaration on Environment and Development*, Rio de Janeiro, 14 June 1992, UN Doc. A/CONF.151/26 (vol. 1); 31 ILM 874 (1992).

[65] Ibid.

[66] *United Nations Framework Convention on Climate Change*, New York, 9 May 1992, in force 21 March 1994, 177 UNTS 107/[1994] ATS 2/31 ILM 849 (1992) [hereinafter UNFCCC].

decisions that seek to prevent climate change and protect biodiversity.[67] Finally, these same principles of participation and recognition of cultural minorities are recognized in the Declaration of Forest Principles.[68]

The strategic litigation project did have a component directly connected to national and international environmental law. GDIP filed a second lawsuit before the Constitutional Court that focused on environmental issues only. In this lawsuit, GDIP questions some articles of the GFL that violated the rights to a healthy environment (Constitution of 1991, Article 79) and sustainable development. This lawsuit also mentions explicitly the right to a healthy environment that is part of the Protocol of San Salvador (Article 11) and the ICESCR (Article 12(b)). The former recognizes the right to a healthy environment as an autonomous right, while the latter recognizes it as a prerequisite for the effective enjoyment of the right to health. Another key argument of the second lawsuit is the principle of progressivity in the application of social rights – in this case, the right to a healthy environment. In the opinion of GDIP and its allies, the GFL was regressive with regard to the levels of protection of the right to a healthy environment already attained under existing environmental legal norms in Colombia.

This second lawsuit was filed a short time after the first, and was regarded as Plan B in case the lawsuit, which was based on the right to prior consultation, failed. Because the right to prior consultation lawsuit succeeded in having the entire GFL declared unconstitutional, the second lawsuit, which only challenged specific provisions of the GFL, was rendered moot. The second lawsuit – namely, the environmental lawsuit – only attacked some clauses of the GFL: those that could be questioned from a constitutional environmental law perspective. GDIP and its allies considered that many clauses of the GFL were questionable from a political, moral, or technical viewpoint. However, they also believed that these clauses could not be considered unconstitutional.

In sum, the impact of the litigation project, which culminated in the decision of the Colombian Constitutional Court declaring the GFL to be unconstitutional, made strategic use of international law on cultural minorities before a national court to defend the interests of indigenous peoples, culturally diverse black communities, and the environment. This litigation also made strategic use of international environmental law in two distinct ways: as the basis of the second claim brought before the Constitutional Court and as a means of enriching the arguments in the successful first claim. The most important consequence of this lawsuit was its contribution to strengthening the voice of cultural minorities in the Colombian public sphere. The Constitutional Court's ruling established a

---

[67] With respect to the first point see Articles 3(1) and 4(1–i) of the UNFCCC, see note 66. With regard to the other two points see e.g. Articles 1 and 8(j) of the *Convention on Biological Diversity*, Rio de Janeiro, 5 June 1992, in force 29 December 1993, [1993] ATS 32 / 1760 UNTS 79 / 31 ILM 818 (1992).

[68] See e.g., Articles 1(a), 2(d), and 5(a) of the Forest Principles, see note 11.

precedent that partially rearranged the relations of power between the national government and cultural minorities. The ruling prohibited the Colombian state from issuing statutes or administrative acts that directly affect indigenous peoples and culturally diverse black communities without consulting them, as it had historically done. In addition, this ruling became a powerful tool to protect the rights of cultural minorities in related cases of great political importance. In subsequent cases, the Court declared other statutes unconstitutional, including the Rural Development Statute[69] and the Mining Code,[70] on which cultural minorities were not consulted despite the fact that these statutes affected them directly.

However, this does not mean that the political and socioeconomic situation of the Colombian cultural minorities has been radically changed. Indigenous peoples and culturally diverse black communities remain at the bottom of the Colombian socioeconomic hierarchy.[71] Likewise, the armed conflict continues to affect them in a disproportionate manner,[72] and the concept of prior consultation continues to be interpreted by government and various national and international companies as a formality that impedes economic development.[73] Undoubtedly, the law has limited capacity to transform social reality. Nevertheless, the legal triumph, although partial, has enabled Colombian cultural minorities to resist the political and legal dynamics that seek to keep their voices marginalized – dynamics that are not only domestic but also international. The North–South divide negatively affects indigenous groups and culturally diverse black communities. They are both impacted by domestic and international forces, multinational and national companies, international institutions such as the IMF and the World Bank, and national and foreign governments that are interested in exploiting the natural resources that can be found within these cultural minorities' territories. The right to prior consultation is a small tool for resisting these forces, albeit a relatively powerful one.

Certainly, we have to be attentive in ensuring that this legal achievement does not bring about the political demobilization of cultural minorities' organizations or their allies in civil society. This is only one of the fronts on which we must work to protect the rights of these communities. Nevertheless, it is worth noting

---

[69] Sentencia C-175 de 2009, M.P. Luis Ernesto Vargas Silva.

[70] Sentencia C-366 de 2011, M.P. Luis Ernesto Vargas Silva.

[71] See e.g. D. Bonilla, "Las comunidades negras en Colombia: entre la diversidad cultural, la diferencia racial y los derechos," in A. Viana (ed.), *Repensar la Pluralidad* (Valencia: Tirant Lo Blanche, 2009).

[72] See e.g. E. Restrepo and A. Rojas (eds.), *Conflicto e (In)visibilidad: Retos en los Estudios de la Gente Negra en Colombia* (Popayan: Editorial Universidad del Cauca, 2004); UNICEF, "Los Pueblos Indígenas en Colombia: Derechos, Políticas y Desafios," www.acnur.org.

[73] C. Rodríguez-Garavito, "Ethnicity.gov: Global Governance, Indigenous Peoples, and the Right to Prior Consultation in Social Minefields" (2011) 18 *Indiana Journal of Global Legal Studies* 263.

that this is a step in the right direction, and one in which international law played an important role. Criticized strongly in the past for its liberal character, its imperial uses, and its exclusionary character,[74] international law on cultural minorities in general, and ILO Convention 169 in particular, was used strategically and efficiently to increase the levels of cultural and environmental justice in Colombia, a country of the global South.

3. THE BLOCK OF CONSTITUTIONALITY, THE NATIONAL COURTS AND THE DEFENSE OF HUMAN RIGHTS: EXPLANATORY ARGUMENTS

The use of international law in national courts is controversial in some legal contexts. The position held on this issue is linked to the monist or dualist view to which countries are committed. Dualists believe that international law and national law are two different and autonomous legal systems and argue that international law has to be incorporated in an explicit way – for example, through statute – in order to make it domestically enforceable. On the contrary, monists argue that international law and national law form a unity. International law, for monists, does not have to be translated into national law to make it internally enforceable. In the United States, for example, there has been notable reticence in accepting that international law may create rights that are judicially enforceable in domestic courts.[75] International treaties are the supreme law of the land in the United States, but only if they are self-executing or if they have been implemented by legislation.[76] In contrast, many countries of the global South are receptive to the use of international treaties by national courts. The examples of South Africa, India, and Colombia are illustrative. Section 232 of the Constitution of the Republic of South Africa 1996 states that customary international law is law in the country provided it does not contradict the Constitution or an Act of Parliament, and Section 233 states that the courts must always favor an interpretation of internal law that is consistent with international law over one that is not. In India, the case law of the Supreme Court of Justice that interprets Article 51(c)

[74] S. Lightfoot, "Indigenous Rights in International Politics: The Case of 'Overcompliant' Liberal States" (2008) 33 *Alternatives: Global, Local, Political* 83; R. Stavenhagen, "Los Derechos Indígenas en el Sistema Internacional: Un Sujeto en Construcción" (1998) 26 *Revista IIDH* 81; A. Xanthaki, "Indigenous Rights In International Law Over the Last 10 Years and Future Developments" (2009) 10 *Melbourne Journal of International Law* 27.

[75] See also, D. Sloss, "When Do Treaties Create Individually Enforceable Rights? The Supreme Court Ducks the Issue in Hamdan and Sanchez-Llamas" (2006) 45 *Columbia Journal of Transnational Law* 29; D. Sloss, "Domestic Application of Treaties," in D. Hollis (ed.), *The Oxford Guide to Treaties* (Oxford: Oxford University Press, 2011), pp. 373–376.

[76] On issues related to extraterritoriality and human rights see *Kiobel* v *Royal Dutch Petroleum Co.*, 133 S. Ct. 1659 (2013) and *Alien Tort Statute*, 28 U.S.C. § 1350 (1976). See also B. Stephens, "Extraterritoriality and Human Rights After Kiobel" (2013) 28 *Maryland Journal of International Law* 256.

522 *International Law, Cultural Diversity, and the Environment*

of the Constitution of India has promoted the application of international law in the internal order as a form of protecting human rights.[77] In Colombia, as discussed in the first part of this chapter, Article 93 of the Constitution and the case law of the Constitutional Court interpreting this article have recognized that international human rights law has the same status as the Constitution or should be used to interpret domestic law.[78] Consequently, in these three countries at least, some aspects of international environmental law (particularly environmental human rights law) can be enforced domestically.[79]

In this section I will present four arguments that, from my perspective, explain why international law may be (and has been) applied by national courts to defend the interests of vulnerable groups in the global South and protect the environment. These arguments are based on the Colombian case study, but are generalizable to other countries of the global South where similar legal and political conditions prevail.

The first explanatory argument is historical. Colombia, like other countries of the global South, has experienced a long history of human rights violations and abuses of power by the state.[80] International law is perceived as a useful and legitimate instrument to stop these transgressions because it is backed by the international community (particularly certain powerful states) and may impose high political costs on violators. These instrumental arguments create incentives that promote the defense of people's rights in the internal order and disincentivize the arbitrary use of power by the State. The legal arguments that explain this perception are directly related to three weaknesses of internal law. First, it does not always have substantive or procedural legal norms that recognize or are able to enforce certain rights. Second, although rules exist, they are no more than paper rules. Third, legal actors do not always trust the existing rules, given that they have been used by the State as a means to violate people's rights rather than protect them.

However, the violation of rights is not the only historical argument that explains why the country has peacefully adopted a form like the block of constitutionality, allowing national courts to apply international law to resolve internal conflicts.

---

[77] S. K. Agarwal, "Implementation of International Law in India: Role of Judiciary," http://dx.doi.org.

[78] The block of constitutionality is explicitly recognized by the constitutions of various Latin American countries. See e.g. Constitution of the Argentine Nation (section 75), Political Constitution of the Republic of Chile (Articles 5-2) and Political Constitution of the Republic of Nicaragua (Article 46).

[79] See M. Anderson and P. Galizzi, *International Environmental Law in National Courts* (London: The British Institute of International and Comparative Law, 2002); D. Bodansky and J. Brunnee, "The Role of National Courts in the Field of International Environmental Law" (1998) 7 *Review of European Community & International Environmental Law* 11.

[80] A detailed history of the violation of human rights in Colombia can be found in Centro Nacional de Memoria Histórica, "Basta Ya, Colombia: Memorias de Guerra y Dignidad," www.centrodememoriahistorica.gov.co.

This phenomenon is also explained by the following arguments. On the one hand, the block of constitutionality was a legal institution that was transplanted from France. Colombia (and the global South in general) is usually described as a weak context for the production of legal knowledge. Consequently, the importation of this institution from a country that is usually described as a strong context for the production of legal knowledge facilitated its rooting and application in the national legal system. The process of importing the "block of constitutionality" was made possible, simple, and fluid given the differences in the legal capital of the importing and exporting countries.

Like much of the global South, Colombia is often considered a weak context for the production of legal knowledge for three interrelated reasons.[81] First, Colombia is considered a minor representative of one of the world's greatest legal traditions: the civil law tradition.[82] The Colombian legal order is usually seen as an iteration of the civil law tradition, the primary sources for which are German and French law.[83] Thus, Colombian law and legal academia are described as spaces of reproduction and dissemination of knowledge created in the centers of power of the global North. This argument is reinforced by the fact that Colombia, even though it does not belong to the common law tradition, has been described over the past decades as an avid receptor and disseminator country of legal products from the United States.[84] Second, Colombian law is usually described as formalist, and therefore as a limited legal space.[85] Thus, the national legal order is described as complete, coherent, closed, and univocal. In addition, this legal system is understood as founded on a thin democratic theory that has as pillars a radically functional interpretation of the principle of separation of powers and a mechanical

[81] D. Bonilla, "Introduction," in D. Bonilla (ed.), *Constitutionalism of the Global South* (New York: Cambridge University Press, 2013), p. 377.

[82] See B. de Sousa Santos, "Three Metaphors for a New Conception of Law: The Frontier, the Baroque and the South" (1995) 29 *Law and Society Review* 579; M. van Hoecke and M. Warrington, "Legal Cultures, Legal Paradigms and Legal Doctrine: Towards a New Model for Comparative Law" (1998) 47 *International* Comparative *Law Quarterly* 498 at 498–499.

[83] D. L. Medina, *Teoría Impura del Derecho: La Transformación de la Cultura Jurídica Latinoamericana* (Bogota: Universidad de los Andes, Universidad Nacional, 2004), pp. 129–233.

[84] See J. H. Merryman and R. Pérez-Perdomo, *The Civil Law Tradition: An Introduction to the Legal Systems of Europe and Latin America* (Stanford: Stanford University Press, 2007), pp. 57, 60; R. D. Kelemen and E. C. Sibbitt, "The Globalization of American Law" (2004) 58 *International Organization* 103; J. H. Merryman, "Comparative Law and Social Change: On the Origins, Style, Decline, and Revival of the Law and Development Movement" (1977) 25 *The American Journal of Comparative Law* 484 at 484–489; K. Ritttich, "The Future of Law and Development: Second-Generation Reforms and the Incorporation of the Social," in D. Trubek and A. Santos (eds.), *The New Law and Economic Development* (Cambridge: Cambridge University Press 2006), pp. 203–252.

[85] See e.g. E. A. Laing, "Revolution in Latin American Legal Education: The Colombian Experience" (1974) 6 *Lawyer of the Americas* 373 at 373–376; R. Pérez-Perdomo, "Rule of Law and Lawyers in Latin America" (2005) 603 *Annals of the American Academy of Political and Social Science* 110.

theory of adjudication.[86] The Colombian legal tradition is therefore seen as a poor source of legal knowledge that should be nurtured from the products generated by other richer and more textured wells of production. Finally, both the Colombian legal system and its legal academy are typically described as ineffective.[87] This argument suggests that social control in Colombia is not really achieved through law, but rather by other means, such as violence or religion. Colombian law is seen as an empty formality that cannot generate the instruments necessary to achieve the most common objectives of law, namely social order, social justice, facilitation of collective action, and the peaceful resolution of disputes. Similarly, the Colombian legal academy (and, by analogy, others in the global South) is deemed to lack the human and financial resources needed to create legal knowledge, such as an adequate number of law journals, appropriate procedures to evaluate the articles received, and dynamic fora to critique and debate the knowledge produced. The result is a dependence on, and a feeling of inferiority with respect to, the academies of the global North.[88]

Paradoxically, this negative representation of the Colombian legal order, despite its important descriptive and normative weaknesses,[89] has permitted the use of international law as an instrument for the defense of the rights of the most vulnerable groups in the country and for the protection of the country's natural resources. This viewpoint, which has been projected from the outside and internalized by a large number of Colombian legal actors, has opened the national legal order to the international community. It has allowed for the use of instruments such as the ILO Convention 169 and the San Salvador Protocol, which includes the right to a healthy environment, in order to ensure that historically disadvantaged groups in Colombia such as indigenous peoples and culturally diverse black communities are able to protect their legitimate interests.

Furthermore, the transplant of the block of constitutionality from France to Colombia has also been fluid and smooth because it has been construed in Colombia as an institutional mechanism to solve problems similar to those addressed by this doctrine in the exporting country, namely the protection of human rights. It is widely recognized that the French Council of Constitutionality created the block of constitutionality in 1971.[90] As the French Constitution of

---

[86] D. Bonilla Maldonado, "El formalismo jurídico, la educación jurídica y la práctica profesional del derecho en Latinoamérica," in H. Olea (ed.), *Derecho y Pueblo Mapuche* (Santiago: Universidad Diego Portales, 2013).

[87] See J. L. Esquirol, "The Fictions of Latin American Law" (1977) 297 *Utah Law Review* 425; J. L. Esquirol, "The Failed Law of Latin America" (2008) 56 *American Journal of Comparative Law* 75 at 94–95.

[88] D. Bonilla Maldonado, "Legal Clinics in the Global North and South: Between Equality and Subordination" (2013) 16 *Yale Human Rights and Development Law Journal* 176.

[89] For an analysis of the normative and descriptive weaknesses of these arguments see note 73, pp. 14–21.

[90] Case D-44, of July 16 1971. For an analysis of the origin of the institution, see E. Carpio Marcos, "Bloque de Constitucionalidad y Proceso de Inconstitucionalidad de las Leyes" (2005) 4 *Revista Iberoamericana de Derecho Procesal Constitucional* 79 at 79–114.

1958 did not contain a bill of rights, this tribunal interpreted the Constitution's preamble to include a referral clause that integrated the Declaration of the Rights of Man and Citizen of 1789 and the preamble of the Constitution of 1946 into the 1958 Constitution.[91] In this way, the Council of Constitutionality incorporated the individual rights of the Declaration into the French Constitution, as well as the principles protecting rights established in the preamble of the Constitution of 1948.[92] Colombia's adoption of the block of constitutionality provides a good illustration of the functionalist theory of comparative law.[93] From this perspective, the journey of a legal institution across national borders is explained because the institution is capable of providing a solution to a problem that exists in both the importing and the exporting countries. The functionalists argue that law can travel because distinct political communities face similar problems and because it is inefficient to create new legal forms when forms already exist that are capable of providing a solution.

The second argument that explains the use of international law by Colombian courts and legal actors is political. International law is an instrument that is utilized to legitimize legal arguments before courts, and serves as the basis for decisions that they issue. Likewise, it is a tool that individuals and institutions involved in controversial and difficult legal cases use to protect themselves from those economic, political, or military powers that may negatively affect them. In Colombia, international law is highly respected due to its origin in the international community, its apparent neutrality in the face of internal conflicts that are argued before courts, its objectives (the protection of human rights and the environment), and its ability to restrain the national authorities' abuses of power. For example, the Colombian Constitutional Court has on several occasions ruled against the state in cases involving Colombia's right to a healthy environment, by invoking the right to health as interpreted by the UN Committee on Economic, Social and Cultural Rights.[94] This reference to international law has also legitimated the Constitutional Court's protection of the right to a healthy environment, recognized by the Colombian Constitution by connecting it to the rights to health and life.[95]

The case of the GFL illustrates this argument very well. The Constitutional Court can argue (to the national government and to the large national and international companies interested in exploiting the country's forest resources) that the unconstitutionality of the statute is a consequence not of a particular

[91] See Uprimny, note 27.

[92] F. R. Llorente, "El Bloque de Constitucionalidad" (2009) 9 *Revista Española de Derecho Constitucional* 27.

[93] See A. Watson, *Society and Legal Change*, 2nd ed. (Edinburgh: Scottish Academic Press, 2001); A. Watson, "Legal Transplants and European Private Law" (2000) 4(4)*Electronic Journal of Comparative Law.*

[94] See e.g. Cases T-851 of 2010, M.P. Humberto Sierra Porto and T-707of 2012, M.P. Luis Ernesto Vargas Silva.

[95] Ibid.

interpretation of a national legal norm but of the application of an international legal norm that has been interpreted by numerous international institutions and national courts. The decision to declare the GFL unconstitutional is therefore a consequence of the application of an order that is perceived as "superior" and which does not have a particular position with respect to the government, forest companies, or the model of development that the GFL promotes. This same rhetorical strategy enabled the GDIP to argue that the unconstitutionality of the GFL was the consequence of a "super-legitimate" mandate stemming from an international instrument that enjoys the support of both the international community and the Colombian state (which approved this treaty). The legitimizing power of international law enhanced the persuasiveness of GDIP's arguments before the Constitutional Court, the national government, and forest companies. It was also useful in protecting its members from criticism received on various political and social fronts – for example, from the Ministry of Agriculture and a number of logging companies.

The third explanatory argument is cognitive. International law, its norms, and its authoritative interpretations reduce the costs incurred by national courts and other legal actors in articulating the necessary arguments on which to base a lawsuit or a ruling. The time, energy, and financial resources necessary to create original arguments that are persuasive for the multiple audiences usually involved in a hard case make the use of international law particularly attractive. The arguments are readily available in the global marketplace of legal ideas; legal actors only have to take them and connect them with the facts and the objectives they hope to achieve. This argument is particularly relevant when the legal actors have a significant workload, as is the case for the Colombian Constitutional Court. Between 2000 and 2012, the Constitutional Court, constituted by nine judges, issued between 1,000 and 1,200 rulings per year.[96] The number of rulings produced by a court like the Colombian one makes it difficult for its members to be able to focus on the creation of new interpretations or legal theories for each of the cases they decide. In addition, many of these cases are highly complex and are politically, economically, and morally controversial. Thus, having a set of solid and legitimate arguments at their disposal facilitates their work enormously.

The fourth and final explanatory argument is strategic: the need to foster alliances among various civil society organizations to ensure that these kinds of lawsuits will be successful. These alliances are critical in enabling efforts to utilize international law in a counterhegemonic manner to be carried out to fruition. The block of constitutionality (which incorporates international law) provides a set of persuasive arguments around which a variety of social organizations and academic institutions can coalesce. These alliances create a critical mass that makes

---

[96] M. Iturralde, "Access to Constitutional Justice in Colombia," in D. Bonilla (ed.), *Constitutionalism of the Global South* (Cambridge: Cambridge University Press, 2013), p. 377.

these kinds of lawsuits visible and makes explicit to the public that these rights are recognized and endorsed by a diverse and broad group of civil society organizations and institutions. These alliances also facilitate the efficient use of scarce resources. Each member of the coalition contributes to the achievement of common objectives. Universities mainly contribute their expertise in particular disciplines. Although the law is a key tool for these types of strategic litigation projects, it is not the only relevant one. Many of these projects require interdisciplinary work to understand the problems that are faced and to articulate arguments that are persuasive to the various audiences involved in the dialogue, such as the courts, public opinion, the local communities, or the executive branch. Disciplines like anthropology, sociology, and political science, to name just three, are important for the success of these kinds of counterhegemonic uses of international law. The various social organizations contribute their capacities for political organization and mobilization, as well as their close contact with the communities that the litigation project aims to serve. Obviously, depending on the case and the characteristics of the universities or social organizations involved, the contributions they make may vary. Some social organizations are more competent in certain disciplines than their partners at the universities, and some academics have noteworthy experience and skills for political organization and mobilization.

The lawsuit was successful to a large degree because it was supported by an alliance among environmental organizations, social organizations that represent the interests of cultural minorities, and academia. The strength of the legal arguments presented, the receptiveness of the Constitutional Court, the public discussion that the case generated, and the subsequent use that was made of the ruling to challenge the constitutionality of other statutes on which cultural minorities had not been consulted are directly related to the diversity of the groups that came together to bring the lawsuit. The Public Interest Law Group contributed the bulk of the legal arguments. The Colombian Commission of Jurists, the National Indigenous Organization of Colombia, and the Process of Black Communities, among other organizations, contributed their capacity to mobilize the bases that they serve and public opinion, as well as their legal knowledge. The strategic litigation project could not have been developed without the joint efforts of these and other social organizations and academic institutions.

4. CONCLUSION

Historically, the dominant theories of international law have had states as their unit of analysis and have concentrated their efforts on the study of the formal sources of international law – that is, the international bodies and courts. The efforts of most doctrinalists and theorists of international law have been focused on the systematization of its norms, the articulation of its historical or philosophical basis, or the creation of normative horizons toward which its norms and practices should be directed. In contrast, critical theorists have sought to make explicit the exclusionary practices, the imperial uses, the ideological character, and the incoherencies of international law and its institutions. However, these theoretical efforts have often paid insufficient attention to counterhegemonic uses of international law by social movements. This kind of critical analysis can obscure international law's potential to contribute to emancipation or social resistance; it may cause a valuable instrument for defending the interests of the countries of the global South in general, and of their disadvantaged groups in particular, to be removed from the tool box available to legal actors. The strategic litigation project examined in this article is an example of international law's emancipatory potential. Describing and analyzing these kinds of cases can also be useful for creating more and better categories that may generate a theoretical framework to help us understand and evaluate what we could call "counterhegemonic international law."

25

The Contours of Energy Justice

Lakshman Guruswamy[*]

1. INTRODUCTION

Globally, around 2.8 billion people (the "Other Third" or "energy-poor") have little or no access to beneficial energy to meet their needs for cooking, heating, water, sanitation, illumination, transportation, or basic mechanical power.[1] The dearth of energy applies to their households; their chances of making a living through agriculture, industry, or crafts; and the hospitals and schools serving their communities.

More than 95 percent of the energy-poor (EP) live either in sub-Saharan Africa or developing Asia, predominantly (84 percent) in rural areas. They cook by burning polluting energy such as biomass, resulting in 3.5 million deaths every year, primarily of women and children.[2] The lack of motive power or mechanical energy for pumping water for domestic and agricultural use, plowing fields, transport, metal works, and agro-processing (such as grinding food), thwarts the possibility of taking up a livelihood requiring energy use. Generating income through small businesses requires energy to transport and distribute goods and services to markets, and for telecommunications. Even the most rudimentary forms of rural agriculture need energy for water-pumping, irrigation, plowing, harvesting, milling, grinding, and processing food. Water treatment plants that provide safe drinking water for communities and schools require energy. Polluted drinking water causes 3.5 million deaths per year, largely among children. The lack of energy impairs functioning of hospitals and schools. Hospitals need energy for refrigerating vital medications and vaccinations; education calls for energy for the

---

[*] This chapter reproduces duly noted past and pending work of the author. I am indebted to Elizabeth Neville for her diligent and perspicacious research.
[1] See text and footnotes in the second section of this chapter.
[2] *The Lancet*, "Global Burden of Disease, Injuries, and Risk Factors Study 2013," July 22, 2013, www.thelancet.com.

530   *The Contours of Energy Justice*

lighting and heating of schools; and a lack of energy for illumination prevents women and children from studying at night and makes life dangerous after dark.

Access to efficient and affordable energy services is also a prerequisite for achieving the Millennium Development Goal (MDG) relating to poverty eradication. The MDGs form a blueprint agreed to by all the world's countries and leading development institutions in the year 2000 to meet the needs of the world's poorest. There are eight MDGs, which range from halving extreme poverty to halting the spread of HIV/AIDS, providing universal primary education, and promoting gender equality, and they were expected to be met by the target date of 2015. They did not, however, institutionalize a right to energy.[3]

Responding to the need for energy, the United Nations (UN) declared 2012 the "International Year of Sustainable Energy for All" and declared the entire decade the "Decade of Sustainable Energy for All." [4] Moreover, the UN announced a goal of universal, primarily electrical, energy access by 2030. While access to electricity must remain the ultimate objective, the daunting additional costs of electricity and the time it will take to do so – realistically, thirty years – will shunt the energy-poor into limbo unless interim measures like those suggested by this chapter are also taken. Beneficial energy, based on appropriate sustainable energy technologies (ASETs), can provide such intermediate energy. ASETs bridge the gap between capital-intensive electricity and the traditional subsistence technologies of the EP. ASETs include: Clean fuels; clean cookstoves; illumination by photovoltaic lights; decentralized mini grids based on solar, wind, and biomass-generated electricity; treadle pumps; improved harnesses and yokes which boost the performance of draft cattle; better axels for transport by cart; simple windmills for pumping water; grain-grinding appliances; and low-cost bicycles.

In 2015 and the years following, the world community will measure and refine the MDGs. As noted, providing access to energy is not discretely set out as one of the MDGs at present, though the Global Conference on Rural Energy Access, hosted by the United Nations in early December 2013, agreed that the reformulation of international economic development goals should include a discrete goal to "make sustainable energy for all a reality, and through this, help to eradicate poverty."[5] The aide memoire of the Global Conference on Rural Energy Access reiterated: "There is a strong nexus between energy and other important development factors such as education, health, gender, environment, economic growth, food security, and water. Sustainable access to modern energy services is a critical input and catalyst for improving the productive capacities and

---

[3] United Nations, "Millennium Development Goals and Beyond 2015," www.un.org.

[4] United Nations, "Sustainable Energy for All," www.un.org.

[5] "Rural Energy Access: A Nexus Approach to Sustainable Development and Poverty Eradication," Global Conference, Economic Commission for Africa, Addis Ababa, Ethiopia, December 4–6, 2013.

welfare of rural isolated communities, leading to poverty eradication and sustainable development."[6]

This chapter aims to integrate the hitherto segmented and fragmented approaches to the challenge of access to energy on the foundations of energy justice. It posits that the needs of the energy-poor must be addressed within the ethical, political, and legal framework of sustainable development (SD). In order that the universally accepted principles of SD be applied in earnest, it is essential that the world accept a rational justification for SD. The great political philosopher John Rawls provides a cogent justification, particularly in the *Law of Peoples*. This article briefly reviews his thesis and arrives at a crucial conclusion: SD, as informed by Rawls, obligates the world to address the needs of the EP.

Part 2 of the chapter demonstrates why energy is the primary determinant of human progress. Part 3 explains the factual and sociopolitical phenomenon of the energy-poor, who lack clean energy for cooking, illumination, sanitation, drinking water, and mechanical or motive power. Part 4 makes the case for using ASETs to supplement the quest for electricity and provide an intermediary source of energy during the transition to electricity. Part 5 restates the conceptual and theoretical grounds found in moral and political philosophy and jurisprudence, positing that the world ought to remedy the lack of access to energy.

2. THE IMPORTANCE OF ENERGY[7]

Energy's presence and influence in the human and social world is essentially ubiquitous.[8] Humans are endlessly engaged in transforming or converting energy found in the environment into energy useful for human purposes.

By the late nineteenth century, energy demand in industrialized countries had grown considerably.[9] This demand was met by the development of electric energy, an incredibly versatile energy source that can be transmitted over vast distances and put to a wide variety of uses. The first electric power plants were hydroelectric facilities relying on flowing water as their energy source, converting mechanical energy to electrical energy. Subsequent power plants have employed fossil fuels, and more recently nuclear fission and geothermal, wind, and solar power, to produce electricity. The development of alternating current technology allowed the transmission of electricity over long distances, enabling the development of regional power transmission grids to distribute the electricity generated

---

[6] Ibid.

[7] This section is based on Chapter 4 of L. Guruswamy, *International Energy and Poverty: The Emerging Contours* (Routledge, 2015, in press).

[8] E. A. Rosa, G. E. Machlis, and K. M. Keating, "Energy and Society" (1988) 14 *Annual Review of Sociology* 149.

[9] J. R. Fanchi, *Energy in the 21st Century* (Singapore: World Scientific Publishing Company, 2011), p. 151.

532 *The Contours of Energy Justice*

across a network of large-scale power plants.[10] By the early twentieth century, electricity had emerged as the favored method for transmitting energy, and researchers responded with a range of products that extended the ways in which humankind could apply this electricity.[11]

3. THE ENERGY-POOR[12]

Conceptually, the sociopolitical world has often been divided into developing and developed countries, or North and South.[13] However, the developing world is not a monolith; there are divisions and distinctions within it. For example, the least developed countries (LDCs) are a subset of nations within the developing world. The LDCs consist of forty-nine countries and 767 million people, located primarily in Africa and Asia. The LDCs have been officially identified by the UN as "least developed" in light of their low income (three-year average gross national income (GNI) per capita of less than US\$992); weak human assets (low nutrition, high mortality, lack of school enrollment, high illiteracy); high economic vulnerability; exposure to natural shocks and disasters; prevalence of trade shocks; economic smallness; and economic remoteness.[14]

A joint report of the United Nations Development Programme (UNDP) and World Health Organization (WHO) articulated some of the differences between LDCs and the rest of the developing world.[15] While 28 percent of people in developing countries lack access to electricity, the corresponding amount in the LDCs is 79 percent.[16]

The plight of the LDCs may be contrasted to other developing countries, sometimes called newly industrialized countries ("NICs"), which have made tremendous economic strides in recent decades.[17] This category includes the BRICS countries of Brazil, Russia, India, China, and South Africa;[18] and the "Asian

[10] Ibid, pp. 152–154.

[11] Environmental Decision Making, Science, and Technology, "History of the Energy System," http://environ.andrew.cmu.edu.

[12] Most of this section is taken from L. Guruswamy, "Energy Poverty" (2011) 36 *Annual Review of Environment and Resources* 139.

[13] The WTO requires countries to self-identify as developing or developed countries: World Trade Organization, "Who Are the Developing Countries in the WTO?," www.wto.org.

[14] UN Office of the High Representative for the Least Developed Countries, Landlocked Developing Countries and Small Island Developing States, "Criteria for Identification and Graduation of LDCs," http://unohrlls.org.

[15] G. Legros, I. Havet, N. Bruce, and S. Bonjour, *The Energy Access Situation in Developing Countries: A Review Focusing on Least Developed Countries and Sub Saharan Africa* (New York: United Nations Development Programme: Environment and Energy Group, and World Health Organization, 2009).

[16] Ibid, p. 10.

[17] These countries are also recognized as "Advanced Developing Countries": U.S. Aid, "List of Advanced Developing Countries," June 2, 2012, www.usaid.gov.

[18] N. A. Thompson, "BRICS: Industrialized Countries with Growing Economic Power," *Latin Post*, January 2, 2014.

Tigers" of Taiwan, Singapore, Hong Kong, and South Korea.[19] It also includes Thailand, Indonesia, Malaysia, and the Philippines, which are following the trajectory of exceptional economic growth and rapid industrialization of the Asian Tigers and have consequently been dubbed "Tiger Cub Economies."[20]

It is therefore necessary at the outset to acknowledge at least two major categories among the developing countries: LDCs and NICs. Many segments within NICs are in fact served by electricity based on fossil fuels. These NICs have advanced up the energy ladder, in contrast to the LDCs who are trapped at the bottom of the energy ladder.

A general lack of access to beneficial energy plays an enormous role in both creating and promulgating the condition of the LDCs, and because the phenomenon of energy poverty is overwhelmingly a problem of the LDCs, the primary focus of this article will be on them.

The current era of globalization is driven by modern innovation and advanced technologies that occur in industrialized countries. These technologies are not necessarily affordable, appropriate, or accessible for the EP. On the other hand, traditional uses of energy, and the technologies surrounding them, are frequently harmful, inefficient, and unproductive. Appropriate Sustainable Energy Technologies (ASETs) seek to bridge the gap between the capital-intensive advanced technologies of the developed world and the traditional subsistence technologies of the EP. The purpose of ASETs is to free the EP from the oppressive impacts of unhealthy and unreliable energy access, and to facilitate sustainable development in the LDCs.

3.1 Cooking

A disturbingly large swathe of humanity is caught in a time warp. They rely on biomass-generated fire as their principal source of energy. These fires are made by burning animal dung, waste, crop residues, rotted wood, other forms of harmful biomass, or raw coal. Smoke from the fire used for cooking leads to the premature deaths by respiratory infection of 3.5 million people annually, primarily women and children.[21] Moreover, fire fails to supply the majority of other basic energy needs. In the LDCs, 715 million people rely on solid fuels for cooking; 703 million of these people rely on traditional biomass, and 615 million of those relying on biomass live in sub-Saharan Africa alone.[22] In the LDCs, the overwhelming

---

[19] R. J. Barro, "The East Asian Tigers Have Plenty to Roar About," *Business Week*, April 27, 1998.
[20] Y. Makabenta, "No Miracle, just a Tiger Cub Economy," *The Manila Times*, May 26, 2014.
[21] Legros et al., note 15. For earlier assessments of mortality, see World Health Organization, "Household Air Pollution and Health," March 2014, www.who.int; Global Alliance for Clean Cookstoves, "Igniting Change: A Strategy for Universal Adoption of Clean Cookstoves and Fuels," November 2011, www.cleancookstoves.org.
[22] Legros et al., note 15.

534 *The Contours of Energy Justice*

majority of people forced to use solid fuels for cooking are rural, and more than 80 percent of rural dwellers rely on solid fuels for cooking, including wood, coal, charcoal, crop residues, and dung; 85 percent of those people rely on wood and its byproducts only.[23] This means that a mere 15 percent of the EP in the LDCs enjoy access to modern fuels for cooking.

The general lack of access to modern fuels and overwhelming reliance on biomass for cooking has a number of adverse consequences for human health, and also for the global phenomenon of climate change. First, the EP that rely on biomass for their fuel for cooking generally cook over an open fire, or with some other form of a traditional stove. This process is exceedingly inefficient, as only about 18 percent of the energy from the fire transfers to the pot.[24] Depending on the type of fuel and stove being used, indoor air pollution can contain a variety of dangerous pollutants, such as carbon monoxide, nitrous oxides, sulfur oxides, formaldehyde, carcinogens (such as benzene), and small particulate matter.[25] Second, 3.5 million deaths per year are attributed to indoor pollution due to combustion of solid fuels worldwide,[26] with more than 99 percent of these deaths in developing countries.[27] Specifically, though the population of the LDCs makes up a mere 12 percent of the global citizenry, it accounts for 30 percent of all deaths caused by indoor pollution.[28] For some perspective, consider the health recommendations of the U.S. Environmental Protection Agency (EPA). The EPA sets a limit of 150 micrograms per cubic meter for small particulates in the United States, yet WHO reports that a typical twenty-four-hour mean level for homes burning biomass fuels is between 300 and 3,000 micrograms per cubic meter.[29] This results in pollution levels that are far more deadly in EP countries than the levels of atmospheric pollution allowed by the developed world. According to WHO, exposure to high concentrations of indoor air pollution presents one of the ten most important threats to public health worldwide, resulting in diseases such as pneumonia, chronic pulmonary disease, lung cancer, asthma, and acute respiratory infections.[30] Furthermore, three published studies suggest that the risk of active tuberculosis is 2.5 times greater for people in homes using wood for cooking than for those who do not, and there is growing evidence suggesting that indoor air pollution causes cataracts.[31]

---

[23] Ibid.

[24] The Lancet, note 2; H. Warwick and A. Doig, *Smoke – The Killer in the Kitchen* (London: ITDG Publishing, 2004).

[25] World Health Organization, *Fuel For Life: Household Energy and Health* (Geneva: WHO Press, 2006), p. 10.

[26] WHO, "Household Air Pollution and Health," www.who.int.

[27] Legros et al., note 15.

[28] Ibid.

[29] The Lancet, note 2; World Health Organization, note 25, p. 10.

[30] WHO, "Indoor Air Pollution Takes Heavy Toll on Health," April 30, 2007, www.who.int.

[31] Warwick and Doig, note 24.

Third, women and children are disproportionately affected by the use of biomass for cooking. Women are traditionally responsible for cooking and childcare in the home, and they spend more time inhaling the polluted air that is trapped indoors. Thus, women and children have the highest exposure to indoor air pollution and suffer more than anyone from these negative health effects.[32] Specifically, the risk of child pneumonia increases by 2.3 times in homes that burn solid fuels for cooking, and women are about twice as likely to be afflicted with chronic pulmonary disease than men in homes using solid fuels.[33] Beyond suffering adverse health effects, women and children are also disproportionately affected by the time constraints needed for collecting fuel. Women are burdened with the majority of the work involved in collecting fuel, which can present other serious hazards such as an increased risk of being raped, as occurred in the refugee camps of Darfur.[34]

Fourth, there are also severe environmental impacts of biomass dependence. The reliance on wood as a fuel source puts considerable pressure on local forests, particularly in areas where fuel is scarce and demand for wood outstrips natural regrowth.[35] Depletion of woodland can lead to soil erosion and loss of a carbon sink.[36] Furthermore, it is well established that burning dung and agricultural residues emits carbon dioxide and methane.[37] Research has identified emissions from the burning of biomass as a significant cause of anthropogenic global warming. For example, according to an article in *Nature Geoscience*,[38] discussed in *Science*,[39] the black carbon emitted by burning biomass is the second largest contributor to current global warming after carbon dioxide emissions. The article concludes that black carbon warms the atmosphere more severely than other GHGs, such as methane, halocarbons, and tropospheric ozone, by absorbing both direct and reflected solar radiation.[40] Unlike GHGs, ambient black carbon dissipates in a very short period of time. Thus, helping to move one third of the global population away from biomass burning will have the effect of reducing global warming more immediately than merely reducing carbon dioxide emissions. Furthermore, removing black carbon would reduce the effects of black soot on

---

[32] Global Alliance for Clean Cookstoves, "Clean Cookstoves Can Save Lives and Empower Women," www.cleancookstoves.org.

[33] Legros et al., note 15.

[34] Cookstove Projects, "Overview," http://darfurstoves.lbl.gov. This is equally the case in other refugee camps such as the Horn of Africa. See L. Shannon, "The Rape of Somalia's Women is Being Ignored," *The Guardian*, October 12, 2011.

[35] WHO, "Broader Impacts of Household Energy," www.who.int.

[36] S. Cairncross, D. O'Neill, A. McCoy, and D. Sethi, "Health, Environment and the Burden of Disease, Guidance Note," Department for International Development, 2003.

[37] A. Sagar, "Alleviating Energy Poverty for the World's Poor" (2005) 33 *Energy Policy* 1367.

[38] V. Ramanathan and G. Carmichael, "Global and Regional Climate Changes Due to Black Carbon" (2008) 1 *Nature Geoscience* 221 at 221.

[39] R. Service, "Study Fingers Soot as Major Player in Global Warming" (2008) 319 *Science* 1745.

[40] Ramanathan and Carmichael, note 38 at 221.

536   *The Contours of Energy Justice*

impairing the albedo, or reflectivity, of polar ice.[41] The presence of overlying black carbon may result in ice retaining more heat, leading to increased melting and further global warming.

The dependence on biomass for cooking can be addressed in two ways. First, agricultural waste or animal dung can be converted to other useable forms of energy, to create better fuels by using biogas digesters. The National Biodigester program, perhaps the best documented and most successful program of its kind, is a joint enterprise between the Cambodia Ministry of Agriculture, Forestry and Fisheries and the Netherlands Development Organisation. Unfortunately, the cost of each biodigester runs into hundreds of dollars, which places it outside the reach of most of the EP.[42] Other forms of fuel pellets or converted fuels have not proven to be practicable and have not gained wide currency.

The other way to address indoor pollution is to increase access to improved cookstoves. The Global Alliance for Clean Cookstoves is an initiative led by the UN Foundation supporting large-scale adoption of clean and safe household cooking solutions as a way to save lives, improve livelihoods, empower women, and reduce climate change emissions.[43] The Alliance's founding partners have set a goal of enabling an additional 100 million homes to adopt clean and efficient stoves and fuels by 2020.

Improved cookstoves can utilize a number of different fuel types, but in general are designed to conduct more efficient combustion and reduce particulate indoor air pollution. For example, Envirofit (a non-profit corporation) has created a stove that can reduce emissions by as much as 80 percent and uses up to 60 percent less fuel, while reducing cooking cycle time by up to 50 percent compared to traditional open fires.[44] The University of California at Berkeley designed a cookstove for refugee camps in Darfur that saves more than 1.5 metric tons of CO^2 per year. In term of CO^2 reductions, this is equivalent to removing two average U.S. vehicles from the road for an entire year.[45] Both of these examples use local solid fuels, such as firewood, in order to facilitate sustainable practices within the community, but there are a number of other stoves that use ethanol, gas, or other forms of liquid fuels to increase combustion efficiency and reduce particulate indoor pollution. Clean cookstoves can cost anywhere from US\$15 to \$150 depending on the model and region in which they are assembled, again demonstrating a relatively low cost–benefit ratio, and presenting a timely opportunity to address the needs of the EP.[46]

---

[41] J. Hansen and L. Nazarenko, "Soot Climate Forcing via Snow and Ice Albedos" (2004) 101 *Proceedings of the Natural Academy of Sciences* 423 at 428.

[42] National Biodigester Programme, "Cambodia," www.nbp.org.kh.

[43] UN Foundation "What We Do: Global Alliance for Clean Cookstoves," www.unfoundation.org.

[44] Envirofit, www.envirofit.org.

[45] Potential Energy, www.potentialenergy.org.

[46] Global Alliance for Clean Cookstoves, "Transformation Strategies," www.cleancookstoves.org.

3.2 Lighting

The EP also lack access to lighting. Lighting is essential to human progress and without it "mankind would be comparatively inactive about one-half of its lifetime."[47] The scorching sun and withering temperatures in the LDCs prevent agricultural labor during the daytime and reduce productivity, and the absence of artificial light severely impedes working at night. Without lighting it is not possible for students to do homework after nightfall. The absence of lighting creates physical insecurity – particularly for women and children – while venturing out in the darkness, and almost entirely prevents commercial activity after dark. Almost 500 million people rely on kerosene for illumination.[48] The hazards of kerosene, such as fires, explosions, and poisonings resulting from children ingesting it, are extensively documented, [49] and children and women are disproportionately affected.[50] There is evidence implicating kerosene in ailments including the impairment of lung function, asthma, cancer, and tuberculosis.[51] The use of kerosene and candles is also costly: Households often spend 10 to 25 percent of their income on kerosene.[52] Over US$36 billion is spent on kerosene annually, US$10 billion of which is spent in sub-Saharan Africa.[53]

3.3 Drinking Water and Sanitation

Lack of access to clean drinking water and sanitation are two interconnected, deadly issues facing the EP. Worldwide, approximately one in eight people – 884 million in total – lack access to safe water supplies.[54] While the MDG on sustainable access to drinking water was successfully accomplished in 2010, with the threshold of 88 percent of the world's population having access to improved water sources reached, the sanitation MDG remains off track, with only 63 percent of people having access to improved sanitation (short of the aim of 75 percent by 2015).[55] In preventing diseases such as diarrhoea, tuberculosis, cholera, and other

---

[47] M. Luckiesh, *Artificial Light: Its Influence Upon Civilization*, 8th ed. (New York: Library of Alexandria, 1920).

[48] N. Lam, K. Smith, A. Gautier, and M. Bates, "Kerosene: A Review of Household Uses and Their Hazards in Low and Middle Income Countries" (2012) 15 *Journal of Toxicology and Environmental Health* 396.

[49] Ibid at 423.

[50] M. D. Peck, "Epidemiology of Burns throughout the World, Part 1: Distribution and Risk Factors" (2011) 37 *Burns* 1087 at 1096.

[51] Lam et al., note 48 at 399–401, 412–423.

[52] "Lighting the Way," *The Economist*, September 1, 2012, p. 14.

[53] Ibid, p. 14.

[54] WHO and UNICEF, *Progress on Drinking Water and Sanitation: Special Focus on Sanitation* (Geneva: WHO Library, 2008).

[55] UN, "Water for Life Decade: Access to Sanitation," www.un.org.

The Contours of Energy Justice

waterborne diseases, basic sanitation is just as important as fresh drinking water.[56] Two and a half billion people lack access to improved sanitation, including 1.2 billion people who have no facilities at all.[57] As a result, 3.4 million people die from water-related disease each year;[58] this number is nearly equivalent to the entire population of Los Angeles, California, and children account for many of these deaths.[59] Other consequences of the lack of clean drinking water and basic sanitation include crop failure in irrigated fields, livestock death, and environmental damage.[60] Energy is necessary to alleviate these problems through collecting, transporting, and distributing clean water, powering water treatment facilities, facilitating in-home water treatment (through boiling, for example), and constructing and powering sanitation facilities.[61] However, ASETs such as small-scale sustainable power grids and water transport mechanisms could help to remediate these issues.

Most of the 2.5 billion people without access to adequate sanitation, including the 1.2 billion people without any facilities at all, live in LDCs in rural Africa and Asia.[62] Accordingly, the sanitation issue currently affects the EP in rural areas more dramatically than those in urban areas. However, the issue is increasingly becoming urban;[63] of the sixty million people added to the world's towns and cities every year, most occupy impoverished slums and shanty-towns with no sanitation facilities.[64]

As with many other issues faced by the EP, children are intensely affected by lack of access to clean drinking water and sanitation facilities. Nearly one in five child deaths – about 1.5 million each year – is due to diarrhoea, which is often caused by unclean drinking water and inadequate sanitation facilities.[65] These deaths occur primarily in LDCs, and the many of the children there who suffer from diarrhoea also suffer from acute malnutrition, a condition that is exacerbated by diarrhoea.[66] Child diarrhoea is a serious global issue, as it painfully kills more young children than AIDS, malaria, and measles combined.[67]

[56] Office of the High Commissioner for Human Rights, "Special Rapporteur on the Human Right to Safe Drinking Water and Sanitation," www.ohchr.org.
[57] WHO and UNICEF, note 54.
[58] A. Prüss-Üstün, R. Bos, F. Gore, and J. Bartram, *Safer Water, Better Health: Costs, Benefits, and Sustainability of Interventions to Protect and Promote Health* (Geneva: WHO Library, 2004, updated 2008), Table 1.
[59] Water.org, "Water," http://water.org.
[60] Ibid.
[61] International Energy Agency, "Water for Energy," www.worldenergyoutlook.org.
[62] Water Supply and Sanitation Collaborative Council (WSSCC), *A Guide to Investigating One of the Biggest Scandals of the Last 50 Years* (Geneva: WSSCC, 2008).
[63] Ibid.
[64] Ibid.
[65] WSSCC, note 62.
[66] UNICEF and WHO, *Diarrhoea: Why Children Are Still Dying and What Can Be Done* (Geneva: WHO Library, 2009).
[67] Ibid.

Energy is necessary to power water treatment and sanitation facilities to provide safe drinking water supplies and adequate sanitation facilities. Within the home, too, clean energy can provide people with the ability to boil water. While extending large-scale electricity grids to rural communities is often impracticable at the outset, decentralized mini grids based on solar, wind, and biomass-generated electricity comprise ASETs that can provide power to the EP for water treatment, sanitation facilities, and in-home water boiling.[68] Another example of an ASET that has been used to combat these issues is the implementation of "dry composting latrines" in Calchuapa, El Salvador by an organization called "Trees, Water, & People."[69] These latrines are fairly simple, inexpensive mechanisms that utilize sawdust in combination with human manure to produce a rich fertilizer that can be used on crops after six to eight months.[70]

Though the MDG for access to clean drinking water has been reached, several factors indicate that the water crisis is going to worsen over time. Over the last century, water use grew more than twice as fast as the population, and this trend is predicted to continue.[71] Population growth and urbanization are two factors stressing the global water supply. Additionally, as the effects of climate change intensify, the water cycle will change and water will become increasingly hard to come by, especially as rainfall is already irregular and water sources are already scarce in many LDCs.[72] Accordingly, it is crucial that ASETs be implemented to reduce the need for clean water and sanitation among the EP.

3.4 Mechanical Power

According to the United Nations Development Programme, "[t]he 2.5 billion people without access to modern energy services still depend on unimproved versions of mechanical power equipment that inefficiently use human or animal power to meet their energy needs."[73] Mechanical power refers to "the transmission of energy through a solid structure to impart motion, such as for pumping, pushing, and other similar needs."[74] In a practical sense, this means either using human and animal power or "modern" energy sources such as wind, solar, gas, or electrical power to complete daily tasks. The energy services that stem from access to

[68] E. Visagie and G. Prasad, *Renewable Energy Technologies for Poverty Alleviation South Africa: Biodiesel and Solar Water Heaters* (South Africa: Energy Research Centre, 2006).

[69] Trees, Water and People, "Dry Composting Latrines," www.treeswaterpeople.org.

[70] Ibid.

[71] D. Zabarenko, "Water Use Rising Faster than World Population," Reuters, October 25, 2011.

[72] M. Brucker, *Climate Change Vulnerability and the Identification of Least Developed Countries* (New York: United Nations Development Programme 2012), p. 1.

[73] L. Bates, S. Hunt, S. Khennas, and N. Sastrawinata, *Expanding Energy Access in Developing Countries: The Role of Mechanical Power* (Warwickshire: Practical Action Publishing Ltd, 2009), p. 2.

[74] Legros et al., note 15.

540 *The Contours of Energy Justice*

mechanical power include agriculture (irrigation, farming, and processing), water-pumping, and small-scale industry.[75] Unfortunately, specific data quantifying exactly how many of the EP in the LDCs lack access to mechanical power is lacking.[76] It is clear, however, that access to mechanical power is a problem for the EP, and that it has begun to receive attention on the international energy agenda.[77]

For the EP, the inability to access modern forms of mechanical energy results in the use of inefficient human and animal power to satisfy their most basic needs. To have water for drinking, women (primarily) must perform the arduous task of walking to the natural source and collecting it for use in the household.[78] Depending on the season, in parts of Africa, this can require spending up to four hours per day collecting water. In Uganda, women spend an average of 660 hours per year (a period equating to about a month) collecting water.[79] Even a very simple ASET, such as a water pump, could drastically cut collection time. Less time spent collecting water will also aid development and gender equality by allowing women to spend the time saved on other productive activities – whether they be economic, educational, or domestic.

While water pumps are widely used in parts of the developing world, they are most commonly operated through the use of human power (by either hand or foot), and in many cases by women and children. Manually operated water pumps are physically demanding and time-consuming, and do not totally remove the burden placed on women and children. In some locations, it may be appropriate to employ windmill, water wheel, or photovoltaic solar technologies to ease the burden caused by manual pumping. Selecting an effective ASET-based pump for lifting potable water requires investigating the groundwater depth, water characteristics, capacity demand, preferred method of operation, and maintenance in the target region. Fortunately, there are numerous non-electric or fossil fuel–based pumps that are up to the task.[80]

Another example of how ASETS can be used to provide useful mechanical energy involves the method for processing grain. Before grain can be consumed or sold, the EP must dry it in the sun or with a handheld fan, and then grind it by hand or with a flail. Because post–harvest processing is "arguably the main factor in helping farmers increase their income," simple technologies such as watermills could drastically cut the amount of physical labor needed, increase production, and improve both food security and profit margins for farmers.[81]

---

[75] L. Bates et al., note 73, p. 2.

[76] As of 2009, only three of the LDCs had data to report on access to mechanical power. Ibid, p. 3.

[77] L. Bates et al., note 73, pp. 11–14.

[78] Ibid, p. 2.

[79] Ibid.

[80] E. Stewart, "How to Select the Proper Human-Powered pump for Potable Water," Masters thesis, Michigan Technological University (2003).

[81] K. Watkins, *Beyond Scarcity: Power, Poverty, and the Global Water Crisis* (New York: Palgrave MacMillan, 2006).

Although improving access to some basic services achieved through mechanical power can be addressed through expanding access to electricity, this energy deficit can also be addressed through non-electric, non-fossil fuel ASETs, such as hand operated grinding and pounding equipment.

A particularly innovative application of ASETs to the EP is the Gravity Goods Ropeways project conducted by Practical Action, Nepal.[82] The project, initiated in 2002, was conducted as a way to reduce the transportation time taken for communities to walk their agricultural produce from the village farmyards in the highlands down to the main roads. The technology was beautifully adapted to fit unique local conditions; it is basically a system of gravity-operated pulleys that can carry up to 130 kilograms of goods in a trolley carriage 1.3 kilometers from an elevated platform to a lower platform, and about forty kilograms of goods from the lower platform to the higher one. The ropeways have reduced transportation costs for farmers by 85 percent, and transportation time from 3–4 hours a day to just five minutes. Each individual pulley is locally managed, and operational costs are funded by use charges. The communities contributed 40 percent of the initial investment and the rest was funded by external sources. In sum, the ropeway required only about US$6,500 of initial external investment. Systems such as this demonstrate the feasibility of applying efficient, simple, and sustainable solutions to the problems of energy poverty.

4. SUSTAINABLE DEVELOPMENT AND THE ENERGY-POOR[83]

4.1 *Right to Sustainable Development and Access to Energy*

International law is the law that governs, and is restricted to relations between legally sovereign co-equal states. Treaties are the primary way in which international law is created. Treaties are written agreements between two or more states, governed by international law, creating or restating legal rights and duties. They are also described as conventions, agreements, protocols, covenants, and pacts. The Vienna Convention on the Law of Treaties (Vienna Convention) deals comprehensively with a number of complex questions concerning treaties.[84] A few are of relevance to this chapter. The first concerns the entry into force of a treaty, or the date on which it officially binds the parties. Even though signed, a multilateral treaty typically does not enter into force until a stipulated minimum

---

[82] *Gravity Goods Ropeway* (Warwickshire: Practical Action, 2010).

[83] This section is excerpted from L. Guruswamy, "Energy Poverty" (2011) 36 *Annual Review of Environment and Resources* 139.

[84] *Vienna Convention on the Law of Treaties*, Vienna, 23 May 1969, in force 27 January 1980, 1155 UNTS 331; (1969) 8 ILM 679; UKTS (1980) 58.

The Contours of Energy Justice

number of states have deposited their ratifications. Ratification is the process by which the respective national governments give legal force to the signatures entered by their representatives.

The problem of access to energy relegates the EP to a life of desperation that affronts international concepts of justice and SD. The concept of SD was originally formulated by the World Commission on Sustainable Development, also known as the Brundtland Commission, as a distributional principle to address the needs of the world's poor while maintaining environmental integrity. SD mandates that global environmental protection must be pursued in tandem with economic and social development. International law, as expressed particularly in the UN Framework Convention on Climate Change[85] (UNFCCC), unequivocally institutionalizes SD.

The UNFCCC is the most important energy convention to date. Having obtained 194 instruments of ratification, it is probably the most extensively adopted treaty in the world. Article 3(1) of the UNFCCC states that the parties have a right to and should promote sustainable development, and that economic development is essential for adopting measures to address climate change, while Article 3(2) affirms that full consideration be given to the special circumstances of developing countries. Parties are required to protect the climate system on the basis of equity and in accordance with their common but differentiated responsibilities and respective capacities. The principle of common but differentiated responsibility, which is found in Principle 7 of the Rio Declaration on Environment and Development[86] and conclusively embodied in Articles 3(1) and 4(1) of the UNFCCC, affirms the responsibility of the developed country parties to take the lead in combating climate change and the adverse effects thereof.

The UNFCCC coalesced with another widely accepted treaty, the Convention on Biological Diversity[87] (CBD), by forcefully and unequivocally expressing the developmental priority of SD. Article 4(7) of the UNFCCC and Article 20(4) of the CBD reaffirm in unison that parties "will take fully into account that economic and social development and poverty eradication are the first and overriding priorities of the developing country Parties." Specifically, therefore, energy poverty can only be addressed within a framework of distributive justice, as part of the overall right to economic and social development established by the foundational norm of SD.

---

[85] New York, 9 May 1992, in force 21 March 1994, 1771 UNTS 107; S. Treaty Doc. No. 102-38; UN Doc. A/AC.237/18 (Part II)/Add.1; 31 ILM 849 (1992).

[86] *Rio Declaration on Environment and Development*, Rio de Janeiro, 12 June 1992, UN Doc. A/CONF.151/26 (vol. I); 31 ILM 874 (1992).

[87] Rio de Janeiro, 5 June 1992, in force 29 December 1993, [1993] ATS 32 / 1760 UNTS 79 / 31 ILM 818 (1992).

4.2 John Rawls and Sustainable Development

John Rawls' concept of international justice provides a moral justification for SD.[88] Rawls discusses a "realistic utopia" grounded in sociopolitical, institutional, and psychological reality.[89] This section attempts to reconcile Rawls's ideas with present realities insofar as they apply to SD and the EP.

Rawls' "original position," a thought experiment expounded in *A Theory of Justice* and developed in numerous other works, envisioned a collection of negotiators from liberal democratic societies. The negotiators assembled behind a veil of ignorance, shorn of any knowledge that might be the basis of self-interested bias – such as knowledge of their gender, wealth, race, ethnicity, abilities, and general social circumstances. Rawls explains that the purpose of such a negotiation was to arrive at legitimate principles of justice under fair conditions – hence "justice as fairness."[90]

In *The Law of Peoples*, concerning justice and international law, Rawls extends his theories from liberal democratic states to "decent" peoples living in non-democratic international societies. Rawls envisions such "well-ordered hierarchical societies" to be "non-liberal societies whose basic institutions meet specified conditions of political right and justice (including the right of citizens to play a substantial role, such as participating in associations and groups making political decisions) and lead their citizens to honor a reasonably just law for the Society of Peoples."[91] Well-ordered societies must satisfy a number of criteria: they must eschew aggressive aims as a means of achieving their objectives, honor basic human rights dealing with life, liberty, and freedom, and possess a system of law imposing bona fide moral duties and obligations, as distinct from human rights. Moreover, they must have law and judges to uphold common ideas of justice.[92]

Rawls demonstrated how the law of peoples may be developed out of liberal ideas of justice similar to, but more general than, the idea of "justice as fairness" presented in *A Theory of Justice*.[93] Just as individuals in the first original position were shorn of knowledge about their attributes and placed behind a veil of ignorance to create principles for a just domestic society, the bargainers in the so-called second original position are representatives of peoples who are shorn of knowledge about their people's resources, wealth, power, and the like. Behind the veil of ignorance, the representatives of peoples – not states, since states lack moral capacity – develop the principles of justice that will govern relations between them: *The Law of Peoples*.

---

[88] J. Rawls, *The Law of Peoples* (Cambridge: Harvard University Press, 2001), p. 106.
[89] Ibid.
[90] Rawls, note 88, p. 3.
[91] Ibid, p. 106.
[92] Ibid, p. 3.
[93] Ibid.

It should be noted at this juncture that there is a difference between John Rawls' theories of domestic and international justice. The principles of domestic distributive justice espoused by Rawls in *A Theory of Justice* did not apply to the international sphere. A pivotal reason for this is that the international community does not possess the basic institutions of a liberal democratic society necessary to institute and implement distributive justice. The machinery of government, consisting of a legislature that can make laws, an executive that implements such laws, and courts with compulsory jurisdiction that interpret and apply the laws of the state, does not exist on a global level. These factors were among the reasons that his book is titled *The Law of Peoples* rather than the law of nations or states.

Rawls emphasized the need for global order and stability over global distributive justice. Once the duty to assist burdened peoples is satisfied, there are no further requirements on economic distribution within Rawls' *The Law of Peoples*. Inequalities across national borders are of no political concern as such. Individuals around the world may suffer greatly from bad luck, and may be haunted by spiritual emptiness. The practical goal of Rawls' *The Law of Peoples* is the elimination of the great evils of human history: Unjust war and oppression, religious persecution, and the denial of liberty of conscience, starvation and poverty, genocide and mass murder. The limits of this ambition mean that there will be much in the world to which Rawls' political philosophy offers no reconciliation.[94]

Rawls seeks to determine the principles of cooperation for such "well-ordered peoples." Rawls posits that non-ideal conditions cannot adequately be addressed unless principles of justice are determined for ideal conditions. Otherwise, it is impossible to know what kind of just society to aim to establish and the necessary means to do so.[95] A "realistic utopia," as Rawls prefers to call his theory, is an aspiration that does not reflect the existing reality of international law and relations.

Rawls emphasizes the crucial importance of peoples rather than states, because of a people's capacity for "moral motives" that is lacking in the bureaucratic machinery of a state.[96] Samuel Freeman correctly observes that a "people" for Rawls is a philosophical construct. It is an abstract conception needed to work out principles of justice for a particular subject – in this case, relations among different well-ordered liberal and "decent" societies.[97] The assumption that states lack moral motives is partially refuted by their acceptance of SD. Nonetheless, Rawls remains trenchant when it comes to the application of SD. Rawls is not talking then about a people regarded as an ethnic or religious group (e.g. Slavs, Jews, Kurds) who are not members of the same society. Rather, a "people" consists of members of the same well-ordered society who are united under, and whose relations are governed

---

[94] L. Wenar, "John Rawls," in E. N. Zalta (ed.), *The Stanford Encyclopedia of Philosophy* (2008) at § 5.6.

[95] Rawls, note 88.

[96] Ibid.

[97] N. Feldman, "Cosmopolitan Law?" (2007) 116 *Yale Law Journal* 1022 at 1038.

by, a political constitution and basic structure. Composed of members of a well-ordered society, a people is envisioned as having effective political control over a territory that its members govern, and within which their basic social institutions take root. In contrast to a state, however, a people possesses a "moral nature" that stems from the effective sense of justice for its individual members. A people's members may have "common sympathies" for any number of non-requisite reasons, including shared language, ethnic roots, or religion. The most basic reason for members' common sympathies, however, lies in their shared history as members of the same society and their consequent shared conception of justice and the common good.

The conclusion most pertinent to SD and the EP is that Rawls elucidates the duty of liberal democratic and decent hierarchical peoples to assist "burdened societies" to the point where burdened societies are enabled to join the "Society of Peoples." It is of particular pertinence that Rawls' duty of assistance does not absolve developing country governments of their obligation to take appropriate action. Rawls' concept of "peoples" has been criticized. Among his more cogent critics, Pogge[98] and Nussbaum[99] question the validity of the distinction between peoples and states, and the difficulties of defining peoples. They claim their criticisms assume importance in any attempt to realize the "Society of Peoples" which Rawls envisions as his realistic utopia. Such criticisms were actually anticipated by Rawls, who pointed out that he eschewed the "state" as a polity because of its historical Hobbesian connotations in "realist" international political theory, which suggests that the power of states can be limited only by the states, and not by moral or legal constraints.[100]

Paradoxically, the legal and political acceptance of SD by the community of nations may be seen as refuting Rawls' distrust of states at the theoretical level, to the extent that the existing international legal framework of SD expressed in the UNFCCC and CBD, for example, lends itself to the Rawlsian ideal. Moreover, Rawls remains relevant at the practical and functional level when it comes to the implementation of SD. As is more fully discussed in the next section, dealing with climate change and SD, the principle of SD has been invoked and erroneously applied to the NICs, while the EP in the LDCs have been ignored.

4.3 Rawlsian Sustainable Development as it Applies to the EP

A starting point for analyzing the international phenomena of the EP must begin with the fact that the EP should be identified primarily as "burdened societies" in

[98] T. W. Pogge, "The Incoherence Between Rawls's Theories of Justice" (2004) 72 *Fordham Law Review* 1739 at 1743.
[99] M. C. Nussbaum, *Frontiers of Justice: Disabilities, Nationality, Species Membership* (Cambridge: Harvard University Press, 2006), pp. 236–244.
[100] Rawls, note 88.

546

The Contours of Energy Justice

the Rawlsian sense.[101] Rawlsian principles will ensure that SD is applied to the EP. Furthermore, their special status as burdened societies must be highlighted rather than hidden. Additionally, it is important to draw attention to Rawls' suggestion as to how the duty of assistance should be discharged, bearing in mind his particular conclusion that merely dispensing funds will not suffice to rectify basic and political injustice.[102]

Rawls' warning that the mere distribution of funds will not rectify the targeted problems now becomes of special relevance. Many rulers, Rawls points out, have been callous about the well-being of their own peoples,[103] and transferring resources to national governments does not ensure that they will be applied to the problems of the EP. For this reason, Rawls advocates that assistance be tied to the advancement of human rights. Tying assistance to human rights will also embrace the status of women, who are often oppressed. It has, moreover, been shown that the removal of discrimination against women has resulted in major economic and social progress.[104]

Such measures almost certainly will be resisted by authoritarian regimes, which will argue this approach amounts to an intrusion into the national sovereignty of a country and violates international law. These rulers might fear that establishing human rights as a condition for helping the EP will expose their own corruption and lack of good governance. Such rulers have reason to fear the granting of human rights where they have not confronted their problems or have demonstrated weak governance. As an example of this, Rawls cites the works of Amartya Sen and Partha Dasgupta, who have demonstrated that the main cause of famine in Bengal, Ethiopia, Sahel, and Bangladesh was government mismanagement rather than shortage of food.[105]

Corruption remains a major problem in many developing countries, where large numbers of complex, restrictive regulations are coupled with inadequate controls. The United Nations Convention on Corruption, which came into force in 2005, was negotiated after *The Law of Peoples* and offers ample contemporary evidence of Rawls' conclusion.[106] It recognized the "seriousness of problems and threats

---

[101] Ibid.

[102] Ibid.

[103] Ibid.

[104] M. Yunus, *A World Without Poverty: Social Business and the Future Capitalism* (New York: Public Affairs, 2007).

[105] A. Sen, *Poverty and Famines: An Essay on Entitlement and Deprivation* (New York: Oxford University Press, 1981); J. Dreze and A. Sen, *Hunger and Public Action* (New York: Oxford University Press, 1989); P. Dasgupta, *An Inquiry into the Wellbeing of Destitution* (New York: Oxford University Press, 1995).

[106] *Convention Against Corruption*, Merida, 9 December 2003, in force 14 December 2005, GA res. 58/4, UN Doc. A/58/422 (2003); 43 ILM 37 (2004) [hereinafter Convention Against Corruption]. As of September 5, 2014, 172 parties have signed and ratified or otherwise acceded to the Convention: United Nations Office on Drugs and Crime, "United Nations Convention Against Corruption: Signature and Ratification Status as of 5 September 2014," www.unodc.org.

posed by corruption to the stability and security of societies, undermining the institutions and values of democracy, ethical values and justice and jeopardizing sustainable development and the rule of law."[107] In his Foreword to the Convention, Kofi Annan, the UN Secretary-General at the time, refers to corruption as an "insidious plague" that has a wide range of corrosive effects on societies. [108] He continues by asserting that:

> It undermines democracy and the rule of law, leads to violations of human rights, distorts markets, erodes the quality of life and allows organized crime, terrorism and other threats to human security to flourish. This evil phenomenon is found in all countries – big and small, rich and poor – but it is in the developing world that its effects are most destructive. Corruption hurts the poor disproportionately by diverting funds intended for development, undermining a government's ability to provide basic services, feeding inequality and injustice and discouraging foreign aid and investment. Corruption is a key element in economic underperformance and a major obstacle to poverty alleviation and development.[109]

In both NICs and LDCs, corruption is a pervasive problem. Not only are official decisions – for instance, the award of government contracts or the amount of tax due – bought and sold, but very often citizens must pay for access to a public service or the exercise of a right, such as obtaining civil documents. The process of allocating political and administrative posts – particularly those with powers of decision over the export of natural resources or import licenses – is influenced by the gains that can be made from them. As these exchanges of privileges are reciprocated by political support or loyalty, the political foundations are cemented.[110] Corruption in turn can have a dramatic effect on a country's economy. It has been estimated, for example, that moving from a relatively "clean" government like that of Singapore to one as corrupt as Mexico's would have the same effect on foreign direct investment as an increase in the marginal corporate tax rate of 50 percent.[111]

Thomas Pogge offers a radical and trenchant criticism of corruption as something ingrained in the international structure of power. According to him, "many developing countries are run by corrupt and incompetent leaders, unwilling or unable to make serious poverty-eradication efforts."[112] Pogge goes on to say that bad leadership, civil wars, and widespread corruption in the developing countries

---

[107] Convention Against Corruption, note 106, Preamble.
[108] Convention Against Corruption, note 106, Foreword.
[109] Ibid.
[110] I. Hors, "Fighting Corruption in the Developing Countries," OECD Observer, April 2000.
[111] S-J. Wei, "How Taxing is Corruption on International Investors?," Williams David Institute Working Papers Series 63, 2007.
[112] T. W. Pogge, World Poverty and Human Rights: Cosmopolitan Responsibilities and Reforms, 2nd ed. (Cambridge: Polity Press, 2008).

548 *The Contours of Energy Justice*

are not wholly homegrown, but strongly encouraged by the existing international rules based on the sovereignty of states.[113]

> As ordinary citizens of the rich countries, we are deeply implicated in these harms. We authorize our firms to acquire natural resources from tyrants, and we protect their property rights in resources so acquired. We purchase what our firms produce out of such resources and thereby encourage them to act as authorized. In these ways, we recognize the authority of tyrants to sell natural resources of the countries they rule. We also authorize and encourage other firms of ours to sell to the tyrants what they need to stay in power – from aircraft and arms to surveillance and torture equipment.[114]

A realistic attempt to remedy energy poverty should be alive to the serious problems posed by sovereignty, and it should try to overcome them. While there are limited ways of bypassing states where they are impediments to energy justice, the irremovable fact is that sovereignty is the basis of international law. Aid, assistance, or empowerment of the energy-poor cannot ignore national sovereignty. Under our present system of international law and governance, SD requires that developed countries play a dominant part in alleviating the condition of the EP. It also invokes the need for action by national governments. Justice requires both that assistance be given and that such assistance be properly administered. The failure of foreign aid has been debated, and better ways of granting assistance must be found. Justice also requires that national governments take on the task of addressing the EP. It is not possible to lay the blame on avaricious rich countries alone.

5. CONCLUSIONS

The most important conclusions may be summarized at this point. First, the inability to access energy both causes poverty and disables impoverished people from developing. The connection between energy and poverty is fundamental to the discourse on sustainable development. Second, the plight of the energy-poor cannot be remedied by relying solely on the states within which they reside. The energy-poor have been glossed over by their identification only as national problems falling within the sovereign jurisdiction of the developing countries within which they reside. They are treated as problems of developing countries and not perceived as a burdened society's call for international action, sometimes independent of those countries.

Third, allowing the EP to languish in their current state violates fundamental concepts of international justice and SD. These concepts are best justified by John

---

[113] Ibid.
[114] Ibid, p. 148.

Rawls, who outlined the duty of developed peoples "to assist burdened societies."[115] Rawls' concepts of duty and distributive justice, though not explicitly articulated, are embodied more generally in the principles of SD and more specifically in the MDGs, which can only be achieved if the need for energy is satisfied.

Fourth, access to energy through electricity remains the ultimate objective. Unfortunately, it is a cost-prohibitive and protracted remedy that will take decades to implement, and does not offer any interim solutions. During the long wait for electricity, large segments of the EP will remain energy-deprived for many decades unless they are offered intermediate solutions based on ASETs. Employing ASETs can begin the journey out of energy poverty.

Finally, there is no doubt that the UN's recent recognition of the need for universal access to energy is a great step forward that acknowledges the connection between energy and poverty and charts a new path for SD. UN recognition of the need for cookstoves indicates that it may be open to more immediately effective forms of development based on ASETs. Such a recognition will offer a new space for formulating appropriate sustainable energy solutions that address the needs of the energy-poor by providing timely, sustainable, and affordable ways to satisfy their energy needs.

[115] Rawls, note 88, p. 106.

PART V

Challenges and Options

26

South–South Cooperation: Foundations for Sustainable Development

Koh Kheng-Lian and Nicholas A. Robinson

1. INTRODUCTION

The global South is a robust theater for cooperation and competition among developing nations. Regional cooperation is expanding through intergovernmental organizations in each southern area. In addition, similarly situated states in different regions often align policy positions globally. In international negotiations, they rally around the principles of "solidarity" and "common but differentiated responsibilities," largely to enhance negotiations with developed nations – the North. When the states of the South strive for capacity-building to achieve Socio-economic development objectives, they have shared goals. They have an office in the Secretariat of the United Nations (UN) devoted to promoting South–South cooperation[1] and an intergovernmental organization, the South Centre,[2] carrying on the work of the South Commission,[3] whose Secretariat is situated in Geneva, Switzerland, to promote Southern states' interests in multilateral and UN organizational settings.

---

[1] UN General Assembly, *Technical Cooperation Among Developing Countries*, 4 December 1974, A/RES/3251 (XXIX).

[2] See South Centre, www.southcentre.int. The South Centre describes itself as having "grown out of the work and experience of the South Commission and its follow-up mechanism, and from recognition of the need for enhanced South-South co-operation. The Report of the South Commission emphasized that the South is not well organized at the global level and has thus not been effective in mobilizing its considerable combined expertise and experience, nor its bargaining power. [...] Broadly, the Centre works to assist in developing points of view of the South on major policy issues, and to generate ideas and action-oriented proposals for consideration by the collectivity of South governments, institutions of South-South co-operation, inter-governmental organizations of the South, and non-governmental organizations and the community at large. [...] [T]he Centre also responds to requests for policy advice, and for technical and other support from collective entities of the South such as the Group of 77 and the Non-Aligned Movement."

[3] See the Report of the South Commission, *The Challenge to the South: The Report of the South Commission* (Oxford: Oxford University Press, 1990).

554   *South–South Cooperation*

But some states of the South are more adept than others in winning development assistance, and competition within the South is a constant also.

South-to-South cooperation was born when the decolonization era ended. The new nations of the UN became a bloc of countries, variously positioned as the non-aligned nations during the Cold War or the Group of 77 (G77). The "solidarity" of this group of nations was able to proclaim a UN "right of development" and proposals were made in 1974 for a New International Economic Order (NIEO).[4] Despite this solidarity having a majority in the UN General Assembly, developed nations saw little need to advance an NIEO, or transfer financial assets to the South. What overseas aid came was perhaps more the result of competition between the USA and USSR to win the support of developing nations in the Cold War and to maintain trade ties between former colonial governments and their former colonies having become independent states, as in the Francophone community or the British Commonwealth. The UN call (which was adopted in 1970) for developed nations to contribute 0.07 percent of their gross domestic product toward developing nations has been met by only two developed states.[5]

In part to compensate for the paucity of international development assistance, nations of the South have found that they can cooperate with each other. This has been most effective when developing Southern states are in contiguous regions. Regionally, the Caribbean states have long promoted such regional cooperation. The Caribbean and Common Market (CARICOM) can act efficiently, given the proximity of its members.[6] The Asian–African Legal Consultative Organization (AALCO)[7] is a UN Observer with a vast membership, but such little funding that its secretariat in New Delhi has accomplished relatively little in inducing South-to-South cooperation. The Organization of African Unity (OAU) became the African Union,[8] and robust engagement in socio-economic integration in Africa is advancing. The Arab League has historically fostered capacity-building across Arab states,[9] but the recent turmoil following the "Arab Spring" has disrupted these activities. Subregionally, the Southern African Development Community (SADEC) takes the process one step further. The Association of South East Asian

---

[4] UN General Assembly, *Declaration on the Establishment of a New International Economic Order*, 1 May 1974, A/RES/3201 (S-VI),

[5] See Millennium Project, "The 0.7% Target: An In-Depth Look," www.unmillenniumproject. org. The UN Millennium Development Goals describe the development assistance target: "0.7 refers to the repeated commitment of the world's governments to commit 0.7% of rich-countries' gross national product (GNP) to Official Development Assistance. First pledged 35 years ago in a 1970 General Assembly Resolution, the 0.7 target has been affirmed in many international agreements over the years, including the March 2002 International Conference on Financing for Development in Monterrey, Mexico and at the World Summit on Sustainable Development held in Johannesburg later that year."

[6] CARICOM, www.caricom.org.

[7] AALCO, www.aalco.int.

[8] African Union, www.au.int.

[9] League of Arab States, www.lasportal.org.

Nations (ASEAN) is perhaps the most elaborated of these southern alliances in political and socio-economic and environmental cooperation: for this reason, ASEAN is discussed here as a case study.

It is beyond the scope of this chapter to describe and analyze all South-to-South cooperation patterns. The end of the Cold War exposed fracture lines in the solidarity of the South. China, aligned with the G77 but preferring to stand apart from that gathering of Southern states, has increasingly taken a leadership position not unlike the roles played by the former USSR or the U.S. China's direct overseas foreign investment in virtually all Southern nations is pervasive and enormous. Chinese state companies are major investors in many Southern states – with the exception of India – including states in South East Asia, the Andes and much of South and Central America, the Pacific, and sub-Saharan Africa. Some states and civil society in Africa and South America complain of China's "land-grabbing";[10] yet China is still perceived as being a developing nation, of the South. Are rich states like the United Arab Emirates or Singapore still a part of the "official" G77 South, or do they constitute a new developed category of states in the South? Can divisions between North African and West Asian Arab States be healed? Or is this part of the South too conflicted for cooperation, either among themselves *(inter se)* or internationally?

This chapter explores several aspects of South–South cooperation. Space precludes examining all the many questions that assess interstate cooperation across the global South, whether in trade negotiations or cooperation on public health or military security. The comparable dynamics in each sector are illustrated by how South–South cooperation (SSC) functions where SSC has shaped one dimension of international law, namely, that of environmental law. Different variants of SSC emerge, despite engaging very different kinds of governments (from pluralistic democracies, to constitutional kingdoms, to autocratic states) and having to accommodate the different interests between competing stakeholders (e.g. commercial enterprises or NGOs). SSC operates actively in implementing multilateral environmental agreements (MEAs),[11] where the states of the South shape their own environmental agenda and then work toward harmonization and global environmental governance regimes. Establishing such cooperation is difficult.

National confidence to engage in SSC also faces a myriad of obstacles. Fourteen main obstacles inhibiting SSC may be identified: (a) historical legacies, such as denial of responsibility from the North, especially colonial masters, for past conduct; (b) lack of political will on the part of Southern states to collaborate; (c) geopolitical power politics, within Southern regions or in tandem with

---

[10] D. Smith, "The Food Rush: Rising Demand in China and West Sparks African Land Grab," *The Guardian*, 3 July 2009.

[11] The MEAs, with selected case studies about how states implement their terms, are set forth in L. Kurukulasuriya and N. A. Robinson, *Training Manual on International Environmental Law* (Nairobi: United Nations Environmental Programme, 2006).

major international powers; (d) corruption and lack of the rule of law domestically, where ruling elites show little interest in investing in sustained cooperation; (e) a lack of agreed norms for cooperation, or shared ethical principles; (f) the economic interests of companies from the North and from multinational companies which are at odds with SSC development interests; (g) situations in which all stakeholders are not "on board," whether in regional or international negotiations, as in failures to engage traditional communities and indigenous peoples in development decisions, or dismissing dialogue with states whose interests are marginal to the issues at hand; (h) excessive deference to sovereignty and non-intervention principles, to defer paying attention to opportunities for cooperation; (i) lack of capacity in civil services, technology sectors, or political leadership of various states; inadequacy of laws, such as regimes for liability (tort law); (j) weak reliance on emerging general principles of international law that serve Southern interests, such as the precautionary principle or the principle of resilience; (l) overly narrow perceptions of self-interests, as when states consider first and foremost only their shot-term interests; (m) lack of trust between South and North, with a view that the North always prefers to enhance its interests ahead of those of states in the South; and (n) a lack of knowledge and need for capacity-building in environmental law. These obstacles appear in the examples of SSC examined below.

SSC will be enhanced by the UN General Assembly's adoption of the "Sustainable Development Goals" (SDGs).[12] The South took the lead in negotiating these SDGs. States with a pronounced distrust of the North, such as Bolivia, resisted adoption of the SDGs, but the overwhelming consensus is that SDGs will foster cooperation across all parties and lead to SSC. The adoption of SDGs by the UN General Assembly provides opportunities to emphasize the importance of the environmental MEAs and international environmental law. The SDGs give substance to the general policies endorsed at the UN Rio+20 Conference in its outcome document, *The Future We Want*.[13] As the UN Open Working Group observed when recommending the draft SDGs to the UN General Assembly, "Rio+20 affirmed the conviction that in order to achieve a just balance among the economic, social and environmental needs of present and future generations, it is necessary to promote harmony with nature."[14]

SDGs are comprehensive. For example, SDG 3 is to "ensure healthy lives," and SDG 3.9 provides that nations shall seek, by 2030, to substantially reduce deaths

---

[12] Report of the Open Working Group of the General Assembly on Sustainable Development Goals, 12 August 2014, http://www.un.org/ga/search/view_doc.asp?symbol=A/68/970&Lang=E

[13] UN General Assembly, *Resolution Adopted by the General Assembly: The Future We Want*, 27 July 2012, A/RES/66/288 [hereinafter *The Future We Want*].

[14] Sustainable Development, "Introduction to the proposal of the Open Working Group for Sustainable Development Goals," 19 July 2014, http://sustainabledevelopment.un.org.

and illnesses from air and water pollution. SDG 11 furthers protection of natural heritage in SDG 11.4. SDG 15 is to "protect, restore and promote sustainable use of terrestrial ecosystems, sustainably manage forests, combat desertification, and halt and reverse land degradation and halt biodiversity loss." SDG 16 mandates strengthening access to justice and the rule of law in SDG 16.3. The SDGs offer a framework for SSC, South–North negotiations, and SSC–North–UN triangular cooperation. The SDGs can stimulate practical projects to enable cooperation among all UN member states and global or regional intergovernmental organizations.

Practical cooperation to realize the SDGs will proceed through the United Nations Development Programme (UNDP) and all other intergovernmental international programs. SDGs do more than simply embrace the 1992 Rio Declaration on Environment and Development;[15] the new UN SDGs reaffirm that environmental protection is the foundation for sustainability. SSC will increase as the UNDP builds states' capacity to protect natural environments and public health and sustain development.

2. THE EMERGENCE OF SOUTH–SOUTH COOPERATION

SSC is a phenomenon that dates back to the late 1960s. In 1974, the UN General Assembly endorsed "the establishment of a special unit within the UNDP to promote technical co-operation among developing countries."[16] One of the aims is to promote, coordinate, and support South-South and triangular/tripartite cooperation (i.e. South–South with UN agencies) globally and within the UN system. SSC has become an important factor in UN negotiations. The UNDP serves as the Secretariat to the High-Level Committee on SSC, a subsidiary body of the General Assembly, which provides policy directives and guidance, and reviews worldwide progress of SSC. In this context, it monitors trends in SSC among UN agencies as well as globally, preparing reports for various intergovernmental bodies, including the report of the Secretary-General on the state of SSC.[17]

States of the global South often perceive that they are better off acting together rather than as allies of the North or the major powers (e.g. the U.S., UK, and France), and the dynamics of their solidarity can be very effective. There is also a "South" within the South (less developed and least developed states), and failure to include these states' interests together with the South bloc erodes inclusiveness

---

[15] *Rio Declaration on Environment and Development*, Rio de Janeiro, 13 June 1992, UN Doc. A/CONF.151/26 (vol. I); 31 ILM 874 (1992) [hereinafter Rio Declaration].

[16] UN General Assembly, *Technical Cooperation among Developing Countries*, 4 December 1974, A/RES/3251 (XXIX), para. 2.

[17] United Nations Office for South-South Cooperation, http://ssc.undp.org.

558   *South–South Cooperation*

in the negotiations within the UN General Assembly or the conferences of the parties of MEAs. Moreover, at the other extreme some states of the South, such as Brazil, China, and India, have become wealthy, with their interests also diverging from the bloc.

Nonetheless, the G77[18], or the "G77 and China," remains the configuration within which SSC functions. Since 2013, the Group of 77 has expanded to include 133 member countries. The G77 has rallied around the principle of "common but differentiated responsibilities," for example for the purpose of refusing cooperation on climate change until the North funds a Green Bank for climate adaptation, and other sustainable development issues. G77 is a robust force in climate change negotiations. At the 19th Conference of the Parties to the UN Framework Convention on Climate Change[19] (UNFCCC) in Warsaw, the G77 and China walked out of the meeting on the issue of loss and damage.[20]

SSC is shaped as much by Southern states' collective development objectives as it is by any perceived shared interests with the North. In the United Nations, this approach found early expression as the "New International Economic Order" (NIEO) set forth in General Assembly resolutions. The NIEO has not attracted support from the North.[21] In April 1992 in Kuala Lumpur, just before the UN Conference on Environment and Development (UNCED) in Rio,[22] the Prime Minister of Malaysia, Dr. Mahathir bin Mohamad, delivered a scathing speech focused on the North–South divide at the Official Opening of the Second Ministerial Conference of Developing Countries on Environment and Development.[23] Observers attended the Kuala Lumpur conference from eleven developed countries, ten international organizations, and nine NGOs, representing thirty-four countries of the South. The Prime Minister summed up the negotiating posture of many Southern states:

> Whether we like it or not, the developed North, having destroyed their heritage, will want to declare that what is left intact in the developing countries also belongs to them. Consequently they are going to insist on having more than just a say in

---

[18] Group of 77, *Joint Declaration of the Seventy-Seven Developing Countries Made at the Conclusion of the United Nations Conference on Trade and Development*, Geneva, 15 June 1964, www.g77.org. The G77 was founded on 15 June 1964 by the "Joint Declaration of the Seventy-Seven Countries" issued at the UNCTAD.

[19] New York, 9 May 1992, in force 21 March 1994, 1771 UNTS 107; S. Treaty Doc No. 102-38; UN Doc. A/AC.237/18 (Part II)/Add.1; 31 ILM 849 (1992).

[20] See *Earth Negotiations Bulletin* for the 19th COP UNFCCC. See ENB Archives at www.iisd.ca/voltoc.html.

[21] UN General Assembly, *Declaration on the Establishment of a New International Economic Order*, 1 May 1974, A/RES/S-6/3201.

[22] *Agenda 21: Programme of Action for Sustainable Development*, Rio de Janeiro, 14 June 1992, U.N. GAOR, 46th Sess., Agenda Item 21, UN Doc. A/Conf.151/26 (1992).

[23] The movement had been initiated by a first ministerial meeting in New Delhi in 1990 and was followed by a meeting in Beijing that same year.

the management of these remaining ecological assets of the world. And when the powerful North speaks, the voice of the individual developing countries will be drowned. It will be different if they speak together with one strong voice in Rio.[24]

This address by an influential national leader articulated forcefully the politically motivated sentiment against the North in advance of the UN negotiations in Rio de Janeiro for the 1992 Earth Summit. The Kuala Lumpur conference expressed deep concern at the lack of progress of negotiations of the draft UN Framework Convention on Climate Change (UNFCCC), which was due to be signed at UNCED. The UNFCCC negotiations placed burdens on all states to abate emissions of greenhouse gases. Since developed nations had caused climate change as a result of the Industrial Revolution and its outcomes, the South demanded[25] that the North take much deeper reductions in emissions. The South argued that it should be accorded a right to development unencumbered by such climate constraints. This was the manifestation of the "common but differentiated" principle at work. The South demanded that Northern countries reduce the emissions of greenhouse gases ahead of any such duty on the South, and that the North help build the capacity of the South to do so.

In a further statement to UNCED in 1992, Dr. Mahathir Mohamad once again raised the issue of the North–South divide. He said that the "poor [are] not seeking [...] charity" but "principles of fairness and equity" for past pollution.[26] This had been the line of argument at all the UNFCCC negotiations, and has continued to the present, as illustrated by the following examples of negotiations under climate and biological diversity treaty regimes.

3. SOUTH–NORTH AND SOUTH-UN NEGOTIATIONS

Virtually all MEAs are at early stages of implementation. The member states of most MEAs have not yet agreed on the specific measures that states must undertake in order to implement their treaty obligations. It is perhaps easier, therefore, for Southern states to rally together and agree on issues of principle, as with the strong assertion of the "common but differentiated responsibilities" principle contained in the UNFCCC and the Convention on Biological Diversity[27] (CBD), both signed at the 1992 Earth Summit. The South's strength of SSC negotiating solidarity can be seen in the negotiations within MEAs. This may be illustrated with reference

---

[24] Dato' Seri Dr. M. bin Mohamad, official opening of the second ministerial meeting conference of developing countries on Environment and Development at Crown Princess Hotel, Kuala Lumpur, 27 April 1992, cited in P. Nguitragoo, *Environmental Cooperation in Southeast Asia: ASEAN's Regime for Transboundary Haze Pollution* (New York: Routledge, 2011), p. 49.

[25] F. Soltau, *Fairness in International Climate Change Law and Policy* (Cambridge: Cambridge University Press, 2011).

[26] Cited in K. Bala, "PM: West Resisting Move to Green the World," *New Straits Times*, 15 June 1992, p. 2.

[27] Rio de Janeiro, 5 June 1992, in force 29 December 1993, 1760 UNTS 79; 31 ILM 818 (1992).

to the Nagoya Protocol to the CBD,[28] and the negotiations over loss and damage in the context of climate disruption under the UNFCCC.

3.1 *The Nagoya Protocol, Article 8*

Following negotiations between the North and South, one of the significant amendments to the Nagoya Protocol [29] was the inclusion of pathogens within the scope of Article 8. The negotiations arose from Indonesia's refusal to give an avian flu virus sample to the World Health Organization (WHO) on the ground that WHO would give the samples to pharmaceutical companies, which would then develop vaccines at a price that Southern countries would not be able to afford.[30] The question of whether such a virus could be considered a "genetic resource" under the CBD arose at the 2010 Conference of the Parties in Nagoya.

The North, together with pharmaceutical companies, attempted to exclude pathogens from the benefit-sharing provision of the CBD. The companies and Northern states were unsuccessful. The South argued that no benefits accrued to them: they would not be given the vaccines on a preferential basis or on concessional terms, nor would they be given access to the technology for making the vaccines in the future. Professor Gurdial Singh Nijar, one of the Southern countries' lead negotiators on access and benefit-sharing, argued that there was no basis to exclude any genetic resource from the Protocol as it was clearly within the scope of the CBD.[31]

The European Union (EU) then proposed a clause on "special consideration relevant to emergency situations." The proposal required countries to provide immediate access to pathogens that also fall under the mandate of relevant international organizations such as the WHO. These pathogens are those of particular public concern for the health of humans, animals, and plants.

The provisions that were finally agreed upon are set out in Article 8 (Special Considerations) and Article 4(3)–(4) (Relationship with International Agreements and Instruments). Article 8(b) provides that, in the development and implementation of access and benefit-sharing legislation or regulatory requirements, each party

---

[28] *Nagoya Protocol on Access to Genetic Resources and the Fair and Equitable Sharing of Benefits Arising from Their Utilization to the 1992 Convention on Biological Diversity*, Nagoya, 29 October 2010, available at http://www.cbd.int [hereinafter Nagoya Protocol].

[29] See chapter 9, J. Cabrera Medaglia, "Access and Benefit-Sharing: North–South Challenges in Implementing the Convention on Biological Diversity and its Nagoya Protocol."

[30] L. Glowka, F. Burhenne-Guimin, H. Synge, J.A. McNeeley, and L. Guntling, "A Guide to the Convention on Biological Diversity", IUCN Environmental Policy and Law Paper No. 030, 1994.

[31] See G. S. Nijar, "The Nagoya Protocol on Access and Benefit Sharing of Genetic Resources: Analysis and Implementation Options for Developing Countries," Research Paper 36, South Centre, March 2011.

shall pay due regard to cases of present or imminent need that can be singled out in the Protocol for special treatment. This provision relates to viruses, and in particular pathogens. At the time the Protocol was being negotiated, the WHO was in the throes of an active debate triggered by the demand by some Southern states that there should be benefit-sharing in respect of pathogens in the global South. The South was concerned that pharmaceutical research in the North would develop medical treatments serving only the North and sought control of pathogens to ensure Southern interests would benefit equitably from the research and cures when found.

3.2 *"Warsaw International Loss and Damage Mechanism" Associated with Climate Change Impacts*

Global climate agreements seek to prevent an irreversible climate change situation and support Southern states as they adapt to climate change conditions and mitigate their emissions of greenhouse gases ("adaptation and mitigation"). The South plays a critical role in enhancing international climate cooperation. The South's role became clear in the highly contested issues of the nineteenth Conference of the Parties (COP 19) to the UNFCCC in Warsaw in November 2013. The South wanted issues of loss and damage due to climate impacts to be covered outside the adaptation framework.[32] On 20 November 2013, the G77 and China walked out of the conference in protest at the North's unwillingness to discuss a mechanism for compensating poor nations for loss and damage due to the impact of severe weather events, and how countries should respond to climate impacts that are difficult or impossible to adapt to, such as Typhoon Haiyan.[33] The North opposed a treaty text that would have provided for compensation based on claims of legal responsibility, where the damage would be much more than any adaptation to climate change, for which the North had pledged a voluntary fund. On the other hand, the South did not want voluntary contributions or any act of charity from the North, but instead insisted that financial payments be linked to industrialized states' responsibility for human-induced climate change.

Climate "losses" include, inter alia, loss of livelihood, damage to property, food security, and climate migration.[34] The damage that Typhoon Haiyan wrought in the Philippines in November 2012 took center stage at COP 19, and nations ended

---

[32] See "Summary of the Warsaw Climate Change Conference," Earth Negotiations Bulletin, 26 November 2013.

[33] Called Typhoon Yolanda in The Philippines, Haiyan occurred during the COP 19 meetings.

[34] See UNFCCC, *Report of the Conference of the Parties on Its Eighteenth Session, Held in Doha from 26 November to 8 December 2012*, 28 February 2013, FCCC/CP/2012/8/Add.1, decision 3/CP.18. Approaches to address loss and damage associated with climate change impacts in developing countries that are particularly vulnerable to the adverse effects of climate change to enhance adaptive capacity, in UNFCCC, *Report of the Conference of the Parties on Its Eighteenth session, Held in Doha from 26 November to 8 December 2012*, 28 February 2013, FCCC/CP/2012/8/Add.1, p. 21.

up with the Warsaw International Mechanism for Loss and Damage Associated with Climate Change Impacts (Warsaw International Mechanism).[35]

The Warsaw International Mechanism in its preamble "acknowledges the contribution of adaptation and risk management strategies towards addressing loss and damage associated with climate change impacts"; it also "acknowledges that loss and damage associated with the adverse effects of climate change includes, and in some cases involves more than, that which can be reduced by adaptation."[36] Northern countries, troubled that they might incur financial burdens to compensate for losses alleged to be the result of climate change, argued that causation for natural disasters provided no basis for making financial claims for damages. The compromise between South and North is reflected in the use of phrases such as "budgetary implications"[37] or "availability of financial resources."[38] The South considered that the Warsaw International Mechanism was a step forward in their demands for agreement on the establishment of a loss and damage compensation mechanism.

4. THE HUMAN RIGHTS CHALLENGE FOR SSC

An overarching question for SSC is how human rights are observed. SSC practice is challenged by aggressive seizures of natural resources in places where the rule of law is weak. In Africa, Asia, and South America, "land-grabbing" is a festering problem, which illustrates why the UN SDGs promote strengthening the rule of law. While land-grabbing is discussed elsewhere in this book,[39] it is emphasized here in the context of SSC. Land-grabbing is unlawful under most national law, and is complex – done both by multinational companies from the North and by Southern corporations from China and elsewhere, often with the connivance of governments of Southern countries.[40] When Southern entities are complicit in land-grabbing, it exposes the failure of SSC.

The ASEAN has tried to advance SSC through measures to observe the rule of law and human rights. However, the persistence of "land-grabbing" in Lao PDR, Cambodia, and Vietnam raises doubts as to the efficacy of the recent ASEAN Human Rights Declaration of 2012 (AHRD). The AHRD extended the traditional concept of human rights to include "the right to adequate and affordable food,

---

[35] UNFCCC COP 19, draft decision-/CP.19, in UNFCCC, *Warsaw International Mechanism for Loss and Damage Associated with Climate Change Impacts*, 22 November 2013, FCCC/CP/2013/L.15.

[36] Ibid, first and second recitals.

[37] Ibid, para. 16.

[38] Ibid, para. 17.

[39] See generally chapter 11, C. Oguamanam, "Sustainable Development in the Era of Bioenergy and Agricultural Land Grab."

[40] M. Kaag and A. Zoomers, *The Global Land Grab – Beyond the Hype* (London: Zed Books, 2014).

freedom from hunger and access to safe and nutritious food."[41] The right to development provides a right of every human person and peoples of ASEAN to "participate in [and] enjoy and benefit equitably and sustainably from economic, social, cultural and political development."[42] Each state's capacity to observe these human rights provisions is uneven across the ASEAN region; nonetheless, to ensure a standard application of the right, the ASEAN Intergovernmental Commission on Human Rights should oversee violations of the human right to food under AHRD.

The issue of land-grabbing in the ASEAN region is compounded by other human rights violations. The disappearance of Dr Sombath Somphone,[43] a "human rights warrior" campaigning against land-grabbing, has become a regional issue. Civil society organizations across South East Asia, and especially in Lao PDR, are demanding that the South take steps to control and eliminate the land-grabbing phenomenon.[44] SSC worldwide has been slow to undertake the enforcement of human rights.

5. SOUTH–SOUTH COOPERATION REGIONALLY

While SSC is problematic in respect of human rights and other social issues, and has a mixed record on trade or security, the SSC record of cooperation on environmental issues is more substantial. The South deals with environmental issues affecting their region within each nation, across borders, and regionally. SSC facilitates the implementation of MEAs. Regional SSC organizations are part of the global environmental governance networks and can play an important role.

SSC is rarely easy. Most states declare that they wish to cooperate, but at the same time decline to act in harmony until all states have formally agreed to do so. The result is inaction until agreement is attained regionally. One state's inability or unwillingness to act is the excuse for all states not to act. The ASEAN[45] illustrates how SSC functions through a regional southern intergovernmental organization. Before examining ASEAN, it is useful to survey other intergovernmental regional organizations of the South. Each merits deeper study in its own right. This chapter identifies patterns evident in SSC, and invites others to undertake comparable studies for other southern regional organizations.

Small island states pose interesting patterns of SSC. In the Caribbean, CARICOM[46] has been a significant regional forum for policy-making and coordinating political and economic decision-making. Although they have sea-coasts along

---

[41] Association of Southeast Asian Nations, "ASEAN Human Rights Declaration", www.asean.org, para. 28(a).
[42] Ibid, para. 35.
[43] L. Hunt, "Missing Sombath Still Dogging Laos," *The Diplomat*, 17 December 2013.
[44] M. Palatino, "Somchai, Jonas, Sombath: Southeast Asia's Missing Human Rights Warrior," *The Diplomat*, 16 April 2013.
[45] Association of Southeast Asian Nations, "History," www.asean.org
[46] Caribbean Community Secretariat, www.caricom.org.

the Caribbean, the states of Meso-America are more focused on their terrestrial environments than the shared marine environment. Nonetheless, these states share common approaches to supporting their legal and institutional capacities. They have cooperated with the UN Environment Programme on agreeing to the Regional Seas Agreement for the Wider Caribbean.[47] But since the U.S. and other participating states have failed to adequately fund this international agreement at necessary levels, it is not well implemented. CARICOM shines in the area of sharing best practices and good relations regionally among its national institutions, whether they are courts or ministries. National well-being is undermined by transnational illicit trade in drugs and the unlawful conduct that it generates.

In the Pacific, the South Pacific Regional Environmental Programme (SPREP)[48] provides a SSC framework for small island states. Because it is a voluntary pact, it has relied on support from European states, Australia, and New Zealand to fund its development undertakings. The traditional societies of small island states tend to have customary law values intact, but a failure to work with customary community norms by overseas aid agencies and investment enterprises weakens the resilience of the local communities to manage their resources and families. The many island states collaborate in operating regional endeavors such as the University of the Pacific, but since each is isolated they cannot aid each other locally so easily.

States from both CARICOM and SPREP have joined to form the Alliance of Small Island States (AOSIS).[49] This coalition has sought to unite states to combat sea-level rise and other climate change phenomena that threaten the very existence of small islands. AOSIS illustrates a problem faced in SSC. Large islands, such as Papua New Guinea, that are not threatened with the existential crises posed by rising sea levels do not share the same political urgency to press the interests of smaller island states. Wealthier states such as the Dominican Republic are threatened by the severe poverty in Haiti. Remote states, such as the Maldives, lack the links and influence with regional groups of neighboring states. AOSIS has found it difficult to shape a cohesive South–South bloc of states.

Beyond the small island states, Southern organizations on large continents face similar challenges. Notwithstanding the shared postcolonial political perceptions of the G77, or the "Cold War" era perceptions of the Non-Aligned "bloc" of nations, merely being a developing nation or being located in the South alone is not a sufficient basis for unity. In the cone of South America, MERCOSUR[50] has made modest progress in shaping cooperation for trade and strengthening

---

[47] This is a UNEP Regional Seas Agreement, see www.cep.unep.org.
[48] Secretariat of the Pacific Regional Environment Programme, www.sprep.org.
[49] Alliance of Small Island States, http://aosis.org.
[50] Mercosur, *Mercado Común del Sur* (Common Market of the South) is an economic integration organization whose founding members are Argentina, Brazil, Paraguay, and Uruguay.

judicial institutions. However, the Andean Pact,[51] with its elaborate set of regional governance agreements, remains little more than just the national regimes of each nation. This is true also of the International Agreement of the Amazon Basin States,[52] who have agreed to set up a regional organization but cannot yet agree on what it should do to conserve the common assets of the wider Amazon.

In South Asia, states have agreed to work together through the South Asian Cooperative Environmental Agreement (SACEP).[53] However, the geopolitics of this region preclude SACEP from becoming effective. Its secretariat is located in Sri Lanka, where civil war has sapped its effectiveness as a seat of cooperation. India has little interest in cooperating with its neighbors on environmental issues, since it is a vast nation in its own right and looks to solving its domestic environmental issues as its first priority. India has asserted its own interest in Ladakh and the balance of the Himalayan region, and there is little environmental cooperation with Nepal or Bhutan. The vastness of the Indian Ocean means that SSC with states in this region is also limited.

The regions of West Asia, through to North Africa, have sound cooperation through affinity organizations such as the Arab League.[54] The Arab League has engaged in cooperative programs for building capacity with respect to land use and planning subjects for Arab states. Financing from Saudi Arabia and other oil-rich states has enabled these capacity-building programs to advance, but the expertise developed does not deeply transform or shape developmental patterns in sustainable ways, since authoritarian regimes within several nations have not been willing to engage the public or deploy trained personnel as needed. Deficiencies in the rule of law have meant that such training and the skills taught were used far too sparingly. More recently, civil strife following the "Arab Spring" has precluded cooperation. In sub-regions, Gulf states cooperate on the protection of the Gulf, and the Kuwait Regional Seas Agreement[55] has played an important role. In North Africa, the Mediterranean Sea's "Barcelona Agreement"[56] has built capacity and cooperation to protect coastal regions and marine environment. Developed states have helped with this capacity-building. However, little SSC has advanced beyond this narrow area for environmental cooperation.

In 2008, Venezuela, Chile and Bolivia became associate members. See MrecoPress, at www.Mercosur.com/about-mercosur.

[51] See V. M. Tafur, "Environmental Harmonization: Emergence and Development of the Andean Community", in Nicholas A. Robinson, Lye Lin Heng, and Elizabeth Burleson (eds.), *Comparative Environmental Law and Regulation* (Westlaw, 2011).

[52] Amazon Cooperation Treaty Organization, www.octa.org.

[53] South Asian Cooperative Environmental Agreement, www.sacep.org.

[54] Arab League Online, www.arableagueonline.org.

[55] *Kuwait Regional Convention for Cooperation on the Protection of the Marine Environment from Pollution*, Kuwait, 24 April 1978, in force 1 July 1979, www.unep.ch/regionalseas/legal/conlist.html.

[56] *Convention for the Protection of the Mediterranean Sea against Pollution*, Barcelona, 16 February 1976, in force 2 December 1978, 1102 UNTS 27.

The SSC in Sub-Sahara Africa is more encouraging. In the post–apartheid region, the Southern African Development Community,[57] with headquarters in Gaborone, Botswana, has guided sustainable development in this region. South Africa's economy is the strong driver, but a collaborative regional approach is fostered as a matter of policy. Less effective collaboration exists in East Africa and in the Francophone states of West Africa. The coastal regional seas programs have not been implemented. The links to colonial economies still drive economic development relationships. The oil wealth of Nigeria has corrupted the rule of law in that nation. In many areas, civil war and civil strife, and now fundamental Islamic paramilitary forces, destabilize societies. Despite all this, the African Union (AU) is a brilliant example of increasingly effective state-to-state cooperation. The African Court on Human and People's Rights has issued influential and progressive judicial decisions on cases before it, though they have been few.

South–South collaboration cannot be forced, but must be encouraged through collaborative and cooperative approaches. Building capacity for SSC is a focus of both the UN University for Peace in Costa Rica and the UN University in Tokyo, which are mandated to encourage SSC. The IUCN Academy of Environmental Law[58] has large membership from universities in the South. However, too often such academic cooperation and capacity-building is not immediately influential with respect to governments. Moreover, if SSC is to advance rigorously, governments will need to enhance their respect for the rule of law and rely more on public participation in environmental decision-making.

ASEAN's experience suggests ways for states to cooperate regionally to build stronger economies, and robust rule-of-law cultures can help strengthen other nations in the same region. This ASEAN approach is criticized as too slow or gradual, and yet, perhaps because it is not forced, it is effective. It may be that the regional approach of the African Union is being driven in this direction, too. Perhaps CARICOM and other regional systems can benefit from the comparative analysis of ASEAN practices, and vice versa. There is virtually no scholarly analysis comparing SSC across regional intergovernmental organizations in different regions in the South. It may be instructive, therefore, to devote more extended attention to ASEAN in this chapter.

6. REGIONAL SOUTH–SOUTH COOPERATION IN SOUTH EAST ASIA

ASEAN was established on 8 August 1967, through the Bangkok Declaration,[59] by its five founding states: Indonesia, Malaysia, Philippines, Singapore, and Thailand. It was subsequently joined by six others in the region, making a total of ten member

---

[57] Southern African Development Community, www.sadc.int.
[58] IUCN Academy of Environmental Law, www.iucnael.org.
[59] ASEAN *Declaration*, Bangkok, 8 August 1967, 6 ILM 1233 (1967).

states (AMCs). The new AMCs are Brunei Darussalam, Cambodia, Lao PDR, Myanmar, and Vietnam. With the exception of Brunei, the other cluster of AMCs, known as "CLMV" (Cambodia, Lao PDR, Myanmar, and Vietnam), are countries in transition, for which the ASEAN Summit Meeting in 2000 launched the "Initiative for ASEAN Integration" (IAI), a framework by which the more developed ASEAN member states could cooperate to build the capacity of the region's less developed states. The CLMV countries are the members in which poor and vulnerable communities are most affected by environmental disasters and degradation. Thus the IAI Strategic Framework[60] seeks to narrow the development gap in ASEAN's integration efforts through additional funding, and special consideration for CLMV participation is built into the design of all ASEAN cooperation programs, projects, and activities, including those under the ASEAN Socio-Cultural Community Blueprint.[61]

Environmental SSC is an ASEAN priority. ASEAN states have collaborated by designating ASEAN Heritage Parks in each country. Three ASEAN members – Indonesia, Malaysia, and the Philippines – have also entered into a tripartite memorandum of understanding relating to the protection of sea turtles.[62] ASEAN environment ministers meet regularly and approve five-year plans for building regionwide capacity for environmental protection. ASEAN is also engaged in the globalized environmental legal system, including facilitation of MEAs. MEA cooperation involves the environmental authorities within each nation, as well as at regional and global levels.

ASEAN's forward-looking governance structure seeks to cultivate new ways to cooperate on environmental and other issues by establishing channels for exchanging views and experiences through what are known as "Dialogue Partners" under Article 44 of the ASEAN Charter.[63] Dialogue Partners include the EU, Australia, Canada, India, and the United States, to mention a few. Meetings with Dialogue Partners stimulate new cooperative efforts within ASEAN.

The principal environmental challenges that the South, including ASEAN, face are climate change, food security, water security, pandemics (e.g. avian influenza and SARS), and climate migration. Severe environmental problems have

---

[60] Initiative for ASEAN Integration (IAI) Strategic Framework and IAI Work Plan 2 (2009-2015), Cha-Am, 1 March 2009, annex to the 2009 Cha-am Hua Hin Declaration on the Roadmap for an ASEAN Community (2009-2015) signed on 1 March 2009 in Cha-am by the Heads of State/ Government during the fourteenth ASEAN Summit, reproduced in K. L. Koh (ed.), *ASEAN Environmental Law, Policy and Governance: Selected Documents*, vol. 1 (Singapore: World Scientific, 2009), pp. 571–592.

[61] 2009 Blueprint on the ASEAN Socio-Cultural Community, 1 March 2009, Cha-am, during the fourteenth ASEAN Summit, reproduced in ibid, pp. 615–650.

[62] Memorandum of Understanding on ASEAN Sea Turtle Conservation and Protection, reproduced in K. L. Koh (ed.), *ASEAN Environmental Law, Policy and Governance: Selected Documents*, vol. 2 (Singapore: World Scientific, 2009), pp. 77–82.

[63] *Charter of the Association of Southeast Asian Nations*, 20 November 2007, www.aseansec.org [hereinafter ASEAN Charter].

568 South–South Cooperation

raised questions not only of human rights but of human "security," particularly among the poor and vulnerable communities, where public health pandemics remain omnipresent threats. "Environmental Human Security" extends beyond ASEAN to what ASEAN calls an "all-of-the-world" approach. ASEAN actively advances the concept of human security,[64] focusing on care for individual humans and the cooperation of states, regional and global organizations, the private sector, NGOs, and other stakeholders.

The ASEAN Political Security Community Blueprint 2009[65] provides a promise of such an approach in addressing transnational challenges, such as food security and land-grabbing. Moreover, since two thirds of the human population in ASEAN will be living in cities by 2050, for ASEAN states to advance the UN SDGs on eradicating poverty, ASEAN aims to accelerate its cooperation at regional, national, subnational, and local levels. SSC can further apply regionally appropriate technologies for transportation or sanitation, as well as tackling social problems such as the land-grabbing phenomenon or the mix of commercial and social issues that cause air pollution from forest fires (the "haze") used to clear land to plant palm oil plantations. The haze pollutes Brunei, Malaysia, Singapore and at times, even south of Thailand and the Philippines.

Social cooperation, however difficult, can produce positive results. Article 1(13) of the ASEAN Charter promotes a people-oriented ASEAN, in which all sectors of society are encouraged to participate to further "the process of ASEAN integration and community building." In furtherance of this Charter provision, and to address land-grabbing and other social problems, in 2011 an Indonesian NGO organized a meeting on South East Asian Human Rights Institutionalism, which adopted the Bali Declaration on Human Rights and Agribusiness in Southeast Asia (Bali Declaration).[66] This Declaration dealt with violations of land rights involving agribusiness. Following the Bali Declaration, on 26 October 2012 the European Parliament called for a moratorium on forced evictions and recommended that the EU suspend tariff-free imports of agricultural goods linked to human rights abuses in Cambodia, with specific reference to the sugarcane plantation industry.[67]

---

[64] K. L. Koh, "The Discourse of Environmental Security in the ASEAN Context," in B. Jessup and K. Rubenstein (eds.), *Environmental Discourses in Public and International Law* (Cambridge: Cambridge University Press, 2012), pp. 218–237.

[65] 2009 Blueprint on the ASEAN Socio-Cultural Community, 1 March 2009 in Cha-am during the fourteenth ASEAN Summit, reproduced in K. L. Koh (ed.), *ASEAN Environmental Law, Policy and Governance: Selected Documents*, vol. 1 (Singapore: World Scientific, 2009), pp. 615–650.

[66] Bali Declaration on Human Rights and Agribusiness in Southeast Asia, adopted by the international meeting of South East Asian Human Rights Institutions on "Human Rights and Business: Plural Legal Approaches to Conflict Resolution, Institutional Strengthening and Legal Reform" hosted by the Indonesian National Human Rights Commission was held in Bali, Indonesia, from 28 November to 1 December 2011, available at www.forestpeoples.org.

[67] European Parliament Resolution of 26 October 2012 on the situation in Cambodia (2012/2844 (RSP)), document T7-0402/2012.

These measures were followed by the 2012 Phnom Penh Workshop on Human Rights and Agribusiness in Southeast Asia, which produced the "Phnom Penh Joint Statement"[68] to give more effective consideration to the Bali Declaration. The Phnom Penh Joint Statement:

> Calls on the governments of the ASEAN region to respect and uphold land rights for local communities and indigenous peoples and to make the right to free, prior and informed consent a mandatory requirement to national laws on land tenure [. . .] [and] on ASEAN to extend the mandate of AICHER (ASEAN Intergovernmental Commission on Human Rights) as an effective and independent human rights mechanism to investigate the violation of farmers' and indigenous peoples' rights and to encourage member states to domesticate the *Voluntary Guidelines on Responsible Governance of Tenure of Land, Fisheries, Forests and in the Context of National Food Security.*[69]

When the regional South tolerates human rights violations, such as Dr Sombard's case, it undermines UN SDGs. The South should not hide behind principles such as state sovereignty or "common but differentiated responsibility" to avoid confronting violations of environmental justice, injuries to public health, and denials of other human rights. One of the greatest challenges to "ASEAN cooperation" lies in how inveterate principles of sovereignty are invoked to resist SSC on grounds that cooperation must observe the ASEAN Way – namely, non-interference in domestic affairs. After twelve years of delay, in 2014 Indonesia finally ratified the ASEAN Agreement on Transboundary Haze Pollution[70] and agreed to combat transboundary air pollution.[71] However, much will need to be done to implement this Agreement. Another example of this problem is the land surrounding Preah Vihear on the South China Sea, where among the states claiming title are four ASEAN countries. The recently established ASEAN Institute for Peace and Reconciliation (AIPR) has modalities to contribute to conflict management. Although AIPR's role is mainly directed to research, it could work on conflict management by promoting socio-economic development in conflict areas, which are mostly economically underdeveloped.

ASEAN's approach to environmental cooperation within ASEAN and with the world, particularly with its Dialogue Partners,[72] is contained in the ASEAN

---

[68] See Forest Peoples Programme, "Statement of the Phnom Penh Workshop on Human Rights and Agribusiness in Southeast Asia: Making the Bali Declaration Effective", 10 December 2012, www.forestpeoples.org.

[69] "Making the Bali Declaration Effective: The Phnom Penh Workshop on Human Rights and Agribusiness in Southeast Asia," adopted by the Committee of the World Food Security, 1 May 2012.

[70] ASEAN Haze Action Online, http://haze.asean.org.

[71] See A. A. Putri, "Indonesia Ratifies Haze Treaty after 12 Years of Stalling," *Jakarta Globe*, 17 September 2014.

[72] ASEAN Charter, note 63, art. 44.

570 South–South Cooperation

Socio-Cultural Community Blueprint.[73] The Blueprint promotes sustainable development objectives through promoting a clean and green environment – protecting the natural resource base by conservation of soil, water, mineral, energy, biodiversity, forest, coastal, and marine resources, as well as improvement in water and air quality for the ASEAN region. Through these regional measures, ASEAN contributes to attaining the objectives of the MEAs and UN SDGs, such as those related to climate change and energy, biodiversity, disaster management, and risk reduction. This cooperation is not only at the horizontal level; it is also vertical. Harmonizing national laws and programs among the ASEAN member states is important given that ASEAN does not have a parliament or a court of justice.

Despite ASEAN's accomplishments, much remains to be done if the UN SDGs are to be attained in the region or internationally. SSC and North–South cooperation are critical to achieving sustainable development, to promote coherence globally in issues such as combating disease or facilitating migration of species. Many gaps in implementation remain.

7. CONCLUSION

Dr Mahathir Mohamad's speech on the North–South divide echoes long after 1992. His rhetoric has been a political rallying point for Southern countries (South–South) in their negotiations with the North about support for their socio-economic development. Attaining the SDGs in the future will require close cooperation between South and North; nonetheless the South continues to stress, through reliance on the principle of "common but differentiated responsibilities," that the North must not forget its development came at the expense of the South. This principle is cited to claim support for southern development through insisting on technology transfer and financial assistance from the North. The UN SDGs can provide a platform for South–South, North–South, and global cooperation. Practical actions can make it so, for example, by cooperating on sea-level rise and other worldwide adaptations to climate change impacts.

One way in which this "new" cooperation can begin is seen in the emergence of triangular partnerships. For example, ASEAN's "Dialogue Partners" provide a framework for ASEAN as a Southern region to engage cooperatively with a Northern region such as the EU, or major states of the North such as the U.S., *together* with the UN, through its specialized agencies. Triangular cooperation exists in some areas of high interdependency, such as disaster management and threat of pandemics in zoonotic diseases. Cooperation through these partnerships has bridged gaps between North and South. A comparable pattern is found in the

---

[73] 2009 Blueprint on the ASEAN Socio-Cultural Community (ASCC or Pillar 3), 1 March 2009, Cha-am during the fourteenth ASEAN Summit, reproduced in K. L. Koh (ed.), *ASEAN Environmental Law, Policy and Governance: Selected Documents*, vol. 1 (Singapore: World Scientific, 2009), pp. 615–650.

relationship of the International Union for the Conservation of Nature (IUCN) and its World Commission on Protected Areas, with parks agencies in states of the South and North alike.

Triangular cooperation is a "whole of the world" approach, which works to dissolve divisions of North and South through practical joint measures. This cooperative model is likely to grow,[74] because as governments perceive that the natural resources and environmental systems they mutually rely upon are under increasing stress, they will find it in their interest to cooperate more closely with other states. Whether due to experiencing pandemics or climate change impacts, governments on each side of the former divide are receptive to North–South cooperation. The UN's role can facilitate and build cooperative triangular relationships with the South's subregional organizations, such as ASEAN. UN specialized agencies, such as the WHO, can be encouraged to expand their work on this model. Triangular cooperation needs to acknowledge its foundations on principles of equity; if Southern countries perceive proposals to cooperate to be favoring large multinationals from the North, the "divide" will re-emerge. The UN, IUCN, WHO, MEAs, international financial institutions (e.g. Asian Development Bank, World Bank or the newly established China – led Asian Infrastructure Investment Bank (AIIB), and other such third parties must mediate North–South relations to be sure equity is observed.

The challenges inherent in South–South cooperation are many. Only some have been highlighted in this chapter. The themes discussed here are an invitation for more comparative study of South–South cooperative relationships. If the UN SDGs are to be attained, building the South's capacity for SSC, as well as for implementation of MEAs, should be given high priority by all states. The North needs to act in practical ways to assist in this process. The South needs to strengthen its regional organizations and network with other Southern regional organizations. The "third parties" need to move into a robust role of bringing about triangular cooperation, and the South and North need to cooperate with them in doing so.

---

[74] The capacity to enhance cooperation in light of both its sociobiological and legal foundations is elaborated in N. A. Robinson, "Evolved Norms: A Canon for the Anthropocene," in C. Voigt (ed.), *Rule of Law for Nature: New Dimensions and Ideas in Environmental Law* (Cambridge: Cambridge University Press, 2014), p. 46.

27

Public Participation in International Negotiation and Compliance

Lalanath de Silva

1. INTRODUCTION

The growth of the civil society[1] sector is largely responsible for claiming more participatory spaces in decision-making at the local, national, regional, and international levels. A handful of government champions have aided and abetted these efforts. What started as a self-serving effort by Northern civil society actors evolved into a benevolent project to bring Southern voices to the table. By the end of the century, there were a significant number of Southern voices making demands for participation on their own behalf. These efforts have resulted in considerable opportunities for civil society participation in international negotiations and compliance, which range from consultative status for civil society organizations with speaking rights to the right to invoke compliance mechanisms.[2] Despite these advances, significant gaps in the rules, institutions, and practices remain.

There is still no uniform international practice code for civil society and public participation in international treaty- and policy-making and compliance. Even within the United Nations (UN) system, each program and agency has its own unique rules and practices, and accreditation systems for civil society organizations vary widely. To this day, some states still contest the right of the public and civil society to participate at the international level. Funding for participation continues to be controlled by Northern bilaterals (governmental aid donors) and foundations, resulting in Northern civil society groups often setting the agenda and dominating

---

[1] For the purposes of this chapter, "civil society organization" is defined as an organization or an aggregate grouping of organizations that have organized themselves to deal with specific interests of society (and are often seen as distinct from the state and business). They are likely to have a central node, office, and representatives. See United Nations Environment Programme, "Report of the Independent Group of Experts on New Mechanisms for Stakeholder Engagement at UNEP," November 11, 2013, www.unep.org.

[2] E.g. the Aarhus Convention provides for a compliance committee to which civil society groups can complain about non-compliance with treaty obligations by states parties.

Lalanath de Silva

the negotiations and compliance processes. This chapter outlines the power and influence of civil society, the benefits and costs of participation, and the rules and practices relating to their participation in international processes. It assesses some of the current gaps in the international system and makes recommendations (with good practice examples) for how those gaps may be closed.

2. POWER AND INFLUENCE OF CIVIL SOCIETY GROUPS

Public participation in international policy- and treaty-making and implementation is largely a phenomenon of the twentieth century.[3] The notion that international treaties were the exclusive domain of states and their authorized representatives effectively came to an end with World War II. While the intergovernmental nature of international treaty negotiations has remained essentially unchanged, civil society participation is now regarded as necessary, if not indispensable. In 1948, the UN listed forty-one groups with formally accredited consultative status.[4] By 2013, there were more than 3,735 non-governmental organizations (NGOs) registered with the UN Economic and Social Council (ECOSOC) and over 30,000 other NGOs working with various UN and other international organizations with varying levels of access to and participation in international proceedings.[5]

The exponential growth in civil society participation in international environmental negotiations can be traced to the 1972 UN Conference on the Human Environment held in Stockholm.[6] Since the 1992 UN Conference on Environment and Development (the "Earth Summit") in Rio de Janeiro, there has been a rapid growth in civil society organizations eager to participate in international proceedings and negotiations.[7] Over 2,400 NGOs and 17,000 people attended the parallel Rio NGO Forum in 1992.[8] The Rio Declaration on Environment and Development (Rio Declaration),[9] Agenda 21,[10] the Statement of Forest Principles,[11] and the two negotiated multilateral environmental agreements

---

[3] S. Charnovitz, "Two Centuries of Participation: NGOs and International Governance" (1997) 18 *Michigan Journal of International Law* 183. Civil society organizations were involved in international negotiations for more than two centuries, albeit at less visible and influential levels than today.

[4] P. J. Simmons, "Learning to Live with NGOs" (1998) 112 *Foreign Policy* 82.

[5] UN Department of Economic and Social Affairs, "NGO Branch," http://csonet.org. The latest list of registered NGOs is available at: http://csonet.org/content/documents/E2012INF6.pdf.

[6] K. Conca, "Greening the UN: Environmental Organizations and the UN System," in T. G. Weiss and L. Gordenker (eds.), *NGOs, the UN, and Global Governance* (Colorado: Lynne Rienner, 1996), pp. 103–119.

[7] Ibid.

[8] UN Conference on Environment and Development, "Earth Summit," www.un.org.

[9] Rio de Janeiro, 14 June 1992, UN Doc. A/CONF.151/26 (vol. 1); 31 ILM 874 (1992).

[10] *Agenda 21: Programme of Action for Sustainable Development*, Rio de Janeiro, 14 June 1992, U.N. GAOR, 46th Sess., Agenda Item 21, UN Doc. A/Conf.151/26 (1992).

[11] UN General Assembly, *Report of the United Nations Conference on Environment and Development: Non-legally Binding Authoritative Statement of Principles for a Global Consensus on*

574   *Public Participation in International Negotiation and Compliance*

(MEAs)[12] that emerged from the Earth Summit have ample references to the important role of civil society in sustainable development.

There are multiple reasons for the rise of civil society groups as stakeholders in international processes, including the advent of information technology and electronic media, greater awareness of global interdependence, the spread of democracy,[13] increasing funding for civil society participation, and improved capacity within civil society groups. UN collaborations with civil society organizations originally emerged from the necessity to implement relief programs, primarily in response to disasters, election monitoring, and human rights protection.[14] Today, interactions span a broader spectrum of activities, including the initiation, negotiation, administration, implementation, and enforcement of MEAs. Civil society and UN agencies alone cannot be credited for this phenomenon. The Unites States and Western European governments in particular have been vocal advocates for increased civil society engagement in international agreements including MEAs.

Many of these governments have included NGO representatives on official state delegations. They also formally and informally work with civil society groups that have solid research capabilities and can provide sound advice on difficult technical issues. At other times, they collaborate closely with groups that command networks and have a field presence capable of delivering results. Because of the high levels of freedoms of speech, expression, press, association, and assembly enjoyed by citizens in these countries, combined with democratic systems of government, civil society groups in Europe and the United States collectively wield considerable power and influence over their governments and politicians. They are a significant force that balances the access and power wielded by business and industry in these countries. For example, large environmental NGOs in the United States have lobbyists who canvass support for their causes in Congress just as corporate sector lobbyists do. Similarly, environmental groups often collaborate with the Green Party in the European Parliament to promote environmental regulations and causes.

On the other hand, governments in the global South have been slow to include NGO representatives on their delegations.[15] NGO representatives on developing

---

the *Management, Conservation and Sustainable Development of All Types of Forests*, 14 August 1992, A/CONF.151/26 (Vol. III).

[12] The *United Nations Framework Convention on Climate Change*, New York, 9 May 1992, in force 21 March 1994, 1771 UNTS 107; S. Treaty Doc No. 102-38; UN Doc. A/AC.237/18 (Part II)/Add.1; 31 ILM 849 (1992) (hereinafter UNFCCC); *Convention on Biological Diversity*, Rio de Janeiro, 5 June 1992, in force 29 December 1993, 1760 UNTS 79; 31 ILM 818 (1992).

[13] B. Gemmill and A. Bamidele-Izu, "The Role of NGOs and Civil Society in Global Environmental Governance," in D. C. Esty and M. H. Ivanova (eds.), *Global Environmental Governance – Options and Opportunities* (Connecticut: Yale School of Forestry & Environmental Studies, 2002).

[14] Ibid.

[15] Personal observation based on the author's experience serving as a member of a developing country delegation and from discussions with other NGO representatives on developing country delegations.

country delegations recount varied experiences. They are marginalized in some delegations while in others they occupy a central place by virtue of their expertise or influence. With varied levels of press freedoms and freedom of association, assembly, and speech, coupled with varying levels of democratic space and opportunity, the influence wielded by civil society groups in the Southern countries is highly variable. Often they are unable to balance the influence of business and industry on these governments and politicians.

There are currently 15,662 organizations from Africa, Asia, and Latin America and the Caribbean registered with the NGO branch of the UN Department of Economic and Social Affairs.[16] In comparison, there are 9,362 organizations registered from North America and Europe.[17] Europe and North America have more than twice as many registered organizations per capita than Asia, Africa, and Latin America and the Caribbean. When this is coupled with the fact that Oceania (consisting mostly of Australia and New Zealand), the Americas, and Europe enjoy the highest levels of philanthropy compared to Asia and Africa,[18] it is not difficult to see that European and U.S. civil society organizations are better represented and funded than developing country organizations. As a result, United States and European civil society groups have greater influence and capacity within the international negotiation process, and their voices tend to be amplified on account of greater receptivity by their own governmental delegations and the media.

The collective impact of these factors is to make European and U.S. civil society organizations far more influential and powerful than Southern groups within the international negotiation processes in which they choose to participate. Because of this, European and U.S. civil society groups influence agenda-setting, negotiations, governance, and eventually implementation of and compliance with MEAs far more than their Southern counterparts. The upshot is that agendas and negotiated outcomes of international processes do not always reflect Southern priorities or challenges and sometimes lead to implementation and compliance failures. For example, because of tighter hazardous waste laws in Northern countries (enacted partly owing to pressure from Northern NGOs), Northern countries and companies have provided financial incentives to Southern countries to accept such waste either for dumping or processing.[19] Southern NGOs and governments were opposed to these moves and often advocated for export bans on such wastes. The Basel Convention on the Control of Transboundary Movements of Hazardous

[16] NGO Branch: UN Department of Economic and Social Affairs, "Integrated Civil Society Organization System," http://esango.un.org.
[17] Ibid.
[18] Charities Aid Foundation, *World Giving Index 2012 – a Global View of Giving Trends* (UK: Charities Aid Foundation, 2012), p. 31.
[19] I. Y. Ajunwa, "The Illicit Transfer and Dumping of Toxic Waste: The Adverse Effects of Toxic and Electronic Wastes on Human Rights," Report to Fourth Session of the United Nations Human Rights Council, 5 March 2007.

576   *Public Participation in International Negotiation and Compliance*

Wastes and their Disposal was negotiated in 1989 and came into effect in 1992.[20] Although the negotiated text allows for export of hazardous waste from one country to another provided the exporting country gets prior informed consent from the importing country, this was not supported by Southern NGOs or governments, and in practice has often failed as a safeguard. With a few exceptions (such as Greenpeace), Northern NGOs were silent on this issue.

Changing this balance requires a two-pronged strategy involving: (a) a seat at the table and a voice in the room in international negotiations for significant and equitable numbers of Southern civil society organizations; and (b) solid capacity–building, increased democratic space, and freedoms and greater influence over Southern governmental decision-making and politicians at the national level for such organizations. While some of these changes can be effected by bilateral and multilateral governmental aid donors, foundation donors, and international organizations, others will require deeper systemic and governance changes at the national level in the Southern countries concerned.

3. THE BENEFITS AND COSTS OF CIVIL SOCIETY PARTICIPATION

Civil society involvement in recent international processes illustrates the increasingly important role it plays in shaping outcomes. The varied functions played by civil society groups in global processes have been well documented. One way to classify them is as: (a) agenda-setters, (b) conscience-keepers, (c) partners, (d) experts, (e) lobbyists, and (f) enforcers.[21] Below is a list of civil society roles compiled by Barbara Gemmill and Abimbola Bamidele-Izu:

- Expert advice and analysis. NGOs can facilitate negotiations by giving politicians access to competing ideas from outside the normal bureaucratic channels;
- Intellectual competition to governments. NGOs often have much better analytical and technical skills and capacity to respond more quickly than government officials;
- Mobilization of public opinion. NGOs can influence the public through campaigns and broad outreach;
- Representation of the voiceless. NGOs can help vocalize the interests of persons not well represented in policymaking;
- Service provision. NGOs can deliver technical expertise on particular topics as needed by government officials as well as participate directly in operational activities;

---

[20] Basel, 22 March 1989, in force 5 May 1992, 1673 UNTS 126; 28 ILM 657 (1989).
[21] F. Yamin, "NGOs and International Environmental Law: A Critical Evaluation of Their Roles and Responsibilities" (2001) 10 *Review of European Community and International Environmental Law* 149. Yamin provides good examples of each of these categories.

Lalanath de Silva

- Monitoring and assessment. NGOs can help strengthen international agreements by monitoring negotiation efforts and governmental compliance;
- Legitimization of global-scale decisionmaking (*sic*) mechanisms. NGOs can broaden the base of information for decisionmaking (*sic*), improving the quality, authoritativeness, and legitimacy of the policy choices of international organizations.[22]

For example, the UN Millennium Ecosystem Assessment was a collaboration between the UN Environment Programme (UNEP), the World Resources Institute (WRI – a leading global environmental think tank), the International Union for the Conservation of Nature (IUCN – a unique organization with government and civil society membership), and other agencies.[23] The assessment filled critical gaps in analysis and knowledge and was an interorganizational collaboration. TRAFFIC is another example of interorganizational collaboration in the implementation of the Convention on International Trade in Endangered Species of Wild Fauna and Flora (CITES).[24] Established in 1976, TRAFFIC is a collaboration between the World Wide Fund For Nature (WWF) and the IUCN.[25] The Convention seeks to protect over 30,000 endangered species, and over 150 countries have ratified the Convention.[26] TRAFFIC helps the CITES Secretariat monitor wildlife trade through twenty-two offices in eight regional programs.[27] Its success lies in solid local investigations, data gathering, and research, coupled with its lobbying power.[28]

On the other hand, civil society involvement in migration issues covered by the International Organization of Migration (IMO) has seen an increase mostly in the past decade, but has not until recently included policy-making.[29] International non-governmental organizations in this field tended to focus on human trafficking or the human rights of migrants and refugees, and not on the entire gamut of international migration phenomena or policy.[30] The challenge of raising funds for broader migration advocacy has been cited as one reason for the lack of civil society engagement on overarching migration policy.[31] Most NGOs working in this field

---

[22] Gemmill and Bamidele-Izu, note 13, p. 7. This list draws on Charnovitz, note 3; D. C. Esty, "Non-Governmental Organizations at the World Trade Organization: Cooperation, Competition, or Exclusion" (1998) 1 *Journal of International Economic Law* 123; D. C. Esty, "The World Trade Organization's Legitimacy Crisis" (2002) 1 *World Trade Review* 7.

[23] Gemmill and Bamidele-Izu, note 13, p. 11.

[24] Ibid.

[25] Ibid.

[26] Ibid.

[27] Ibid.

[28] Ibid.

[29] C. Thouez, "The Role of Civil Society in Shaping International Migration Policy," Duke University, Sanford School of Public Policy, 2003.

[30] Ibid.

[31] Ibid.

were involved in operational activities providing relief to refugees or undertaking advocacy at the national level to improve the human rights of migrant workers.[32] In 2003 there were few, if any, focused on international migration policy. This gap has been closed today, with more NGOs taking on international migration policy advocacy.

In contrast, climate change negotiations have attracted hordes of civil society groups to the meetings. In December 2009 nearly 1,300 civil society organizations registered to attend the 15th Conference of the Parties (COP 15) to the United Nations Framework Convention on Climate Change[33] (UNFCCC) held in Copenhagen, Denmark.[34] In freezing weather, they stood in long lines waiting to obtain their credentials and badges in order to enter the meeting areas. Space requirements had been underestimated, which ultimately led to a showdown with the UNFCCC Secretariat.[35] During the negotiations, civil society groups proposed revisions to the negotiating text of the conference.[36] Others, such as think tanks and business associations, worked behind the scene to influence and advise government delegates on such revisions. Still others were involved in advocacy, including demonstrations.[37] The rising expectation of civil society groups that they will participate in international negotiations is nowhere more evident than in the climate talks.[38] By COP 18, in 2012, there were 1,621 NGOs registered to participate in the proceedings.[39]

A closer examination of civil society groups registered with the UNFCCC reveals that there are far more groups from the United States and Europe than from the global South. Business and industry associations are also included among the registered groups. Melanie Müller, commenting on civil society groups from the North and South that participate in the negotiations, states that "equal rights to participate do not guarantee that organisations have equal opportunities to participate."[40] Based on UNFCCC statistics, she concludes that "many of the organisations involved are from Europe, the USA and other rich countries where NGOs tend to have more resources than those of poorer nations."[41] Referring to the Durban COP, she states that "more than 120 German organisations and 50 French organisations have registered," whereas the "respective numbers for Brazil and

---

[32] Ibid.
[33] UNFCCC, note 12.
[34] A. Spain, "The Rise of Civil Society," March 2012, www.mediate.com.
[35] Personal knowledge.
[36] Spain, note 34.
[37] Ibid.
[38] For a graph showing participation in UNFCCC COPs prepared by the UNFCCC Secretariat see UNFCCC, "Participation Breakdown," http://unfccc.int.
[39] UNFCCC, "Cumulative Admissions of Observer Organizations in Civil Society and the Climate Change Process," http://unfccc.int.
[40] M. Müller, "The Myth of a Global Civil Society" (2011) 9 *Development and Cooperation* 52.
[41] Ibid.

Kenya are around 25 and 17" and "Bangladesh, one of the countries that are likely to be worst hit by climate change, managed to rally only eight organisations."[42]

On many climate change issues, civil society groups from the North and South have conflicting positions. Although most may agree that global warming should be limited to two degrees Celsius, Northern and Southern NGOs often differ on how that goal should be achieved, as well as on how the burdens of achieving the goal should be shared and whether market mechanisms alone will suffice. For example, Northern NGOs are increasingly downplaying the concept of common but differentiated responsibility (CBDR), whereas southern NGOs advocate upholding it. This difference of views often plays out in discussions concerning the responsibilities of India, China, and Brazil (emerging economies) to reduce greenhouse gas emissions.

NGOs involved in global processes such as the climate negotiations face the same dilemmas and structural problems as those of official government delegations.[43] A host of issues are at stake. Who gets a seat at the table? Whose voice will be heard in the room? Is it even possible to develop a common position in the midst of "extremely heterogeneous interests"?[44] How should tasks be divided among such a large group of actors?[45] Where will resources come from and how best can they be put to use? Who gets included and excluded from international negotiations often turns on who can raise the funds for travel and hotel accommodation. The more serious and consistent NGO actors in the climate negotiations have a well-developed strategy for fundraising, while many Southern NGOs that attend are at the mercy of larger civil society networks or other groups that make an effort to increase Southern participation. There is also a concern that some NGOs attending negotiations are mere proxies for governments who fund them and facilitate their attendance. As a result, "the NGO community has experienced a split, which divides the more hierarchically structured 'global players' from other NGOs with fewer resources and spontaneously organized grassroots organizations and social movements."[46]

As the numbers of participating civil society groups at the climate negotiations increase, "[c]onflicts of interest are becoming more and more visible, between Northern and Southern NGOs, between NGOs and social movements, and between environmental and development organizations."[47] Just as commercial interests capture regulators, governments capture NGOs that are more comfortable working with them, in order to increase the NGOs' own influence over the process.

---

[42] Ibid.
[43] B. UnmIbidüßig, "NGOs and Climate Crisis: Fragmentation, Lines of Conflict and Strategic Approaches," 9 June 2011, www.boell.de.
[44] Ibid.
[45] Ibid.
[46] Ibid.
[47] Ibid.

580   *Public Participation in International Negotiation and Compliance*

Bigger NGOs that want to influence real political processes sometimes lose touch with the public interest, becoming preoccupied with what donors want or their own narrow project interests. The conflicts may be classified into three groups, namely: (a) local vs. international, (b) market mechanisms vs. system change, and (c) burden-sharing between North and South.[48] For example, local Southern NGOs may well see an eviction of indigenous people from a new protected area as a violation of human rights, whereas some international Northern NGOs may see it as a necessary step to ensuring the integrity of the protected area. Northern NGOs may advocate market incentives in the form of tax credits or pollution permit trading as a means of pollution control, whereas Southern NGOs may advocate for strengthening institutional capacity for enforcing pollution control laws or changes to the laws themselves. Without a more open and concerted effort to improve global communication among the growing civil society groups and some "structural adjustments" to the donors that fund NGOs and distribute resources, it is unlikely that civil society groups will be able to agree on common positions in the climate negotiations. That in no way diminishes their role as watchdogs or fire alarmists. In this sense, they will remain a counterbalance to political power and vested interests that can otherwise skew outcomes from the international climate process.

Despite these drawbacks, civil society groups have influenced international environmental negotiations in the ways outlined above. Agenda-setting and framing are two critical roles that NGOs have played in this arena. For example, NGOs transformed the landmine issue from a military and security issue to a humanitarian one.[49] Through their research and advocacy they offer models and solutions to what may seem challenging problems.[50] They expose vested interests and lay bare conflicts of interests. All these facets make their role valuable. Yet in the final analysis, much of the time, the more effective and successful civil society groups are those from the United States and Europe. Exceptionally, a Southern country group, such as the Third World Network,[51] might emerge to become a champion, largely because such organizations have mastered fundraising, undertake good research, and have sharpened their advocacy and media presence.

---

[48] Ibid. The article contains an informative discussion of each of these tensions with illustrative examples.

[49] K. R. Rutherford, "The Evolving Arms Control Agenda: Implications of the Role of NGOs in Banning Antipersonnel Landmines" (2000) 53 *World Politics* 110. For a contrary view see K. Anderson, "The Ottawa Convention Banning Landmines, the Role of International Non-Governmental Organisations and the Idea of International Civil Society" (2000) 11 *European Journal of International Law* 91 at 119, 120.

[50] J. Braithwaite and P. Drahos, *Global Business Regulation* (Cambridge: Cambridge University Press, 2001), pp. 585–593. In terms of Braithwaite and Drahos' typology of modelers, civil society groups are model mongers, model missionaries, and model modernizers – experimenting with, developing, improving, and promoting models of solutions to problems that governments are seeking to tackle through international processes.

[51] The Third World Network is a focal point for many Southern NGOs: see Third World Network, www.twnside.org.sg.

4. CIVIL SOCIETY PARTICIPATION: RULES AND PRACTICES

Even though two decades have gone by since the Earth Summit, there is no uniform international code of practice or rules for engagement with civil society in international environmental negotiations or compliance. Each international organization and UN agency and program has its own rules and practices. For example, the United Nations Environment Programme has its own rules, which are now under revision;[52] on the other hand, the UNFCCC has a different set of rules for civil society participation.[53] While many have attempted to harmonize or adopt similar rules, there are also significant differences. While Northern civil society groups that are better resourced and experienced have mastered these rules and practices and have learned to work the system, Southern civil society groups, especially those who are new to the process, are often confused and befuddled by them.

The international process leading to the Earth Summit in 1992, and Agenda 21, which emerged from that meeting, acknowledged that sustainable development could not be achieved by governments alone and that there were other stakeholders who needed to be involved.[54] Following the Earth Summit, the UN Commission on Sustainable Development (CSD) was established, and civil society participation in the work of the CSD was organized around nine major groups.[55] The nine major groups are: business and industry; children and youth; farmers; indigenous peoples; local authorities; non-governmental organizations; the scientific and technological community; and women.[56] Each international organization has its own eligibility criteria and registration/accreditation system for civil society organizations. For example, the UN relies on the United Nations Economic and Social Council (ECOSOC) system for accrediting civil society organizations. International, regional, and national NGOs and non-profit public or voluntary organizations are eligible to obtain consultative status with ECOSOC.[57] Many other UN agencies and programs recognize ECOSOC accreditation and permit such organizations to participate in proceedings. In addition, UN and other international agencies may have their own registration system as well, largely because ECOSOC rules for accreditation are onerous and take significant time to complete.[58]

---

[52] United Nations Environment Programme, note 1.

[53] UNFCCC, "Civil Society and the Climate Change Process," http://unfccc.int.

[54] UN Sustainable Development Knowledge Platform, "Major Groups," http://sustainabledevelopment.un.org.

[55] The nine major groups were first identified in Agenda 21, note 12, Chapters 24–32.

[56] Ibid.

[57] NGO Branch: UN Department of Economic and Social Affairs, "Consultative Status with ECOSOC and Other Accreditations," http://esango.un.org.

[58] M. Kamiya, "A Study of Formal Relationships between Civil Society and Multilateral Bodies: Accreditation and Other Consultative Modalities," Working Paper, Forum International de Montreal and Heinrich Boll Foundation, 2007.

582 *Public Participation in International Negotiation and Compliance*

This is also true for international processes on the environment. For example, the United Nations Environment Programme (UNEP) has its own major groups and stakeholder branch in Nairobi, adopts the nine major groups approach, and has its own rules of registration (in addition to ECOSOC) for meetings.[59] These mechanisms and rules are now under review following a mandate from Rio+20 to upgrade UNEP.[60] The Convention on Biological Diversity follows a similar procedure and has adopted the nine major groups approach.[61] On the other hand, the UNFCCC has its own registration system for admission of NGOs as observers.[62] The criteria for admission of UNEP and UNFCCC are not identical. In all of these organizations, NGOs can obtain observer status, which also means they may not directly participate in meetings and proceedings except at the discretion of the chair.

Over time, traditions have developed in UNEP and UNFCCC that regulate engagement with civil society organizations. For example, at the Governing Council meetings of the UNEP, two representatives each from the nine major groups were allocated seats in the main room.[63] They could raise their flag and ask to speak on agenda items during meetings, at the discretion of the chair. However, when a task was allotted to a committee or subcommittee, the issue of civil society participation became precarious. The chair of a committee or subcommittee had discretion to allow NGO observers into a session. An objection from a state delegate quietly passed on to the chair could result in exclusion of civil society – with no means to challenge the reasons or decision or assess the views of other government delegates. Even when permitted to attend, NGO observers were rarely allowed to speak and could only pass notes to or whisper with government delegates, who occasionally became their voices. Hopefully, these restrictive and archaic practices will change with the new UNEP rules now being drafted.[64] States have repeatedly affirmed the basic notion that sustainable development can only be achieved by all stakeholders (government, business, and civil society) working together in a robust partnership. Such a partnership will remain a distant dream unless all stakeholders are allowed to fully and effectively participate in sustainable

---

[59] UNEP, "Major Groups and Stakeholders," www.unep.org.

[60] UNEP, "Developing New Modalities for Stakeholders Engagement in UNEP," www.unep. org. The author served as a member of an expert group established by UNEP to review and recommend mechanisms for stakeholder participation. The expert report was published in October 2013, http://www.unep.org/civil-society/Portals/24105/documents/MGFC/Report% 20of%20the%20expert%20group%20to%20UNEP%20-%2024%20October%202013.pdf.

[61] Convention on Biological Diversity, "Thematic Programme and Cross-Cutting Issues," www. cbd.int.

[62] UNFCCC, "Civil Society and the Climate Change Process," http://unfccc.int.

[63] UNEP, "GC/GMEF Processes and Major Groups and Stakeholders: A Guide on How to Participate in the GC/GMEF Sessions," www.unep.org, para. 2.1.

[64] Governing Council of the United Nations Environment Programme, *Proceedings of the Governing Council/Global Ministerial Environment Forum at Its First Universal Session*, 18–22 February 2013, UNEP/GC.27/17, II.D, para. 26.

development decision-making. Yet, in closed-door meetings of the G77 and China (the grouping of developing country delegations), government delegates are sometimes heard to make statements challenging the need for civil society involvement, manifesting a profound ignorance of the role of civil society as a stakeholder in sustainable development.[65]

From the perspective of Southern civil society, these rules and practices are oppressive, complicated, and intimidating; oppressive because the rules and practices are often skewed in favor of better resourced civil society groups; complicated because they are unclear, vary from one international organization to another, are not written down, and are known only to seasoned delegates, including NGO observers; intimidating because when they are enforced they cause embarrassment and frustration to Southern NGOs who are probably attending for the first time or who do not speak the language of the meeting or are not part of the inner circle of knowledge. Leaders of indigenous peoples or farmers attending such meetings can hardly be expected to speak in diplomatic language or style. Nor can they be expected to be well versed in the unwritten and poorly disseminated rules of engagement of international institutions often buried in small print in some archived document. Over time, these rules and practices ensure the exclusion of social movements and people affected by decisions of such agencies from raising their voices or holding decision-makers accountable. The absence of these stakeholders from negotiations and compliance mechanisms leaves a vacuum that is quickly filled by the better resourced Northern civil society groups, who have their own agendas but often profess to speak on behalf of the absent constituents. Socialized within the international agency's own culture and systems, these civil society representatives – who are "regulars" – develop close relationships with diplomats and government delegates, engage in negotiations, make and break deals, and influence the decision-making in significant ways. Southern civil society groups often have to make alliances – sometimes not entirely to their benefit – with Northern civil society groups to have any success at advocacy, lobbying, and influence. The larger question as to who gets seats at the table and whose voices are heard in the international environmental negotiating rooms continues to remain a live issue for most Southern civil society and constituency groups.

But there are hopeful signs of change. The civil society participation rules and mechanisms in the Aarhus Convention and the Civil Society Mechanism (CSM) of the Committee on World Food Security deserve spotlighting. The Convention on Access to Information, Public Participation in Decision-making and Access to Justice in Environmental Matters, better known as the Aarhus Convention, has rules and procedure worthy of emulation.[66] It is a convention of the UN Economic

---

[65] Author's personal knowledge as a developing country delegate at environmental negotiations.

[66] Economic and Social Council, *Rules of Procedure of the Meeting of the Parties to the Convention on Access to Information, Public Participation in Decision-making and Access to Justice in Environmental Matters*, 2 April 2004, ECE/MP.PP/2/Add.2, Annex.

584   *Public Participation in International Negotiation and Compliance*

Commission for Europe but is open to accession by non-European states as well.[67] It is the only convention that establishes legal rights for citizens of state parties to the convention – rights of access to information, public participation, and access to justice.

Based on Principle 10 of the Rio Declaration, which affirms that environmental issues are best handled with the participation of all relevant stakeholders supported by access to information and justice, the Aarhus Convention spells out in some detail the content of those rights and sets up a compliance mechanism that can be invoked by any citizen of the states parties to the Convention.[68] Under the rules of procedure, any NGO can register and participate in the proceedings of all the meetings under the Aarhus Convention, but has no right to vote.[69] NGOs can only be excluded if one third of the states parties object to their participation.[70] This has never happened in the Convention proceedings. Proceedings are open to the public and where all the attending public cannot be accommodated, the proceedings are required to be relayed to the public in a separate location.[71] Additional provisions guarantee that civil society groups can propose and have input into agenda-setting and have access to all the documentation generated under the Convention. Accountability to the legal obligations under the Convention is assured through a compliance committee, which can accept and process complaints from citizens of states parties.[72] These provisions have led to robust civil society participation in the Convention and its many treaty bodies and task forces. In the early years (2004 onwards), most of the cases before the Compliance Committee were from eastern European and Central Asian countries such as Kazakhstan, Ukraine, Armenia, Poland, and Lithuania.[73] This trend has shifted in recent times (from 2008 onwards), with many more cases being filed against Western European countries such as the United Kingdom, Spain, Austria, and France, as well as the European Community.[74] The main weakness of this compliance mechanism is that corrective action by states parties in response to the Committee's findings on cases has been mixed.[75]

---

[67] *Convention on Access to Information, Public Participation in Decision-Making and Access to Justice in Environmental Matters,* Aarhus, 28 June 1998, in force 30 October 2001, 2161 UNTS 447; 38 ILM 517 (1999), art. 19(2) [hereinafter Aarhus Convention].

[68] Ibid.

[69] Rules of Procedure, note 66, rr. 6(2)–(3).

[70] Ibid.

[71] Ibid, rr. 7(1)–(2).

[72] *Aarhus Convention,* note 67, art. 15.

[73] A. Andrusevych, T. Alge, and C. Konrad (eds.), *Case Law of the Aarhus Convention Compliance Committee (2004–2011),* 2nd ed. (Lviv: RACSE, 2011).

[74] Ibid.

[75] S. Kravchenko, "Giving the Public A Voice in MEA Compliance Mechanisms," in *Compliance and Enforcement in Environmental Law: Towards More Effective Implementation* (London: Edward Elgar, 2011).

Another civil society participatory mechanism worthy of mention is the Civil Society Mechanism (CSM) of the Committee on World Food Security (CFS). The CFS was first established by the World Food Conference of 1974. It underwent major reforms in 2009 largely as a result of the 2008 food crisis, which manifested significant gaps in world food governance. The reform process was promoted and supported by a large number of civil society groups, including small-scale producers' organizations, indigenous peoples, and other organizations, together with many governments. The thrust of the reforms was directed at making the CFS an inclusive forum for global policy-making on inequality, poverty, and the human right to food. A nine-month process unfolded in Rome involving discussions among governments, UN agencies, and non-state actors. What was perhaps unique in the reform process was the participation of peoples' organizations and networks and social movements through their umbrella network, the International Planning Committee for Food Sovereignty (IPC).

The reforms resulted in redefining the CFS as "the foremost *inclusive* international and intergovernmental platform for all stakeholders to work together in a coordinated way to ensure food security and nutrition for all."[76] Participation in the CFS is open to UN member states as well as "representatives of UN agencies and bodies, civil society and non-governmental organizations and their networks, international agricultural research systems, international and regional financial institutions and representatives of private sector associations and private philanthropic foundations."[77] These reforms brought civil society (especially social movements from developing nations) into the decision-making and implementation process as full participants. It is still too early to assess the strengths and weaknesses of this innovation.

The reform document discusses how any civil society organization working on food security issues can obtain observer status.[78] The document states that the quota of seats "assigned to civil society organizations and NGOs will be such as to ensure their visible and effective participation, equitable geographic representation," with particular attention to "representing smallholder family farmers, artisanal fisherfolk (*sic*), herders/pastoralists, landless, urban poor, agricultural and food workers, women, youth, consumers, Indigenous Peoples, and International NGOs whose mandates and activities are concentrated in the areas of concern to the Committee."[79] The document established the principle that civil society was entitled to autonomously organize its own facilitating body (CSM).[80] The CSM

---

[76] Food and Agriculture Organization of the United Nations, "The Committee on World Food Security," www.fao.org (emphasis added).

[77] Ibid.

[78] Committee on World Food Security, *Reform of the Committee on World Food Security*, 14, 15, and 17 October 2009, CFS:2009/2 Rev.2, agenda item III, paras. 13-15.

[79] Ibid, paras. 11(ii), 15.

[80] Ibid, para. 16.

586   *Public Participation in International Negotiation and Compliance*

was mandated to "also serve inter-sessional global, regional and national actions in which organizations of those sectors of the population most affected by food insecurity, would be accorded priority representation."[81] Separately, "(p)rivate sector associations, private philanthropic organizations and other CFS stakeholders active in areas related to food security, nutrition, and the right to food are encouraged to autonomously establish and maintain a permanent coordination mechanism for participation in the CFS and for actions derived from that participation at global, regional and national levels."[82] The CSM has a trust fund of its own, managed by civil society members. Donors contribute directly to the trust fund to facilitate participation and other work related to the CSM.

The resulting participation of civil society groups in the Aarhus Convention and the CSM of the CFS are inspiring examples of how stakeholders participation, including civil society and social movements from the South, can enhance and enrich international decision-making in areas such as the environment and food security, and how mechanisms can be successfully established, funded, and operated in such a context. These pioneering efforts have paved the way for a sea-change in the way civil society and other stakeholder participation ought to be reformed in international processes, including those related to the environment.

5. CLOSING THE GAPS

This concluding section identifies the gaps in civil society participation in international negotiations and compliance and proposes recommendations for closing them. The key gaps in participation, and some solutions, may be catalogued? as follows:

i.   The recognition that the current rules in the UN and other international organizations governing civil society participation are archaic, out of step with the rise and increasingly important role of modern civil society and rapid advance of communications technology, and need urgent reform. These rules do not embody the positive experience from successful good practices such as the Aarhus Convention and the Civil Society Mechanism of the Committee on World Food Security;

ii. The need to develop a uniform model code of practice on civil society participation for the UN and international organizations that is transparent, inclusive, accountable, and easy to comprehend and administer; recognizes the autonomous nature of civil society; and is fair and equitable to Southern civil society groups, especially social movements;

iii. The need for Northern donors to proactively balance their funding for Northern NGOs with funding for Southern NGOs, including for

---

[81]   Ibid.
[82]   Ibid, para. 17.

building their research and advocacy capacity to interact with international negotiations and compliance processes;[83]

iv. The need for Northern donors to be sensitive to the perspectives and advocacy positions of Southern NGOs, which sometimes differ from those of Northern NGOs;

v. The need for Southern governments to recognize the importance of Southern civil society inputs and to proactively include civil society in their official delegations and to change bureaucratic culture to actively bring them into the delegation's decision-making processes;

vi. The recognition that civil society is heterogeneous and that grouping business and industry and local government institutions as part of civil society in participation rules is problematic, glosses over and hides conflicts of interests between these groups (including tensions between North–South and South–South NGO groupings), and reduces the chances of the development of common advocacy positions;

vii. The understanding on the part of Southern NGOs that if they are to effectively influence international negotiations and take advantage of compliance mechanisms, they need to engage in a concerted effort to improve their research and advocacy capabilities and raise funds, if necessary through educating Northern donors;

viii. The recognition by Northern NGOs that while their research and advocacy on behalf of developing country issues is currently filling a gap, they owe a duty to proactively engage in capacity-building and bring Southern civil society groups to the negotiating table, enabling Southern groups to research and do their own advocacy according to the priorities and outcomes they see as most suitable.

Many of these reforms will require political commitment and concerted civil society action. Inertia within the international system and the international bureaucracy, as well as resistance from some governments, will need to be overcome. Nevertheless, reform of civil society participation norms in international negotiation processes is long overdue, and the question of when it will happen is a case not so much of "if" but of "when." Timing of reform is most likely to be driven by the advancement of technology, the governmental open data movement, changed priorities and modalities of donors in favor of Southern civil society, increasing transparency and democracy in Southern nations, and the growing loss of confidence in the international negotiation and compliance processes.

---

[83] In this regard the "Think Tank Initiative" of a group of donors is worthy of mention. Its goal is to identify, fund, and support capacity development of Southern think tanks.

28

Access to Remedies in Environmental Matters and the North–South Divide

Jona Razzaque

1. INTRODUCTION

A breach of an international obligation leads to a duty to provide a remedy[1] and the purposes of remedies are many: to provide injunctive relief to stop harmful environmental activities; to award damages to compensate for the harm suffered, restitution or remedial measures; and to award litigation costs and fees.[2] Remedies against non-compliance must be adequate to encourage effective implementation of treaty obligations. While states have an obligation to uphold the rule of law and fulfill their treaty obligations in good faith, the global South in many instances lacks financial and technical capacity to comply with the provisions of multilateral environmental agreements (MEA). Also, there are substantive weaknesses as well as procedural[3] flaws in the compliance mechanisms of some MEAs. A weak remedies structure with lack of provisions on sanctions, compensation or retaliation creates further problems for MEA compliance.[4]

If the purpose of remedies in environmental matters is to provide redress to victims, implement obligations, promote restoration, reinforce the rule of law, and encourage sustainable development, the remedies available under international environmental law fail to achieve these objectives. While several MEAs[5] include

---

[1] International Law Commission, *Draft Articles on Responsibility of States for Internationally Wrongful Acts*, 3 August 2001, 53 UN GAOR Supp. (No. 10) at 43, UN Doc. A/56/10 (2001) [hereinafter ILC Draft Articles].

[2] "Remedy is the means by which the violation of a right is prevented, redressed, or compensated", H. C. Black, *Black's Law Dictionary*, 2nd ed (St. Paul: West Publishing Company, 1995).

[3] For example, lack of participation of the South during negotiation and in the implementation of the MEA provisions.

[4] D. Bodansky, *The Art and Craft of International Environmental Law* (Cambridge: Harvard University Press, 2011), p. 225.

[5] *United Nations Framework Convention on Climate Change*, New York, 9 May 1992, in force 21 March 1994, 1771 UNTS 107; S. Treaty Doc No. 102-38; UN Doc. A/AC.237/18 (Part II)/

compliance review mechanisms, the remedies for breach of these provisions remain weak.[6] There are some exceptions: for example, the Compliance Committee of the Aarhus Convention[7] plays a crucial role in assessing and evaluating compliance with the convention obligations. Some MEAs provide mechanisms for civil and/or criminal damages that the member states can impose at the national level through national law.[8] The MEA secretariats can also take action in some instances.[9] However, these mechanisms are the exception rather than the rule; in general, the remedies offered by international environmental law are still at a nascent stage.[10]

The aim of this chapter is not to provide an overview of remedies available in international environmental law. Rather, the focus is on issues where the North–South divide adds to the already existing concerns regarding the weak remedial regimes of environmental law. The chapter first briefly highlights that state responsibility in international law offers inadequate remedies in relation to environmental pollution. Second, the priority given to economic interests in trade and investment fora sidelines the concerns of the South and affected individuals (or communities) in cases of environmental pollution. In the third and fourth sections, the discussion is focused on the World Trade Organization's (WTO) dispute settlement body that deals with trade disputes between states, and the International Centre for the Settlement of Investment Disputes (ICSID) tribunal that adjudicates investor–state investment disputes. The structure and operation of the WTO dispute settlement body were questioned by the South during and after the Seattle Ministerial Conference in 1999.[11] Since then, with concerns mounting about significant costs, the duration of proceedings, and uncertain benefits of participation by the global South, the sense of distrust has increased, as the global North is in a much better

---

Add.1; 31 ILM 849 (1992); *Convention on Biological Diversity*, Rio de Janeiro, 5 June 1992, in force 29 December 1993, 1760 UNTS 79; 31 ILM 818 (1992); *Convention on International Trade in Endangered Species of Wild Fauna and Flora*, 3 March 1973, in force 1 August 1975 [hereinafter CITES].

[6] P. Birnie, A. Boyle and C. Redgwell, *International Law and the Environment* (New York: Oxford University Press, 2009).

[7] *Convention on Access to Information, Public Participation in Decision-Making and Access to Justice in Environmental Matters*, Aarhus, 28 June 1998, in force 30 October 2001, 2161 UNTS 447; 38 ILM 517 (1999) [hereinafter Aarhus Convention].

[8] For example, Article 5 of the *Nagoya-Kuala Lumpur Supplementary Protocol on Liability and Redress to the Cartagena Protocol on Biosafety* (2010).

[9] For example, the Review of Significant Trade process in the CITES can bring remedial action if certain listed species (in Appendix II) are being traded in breach of CITES provisions. See CITES, "Review of Significant Trade in Specimens of Appendix-II Species," www.cites.org.

[10] See generally P. Birnie, A. Boyle, and C. Redgwell, note 6; P. Sands, J. Peel, A. Fabra, and R. MacKenzie, *Principles of International Environmental Law* (New York: Cambridge University Press, 2012).

[11] The Southern countries have been vocal about more participation in WTO negotiations since 1986 when Uruguay Round Trade Negotiation commenced. See H. T. Phamd, "Developing Countries and the WTO: The Need for More Mediation in the DSU" (2004) 9 *Harvard Negotiation Law Review* 331.

590   *Access to Remedies in Environmental Matters*

position to take advantage of the WTO dispute settlement mechanism and of the investor-to-state arbitration under the ICSID Convention. The chapter then assesses major challenges and strategies that the victims of environmental pollution in the South have used to expedite access to remedies and to address the increasing environmental abuses by corporate entities.

2. STATE RESPONSIBILITY AND REMEDIES

If one state commits an internationally unlawful act against another, this conduct establishes international responsibility between the two states.[12] However, the global nature of environmental problems, the diversity of victims, the diffuse nature of pollution, and the challenge of allocating costs, make it difficult to assess the level of responsibility of states, develop appropriate remedies, and apportion liability.[13] In environmental cases, a breach of any treaty obligation or customary international law would give rise to state responsibility.[14] The *Trail Smelter Arbitration* shows that states do not have absolute territorial sovereignty and "no state has the right to use or permit the use of territory in such a manner as to cause injury by fumes in or to the territory of another."[15] Principle 21 of the Stockholm Declaration[16] and Principle 2 of the Rio Declaration on Environment and Development[17] create a general duty of states "to ensure that activities within their jurisdiction or control do not cause damage to the environment of other states." However, this duty does not impose a threshold level of environmental harm required to trigger responsibility,[18] and requires that the sovereign right to exploit resources be balanced by the obligation not to cause environmental damage.

Under state responsibility, only a state is liable for damage and only a state can claim damages. Individuals who are often the victims of environmental pollution cannot rely upon state responsibility, unless the state is willing to take up the claim on their behalf. Still, a state can be held responsible for the activities of private individuals and corporations within its jurisdiction if the state has failed to stop or control the activity in accordance with the rules of international law. Thus, if the actions of a private actor in one state cause significant damage to the environment

---

[12] M. Shaw, "International Courts, Responsibility and Remedies," in M. Fitzmaurice and D. Sarooshi, *Issues of State Responsibility Before International Judicial Institutions* (Oxford: Hart Publishing, 2004), p. 19. See also ILC Draft Articles, note 1.

[13] L. A. de La Fayette, "International Liability for Damage to the Environment," in M. Fitzmaurice, D. Ong, and P. Merkouris (eds.), *Research Handbook on International Environmental Law* (Cheltenham: Edward Elgar, 2010).

[14] P. Birnie et al., note 6.

[15] *Trail Smelter* (USA v Canada) Award of 1941, III RIAA 1911 at 1965.

[16] *Declaration of the United Nations Conference on the Human Environment*, Stockholm, 16 June 1972, UN Doc. A/Conf.48/14/Rev. 1(1973); 11 ILM 1416 (1972).

[17] *Rio Declaration on Environment and Development*, Rio de Janeiro, 13 June 1993, UN Doc. A/CONF.151/26 (vol. I); 31 ILM 874 (1992) [hereinafter Rio Declaration].

[18] G. Handl, "International Accountability for Transboundary Harm Revisited: What Role for State Liability?" (2007) 37 *Environmental Policy and Law* 116.

in another state, the state which has jurisdiction over the private actor could be liable for the damage if it has failed to implement or enforce environmental law consistent with customary international law or treaty law.[19]

The no-harm rule imposes restrictions on state sovereignty, including a duty not to cause significant injury[20] and to minimize risk of injury to the extent possible. Based on the no-harm rule, Palau, a low-lying small island state in the Pacific, has requested the United Nations (UN) General Assembly to seek an advisory opinion from the International Court of Justice (ICJ) that the greenhouse gas emissions of the United States are causing harmful impacts due to climate change in Palau and that United States failure to apply the due diligence obligation to minimize the risk of climate change-related damage constitutes a breach of the no-harm rule.[21] However, it will be difficult to show the causal link between the damage caused to human health and the environment and the anthropogenic emissions of the United States. Apart from that, the level of risk and liability (e.g. strict or fault-based) is uncertain and reparation for environmental damage remains inadequate.[22] In the *Gabčíkovo-Nagymaros Case*, the ICJ noted the "irreversible character" of environmental damage and the "limitations inherent in the very mechanisms of reparation of this type of damage."[23] For instance, compensation is not adequate to provide redress for the loss of a species or irreversible environmental damage, which may have an impact on present as well as future generations. How can compensation adequately redress small island states and their people for loss of territory, nationality, and culture? Moreover, countries of the global South may be unwilling to bring cases against big polluting nations of the North as this may adversely affect their financial (e.g. access to funds, aid) or economic (e.g. market access) gains. Despite the *Trail Smelter Arbitration*,[24] the Nuclear Weapons Advisory Opinion,[25] the Stockholm Declaration, and the customary status of the no-harm rule, island states such as Tuvalu and the Maldives have opted to use diplomatic channels rather than initiating claims in the ICJ.[26]

---

[19] *Pulp Mills on the River Uruguay* (Argentina v Uruguay), Judgment, ICJ Reports 2010, p. 14. *Advisory Opinion, Responsibilities and Obligations of State Sponsoring Persons and Entities with Respect to Activities in the Area*, ITLOS, case No. 17.

[20] International Law Commission, *Draft Articles on the Prevention of Transboundary Harm from Hazardous Activities*, Geneva, 11 May 2001, UN Doc. A/56/10.

[21] "Palau Seeks UN World Court Opinion on Damage Caused by Greenhouse Gases," UN News Centre, 22 September 2011, www.un.org; K. Boom, "See You in Court: The Rising Tide of International Climate Litigation," 27 September 2011, http://theconversation.com.

[22] *Gabčíkovo-Nagymaros Project* (Hungary/Slovakia), Judgment, ICJ Reports 1997, p. 7.

[23] Ibid, para. 140.

[24] *Trail Smelter Arbitration (United States v Canada)*, Special Arbitral Tribunal, 3 U.N. Rep. Int'l Arb. Awards 1905 (1941).

[25] *Advisory Opinion of the ICJ on the Legality of the Threat or Use of Nuclear Weapons*, ICJ Reports 1995, p. 226.

[26] K. Boom, "The Rising Tide of International Climate Litigation: An Illustrative Hypothetical of Tuvalu v Australia," in R. Abate and E. A. Kronk Warner (eds.), *Climate Change and Indigenous Peoples: the Search for Legal Remedies* (Cheltenham: Edward Elgar, 2013), p. 410.

3. SETTLING DISPUTES AT THE WTO AND THE SAGA OF INEQUALITY

The dispute settlement body (DSB) offers an alternative remedial framework based on the norms of neoliberal globalization.[27] During the Uruguay Round talks and since the WTO's establishment in 1994, the South has expected that the dispute settlement process would help weaker trading partners enforce the rights and obligations under various WTO agreements. The Dispute Settlement Understanding (DSU)[28] was supported by the South as it offered trade certainty, quasi-automatic process of adjudication, strict timelines, and reduction of the threats of unilateral trade measures by the North.[29] However, the cases brought before the DSB up to 2011 reveal that the majority of consultations were requested by the North, and that the United States and the European Union (EU) have initiated the largest number of cases. Measures imposed by the North have been disputed in 58 percent of the cases.[30] Most complaints were brought against the United States or the EU;[31] in a very few instances, the South as a complainant brought cases against other industrialized countries of the North apart from the United States or EU.[32] Compared with other countries of the South, China, Brazil, and India have used the DSB more frequently. It is interesting to note that disputes involving the South focus mainly on agriculture, beverages and seafood products, along with textiles, apparel, and other manufacturing, while disputes initiated by the North include intellectual property-intensive sectors as well as capital-intensive industries.[33]

3.1 The North–South Power Imbalance

The difference in capacity and wealth between the North and the South has led to a power imbalance in initiating and continuing the litigation process.[34] Generally,

---

See chapter 20, M. Burkett, "A Justice Paradox: Climate Change, Small Island Developing States, and the Absence of International Legal Remedy."

[27] J. A. Scholte, "The Sources of Neoliberal Globalization," UN Research Institute for Social Development, Programme Paper 822, 2005.

[28] DSU provides for four different methods to settle disputes between WTO Members: Consultations or negotiations (Article 4); adjudication (Articles 6 to 20); arbitration (Articles 21.3(c), 22.6 and 25); and good offices, conciliation and mediation (Article 5).

[29] C. Raghavan, "The World Trade Organization and Its Dispute Settlement System: Tilting the Balance against the South," Trade and Development Series No. 9, 2000.

[30] R. A. Torres, "Use of the WTO Trade Dispute Settlement Mechanism by the Latin American Countries – Dispelling Myths and Breaking Down Barriers," Staff Working Paper ERSD-2012-03, World Trade Organization Economic Research and Statistics Division, February 2012.

[31] Ibid.

[32] J. François et al., "Trading Profiles and Developing Country Participation in the WTO Dispute Settlement System," ICTSD Issue Paper No. 6, 2008.

[33] WTO, "Chronological List of Dispute Cases," www.wto.org.

[34] Raghavan, note 29.

the dispute settlement process is expensive for Southern countries, as they may have to retain trade lawyers based in the North. In addition, countries with permanent WTO missions in Geneva are more likely to bring cases because of their easy access.[35] The relief granted by the DSB may take a while to be enforced, and this may cause severe economic hardship to the country initiating the DSU process. During the DSU Review negotiations in 2002, the "inadequacies and structural rigidities of the remedies available to poor countries" were highlighted as reasons for non-participation in the DSB.[36] Of the total requests for consultations in the WTO DSB in 2012, only one complainant was from the global South – Bangladesh, a least developed country (LDC) – and this claim was settled outside the DSB.[37]

To assist countries of the South, especially the LDCs, with their participation in the DSB, a group of states established the Advisory Centre on WTO Law (ACWL) in 2001.[38] The ACWL's role is to assist the complainant country, and a recent study shows that it has helped the respondent in three cases.[39] With a very limited work program, the ACWL has received a mixed reception, with some positive views on its ability to provide technical assistance to LDCs.[40]

The South is also concerned about the right of an amicus[41] to participate in the WTO proceedings. Similar to the ICSID forum discussed later in the chapter, the issues raised in WTO disputes often generate considerable public interest, particularly when they include issues of public health and safety, the environment, and the protection of animals. To increase the transparency of the DSB, the North (the United States, EU and Canada) called for the opening of dispute hearings to the public and for giving outside parties the opportunity to present amicus curiae briefs.[42] Several NGOs from the South and the North urged transparency of WTO proceedings[43] and actively promoted the right to present such briefs to the DSB. When the proposal to allow amicus briefs was raised in the WTO, some Southern countries feared that amicus curiae briefs in the DSB would open the floodgates to Northern NGOs who will seek to protect the interests

---

[35] WTO, "The History and Future of the World Trade Organization," www.wto.org.

[36] TN/DS/W/17 (9 October 2002), para. 12.

[37] *India – Anti-Dumping Measure on Batteries from Bangladesh*, WT/DS306.

[38] Thirty countries of the South are entitled to ACWL services, as are LDCs.

[39] Calculated from ACWL 2012.

[40] C. P. Brown and R. McCulloch, "Developing Countries, Dispute Settlement, and the Advisory Centre on WTO Law," (2010) 19 *Journal of International Trade and Economic Development* 33.

[41] An amicus is a bystander who, without any direct interest in the litigation, intervened in his own initiative to make a suggestion to the court on matters of fact and law within his knowledge. J. Razzaque, "Changing Role of the Friends of the Court in the International Courts and Tribunals" (2002) 1(3) *Non State Actor and International Law* 169.

[42] "US Recommends Prompt Compliance, Transparency to Reform WTO Process," *International Trade Reporter*, 11 November 1998.

[43] B. Duncan, "Private Actors in Public International Law – Amicus Curiae and the Case for the Retention of State Sovereignty" (2002) 25(2) *Boston College International and Comparative Law Review* 235.

of the North.[44] Despite the divisions among member states, the WTO Appellate Body (AB) permitted amicus curiae briefs to be submitted[45] and affirmed this decision in several subsequent cases.[46] The AB also established a procedure in 2000 for accepting amicus curiae briefs,[47] which outraged a number of WTO members.[48] Some of the Southern countries were of the opinion that the decision on amicus participation should have been made at the political level by the WTO members and not by the AB. By January 2013, the DSB had received amicus curiae briefs in thirty-six disputes.[49] While a majority of these briefs were from Northern NGOs, a number of southern NGOs have also participated in submitting amicus briefs.[50] Amicus briefs submitted in several WTO disputes show that some Northern NGOs, being aware of the concern over their possible overrepresentation, work in partnership with southern NGOs.[51]

3.2 Trade and Environment in the DSU

As predominantly a trade body, the WTO has often sidelined environmental issues.[52] Efforts by Europe and the United States to include "environment" in Article XX of the General Agreement on Tariffs and Trade (GATT) were dismissed by Southern countries that wanted to include "development" or "sustainable development" as an exception.[53] Recent WTO jurisprudence shows that many cases brought before the WTO DSB impinge on environmental concerns including climate change measures, energy subsidies, and export restrictions. The trade and environment debate emerged more than two decades ago, with a number of

---

[44] For example, Mexico, Malaysia, the Philippines, and Egypt strongly resisted the admission of amicus curiae briefs. General Council, *Minutes of the Meeting of 22 November 2000*, WT/GC/ M/60.

[45] U.S. – *Import Prohibition of Certain Shrimp and Shrimp Products*, WT/DS58/AB/R.

[46] *(US – Shrimp) Appellate Body Report, United States – Import Prohibition of Certain Shrimp and Shrimp Products*, WT/DS58/AB/R, adopted 6 November 1998, DSR 1998: VII, paras. 104–6,110. *Imposition of Countervailing Duties on Certain Hot-rolled Lead and Bismuth Carbon Steel Products Originating in the United Kingdom*, Report of the Appellate Body, 7 June 2000, DSR 2000: V, 2601, paras. 39–42. *Measures Affecting Asbestos and Asbestos-containing Products*, Report of the Appellate Body, 5 April 2001, DSR 2001: VII, 3243 (paras. 51–5). WTO, "Repertory of Appellate Reports: Amicus Curiae Briefs," www.wto.org.

[47] WT/DS135/9, 8 November 2000.

[48] "WTO Appellate Body Under Fire for Move to Accept Amicus Curiae Briefs from NGOs," WTO Reporter, ICTSD Internal Files, 27 November 2000. ICTSD, "WTO General Council Slaps Appellate Body on Amicus Briefs," *Bridges Weekly Trade News Digest*, 28 November 2000.

[49] S. Bashir, "WTO Dispute Settlement Body Developments in 2012," www.wto.org.

[50] L. Butler, "Effects and Outcomes of Amicus Curiae Briefs at the WTO: An Assessment of NGO Experience," Amicus Curiae Briefs and NGOs, 8 May 2006.

[51] Ibid.

[52] The Preamble of the *Agreement Establishing the World Trade Organization*, Marrakesh, 15 April 1994, in force 1 January 1995 mentions "sustainable development." The *Declaration on TRIPS Agreement and Public Health*, Doha, 14 November 2001, WT/MIN(01)/DEC/2 furthered the notion that trade liberalization should contribute to sustainable development.

[53] S. Charnovitz, "Exploring the Environmental Exceptions in GATT Article XX" (1991) 25 *Journal of World Trade* 37 at 38–47; Raghavan, note 29.

disputes that emphasized the tension between the competing goals of trade liberalization and environmental regulation.[54] While import bans based on environmental concerns were supported by Northern environmental NGOs,[55] Southern countries were worried that extraterritorial environmental regulations (such as United States bans on shrimp and tuna harvested in ways that harmed certain non-target species) would place their domestic producers at a competitive disadvantage. The South denounced these restrictions as protectionism, attacked the restrictions as illegal under trade law, and challenged the environmental conditions before the GATT and its successor, the WTO. In the *Tuna/Dolphin*, *Shrimp/Turtle* and *US-Gasoline* cases, the GATT/WTO ruled in favor of the South.[56] For instance, in the *Shrimp/Turtle case*, the AB ruled that Article XX(g) of GATT allows measures taken to conserve exhaustible natural resources, living or non-living. While the United States, in this case, had a legitimate interest to protect the endangered migratory sea turtles, its failure to negotiate with relevant WTO members – India, Malaysia, Pakistan, and Thailand – was held to be discriminatory and unjustifiable. However, the AB's approach in *Shrimp/Turtle* opened the door for the North to impose trade restrictive measures to protect health as well as the environment. Thereafter, several cases have highlighted the North as protector of the environment in the WTO,[57] completely obscuring the North's role in global environmental degradation through its overconsumption of the planet's resources.[58] At the same time, the North's environmental standards (e.g. certification) shift the costs of environmental protection to the South, which must comply with Northern product standards or lose export markets. This further exacerbates the North–South divide because the South does not have the resources and technology to facilitate compliance.

In recent years, cases have been brought by some Northern (e.g. United States, EU) and Southern (e.g. China) countries against national measures that promote renewable energy and environmentally friendly technologies.[59] Such measures to

---

[54] Panel Report, *US-Restrictions on Imports of Tuna*, DS21/R-39S/155 (3 September 1991). Appellate Body Report, *US – Import Prohibition of Certain Shrimp and Shrimp Products*, adopted 12 October 1998, WT/DS58/AB/R. *US – Standards for Reformulated and Conventional Gasoline*, adopted 20 May 1996, WT/DS2/9.

[55] A. Mattoo and P. Mavroidis, "Trade, Environment and the WTO," in E.-U. Petersmann (ed.), *International Trade Law and the GATT/WTO Dispute Settlement* (New York: Kluwer Law International, 1997).

[56] *US – Import Prohibition of Certain Shrimp and Shrimp Products*, DS58/R (15 May 1998).

[57] *EC – Measures Affecting the Approval and Marketing of Biotech Products*, Panel Report, 21 November 2006, WT/DS291/R, WT/DS291/R & WT/DS293/R; *EC – Measures Affecting Asbestos and Products Containing Asbestos*, Report of the Appellate Body, 12 March 2001, WT/DS135/AB/R; *Brazil – Measure Affecting Imports of Retreaded Tyres*, Report of the Appellate Body, 3 December 2007, WT/DS332/AB/R.

[58] C. Gonzalez, "Beyond Eco-Imperialism: An Environmental Justice Critique of Free Trade" (2001) 78 *Denver University Law Review* 979 at 1007–1012.

[59] M. Wu and J. Salzman, "The Next Generation of Trade and Environment Conflicts: The Rise of Green Industrial Policy" (2014) 108 *Northwestern University Law Review* 401.

promote renewable energy put most Southern countries at a disadvantage because they lack the resources to support their own renewable energy industries and are thereby rendered dependent on the North or China for technology.

The South has also been affected by trade remedies that permit import restraints or relief from imports that are deemed to compete unfairly with domestic industries.[60] Brought against foreign companies in domestic administrative proceedings, these trade remedy cases allow importing countries to impose higher tariffs or other forms of protection to make the importing market less attractive to foreign producers.[61] According to the 2001 Declaration by the G77 and China, these trade remedies have had a "serious negative impact on the trade and development prospects of the developing and least developed countries."[62] To many, these trade remedies are being used by some Northern and Southern countries as a tool to protect domestic industries against foreign competition.[63] Since 1995, there has been a significant increase in the amount of anti-dumping duties implemented by the South. India, Argentina, and China are the main countries that have utilized anti-dumping measures – a large number of these cases are against Northern countries.[64] While exports from the South remain the main target for anti-dumping measures implemented by the North, Latin American countries faced with cheap Chinese imports have initiated numerous anti-dumping investigations and trade measures against China.[65] Trade remedies are a North–South issue, as the North tries to enhance its power at the expense of the South, as well as a major South–South issue, as some Southern countries try to protect their industries from inexpensive imports.

4. ICSID AND THE RECALIBRATION OF SOVEREIGNTY BY THE GLOBAL SOUTH

With the growth of foreign investment in the past decade and the proliferation of international investment agreements (IIAs), the number of investment disputes has increased notably. Some Southern countries have raised concerns about the

---

[60] Trade remedies include actions against dumping, subsidies and special countervailing duties to offset the subsidies, and emergency measures to limit imports temporarily, designed to safeguard domestic industries.

[61] "Trade Remedies and the WTO," WTO E-Learning, May 2012, p. 86.

[62] The G77, "Declaration by the Group of 77 and China on the Fourth WTO Ministerial Conference at Doha, Qatar," 22 October 2001, www.g77.org, para. 6.

[63] T. P. Stewart, "Trade Remedy Actions by WTO Members: A Cause for Concern or a Reflection of Improved Market Access?" (2013) 8(6) *Global Trade and Customs Journal* 159.

[64] Between 1995 and 2012 the South implemented 67 percent of all anti-dumping measures, while the North accounted for only 33 percent of all final anti-dumping duties: W. Viljoen, "Trade Remedies and Safeguards in BRICS Countries," Tralac Working Paper, 22 February 2013.

[65] C. G. Gonzalez, "China's Engagement with Latin America: Partnership or Plunder?," in E. Blanco and J. Razzaque (eds.), *Natural Resources and the Green Economy: Redefining the Challenges for People, States and Corporations* (London: Brill, 2012), pp. 52–55.

benefits of such arbitration, being skeptical about its legitimacy and its respect for host state sovereignty. Many resource-rich countries of the South lack the economic capacity to develop their resources and need to attract foreign capital and technologies to develop, explore, and exploit natural resources. Countries have tried to retain ownership of these resources despite intense privatization and liberalization pressures in different eras of the twentieth century. Due to economic crises and the continued violation of environmental and human rights standards by multinational companies, we have seen a wave of expropriation and nationalization in the South that allowed the host states to impose national controls on resource extraction.[66] Thus, it is not surprising that the relationship dynamics between sovereign rights of host states in relation to their natural resources and investor–state arbitration are going through a transformation. The North–South tension is visible in the disputes concerning the fair and equitable treatment of investors (discussed in section 4.1) and in the growing number of amicus curiae applications at the International Centre for Settlement of Investment Disputes (ICSID) panel (discussed in section 4.2).

ICSID is a preferred forum in many investment agreements as it provides protection to foreign investors by allowing the investors or the host state[67] to seek compensation in cases of breach of contractual obligations or IIA provisions.[68] ICSID arbitration also permits the investor's home state to take over the investor's claim and pursue this claim against the host state in lieu of diplomatic protection or of litigation in the home or host state.[69] Parties generally opt for a third country to hold arbitral proceedings in order to ensure impartiality.[70] As ICSID proceedings are not regularly held in Southern countries, in many instances this restricts the participation of the claimants from the South.[71] Moreover, the South often lacks experts with sufficient knowledge and skills to be appointed as international arbitrators.[72]

---

[66] P. Andrews-Speed, *International Competition for Resources: The Role of Law, the State and of Markets* (Dundee: Dundee University Press, 2008).

[67] G. Laborde, "The Case for the Host State Claims in Investment Arbitration" (2010) 1(1) *Journal of International Dispute Settlement* 97.

[68] To resolve investment disputes, parties may take recourse to the arbitral proceedings of the ICSID or UNCITRAL and other arbitration forums such as the International Chamber of Commerce, the Stockholm Chamber of Commerce, and other ad hoc arbitration.

[69] *Convention on the Settlement of Investment Disputes between States and Nationals of Other States*, Washington, 18 March 1965, in force 14 October 1966, 17 UST 1270, TIAS 6090, 575 UNTS 159.

[70] P. Di Rosa, "The Recent Wave of Arbitrations Against Argentina Under Bilateral Investment Treaties: Background and Principal Legal Issues" (2004-2005) 36 *University of Miami Inter-American Law Review* 41.

[71] L. Cotula, *Human Rights, Natural Resources and Investment Law in a Globalised World – Shades of Grey in the Shadow of the Law* (New York: Routledge, 2012). A. R. Johnson, "Comment, Rethinking Bilateral Investment Treaties in Sub-Saharan Africa" (2010) 59 *Emory Law Journal* 919.

[72] A. A. Asouzu, "Some Fundamental Concerns and Issues about International Arbitration in Africa" (2006) 1 *African Development Bank Law Development Review* 81.

4.1 ICSID Arbitration, Legitimacy and Fair Treatment

IIAs establish obligations of states through "broad standards" and "open-ended" provisions, which can lead to a discretionary interpretation of the provisions, with unpredictable outcomes in investor–state arbitrations.[73] Host states may end up paying large amounts of compensation to investors due to the expansive interpretation of provisions such as fair and equitable treatment. This, coupled with effective enforcement mechanisms (e.g. seizure of overseas assets of the host state), can significantly constrain the ability of the host state to protect its own environment or public health standards, which may adversely affect commercial investments as well as environmental quality, public health, and well-being.[74] The risk of having to compensate the foreign investor can chill environmental regulation when governments fear that environmental and human rights regulations may hamper economic competitiveness. The contract-based interpretation of the IIAs usually favors the investors and sidelines public interest concerns of host states.[75] Moreover, the divergent and contradictory findings by arbitral tribunals on similar investment provisions trigger uncertainty in Southern host states with regard to their obligations under IIAs.[76] In addition, the outcomes may be different depending on whether the arbitrator comes from the South or the North.[77] Thus, a crisis of legitimacy of the system has arisen.[78]

There is a concern as to whether ICSID arbitration adequately addresses the economic and social interests of Southern host states. The fear of losing sovereign rights over natural resources resonates with the position taken by the South in relation to the New International Economic Order,[79] the Declaration on the Permanent Sovereignty of States over Natural Resources,[80] and the Charter of Economic Rights and Duties of States.[81] The primary sovereignty concern is that provisions regarding expropriation, fair and equitable treatment, and even national treatment may restrict the ability of Southern states to protect the environment and

---

[73] J. Hueckel, "Rebalancing Legitimacy and Sovereignty in International Investment Agreements" (2012) 61 *Emory Law Journal* 601.

[74] L. Cotula, "Law at Two Speeds: Legal Frameworks Regulating Foreign Investment in the Global South," Vale Columbia Center on Sustainable International Investment, 2012.

[75] M. Sornarajah, "Mutations of Neo-liberalism in International Investment Law" (2011) 3(1) *Trade Law and Development* 203.

[76] C. N. Brower and S. W. Schill, "Is Arbitration a Threat or a Boon to the Legitimacy on International Investment Law" (2009) 9 *Chicago Journal of International Law Review* 471.

[77] Ibid.

[78] S. D. Frank, "Development and Outcomes of Investment Treaty Arbitration" (2009) 50 *Harvard International Law Journal* 435.

[79] UN General Assembly, *Declaration on the Establishment of a New International Economic Order*, 1 may 1974, A/RES/s-6/3201.

[80] 14 December 1962, GA res. 1803 (XVII), 17 UN GAOR Supp. (No.17) at 15, UN Doc. A/5217 (1962).

[81] 12 December 1974, GA Res. 3281(xxix), UN GAOR, 29th Sess., Supp. No. 31 (1974) 50; 14 ILM 251 (1975); 69 AJIL 484 (1975).

the rights of people directly affected by the investment. The investors' demands to include provisions on national security, labor and health standards, and environmental safeguards in the IIAs pose difficulties for the South, as these standards restrict the sovereign right of the host states to impose their own national standards.[82] In some cases, these provisions restrict the power of the host state to expropriate.[83]

The structural and functional weaknesses of arbitration proceedings have given rise to the recent surge in "economic nationalism."[84] As a protection measure by the South, we see the revival of the Calvo doctrine,[85] which highlights the deep-set distrust toward investor countries of the North. Under this doctrine, "foreign investors are subject to a host government's legal system and are not entitled to enhanced treatment, including external fora for resolving disputes."[86] For example, Latin American states such as Ecuador, Chile, and Venezuela show a trend to limit the effect of investment treaty arbitration on host states and bring them under national jurisdiction.[87] During the 1980s wave of economic globalization, Latin American countries started signing BITs and accepted the ICSID Convention that restricts the application of the Calvo doctrine. In 2009, the President of Ecuador, Rafael Correa, denounced the ICSID.[88] Venezuela and Bolivia withdrew from ICSID, asserting that it is ideologically, procedurally, and functionally deficient to protect host states' interests and is biased toward Northern states.[89] Major investment economies such as Brazil, South Africa, and India are not parties to ICSID.[90] The effect of this revival of the Calvo doctrine is important for the investor countries of the North as well as the BRIC countries that are engaged in exploiting the natural resources in the South.

[82] M. Sornarajah, *International Law on Foreign Investment* (New York: Cambridge University Press, 2004), p. 397.

[83] K. Gordon and J. Pohl, "Environmental Concerns in International Investment Agreements: A Survey," OECD Working Papers on International Investment, No. 2011/1, 2011.

[84] W. Shan, "From North–South Divide to Private–Public Debate: Revival of the Calvo Doctrine and the Changing Landscape in International Investment Law" (2007) 27(3) *Northwestern Journal of International Law and Business* 654.

[85] M. Sornarajah, "Mutations of Neo-Liberalism in International Investment Law" (2011) 3(1) *Trade Law and Development* 203; W. Shan, "Calvo Doctrine, State Sovereignty and the Changing Landscape of International Investment Law," in W. Shan, P. Simons, and D. Singh (eds.) *Redefining Sovereignty in International Economic Law* (Oxford: Hart Publishing, 2008) p. 248.

[86] K. M. Supnik, "Making Amends: Amending the ICSID Convention to Reconcile Competing Interests in International Investment Law" (2009) 59 *Duke Law Journal* 343.

[87] UNCTAD, "Recent Developments in Investor-State Dispute Settlement, Updated for the Multilateral Dialogue on Investment," 1 May 2013, http://unctad.org.

[88] "ICSID in Crisis: Straight-Jacket or Investment Protection?," 10 July 2009, www.brettonwoodsproject.org.

[89] Supnik, note 86 at 355. See also "Venezuela Finally Leaves ICSID on Wednesday, July 25," El Universal, 24 July 2012.

[90] ICSID, "List of Contracting States and Other Signatories of the Convention," https://icsid.worldbank.org (as of 1 November 2013).

600   *Access to Remedies in Environmental Matters*

The IIAs obligations are primarily imposed on the host states and there are no corresponding international obligations imposed on foreign investors, or on the investors' home state, to require that its nationals comply with standards in their operations abroad.[91] As IIAs are unable to adequately protect the rights of the host states and the affected communities of the South, new models of IIAs have been proposed by several non-state actors. For instance, the IISD Model International Agreement on Investment for Sustainable Development,[92] based on the OECD Guidelines for Multinational Enterprises,[93] aims to address the balance of interests among foreign investors, the host states, and the home state. The UN Conference on Trade and Development is promoting an Investment Policy Framework for Sustainable Development.[94] Some host countries of the South are also becoming more assertive in investment treaty-making.[95] Moreover, the Southern African Development Community has developed a model investment treaty to balance investment protection with sustainable development goals.[96]

4.2 *The Procedural Gap*

Investment arbitration tribunals initially refused to allow amicus submissions on account of the inherent difference between arbitration proceedings and cases before domestic or international courts. Due to the confidential nature of the tribunal, an amicus, generally an NGO,[97] needs permission of the tribunal to participate. For example, in *Aguas del Tunari SA v Bolivia*,[98] which took place pursuant to the provisions of the Netherlands–UK BIT, the tribunal denied citizens and environmental groups standing due to the parties' unwillingness to consent to

---

[91] A. Newcombe and L. Paradell, *Law and Practice of Investment Treaties: Standards of Treatment* (New York: Kluwer Law International, 2009), pp. 63–64. This concern is linked to the debates on the international obligations of economic actors and corporate social responsibility. For example, Benin–Canada BIT refers to corporate social responsibility standards but does not create enforceable obligations for investors.

[92] H. Mann, "IISD Model International Agreement on Investment for Sustainable Development" (2005) 20 *ICSID Review: Foreign Investment Law Journal* 91.

[93] OECD, "OECD Guidelines for Multinational Enterprises, 2011 Edition," 2011, www.oecd.org.

[94] UNCTAD, "Investment Policy Framework for Sustainable Development," http://unctad.org.

[95] X. Carim, "Lessons from South Africa's BITs review, Perspectives on Topical Foreign Direct Investment Issues," Vale Columbia Center on Sustainable International Investment, 25 November 2013.

[96] Established in 1980, the main objectives of SADC are to achieve development and economic growth to alleviate poverty and enhance the standard and quality of life of the peoples of Southern Africa. See "SADC Model Bilateral Investment Treaty Template with Commentary," South African Development Community, July 2012.

[97] It can also be a state. For example, the United States' petition under Rule 37(2) of ICSID in *Siemens AG v The Argentine Republic*, ICSID Case No. ARB/02/8.

[98] *Aguas del Tunari, SA v Republic of Bolivia*, ICSID Case No. ARB/02/3.

their participation. However, concerns were raised regarding the transparency of these proceedings as they impinge on human rights; environmental policy; privatization of public services such as water, oil, and gas; waste management; and fiscal policy of the host state.[99]

Since ICSID Rules have been amended to provide tribunals with the discretion to allow amicus to make written submissions in arbitral proceedings,[100] ICSID tribunals have accepted such briefs only in a few cases.[101] In two recent cases[102] the tribunal rejected a petition for leave to submit a joint amicus curiae brief by the European Center for Constitutional and Human Rights and four indigenous communities in Zimbabwe because they did not satisfy any of the criteria under Rule 37(2) of ICSID Arbitration Rules.[103] The tribunal noted that the circumstances of the amici's application gave rise to legitimate doubts as to their independence or neutrality as the amici did not have a "significant interest in the proceeding." This decision highlights that the current approach to granting amicus standing is largely ad hoc and discretionary. Those who favor less transparency are ruled by a fear that such public involvement could potentially politicize investment disputes leading to a loss of investor confidence in the arbitration mechanism. Given the public interest in the proceedings, a fine balance is needed between the confidential nature of the proceedings and the level of public involvement that promotes transparency. Both North–South and South–South investment flows have policy implications that favor the involvement of amici in arbitral proceedings.

5. HUMAN RIGHTS REMEDIES AND ENVIRONMENTAL POLLUTION

Human rights law seeks to protect rights-holders against arbitrary interference by their state and provide access to remedies. Environmental degradation often leads to human rights violations, and this inseparable link between human rights and the environment[104] was acknowledged by Judge Weeramantry of the ICJ in

---

[99] E. Levine, "Amicus Curiae in International Investment Arbitration: The Implications of an Increase in Third-Party Participation" (2012) 29(1) *Berkeley Journal of International Law* 200.

[100] Rule 37(2) of the ICSID Rules of Procedure for Arbitration Proceedings (Arbitration Rules).

[101] *Aguas Argentinas, SA, Suez, Sociedad General de Aguas de Barcelona, SA and Vivendi Universal, SA and the Argentine Republic*, ICSID Case No. ARB/03/19, Order in response to a petition for transparency and participation as amicus curiae, 19 May 2005 (paras. 17–29). *Aguas Provinciales de Santa Fe SA and Others v Argentina* (17 March 2006), Order in Response to a Petition for Participation as *Amicus Curiae*, ICSID Case No. ARB/03/17. *Biwater Gauff (Tanzania) Ltd v Tanzania*, ICSID Case No. ARB/05/22.

[102] *Bernhard Von Pezold and others v Zimbabwe* (ICSID Case No. ARB/10/15) and *Border Timbers Limited et al v Zimbabwe* (ICSID Case No. ARB/10/25), Procedural Order No. 2, 26 June 2012. The cases were conjoined and the ICSID Tribunal produced a combined Procedural Order.

[103] Paras. 56, 59, 61.

[104] See chapter 8, L. J. Kotzé, "Human Rights, the Environment, and the Global South".

602 *Access to Remedies in Environmental Matters*

his separate opinion in the *Gabčíkovo-Nagymaros* case[105] and established at the national level through constitutional rights.[106] The link between human rights and environmental degradation is not new[107] and the duty to protect the environment applies to states as well as non-state actors.[108] The universal and inalienable nature of human rights makes it a perfect candidate to deal with serious, large-scale damage to the environment, as well as with the adverse impacts of climate change.[109] An example is the Inuit petition to the Inter-American Commission on Human Rights in 2005, where the Inuit referred to the adverse effects of climate change on their protected rights, including the right to life.[110] This petition highlights that the right to a healthy environment is a basic condition of the right to life and the deterioration of environmental quality can impair the fulfillment of other human rights, such as the right to health, right to family life, and right to property.[111] While the Inter-American Commission did not elaborate on the reasoning,[112] it is likely that they were concerned about the weak causal links between the actions of the U.S. government and the harm experienced by the Inuit.

In a number of cases, the regional human rights bodies have examined alleged violations of human rights and environmental degradation and discussed the link between human rights and the environment.[113] For instance, within the European

---

[105] *Gabčíkovo-Nagymaros Project* (Hungary/Slovakia), Judgement, ICJ Reports 1997, p. 7, paras. 91–92 (Separate Opinion of Vice-President Weeramantry).

[106] A. Boyle, "Human Rights or Environmental Rights? A Reassessment" (2007) 18 *Fordham Environmental Law Review* 471.

[107] UN Economic and Social Council, *Review of Further Developments in Fields with which the Sub-Commission has Been Concerned, Human Rights and the Environment: Final Report Prepared by Mrs. Fatma Zohra Ksentini, Special Rapporteur*, 6 July 1994, E/CN.4/Sub.2/1994/9; UN General Assembly, *Report of the Independent Expert on the Issue of Human Rights Obligations Relating to the Enjoyment of a Safe, Healthy and Sustainable Environment, John H. Knox*, 24 December 2012, A/HRC/22/43.

[108] *Guiding Principles on Business and Human Rights: Implementing the UN "Protect, Respect and Remedy" Framework*, 21 March 2011, UN Doc. A/HRC/17/31, p. 17 [hereinafter Guiding Principles on Business and Human Rights]. See also, United Nations Global Compact, "The Ten Principles," www.unglobalcompact.org, Principles 1–2, 7–9.

[109] Human Rights Council, *Human Rights and Climate Change*, Resolution 7/23, 28 March 2008; J. H. Knox, "Climate Change and Human Rights Law" (2009) 50(1) *Virginia Journal of International Law* 1. For criticisms of the human rights approach, J. H. Knox, "Climate Ethics and Human Rights" (2014) 5 *Journal of Human Rights and the Environment* 26.

[110] "Petition to the Inter-American Commission on Human Rights Seeking Relief from Violations Resulting from Global Warming Caused by Acts and Omissions of the United States," 7 December 2005, www.ciel.org, p. 90.

[111] Ibid, p. 82.

[112] A. E. Dulitzsky, Letter to Paul Crowley, Legal Representative of Sheila Watt-Cloutier et al. regarding Petition No P-1413-05, http://graphics8.nytimes.com/packages/pdf/science/16com missionletter.pdf; J. H. Knox "Diagonal Environmental Rights," in R. Lemarchand (ed.), *Forgotten Genocides: Oblivion, Denial, and Memory* (Philadelphia: University of Pennsylvania Press, 2011), pp. 90–91.

[113] Boyle, note 106 at 471.

Court of Human Rights,[114] the claims for environmental protection are primarily based on the violation of the right to private life and home.[115] However, the application of this right does not include a general right to protect the environment.[116] In addition, Article 8 of the European Convention on Human Rights (which protects private and family life) can be restricted if the activity falls under Article 8(2) (e.g. authorized economic activity) – but only if the economic activity in question has a legitimate aim and is lawful and proportionate to the legitimate aim pursued.[117]

A bolder approach has been taken by the African Commission on Human and Peoples' Rights in its interpretation of Article 24 of the African Charter, which expressly includes a substantive right to a satisfactory environment. In the *Ogoniland* case,[118] which involved the disposal of toxic waste causing soil and water pollution and affecting human health, the Commission noted that Article 24 "imposes clear obligations upon a government," requiring the state "to take reasonable and other measures to prevent pollution and ecological degradation, to promote conservation, and to secure an ecologically sustainable development and use of natural resources."[119] While the Commission found the Nigerian government liable for violation of human rights provisions and appealed the government to ensure "adequate compensation" to victims of human rights violations,"[120] the Commission's decisions are not binding and have very little impact on the ground. Here, it is worth noting that although there is an African Court on Human and Peoples' Rights, a number of African states are not parties to the Protocol on the Establishment of an African Court on Human and Peoples' Rights.[121]

These cases have enforced substantive rights (e.g. the *Ogoniland* case) and developed remedies for violations of environmental rights such as remedial action or compensation (e.g. the *Hatton* and *Awas Tingni* cases[122]). They highlight the

---

[114] For example, *López Ostra* v *Spain*, 20 Eur Ct HR 277 (1994); *Guerra* v *Italy*, 26 Eur Ct HR 357 (1998); *Öneryildiz* v *Turkey*, 41 Eur Ct HR 20 (2004); *Taskin* v *Turkey*, 42 Eur Ct HR 50 (2004); *Fadeyeva* v *Russia*, 45 Eur Ct HR 10, 88 (2005).

[115] *Convention for the Protection of Human Rights and Fundamental Freedoms*, Rome, 4 November 1950, in force 3 September 1953, ETS 5; 213 UNTS 221, art. 8 [hereinafter European Convention on Human Rights].

[116] Birnie et al., note 6, pp. 282–285.

[117] *Hatton and Others* v *The United Kingdom* (GC) 2003, 37 EHRR 28.

[118] Decision regarding Communication 155/96 (Social and Economic Rights Action Center/ Center for Economic and Social Rights v. Nigeria), Communication No. ACHPR/COMM/ A044/1 (27 May 2002), available at www.cesr.org/downloads/AfricanCommissionDecision.pdf.

[119] Ibid, para. 52.

[120] Ibid, p. 15, para. 69. See chapter 8, L. J. Kotzé, "Human Rights, the Environment, and the Global South."

[121] Protocol to the African Charter on the Establishment of the African Court on Human and Peoples' Rights, 10 June 1998, in force 1 January 2004, OAU/LEG/MIN/AFCHPR/PROT.1 rev.2 (1997). See list of ratification: www.achpr.org/instruments/court-establishment/ratifica tion.

[122] *Mayagna (Sumo) Awas Tingni Community* v *Nicaragua*, Judgment of 31 August 31 2001, Inter-Am Ct HR, (Ser C) No. 79 (2001).

604   *Access to Remedies in Environmental Matters*

need for express inclusion of environmental quality in binding instruments (e.g. the African Charter and the San Salvador Protocol to the American Convention on Human Rights)[123] to hold states and private actors responsible for their action or inaction resulting in environmental degradation. Indeed, the express recognition of a right to a healthy environment may make it easier for affected individuals to bring a claim in court.

6. CHALLENGES AND CONCERNS

Transnational corporations and NGOs play a crucial role in natural resource management – sometimes being even more powerful than individual states. This highlights the need for effective remedies to deal with environmental degradation caused by MNCs, for instance in Bhopal (India), Niger Delta (Nigeria), or Ok Tedi (Papua New Guinea), that severely impact human rights, such as the rights to life, food, water, and health.[124] Remedies available under state responsibility, the WTO, and investment agreements fail to protect individuals and communities affected by environmental damage caused by corporate activities. While the human rights jurisprudence creates substantive and procedural obligations for the state in relation to the environment, it covers only those environmental harms that infringe human rights.[125] Thus, human rights law cannot protect the environment, except indirectly. Southern countries often fail to meet these human rights obligations by allowing excessive levels of pollution or failing to provide full and equal access to information and justice. The failure of Southern states to take necessary measures to safeguard individuals or communities within their jurisdiction from infringements of human rights by private actors gives rise to several alternative avenues that may provide some remedies to victims in the South.

First, it is possible to bring an action under tort law in the home country of the MNCs, mostly in the North, for corporate abuse. For example, the Alien Torts Claims Act (ATCA) in the United States[126] and the tort obligations of negligence in the UK[127] have been used by individuals or communities in the South to bring an

---

[123] *Additional Protocol to the American Convention on Human Rights in the Area of Economic, Social and Cultural Rights*, San Salvador, 17 November 1988, in force 16 November 1999, OAS Treaty Series No. 69; 28 ILM 156 (1989).

[124] For examples of these disasters, see Business and Human Rights Resource Centre, "Lawsuits: Selected Cases," http://business-humanrights.org.

[125] G. Handl, "Human Rights and Protection of the Environment: A Mildly "Revisionist" View," in A. A. C. Trindade (ed.), *Derechos Humanos, Desarrollo Sustentable y Medio Ambiente* (San Jose: Instituto Interamericano de Derechos Humanos, 1995).

[126] *Alien Tort Claims Act 1789*, 28 USC § 1350 (2000). ATCA applied in, e.g., *Doe I v Unocal*, 395 F 3d 932 (9th Cir 2002); *Wiwa v Royal Dutch Petroleum Co*, 226 F.3d 88 (2d Cir. 2000); *Kiobel v Royal Dutch Petroleum Company*, 133 S.Ct. 1659 (2013).

[127] Cases brought under negligence in the UK include: *Connelly v RTZ Corporation Plc & Another* 1998 AC 354 (HL); *Sithole & Others v Thor Chemicals Holdings & Desmond Cowley* 2000 WL 1421183; *Lubbe & Ors v Cape Plc* 2000 1 WLR 1545 (HL).

action against the MNCs. In *Wiwa v Royal Dutch Petroleum*,[128] a claim brought under ATCA, it was alleged that Shell was complicit in supporting military operations against the Ogoni and the company actively pursued the convictions and execution of the Ogoni Nine, including by bribing witnesses against them. In 2009, Shell agreed to settle for US$15.5 million, including US$5 million which the plaintiffs donated to a trust to benefit the Ogoni people.[129] A separate case was brought in 2002 against Royal Dutch Shell in U.S. federal court by a group of Ogoni people claiming that the company, through its subsidiary, was complicit in the commission of torture, extra-judicial killing, and other violations in Nigeria pursuant to the ATCA. In this case, the Supreme Court held that ATCA does not apply to conduct outside of the United States and dismissed the case.[130] While this decision restricts the application of ATCA,[131] a case may still survive if directed against U.S. corporations "where some of the acts alleged to have violated international law occurred in the US."[132]

Second, because pollution is likely to cause serious and long-lasting damage to the environment, criminal law of the host state may play a role, albeit less prominently, in dealing with environmental disasters of this nature. For example, the Gulf of Mexico Oil Spill case in the United States shows some use of criminal law where British Petroleum agreed to pay US$4.5 billion in penalties and plead guilty to manslaughter and other criminal charges related to the spill.[133] While there are calls for increased use of criminal law for corporate manslaughter,[134] bribery,[135] and criminal negligence,[136] a soft approach to corporate crime is evidenced through a lack of environmental prosecutions and a low level of criminal penalties in the South.[137]

Third, the affected community can make use of public interest litigation (PIL) to seek redress against a violation of a legal or constitutional right. This has been widely used to uphold environmental law.[138] Although such litigation for environmental

---

[128] *Wiwa v Royal Dutch Petroleum Co*, 226 F.3d 88 (2d Cir. 2000).

[129] "Shell Settles Nigeria Deaths Case," BBC News, 9 June 2009.

[130] *Kiobel v. Royal Dutch Petroleum Co*, 133 S.Ct. 1659 (2013).

[131] The effect of Kiobel can be seen in the decision of *RioTinto, PLC v Sarei*, No. 11-649, 2013 WL 1704704 (22 April 2013) where the Supreme Court wants to further consider the case in light of *Kiobel*.

[132] L. S Weiss and W. B Panlilio, "Defending Against Alien Tort Statute Cases post-Kiobel: What Are the Key Defenses?," The American Law Institute, Continuing Legal Education Seminar, 2013.

[133] T. J. Schoenbaum, "Liability for Damages in Oil Spill Accidents: Evaluating the USA and International Law Regimes in the Light of Deepwater Horizon" (2012) 21(3) *Journal of Environmental Law* 403.

[134] *Corporate Manslaughter and Corporate Homicide Act* 2007 (UK), c. 19.

[135] *Bribery Act* 2010 (UK), c.28.

[136] For example, the U.S. Clean Water Act 33 USC §1251 et seq. (1972); the EU Directive 2008/99/EC on the protection of the environment through criminal law, L 328/28 (6.12.2008).

[137] M. G. Faure, "Instruments for Environmental Governance: What Works?," paper presented at the Annual Colloquium of the Academy for Environmental Law of the IUCN, Wuhan, 2009.

[138] J. Cassels, "Judicial Activism and Public Interest Litigation: Attempting the Impossible?" (1989) 37 *American Journal of Comparative Law* 498.

606 *Access to Remedies in Environmental Matters*

causes originated in the United States,[139] PIL has been used in numerous jurisdictions of the South, most notably in India.[140] The historical development of PIL in India shows that the judiciary has been very active in relaxing the standing rules giving access to marginalized communities and interpreting the constitutional rights in a liberal manner in order to enhance the rule of law.[141] Critics have highlighted some negative aspects of PIL: that such legal proceedings can be lengthy and time-consuming; that many countries provide no legal assistance to bring environmental cases and no specific guidelines on the recovery of attorney fees and costs; that there is a lack of implementation of the judgments[142] and inadequate penalty for "contempt of court" (i.e. when the polluting companies or government agencies ignore the court's decision). In addition, judicial decisions can be influenced by political or extra-institutional pressures (e.g. economic actors, lobbies) and depend on professional capabilities and independence. Thus, access to courts by the victims in the South may not always ensure justice.

Fourth, local people of Southern countries affected by World Bank-financed projects can make complaints to the World Bank Inspection panel to ensure that the Bank adheres to its operational policies and procedures in the design, preparation, and implementation of such projects.[143] Both internal[144] and external[145] pressure provided the momentum for the creation of the Panel. During the 1980s, the Bank had engaged in a number of projects (e.g. the Narmada dam project in India) that had devastated local populations and caused significant environmental damage. There was pressure from transnational activists and project-affected communities who questioned the social and environmental impact of projects financed by the Bank. The Panel was initiated in 1993 to help the Bank prevent or correct poor project design and costly mistakes; improve project quality, environmental

---

[139] J. Sax, *Defending the Environment: A Handbook for Citizen Action* (New York: Vintage Books, 1970).

[140] J. Razzaque, *Public Interest Environmental Litigation in India, Pakistan and Bangladesh* (New York: Kluwer Law International, 2004).

[141] R. Dhavan "Whose Law? Whose Interest?," in J. Cooper and R. Dhavan (eds.), *Public Interest Law* (Oxford: Blackwell, 1986), p. 21.

[142] Ibid.

[143] The Compliance Advisor Ombudsman is another non-judicial forum for affected people to bring their complaints against IFC and MIGA. The WB Inspection panel investigates projects the IBRD and the IDA. The Panel so far has ninety one cases – the majority of these complaints are from Southern countries.

[144] On the Morse Commission report (1992), see B. Morse and T.R. Berger, *Report of the Independent Review* (Ottawa: Resource Futures International, 1992); on the Wapenhans Report (1992), see The Whirled Bank Ground, "The Willi Wapenhans Report," www.whirled bank.org.

[145] For instance, in 1993, the U.S. Congress called for establishing an accountability mechanism to ensure the Bank's social and environmental sustainability. Also, the Rio Declaration addresses interrelated issues of social development, economic development, and environmental protection. See generally D. Hunter and L. Udall, "The World Bank's New Inspection Panel: Will It Increase the Bank's Accountability?," CIEL Brief No. 1, Washington DC Center for International Environmental Law, 1994.

assessments, public consultation, and resettlement plans; and apply social and environmental standards to infrastructure projects.[146] A study shows that Southern civil society actors have generated the most claims submitted to the Panel so far[147] and that as a result of a Panel decision, a dam project in Nepal was cancelled.[148] However, critics question whether the Panel truly increases the accountability of the Bank, as it has a limited substantive mandate to investigate claims against the Bank's actions or inaction, rather than against borrower states.[149] Also, the Panel does not propose remedial measures and it "does not have the power to issue an injunction, stop a project, or award financial compensation for harm suffered."[150]

Fifth, primarily out of concern about the conduct of MNCs abusing human and environmental rights, CSR[151] has been included in various voluntary codes of corporate conduct. Codes of conduct on a range of topics perform public functions through soft or informal instruments that are created by a set of public and private actors.[152] In a way, these initiatives are emanations of free market philosophy and neoliberal ideology that aim to fill up the regulatory vacuum created by weak international and national laws regulating business actors.[153] The Ruggie Framework for Business and Human Rights states that the responsibility to respect human rights applies to all company activities and through its relationships with other stakeholders, such as suppliers, communities, non-state, and state actors.[154] The OECD Guidelines provide for National Contact Points (NCP) that bring parties together to mediate a solution to complaints brought against MNCs in the host states by victims of corporate abuse.[155] However, there are no sanctions or penalties attached to NCP decisions. Sadly, the amendment to the OECD Guidelines in 2011 did not bring any substantive changes to the operation of the NCP.[156] By signing up to voluntary guidelines, companies do not necessarily raise their

[146] D. Hunter, "Using the World Bank's Inspection Panel to Defend the Interests of Project-Affected People" (2001) 4 *Chicago Journal of International Law* 201.

[147] D. Clark, J. Fox, and K. Treakle (eds.), *Demanding Accountability: Civil-Society Claims and the World Bank Inspection Panel* (Lanham: Rowman and Littlefield, 2003), p. 257.

[148] Nepal-Arun III Hydroelectric Project.

[149] K. Treakle and E. D. Pena, "Accountability at the World Bank: What Does It Take? Lessons from the Yacyretá Hydroelectric Project, Argentina/Paraguay," in D. Clark, J. Fox, and K. Treakle (eds.), *Demanding Accountability: Civil-Society Claims and the World Bank Inspection Panel* (Lanham: Rowman and Littlefield, 2003), pp. 78–79.

[150] E. R. Carrasco and A. K. Guernsey, "The World Bank's Inspection Panel: Promoting True Accountability through Arbitration" (2008) 41 *Cornell International Law Journal* 3.

[151] The European Commission defines CSR as "the responsibility of enterprises for their impacts on society", Communication from the Commission, A renewed EU strategy 2011–14 for CSR, Brussels, COM(2011) 681 final. 25.10.2011.

[152] J. Razzaque, "Corporate Responsibility in Tackling Environmental Harm: Lost in the Regulatory Maze?" (2013) 16(2) *Australasian Journal of Natural Resources Law and Policy* 197.

[153] S. R. Ratner, "Corporations and Human Rights: A Theory of Legal Responsibility" (2001) 111 *Yale Law Journal* 443.

[154] Guiding Principles on Business and Human Rights, note 108.

[155] OECD, note 93, para. 11 (Concepts and Principles (I)).

[156] OECD, note 93.

608 *Access to Remedies in Environmental Matters*

performance standards; nor do these guidelines assist the victims of environmental harm. Nevertheless, these guidelines may influence corporate activities to move "beyond the law" in a direction that complements government regulations, engages non-state actors in setting standards, and involves consumers to push the company to behave sustainably.[157]

While victims of environmental harm may have alternative avenues to seek redress, these are not necessarily effective. Thus, the challenge for the South and the victims of the South (and the North) remains. State responsibility needs to converge with individual and business accountability to provide effective remedies for victims of environmental harm. Moreover, we need to revise the rather bilateral nature of state responsibility principles to accommodate global issues such as climate change.

---

[157] D. McBarnet, "Corporate Social Responsibility Beyond Law, Through Law, For Law: The New Corporate Accountability," in D. McBarnet, A. Voiculescu, and T. Campbell (eds.), *The New Corporate Accountability: Corporate Social Responsibility and the Law* (Cambridge: Cambridge University Press, 2007), pp. 9–58.

29

Sustainable Development versus Green Economy: The Way Forward?

Shawkat Alam and Jona Razzaque

1. INTRODUCTION

Sustainable development (SD) is an inherently dynamic, indefinite, and contested concept. Its outcomes are heavily dependent on the pathways and operations of each country. The implementation of SD varies depending on the different levels of development and strategic priorities of each country.[1] As stressed by the G77 and China: "[r]egarding sustainable development [...] each country has the sovereign right to decide its own development priorities and strategies and consider that there is no 'one size fits all' approach."[2] Southern and Northern countries differ over the interpretation and implementation of SD, and the narrative of SD can be perceived as just a "'diplomatic trick' to bring all stakeholders under a common banner" to pursue coherent actions on SD.[3] So far, the "state-centric talk fests" have not managed to bring any "meaningful change" to unsustainable practices.[4] Thus, political pragmatism remains a significant element for the future progression and operationalization of SD within international environmental law.

We are grateful to Professor Carmen Gonzalez and Sumudu Atapattu for their helpful comments on earlier drafts.

[1] UN, Rio+20 UN Conference on Sustainable Development, *The Future We Want*, 20-22 June 2012, A/CONF.216/L.1; Sustainable Development, "Introduction to the Proposal of the Open Working Group for Sustainable Development Goals," http://sustainabledevelopment.un.org, paras. 12, 13, 18.

[2] The Group of 77, "Statement on Behalf of the Group of 77 and China by H.E. Mr. Sacha Llorenti, Ambassador, Permanent Representative of the Plurinational State of Bolivia to The United Nations, Chair of the Group of 77, At the Closing Session of the Open Working Group on Sustainable Development Goals (New York, 19 July 2014)," www.g77.org.

[3] J. E. Vinuales, "The Rise and Fall of Sustainable Development" (2013) 22(1) *Review of European Community and International Environmental Law* 3 at 4.

[4] M. Halle, A. Najam, and C Beaton, *The Future of Sustainable Development: Rethinking Sustainable Development after Rio+20 and Implications for UNEP* (IISD, 2013), p. 3.

610 *The Way Forward?*

The UN Conference on Sustainable Development, 2012 (Rio+20) identified "a green economy in the context of sustainable development and poverty eradication"[5] as one of its main themes. The concept of "green economy" came to prominence following the Rio+20 conference, and promised a new paradigm of environmentally responsible growth.[6] The outcome document of Rio+20 did not provide a definition of 'green economy'[7] and encouraged "each country to consider the implementation of green economy policies in the context of sustainable development and poverty eradication, in a manner that endeavours to drive sustained, inclusive and equitable economic growth and job creation."[8] The key aim for a transition to a green economy is to enable economic growth and investment while increasing environmental quality and social inclusiveness.[9] It is hailed by international institutions (e.g. the United Nations Environment Programme and the World Bank) as a great enabler for economic rebalancing between the North and the South, leaving aside questions as to who reaps the benefits of unsustainable economic activity and who bears the burden of resource depletion and pollution.[10] While SD remains the highest priority of the international and national development agenda, moving toward a green economy is considered a multifaceted pathway to achieving SD.[11]

A green economy is not intended to replace sustainable development and the implementation of a green economy must be consistent with the principles identified in the Rio Declaration on Environment and Development[12] and the Johannesburg Declaration on Sustainable Development (Johannesburg Declaration).[13] These include justice, dignity, social inclusion, good governance

---

[5] UN General Assembly, *Resolution Adopted by the General Assembly: The Future We Want*, 27 July 2012, UN Doc A/RES/66/288, para. 12 (hereinafter *The Future We Want*).

[6] U. Brand, "Green Economy – the Next Oxymoron?" 21 (2012) *GAIA* 28.

[7] United Nations Environment Programme (UNEP), *Green Economy Report: A Preview* (United Nations Environment Programme, 2010), p. 3. The United Nations Environment Programme provides the following definition: "[a] Green Economy can be defined as an economy that results in improved human well-being and reduced inequalities over the long term, while not exposing future generations to significant environmental risks and ecological scarcities."

[8] Ibid, para. 62.

[9] UNEP, *Towards a Green Economy: Pathways to Sustainable Development and Poverty Eradication* (UNEP, 2011). UNEP is one of the leading environmental organizations that is spearheading the "green economy" concept.

[10] Ibid. World Bank, "Inclusive Green Growth: The Pathway to Sustainable Development," May 23, 2012, http://issuu.com/world.bank.publications. See also UNESCAP, "Low Carbon Green Growth Roadmap for Asia-Pacific," January 1, 2012, www.unescap.org; "Green Economy in Action: Articles and Excerpts that Illustrate Green Economy and Sustainable Development Efforts," United Nations Development Program, August 2012.

[11] C. Y. Ling and S. Iyer, "Developing Countries Raise Concerns on 'Green Economy' as Rio +20 Begins," South Bulletin, vol. 47, 2010.

[12] Rio de Janeiro, 13 June 1992, UN Doc. A/CONF.151/26 (vol. I); 31 ILM 874 (1992).

[13] Johannesburg, 4 September 2002, UN Doc. A/CONF. 199/20), Resolution 1, Annex.

and accountability, resilience, and inter- and intragenerational equity.[14] However, to many, the green economy is an instrument for the advancement of corporate interests, as it emphasizes markets and businesses as a solution to environmental and economic problems.[15] According to Simons, corporate human rights impunity is deeply embedded within the structures of the international legal system, allowing powerful states to create a globalized legal environment that fosters further corporate impunity.[16] Therefore, enhancing economic interests of Transnational Corporations (TNCs) based in the North at the expense of human rights and environmental sustainability in the global South is a systemic issue, not simply the result of globalization creating governance gaps, as Ruggie argues.[17] Hence, the green economy is not a panacea for global economic, social, and environmental inequity.

The Rio+20 outcome document[18] acknowledges the disparities in policy and institutional frameworks, political circumstances, levels of development, and economic and environmental interdependencies in the global community. Thus, for the future implementation of SD, different Southern countries face different challenges, opportunities, and outcomes.[19] To operationalize SD, one of the outcomes of the Rio+20 conference was an agreement to launch a process to develop a set of Sustainable Development Goals (SDGs).[20] These goals are built upon the Millennium Development Goals (MDGs) and converge with the post–2015 development agenda. Certainly, it will not be an easy task for the SDGs to reflect various national realities, capacities, and development priorities.[21] An integrated approach to sustainable development would, nevertheless, assist collaboration across various fields, sectors and scales by drawing connections between social, economic, and environmental spheres; facilitating appropriate policy frameworks for diverse states; and

---

[14] *The Future We Want*, note 5, paras. 15–18.

[15] Friends of the Earth International, "Reclaim the UN from Corporate Capture," June 1, 2012, www.foei.org.

[16] P. Simons, "International Law's Invisible Hand and the Future of Corporate Accountability for Violations of Human Rights" (2012) 3 *Journal of Human Rights and the Environment* 5 at 5.

[17] Ibid.

[18] *The Future We Want*, note 5, para. 246.

[19] OECD, *Towards Green Growth* (Paris: OECD, 2011), p. 10.

[20] The outcome document of the Rio+20, entitled *The Future We Want*, sets out a mandate to establish an open working group to develop a set of sustainable development goals. Rio+20 did not elaborate specific goals but stated that the SDGs should be limited in number, aspirational, and easy to communicate. The goals should address, in a balanced way, all three dimensions of sustainable development and be coherent with and integrated into the UN development agenda beyond 2015. The Report of the Open Working Group of the General Assembly on Sustainable Development Goal was submitted to the UN General Assembly on August 12, 2014: see UN General Assembly, *Report of the Open Working Group of the General Assembly on Sustainable Development Goals*, 12 August 2014, UN Doc. A/68/970.

[21] The Group of 77, "Statement on Behalf of the Group of 77 and China by its Chairman, Ambassador Peter Thomson of Fiji, at the Second Session of the General Assembly Open Working Group on Sustainable Development Goals (SDGs) (New York, 17 April 2013)," www.g77.org.

recognizing the need to engage local communities.[22] However, the magnitude of the disparity between the needs and priorities of the global North and South complicates matters.

Poverty alleviation, sustainability (economic, social, and environmental), and participation are the three fundamental objectives of the SD paradigm. However, the concepts of sustainability and participation are poorly articulated, making it difficult to determine whether a particular development project actually promotes a particular form of sustainability, or what kind of participation will lead to a particular social outcome. [23] On the one hand, "[g]ood governance and the rule of law at the national and international levels are essential for sustained, inclusive and equitable economic growth, sustainable development and the eradication of poverty and hunger."[24] Moreover, there is a need to "ensure enhanced representation and voice of developing countries in decision making in global international economic and financial institutions in order to deliver more effective, credible, accountable and legitimate institutions."[25] Even the proposal from the Open Working Group of the General Assembly on Sustainable Development Goals[26] showed a rift between the North and the South. Venezuela objected to some provisions in the document because of their "interventionist character in the State public policies."[27] Both Bolivia and Venezuela used similar language to convey that they are unwilling to accept "any kind of evaluation, monitoring, reporting and review" of national policies and measures as it will affect their sovereign rights. However, France, Germany, and Switzerland urged countries to refrain from revisiting texts that were the subject of extensive compromises.[28]

Indeed, without embracing equity as the central tenet of SD, there can be no wholesale adoption of the SDGs across the North and the South. At the same time, there are diverse opinions and priorities not only between the global South and the global North, but also among the nations of the global South. Thus, the future progression and implementation of SD requires a discussion from the perspectives

---

[22] J. Robinson, "Squaring the Circle? Some Thoughts on the Idea of Sustainable Development" (2004) 48 *Ecological Economics* 369 at 369.

[23] S. M. Lele, "Sustainable Development: A Critical Review" (1991) 19(6) *World Development* 642.

[24] Sustainable Development, note 1, para. 12.

[25] Ibid, Goal 10.6.

[26] UN, note 1, para. 248. A thirty-member Open Working Group (OWG) of the General Assembly is tasked with preparing a proposal on the SDGs. The Open Working Group was established on January 22, 2013 by decision 67/555 (see UN General Assembly, *Draft Decision Submitted by the President of the General Assembly: Open Working Group of the General Assembly on Sustainable Development Goals*, 15 January 2013, A/67/L.48/Rev.1) of the General Assembly.

[27] Sustainable Development, "Statement by Cristiane Engelbrecht, Counsellor, Permanent Mission of the Bolivarian Republic of Venezuela to the United Nations," http://sustainable development.un.org.

[28] Sustainable Development, "Statement by France, Germany and Switzerland, OWG13," http://sustainabledevelopment.un.org.

of integration (discussed in section 2)[29], responsibility (discussed in section 3) and cooperation (discussed in section 4).

2. BALANCING INTEGRATION OF THE THREE PILLARS OF SD

Sustainable development[30] is considered an umbrella concept encompassing both substantive and procedural components. It integrates three essential pillars: social development; environmental protection; and economic development.[31] At the 1972 UN Conference on the Human Environment, the South expressed concern over the priority given to environmental issues[32] and the possibility that this would perpetuate "existing unequal economic relations and technical dependence, miring them in poverty forever."[33] During the 1970s, the South questioned not only the relative importance of environmental policies but also the very legitimacy of global environmental governance. This critique has had a lasting impact on the SD agenda, including at Rio in 1992 and Johannesburg in 2002.[34] The South came to Johannesburg eager to discuss how global environmental governance could be implemented more effectively.[35] In retrospect, the Southern demands for global environmental governance priorities have had considerable, even remarkable, influence on the transformation of the environmental agenda into a SD agenda.[36]

---

[29] B. Giddings, B. Hopwood, and G. O'Brien, "Environment, Economy and Society: Fitting Them Together into Sustainable Development" (2002) 10(4) *Sustainable Development* 187 at 195.

[30] Sustainable development is defined in the *Brundtland Report* as development that "meets the needs of the present, without compromising the ability of future generations to meet their own needs": World Commission on Environment and Development, *Our Common Future* (New York: Oxford University Press, 1987), p. 8.

[31] P. Birnie, A. Boyle, and C. Redgwell, *International Law and the Environment* (New York: Oxford University Press, 2009), p. 116. P. Sands, J. Peel, A. Fabra, and R. MacKenzie, *Principles of International Environmental Law* (Cambridge: Cambridge University Press, 2012), p. 215.

[32] W. Rowland, *The Plot to Save the World: The Life and Times of the Stockholm Conference on the Human Environment* (Toronto: Clarke, Irwin and Co., 1973); Founex, *Development and Environment: Report and Working Papers of Experts Convened by the Secretary General of the UNCHE* (Mouton: Paris, 1972); R. Clarke, *Stockholm Plus Ten: Promises, Promises? The Decade Since the 1972 UN Environment Conference* (London: Earthscan, 1982). See also chapter 5, K. Mickelson, "The Stockholm Conference and the Creation of the South–North Divide in International Environmental Law and Policy."

[33] Rowland, note 32; S. Hecht and A. Cockburn, "Rhetoric and Reality in Rio" (1982) 254(24) *The Nation* 848.

[34] See chapter 3, R. Gordon, "Unsustainable Development." See also A. Najam, "Developing Countries and Global Environmental Governance: From Contestation to Participation to Engagement" (2005) 5 *International Environmental Agreements* 303.

[35] J. Wilson and V. Munnik, *The World Comes to One Country – An Insider History of the World Summit on Sustainable Development* (Berlin: Heinrich Boll Foundation, 2003).

[36] See generally M. C. Segger and A. Khalfan, *Sustainable Development Law: Principles, Practices and Progress* (Oxford: Oxford University Press, 2004).

614 *The Way Forward?*

The concerns of the South remain substantially different from those of the North. The North tends to highlight the environmental aspects of SD while the South tends to be far more concerned about the poverty alleviation and economic development aspects.[37] The tension involved in balancing the three pillars of SD is evident in Rio+20's qualified references to the green economy "in the context of sustainable development and poverty eradication."[38] During the negotiation of the Rio+20 outcome document, it became clear that the global South was concerned that the North will use the green economy to promote "green protectionism" or to sideline the poverty alleviation issues.[39] Even the "zero draft" [40] that compiled inputs from states and other stakeholders highlighted the priorities of poverty eradication and the importance of "sustained, inclusive and equitable growth,"[41] and thereafter, the Rio+20 outcome document recognized the need to enhance social inclusion.[42]

The North's disproportionate contribution to global environmental degradation and its ongoing interest in ensuring that international power structures remain skewed toward its benefit has added fuel to the "North-South divide" fire.[43] The challenge is to assess how the interdependent relationship among the social, environmental, and economic pillars of SD impacts on the *quality* of each pillar. Inadequate integration of environmental issues can have a detrimental effect on social concerns such as poverty alleviation and food and energy security,[44] while a failure to ensure that environmental imperatives are factored into economic development initiatives can result in long-term constraints on future economic opportunities, such as eco-tourism, which relies on a pristine environment for its viability. Although at Rio+20 both Northern and Southern countries agreed that

---

[37] A. Najam, "The Unraveling of the Rio Bargain" (2002) 21(2) *Politics and the Life Sciences* 46; W. Sachs et al.(eds.), *The Jo'burg Memo: Fairness in a Fragile World* (Berlin: Heinrich Boll Foundation, 2002).

[38] Rio+20 United Nations Conference on Sustainable Development, "Green Economy in the Context of Sustainable Development and Poverty Eradication," www.uncsd2012.org.

[39] E. Morgera, "The Conceptual and Legal Perspective on the Green Economy" (2013) 22 *Review of European Community and International Environmental Law* 21. See also Rio+20 United Nations Conference on Sustainable Development, "Compilation Document Submissions from Member States," www.uncsd2012.org.

[40] Circulated by the Preparatory Committee of the UN Conference on Sustainable Development, the zero draft was intended to serve as the basis for negotiations prior to the Rio+20 Conference. The Draft was based on the recommendations of delegates at the Second Intersessional Meeting of the Rio+20 Conference: see Sustainable Development Policy and Practice, "UNCSD Bureau Releases 'Zero Draft'," http://sd.iisd.org.

[41] UN, "The Future We Want: Zero Draft of the Outcome Document of the UN Conference on Sustainable Development," www.uncsd2012.org.

[42] Ibid, paras. 56, 58(j), 58(k).

[43] See chapter 3, R. Gordon, "Unsustainable Development'; chapter 2, R. Islam, "History of the North-South Divide: Colonial Discourses, Sovereignty, and Self-Determination."

[44] W. M. Adams, *The Future of Sustainability: Re-thinking Environment and Development in the Twenty First Century* (Gland: International Union for Conservation of Nature, 2006, pp. 12–13.

the SDGs should be universal and should integrate and balance the three pillars of SD and address unsustainable and unjust patterns of consumption and production,[45] North–South tensions were apparent.

First, the divergence between the South and the North relating to the green economy remained unchanged.[46] Southern countries were concerned that the "green economy" would replace "sustainable development," eroding the consensus reached at the Rio Conference in 1992, including international commitments on finance and technology transfer. Southern countries, however, cautioned that any global roadmap on the global economy might not respect developmental and economic diversity and any external timeline determining the pace of countries' transition to a green economy would potentially limit their economic growth.[47] During the Rio+20 process, the debate on the green economy seemed to focus on whether all countries should prioritize environmental protection measures to achieve economic development, or "whether only countries at an advanced level of economic development should be required to do so."[48] Although the multifaceted vision of green economy policies takes into account different circumstances and priorities of various countries at different stages of development, the notion of the green economy has failed to attract widespread consensus, as it encourages transforming natural capital into economic assets and promotes the resource-intensive production and consumption patterns of the global North.[49] Moreover, the global North (e.g. the EU) has prioritized the role of the private sector in "promoting and adopting a sustainable business model" and in "including environmental and social concerns in their investment decisions."[50]

The challenge here is how to promote economic growth that is consistent with the preservation of the natural resource base in the context of the Northern-style economic model that promotes privatization and consumerism. Ruth Gordon, for instance, points out that the planet's resources are incapable of supporting a global standard of living equivalent to that currently enjoyed by the North.[51] Transforming

---

[45] Third World Network, "United Nations: Varying Visions and Priorities at SDG Working Group," March 20, 2013, www.twnside.org.sg.

[46] A. Cutter and R. Kuusipalo, "Briefing Note: Principles for a Green Economy," www.stakeholderforum.org.

[47] Ibid; A. Chasek, "Incorporating Regional Priorities into Global Conferences: A Review of the Regional Preparatory Committee Meeting for Rio+20" (2012) 21 *Review of European Community and International Environmental Law* 4 at 6.

[48] E. Morgera and A. Savaresi, "A Conceptual and Legal Perspective on the Green Economy" (2013) 22 *Review of European Community and International Environmental Law* 14.

[49] Ibid. See also J. A. Ocampo, "The Transition to A Green Economy: Benefits, Challenges and Risks from A Sustainable Development Perspective. Summary of Background Papers," in *Report by a Panel of Experts to Second Preparatory Committee Meeting for United Nations Conference on Sustainable Development* (2011).

[50] Ibid, p. 22. See also Rio+20 United Nations Conference on Sustainable Development, "European Union and its Member States," www.uncsd2012.org.

[51] See chapter 3, R. Gordon, "Unsustainable Development'; chapter 2, R. Islam, "History of the North–South Divide: Colonial Discourses, Sovereignty and Self-Determination."

616 *The Way Forward?*

markets (e.g. agricultural markets, energy markets, and financial markets) to facilitate more sustainable practices will require the growth of certain industries which have a minimal ecological footprint, encouraged through the use of government actions (e.g. taxation policies and other incentive schemes) and developing fundamental rules in the market – for instance, standards, transparency, and reporting requirements.

Second, identifying *where* the change is occurring is crucial for the future progression and implementation of sustainable development as well as SDGs. To this extent, high-level strategic fora that have traditionally been associated with other development concerns (e.g. the World Economic Forum) are now engaging with the notion of SD. These fora (including the WTO) play an important role in translating the central tenets of SD into their dialogue and discourse.[52] However, the demise of the Commission on Sustainable Development[53] shows that a strong institutional platform for SD at the international level is lacking:

> United Nations system organizations and major groups came to the conclusion that the Commission had progressively lost its lustre and effectiveness, pointing to several shortcomings, including its lack of impact on the implementation of sustainable development policies; the ineffectiveness of its role in integrating economic, social and environmental dimensions of sustainable development in the work of the United Nations system; and its cumbersome decision-making processes and unclear outcomes.[54]

The dynamic relationship that emerges when different institutions converge through enhanced policy integration could potentially lead to the sort of strong collaborative and communicative process that is crucial for the realization of SD. However, there are several concerns. First, the various substantive and procedural components and the three pillars of SD are not effectively integrated within the legal and policy framework of international financial institutions (e.g. the World Bank and IMF) and the WTO.[55] Moreover, the remedies structure of such financial institutions are unable to offer justice to the victims of the global South affected by the projects funded by these institutions. Examples from the WTO show that the North's environmental standards shift the costs of environmental protection to the South. This exacerbates the North–South divide because the South is not provided with the resources and technology to facilitate compliance.[56]

---

[52] See Chapter 6, V. P. Nanda, "Global Environmental Governance and the South'; Chapter 7, B. H. Desai and B. K. Sidhu, "Quest for International Environmental Institutions: Transition from CSD to HLPF."

[53] SciDevnet, "UN Launches New Sustainable Development Body," October 3, 2013, www. scidev.net.

[54] UN General Assembly, *Lessons Learned from the Commission on Sustainable Development*, 26 February 2013, A/67/757, para. 3.

[55] See chapter 14, S. Alam, "Trade and the Environment: Perspectives from the Global South."

[56] See chapter 28, J. Razzaque, "Access to Remedies in Environmental Matters and the North–South Divide."

Second, collaboration is affected by weak interaction between institutions. Also, a lack of institutional transparency and weak participatory mechanisms inhibit accountability and civil society inputs, and impede Southern leadership that can drive the SD agenda. Thus, there is a need to "ensure enhanced representation and voice of developing countries in decision making in global international economic and financial institutions in order to deliver more effective, credible, accountable and legitimate institutions".[57] In addition, subnational and local governments can play a pivotal role in achieving SD (and SDGs). Active engagement with these stakeholders can encourage different forms of leadership and a "bottom-up" approach[58] that may influence local participants (e.g. grassroots sustainable development leadership such as Local Agenda 21, a scheme aiming to foster community-level sustainable development).

3. REORIENTING THE PRINCIPLE OF COMMON BUT DIFFERENTIATED RESPONSIBILITIES

The CBDR principle[59] has been regarded as an essential tool to achieve SD since its adoption at the Rio Conference in 1992 and reaffirmation at Rio+20.[60] However, this principle is mired in conflict and tensions between the North and South.[61] For example, concerned about the fact that the proposed SDGs do not refer to concrete actions of Northern countries, G77 and China stated that:

> [...] the very notion of "means of implementation" means that the mix of financial resources, technological development and transfers as well as capacity building must be supported by actions from developed countries at the international level. This refers to time-bound financing targets; associated trade and economic policies; technology transfer and other resources to assist and enable developing countries efforts.[62]

---

[57] Sustainable Development, note 1, Goal 10.6.

[58] UN General Assembly, note 54, para. 66.

[59] See L. Rajamani, *Differential Treatment in International Environmental Law* (Oxford: Oxford University Press, 2006); T. Deleuil, "The Common but Differentiated Responsibilities Principle: Changes in Continuity after the Durban Conference of the Parties" (2012) 21(3) *Review of Europe Community and International Environmental Law* 271.

[60] *The Future We Want*, note 5, paras. 15 and 191. See also UN General Assembly, note 54, para. 5.

[61] D. French, "Developing States and International Environmental Law: The Importance of Differentiated Responsibilities" (2000) 49(1) *International and Comparative Law Quarterly* 35 at 36.

[62] Sustainable Development, "Statement on Behalf of the Group of 77 and China by H.E. Mr. René Orellana, Ambassador on Environment and Development Issues of the Plurinational State of Bolivia, at the 11th Session of the Open Working Group on Sustainable Development Goals (SDGs) On 'Means of Implementation and Global Partnership for Sustainable Development' (New York, 9 May 2014)," http://sustainabledevelopment.un.org.

618   *The Way Forward?*

The application of the CBDR principle has certain essential criteria.[63] First, it requires all concerned states to take part in international response measures aimed at tackling environmental problems. Second, it leads to the adoption and implementation of environmental standards that impose different commitments for different states. Overall, this principle suggests that all states bear a responsibility for protecting the environment, but the global North should take the lead due to its superior technological and greater financial resources, along with its greater historic contribution to environmental harm. According to the South, CBDR requires that the North take responsibility for current and historic environmental harm incurred during its progression toward and maintenance of a higher level of development. As the recent observations from some Southern countries highlight, such differentiation is integral to global partnership as it is "principally between governments of developed and developing countries, with the developed countries taking the lead in providing resources and the means of implementation."[64] However, to some Northern countries:

> CBDR as set out in Rio Principle 7 in 1992 cannot apply as an overarching principle to a holistic agenda and does not integrate the idea of dynamic differentiation as stated in the Rio 2012: depending on realities, capacities and levels of development of countries. Moreover, it is worth recalling that Rio Principle 7 has a clear limitation to [the realm of] environmental degradation.[65]

While the purpose of this principle is to ensure fairness in environmental regimes, the current categorization of countries as "developing" and "developed" challenges the fair and effective application of the principle in practice, particularly in relation to climate change.[66] Undoubtedly, the CBDR principle remains an important cornerstone in the implementation of SD and the achievement of SDGs. At Rio+20, the G77 and China proposed the reaffirmation of the CBDR principle, which brings "equity" to the center of obligations.[67] The South feared that without equity as the cornerstone, the basis for international cooperation and development assistance would be threatened.[68] However, some have argued that certain Southern countries have benefited at the expense of others under this principle.[69]

---

[63] See chapter 4, S. Atapattu, "The Significance of International Environmental Law Principles in Reinforcing or Dismantling the North–South Divide"; A. Khalfan, "The Principle of Common but Differentiated Responsibilities: Origins and Scope," for the World Summit on Sustainable Development 2002, Johannesburg, August 26, 2002.

[64] Sustainable Development, note 62, para. 10.

[65] Sustainable Development, "Proposal for Statement by France, Germany and Switzerland, OWG 11, Focus Area 15: Means of implementation/Global Partnership," http://sustainablede velopment.un.org

[66] Rajamani, note 59, p. 165.

[67] M. Khor, "Rio+20 Summit: The Key Issues," South Center Briefing Paper, 2012.

[68] Ibid. See Sustainable Development, note 1, para. 8.

[69] See chapter 10, R. Maguire and X. Jiang, "Emerging Powerful Southern Voices: Role of BASIC Nations in Shaping Climate Change Mitigation Commitments"; T. Deleuil, "The

While both the North and the South are demanding a more active contribution from the other group, they are at the same time afraid of sacrificing too much for the benefit of others. This may be to avoid adjustment and transaction costs and prevent the amplification of negative environmental externalities.[70] For instance, according to Cuba, "[w]ith the green economy, the developed countries are attempting to forget their ecological debt to mankind and the principle of common but differentiated responsibilities according to levels of development, and greening their new ploy to oblige developing countries to adopt economic programmes that limit their development, such as the concept of low-carbon economies."[71] These divergent approaches of the North and the South, and the trade-offs among the three pillars of SD (i.e. weak versus strong sustainability), underscore the need for indicators or goals (e.g. SDGs) to evaluate policy responses to SD. The challenge is to integrate sustainable development into policy frameworks by providing national governments with guidelines for policy design and adaptation that seek to alleviate poverty, ensuring equitable participation and access to justice, eliminating market distortions, facilitating market access, restructuring taxation, and monitoring the implementation and impacts of SDGs.

With equity at its core, SD involves not only an integration of the three pillars, but also the integration of different stakeholders and decision-makers. This includes public and private institutions, as well as marginalized stakeholders (including ethnic minorities, women, and indigenous peoples) to ensure effective policy development and the prevention of environmental degradation. The centrality of equity and the need to incorporate marginalized stakeholders through consultation is recognized in the 2002 Johannesburg Declaration and the MDGs. However, despite this recognition, policy development and government action to date lack such inclusiveness. Without the integration of marginalized communities and a genuine effort for an inclusive approach in policy design and consultation, the international community will fail to address the root causes of unsustainable behaviors. These roadblocks are the result of an omnipresent postcolonial "hangover" within the governance structures of international institutions, including a lack of mechanisms to mitigate the power of the Northern states, transnational corporations, and institutions, such as the World Bank, from unsustainable development and dispossession of marginalized peoples. Even the Rio+20 outcome document does not make any reference to the various international initiatives

Common but Differentiated Responsibilities Principle: Changes in Continuity after the Durban Conference of the Parties" (2012) 21(3) *Review of Europe Community and International Environmental Law* 271.

[70] T. Voitureiz, P. Ekins, H. Blanco, I. von Homeyer, and D. Scheer, "Trade SIAs and the New Challenges of Trade Liberalisation," in P. Ekins and T. Voitureiz (eds.), *Trade, Globalisation and Sustainability Impact Assessment* (London: Earthscan, 2009), pp. 92–94.

[71] Rio+20 United Nations Conference on Sustainable Development, "Cuba: Inputs by Cuba to the Preparatory Process for the United Nations Conference on Sustainable Development (Rio +20)," www.uncsd2012.org.

620   *The Way Forward?*

(e.g. UN Global Compact and UN Guiding Principles on Business and Human Rights)[72] that promote corporate accountability – rather, it simply "invite[s] business and industry as appropriate and in accordance with national legislation to contribute to sustainable development and to develop sustainability strategies that integrate, *inter alia*, green economy policies."[73] Although these international initiatives are not without criticism,[74] they underscore the corporate responsibility to respect human rights.

4. PROMOTING PARTICIPATION AND ALLIANCE

One of the major challenges for international cooperation is how to reconsider the traditional division between the North and the South.[75] According to the Open Working Group on Sustainable Development Goals, North–South partnerships can: implement programs and policies that encourage "pro-poor and gender sensitive development strategies," "technology development," "international cooperation and capacity building"; facilitate "sustainable and resilient infrastructure development"; enhance "representation and voice of developing countries in decision making in global international economic and financial institutions"; and strengthen "resilience and adaptive capacity to climate related hazards."[76] The Open Working Group Proposal for Sustainable Development Goals requests countries to "enhance international support for implementing effective and targeted capacity building in developing countries to support national plans to implement all sustainable development goals, including through North-South, South-South, and triangular cooperation."[77]

However, neither North nor South has ever been homogenous, especially where Southern countries have achieved significant economic development (e.g. Singapore, Mexico, India, Brazil, and China) and a number of countries of the North are facing an economic crisis.[78] With the emergence of the BASIC coalition[79] and the

[72] UN Global Compact, www.unglobalcompact.org; Office of the High Commissioner for Human Rights, "Guiding Principles on Business and Human Rights," www.ohchr.org.
[73] *The Future We Want*, note 5, para. 69.
[74] See e.g. Simons, note 16, for criticisms of the UN Guiding Principles on Business and Human Rights.
[75] J. Pauwelyn, "The End of Differential Treatment for Developing Countries? Lessons from the Trade and Climate Change Regimes" (2013) 22 *Review of European Community and International Environmental Law* 29 at 41; K. A. Hochstetler, "The G-77, BASIC, and Global Climate Governance: a New Era in Multilateral Environmental Negotiations" (2012) *Revista Brasileira Politica Internacional* 53 at 59.
[76] See generally Sustainable Development, note 1.
[77] Sustainable Development, note 1, Goal 17.9.
[78] Pauwelyn, note 75 at 29; P. Cullet, "Common but Differential Responsibilities," in M. Fitzmaurice, D. Ong, and P. Merkouris (eds.), *Research Handbook on International Environmental Law* (Cheltenham: Edward Elgar, 2010), pp. 161, 174–176.
[79] These countries are Brazil, South Africa, India, and China – four of the largest and/or fastest growing developing states joined together for the first time as the BASIC group in Copenhagen in 2009.

New Development Bank,[80] South–South cooperation has the potential to boost Southern influence in global environmental negotiations. However, huge disparities remain among the countries of the global South.[81] Least developed countries certainly cannot be treated the same way as the BASIC group.[82] Countries with emerging economies are seen as "the elephants hiding behind mice" by the North,[83] and some countries of the South argue that the BASIC countries are taking advantage of their exemption from emission reduction obligations in relation to climate change and other trade-related differentiated responsibilities, such as trade liberalization and market access.[84] Such South–South divisions may lead to the disintegration of the global South by potentially diminishing the overall bargaining position of the South.[85] Despite BASIC countries' desire to remain in the G77 and China group, the 2009 Copenhagen conference saw the split widening between them as some of the most vulnerable countries challenged the BASIC countries to do more to reduce emissions.[86] At the same time, increased recognition of the internal South–South divide may serve as an argument for more development assistance (e.g. climate funding and technology transfer) from the BASIC countries to the G77.[87] Policy alliances among the countries of the South are needed in order to address implementation challenges of SD (and SDGs) collectively.

In this respect, creating effective strategic coalitions must reflect the core principles espoused by SD. Specifically, strategic coalitions must adopt an ecosystem approach, coupled with shared economic and social realities, to provide a strong voice for sustainable development issues among the global South. To illustrate, the coalition of small island developing states (SIDS) is becoming a strong voice calling for immediate action against anthropogenic climate change and associated sea-level rise. The emergence of a policy coalition that shares similar environmental, social, and economic realities will focus attention on specific development

---

[80] Formerly known as the BRICS Development Bank, New Development Bank was agreed to by BRICS leaders at the Fifth BRICS Summit held in Durban, South Africa on March 27, 2013.

[81] See chapter 26, K. L. Koh and N. A. Robinson, "South–South Cooperation: Foundations for Sustainable Development."

[82] See chapter 20 for M. Burkett, "A Justice Paradox: Climate Change, Small Island Developing States, and the Absence of International Legal Remedy"; chapter 21, E. A. Kronk Warner, "South to South: Examining the International Climate Regime from an Indigenous Perspective"; chapter 23, R. R. M. Verchick and P. Govind, "Natural Disaster and Climate Change"; chapter 10, R. Maguire and X. Jiang, "Emerging Powerful Southern Voices: Role of BASIC Nations in Shaping Climate Change Mitigation Commitments."

[83] S. C. Schwab, "After Doha: Why the Negotiations are Doomed and What We Should Do About It" (2011) 90(3) Foreign Affairs 107.

[84] Pauwelyn, note 75 at 38.

[85] Ibid at 39.

[86] See chapter 10, R. Maguire and X. Jiang, "Emerging Powerful Southern Voices: Role of BASIC Nations in Shaping Climate Change Mitigation Commitments"; Hochstetler, note 75 at 58.

[87] Ibid.

622   *The Way Forward?*

issues despite the relative political obscurity of SIDS in the international arena. Creating policy coalitions that integrate the three pillars of SD allows discussion, action, and solutions to be appropriately channeled in resource-constrained Southern countries. However, there is still the risk of negative developments, with BASIC countries replicating the global North's development trajectory by, for example, engaging in land grabs for biofuel development.[88]

Notwithstanding emerging South–South coalitions, policy implementation to promote sustainable development must bridge the North–South divide. Without addressing fundamental issues pertaining to equity and poverty, SD will remain an exercise in idealism rather than resulting in tangible development outcomes. Economic prosperity is tied intrinsically to the principles of social equity and environmental integrity. In this respect, SD must re-emphasize the importance of effective capacity-building in Southern countries, which includes, inter alia, appropriate measures for technology transfer and improving Southern countries' capacities for critical analysis, as well as enabling the development of adequate measures for much needed monitoring and reporting pursuant to existing international environmental obligations. In addition, responsibility is also placed on Southern countries to ensure that appropriate legislative frameworks, governance structures, and political environments exist in order to ensure capacity-building and, subsequently, sustainable behavior. This includes sustained endeavors to address corruption and ensure accountability, transparency, and appropriate consultation procedures that reflect the views of the affected, and in particular marginalized communities.

In this respect an important exercise to improve governance within the global South is to decentralize power from national to municipal levels in what Hamdouch and Depret describe as a "vertical" process.[89] Not only does this prevent governments from exercising a disproportionate influence in policy design; it also presents an effective strategy to ensure power relations are accountable and reflect local interests.[90] In addition to state actors, intergovernmental and nongovernmental organizations play an important role in facilitating this process. Civil society groups and the media provide external measures of accountability and place pressure on governments to ensure that adequate systems and regulatory frameworks are in place to move toward achieving sustainable development.[91] It is crucial to note that intergovernmental institutions, such as the IMF and the WTO, have

---

[88] See chapter 19, C. G. Gonzalez, "Food Justice: An Environmental Justice Critique of the Global Food System"; chapter 11, C. Oguamanam, "Sustainable Development in the Era of Bioenergy and Agricultural Land Grab."

[89] See A. Hamdouch and M-H. Depret, "Policy Integration Strategy and the Development of the Green Economy: Foundations and Implementation Patterns" (2010) 53(4) *Journal of Environmental Planning and Management* 473 at 483.

[90] See G. S. Cheema and D. Rondinelli, *Decentralizing Governance: Emerging Concepts and Practices* (Washington, DC: Brookings Institution Press, 2007), p. 240.

[91] See note 89.

historically served as obstacles to the achievement of sustainable development. These institutions are dominated by Northern interests and lack proper mechanisms that reflect the concerns of the global South. Furthermore, some Southern nations have asserted that these institutions impose conditionalities that are unfair and infringe upon state sovereignty. As a result, these institutions fail to adequately reflect the interests of the world's poor or harmonize Southern perspectives in the SD agenda. The tensions surrounding the green economy debates highlight the increasing level of corporate influence within the UN that creates a power imbalance, exacerbates the distrust between the North and the South, and hinders effective strategic alliances.[92]

Instead of creating insiders and outsiders or winners and losers, the challenge is to enable the global North and the South to cooperate with one another to initiate change, not only for the implementation of SDGs, but also to move toward global justice. The global South demands that the benefits of the global economic order be equitably distributed, the standard of living of the poorest be enhanced, and the processes by which the rules are made be fair and equitable. However, this will not be an easy task. International law fails to control corporate power, national regulations and enforcement mechanisms remain weak to protect natural resources; and the global South is unable to resist the temptation of new markets (e.g. biodiversity or ecosystems). The Northern and Southern countries are not willing to openly challenge the foundational concepts of the Northern development model. Yet, this model is fundamentally unsustainable, deepening the divide between the globalized rich and the localized poor.[93] This is exemplified by the simple fact that 80 percent of the world's resources are consumed by only 20 percent of the world's population.[94] Hence, sustainable development will not be possible unless we radically change the current economic structure and rethink GDP as a proxy for human flourishing, trade liberalization as the engine of better living conditions, and the myth of unlimited economic growth. International economic law must be engaged in this critical reevaluation, as it has historically maximized the power of transnational corporations by limiting state regulation and public accountability. Now the South must instead emphasize that a sustainable economic order is not possible unless the benefits of the global economic order are equitably distributed, the standard of living of the poorest is enhanced, and the process by which the rules are made is fair and equitable.

---

[92] Friends of the Earth International, note 15; "Rio+20 Summit: Whose Green Economy?," Supporter Briefing, World Development Movement, May 2012.

[93] W. Sachs et al., "Fairness in a Fragile World: A Memo on Sustainable Development" (2002) 19 *New Perspectives Quarterly* 8 at 9.

[94] Ibid at 12.

Index

Aarhus Convention (Convention on Access to Information, Public Participation in Decision-making and Access to Justice in Environmental Matters), 107, 176, 583–4, 586, 589

Abidjan disaster, 256, 269, 273

Access and Benefit Sharing (ABS). *See* Benefit sharing

Access to information, 134, 174, 250, 583–4, 604

Access to remedies, 588

Africa, 5–6, 61, 77, 105, 173–4, 178–80, 182–4, 186, 188, 196, 201, 222, 231, 239–40, 242–4, 246, 248, 250, 256, 258–60, 264–6, 270, 274, 283, 307, 324–5, 330, 385, 401, 411, 419–21, 452, 456, 529, 532–3, 537–8, 540, 554–5, 562, 565–6, 575, 600, 603

African Charter on Human and Peoples' Rights, 176, 179, 604

African Commission on Human Rights (ACHR), 182–4, 189

Agenda 21, 66–7, 125, 133, 137, 155, 158–60, 163–4, 298, 300, 383, 387, 573, 581

Alien Tort Claims Act, 436, 440, 604–5

Alliance of Small Island States, 11, 216, 231, 233–4, 236, 502, 564

American Convention on Human Rights, 176, 186, 371, 458, 513

American Declaration of the Organization of American States (American Declaration), 461–2

Amicus Participation, 594

Annex I countries, 95, 218–19, 229, 234

Anthropocene, 171, 179

Anti-privatization, 469–70, 478, 481, 483, 486, 489

Appropriate sustainable energy technologies (ASETs), 530–1, 533, 538–41, 549

Arctic Council, 108

Argentina, 105, 229, 243, 278, 414, 470–3, 489, 596

ASEAN, 555, 562–3, 566–71

Asian Cities Climate Change Resilience Network (ACCCRN), 505

Bamako Convention, 264–5, 270–1, 276

Bandung Conference, 7

Basel Ban, 266, 270, 274, 276

Basel Convention, 256–7, 259–60, 264–6, 268–71, 273, 275, 575

BASIC Climate Negotiating Bloc, 220

BASIC countries (Brazil, South Africa, India, and China), 11, 19, 216, 221, 223, 225–7, 235–6, 621–2

Beef Hormones case, 105

Belgrade Process, 137

Benefit sharing, 79, 84, 95, 98, 101, 192–3, 195–200, 202–12, 561

Best Practices, 148–9, 253–4, 365, 372, 386, 564

Beyond the Limits of National Jurisdiction, 82–4

Bilateral Investment Treaties (BITs), 46, 321, 328, 331, 335, 391, 422, 432, 470, *See* also International Investment Agreements (IIAs)

Bioenergy/Biofuel, 2, 237–41, 243–5, 247–9, 252, 254, 418–19, 422, 431, 454, 622

Biopiracy, 82, 102, 196, 202–3, 416

Biosafety Protocol, 102, 105

Bolivia, 129, 179, 231, 282–3, 336, 470, 475, 477, 480, 489, 556, 599, 612

Bonn Guidelines on Access to Genetic Resources and Fair and Equitable Sharing of the Benefits, 101, 193

Brazil, 11, 26, 72, 95, 105, 108, 117–18, 123, 155, 162, 185, 198, 216, 220, 225–6, 228–9, 234–5, 239,

626   *Index*

241, 243, 249, 278, 302, 335, 397–8, 414, 420,
451, 455, 464, 466, 532, 558, 578, 592, 599, 620
Brundtland Commission (World Commission on
Environment and Development), 60, 79,
121–2, 542
Brundtland Report (Our Common Future), 14,
50, 61–2, 64–6, 122, 124, 155, 252, 297–8, 300,
382, 384

Cairo Guidelines, 259
Canadian International Development Agency
(CIDA), 111
Caribbean Community (CARICOM), 554, 563–4,
566
Charter of Economic Rights and Duties of States
(CERDS), 33, 36–8, 59, 598
Charter of the United Nations, 28, 81–2, 389, 425–6
China, 2, 5, 71–2, 77, 95, 178, 188, 215–16, 220–4,
228–9, 233–6, 241, 243, 245, 258, 274, 359, 398,
414, 419, 446, 498, 532, 555, 558, 562, 579, 592,
595–6, 620
Civil Society, 322, 334–6, 390, 419, 423, 432, 469,
476–7, 479, 490, 496, 520, 526–7, 555, 563,
572–87, 607, 617, 622
Civil Society Mechanism (CSM), 583, 585–6
Class Action, 437, 444–7
Climate change, xix, 2–4, 6, 10–12, 15–19, 51, 65,
69, 72, 87, 91, 94–5, 97, 108, 123, 129, 131–2,
214–15, 217–18, 220–6, 228, 233–4, 237, 239,
242, 245–6, 297–8, 352, 373–4, 401, 405, 410,
417, 435–9, 442–4, 447–55, 457–64, 467–8,
491–2, 494–9, 501–5, 510, 519, 534, 536, 539,
542, 545, 558–9, 561–2, 564, 567, 570, 578–9,
591, 594, 602, 608, 618, 621
Climate change adaptation (CCA), 411, 491–2,
494–5, 500–1, 503, 507
Climate justice, 13, 403, 510
Climate resilience, 492, 496, 501, 503, 505, 507
Cocoyoc Declaration, 118–19, 121
Colombian Constitution of 1991, 511
Colombian General Forestry Law, 508, 511–13,
519, 525–6
Colonialism, 24, 26–30, 32, 47, 102, 178, 195, 258,
264, 398, 407, 456, 460
Commission on Permanent Sovereignty over
Natural Resources, 80
Commission on Sustainable Development
(CSD), 152–63, 165–7, 383, 386, 581
Committee on World Food Security (CFS),
585–6
Commodity speculation, 418, 422
Common but differentiated responsibilities and
capabilities (CBDR), 14, 18, 91, 93–4, 96, 217,
233–4, 301, 310, 498, 503, 579, 617–18

Common concern of mankind, 86, 99–100
Common heritage of mankind principle
(CHMP), 83, 98–100
Comparative Law in the Global South, 283, 525
Compliance measures, 203, 209, 211
Comprehensive Environmental Response,
Compensation, and Liability Act
(CERCLA), 106
Constitutional Environmental Law, 519
Constitutional Review, 292, 486–7
Constitutional Rights, 288–9, 291–2, 602, 606
Convention Concerning Indigenous and Tribal
Peoples in Independent Countries (ILO
169), 459–60, 467–8, 511, 513, 521, 524
Convention on Access to Information, Public
Participation in Decision-making and Access
to Justice in Environmental Matters. *See*
Aarhus Convention
Convention on Biological Diversity (CBD), 98,
100–2, 104, 192–3, 195–7, 199, 201–2, 204,
207–8, 542, 545, 559–60
Convention on International Trade in
Endangered Species of Wild Fauna and
Flora (CITES), 577
Copenhagen Accord, 95, 227–8
Corrective justice/injustice, 91, 259, 279, 403, 405,
423
Customary/indigenous laws, 180, 210, 213

Debt crisis, 7, 44, 122, 340, 411
Declaration of Principles Governing the Sea-Bed
and the Ocean Floor and the Subsoil
Thereof, 83
Deep seabed mining, 42, 84
Derivatives, 198–200, 210, 212, 418
Disaster funding, 493
Disaster management, 495–7, 570
Disaster resilience, 503, 507
Disaster risk reduction (DRR), 491, 495–6,
498–504, 507
Distributive justice/injustice, 23, 91, 259, 279, 403,
405, 423, 542, 544, 549
Doctrine of Discovery, 24
Doha Development Round, 300
Dualism, 377, 521
Due diligence, 207, 322–3, 360, 368, 371–3, 396,
427, 591
Durban Platform for Enhanced Action, 214, 232

Earth Summit (1992). *See* United Nations
Conference on Environment and
Development (UNCED or Earth Summit)
Ecocentrism, 179
Ecological debt, 10, 619

Index

Ecological footprint, 10, 67–8, 254, 616
Economic and Social Council (ECOSOC), 156, 158–9, 162–3, 166, 573, 581
Economic and Social Rights, 183
Energy Independence, 238, 245
Energy justice, 529, 531, 548
Energy poor (EP), 529–34, 536–43, 545–6, 548–9
Environmental Greening, 238
Environmental Impact Assessment (EIA), 333
Environmental Justice/injustice, 13–15, 17, 19, 179, 191, 256, 258–60, 265, 267–8, 275, 278, 281, 293, 380–1, 387, 389, 394–5, 397–9, 401–5, 423, 434, 517–18, 521, 569
Environmental requirements, 10, 299, 302–3, 305, 307–8, 314–15
Environmental rights, 173–7, 179–82, 185–6, 189, 392–4, 603, 607
Environmental, social and governance issues (ESG), 360, 368, 373–4
Environmentally sound management (ESM), 260–3, 267, 272
Equator Principles, 354, 395
Equity, 14, 71, 79, 91–2, 97, 110, 128, 154, 179, 187, 189, 215, 217, 222, 236, 239, 241, 246, 313, 324–5, 340–1, 469, 475, 480, 510, 542, 559, 571, 612, 618–19, 622
Eurocentrism, 25–7, 33, 49
Extralegal retaliation, 442

Food justice, 401–5, 411, 423, 425–6, 431–4
Food regime, 407, 411–12, 432, 434
Food security, 10, 203, 206, 237–8, 245, 247, 253, 404, 432, 454, 530, 540, 561, 567–9, 583, 585–6
Food sovereignty, 403–5, 432, 585
Foreign Direct Investment (FDI), 37, 46–7, 319, 322, 328, 330, 335
Founex Report on Development and Environment, 113, 117, 121
Fourth World, 456–7, 463, 466–7
Free, prior and informed consent (FPIC), 79, 98–103, 108, 193, 197–8, 203, 205–8, 210–13, 241–2, 260, 262–4, 271–2, 276, 342, 348, 391, 459, 465, 467, 511–13, 516–17, 519–20, 576

G-77 plus China, 2, 5, 7, 96, 166, 215, 555, 558, 561, 583, 596, 609, 617–18, 621
Gabcikovo Nagymaros Project, 75
Gandhi, Indira, 115, 117
General Agreement on Tariffs and Trade (GATT), 6, 8, 45, 299, 301–5, 314, 320, 408, 509, 594–5
Genetically modified crops (GM crops). See Genetically modified organisms (GMOs)

Genetically modified organisms (GMOs), 102, 108, 415–17
Global commons, 83, 85
Global Environment Facility (GEF), 133, 135, 137, 139, 148, 152, 157
Global Environment Outlook: Environment for Development (GEO-4), 131–2
Global environmental governance (GEG), 15, 130, 139, 555, 563, 613
Global food crisis, 241, 245
Global land rush. See Land grab
Global Ministerial Environment Forum (GMEF), 134, 136, 139, 147
Global South, xxi, xxii, 2, 5–6, 9–12, 46, 51–2, 54–6, 59–66, 68, 70–2, 77, 89, 91, 98, 103, 110, 114, 121, 130–1, 145, 153–5, 158–9, 163–6, 168, 171–4, 177–80, 182, 188–91, 195, 214, 224, 237, 240–1, 244–5, 247, 256, 259, 262, 266, 276–9, 281, 293, 297, 299, 318, 338–40, 351, 356–9, 361, 366–9, 373–4, 377, 380–1, 387, 390, 398, 401–3, 405–9, 412, 414–19, 422–3, 426, 430–1, 446, 456–7, 463, 467–71, 489, 491, 499–503, 508–11, 518, 521–4, 528, 555, 557, 561, 574, 578, 588–9, 591, 593, 596, 611–12, 614, 616, 621–3
Green economy, 48, 128–9, 239, 387, 609–11, 614–15, 619–20, 623
Green Revolution, 407, 409–10, 416
Gross National Product (GNP), 55, 114, 164, 265, 432

Hazardous waste, 10, 15, 106, 150, 154, 256–76, 383, 401, 403, 575–6
    Management and disposal, 256, 393
    Transboundary movements, 260–2, 267, 276, 575
High Level Political Forum (HLPF), 152–4, 158–9, 162–8
Human rights, 9, 14, 17, 19, 29, 35, 40–1, 45, 75, 92, 120, 171–6, 178–9, 183–4, 189–90, 212, 241, 244, 253, 255, 278, 281–2, 289, 317–19, 321–5, 327, 329–37, 354, 362–4, 369, 371–3, 377–8, 380–1, 384, 386, 388–94, 396–8, 422–3, 425–8, 432, 447–8, 458, 460–1, 476, 513, 521–2, 524–5, 543, 546–7, 562–3, 568–9, 574, 577–8, 580, 597–8, 601–4, 607, 611, 620
Hyogo Framework for Action (HFA), 494–5, 499, 502–3

ILO Convention 169. See Convention Concerning Indigenous and Tribal Peoples in Independent Countries (ILO 169)
Imperialism, 7, 28–9, 312, 470
Import substitution industrialization (ISI), 44

628   *Index*

Independent Expert on Human Rights and the Environment, 425

India, 2, 72, 75, 95, 103, 107, 115, 118, 144, 177, 185, 188–9, 216, 220, 225, 228–9, 234–5, 243, 245, 260, 267, 274, 278, 283, 318, 328, 331, 336, 361, 398, 412, 419, 446, 452, 492–3, 498, 501, 504, 506, 521, 532, 555, 558, 565, 567, 579, 592, 595–6, 599, 604, 606, 620

Indian Supreme Court, 75, 107, 283

Indigenous and Local Communities, 99, 101, 193, 197, 202, 205–6, 248–9

Indigenous environmental knowledge (IEK), 455, 463, 465, 468

Indigenous Peoples, 6, 17, 25, 34–5, 102, 185–6, 212–13, 325, 328, 348, 381, 386, 391–3, 395, 398, 401, 433, 451, 453–5, 457–60, 462, 464–7, 510–11, 516, 518–20, 524, 556, 569, 580–1, 583, 585, 619

Industrial Revolution, 30, 50, 52–3, 559

Institutional arrangements of the environmental governance system, 136

Inter-American Commission on Human Rights (IACHR), 182, 184–6, 371, 461

Inter-American Development Bank (IDB), 345–6

Interest Convergence, 447–9

Inter-generational equity, 75, 79, 81, 91–2, 187, 303, 405

International Center for the Settlement of Investment Disputes (ICSID), 46, 327, 335, 474, 477, 481, 489, 589, 593, 596–9, 601

International Court of Justice (ICJ), 29, 31–2, 75–6, 370, 436, 440, 442, 591, 601

International Covenant on Civil and Political Rights (ICCPR), 424

International Covenant on Economic, Social and Cultural Rights (ICESCR), 255, 281–2, 424–5, 427, 519

International environmental governance, 131, 133–4, 137–9, 143, 145, 150, 157, 168, 356, 364

International environmental norms, 51, 365, 368

International Finance Corporation's Sustainability Framework, 394

International Human Rights Law, 14, 18, 75, 107, 354, 425, 440–1, 513, 522

International Institute for Sustainable Development, 329, 600

International Investment Agreements (IIAs), 321, 327, 330–1, 334–5, 337, 596, 598–600

International Investment Disputes, 327

International Investment Law, 9, 317, 319, 326, 334, 336, 421

International Labor Organization (ILO), 145, 323, 330

International Law Commission's Draft Articles on the Responsibility of States, 369

International Monetary Fund (IMF), 6, 43–4, 47, 55, 65, 165, 405, 411–13, 423, 425–6, 429–30, 470, 482, 489, 509, 520, 616, 622

International Policy Framework for Sustainable Development (IPFSD), 330–1

International Seabed Authority (ISA), 41

International sustainable mineral development law, 380–1, 387

Internationally Wrongful Acts (ILC Draft Articles). *See* International Law Commission's Draft Articles on the Responsibility of States

Intra-generational equity, 79, 91–2, 301, 303, 313, 316, 325, 336, 339, 405

Inuit Circumpolar Council (ICC) Petition, 460–3

Investor-state arbitrations, 598

Investor-State Dispute Settlement System, 327–8

Johannesburg Declaration, 14, 87, 90, 125, 619

Johannesburg Plan of Implementation (JPOI), 136, 163

Johannesburg World Summit on Sustainable Development (WSSD), 110, 125–8, 131, 134, 136, 194, 384, 389

Joint Statement, Leaders of Pacific Islands Forum and the UN Secretary General, 439

Judicial review, 287, 332, 375, 377

JUSCANZ group (Japan, US, Canada, Australia, and New Zealand), 12

Justice in Environmental Matters, 176, 583

Kuala Lumpur Supplementary Protocol on Liability and Redress, 106

Kyoto Protocol, 95, 215–16, 218–20, 227, 375

Land acquisition. *See* Land grab

Land grab, 237–8, 240–7, 249–55, 418–20, 426–7, 432, 555, 562

Land speculation, 241

League of Nations (LN), 28–9

Least developed countries (LDCs), 216, 222, 231, 234–6, 301, 310, 325, 331, 532–5, 537–40, 545, 547, 593

Limited Liability, 341, 345, 348

Loss and damage, 216, 492, 501–3, 560–2

Low Income Countries (LICs), 51

Maastricht Principles on Extraterritorial Obligations of States in the Area of Economic, Social and Cultural Rights, 427

Malmo Declaration, 134

Mandate system, 28

Index

Market access, 31, 128, 299–300, 314, 316, 429, 591, 619, 621

Millennium Development Goals (MDGs), 14, 125, 154, 277, 361, 530, 549, 611, 619

Minimum Core, 279–81, 287–8, 290–3

Monism, 521

Moon Treaty, 85–6

Multicultural Constitution (Colombia), 516

Multilateral environmental agreements (MEAs), 134–6, 138, 142, 145–8, 150–2, 157, 555–6, 558–9, 563, 567, 570–1, 574–5, 588–9

Multinational corporations (MNCs), 34, 46–7, 604, 607, See also Transnational corporations (TNCs)

Mutual recognition agreements (MRAs), 310–11

Mutually Agreed Terms (MATs), 99–101, 193, 197, 200, 202, 204–7, 210

Nagoya Protocol on Access to Genetic Resources (NP), 101, 194–213

National Treatment Principle, 299, 327

Nationally Appropriate Mitigation Action (NAMA), 228–9, 234–5

Natural Disasters, 131, 230, 491–3, 495–7, 499–500, 507

Neo-colonialism, 118, 178

Neoliberalism, 240, 339, 343–4, 349, 353, 411–12, 471, 475, 478, 483, 489, 592, 607, See also Washington Consensus

New International Economic Order (NIEO), 7, 36–8, 118, 120–1, 554, 558

New Zealand Superannuation Fund (NZSF), 357, 366–9, 371, 374–8

Newly industrialized countries (NIC), 532–3

Non-Annex I countries, 94, 216, 219, 221, 228–9, 234

Non-state actors, 3, 363, 370, 427, 585, 600, 602, 608

Non-tariff barriers (NTB), 299, 303–5, 315

North-South transfers of hazardous waste, 276

Norwegian Government Pension Fund – Global (NGPF-G), 357, 361–5, 368–9, 371, 374, 377

OECD Guidelines for Multinational Enterprises, 323, 330, 600

OPEC Oil Embargo, 238

Organization for Economic Co-operation and Development (OECD), 106, 267, 274–6, 303, 320, 386, 395–7

Organization for Economic Co-operation and Development (OECD) Principles of Corporate Governance, 365

Organization of African Unity (OAU), 264–5, 554

Overseas Development Assistance (ODA), 164

Pacific Islands Forum to the Secretary General, 439

Participatory rights, 75, 79, 107, 206, 326, 392

Peremptory norm of international law, 85

Permanent sovereignty of states over natural resources, 7, 34, 36, 38, 47, 79–81, 92, 321, 326, 389, 433, 598

Polluter pays principle, 75, 79, 106, 189, 498, 503

Pogge, Thomas, 9, 547

Poverty and Environment Initiative (PEI), 151

Poverty eradication, 48, 90, 99, 128, 166, 234, 509, 530–1, 542, 610, 614

Precautionary principle, 75, 79, 99, 102, 104–5, 189, 307–8, 333, 556

Principle of good neighborliness, 75, 82

Principles of international environmental law, 7, 189

Prior informed consent (PIC). See Free, prior and informed consent (FPIC)

Procedural fairness, 91, 314, 376

Procedural justice/injustice, 259, 279, 405, 423

Programme for the Further Implementation of Agenda 21 (PFIA21), 163

Project Finance, 9, 16, 338–42, 345, 350–5

Proportionality, 281, 288–93

Protocol on Liability and Compensation to the Basel Convention, 268, 276

Public Interest Litigation, 331, 337, 446, 449, 486, 606

Quantified Emission Limitation and Reduction Objectives (QELRO), 234–5

Rawls, John, 531, 543–4, 549

Reasonableness, 279–81, 286–8, 290–3

Recycling loophole, 266, 276

Reducing Emissions from Deforestation and Forest Degradation (REDD), 12, 452, 455, 459–60, 463–7

Renewable Fuels Standards, 419, 431

Resolution 1803 (XVII) on Permanent Sovereignty over Natural Resources, 34, 36–7

Responsible Agricultural Investment, 253–5, 326

Right to Development, 7, 92, 124, 225, 324, 433, 458, 465, 559, 563

Right to Food, 255, 323, 405, 423–6, 430–4, 563, 585–6

Right to participate in the decision making process, 107, 174, 209, 212, 459

Right to Prior Consultation. See Free, prior and informed consent (FPIC)

Right to Water, 277–85, 287–8, 290, 292–3, 393, 470, 481, 489

Rio Declaration on Environment and Development, 86–7, 89–90, 94, 104–6, 123, 125, 133, 174, 298, 300, 324–5, 335, 383, 387, 390, 518, 542, 557, 573, 584, 590, 610

630 Index

Rio+20 Conference on Sustainable Development. *See* United Nations Conference on Sustainable Development (UNCSD or Rio+20)

Rio+20 Outcome Document, 141, 143–4, 149–51, 162, 164, 175, 387, 556, 610–11, 614, 619

Risk assessments, 306

San Salvador Protocol to the American Convention on Human Rights, 604

Santiago Principles, 358, 372–4, 378–9

sic utere tuo ut alienum non laedas, 82

Small Island Developing States (SIDS), 215–16, 222, 235, 325, 435–9, 441, 443–4, 449–50, 621–2

Social justice/injustice, 14, 57, 245, 253, 259, 278, 283, 339, 356, 403, 405, 423, 524

Socially Responsible Investing (SRI), 356–69, 372–4, 377–9

Soft law, 9, 33–4, 37–8, 75, 88, 177, 311, 331, 358, 362, 374, 386

South Africa, 29, 103, 179, 181, 186–7, 216, 220, 226, 228, 230, 232, 243, 278–9, 281, 283, 286, 292, 328, 335–6, 361, 385, 398, 420, 470–1, 482–4, 487–8, 521, 532, 566, 599

South-North Environmental Discussions, 109–10, 112, 115, 117, 123–4, 128, 557, 559

South-South Cooperation, 18, 147, 163, 167, 553, 555–9, 562–71, 621

Sovereign Wealth Funds (SWFs), 356–61, 367–70, 372–4, 378–9

Sovereignty, 6, 23–4, 26–7, 34, 36, 39–40, 43–4, 46–8, 59, 79–82, 84–5, 100, 152, 154, 192, 195, 273, 297, 321, 324, 389, 509, 546, 548, 556, 569, 590–1, 596–8, 623

Special and differential treatment, 7–8, 301, 312, 331, 408

Special Purpose Entity, 340–1, 351–3

Standards, labelling, packaging and certification, 299

State responsibility, 75, 369, 372, 503, 589–90, 604, 608

State Responsibility for Transboundary Harm, 440–1

Stockholm Conference on the Human Environment, 1, 76, 173, 382

Stockholm Declaration, 50, 58–9, 75, 81, 117, 173–4, 326, 382, 590–1

Strong, Maurice, 111, 131

Structural Adjustment, 7, 44, 65, 340, 411–14, 429, 475, 478, 483, 580

Subsidies, 8, 106, 238, 303, 407–9, 412–14, 426, 429–30, 484, 594

Sustainable agriculture, 249, 410, 420, 430

Sustainable Development, 14, 16, 18–19, 35, 47–8, 50–2, 58, 60, 62–6, 75, 77, 79, 81–2, 86–93, 96, 106, 121–8, 130–1, 134, 137, 139, 141–4, 150, 157, 159–68, 180, 183, 187, 189, 237–9, 241, 244, 247–52, 297–301, 303, 305, 307, 310, 314, 316, 319, 321, 324–7, 329–35, 338–40, 342, 350, 355, 357–8, 361–2, 364–5, 367, 374, 378–9, 381–8, 394, 430, 499, 510, 518–19, 531, 533, 541–3, 545, 547–8, 553, 558, 566, 568, 570, 574, 581–2, 588, 594, 600, 603, 609–17, 620–3

Sustainable Development Goals (SDGs), 319, 350, 556–7, 562, 568–71, 611–12, 615–19, 621, 623

Sustainable Energy for All (SE4ALL), 530

Sustainable livelihoods, 389, 402, 434

Tariffs, 8, 408, 411, 413, 426, 429, 472, 474–5, 596

Tax incentives, 421

Technical assistance, 146, 149, 300, 309–10, 344, 593

The Future We Want, 127–8, 132, 139, 144, 162, 164, 326, 387, 389, 556

Third World Approaches to International Law (TWAIL), 12, 19

Toxic colonialism, 11, 256, 258, 276, 401

Trade and the Environment, 297, 300, 316

Trade facilitation/capacity building, 136, 141–2, 145–6, 166, 275, 298, 300, 303, 310, 313, 331, 384, 386, 397–8, 553–4, 556, 565–6, 576, 617, 620, 622

Traditional knowledge, 98–103, 193–4, 196–8, 201, 203–8, 211, 248, 315, 352, 416–17

TRAFFIC, 577

Trail Smelter Arbitration, 590–1

Transnational corporations (TNCs), 3, 8, 16, 19, 243, 321, 336, 372, 380, 398, 402, 407, 409, 411, 414–16, 418–19, 423, 426–8, 604, 611, 619, 623, *See* also Multinational corporations (MNCs)

Transnational mining governance framework, 394

Triangular Cooperation, 167, 557, 570–1, 620

Ul-Haq, Mahbub, 111

United Nations Committee on Economic Social and Cultural Rights (CESCR), 424

United Nations Conference on Environmental Development (UNCED or Earth Summit), 66, 98, 109, 121, 123–4, 128, 131, 155–6, 163, 558–9, 581

United Nations Conference on Sustainable Development (UNCSD or Rio+20), 1, 110, 127–9, 139, 141–4, 150–1, 162, 165–6, 175, 326, 556, 582, 610–11, 614–15, 617–19

United Nations Conference on Trade and Development (UNCTAD), 119, 252, 321, 327, 420, 428

United Nations Declaration on the Rights of Indigenous Peoples (UNDRIP), 459–60, 465–8

Index

United Nations Development Programme (UNDP), 148, 151, 277, 532, 557

United Nations Environment Programme (UNEP), 50, 119, 121, 128, 130–53, 156–60, 166, 232, 239, 260, 273, 577, 582

United Nations Food and Agriculture Organization (FAO), 241, 252, 406

United Nations Framework Convention on Climate Change (UNFCCC), 74, 86, 95, 217–19, 221–3, 225–7, 230–1, 233, 236, 438, 441, 445, 492, 495, 498–503, 542, 545, 558–9, 561, 578, 581–2

United Nations General Assembly, 7, 439, 459

United Nations Guiding Principles on Business and Human Rights, 322, 620

United Nations Human Rights Council (UNHRC), 175

United Nations Law of the Sea Convention (UNCLOS), 31, 41–2, 84, 86, 95, 98, 440

United Nations Principles for Responsible Investing (UNPRI), 360, 368, 374, 378

United States Environmental Protection Agency (EPA), 534

Universal Declaration of Human Rights, 173, 281, 323–4, 331, 424, 458

Uruguay, 105, 112, 283, 303, 320, 470, 478–81, 489, 592

Voluntary Codes of Corporate Conduct, 365, 607

Ward Barbara, 111, 119

Warsaw International Mechanism (WIM), 495, 501–2

Warsaw Loss and Damage, 495, 501, 558, 562

Washington Consensus, 7–8, 339, See also Neoliberalism

Water, 132, 165, 188, 224, 242, 247–9, 254, 257, 272, 277–88, 290, 292–3, 318, 332, 352, 365, 393, 403–4, 406, 411, 419–22, 424, 431, 435, 438, 469–81, 483–9, 506, 529, 537–40, 567

Westphalia Treaty, 26–7

Wind Energy Development / Wind Farms, 342–4, 352

World Bank, 6–7, 43–4, 46–7, 55, 65, 82, 112, 148, 164–5, 241–2, 244, 252, 327, 342, 344, 348, 394, 405, 411–13, 423, 425–6, 429–30, 464, 470–1, 473–5, 477–8, 489, 509, 520, 571, 606, 610, 616, 619

World Bank Inspection Panel, 606

World Bank International Finance Corporation (IFC), 342, 344–5, 352, 394–5, 397

World Commission on Environment and Development (WCED), 62, 66, 86–90, 155, 382

World Health Organization (WHO), 284, 287, 532, 560, 571

World Summit on Sustainable Development (WSSD). See Johannesburg World Summit on Sustainable Development (WSSD)

World Trade Organization (WTO), 8, 40, 45, 47, 105, 137, 145, 164, 208, 273–4, 299, 301–2, 304–6, 308–9, 312–13, 315, 320–1, 405, 413, 415, 423, 429, 442, 447, 589, 592–5, 604, 616, 622

WTO Agreement on Agriculture (AoA), 45, 413–14

WTO Agreement on the Application of Sanitary and Phytosanitary Measures (SPS Agreement), 305–10, 312, 315–16

WTO Agreement on Trade Related Aspects of Intellectual Property Rights (TRIPS), 40, 45, 208, 320, 415

WTO Appellate Body, 594

World Trade Organization Dispute settlement regime, 442, 592–4

WTO Dispute Settlement Understanding, 592

For EU product safety concerns, contact us at Calle de José Abascal, 56–1°,
28003 Madrid, Spain or eugpsr@cambridge.org.

www.ingramcontent.com/pod-product-compliance
Ingram Content Group UK Ltd.
Pitfield, Milton Keynes, MK11 3LW, UK
UKHW020347060825
461487UK00008B/562